**WORLD YEARBOOK
OF EDUCATION 1980**

World Yearbook of Education 1980
Professional Development of Teachers

Edited by **Eric Hoyle** *(Consultant Editor)*
University of Bristol

and **Jacquetta Megarry** *(Series Editor)*
Jordanhill College of Education

US Consultant Editor **Myron Atkin** *Dean of Education,*
Stanford University

**Kogan Page, London/Nichols Publishing
Company, New York**

First published 1980
by Kogan Page Limited,
120 Pentonville Road, London N1 9JN

ISBN 0 85038 287 4
ISSN 0084-2508

First published in the USA
in 1980 by Nichols Publishing Company,
PO Box 96, New York, NY 10024
ISBN 0-89397-084-0
LC Catalog Card No 32-18413

Printed and bound in Great Britain
by Billing and Sons Limited

Contents

List of Contributors

Professor Donald Orlosky, Professor of Education, University of South Florida   *Chapter 19*

Mrs Pauline Perry, Staff Inspector, Department of Education and Science, London   *Chapter 9*

Dr John Raynor, Senior Lecturer in Education, Open University   *Chapter 16*

Dr William Smith, US Commissioner of Education, Department of Health, Education and Welfare, Washington, DC   *Chapter 15*

Dr William Taylor, Director, Institute of Education, University of London   *Chapter 23*

Professor Richard Tisher, Professor of Education, Monash University, Australia   *Chapter 4*

The above affiliations do not imply identification with the views expressed by the authors, who are writing as individuals.
The Editors would like to thank Iris Megarry for her skilful editorial assistance.

Preface

'The strength of an education system must largely depend upon the quality of its teachers' (YBE 1963: xii). In these words, George Bereday and Joseph Lauwerys introduced the *Year Book of Education 1963: the Education and Training of Teachers*. The words are as apposite in 1980 as they were in 1963, and much of the introductory material — both theirs and Brian Holmes' — not only still reads well today, but also bears quotation again in this Preface. However, in education as in human development, 17 years is a long time, and teacher education has seen major change and upheaval in the last two decades, as Bone documents vividly in Chapter 3. No apology is needed for revisiting this theme.

Parts of the *YBE 1963* offer instructive reminders of some of these changes. Recurring mention of acute teacher shortage, emergency training measures, rising birth-rates and falling death-rates all serve to underline the expansionist mood of the 1960s. Holmes identified three traumatic post-war changes which influenced this development. The inflated expectations — of political independence, higher living standards, and universal primary education — in developing countries were paralleled by demands for universal extended secondary and higher education in the developed countries, especially the United States. Second, demographic changes and rising birth-rates led in turn to rapid expansion of the school-age population. Third, the remarkably rapid progress in the application of technology, especially in science and mass communications, made 'the simple literacy of the nineteenth century — the three Rs — now as outmoded as the horse and buggy in the jet aircraft age' (YBE 1963:2).

Painful contraction of teacher education, including college closures, compulsory redundancies, or at best diversification and consolidation, has since occurred in most countries. The extent to which this has been caused by worldwide economic recession and political pressures, rather than by any diminution of the demand for education, and hence for teachers, is highlighted by Holmes' analysis. For although the world population growth-rate is declining, and the birth-rate in 14 European countries has dropped below replacement level, worldwide the total population is still increasing rapidly. The school-age population is increasing faster still in countries which are progressively extending the years of compulsory schooling. Even those countries which have reached, if not exceeded, the prudent maximum for compulsion, and whose school-age population is actually declining, have seen a continuing growth in the demand for higher, further and continuing education. All the evidence is that higher living standards and increased educational opportunity fuel rather than extinguish the demand for more.

The increasing momentum of technological change has brought revolutionary developments in electronics, telecommunications and automation. Its possible implications for employment, education and life-style are only now being realized. The results of the expected increase in leisure time should be of particular interest to educators at all levels. In Chapter 18, I have explored the consequences of this for teacher education; here I want only to emphasize that the microelectronic revolution must elevate the value of uniquely human skills at the expense of those which are easily automated or computerized. Together with the need for education (or re-education) for versatility in employment and leisure, we will need more purely academic education, not less, and teachers who are better-equipped to provide it than are available at present.

Microprocessors will not go away just because teachers and educators pay no attention to them, or wish that they had not been invented. But if teachers *can* accept the possibilities of the new technology without being overwhelmed or paralysed by it, the microelectronic revolution *need* not lead to the decline of the teaching profession that has been prophesied. Everything depends on how the teaching profession responds to the challenge. The *YBE 1963* was prescient on this topic: 'Teachers may have to accept that new teaching devices…will replace them as a major source of information' and earlier it predicted that 'new technological media promise to revolutionise concepts of classroom instruction, if indeed not concepts of learning itself. Teachers of the future will need to be prepared to be flexible enough to adapt themselves to this revolution.'

Profound demographic and economic changes since 1963 have led to a contraction in teacher education caused by the decline in numbers of students embarking on initial training. This results from a decline in the demand for newly trained teachers and reflects a loss of confidence among school-leavers in teaching as a secure job. Teacher educators have responded by arguing that a reduction in the pre-service load allows more scope for expansion into the in-service field. The educational arguments for this have no doubt been sharpened by expediency; widespread threats to teacher education budgets, lecturers' jobs, and even to the continued existence of small teachers' colleges have reinforced the case for distributing a teacher's professional education throughout his career.

The theme of last year's *WYBE — Lifelong Learning and Recurrent Education* — is not unrelated to the present one. Just as youth is not necessarily the best time for a person's whole lifetime input of education, so the year(s) immediately prior to service are not the ideal time in his career for the intending teacher's total lifetime allocation of teacher education. Bush argues forcefully in Chapter 25 that the early years of teaching pose special problems, and Tisher considers the case for induction schemes which try to solve them in Chapter 4. In general, the needs of the beginning teacher are different from those of the teacher in mid-career, and of the teacher approaching retirement, as Bolam indicates in Chapter 5. Moreover, the demands made of classroom teachers are changing and promise to change further in the future. Thus, the last two decades have been marked by a major expansion of in-service education for teachers, though many would deny the adequacy of the present levels. It is one thing for a committee to recommend one term for in-service in every seven years of a teacher's career, and quite another for teachers' employers to provide the resources to implement it. In-service education should not, of course, be conceived of as narrowly vocational. As Raynor comments in Chapter 16, teachers have been avid consumers of lifelong education as well as purveyors of it. It would be a poor advertisement for the value of education were they otherwise.

The difference between the terms used in the 1963 and 1980 approaches to the theme is a telling one. In the *YBE 1963* the editors permitted their contributors the use of both the terms 'teacher education' and 'teacher training' as suited the context, and noted that the terms were used interchangeably in some countries. It is noticeable that the term 'teacher education', with its less narrowly vocational connotations, is far more popular among *WYBE 1980* authors than their predecessors. In entitling the volume *Professional Development of Teachers* we have broadened the scope still further, and yoked together two meanings — the development of teaching as a profession and the professional development of teachers as individuals.

Many of the contributors, and especially Hoyle in Chapter 2, have explored the meanings, criteria, and connotations of the epithet 'profession'. I shall not attempt to summarize or reconcile their comments. Readers who cannot agree on a stipulative definition will nevertheless probably recognize the same examples. Doctors are professionals, dockers are not. Teachers would like to be regarded as professionals by the rest of the world but their hopes are not generally realized. In Chapters 24 and 26, Judge and Bloomer discuss various reasons for this, including the financial one. Teaching is a mass occupation; the more teachers insist on lower class sizes and higher teacher/pupil ratios, the more surely they guarantee that it must remain so. As the *YBE 1963* said, 'Mass education eroded the former position of teachers, whose professional status has yet to be regained.' No society can afford to pay top professional salaries to a large occupational group; the arithmetic is brutally simple. This does *not* amount to an assertion that teachers are adequately paid at present. Even for their *minimal* social/economic function — that of child-minders — teachers' remuneration falls below the current rate for the job, at least in Britain. Low salary brings low status as its companion. To alter either radically may require a drastic revision of our assumptions about the labour-intensive nature of education, the role of technological aids and the acceptable level of teacher/pupil ratios.

The history of technological aids in education is that of innovations like programmed learning, computers and audio-visual aids which have falsified prophesies that they would replace teachers. Instead, they have increased and altered the nature of the demands on teachers without altering the accepted ratios of teachers to pupils. Put crudely, such aids have made education more expensive, though enthusiasts seek to justify them by the claim that they have also made it more effective. Politicians are unlikely to finance any significant improvement in teacher/pupil ratios and the teachers' unions seem unlikely to contemplate the decline in such ratios which would be necessary to counterbalance the additional expense of major investment in technological aids.

Full professional status will also require a change of heart by teachers themselves. For would-be professionals, they have been surprisingly indifferent to evaluating their own success, notably incurious about the nature of classroom transactions and generally impatient of both the demands and findings of educational researchers. No medical student would betray similar attitudes to medical research if he hoped to impress his examiners, and society would never tolerate such a low proportion of the medical budget being spent on research as is the case in education. As the *YBE 1963* said, 'A profession can advance no faster than the scientific and instructional theories on which it must rely'; teachers should be concerned about the weakness of the knowledge base upon which their art depends.

Teachers are not, of course, solely to blame for the low status and weak impact of educational research. Part of the problem derives from the inconclusive nature of its findings; these reflect the inappropriate models of research which have been used and partly underlines the naivety of expecting 'conclusive results' in such a complex and context-bound field. In Chapter 21, McIntyre throws light on what teacher education can and cannot realistically expect of research. Human learning is not susceptible to miracle drugs; placebos may even be more effective if taken with the right attitude. The whole rhetoric of comparative experiments, input and output measures, replication and measurement implies a quasi-scientific approach which is often inappropriate. As McIntyre and Elliott demonstrate, there are encouraging signs that more fruitful and appropriate models and styles of educational research are developing. The emergence of the classroom as a legitimate subject for research is surprisingly recent, and they document some promising approaches which have already been developed.

In particular, as several contributors note, the erosion of the artificial barrier between teacher and researcher is a hopeful sign. Not only do teachers need to be intelligent *consumers* of educational research, they should also contribute to it. Many doctors combine clinical practice with academic research, and teacher-researchers will contribute not only to their own professional development as individuals but also to the development of the teaching profession.

A change of attitude to teacher educators and their work in the professional preparation of teachers will also be necessary. Schoolteachers have been traditionally sceptical of the value of initial training, let alone of more ambitious or sustained initiatives in in-service education. This stems partly from professional jealousy of college and university lecturers who tend to be 'promoted' out of the ranks of classroom teachers never to return; it is exacerbated by the knowledge that their salaries, status and working conditions are better than those of schoolteachers. It partly results from a belief that teacher educators are refugees from their own inability to cope with classroom realities — a belief which is much more often repeated than substantiated. It comes as no surprise to read in Joyce's chapter that teachers in the US credit teacher educators with far less teaching experience and competence than they actually possess.

However, there are faults on both sides, and some of the scepticism is undoubtedly well-founded. Teacher education has suffered from unjustified complacency; it has displayed excessive conservatism in its content and organization, has profited little from research and conducted less. and has relied upon traditional and unsystematic training methods. Its credibility has been undermined by the failure of teacher educators to employ in their own teaching the innovative methods which they have repeatedly advocated to impending teachers — a point I develop in Chapter 18. It has been weakened by the great divide between low-level 'tips for teachers' and high-level theory of obscure relevance.

Especially in North America, there has been considerable recent interest in attempts to professionalize teacher education by basing it on a rigorous 'scientific' model, for example by using competency-based approaches. This has been reinforced by the change in the general climate toward greater public participation, and the demand for accountability has been heard in teacher education as well as in education at large. Above all, there has been perennial criticism of the isolation of theoretical professional studies in psychology and education from practical advice on teaching methods, and of the persistent failure to relate the theoretical notions presented at the training institution to the classroom events encountered by intending and practising teachers. One response to such criticisms has been a shift of emphasis from academic 'disciplines' toward classroom issues, accompanied by the development of alternative methods — including microteaching and simulation for example (see Chapters 18 and 19).

A more radical response has been to question the *locus* of provision, and especially that of in-service education: should it be school-based, school-focused, or provided at a teachers' centre, college or university? Many of the *WYBE 1980* contributors explore this issue — notably, Hoyle, Bolam, Perry and Baker; and Kolawole describes a programme in which teacher trainers are itinerant. The current trend is certainly toward basing in-service education on the user's institution rather than the provider's. Indeed, the clear distinction between user and provider has come to be questioned. As Joyce remarks in Chapter 1, other teachers are and perhaps always have been a major source of advice and help for their colleagues. How far this argument will be applied to pre-service training remains to be seen; many would view a move to make teacher preparation school-based as risking a return to a system of apprenticeship rather than professional education, and therefore would see it as a retrograde step.

In the past, the willingness of schools to co-operate over teaching practice arrangements has been taken for granted; schools have had little influence on the training courses for which their facilities have provided an integral part. Gradually, telling signs are emerging that the teacher educators would like to develop a partnership with teaching practice schools, though clearly with the schools as junior partners. Thus, teachers are being asked to participate more in the assessment of students, and even in academic decision-making in teacher training institutions. However, partnership in teacher education, as in marriage or business, presupposes not only common aims but also mutual understanding, respect and trust; good communications are not enough. Continuing collaboration, sharing and even exchange of jobs (both part-time and long-term) are needed if teachers and tutors are to develop and maintain awareness of each others' day-to-day realities. However it is caused, the suspicion and mistrust with which teachers regard teacher trainers is to the credit of neither, and steps must be taken to break down these barriers before talk of a partnership in professional preparation is more than mere rhetoric.

Whatever the criticisms that may fairly be made of the content, method, career patterns and organization of teacher education, it must be said that many intending and practising teachers have never really taken to heart the idea that people need to *learn* how to be teachers. The concept of the 'born' teacher has been used to justify lack of training. Langeveld effectively demolished this notion in his *YBE 1963* chapter on the psychology of teachers and the teaching profession. It opens 'The idea that any person is exclusively fit for a particular profession is an illusion...'; later (pp 400-1) he notes that 'the "born" teacher must receive first of all a good training in the skills of his occupation...' and also that 'the "born" teacher may be "born" for teaching in one situation and not do nearly so well in another'.

We are all *amateur* teachers. In the family, around the house, at the workplace, on the street, through the media, in casual conversation, on the sportsfield or in our leisure pursuits, we are constantly teaching and learning informally. No one would deny or want to over-organize these activities. But if young people are deprived of their liberty in order to be educated in schools, or if an adult student pays hard-earned money in course fees for further and higher education, they are surely entitled to expect professional skills to be available in professional conditions. Teachers who attack teacher education, instead of offering constructive criticism and saying how it should be improved, do not seem to realize that they undermine their own claims to professional status. For if one does not need training to be a teacher, if anyone can learn to teach just by doing it, then what possible claim can teachers have to occupational identity, let alone to the status and salary of professionals?

Even if 'born teachers' exist, they are unlikely to be born fully-fledged. Undoubtedly there are skills required by teachers today which *can* be learned and *should* be practised under appropriate feedback conditions. These include projecting the voice, loading a video-cassette, asking higher-order questions, establishing and maintaining eye contact, non-directive counselling, writing objective-type test questions, evaluating a multi-media kit, preparing, running and debriefing a simulation game, designing effective work-cards, establishing rapport, designing a computer-based simulation, running an open-ended discussion, making and analysing a tape transcript. The fact that some intending teachers possess such skills to a greater extent than others at the outset is undeniable but irrelevant. That most people, given sufficient time and persistence, could learn most of them, is also beside the point. Teachers — even 'born teachers' — require training in skills and professional education on a broad front. This is as true if their charges are infants or university graduates. It is unfair to students of any age that untrained teachers should learn 'on the job' or by 'apprenticeship', and signs are at last emerging that the argument is beginning to be accepted even in higher education, where hitherto the curious assumption has prevailed that lecturers should be appointed for their research or publications record and that their teaching abilities either did not matter or would, by some mysterious process, be automatically guaranteed.

Teachers' attempts to improve their professional status have been handicapped by the legacy of a divisive history. The old distinction died hard between 'elementary school teachers' — with low qualifications and a college training — and 'secondary school masters' — university graduates whose academic qualifications were presumed to substitute for their lack of any special professional preparation. In Chapter 24, Judge traces the lines between the dual system of curriculum and schooling and the dual system of teacher training to which it gave rise. As Holmes noted (*YBE 1963*: 120): 'Few people have been quite sure whether all teachers should be regarded as members of the same profession and trained accordingly, or even whether some of them needed any training at all.'

In many countries, both the organization of teacher training and the demarcation of teacher trade unions by sector have reflected this uncertainty. Separate unions, salary structures and training schemes for primary and secondary teachers have been deeply and lastingly divisive. Greater professional unity would strengthen the profession in its attempts to improve its practice and its public esteem.

Professionalization, as Hoyle explains in Chapter 2, involves the improvement both of status and practice. Two approaches are discernible: one is toward organized trade unionism — with a stress on professional unity, solidarity with the labour movement and the use of industrial action — and the other toward imitation of the 'established' professions — emphasizing higher entry standards, longer training periods and greater professional autonomy. In Chapter 11, Kemble traces the identification of the two major American teacher organizations with the two approaches — and argues that 'professionalism is not possible without unionism'. Taylor also comments in Chapter 23 on the long-standing debate within the teaching profession about which route is more likely to be successful.

Paradoxically, teachers in Scotland seem to be pressing *both* sides of the argument harder than their English counterparts. Having trained and practised as a teacher and educationist North of the border after having been educated in the South, I find the contrasting images and policies of the two teaching forces fascinating. (To avoid circumlocution I shall subsume Wales with England, like Judge in his chapter, and hope not to be misunderstood.) Unlike those in England, Scottish secondary teachers, no matter how scarce are teachers in the subject they profess, must *all* be professionally trained, and only university graduates are eligible (other than those professing practical or aesthetic subjects). Two probationary years, not just one, follow the training period, which for college-trained primary teachers was a year longer in Scotland than in England for many years — though England is now leading the British move toward an all-graduate profession.

More fundamentally, the whole registration procedure in Scotland is conducted and monitored by a General Teaching Council, which was established in 1965 to allow practising teachers — who constitute a majority of this body — to control access to the profession, to take disciplinary action where necessary, and to make recommendations to the government on supply and training. With regard to teacher education, the relative standing of the colleges of education *vis-à-vis* the universities is also different in the two countries. In England, the prestigious work of training graduates for secondary education is carried out by the university institutes and schools of education; this reinforces the dualistic approach to training. In Scotland, by contrast, (with the unique exception of Stirling) the universities cannot certify teachers, and the fact that teachers may be trained for primary, secondary and further education by the same lecturers at the same college perhaps assists the cause of professional unity among teachers and their educators.

If comparison of professional autonomy and standards of entry and training favours Scotland, it is perhaps surprising to find that Scottish teachers have also pursued trade unionist tactics more successfully. Since the early 1960s, industrial action has been employed frequently, both to improve pay and to protect conditions of service; while this new-found militancy may seem mild when judged by international standards (by comparison with the activities of Australian teachers, for example) it was unprecedented in the history of British teacher politics. English teachers have no counterpart to the Scots' contract of service which, among other safeguards, specifies maximum class sizes at all levels. This was campaigned for in the early 1970s, when teacher shortage allowed employers to allocate teachers to classes of 40 or 50 pupils; it will also be a useful protection for jobs in time of surplus when compulsory redundancies are threatened. English teachers have been ambivalent about the notion of a contract and their current efforts to secure one seem unlikely to meet immediate success. They are, of course, handicapped by the fragmentation and diversity caused by competing unions. The largest single union in England claims only just over half the total number of teachers as its members, whereas in Scotland the corresponding figure is over 85 per cent. Whatever the reason, the teaching profession in Scotland has displayed an 'aggressive striving for professionalism' (to use the terms which Kemble applies to the American scene) through the trade union route with greater success. Perhaps the greater proportion of male teachers in Scotland, in primary as well as secondary schools, has contributed to stronger trade union consciousness?

It has been argued on other grounds that it is undesirable for teaching to become exclusively women's work. Writing in the *YBE 1963*, Langeveld put this idea in words which would today run the risk of being accused of sexism: 'no country should pride itself on its educational system if the teaching profession has become predominantly a world of women'. Whether or not a statistical preponderance of women is always or inevitably associated with a lack of professionalism and career-mindedness must be doubted. Even if there once was a connection, it may be weakening as the role of women in the workforce and in daily life is unquestionably changing.

In any event, the question is not what the sex ratio should be in the profession, but what should be the attitude of its members. From nursery teachers to university professors, the profession can and should include both male and female, united in a desire for self-improvement, both at a personal and at a professional level. Important as it is to recruit suitable people, it is even more essential to encourage professional attitudes through appropriate training and induction, and maintain them through continuing professional education. Personal growth and professional development should not be set in opposition but combined. Only by improving the status and practice of the profession can we expect to increase its attractiveness to future generations. To end with a final quotation from the *YBE 1963*:

> There is therefore no more important matter than that of securing a sufficient supply of the right kind of people to the profession, providing them with the best possible training and ensuring to them a status and esteem commensurate with the importance and responsibility of their work.

It is to these important problems that the 26 *WYBE 1980* contributors have addressed themselves in the pages that follow.

Jacquetta Megarry
WYBE Series Editor
Glasgow, January 1980

Part 1: Basic Issues

1. The ecology of professional development

Bruce Joyce

Summary: This chapter is based on the assumption that a comprehensive programme of professional development should fulfil three functions: the provision of an adequate system of in-service training for teachers; the provision of support to schools which will enable them to improve their programmes; and the creation of contexts in which teachers are enabled to develop their potential. The barriers to an effective programme of professional development are considered, including those arising in relation to resources, structures, the nature of schools as social systems, and the work situation of teachers. A need for a comprehensive model of professional development is urged, and as a contribution to this the chapter offers three partial models. One deals with methods of in-service training, a second explores patterns of governance involving grass-roots democracy which equalizes professionals and community members, and a third examines the potentiality of programmes of professional development and school renewal as a continuous process. These partial models are illustrated by reference to various research and development programmes. The chapter ends with a set of propositions for improving professional development.

The purpose of this chapter is to consider the movement toward professional development, which however sporadic, confused and complicated by political considerations, is, I believe, now emerging. Specifically, I shall discuss its aims and the effectiveness of existing efforts to initiate the changes in the naturally occurring patterns or social 'ecology' of schooling necessary for progress. Useful models of the likely results of suggested action will also be considered.

The political issues are by no means resolved. Much conflict still exists, and the lack, until very recently, of any quantity of relevant good general literature has hindered the construction of a conceptual framework for further advance. For example, professional development literature from 1957-77 included only half a dozen items suitable for this purpose. This scarcity reflects the fact that there exists at present no agreed procedure for examining professional development and its problems. In this chapter, I wish to present a structure for this study from the point of view of its social ecology.

The substance of this paper is derived from an examination of a series of investigations into professional development and related fields which have been conducted in recent years. These are:

1 . A nation-wide survey of pre-service teacher education (Joyce, Howey and Yarger, 1977a, 1977b).
2 . A study of in-service teacher education in which the literature referred to

above was reviewed exhaustively, interviews were conducted with more than 1500 persons concerned with professional development and 30 position papers were commissioned and analysed (Joyce, Howey and Yarger, 1976).

3. A study of the National Urban/Rural School Development Programme which capitalized on the energy of school community councils to generate plans and professional development activities to accompany them (Joyce, 1978a).

4 . An extensive series of studies of teachers' thinking in classrooms (Joyce, 1978b).

5 . A series of surveys of in-service teacher education practices in several states (Yarger, Howey and Joyce, 1980).

6 . Case studies of a set of professional development projects (Joyce *et al*, 1979a).

7 . A study of initiatives in professional development at the federal and state levels and the impact of those initiatives in several local school sites in California (Joyce *et al*, 1979b).

8 . Investigations into the relationship between teachers' psychological states and their use of professional development activities (McKibbin and Joyce, 1980).

9 . The literature on pre-service and in-service training research (Joyce and Showers, 1980).

10. The literature on organizational and curricular change in education (Joyce, 1980).

The list by itself indicates the complexity of professional development. From some vantages, the issues in professional development are questions of training and how to generate and implement effective training. (What conditions are necessary for professional learning?) From another perspective its major issues are ones of governance. (Who should be involved and how should they be involved?) From a third perspective it is a matter of implementing plans for school improvement whether generated within or outside the school district or individual school site.

In this chapter, these sources have been blended with clinical experience in an attempt to develop a structure for examining professional development and to describe and evaluate models for generating comprehensive programmes.

The three purposes of professional development

Professional development must fulfil three needs, which, in spite of apparent diversity, have much in common: the social need for an efficient and humane educational system capable of adaptation to evolving social needs; the need to find ways of helping educational staff to improve the wider personal, social and academic potential of the young people in the neighbourhood; and the need to develop and encourage the teacher's desire to live a satisfying and stimulating personal life, which by example as well as by precept will help his students to develop the desire and confidence to fulfil each his own potential. The first need concerns the society in which the teacher is functioning. The second, the spirit and morale of the school in which the teacher is employed. The third, and perhaps most important, concerns the calibre of the teachers selected for training and employment.

Planning professional development programmes raises serious questions about the quality of life not only within schools but throughout society. Education is a massive social institution. In economic terms it consumes about 8 per cent of the resources generated by the United States each year. Over two and a quarter million persons hold professional positions in public education. Nearly 18,000 boards of education are elected or appointed, and most home owners vote regularly for or against taxation to provide resources for the schools of their communities. This mammoth institution has responsibility for from 12 to 15 years of the lives of each human being in the society. The quality of life of childhood and adolescence — nearly a quarter of the life span of each individual — is directly influenced by the quality of our schools. Moreover, what happens to people during those years greatly affects the quality of the rest of their lives.

The relationship between school and society transforms the problems of schooling into those of society. Hence, behind the issues about the success or failure of professional development programmes are the questions, 'Do we care enough about society to invest sufficient resources and imagination in the improvement of schools?' 'Do we care enough about each one of our schools to see that they have the resources to increase the dynamism, creativity, and skill of the people who work with children?' Finally, 'Do we care enough about teachers to provide the means that they can use to stay vital and to reach out for continuous growth?'

The teacher at the centre

Whether we approach professional development from the orientation of society, school or individual, the focus of activity is on the lives of teachers. Most beginning teachers are woefully unprepared for the complex and demanding tasks of the classroom. Pre-service teacher education is pathetically weak and beginning teachers must learn on the job, helping one another as best they can. Professions based on the 'hard sciences' provide a very different setting for entry to practice. For example, the physician is backed by a complex science, traditions of considerable professional authority, powerful treatment institutions, and personal wealth. Also the mission of medicine is quite clear. Unlike the physician, the teacher receives a very small amount of initial training, is thrust into a complex job with little formal help available, has little prestige but much criticism, and can turn to no powerful institutions or highly trained specialists to help solve the daily problems of relating to students. Teachers are scrutinized continuously, pressed toward 'accountability', and find their innovations greeted with suspicion by many community members. The aims of education are debated widely. The teacher is admonished to 'be humane and personal, but teach the basic skills', and to 'treat everyone as an individual, but make sure everyone receives the standard imprint of education'.

Changes in all these contexts will be complex and, to be successful, will involve the reorganization not only of the formal training process, but also of employment conditions; constant monitoring of performance of both teachers and taught; ready access to further information concerning new developments in teaching aids and training in their use; greater involvement in the community surrounding the school. At present, professional development is supposed to be initiated by legislation and executive action; these initiatives frequently have little impact in practice. This discrepancy needs to be understood and analysed. Thus, the establishment of effective professional development demands the creation of a very different kind of social system.

The reality of size

Although there is currently great dissatisfaction about the present structure of in-service teacher education, there does exist a large and complex organization of resources which has attempted to deliver services to education professionals (Joyce *et al*, 1976). Partly because incentives are provided by certification requirements, salary increments, and opportunities for professional advancement, a large proportion of teachers and school administrators have attended universities and received considerable education beyond the bachelor's degree; many have received masters or doctorates. (In a recent case study of one school in California it was discovered that the entire staff had at least 75 credits beyond the bachelor's degree.) Many of the more than 1400 institutions which offer pre-service teacher preparation also offer courses which are taken by in-service personnel and there are presently more than 45,000 education professors who do or potentially could render such service. About an equal number of supervisors and curriculum consultants are employed by public school districts, part of whose function is also to render service. Combined, there are close to 100,000 professors and curriculum consultants and about two million classroom teachers, or, approximately one professor and consultant for every 20 teachers. To be sure, the professor/consultant group does not work full-time to provide services, but nonetheless there is a large array of persons who bear a service relationship to education personnel. As we shall see later, there is considerable dissatisfaction with the services presently being rendered by both university and school personnel, but the number of personnel and the *potential* service they render cannot be denied.

In addition there are about 100,000 principals and vice-principals employed in the 17,000 school districts in the nation, which is one for about every 20 classroom teachers. From the point of view of many in-service experts, one of the major tasks of administrators is to assist teachers to grow in professional competence or to help teachers organize staff development programmes tailored to their needs. While in-service education has not been a major assignment of many administrators, if they only spent 10 per cent of their time in professional development related activities, the total effort would be enormous.

Finally, we must consider the nearly 50,000 non-supervisory instructional personnel, such as reading instructors, media and communication experts, mental health specialists and department chairmen who are also expected to act at least in part as support personnel for teachers. Thus, aside from classroom teachers themselves there may be as many as a quarter of a million persons who engage at least part-time as instructors in some form of in-service education activity. Potentially this is at least one person for every eight teachers. In addition, teachers can provide services to one another and to administrators; although there are no hard figures on this subject, it is probably that as many as 25,000 teachers each year serve their fellow teachers and others through service given in courses, workshops, and informal activities.

The formulation of models to improve the in-service arena is further complicated by the problems of language. Joyce, Howey and Yarger (1976) comment that 'the formulation of definitions in ISTE is especially difficult, as is revealed by the many languages used in the position papers and interviews. Terminology ran riot. With the exception that nearly everyone spoke negatively about ISTE there was relatively little agreement about definitions or how it should be carried on.'

Thus, speaking only of resources provided through universities and school districts, the area of professional development is considerable but is marred by widespread dissatisfactioin with the traditional channels of service and a considerable lack of agreement about terminology and problems.

In addition to the investment which has been made in universities and school districts, in recent years a large number of initiatives have been made by federal and state governments to make energy available to improve staff development activities. A recent study by Joyce *et al* (1979b) has mapped these for the state of California to develop a picture of initiatives in that state and to identify how they affect local school sites, using case studies and professional development profiles.

1. *Agency-building and strengthening efforts.* For example, both state and federal funds are used to create new agencies called 'teacher centres'. Legislation such as the School Improvement Programme is designed to *strengthen* the ability of schools to improve educational programmes, partly through in-service activities.

2. *Programmatic efforts in specific curriculum areas.* State and/or federal funds are authorized to bring attention to specific curriculum areas. Examples include initiatives from the Women's Equity Act at the federal level. Under this act, programmes are designed to increase consideration of creating sex-fair curricula whereby neither women nor men are advantaged or disadvantaged by what is taught, how it is taught, or in access to any kind of general or vocational training. Another example is in mathematics education where authorizations at the federal level have provided funds to develop procedures for increasing teachers' and hence students' understanding of the metric system and ability to use metric measurement.

3. *Programmes with a proportion of their funds allocated to professional development.* The third category consists of authorization to spend to provide certain kinds of educational services to children with the provision that a proportion of the authorized funds be used to educate teachers in the area of concern. The exact proportion may or may not be stated in the legislation. Wide latitude is generally left to state and local administrators. We refer to these as *proportional* programmes simply because a portion of the authorized monies is for professional development. Special education, bilingual education and the Regional Occupational Programme are examples.

The initiatives vary in emphasis, the amount of funding allocated, the proportions which were to be given to professional development, the means of funding (whether funds were to be provided to counties, districts, or through competitive proposals), and the kinds of services which were expected to be delivered. Several of the proportional programmes (special education, vocational education, bilingual education and the Regional Occupation Programme) have large funding levels, substantial proportions of which are theoretically for professional development. (*See also Chapter 8.*) In each case it is generally agreed that, in practice, lesser proportions are devoted to professional development. The potential, however, is great.

Additionally, it is worth noting that nearly all the efforts have a relatively small funding base and are organized at state level. Thus, relatively small agencies are attempting to provide services to an enormous number (about 170,000) of teachers working in a very large number of schools.

It is also interesting to note that nearly all of the programmes have relatively low funding levels per teacher. That is, if the efforts are distributed widely, they can buy very few services for any individual person. If we accumulate all the agency-building authorizations (aside from the School Improvement Programme) and assume that maximum funds were devoted to professional development, the amount would only be about $25 per teacher per annum.

The initiatives received considerable publicity at the national level. Compared with the considerable investment in the traditional channels (the university and the curriculum consultant corps) they are relatively small, yet they are also extremely important because they represent attempts to generate innovative structures, because they are accompanied by evaluation and because many of them represent models for change which are currently being tested in practice.

The practitioner's view of in-service teacher education

In an extensive survey of community members, higher education personnel and teachers in California, Michigan and Georgia, Joyce, Howey and Yarger (1976) attempted to synthesize the views of these groups about the present state of in-service education and its problems. Interestingly enough, the three role groups had similar perceptions both of the state of in-service education and its problems, although teachers and higher education personnel in particular generally believe that they have different perceptions.

All three role groups are generally agreed that there is at present a low level of in-service teacher education. Teachers report that they received very little help when they were beginning to teach and are presently receiving very little. Teachers' usage of higher education institutions appears to be decreasing sharply and presently does not touch the lives of many teachers at all. (In California, for example, nearly a third of the teachers have not been to a higher education institution for any kind of in-service education during the past three years.) There were very few differences between the three states; the reported level of in-service education of all kinds was very similar across all three states, with very few differences between urban and rural areas, or between rich and poor school districts; nor did the age or experience of the teachers appear to make any real difference.

Teachers on the whole do not visit one another and observe each other while teaching and very few teachers receive much feedback about their performance. In addition, few teachers receive help from the strongest training options, that is from researched and developed instructional systems. What little analysis of teaching there is, is concentrated in relatively few places. Teachers believe that the major help they received, when they began to teach and were oriented to their present roles, and later in helping them to maintain and improve their present skills, was delivered by other teachers. This is especially interesting, since nearly all of the present formal investment in in-service education is in higher education institutions and the supervisory corps of school districts. If teachers are, in fact, receiving their major help from other teachers, then the chief formal systems of in-service education are not seen to be providing, at least by the teachers, as much service as the informal system of teachers working in the same context. In other words, it appears clear that the present investment of school district and higher education resources is not nearly as effective as the informal system which operates automatically within any given situation. However, teachers do not appear to be receiving much service from one another; in many situations the informal system does not seem to be particularly effective either, especially since very few teachers see each other teach.

One difference between higher education faculties and teachers is that faculty members believe that they are much more competent to help teachers than the teachers believe. Professors have had much more experience in the public schools than teachers think. (Their actual experience averages about ten years, whereas teachers believe that they have had little or none.)

About three quarters of the respondents from all three states believe that in-service teacher education is in relatively poor health. Nearly half of the teachers in all three states have been in the same school building for ten years or more, which makes it all the more curious that the informal system is relatively ineffective.

It appears quite clear that vast investment in university and consultative services is not paying off, at least in the perceptions of the clients of those services, and that the informal system is more effective. However, the informal system itself does not appear to be providing adequate service, at least in the opinion of most clients. Furthermore, teachers, administrators, consultants, and higher education personnel are apparently relatively inexperienced in the use of most of the well-researched approaches to in-service education that have been developed during the last few years (eg the use of microteaching, structured feedback, simulation, and clinical supervision).

A closer look at the ecology of some schools

Under the auspices of the California State Department of Education, case studies have been conducted of a number of schools, districts, and county offices in an attempt to understand better the dynamics of the county and district organizations responsible for professional development services, and the kinds of services which are actually delivered to individual schools. In addition, the 'professional ecology' of those schools was studied and an attempt made to understand the kinds of activities which teachers engage in to increase their professional competence, knowledge of subject matter, and personal development.

The study (Joyce, 1978a) clearly shows that staff development is a complex area and that initiatives to improve it enter a field of forces which is not easily understood but which has to be taken into account in planning, providing for, and evaluating efforts. In a simpler world, planning of in-service education could be approached in logical sequence. First, initiatives which authorize the expenditure of funds for certain kinds of activities would be identified. Second, documentation could indicate the magnitude and probably quality of those activities. Third, an assessment could be made of the effects of the activities on teacher behaviour. Finally, a direct effort could be made to determine whether those changes in teacher behaviour were associated with improved pupil achievement of various kinds.

Unfortunately, the situation in the real world of professional development does not permit such programme planning and implementation. The study revealed an elaborate set of largely separate initiatives which connect variously with counties and local schools and make uneven connections with districts and the lives of teachers. Professional development turns out to be a maze whose paths need to be charted with care.

The major lessons from the study deal with the ecology of professional development, and are summarized below.

There is at present no smoothly operating professional development organization. As a result, many teachers are engaged in almost no formal or informal professional development activities. This statement should not be taken to mean that there are no school districts which have good professional development programmes. Clearly, there are some schools with excellent programmes and some district organizations which are very effective. However, there is no general system which pervades the profession in an organized way so that giving and receiving service is habitual and affects most if not all personnel. Because there is no 'professional development organization' as such, in-service activities are generally planned on an *ad hoc* basis. Teachers are rarely visited by administrators, consultants or other teachers who work near them and could help them in their teaching. There are many barriers between professional development centres at any level (the state, universities and colleges, counties, and districts) and local teacher centres and the lives of teachers. Thus, initiatives to improve staff development do not fall on fertile ground. All over the United States we are at the very beginning of efforts to plan and institutionalize a permanent professional development organization which is realistically based on an understanding of the lives of teachers and a clear understanding of the skills teachers need in order to do their jobs more effectively. Until recently, job-embedded professional development has simply not been a high priority and the results can be seen in the relatively small amount of encouragement teachers receive to improve their competence. In addition, relatively little information is available about the capability of states, counties, districts, and local centres to deliver services to teachers.

Given the efficient organization of professional development, the progress of a new initiative (say to increase the capability of teachers to operate more effectively within a given curriculum area) could be traced relatively easily. It would be simple to find out what kinds of activities resulted from the initiative, how they affected teacher behaviour, and whether student achievement was improved in the area concerned. However, in reality the situation is much more complex.

The matter is further complicated in that the formal and informal systems of the school and the sets of activities that constitute professional development opportunities within schools are interdependent: each part affects all the other parts. Changes in one aspect, depending on how they interact within the totality of the system, can be magnified or diminished tremendously. Fortuitous events such as changes in one or two staff members, morale, and a single administrator, all substantially affect the other dimensions of the system of delivery. Unplanned as well as planned events can have profound effects. Although in most schools levels of professional development are relatively low, in some there is a very high level of professional development, which appears to result from a complex of seemingly chance occurrences that interact with each other and with the social system of the school to improve greatly the employment of resources in those schools, compared with others in the area. Professional development is composed of patterns of behaviour operating within a system. It is the patterns of learning and/or opportunities to learn that are present in the lives of teachers and other educational personnel.

These patterns take shape partly as a result of the formal organizational properties of the school and partly as a result of the informal properties of its social organization. Thus, without a considerable increase in knowledge about the nature of the lives of teachers, about the conditions that provide them with opportunities to learn and how those conditions can be changed, it will be virtually impossible to generate valid models of in-service activities and initiatives. Hence to understand professional development requires also an understanding of both the formal and informal organization of the schools within which teachers work, and the interaction between the organizational systems of those schools and the external forces which impinge upon them.

Not only has the study of in-service education been relatively neglected as a part of life in schools: there are very few local instances where formative evaluation of professional development has been firmly established. Studies of professional development for the most part pose questions which are not usually raised in any systematic way within school organizations. It will not be possible to mount systematic studies of the area unless most of the documentation activities are carried out at the local level. Intensive, formative and summative evaluation efforts will require a considerable change in the habits of local personnel to increase their willingness to document and to develop effective local evaluation systems.

To map initiatives at all levels, whether federal, state, county-wide, district-wide, or at the local school level is very difficult because of the varieties of *ad hoc* structures and idiosyncratic social organizations. Even to ascertain funds spent, activities carried out, and portions of personnel actually assigned to professional development, requires extensive and specific studies. Individual sites can only be understood through in-depth analysis of their patterns of organization, social environments, and the kinds of professional development activities which usually take place.

Most of the heavily researched methods for training teachers are rarely employed and in fact are unknown to most of the personnel who might be using them, whether teachers, administrators, supervisors, county officials, or teacher centre personnel. Consequently most of the people responsible for professional development are unaware of many of the technological improvements of the field, inexperienced in using them, and untrained in applying them to professional development. The design study confirmed the results of recent surveys in this respect.

The lives of teachers: varieties

Studies of the lives of teachers reveal that small differences in the work situations and lives of each teacher may have a large effect on the in-service activities the teachers and other professionals engage in. Teachers are candid about this and are exceedingly good informants about the details of their professional work and the kinds of opportunities for learning that are available to them. Teachers differ considerably from one another, in their perceptions of the demands of their job, their relationships to the context of the schools in which they work, and the effects on them of the activities in which they engage.

The organizational patterns of the state departments of education, counties, districts and individual schools are such that many elements within each of these organizations exist in considerable isolation from one another. Administrators and supervisors are isolated from one another within the same organizational unit. Teachers can be extremely isolated from each other and from service agencies, even when such agencies are located close to them.

Problems of co-ordination are not simply ones of developing the administrative ability to co-ordinate initiatives. The solution to these problems may indicate basic structural change in units.

The treatment of beginning teachers is illustrative. We discovered that it is possible for a newly employed teacher to receive no help at all from any kind of initiative and little through the informal system of the school, although he or she is working in a matrix in which there are other teachers, department chairmen, principals, supervisors, county officials, professional development centres, and universities, all fuelled by various initiatives at the federal, state, county, and local levels.

People working in professional development functions are isolated from one another organizationally and programmatically. Although there are many organizational elements which deal with professional development at the district, county and state levels, there is little co-ordination. At each level, professional development co-ordinators find that their functions are defined so narrowly that they do not include the chief elements (eg curriculum change and its agents) which are operating in professional development.

Many of the resources which are ostensibly authorized for professional development under proportional allocations are not actually used to generate professional development activities. Counties and districts work under difficult budgetary constraints. Because county budgets are not implicitly structured to provide for professional development categories as such, authorizations have to be received from a variety of other budget lines. Thus, each authorization results in a separate programmatic budget and concomitant organizational structure dealing with that authorization. This also exacerbates the isolation of organizational elements from one another.

There are important differences in the types of in-service education which occur at elementary and secondary levels and in urban and rural organizations. The magnitude of resources needed to effect change, the kinds of organizations which are likely to be effective, and the essential nature of co-ordination among agencies, are likely to vary by setting and may be by no means a linear function of size. Thus it is probable that initiatives which fail to recognize differences in level and population concentration will not be uniformly effective. A clear understanding of the effects of setting should be very useful at both policy and operational levels.

When we consider the school as an 'internal system' of people, practices, and organizational structures we find that it interacts with and is strongly affected by what we can term its 'external systems' (the community, the organizational structure of the school district, and the interfaces between the school and initiatives which can provide resources for its improvement). The external system is so powerful that small variations in it can have a considerable impact. For example, in one school a single board of education member (as it happens a principal of a nearby school) was generating opposition to what others regarded as one of the most positive and powerful factors in that school, both for the improvement of the staff and the educational programme for the children. A single change in board membership would greatly affect the social context of that school. Many important aspects of schools cannot be understood without consideration of the relevant external systems.

The principal continues to be a powerful force in energizing programmes, even when playing a non-directive role. His personal style, level of activity, competence, and relationships with faculty and community, all interact with his ideas for improving the school, to make him a powerful determinant of what will happen as a result of any initiative. Potentially the principal is an organizer of professional development, a facilitator to the faculty, and a negotiator of resources for the school. His skill in performing these functions will have much to do with the fate of any given initiative in his school.

The experience of special programmes which have involved parents and other community members in productive roles has been one of increased productivity in professional development. But in most schools there is an extremely low level of parental involvement in professional development activities. Lack of experience in organizing the involvement of parents and community members must be taken into account in the implementation of many initiatives, some of mandated community involvement.

As indicated earlier, meagre use is made of the best-researched staff training methods. Even tools being used to carry out assessments of needs and to translate them are often simplistic and out-of-date, eg questionnaires are being used to identify needs, where the development of problem-solving approaches would be more appropriate. Organizations at all levels appear to be a long way from the development of well-established problem-solving groups who can address fundamental curriculum issues and develop powerful local professional development programmes. Because of insufficient vigorous professional activity, various commercial interests are moving into the territory, such as makers of educational products, and developers and purveyors of specific approaches to teaching. They are offering to fill a void which could be filled by universities, county organizations, and professional centres.

Most initiatives at present simply fail to develop. The first question we have to face is how to create an environment which will be more congenial to efforts to put energy into the system. To do so, the social environment of education, as well as the structural properties of professional development efforts, need to be better understood.

Teaching as a normative, bureaucratic activity

The nature of teaching is important to in-service education for two reasons. One is that teaching should be improved by investments in professional development. All parties concerned agree on this. It is surprising, therefore, that there is so little discussion of the nature of teaching in connection with the discussions about in-service education itself. There is concern about governance and relevance and increasing the proportion of teacher education which goes on in schools themselves, but there is remarkably little discussion about the nature of the act which everyone is intent on improving.

I attribute the nature of teaching to the nature of its institutional life. We have to ask what can be done to those institutions to enable people to become the creative decision-makers which education in the best sense would seem to require. Let us reflect on the kind of life that is lived in most schools. The teacher in the self-contained classroom has a mind-boggling job. For 30 hours a week he has to tend to the academic, emotional and social well-being of 25 to 35 children, attempting to teach an impossible variety of subjects with very little assistance or support. The teacher in a departmentalized organization is no better off. He works in time-modules of 40 to 50 minutes which inhibit many kinds of instruction. He faces one group of children after another and generally works alone. If he were an average English teacher and he chose to ask children to write a theme, paper, or short story a week, he would be grading more than four to five thousand themes each year! Studies of teaching indicate that the average teacher is responding to as many as 500 verbal stimuli an hour (and countless more non-verbal stimuli).

In the previous section I may have given the impression that teaching styles are immutable. This is not the case at all. A vast variety of investigations have demonstrated again and again that teachers can respond to training very quickly, whether it be feedback or direct instruction in skills and strategies, and that they can very quickly reach proficiency in a wide variety of educational alternatives.

In our own work, we have found no relationship between natural teaching styles and the acquisition of particular models of teaching. That is, teachers who seem to be more non-directive do not appear to pick up on non-directive models any more rapidly than teachers who are relatively directive. Further, teachers appear to be able to acquire a repertoire of skills relatively easily. They can learn to implement a dizzying variety of curricula when given the opportunity, and also to make radical changes in school organization. Where there has been a concerted effort, change has taken place with great rapidity. It often disappears, being swallowed up by the great normative structure of the business. But that should not dismay us. The fact is that teachers can very rapidly create new educational forms.

One of the problems in the assessment of training has been the belief that training, in order to be judged effective, has to control the teaching style of a person. When we teach someone a Rogerian model of teaching, an observer watching that person teach afterwards often remarks, 'I was in his/her classroom the other day and he/she was doing something else. Your training was ineffective.' But of course he was doing something else. We did not intend to make him solely Rogerian, unable to do anything else in his teaching.

A serious error in many conceptions of training is that teaching style is viewed as a dependent variable of training. It appears to be much more sensible to aim at increasing the repertoire, thus enhancing the ability to choose alternative models of education and to act on them, to develop better content and to expose children to it. It should be the goal of training to create an available reservoir of alternatives, rather than the monolithic implementation of one teaching method.

We have available to us a variety of modes for helping teachers to change themselves. Where direct and clear training has been provided, where teachers have had the opportunity to generate their own ways of helping one another, the results have been consistently impressive, whether the focus has been feedback, skill and strategy training, curriculum implementation, or staff reorganization.

If teachers can learn so rapidly, then what is the problem? For the answer we have to refer to previous sections. The nature of schools makes most of the current objectives of teacher education and re-education simply irrelevant.

The amazing thing is that teachers can respond to all sorts of training and become more powerful almost immediately. The problem is that the present types of in-service education rarely offer teachers the opportunity to receive feedback, skill training, training in teaching strategies, or curriculum training, in ways that are closely enough allied to their functions to permit these to be powerfully effective.

The structural problems of professional development

When we say that ISTE has structural problems, we mean that its structure is formed by several dimensions which interact with one another, and that the effectiveness of the enterprise depends on the productive interaction of the dimensions. Weakness in one dimension is magnified because it undermines the power of the other dimensions, but improvement of one dimension alone will not appreciably improve ISTE — the dimensions must be effectively meshed. Several dimensions of ISTE are seriously flawed at present, and the relationship between the dimensions is far from optimal. The general structural problem overshadows specific problems, making narrow remedies of doubtful value. The following quotation from *Issues to Face* summarizes one attempt to define the dimensions of professional development.

> It appears at present that there are four major dimensions that take the form of systems that link together to form the operating structure which is ISTE. The four systems are:
>   1. The Governance System
>   2. The Substantive System
>   3. The Delivery System
>   4. The Modal System
> The governance system is composed of the decision-making structures which legitimize activities and govern them. The substantive system is composed of the content and process of ISTE and deals with what is learned and how it is learned. The delivery system is made up of incentives, interfaces between trainees, trainers, training, and staff. It deals with motivation, access, and relevance to the role of the individual professional. The modal system consists of the forms of ISTE, ranging from sabbaticals abroad to intensive on-site institutes. These modes are the envelopes in which ISTE is delivered. The figure below depicts the four interlocking systems of ISTE.

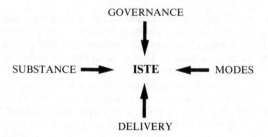

Figure 1 *The systems of ISTE*

Decisions (governance) result in substance (and process), modes (selected from varieties), and delivery (incentives, interfaces, staff). Thus, a school faculty, authorized by a grant from a district, may decide (governance) to develop a workshop (mode) in which mathematics is explored with a hands-on approach (substance and process) during released time, on the premises, with the teachers themselves as staff (delivery).

It is this complex structure of interlocking systems which needs to be studied and improved. Many present proposals to study ISTE are fragmentary, in the sense that they emphasize only one aspect of ISTE. If ISTE is to be improved, it must be studied as a system composed of at least four sub-systems. For example, cost and finance is only one facet of governance, and any facts about costs are relatively uninformative unless examined in the context of other facets of governance, and substance modes, and delivery. Incentives are an important aspect of delivery, but study of incentives alone will tell us little. We must ask incentives for what, how, and under what governance system. Thus, any study aimed at changing ISTE requires exploration of the whole structure of ISTE, not merely of its parts.

To treat the problems of in-service education as structural is to suggest that what is needed is not a pasting-up of the old machine, but a building of a new one. There is something wrong with too many of the major dimensions of in-service education as it is presently being practised, and partial or small solutions will probably have very little effect in the long run. The teacher centre movement for example, is a very important one and teacher centres in some cases represent something close to new structural innovations in in-service education. The vast majority of them, however, are likely to be costly relative to their effects and many of them will probably cease to exist once short term infusions of funds and staff are withdrawn unless the efforts to institutionalize them are based on a knowledge of the structure and take into account the structural problems. (Joyce *et al*, 1976)

In summary, we need better substance for in-service education, a more appropriate use of correct modes, and more effective types of delivery, all under more integrative governance systems which permit teachers and others to have a powerful influence on the kinds of things that are done. The present structure separates teachers and trainers, alienates them from one another, reduces the effectiveness with which they can work with one another, and treats in-service education as something apart from the every-day process of teaching and living. Teacher education has to become relevant to the roles which teachers actually play. University professors, curriculum consultants, community members and teachers need to work together in schools to create more vital, flowing and divergent teacher training programmes.

What are our alternatives?

Quite clearly, we need to develop more collaborative governing structures for in-service education and to develop the notion that in-service education is a support system for teachers. We need to face the problems of reconciling the individual's need for training on his own terms and the needs of the system through which he works for the education of children.

Fundamentally, we need to recognize that life in schools is real life. Teachers working in the kind of structures in which they live with the kind of alienated support services which they have, become increasingly alienated and frustrated.

We need to develop a different kind of technology of design that will enable teachers to stretch out as they need to and to become more comfortable with the kinds of problems that they have to deal with. Most important, we need to restructure the school so that it becomes a place where everyone, teachers and students alike, can grow more effectively.

Construction of models of in-service education

At least in the near future, it is unlikely that a model can be designed for any school which is both comprehensive and specific enough to be useful. Such a model, if it emerges, will demonstrate that present patterns are culturally determined and are organically related to our political and economic, as well as educational, institutions. In this sense, a comprehensive model will be akin to a model for changing the political or economic system. The difficulties inherent in generating social change models are enormous. This can be seen clearly in the area of economics. Models for changing the patterns of behaviour attendant on an economic indicator such as inflation are very difficult to manipulate and certainly not yet perfected. However, by recognizing the multi-dimensional character of professional development, we can ensure that the degree of comprehensiveness of models is ascertained and that we can use those which may apply to one dimension alone rather than attempt to rebuild the entire system.

We need to consider very carefully the ground on which comprehensive models can be built, however. In the next pages two sources are described, which together can be seen to generate partial models which have a grounding in the study of innovative practice. The first is from the study of training research, the second from the study of the Urban/Rural School Development Programme. A third source, from the study of Teacher Corps, is described by Smith in Chapter 15.

Training ourselves to teach: the messages of research

From the analysis of research on training we can build and test training modes and in-service programmes. Although a very powerful training model can now be built, it is quite clear that it does not demonstrate all the problems that beset in-service education. Let us examine first a governance-oriented approach.

Over the last 20 years a number of relatively efficient teacher training methods have been developed and researched, although none of them is in general use today. These methods represent the current 'best practice' in self-instructional and 'taught' pre-service and in-service techniques. Research on them contributes to our present fund of knowledge about ways to improve teaching through direct training. The analysis is based on more than 200 studies in which researchers investigated the effectiveness of various kinds of training methods, from which were developed working hypotheses which we can use to design school improvement programmes which incorporate training. This material is based on a report by Joyce and Showers (1980).

Two purposes of training:'tuning' our present styles and mastering new strategies

Improving our teaching can be based on 'tuning' our present skills — learning to do better what we do already — or on learning new ways of teaching. When tuning our skills, we try to become more affirmative, involve students more, manage logistics more efficiently, ask more penetrating questions, induce students to be more productive, increase the clarity and vividness of our lectures and illustrations, understand better the subject matter we teach — in short we work on our craft. Training oriented toward fine-tuning consolidates our competence and is likely to increase our effectiveness and attractiveness.

To master new teaching strategies or models, or to substitute one curriculum for another, is quite a different operation. To develop a new approach we need to explore and understand its rationale, develop the ability to carry out new teaching strategies, and master fresh content.

Generally speaking, it is easier to 'fine-tune' our existing approaches than it is to design and implement new ones. This is simply because the magnitude of change is greater and more complex when we change our repertoire than when we refine an already mastered teaching strategy. We have to learn to think differently, to behave differently and to help children adapt to and become comfortable with the new approaches. Analysis of the training literature leads to the belief that the mastery of new approaches requires more complex combinations of training elements than does the fine-tuning of our present styles. Both methods require training that relates directly to the clinical acts of teaching. Teaching skills and strategies and curriculum implementation are part of our clinical performance as professionals. Training in those areas is also directly connected to potential effectiveness in the classroom. If the objective of training is achieved, our teaching behaviour is changed in a way which will probably improve it, whether that be the refinement of our style or the mastery of the new approaches.

Whether we teach ourselves or whether we have the help of a training agent, improvement in our skills occurs at several levels: the first is awareness, the second is the acquisition of organized knowledge, the third is the learning of principles and skills, and the fourth is the ability to apply those principles and skills to problem-solving activity.

Components of training

Most of the training literature consists of investigations in which training elements are combined in various ways, whether they are directed toward the fine-tuning of styles or the mastery of new approaches. From our analysis of this quite diverse literature we were able to identify many training components which have been studied in a number of ways. Alone and in combination, each of these training components contributes to the impact of a training sequence or activity. When used together, each has much greater power than when used alone. The major components of training are:

1. presentation of theory
2. modelling or demonstration of skills or models
3. practice in simulated and classroom settings
4. structured feedback
5. open-ended feedback
6. coaching for application.

It appears wisest to include several and perhaps all of the above training components in the development of pre-service and in-service activities. In fine-tuning of style, modelling, and practice under simulated conditions and in the classroom combined with feedback, will probably result in considerable changes. Where using a new approach is the desired outcome, theory, presentations of discussions of theory and coaching for application are probably necessary as well. The theory of a new approach must be well presented and demonstrated; followed by practice in simulated conditions with careful and consistent feedback; then used in the classroom with further coaching and feedback. If all these stages are carried out, it is likely that maximum improvement in staff skills and satisfactions will follow. Omission of any of these training methods will weaken the effect of the whole process, notably on the teacher's own performance. The potency of promotion prospects in the process of improving education will encourage most teachers to co-operate whole-heartedly in such in-service programmes.

The Urban/Rural School Development Programme

The Urban/Rural School Development Programme was a federally-sponsored effort to involve community members and school staff from 25 extremely poor neighbourhoods in equal decision-making; the use of staff development to improve the quality of education in those areas was a crucial feature. In the School-Community Councils, from 1970 to 1977, lay persons and education professionals laboured to analyse local educational needs and find the means to help teachers become more vital forces in the lives of their children.

The social intent of the Programme

The major purpose of the Urban/Rural Programme was to improve the social process of educational decision-making in several ways:

1. By reducing alienation.
2. By increasing efficacy within the social system.
3. By increasing the extent to which teachers and community members relate to one another in the determination of staff development activities.
4. By integrating the reduction in alienation, the increased feelings of efficacy, and an increase in power to produce a greater flow of community energy toward the improvement of education.
5. By making local needs the focus of action.

The Urban/Rural School Development Programme, then, was an experiment in grassroots democracy to establish a condition of parity between education professionals and community members, with the purpose of generating staff development activities through collaborative decision-making and the assessment of local needs.

What were the sites like?

13 sites were urban and 12 were rural. The urban sites were concentrated primarily in the northeastern United States, while the rural sites were more scattered throughout the country. Several sites exhibited characteristics of both urban and rural areas. Seven communities were predominantly Black; four had large populations of peoples with Spanish surnames; six were generally White and rural; two were largely Native American communities; and six included broad mixtures of ethnic groups. Most of the major geographical regions of the country were included, with six sites in the Northeast, seven in the Midwest, five in the Southeast, three in the Southwest, three in the Plains States or Far West, and one in the Commonwealth of Puerto Rico.

In five sites, the Urban/Rural services were concentrated on one single school's staff, community, and student population. The others provided services to a cluster of schools (from two to ten). The schools served approximately 47,000 students altogether. (The student body of the smallest school was about 300 children, the largest nearly 6000.) The Urban/Rural schools were staffed by some 2500 teachers, with a range of 20 to 254 teachers per site. These projects have successfully experimented with a model which depends on joint decision-making by teachers and community members under the guidance of the Board of Education and the local school district officials.

A model for community involvement

At the core of the Urban/Rural concept is a School-Community Council (SCC), consisting of an equal number of education professionals and community members, whose responsibility it is to make decisions about staff development for a particular local school or for a group of schools. Council members are elected by the professional staff of each project school and by members of the community the school serves. The essential concept is one of parity. Structurally, parity means equal representation in decision-making. Procedurally, it means equal input from professionals and community members in the determination of staff development activities to improve school practices. Organizationally, it is embedded in the council.

In 1970 and 1971, SCCs were set up in each of the Urban/Rural sites. Each one elected a council chairperson and hired a team manager (project director) as administrator of the project. In varying degrees, the council and team manager employed staff members who were to be responsible for implementing the programme (such as resident professors, community co-ordinators, and curriculum and training specialists).

THE NEEDS SURVEY. Each council was responsible for conducting a needs survey of the school and the community. This was accomplished in diverse ways — through meetings, questionnaire surveys, studies by outside consultants, and consultations with school administrators. One community employed a network of 300 'outreachers' to ensure broad input through interviews. The needs thus identified were analysed by the SCC to determine the chief areas on which professional development activities would concentrate.

TRANSLATION OF NEEDS INTO PROGRAMME. The councils then endeavoured to translate needs into professional development activities which would further the education of children. Across the country, the needs varied widely, as did their interpretation in programmes. Some schools were grappling with integration problems and concentrated on helping teachers to relate more effectively to children and other community members. Others chose specific problems of the schools. In several cases, communities focused on their heritage and generated programmes to help teachers and other community members to work with students and parents to develop and to interpret the heritage of the community more effectively. Emphasis on cultural pluralism was recognized as a general need even in projects which were not embedded in communities characteristically comprised of racial or ethnic minorities.

IMPLEMENTATION. Each of the projects then dealt with the kinds of workshops, courses, and other experiences considered to be most relevant to the diverse school and community needs. One Urban/Rural project combined with other community agencies to develop a radio station to help unify the community and make all members more aware of their heritage. Some projects concentrated heavily on professional development activities, and as many as 300 workshops and other in-service teacher education experiences have been generated by individual projects. Some projects concentrated on the recruitment, training, and usage of classroom aides. The projects were responsible not only for implementing the programmes in communities but for evaluating the programmes as they progressed. Sometimes the evaluation was accomplished through survey methods (chiefly interviews and questionnaires); at other times it took the form of assessing pupil achievement with respect to the in-service training provided for teachers.

THE LOCAL EDUCATION AGENCY: INDEPENDENCE OF THE COUNCIL. The projects were funded through the local education agencies by the US Office of Education; however, decisions about the expenditure of funds were made by the councils. Thus, the local education agency was able to maintain control over accounting and budgeting procedures, but the SCC was responsible for programmes; the team manager reported directly to the council. In most cases, the team manager and council chairperson worked as peers in the administration of the projects. Since team managers typically were drawn from professional ranks, and council chairpersons from the local community, this arrangement reinforced the parity concept by providing a formalized council leadership structure which reflected and safeguarded the interests and needs of both education professionals and community members. Based on a conviction that schooling can be improved through co-operatively worked professional development programmes, the division of formal leadership affirmed the potential contributions new educational partnerships can make to the in-service teacher education enterprise. While the local education agency was assured of a proper expenditure of funds and reporting, neither school board members nor administrators were in a position to control the decision-making process.

The councils were formed with relative speed. It took much longer, however, for SCCs to develop effective processes. Communities needed to learn how to organize and elect members. Although the education professionals had less difficulty electing their representatives, all council members needed to work together, and it took councils as long as a year or more to achieve process parity. Once parity was achieved, however, councils were able to proceed with an actual equality of decision-making, with comfortable input by professionals and community members, a realistic appraisal of the needs of the community and the school, and the design and implementation of programmes that could serve them best.

How successful were the programmes?

We can draw together a number of generalizations from the Urban/Rural experience:

1. Over the programme as a whole, a relative equality of community and professional input was achieved. Councils took from one to two years to become organized but, once organized, did an effective job of translating local needs. The greater the level of equality achieved, the more active were the teacher education programmes generated.

2. The effect of participation seems to have been to reduce alienation and to increase feelings of efficacy among community members and professionals alike.

3. The more the participants were involved in the planning process, the greater were their feelings of co-operation with other groups and the greater their perception of project impact on their local situation.

4. It appears possible for teachers and community members to assess local needs and take action to satisfy them.

5. Many projects managed to capture and focus the energy of community members and professionals on important problems in their areas. Urban/Rural appeared to fill a void where community members and others were seeking participation and had previously lacked the channels for it. From findings in the comparison sites of Georgia, Michigan, and California, it appears that many

community members throughout the United States would like to participate more in educational decision-making and are willing to put time into that enterprise. The more they desire this, the more favourably they regard attempts to solve the harder problems of creating vital schools and supportive professional development programmes.

6. Urban projects, on the whole, will be more expensive than rural projects and generally will provide less output for the dollar. This differential, we believe, is the price of the complexity of an urban society.

The Urban/Rural Programme was a relatively simple and unambitious attempt to persuade teachers and community members to work more closely together on equal terms in governing their communities. The National Teacher Corps Programme, described by Smith in Chapter 15, was a more comprehensive, larger-scale attempt to make lasting changes in the processes by which school improvement and professional development are not only improved in the short run, but continuously renewed.

Profiting from the past

The multi-dimensional nature of professional development presents serious problems for the generation of models for its organization and improvement. The area is beset by such serious difficuties that mildly revisionary reforms are not likely to make a substantial improvement. We need to provide for the study development of professional skills, continuing systems of school improvement, and opportunities for personal growth and enrichment by the individual practitioner. It is very unlikely that a single form of professional development will achieve all these goals and conditions. Most effective methods for achieving any radically different form will require considerable changes in the institutional framework within which educationalists work. In other words, most of the promising forms of in-service education do not easily fit into the present institutional structure. Thus, comprehensive reform will require major changes in the very nature of the social institution of the school. Furthermore, the multi-dimensional nature of professional development makes it unlikely that models addressed to one aspect alone will have much impact. Good governance models are unlikely to make much difference unless opportunities for training are made more effective. Similarly, first-class training models do not comfortably fit an unfavourable social system within the school or school district. Tested models are rare — systematic and cumulative research is of relatively recent origin. Nonetheless, there are many areas of knowledge and experience which can be built on systematically. The following propositions are based partly on the existing knowledge base and partly on an analysis of the structural problems of the field.

Conclusion: propositions for the improvement of professional development

Here are 11 propositions for the improvement of professional development, drawn from the foregoing analysis.

1. Ultimately the task is to build a continuing in-service system which can serve the regular development of professional competence, the improvement of

schools, and the enrichment of the life of the individual teacher.

2. There are many forms of in-service education which can serve those purposes. These require different conditions for effective delivery. For example, the governance of job-embedded and job-related education is likely to be very different from that of credential-oriented and/or personal development oriented work.

3. Many well-researched and quite powerful training methods are seriously under-used in the present in-service system.

4. Training research, however, lends support to the idea that teachers are capable of acquiring wide repertoires of teaching skills and models, provided that proper conditions are created.

5. The lack of experience of the stronger training options of most education personnel implies that a massive profession-wide retraining would be necessary in order to operate them on any wide scale.

6. However, teachers can be very effective trainers of other teachers, so there is no manpower problem, in the sense that there are plenty of people in the schools who have teaching capability, including the ability to teach other adults.

7. Probably many potentially effective resources are being under or wrongly used at present. For example, university personnel are presently attempting to deliver services directly to teachers that teachers might better deliver themselves. University personnel might be better employed helping people to learn how to train one another rather than trying to provide in-service education which they have no way of following up.

8. The ecologies of schools differ widely and generate very different combinations of options for their staffs. In some situations there is a productive atmosphere which 'pulls' nearly everyone into developmental activities; in others, the converse applies.

9. There are wide differences in the extent to which individuals take advantage of opportunities in their environments. McKibbin's excellent study (1980) showed strong correlations between teachers' self-esteem and their practical efforts to improve their performance through using available opportunities for professional development. Yarger, Howey and Joyce's surveys (1980) of teachers' participation in and preferences for in-service options also supports the contention that the individual wish for self-growth is a powerful force. People who participate actively in one kind of staff development tend to do so in other kinds as well, and have more favourable attitudes toward the options which are offered. In other words, the most active people tend to be active across the board, and feel better both about themselves and the system which is attempting to deliver services to them.

10. Collaborative governance within districts, between school and community personnel, and between institutions, appears to generate greater levels of activity and more positive feelings towards self and others. The issue is not so much whether one adopts a 'top-down' or 'bottom-up' approach to decision-making, but whether collaboration and co-operation are developed. Administrators, teachers, community members, university personnel, and technical assistants, all appear to be vital to the generation of a favourable ecology, and their involvement is evidently crucial.

Effective on-site in-service education appears to be essential if teachers are to transfer what they learn from any source into their own jobs. Transferring new skills into the classroom is an extremely difficult process. It is possible to develop a high degree of skill and knowledge and be unable to apply it unaided.

11. The nature of the teaching job generates normative forces. Teachers begin to think along lines which are heavily influenced by the way they teach and they are prone to perpetuate familiar approaches to teaching. Without an environment in which teaching is analysed and discussed, in which teachers work to help each other to experiment with their behaviour, very little innovation is likely to be generated or to persist.

Thus, it has to be recognized that fresh professional development models will be exceedingly difficult to develop. A comprehensive model has to serve as the model for the improvement of a major social institution and to indicate the necessary changes in the conditions of life of the people who live and work within it. It is unlikely that any single unitary approach will develop in the near future which can apply to all dimensions of in-service education; but combinations of approaches can be used as a basis for broad reform.

In this chapter, I have described some of the potential material for partial models based on training, research, on the study of a community-based effort, and on the study of an effort dependent upon collaboration among institutions. All three provide bases on which success can be built. But the ultimate model will have to take into account all four dimensions of ISTE (p 31) simultaneously. In so doing, it must blend and build upon a body of research and experience, which must be constantly replenished.

References

Hunt, D and Joyce, B (1967) Teacher trainee personality and initial teaching style *American Educational Research Journal* **4** 3:47-63

Joyce, B (ed) (1978a) *Involvement: A Study of Shared Governance in Teacher Education* National Dissemination Center: Syracuse University

Joyce, B (ed) (1978b) From thought to action *Education Research Quarterly* **3** 4

Joyce, B (ed) (1980) *Lessons Learned from the History of Change in Education* The University of Nebraska Press: Omaha, Nebraska

Joyce, B, Bush, R, Marsh, D and McKibbin, M (1979a) *The California Staff Development Study* Office of Program Evaluation and Research of the California State Department of Education: Sacramento, Ca

Joyce, B, Bush, R, Marsh, D, Meyers, H and Birdsall, L (1979b) *Recommendations for the Evaluation of Staff Development in California: Report of a Preparatory Study* Office of Program Evaluation and Research, California State Department of Education: Sacramento, Ca

Joyce, B, Howey, K and Yarger, S (1976) *Issues to Face* ISTE Report I (first of 5 volumes) National Dissemination Center: Syracuse University

Joyce, B, Howey, K and Yarger, S (1977a) *Preservice Teacher Education* Consolidated Press: Palo Alto, Ca

Joyce, B, Howey, K and Yarger, S (1977b) Preservice teacher education: impressions from a national survey *Journal of Teacher Education* **19** 1

Joyce, B and Showers, B (1980) Training ourselves: the message of research *Educational Leadership* **37** 4

Joyce, B, Wald, R and Weil, M (1972) Content for the training of educators: a structure for pluralism *Teachers College Record* **73**: 371-92

McKibbin, M and Joyce, B (1980) Psychological states and staff development *Theory into Practice* (forthcoming in **19** 4)

Nicholson, A and Joyce, B (1976) *The Literature on Inservice Teacher Education* ISTE Report III National Dissemination Center: Syracuse University

Yarger, S, Howey, K and Joyce, B (1980) *Inservice Teacher Education* Consolidated
  Press: Palo Alto, Ca

Note

*The material in this chapter is partly drawn from Joyce, Howey and Yarger (1976) and
Joyce and Showers (1980).*

2. Professionalization and deprofessionalization in education

Eric Hoyle

Summary: Professional development assumes the increased professionalization of teachers. However, although this may be in the interests of the members of a profession, it is legitimate to question whether it is in the interests of clients. Critics of professionalization argue that the alleged need for professional practice to be based on a body of systematic theoretical knowledge is greatly exaggerated, since most of the time, practice is conducted according to intuition, experience and common-sense knowledge. This view is supported by recent developments in the sociology of knowledge as well as by research on how teachers see their task. However, although there is no clear evidence that theoretical knowledge influences practice, neither is there convincing evidence that it could not do so. There is therefore a case for continuing the professional development of teachers but in contexts in which the teacher's own epistemological assumptions are taken seriously by researchers and theory builders. Such contexts would include, for example, programmes of participatory research and school-focused in-service training.

Professional development is the process by which teachers acquire the knowledge and skills essential to good professional practice at each stage of a teaching career. The contents of this *World Yearbook* attest to the fact that in many societies there is growing interest in the process of developing the professional competence of teachers and a steadily increasing commitment to the institutions and activities which promote it, including the induction of new teachers, in-service education and training, and staff development programmes. Professional development is regarded as an unquestionably desirable activity for the state to support and the questions tackled in most of the contributions to this Yearbook are 'how?' questions rather than 'why?' questions. Like all the other contributors, I have a personal commitment to the professional development of teachers but wish here to explore some of the arguments against the professionalization of teachers, before proceeding to reaffirm the need for professional development in the light of these criticisms.

The case for the deprofessionalization of teachers

The professional development of teachers implies a process whereby teachers may be helped to become more professional. This, in turn, implies a model of professional practice to which teachers should aspire, and it is the validity of this model for both developed and developing countries which critics of the process of professionalization query. In order to understand this criticism it is necessary to explore the connotations of the concept of *profession* and three associated concepts: *professionalization, professionality* and *professionalism*.

Broadly speaking, there are two views of the function of the concept of a *profession*. One treats it as a descriptive term, the other as a term which always carries a symbolic or ideological connotation. The exploration of *profession* as a descriptive category has a history of at least 70 years. The general approach has been to try to identify the characteristics of occupations like medicine and law — traditionally designated professions — which distinguish them from other occupations. There is a voluminous literature on this topic and numerous lists of criteria have been produced. Examples of characteristics of a profession which appear in many of these lists include: their practice is underpinned by a body of theoretical knowledge; practitioners undergo a relatively long period of training; there is a code of ethics governing practitioner behaviour; practitioners enjoy a relatively high degree of autonomy; and the profession itself is responsible for admission of new members. Initially, occupations were dichotomized between professions and non-professions, but it is now more common to arrange occupations on a continuum, at one end of which are the 'ideal type' professions. These meet all the criteria, not surprisingly since the criteria were derived from these occupations in the first place. Along the continuum from these are ranged what have variously been called semi, quasi, or emergent professions, which have some, but not all of the characteristics of a profession, and further along still are the trades, crafts and routine non-manual occupations which meet only some of the main criteria of a profession, and these only to a limited degree. As we shall see later, this ostensibly 'descriptive' approach embodies certain built-in value assumptions.

The alternative approach to the concept of profession starts from the assumption that it is a value-laden term and explores how it is thus used. Hughes (1958) notes that *profession* is a term which is a 'symbol for a desired conception of one's work and hence of one's self'. Radical critics of the professions, whose views will be considered later, hold that it is an ideological term used as a bargaining position in an occupation's efforts to improve its status, rewards and conditions of work.

The concept of profession has reference both to the individual practitioner and to the occupation as a whole, and the criteria may embrace both dimensions. For example, the criterion of knowledge base implies the existence of a body of systematic knowledge on which professional practice is based, and also refers to the degree to which individual practitioners possess this knowledge. Similarly, autonomy can refer to the relative independence of the profession as a whole from political control and also to the individual practitioner's relative freedom from external control over his day-to-day professional practice. This distinction between the collective and individual dimension is important in any consideration of the second concept, that of *professionalization*.

Professionalization has two major dimensions: the improvement of status and the improvement of practice. The first of these dimensions involves those efforts of the organized profession to meet the criteria which characterize the ideal type profession or, in the case of an established profession, to maintain or even improve its privileged position. This dimension of professionalization will vary from society to society, but some of its components are: an increasingly lengthy period of training, a qualified membership with a strong boundary between those who are legitimately entitled to practise and those who are not, an increasing control over the activities of the profession (eg control over the curriculum, in the case of teaching), control over the training and licensing of future members of the profession and so forth. Professionalization as the improvement of practice involves the continuous improvement of the knowledge and skills of practitioners. In this sense, professionalization can be equated with professional development.

There is clearly a potential congruence between the two components of professionalization. One would anticipate a positive relationship between the extension of the period of initial and in-service training and an improvement in the knowledge and skills of the practitioner. One might assume that this would be true where increasingly stringent demands are set for those who wish to enter the profession. It might further be assumed that professional practice would be enhanced to the degree that it was controlled by professionals themselves. However, it might be argued, and indeed is argued by protagonists of deprofessionalization, that the improvement of status and the improvement of the service to clients may well be inimical to each other, with the quest for status taking priority over the improvement of service.

This divergence is reflected in the final pair of concepts to be considered. *Professionalism* is used in this context to refer to a commitment among members of an occupation towards increased professional status and the strategies used, particularly by associations or unions, to achieve this. *Professionality* is reserved for the attitudes towards professional practice among the members of an occupation and the degree of knowledge and skill which they bring to it. The relationship between professionalism and professionality is complex. It could be close but, on the other hand, there could be a disjunction between them. One difficulty in disentangling the relationship is that the professionalism pursued by associations is often expressed in terms of client interest. Professional associations tend to use rhetoric combined with union strategy. In other words, their efforts to get governments to enact certain policies, or to prevent them from enacting policies of which the associations disapprove, will often be expressed in terms of the ostensible interests of clients; but if governments should not prove amenable to such arguments, militant action may be threatened or actually taken.

Professionalism obviously has much in common with trade unionism, but it cannot be equated with it because service to the client will often involve more than mere rhetoric in that the client, as well as the practitioner, will benefit from the policies proposed. It is very difficult to answer with any certainty the question: *cui bono?* If a teachers' union presses for a longer period of training, this could obviously benefit the pupils as well as enhance the status of teaching by bringing it closer in length of training to that undergone by entrants to the established professions. Or, if a teacher union resists the use of auxiliaries in the classroom, this could be in the interests both of the pupils, if exposure to non-professional staff were considered to be detrimental, and of the profession as a whole, by preventing dilution. On the other hand, the use of auxiliaries might enhance the service offered and contribute to the professionality of the teacher, in which case the causes of professionality and professionalism would converge. Thus the rhetoric of professionalization emphasizes the enhancement of the professionality of teachers and hence the improvement of the education of the pupils. But the critics of deprofessionalization suggest that professionality is *not* enhanced and that the pupils do *not* benefit from the process of professionalization. Before considering the arguments of those who advocate deprofessionalization, we can examine the values inherent in the concept of a profession.

One view of the concept *profession* treats it as a descriptive category and seeks to identify the criteria by which an occupation can be so categorized. Such an approach is not solely descriptive but has built-in value assumptions; these assumptions are as follows.

1. A profession is an occupation which performs a crucial social function.
2. The exercise of this function requires a considerable degree of skill.
3. This skill is exercised in situations which are not wholly routine but in which new problems and situations have to be handled.
4. Thus, although knowledge gained through experience is important, this recipe-type knowledge is insufficient to meet professional demands and the practitioner has to draw on a body of systematic knowledge.
5. The acquisition of this body of knowledge and the development of specific skills requires a lengthy period of higher education.
6. This period of education and training also involves the process of socialization into professional values.
7. These values tend to centre on the pre-eminence of clients' interests and to some degree they are made explicit in a code of ethics.
8. Because knowledge-based skills are exercised in non-routine situations, it is essential for the professional to have the freedom to make his own judgements with regard to appropriate practice.
9. Because professional practice is so specialized, the organized profession should have a strong voice in the shaping of relevant public policy, a large degree of control over the exercise of professional responsibilities, and a high degree of autonomy in relation to the state.
10. Lengthy training, responsibility and client-centredness are necessarily rewarded by high prestige and a high level of remuneration.

The above is, of course, something of a caricature of a professional ideology, but it highlights the position against which the forces for deprofessionalization are gathered. There are two main thrusts to this anti-professional argument. One is against the notion of a body of theoretical knowledge as essential to the welfare of clients; this is obviously the element most relevant to the question of professional development. The other is the question of practitioner and occupational autonomy which is less directly relevant to the question of professional development but is nevertheless a contextual factor of some interest.

The professionalization of teachers in most developed societies has included the enhancement of knowledge. Taking Britain as an example, we can note that since the Second World War, the period of training in colleges of education increased from two to three years and thence to a four year course. Accompanying this process has been a movement towards a graduate profession in which all entrants will have undertaken a four year BEd course or a three year degree course followed by a year of teacher training leading to the postgraduate certificate in education. In Britain, all graduates have to undergo training, except, in England and Wales, for those with degrees in shortage subjects such as mathematics and science, for whom training is still optional. With the extension of the training course in the colleges and polytechnics, students have been exposed to a lengthier period of induction into educational and curriculum studies. There also appears to have been a growth in the provision of in-service education in many countries and there is an increasing interest in the potential for professional growth through programmes of staff development. In the same period, there has been a considerable increase in the educational literature. The library sections containing books on the history, philosophy, sociology and psychology of education have expanded enormously. Large numbers of new journals on all aspects of education have been published. There has also been a considerable expansion of the superstructure of educational research and development, through the specialized agencies which have been created for the funding, prosecution and dissemination of educational research and curriculum development. The educational enterprise has experienced its own knowledge explosion.

The argument for deprofessionalization has been mounted by a number of radical critics of the professions. The broad position taken attacks the functionalist rationale at almost every point. It is argued that:

1. the functions of practitioners are no more crucial to the well-being of members of society than those of many other occupations;
2. the skills required, and particularly the need for a systematic body of knowledge, have been greatly exaggerated by the protagonists of professionalization;
3. the values of the professions are no less self-interested than those of other occupations;
4. the autonomy claimed for the profession as a whole, and for individual practitioners, is unnecessary and is proposed only as a means of avoiding accountability to society in general and to individual clients in particular;
5. the high prestige and rewards enjoyed by the professions have not been bestowed by a grateful society but have been acquired by the professions through the exercise of power and influence.

These issues cannot all be considered equally, and the argument will focus on the alleged need for a systematic body of theoretical knowledge. Apart from the writers on de-schooling, the protagonists of deprofessionalization tend not to deal specifically with the educational knowledge required by teachers. Hence one has to make assumptions about what their view might be on educational theory and on knowledge of subject areas.

The basic argument of the critics of the professions, including many moderates who would like to see some changes though not wholesale deprofessionalization, is that for the professions which deal with people, intuitive, experiential and common-sense knowledge is much more in the client's interest than the bogus attempt to use cognitive, systematic, theoretical knowledge. The following are some representative views.

Halmos (1965, 1970, 1971), a moderate critic of the professions, argues that although systematic knowledge has a place in professional practice, it must remain subordinate to the quality of the relationship between practitioner and client and to the values which should inform that relationship. He summarizes these values as the ideology of counselling, which is caring, supportive and therapeutic. He advances an argument for the relationship between sociology as a discipline and social work as a practice by drawing our attention to the potential conflict between the value systems of the personal service professions and the social sciences in which those professionals are often trained. In emphasizing methodical rigour, objectivity, scepticism and neutrality, the social sciences run counter to the subjectivist, optimistic, personal involvement which he believes to be essential to good professional practice in those professions which are concerned with the welfare of people (Halmos, 1971). Of course, he is here indicating only the 'positivistic' paradigm of social science and, as we shall see below, a newer, more interpretative paradigm is more in tune with professional practice of the kind which Halmos is concerned to promote. Nevertheless, the conflict which he highlights exists. In education it finds its expression in the jibes which teachers make about psychologists and sociologists who are more concerned with the academic purity of their research than with the 'real' needs of pupils.

Reiff (1971), like Halmos, does not wholly dismiss the importance of professional expertise, yet he points out that it represents only a relatively small element in the exercise of professional practice, compared with the common-sense knowledge which practitioners share with laymen. He writes:

> Every professional occupation includes a large component of non-professional knowledge and technology in its professional practice — intuition, common sense, folkways, and cultural and moral values. There is no reason to believe that professionals are more effective or better equipped in their use of this non-professional knowledge and skill because of their more professional (ie esoteric) knowledge. In fact, they tend to organize their use of non-professional knowledge and skill for their own purposes rather than the client's. They aggrandize non-professional knowledge, pretending to have a much greater range of professional esoteric knowledge and skill than, in fact, exists.(Reiff, 1971: 63)

Benne (1970) distinguishes between 'expert' authority and 'pedagogical' (or 'anthropogogical' authority as he chooses to call it since it relates as much to authority relationships between adults as between adults and children). The exercise of 'expert' authority is characterized by the objectivity of the professional and an inevitable differentiation between practitioner and client. The doctor tackles the problem of his patient's illness as a scientific problem independently of the wishes or intentions of the patient who, to some extent, is treated as an 'object'. Moreover, the distance between doctor and patient is maintained. However, in a situation of pedagogical (or anthropogogical) authority the intention of the professional is to reduce the distance between himself and his client. The differentiation of function disappears and both come to work more closely together in the interests of resolving the client's problems. And, of course, in this relationship the client is treated as an individual and his wishes, intentions and aspirations are taken into account in the relationship.

These examples are perhaps sufficient to give some indication of the approach of those writers who question the relevance of theoretical knowledge of the professional-as-expert. More radical critics of the professions (eg Bennett and Hockenstad, 1973; Haug, 1973) foresee a time when professional credentialism will be reversed; more people will be involved in what are currently professional activities and they will undertake this work in a wider variety of settings, with less specialization, and with their clients becoming more participative, more authoritative and less socially distanced. Paradoxically, as some writers have pointed out, an advanced technology which permits medical diagnosis and the tracing of legal precedent by computer might well further such a trend. In Chapter 18 Megarry points to some of the implications of advancing technology for changing relationships between teacher and taught.

There has been no sustained critique of the professional knowledge of teachers apart from the well-known arguments of the de-schoolers, hence one has to infer what such criticisms might be from the general body of radical and reformist writings on the professions. Three points may be made. The first is that the knowledge base remains weak. In spite of the increase in research and development activity there is still little consensus on the validity of the knowledge so acquired. Another point is that there remains a considerable gap between theory and practice. Insofar as there is general agreement about a particular area of educational theory, this does not necessarily inform policy or practice. A third criticism, which follows from the second, is that for various reasons, teachers have by and large failed to internalize the bodies of theory and research which have been generated. The response to these criticisms of those who seek to professionalize teaching is to argue for more research, particularly as it relates to practice, and for more training of teachers so that they may better acquire and make use of this growing body of professional knowledge. The arguments of the deprofessionalizers, on the other hand, are in quite the other direction. They regard the pursuit of an improved knowledge base as misguided, since, they would argue, there can be no systematic body of knowledge on which teachers can draw effectively.

The epistemological assumptions of the advocates of professionalization and deprofessionalization are thus fundamentally different. The advocates of deprofessionalization argue that the rationalistic assumptions of much theory and research in education are inappropriate. In their view, the methods of training appropriate to teachers are quite different from the natural science assumptions which researchers and theorists have sought to meet in the past, and into which those responsible for the education of teachers have failed to redirect them. Elliott's chapter in this volume offers a cogent and well-illustrated critique of assumptions of teacher causality based on a division of labour between the researcher who produces causal knowledge and the teacher who applies it.

A poignant attack on the dubious relationship between theory and practice has been offered by McNamara, a university lecturer in education who spent sabbatical leave teaching in two primary schools. He writes:

> I have always been fascinated by the problems involved in theorizing about and researching into education. Thus I was taken aback by my reaction to these activities when I returned to the classroom. Once working again as a teacher I lost all desire to keep up to date with the literature. This was not because my mind went soggy or because I became too involved with the minutiae of day-to-day problems. It was simply that the world of the academic journals seemed completely irrelevant to classroom life. Inherent in the nature of social science and educational research is a propensity to generalize and develop second order abstractions from the concreteness of particular examples. In addition, such activities are conducted in an ambience of intellectual detachment and scepticism. But as a teacher I had to act in particular and concrete situations and, moreover, be committed to and believe in what I was doing. (McNamara, 1976: 155)

Deprofessionalization and phenomenology

The views on knowledge held by some, but by no means all, critics of the professions approximate to the 'sociology of knowledge' perspective adopted by sociologists of education of a phenomenological persuasion. This approach questions many assumptions made about the validity of the objectivity of knowledge. Drawing on a variety of sources, particularly the phenomenology of Alfred Schutz (1967) and the philosophy of science of Thomas Kuhn (1970), these writers argue that knowledge is a social construct which is generated through social interaction. Hence their view of educational knowledge and of the actual curriculum itself is that both have been socially constructed and are sustained in the interests of particular groups in society, amongst which are the organized professions. They therefore advocate a demystification of this knowledge and the challenging of the taken-for-granted assumptions embedded in it. Educational theory is rejected insofar as it is a body of inert knowledge with little relevance to practice. They argue for its removal from courses of teacher education in favour of a critical analysis of classroom activities and of existing curricula and the adoption of a reflexive approach towards the student's or teacher's classroom practice. As far as the school curriculum is concerned, these writers emphasize the importance of the common-sense knowledge which children bring to school and the importance of the teacher working with this knowledge rather than taking for granted the alleged importance of the traditional academic subjects. The educational encounter is seen as itself a process wherein knowledge is negotiated (see, for example, Young, 1971; Whitty and Young, 1976; Gleeson, 1977).

Followers of this phenomenological approach to educational knowledge support the critics of the professions in their view that it is unimportant for teachers to acquire either a systematic body of educational theory or an academic knowledge of subject matter. The call for increased professionalization is seen by them as serving to exaggerate the knowledge which teachers require to maintain an arbitrary distance between teacher and taught, to mystify the public and hence to act as a protection against accountability, and to gain influence and prestige in society generally.

The professionality of teachers

The strictures of critics of the professions lead one to raise questions about the professionality of teachers. What, generally speaking, is the present nature of teacher professionality? What are the prospects for a process of professional development in improving the quality of professionality? Do the arguments of the advocates of deprofessionalization lead one to the conclusion that the attempted improvement of teacher professionality is misguided?

In pursuing answers to these questions, the author will draw upon a distinction made elsewhere between *restricted* and *extended* professionality (Hoyle, 1974). This distinction is derived from various sociological and educational writings and is used here for heuristic purposes; it remains empirically untested. By *restricted* professionality I mean a professionality which is intuitive, classroom-focused, and based on experience rather than theory. The good restricted professional is sensitive to the development of individual pupils, an inventive teacher and a skilful class manager. He is unencumbered with theory, is not given to comparing his work with that of others, tends not to perceive his classroom activities in a broader context, and values his classroom autonomy. The *extended professional*, on the other hand, is concerned with locating his classroom teaching in a broader educational context, comparing his work with that of other teachers, evaluating his own work systematically, and collaborating with other teachers. Unlike the restricted professional, he is interested in theory and in current educational developments. Hence he reads educational books and journals, becomes involved in various professional activities and is concerned to further his own professional development through in-service work. He sees teaching as a rational activity amenable to improvement on the basis of research and development.

If this broad distinction has any validity, basic questions inevitably arise. Is extended professionality just a form of restricted professionality with added dimensions, or are the two different and irreconcilable perspectives on teaching? If restricted professionality can be extended, by what methods is this likely to be achieved if the strengths of restricted professionality are not to be lost? On the basis of the case for deprofessionalization, is there an argument for attempting to move teachers from restricted to extended professionality but also encouraging trends in quite the opposite direction by emphasizing the interpersonal aspect of this form of professionality, by reducing the level of credentials needed to enter teaching thus admitting the intuitive but unqualified, and by abandoning the research and development infrastructure which only serves to mislead teachers and perhaps to induce in them a sense of guilt?

One of the studies most relevant to a discussion of these questions is Philip Jackson's *Life in Classrooms* (1968) which includes a study of views on teaching held by a group of American elementary schoolteachers who had been identified as good practitioners by their superiors. Some of Jackson's main findings indicate that these teachers were more 'restricted' than 'extended' in the terms outlined above. Their approach to teaching was intuitive. They had knowledge of some of the concepts to be found in educational theory but these were interpreted to fit with their own common-sense notions of pupil development. Their satisfaction came from the immediacy of events, the here and now reality of the classroom. They valued their autonomy and their personal relationship with their class. They did not appear to be interested in evaluating their work in any objective manner. They answered questions on evaluation in terms of the immediate feedback from pupils, 'the expression on their faces'. Educational objectives had little relevance for them. Jackson writes:

> Sometimes teaching is described as a highly rational affair. Such descriptions often emphasize the decision-making function of the teacher, or liken his task to that of a problem-solver or hypothesis tester. Yet the interviews with elementary teachers raise serious doubts about these ways of looking at the teaching process. The immediacy of classroom life, the fleeting and sometimes cryptic signs on which the teacher relies for determining his pedagogical moves and for evaluating the effectiveness of his actions call into question the appropriateness of using conventional models of rationality to depict the teacher's classroom behaviour.

It could be inferred from this study that restricted and extended professionality *are* fundamentally different perspectives or, at least, that any policy of extending teacher professionality could lead to a loss of job satisfaction and perhaps of teaching skill. An advocate of deprofessionalization might argue that insofar as these teachers have had a systematic professional training, it does not appear to have impinged greatly on their practice and hence might well have been unnecessary. There is at least a case to answer here.

Continuing professional development

Is the anti-professional critique so devastating that we should abandon the professionalization of education and the professional development of teachers? In my view the answer is 'no'. The critique is highly salutary to the teaching profession itself and to those concerned with the preparation of teachers. While we should profit from it, its claims are too wide-sweeping. It should teach us not to make easy assumptions about the relationships between knowledge and practice. Where we are still hoping to bring together knowledge and practice in professional development, we should learn to reconsider the context of learning and pay serious attention to two elements which inform our theories about educating children: the centrality of experience and the validity of different ways of knowing.

The arguments of the critics of the professions may have force in relation to 'pre-industrial' societies; I believe that they should inform the educational policies of developing societies which appear likely to become afflicted with the 'diploma disease'. However, in industrialized societies, a strong link has been established between schooling and occupation at the individual level and between education and the economy at the system level. The link has certainly been exaggerated, particularly in the manpower arguments of the 1960s, but it exists nevertheless. Schooling may not 'make a difference' in terms of transforming the class structure, but it makes a difference to the individual whether he attends school or not. The arguments of the critics would have greater cogency if there were a general political will to return to a simpler society in which education for life in the local community would be sufficient; but there is no sign of such a will. Hence, as new knowledge is created and as innovations in curriculum, pedagogy and organization are generated, there remains a need to help teachers to cope with these in some way.

In spite of a perennial debate about the relationship between theory and practice amongst educationists, the more fundamental and radical questions about the relationship between knowledge and action have remained relatively unexplored. They have, of course, been treated philosophically, but at the sociological level the issues have been touched upon only by the phenomenologically-inclined critics of the curriculum as part of a more general critique of contemporary schooling. Perhaps one of the best approaches to the problem has been taken by Eliot Freidson in *Profession of Medicine* (1970). He addresses himself to such questions as 'In what areas is expertise absolutely necessary and what not? In what areas where expertise is necessary does expertise which is demonstrably superior to common opinion actually exist? And where there is expertise, what are its limitations? Freidson argues that there is, in fact, a considerable gap between expert knowledge and expert practice. He is worth quoting on this distinction:

> But what are the referents of 'knowledge' and 'expertise'? Obviously, they refer to a body of putative facts ordered by some abstract ideas or theories: we may expect to find them embodied in the treatises and textbooks which provide the formal substance of what experts learn in professional schools and what they presumably know thereafter. However, such knowledge or expertise is extremely limited as a reality: it is locked up in books or heads, and as it is defined it has no link with the activities of consulting, treating, advising, or otherwise working at 'being' an expert. A practicing or consulting expert engages in activities, and activity is not, after all, knowledge. The lack of equivalence between knowing and doing requires us to either redefine 'knowledge' as that which knowledgeable people do, or to distinguish knowledge as such and to analyze its relationship to what reputedly knowledgeable people do.
>
> Because some kinds of people devote themselves to contributing to the body of knowledge while others devote themselves to applying that body of knowledge to human affairs, it seems appropriate to distinguish the body of knowledge as such from the human activities of either creating that knowledge (research) or applying it (practice). The activities can be judged by their faithfulness to the knowledge and by the degree to which they are founded upon that knowledge. To evaluate the expert and his expertise, then, one does not only evaluate the knowledge of his discipline as such but also the relationship of his activity of being an expert to that

knowledge. Thus we must ask, what is the substance of the expert's work as well as of his knowledge? Is systematic and reliable knowledge involved in every facet of his work? Is objective knowledge involved rather than moral or evaluative preference? The answers to such questions allow us to determine the degree to which the work of the expert is justifiably and appropriately protected from the evaluation and influence of laymen. (Freidson, 1970)

The parallel with educational research and theory and its relationship with educational policy and teaching practice can be drawn.

The anti-professional critique of knowledge is cogent but does not entirely dispose of the problem. Just as there is little indication that research influences theory and practice there is little indication that it does *not*. The distinction drawn by Freidson is a valuable one and the questions posed are important. We certainly need to explore further the relationship between knowledge and practice, and there are different epistemologies of those located in different parts of the system: researchers, administrators, teachers, and a host of other stakeholders. But, above all, we have to rethink the contexts and methods of staff development in the light of the anti-professional critique.

This involves rethinking the roles of researcher, theorist and teacher educator at initial and in-service levels. However participatory their actual teaching strategies, the prevalent stance has been for these experts to impose on teachers their bodies of systematized knowledge, categorized in their terms and based on their epistemological positions and disciplinary paradigms. There are, however, signs of change, and three trends can be noted: the adoption of a phenomenological approach to the definition of school problems, an increased participaton in research by teachers (with the problems being identified by the teachers themselves) and an expansion of school focused in-service training.

The functional distinction between the producers of educational knowledge via research and the assumed users of such knowledge has been quite marked, as Freidson noted. But there are trends whereby the users of knowledge — the teachers — are being brought more into the process of knowledge production, and on their own terms. This is taking place in universities and colleges where, via teacher research groups, teachers bring their problems and obtain help in researching these problems in a practical way. The aspiration here is for the academic researcher to try as far as possible to help teachers to research the problems as they define them. These definitions will not always accord with the academic researcher's traditional notions of what is feasible. But while researchers can to some degree control their variables — or get rid of them — in pursuit of an elegant design, teachers cannot control *their* variables; they have to live with them. Thus although the teacher learns that global problems cannot easily be reduced to a researchable form, it is important that the researcher learns to meet the teacher more than half-way, even if the outcome is less-than-pure research.

Surely we now know the importance of teachers' definitions of the situation for their actions not to feel too perturbed by the idea of involving teachers in research. Curricula, methods, and forms of organization are only successful to the degree that teachers define them as likely to be successful. There may be little about teaching which can be said to be 'successful' or otherwise on the basis of research which is independent of teacher values. Without arguing for the complete abandonment of detached, positivistic research, one can at least argue that teachers' definitions have to be taken seriously, and the more these definitions can be shaped by systematic enquiry the better. In Chapter 21, McIntyre outlines a number of ways in which action and integration studies might make a contribution to teacher education. There may well be a need for academic researchers to involve themselves as consultants in the school's attempt to resolve its own problems of curriculum or organizational development, even though the research or systematic enquiry which they guide does not conform to traditional patterns (eg Richardson, 1973).

Finally, a number of countries are developing patterns of school-focused in-service training as an alternative to, but not necessarily a total replacement for, the traditional pattern of in-service training whereby individual teachers attend courses away from their school, to engage with problems in the terms dictated by lecturers in institutions of teacher education or other agencies. Emerging patterns emphasize that in-service training should be, to a greater extent than in the past, focused upon substantive school problems, take functioning groups of teachers as its target and work with the definitions provided by those teachers. Such training should enjoy the support of external agencies which would accept, or at least negotiate, the knowledge and skills which teachers claim to need for solving the problems of their school and it should provide as much support as possible (for a discussion of possible approaches, see Hoyle, 1973 and Chapters 5 and 13).

Conclusion

The writings of the critics of professionalization have to be taken very seriously by educationists. Although the critique has not been systematically developed at the epistemological, sociological and political levels, there are pointers to suggest that much that is now offered and undertaken as staff development may have little impact upon the practice of teaching and may, indeed, be more related to self-interest than client interest. Yet the strictures are too radical and perhaps underestimate the indirect influence of systematic research and theorizing on practice. To abandon the professional development of teachers entirely would be to throw out the baby with the bathwater. What educational theorists and researchers, on the one hand, and teachers and policy makers, on the other, now need to do is explore ways of furthering the professional development of teachers through approaches which take as their starting point the teacher's definitions of his problem.

References

Benne, K (1970) Authority in education *Harvard Educational Review* **40** 3: 385-410

Bennett, W S Jr and Hockenstad, M C Jr (1973) Full time people-workers and concepts of the 'professional' *in* Halmos, P *Professionalization and Social Change* The Sociological Review Monograph 20, University of Keele: Keele

Freidson, E (1970) *The Profession of Medicine* Dodd, Mead and Co: New York

Gleeson, D (1977) *Identity and Structure: Issues in the Sociology of Education* Nafferton Press: Driffield

Halmos, P (1965) *The Faith of the Counsellors* Constable: London

Halmos, P (1970) *The Personal Service Society* Constable: London

Halmos, P (1971) Sociology and the personal service professions *in* Freidson, E (ed) *The Professions and their Prospects* Sage Publications: Beverly Hills

Haug, M R (1973) Deprofessionalization: an alternative hypothesis for the future *in* Halmos, P *Professionalization and Social Change* The Sociological Review Monograph 20, University of Keele: Keele

Hoyle, E (1973) The strategies of curriculum change *in* Watkins, R (ed) *In Service Training: Structure and Content* Ward Lock Educational: London

Hoyle, E (1974) Professionality, professionalism and control in teaching *London Educational Review* 3 2:15-17

Hughes, E C (1958) *Men and their Work* Free Press: New York

Jackson, P (1968) *Life in Classrooms* Holt, Rinehart and Winston: New York

Kuhn, T S (1970) *The Structure of Scientific Revolutions* (2nd edition) Chicago University Press: Chicago

McNamara, D (1976) On returning to the chalk face: theory not into practice *British Journal of Teacher Education* 2 2:147-60

Reiff, R (1971) The danger of the techni-pro: democratizing the human service professions *Social Policy* 2 82-4

Richardson, E (1973) *The Teacher, the School and the Task of Management* Heinemann: London

Schutz, A (1967) *The Phenomenology of the Social World* Northwestern University Press: Evanston, Ill

Whitty, G and Young, M F D (eds) (1976) *Explorations in the Politics of School Knowledge* Nafferton Press: Driffield

Young, M F D (ed) (1971) *Knowledge and Control* Collier-Macmillan: London

Part 2: Current Trends

3. Current trends in initial training

Tom Bone

Summary: Teacher education was under attack during most of the 1970s, and this chapter begins by examining the sources of the pressures to which it was subjected, both those resulting from the fall in birth-rates and the decline in the need for teachers, and those associated with the failure of education to meet exaggerated public expectations, and the consequent criticism of the preparation of teachers.

In the developing countries criticisms were growing that the nature of the education provided in schools was often irrelevant to the needs of the community served, and the teacher training institutions were required to produce teachers of a new kind. The nature of the problem is discussed and some approaches to its solution described.

In the developed countries the response to pressure has come partly through structural change and partly through revision of curriculum and methods. Examples of the former are looked at, and there is some detailed examination of the most frequently adopted changes of the latter kind. An attempt is made to assess the position at the beginning of the 1980s with regard to microteaching, the competency-based approach, techniques of mastery learning, and alterations in the arrangements for teaching practice to give the schools a greater part to play in teacher preparation.

The chapter sees teacher education as having lost the complacency which was common in the 1960s, and having been strengthened, if also scarified, by the attacks of the 1970s. Institutions which train teachers all over the world are now much more conscious of the need to engage themselves in the frequent revision of courses, and much more willing to enter into partnership with other agencies in the work of training. It is here that their best hope lies, for the training institutions should no more stand alone than should initial training itself be separated from the rest of the continuing professional development of teachers.

Teacher education under attack: the pressures in the developed countries

In the developed countries, the period of the 1960s was generally one in which teacher training systems had to expand rapidly to provide the additional teachers required by rising birth-rates. At the same time, there was a widespread move to give the individual training institutions more prestige and autonomy by freeing them from the tight supervision of state education departments; Australia and Scotland provided good examples. By the early 1970s, however, birth-rates were falling rapidly, and, although the timing of the process has varied from country to country, by the end of the 1970s teacher training systems and individual institutions have had to be severely contracted by state control. An excellent account of the process as it affected England and Wales is given by Lynch (1979:33-49).

Economic difficulties have meant that the developed countries have had to search for areas in which public expenditure could be reduced, and, with the need for teachers receding, initial training has been an obvious target. Common solutions have been for individual colleges to be closed, for groups of colleges to be amalgamated, or for one or more to become part of another larger institution like a polytechnic.

There have been pressures of other kinds too. The failure of education as a whole to meet the high expectations which had been set for it led in the 1970s to a reduction in public confidence in schools, seen partly in the search for alternative forms of education (Illich, 1971) and partly in the demand for accountability (Atkin, 1979). There were complaints about declining standards in education (persistent even when refuted by statistics), criticisms from the lay public of innovations which were misunderstood, and further criticisms from ratepayers and taxpayers that other innovations were not being sustained by teachers after they had cost a great deal of money to introduce. Discussion of the weaknesses of teachers led quickly to criticism of their training; they were often not sufficiently well prepared for the innovations they were expected to implement. This was, for example, one of the causes (although not the decisive one) of the relative failure of open-plan education in many parts of Australia, Canada, the United States and the United Kingdom. The teacher trainers said that teacher attitudes were vital in such matters, and, hard pressed by their critics, they discovered that the most important time for forming the future behaviour and attitudes of teachers was the first year after initial training had been completed, the year in which, under pressure of new and taxing responsibilities, they were most susceptible to the advice and influence of colleagues. However, it was difficult to admit this without diminishing the importance of initial training itself in the eyes of others.

The shape and content of training programmes had in many places changed considerably in the late 1960s and early 1970s, consequent upon the greater freedom of institutions, but students continued to complain about being over-taught and under-stretched intellectually, and sometimes drew attention to the unwillingness of most of their trainers to refresh or renew their own experience by a return to the classroom (Taylor, 1978). Research studies continued to show that the theoretical part of training programmes had made relatively little impact on the thinking or behaviour of teachers who had followed those programmes a few years earlier (Nisbet et al, 1977). Argument continued on the comparative merit of concurrent or consecutive training (Goldman, 1976), and although the teacher trainers tended almost universally to believe that the former was preferable, they found this very difficult to prove in terms of the effectiveness of practising teachers. Consequently, there was the obvious danger that initial training could be reduced to one year courses after the gaining of other qualifications elsewhere. Although it has not gone as far as that, one of the marked trends in England and Wales in the second half of the 1970s was towards consecutive traning (Lynch, 1979), and there are signs of a similar tendency in other countries.

Another pressure came, in many countries, from the representatives of the teaching profession, who felt that practising school-teachers should have influence over the courses which gave entry to their ranks. Scotland took an early step in establishing a General Teaching Council in 1965, registration with which became a condition of employment as a teacher. The Council, in making requirements for registration, has been able to exert considerable influence over the colleges of education (Bone, 1976).

A more widespread development was that teacher associations became discontented by the way in which major changes could be made in preparation for entry to their profession without their being consulted at all, an example being the way in which the new BEd degree courses were established in the United Kingdom in the mid-1960s. In those cases where universities were validating new college courses it tended to be assumed that teachers would be so pleased with the opening up of degree possibilities that they would accept the universities' requirements without question. However, teachers' associations sometimes felt that the academic requirements of the degree took undue precedence over the arrangements for teaching practice, and by the time further changes were being made in the mid-1970s the teachers were less willing to accept this. Without a teaching council on the Scottish model, their opportunities to exert influence have tended to depend on the process of validation, which in England and Wales has been through the Council for National Academic Awards. That Council, to which, with government encouragement, many teacher training institutions turned in the 1970s, has ensured that there have always been school-teacher members on the visiting parties which have examined course proposals, as well as on the committees within the institutions which have devised these proposals. Lynch (1979) again provides a good account of the process, and it is certainly true that the influence of teachers on training all over the United Kingdom is very much greater in 1980 than it was ten years ago. And this is not merely a British trend; it is one which is noticeable throughout the developed world, although the forms of influence vary from country to country.

In this discussion of external pressures on training in the developed countries it may seem that undue emphasis has been placed on the United Kingdom, but that is probably where the process of contraction has been most clearly seen and best documented. That the general trend of the pressures has been much the same elsewhere can be shown by a brief look at the McGregor Report on 'The Education and Training of Teachers in British Columbia' (1978). This is the report of a B C Government Committee which, whether it is implemented or not (and resistance to it will be strong), makes recommendations which are a typical response to the pressures identified in this chapter. Its main suggestion is the establishment of a new Council for the Education of Teachers which would recommend policy concerning the preparation of teachers, monitor existing programmes, and approve all new programmes. This Council would be composed of locally elected trustees, members of the lay public, teachers in service, and a representative of the government, with the deans of the three universities being present but having no vote.

The McGregor Committee also felt that this was 'an opportune time for standards of admission to be raised' and recommended that there be no direct admission from secondary school to a university faculty of education, but that the completion of at least one academic year in another faculty with an average of 70 per cent be prerequisite. There would, in addition, be a test in English usage. All elementary teachers should complete a five year degree course, three being devoted primarily to academic education, and two primarily to professional training, with at least sixteen weeks being spent on teaching practice during the last two years. Secondary teachers would similarly require five years of study, of which four would be devoted to academic education and one to professional training, with a minimum of twelve weeks' teaching practice. Those who trained the teachers in the universities 'should themselves be models of excellence in the classroom', seeing teaching as their primary obligation and regarding research as a valid but secondary activity.

Whether it ultimately proves influential or not, this McGregor Report manages in 25 pages to provide excellent documentation of the pressures and criticisms being directed toward the initial training of teachers at the end of the 1970s.

Pressures on training in the developing countries, and the response

The pressures for change which came to be exerted on teacher training institutions in the developing countries in the 1970s were based upon a common recognition that the training systems served to support forms of education which were ill-suited to the needs of the countries themselves. This was seen most clearly in areas formerly ruled by colonial powers, which encouraged education systems that were Western in values, objectives, content, methods and language (Hercik, 1976). It might have been expected that when these countries achieved political independence they would have recognized the need to provide education related to the overall needs and priorities of the population; instead, they tended at first to increase provision of the traditional kind of education which parents demanded of their children.

However, doubts about the usefulness of inherited educational patterns were soon voiced in the 1960s. For example, the conference of African states on the development of education in Africa (held at Addis Ababa in 1961) called for a reform of curricula, text books and methods of teaching 'so as to take account of African environment, child development and cultural heritage', and sought a more practical orientation for universal primary education. Targets for advance were set, but at a similar conference in Nairobi in 1968 it had to be admitted that these had not been reached except in the field of higher education. Doubtless there were a variety of reasons for this, but it is interesting that one given frequently at the conference was the failure of teachers to adapt to the new curricula and methods.

Thus what happened in the developing countries in the 1970s, although occurring at differing rates from area to area, was that there came to be pressure on the teacher training institutions of an even more fundamental kind than that described in the previous section as affecting their developed counterparts. They had been producing teachers fitted for a role which was no longer wanted, and what they now had to do was to train teachers who could bring the schools closer to the communities they served. They also had to train far more of them. UNESCO gave technical and financial assistance; new colleges were built to provide more teachers; and a number of projects were set up to provide for a reorientation of training. The Gandhi Shikshan Bhavan and the Hansraj Jivands College, both in Bombay, provide examples of how teachers in training have been required to spend part of their course on manual work, and part in organized assistance to slum dwellers (Cropley and Dave, 1978).

In Tanzania, primary education concentrates upon the achievement of literacy and numeracy, the fostering of good citizenship, the encouragement of a spirit of self-help, and the study of community activities. The pupils play their part in the development of their village by working on farms, digging canals, etc, and students training as teachers pay regular visits to such schools to provide help and to acquire the necessary skills for this kind of work themselves.

As in the previous section, it may be helpful to end with one example given in a little more detail. In Bangladesh, an education system which has produced large numbers of unemployed graduates, and which has seemed irrelevant to the lives of the vast majority of the population, is now being radically altered. The administrators there are trying to produce a system in which children are not expected to attend school continuously, but can alternate schooling with actual work, and in which that schooling is much more closely related to their ordinary lives. There is to be a wide variety of courses, formal and non-formal, full-time and part-time, to fit the varying needs of individuals and their occupations, for the overall intention is that education will be work-oriented, with easy movement between study and employment. Higher education is to be available only to those who have already obtained employment, thereby eliminating the wastage of resources which has occurred so frequently in the past (Huq, 1977).

Perhaps the greatest problem in all this, however, is that of finding the teachers who can provide the new form of education. The existing teachers of Bangladesh, poorly trained and perhaps even more poorly paid, have not in the past been noted for their flexibility, inventiveness, or willingness to adopt a practical approach.

The training institutions are therefore now seeking to move over rapidly to the preparation of teachers for this kind of work. In addition, the government is trying to inject a new force into the situation through plans for the establishment of a national development corps, a form of 'national service' which may be made compulsory for everyone who seeks entry to higher education and who wishes to obtain a job in government service. This would involve young people in two years' work on a subsistence wage, spent mainly in practical activities in the rural areas. One of the requirements might be that they would help school-teachers to implement the new ideas for education. It is hoped that, even with a relatively short training, their youth and vigour may help to bring about the necessary changes.

As in so many of the developing countries, the task is enormous, but it is only through imaginative approaches of this kind that advances are likely to be achieved with any speed.

Structural changes in the developed countries

Although teacher training systems vary quite considerably within the developed countries, there have been certain common trends in their responses to the pressures described in the first section of this chapter. First, and not surprisingly, when it became clear that fewer teachers were needed, the training institutions argued that it was time to strengthen their courses by making them longer, thereby to equip teachers more fully for the demands of their future work. This process has been seen in Australia, Canada and several parts of Europe within the 1970s. It has occurred both where training has been concurrent with the higher education of the students, as in primary training in Western Canada, and where it has been consecutive, following a lengthy period of higher education elsewhere, as in secondary training in Norway. To take the latter country as an example, professional training has always been very short (15 weeks), and it is now hoped that the institutions will persuade the government to double that period.

The lengthening and strengthening of courses has been accompanied by a process in which a much higher proportion of the teacher population comes to have a degree, and the international trend is certainly towards degrees for all teachers. England and Wales, where for a long time non-graduates were allowed to teach in secondary schools, are now moving over almost completely to degree courses; courses leading to diplomas have not been offered since 1978, even to primary teachers. Since 1979, teachers in those countries will work either for BEd degrees or for a postgraduate certificate following a degree course elsewhere. In countries like Scotland where that position has not yet been reached, the colleges of education have been arguing for it strongly, and their lack of success to date is only due to the reluctance of governments to incur additional expenditure.

The coming of degrees for all teachers removes what has been perhaps the most obvious difference in their qualifications. It not only brings primary and secondary teachers closer together, but also makes it easier to abandon the traditional differences in training among secondary school teachers which have existed in many parts of Europe. This is increasingly important as more and more European countries move over to a fully comprehensive system of schooling.

In the United States, perhaps the most obvious change has been the increase in state control of training, through certification. Now, in many states, the education authority evaluates training courses, often through visits to universities and meetings with faculty, students, former students and school-teachers. If this makes the universities more accountable to the public, it also increases the cost of the process, besides making training more susceptible to fluctuations in political thinking (Atkin, 1979).

Another response to the pressures of contraction is that training institutions everywhere have tried to become much more selective when dealing with applications. As fewer teachers have been needed it has been hoped that the teaching profession would be able to recruit from the same ability cohorts as do other professions (Taylor, 1978). Unfortunately, the increased level of selection has only been accompanied by a fairly limited increase in the average educational standards of entrants, since the publicity given to teacher unemployment has tended to produce a falling-off in applications for courses. Indeed, in England and Wales in 1977 and 1978, when institutions were moving over to degree courses and thereby requiring a higher standard of entrant, quite a number found it difficult to achieve the quotas set for them by the government, even when those quotas were much smaller than the numbers they had been training only a year or two previously.

With employment less certain for trained teachers than in the past, naturally much thought has been given to alternative destinations for those on training courses. Thus, in 1972, the Committee of Inquiry led by Lord James advocated the establishment of a new Diploma in Higher Education which could be awarded at the end of a two-year course in a college (DES, 1972); this could be an end-product in itself or alternatively it could be the first part of either a BEd course for a teacher or a BA course for someone with other intentions. This allowed students to keep their options open for the first two years, and the idea was taken up by many institutions in England (Porter, 1977), thereby increasing the extent of consecutive training. The new DipHE qualification has not been as successful as was hoped, however, and critics have said that the training of the great majority who would take BEd degrees has been distorted, since in such places all the teaching practice comes in the final year along with heavy degree studies.

This chapter is concerned with initial, rather than in-service training; however, one of the most important changes in teacher education in the 1970s was the extent to which those engaged in pre-service training have also come to be involved in working alongside experienced teachers in school-focused in-service work. This has obviously made them more aware of current developments in the schools, and has gone some way towards removing previous weaknesses.

While it is true that teacher training has suffered severe contraction, with closures of colleges in Britain and threats of closures in certain other countries like Australia, it would nevertheless be wrong to present a pessimistic view of the effects of structural changes. What has emerged from the crisis of the 1970s has in most cases been the establishment of stronger units of training, even if they are fewer in number.

Attempts to bring training institutions to work together have usually been accompanied by difficulties, as can be seen in the story of the establishment of the Atlantic Institution of Education in the maritime provinces of Canada (Anderson and Lauwerys, 1978). In England and Wales the process was particularly traumatic, leading to widespread criticism of the government (Hencke, 1978), but the institutions have now become less firmly wedded to traditional practices, and more concerned with regular revision of their courses.

Curricular and methodological change in the developed countries

It was in the 1970s that the world accepted the need for the continuing education of teachers. Even if in-service training expanded less than had been hoped because of the economic recession, it was natural to limit the range of work covered in initial training. Where a further period of training could be expected, institutions could abandon the attempt to provide the type of broad but superficial coverage of which students had complained so bitterly. Thus, at the beginning of the 1980s, initial training is no longer designed to produce a complete teacher, but rather to prepare students for their first teaching post. At its narrowest, this is seen as the provision of 'survival skills', and implies some retreat from professional education towards basic training. Nevertheless, it is true that much of what has traditionally been regarded as the appropriate course content was presented prematurely.

In the teaching of skills, significant but rather limited use has been made of one technique which, only about ten years ago, appeared likely to revolutionize training. This is micro-teaching, and the story of its application to teacher training is a disappointing one. It appears to have several potential advantages over conventional training: it provides a learning environment less complex than the classroom, and therefore one in which the trainee has greater opportunity to practise skills; it offers him an opportunity to concentrate on his own learning rather than on coping with the needs and demands of his pupils; it allows him to analyse his own practice systematically and to make his own evaluations of it; and it allows for repeated practice until a particular skill has been fully mastered (McIntyre, Macleod and Griffiths, 1977). But less use has been made of this instrument than one would have expected, especially in Europe and Australia, because of the resistance of the traditional training departments and the existence of genuine (but perhaps exaggerated) logistical difficulties. The trend is towards its decline, largely because it is so difficult to provide trained and skilled supervision for each student on a one-to-one basis where large numbers exist, and institutions have resorted to the use of untrained supervision or the use of peer groups as evaluators. These are both expedients which, as research has shown, reduce the effectiveness of such training (Perrott, 1977). Partly for this reason, it is now being used more in in-service training, where the numbers of students tend to be smaller, and where their capacity for self-evaluation is greater.

By contrast, a moment which *has* had very great impact on teacher education, especially in the United States, is the competency-based approach. Supported by behaviourist psychology and the drive for accountability, this has spread so rapidly that now, at the beginning of the 1980s, it is not so much an innovation as the established method of teacher training in North America. In many states teacher certification procedures are founded upon competency-based programmes, and New York State, for example, is moving over entirely to this approach (Burton, 1977). Dissatisfied with the effectiveness of previous methods of training, New York has rejected the 'assumption that completion of didactic courses is automatically translated into competent practice', and says that 'the basis for certification should be demonstrated competence germane to the field of certification' (State Education Department of New York, 1975).

Briefly, in this approach the required competencies are identified in behavioural terms, with assessment criteria specified and made public. Student teachers are trained to acquire the necessary skills (or knowledge, or attitudes), and given an opportunity to practise them, first in controlled situations (often with the use of technology, sometimes micro-teaching), and later in normal school situations. In the early versions of the model, the pupils taught by the student teachers were then tested for their acquisition of the skills or knowledge thought to have resulted from the teaching. However, the impossibility of relating pupil learning to any specific teaching behaviour has brought about a retreat from that position, so that what now happens is that the student teachers are required to demonstrate in schools that they can employ the skills assumed to produce desirable learning (Magoon, 1976).

The competency-based approach has aroused fierce opposition from educational philosophers who condemned it as too mechanistic. 'The most important attitudes and values developed through a liberal education resist such codification' (Shugre, 1973). There has also been political opposition from within the training institutions, whose authority is undermined by the participation of school districts, teacher unions, etc, which accompanies the competency approach. Finally, while this approach has been welcomed by those concerned about accountability because they believe they can measure what the courses achieve, the actual costs of the competency-based approach may be high, since it is said to call for additional faculty members working closely with students, a large amount of paid release time for teachers, and sophisticated computerized management systems (Burton, 1977). If the movement has had 'remarkably little impact upon Europe' (Taylor, 1978), it may be because in that continent there has been less money available for teacher education, less demand for accountability, and slightly more attention paid to educational philosophers.

As indicated in the first section of this chapter, dissatisfaction in the 1970s was not confined to teacher education; it was evident in relation to the whole process of schooling. Just as the competency-based approach supplanted traditional methods in teacher education in many places, so in the schools a new slogan has gathered strength — mastery learning. With Bloom as its standard bearer, and such others as Block, Anderson, Burns and Galloway as its evangelists,* this movement has gained considerable ground among theoreticians, and has been implemented in a number of North American schools (eg Lethbridge, Alberta). It would not be appropriate to consider it in any detail in this chapter, but inevitably it has implications for teacher training.

Briefly, mastery learning is based on the belief that, under appropriate instructional conditions, virtually all students can learn well and 'master' most of what they are taught, and that teachers can and should teach in such a way that students achieve this mastery. There are two main strategies: the first, which applies mostly to schools, is Bloom's own 'Learning for Mastery' which, with a relatively fixed time for the instruction, gives each pupil/student differentiated treatment according to aptitude, with the teacher devising a variety of alternative instructional procedures so that each student reaches the level of mastery specified in advance; the second, called the 'Personalised System of Instruction' (PSI), was developed by Keller (1968, 1974) for higher education where time is more fluid. Students proceed at their own pace, but they can only advance to new material when mastery has been displayed to a 'proctor', who may be an advanced student or a classmate.

The success of this movement would depend on teachers being trained to apply it, and a number of projects have developed with that intention (eg at Bloomington, Indiana). The Keller Plan has been received with enthusiasm in a number of institutions, but, nevertheless, at the beginning of the 1980s, mastery learning is still used relatively little in teacher training. This is partly because it is open to objections similar to those aimed at the competency-based approach. Thus, those who reject the latter reject mastery learning also, while those who employ the competency-based approach can feel that they have no need to go further towards mastery learning. Yet there is a difference: in the competency-based approach students may receive different grades and some may even fail; in mastery learning, ideally, all students receive the grade A.

A sharp contrast to all this is presented by the growing interest, again in North America, in human relations training for teachers. Based upon the work of Carl Rogers, this is emphasized in some institutions as a necessary complement to the focus on 'mechanically' acquired competencies. In the early 1970s it was limited mostly to in-service training, since it required expert group leaders, of whom there were relatively few, but at the end of the 1970s it was being more widely used in pre-service training, with short programmes for all trainees on certain courses. The Thiokol Interaction Laboratory for Teacher Development is one of the sets for exercises used in such places, with the students actively involved in role playing, simulation games and action-oriented problem solving (Thiokol Chemical Corporation, 1977).

This approach centres upon the belief that the success or failure of teachers will depend just as much on their ability to interact successfully with other people as upon any other skills or knowledge which they may possess. The whole aim is to increase that ability in each of the learners; the approach is humanistic in that it concentrates on understanding of oneself and of others in person-to-person interaction. The programmes tend to be relatively short, since this is still a

* For references, see Bloom (1968, 1976), Block and Anderson (1975), Block and Burns (1976) and Galloway (1976).

developing discipline, but interest in it is increasing, and the students who follow such programmes appear to find them highly beneficial. This humanistic approach is also to be found in some places outside North America, eg Melbourne (Dow, 1979), and perhaps it is now spreading. If so, it should be seen not as an alternative to the competency-based approach, but as a desirable complement to it.

It is only in the field of teaching practice, however, that trends are observable which are common to almost every developed country. The first has been a general recognition of the need to bring the part of initial training which takes place in colleges and universities into a much closer relationship with the part which takes place in schools. The lack of such a close and planned relationship was one of the most frequent complaints of the early 1970s (eg Stones and Morris, 1972), and during the 1970s there was a movement in North America, Australasia and Europe to make the practical work carried out in schools build upon and reinforce more strongly the theoretical work of the training institution.

This has usually involved the appointment of a specific person within the staff of the school to take responsibility for the general oversight of the students' practice, and to ensure the implementation of a programme planned jointly with the college or university. The title varies (eg in Scotland they are 'regents' while in California they are 'resident teachers'), and in some places such persons have responsibility for the in-service induction of new teachers rather than for the pre-service training of students (eg the 'teacher tutors' in pilot schemes in Liverpool and Northumberland). Common to them all, however, is a need to work in close co-operation with colleagues in the training institution. One of the most fully-fledged schemes of this kind is set out in the Sneddon Report (1978) produced by the Scottish General Teaching Council.

An example of the new approaches is provided by Jordanhill, the largest college of eduction in Britain, where the one year course for students qualifying for secondary school teaching has been reorganized to provide both more sustained contact with particular schools and closer relationships between professional studies (educational theory and psychology), methods work and practice. The latter comes partly through a 'co-ordinated day' each week in college, with three major topics (discipline, assessment, and social education) providing the focus of study, and partly through arrangements whereby the school regents conduct seminars relating these topics to features of the teaching practice experience. Thus it is planned that the theoretical and practical work reinforce each other.

The general trend, however, is toward some reduction in the theoretical part of initial training, partly because it has been criticized so much and partly because it is felt that some of it can be provided more relevantly at a later in-service stage. As a consequence, the periods of teaching practice are tending to become longer, with students being assessed less on their ability to teach a single lesson in front of the college tutor, and more on their effectiveness in carrying out a programme with a class which is sustained over a number of weeks, or even a term or semester.

An interesting example is provided by British Columbia. There the University of Victoria has entered into an arrangement with the Saanich School District whereby some final year students are contracted on salary to spend half of each day for the entire year in particular Saanich schools. There they take full responsibility for teaching one secondary class and assist an experienced teacher in the teaching of another. Besides teaching, they become heavily involved in assisting with extra-curricular work and other school activities, thus becoming active members of the school community. In the other half of the day they do methods work and theoretical work in the university, where the relationship with the schools has been strengthened by the involvement of outstanding school teachers in the methods course. The university pays these teachers a part-time salary and also pays substitute time to release them from some of their school work. It is claimed that the arrangements make for a constant interaction between theoretical and practical considerations, and that this is one of the great strengths of the programme (Harker, 1979).

Another trend, found mainly in North America, but not exclusively (also in Melbourne, for instance — Dow, 1979), has been towards a greater measure of self-assessment by students while working in schools. Typically, as in some universities in California, there is an assessment schedule which contains a large number of items, and towards the middle and end of each practice the students are invited to assess themselves on these points in conference with their supervisors. Those with experience say that a remarkable consistency develops between the scoring of the supervisors and that of the students, and one of the great advantages is that the students seem able to discuss their own abilities and experiences in a more realistic and responsible way than is typically found in institutions where assessment is carried out entirely externally. Self-involvement reduces the negative connotations of assessment, and brings it nearer to what Cope (1975) calls a 'process of intensifying student learning'.

Perhaps that is a good note on which to end this chapter, for intensifying student learning is the intention behind all the developments of recent years. At the beginning of the 1970s, teacher training was said to be too diffuse, too superficial in its coverage, insufficiently professional in its own approaches, and too haphazard in relation to teaching practice. Now, after a period which has been difficult in most countries and quite traumatic in some, it is common to find new forms of organization and new patterns of training in existence. These have usually been devised too recently for the teacher trainers to be completely confident that their problems have been solved; indeed one result of the traumas of the mid-1970s may be that it will be a long time before they are fully confident again. It may, however, be no bad thing that the complacency of the 1960s has gone, and that there is, almost everywhere in the world, an increased willingness to question existing practices, and to enter into partnership with other agencies. Just as teacher training is itself seen as only one part of the process of professional development of teachers, so the teacher training institutions no longer can or should stand alone.

References

Anderson, G J and Lauwerys, J A (1978) *Institutional Leadership for Educational Reform: The Atlantic Institute of Education* UNESCO: Paris

Atkin, J M (1979) Educational accountability in the United States *Educational Analysis* 1 1

Block, J H and Anderson, L W (1975) *Mastery Learning in Classroom Instruction* Macmillan: New York

Block, J H and Burns, R B (1976) Mastery learning *in* Shulman (1976)

Bloom, B S (1968) *Learning for Mastery* UCLA-CSEIP: Centre for the Study of Evaluation of Instruction Programs, University of California at Los Angeles

Bloom, B S (1976) *Human Characteristics and School Learning* McGraw-Hill: New York

Bone, T R (1976) Current developments in teacher education in Scotland *in* Lomax. (1976)

Burton, A (1977) Competency-based teacher education in the USA *Compare* 7 1

Commonwealth Foundation (1977) *Education for Development* Occasional Paper XLIV: London

Cope, E (1975) *Research into the Practical Elements of Teacher Training, with Special Reference to the Supervisory Process and Student Learning* Society for Research into Higher Education: Surrey

Cropley, A J and Dave, R H (1978) *Lifelong Education and the Training of Teachers* Pergamon Press and the UNESCO Institute for Education: Oxford

Department of Education and Science (1972) *Teacher Education and Training* (The James Report) HMSO: London

Dow, G (1979) *Learning to Teach: Teaching to Learn* Routledge and Kegan Paul: London

Galloway, C (1976) *Psychology for Learning and Teaching* McGraw-Hill: New York

Goldman, R J (1976) Innovations in teacher education in Australia *in* Lomax (1976)

Harker, W J (1979) The Saanich Teacher Training Programme *Innovation* (March 1979) UNESCO: Geneva

Hencke, D (1978) *Colleges in Crisis* Penguin Books: Harmondsworth

Hercik, V (1976) European models of teacher education in developing countries *in* Lomax (1976)

Huq, M S (1977) Social, economic and political realities and the structure of education in South-East Asia *in* Commonwealth Foundation (1977)

Illich, I (1971) *De-Schooling Society* Calder and Boyars: London

Keller, F S (1968) Goodbye Teacher... *Journal of Applied Behaviour Analysis* 1: 79-88

Keller, F S and Sherman, J G (1974) *The Keller Plan Handbook* W A Benjamin: Menlo Park

Lomax, D E (ed) (1976) *European Perspectives in Teacher Education* John Wiley and Sons: London

Lynch, J (1979) *The Reform of Teacher Education in the United Kingdom* Society for Research into Higher Education: Surrey

Magoon, A J (1976) Teaching and performance-based teacher education *in* Lomax (1976)

McGregor Report (1978) *The Education and Training of Teachers in British Columbia* Government of British Columbia: Victoria

McIntyre, D, Macleod, G and Griffiths, R (eds) (1977) *Investigations of Microteaching* Croom Helm: London

Nisbet, J, Shanks, D and Darling, J (1977) A survey of teachers' opinions on the primary diploma course in Scotland *Scottish Educational Studies* 9 2

Perrott, E (1977) *Microteaching in Higher Education: Research Development and Practice* Society for Research into Higher Education: Surrey

Porter, J (1977) Further and higher education: the future of teacher education *Journal of Further and Higher Education* Summer 1977

Scottish Education Department (1978) *Learning to Teach* (The Sneddon Report) HMSO: Edinburgh

Shugre, M E (1973) *Performance-based Education and the Subject Matter Fields* American Association of Colleges for Teacher Education: Washington, D C

Shulman, L S (ed) (1976) *Review of Research in Education, 1976* American Educational Research Association, Peacock: Itasca, Ill

State Education Department of New York (1975) *Teacher Education Programme Proposals* New York

Stones, E A and Morris, S (1972) *Teaching Practice: Problems and Perspectives* Methuen: London

Taylor, W (1978) *Research and Reform in Teacher Education* National Foundation for Educational Research for the Council of Europe: Oxford

Thiokol Chemical Corporation (1977) *Interaction Laboratory for Teacher Development* PO Box 1000, New Town, Pennsylvania 18940

4. The induction of beginning teachers

Richard Tisher

Summary: This chapter on teacher induction considers the planned professional support provided for new teachers during their first teaching year. The provisions made by various educational authorities are discussed under the three headings of provisions during entry, school-based activities and system-based activities. It is noted that although there are a variety of provisions for new teachers they are not always as well served as might be expected. Also, as induction is a complex process it is not possible to argue for the superiority of any one induction practice; all those reported have a place.

However, in order to improve the quality of induction it is suggested that those persons responsible for induction programmes and policies could well explore certain directions with some profit. Included in these are an extension of the purposes of induction as presently conceived, the training in counselling skills of those experienced teachers who have special responsibilities for induction, basing induction practices in the school where the new teacher is a staff member, altering the teaching conditions under which beginning teachers start their career, and changing expectations regarding induction on the part of schools, training institutions and beginning teachers. It is also argued that any proposals for the better induction of teachers need to take cognizance of the dual aspect of teacher development — the professional and the personal.

Introduction

Why an interest in induction?

Although in the last few years there have been fewer new teachers entering the profession in most nations, the issues and challenges associated with their entry appear to remain the same. For example, there is still an almost overnight change in responsibilities for learning; from being students responsible only to themselves for their own learning they become fully responsible for the instruction of numerous pupils from the first working day. In fact, as Lortie (1975) notes, there seems to be a general expectation that they should perform the same tasks as a 25 year veteran. However, there is not a comparable expectation that they will perform the tasks as competently as their more experienced colleagues.

Information from a variety of sources in different countries (eg, national research teams in the UK and Australia, school principals, superintendents of school districts in the USA) combine to indicate that the rapid change from being a trainee to being a teacher can produce a range of reactions; these include a disenchantment with pre-service programmes, a temporary jettisoning of some educational ideals such as the encouragement of individual, self-propelled learning in pupils, and a tendency to resort to lecturing in class. New teachers and their principals admit there are a number of things that beginning teachers manage less than adequately, for example teaching immigrants, slow learners and groups with a wide ability range (Tisher, Fyfield and Taylor, 1979). There is also a prevalent belief among principals that beginning teachers are not finished products at the conclusion of their pre-service education, and that they can still learn more from others, including their experienced colleagues. It is no wonder, then, that state employing authorities, local educational authorities, teachers' centres, principals' organizations and teachers' associations have evinced concern both about the quality of new recruits to teaching and with how they manage during their first year, as well as with the type of professional support they receive as they learn to cope with their new job. In several countries national and state resources have been made available to improve the mode of new teachers' entry to teaching. The terms 'teacher induction' or 'induction of beginning teachers' are generally used to refer to this entry and to the planned support the new teachers receive as that occurs.

There is also an implied expectation that during induction new teachers will become, at a basic level, professionally competent and professionally at ease in their job. As a consequence it is difficult to state precisely when induction ends. Some teachers become quite competent and at ease within several months of taking an appointment, whereas others may require several years. Nevertheless a number of education authorities (particularly in the UK and Australia) are especially interested in the first year of teaching and for the purposes of the present discussion attention will be concentrated on the planned provisions for beginning teachers during their first teaching year. This concentration on planned provisions is not intended to imply that informal professional support for new teachers has no value or is necessarily of less significance than the more formal provisions. On the contrary, it is recognized that it can be extremely effective. Unfortunately it is difficult to document the occurrence, nature and frequency of informal procedures as precisely as the formal ones. Furthermore, the provision of informal support is a chance affair very much dependent upon the ability and willingness of experienced teachers to give time and counsel to their new colleagues. If it is accepted that induction into teaching is one of the crucial stages in the overall process of professional development and socialization of teachers then it cannot be left to chance.

Sources of information

What then is being done for new teachers? Can its quality be improved? These are questions to be addressed in the following sections. Ancillary questions are: When special provisions are made for beginning teachers what proportion of them receive these? and What types of professional support do beginning teachers require and recommend? The information which follows has been culled from a number of sources in several countries: acknowledgements appear at the end of the chapter. The greatest amount of published information on what is done formally by national, state, regional and school authorities seems to be available in the UK and in Australia where national agencies have funded studies of teacher induction.

In Australia the Education Research and Development Committee, a federally funded committee established to foster research in education, provided money during 1976-1978 for a national survey of induction practices.

This project involved two stages; first, a descriptive survey of what state, regional and school authorities claimed was done to support the entry of beginning teachers to the profession, and secondly, a systematic national survey of what beginning teachers actually experienced. The second stage was executed in three phases. After the first few months of teaching (late March) a systematic, representative sample of new teachers in all states and territories was surveyed by a mailed questionnaire. At the same time the principals of the schools to which the sample had been appointed also responded to a questionnaire, some items of which were identical to ones in the teacher's document. In mid-year (June-July) a selected number of beginning teachers in inner-city industrial, outer metropolitan, country-urban, and remote areas of the nation were interviewed. Finally, towards the end of their first year (October) another questionnaire was mailed to a systematic representative sample of new teachers throughout the nation. Over 1,600 teachers completed the first questionnaire and 1,300 the second. About 700 principals or their nominees completed the principals' questionnaire. The findings which are now available in two published reports (Tisher, Fyfield and Taylor, 1978, 1979) were first disseminated personally by the research team to state, territorial and school authorities as well as to training institutions, principals' associations and teachers' unions.

In the UK, there was an extensive survey of beginning teachers by Taylor and Dale (1971) of the Bristol University School of Education Research Unit; these findings, coupled with an increasing national awareness of the problems of these teachers, prompted the Department of Education and Science to fund a research and development project to study the needs, problems and advantages associated with the mounting of in-service courses for new (probationary) teachers in a variety of urban and rural settings. The project began in the 1968-69 school year with pilot courses for beginning teachers, conducted in an urban Local Education Authority (LEA). During 1969-70 more detailed experimental courses were conducted in another four LEAs and the impact of these was assessed through questionnaires and interviews. In the latter part of 1971 the Department of Education and Science funded a programme to disseminate the findings and recommendations (see Bolam, 1973). A series of lectures and seminars were arranged throughout the country for teachers, administrators, and lecturers from colleges and universities so that all those interested in induction procedures could be made aware of the practical outcomes of the research project. Another initiative was taken sometime after the publication of the James Report on Teacher Education and Training in 1972 when full scale induction schemes were monitored and evaluated in the Liverpool and Northumberland LEAs (Bolam and Baker, 1975) during 1974-78. Other developments have occured since then and reference will be made to these in appropriate places in the ensuing text.

There appear to be no comparable reports in other countries of national surveys of induction like the Australian ones, or of sponsored, monitored and evaluated action research projects like those in the UK. Some programmes have been established within the United States but they are few and far between; only one state pilot scheme is reported within the past seven years (Zeichner, 1979). It was initiated in seven school districts in Alabama and involved university lecturers, state education consultants and local authority programme co-ordinators, each of whom assisted beginning teachers with their daily tasks. A number of local USA education authorities state that beginning teachers certainly do receive help informally within schools from experienced colleagues, but this is not substantiated by precise data or by clear official policy statements.

In fact, a prevalent view of the USA delegates who attended a national conference on Research in Teacher Education in Austin, Texas, in January 1979 was that very little attention was being given to the induction of new teachers in their country. Only further research will tell whether this is actually the case. It may be that the subsequent findings will mirror those of a recent research report in New Zealand on the professional development of beginning teachers (Murdoch, 1978). Those findings suggest that beginning teachers do not fare very well with respect to help received from within or without their school.

From an inspection of various local and national documents and from comments received from a number of correspondents there seems to be a general consensus of opinion that comparable induction issues exist for all countries and that there are remarkable similarities with respect to the professional support required by beginning teachers in different countries. Bold assumptions, no doubt, but ones that each reader can test against the information available to him regarding his own country and local education authority.

When new teachers take up their first appointment they enter areas of competing pressures (Fenstermacher, 1979; Lortie, 1975) where they must adopt or create appropriate social strategies to help them cope with the social situation confronting them. By this time they have already acquired a 'latent culture' (Lacey, 1977) which includes skills, values, attitudes and perspectives obtained during pre-service education. It is of value to assess how well various groups capitalize on this latent culture, which will be activated differently depending on what is done for new teachers as they come progressively under the influence of their employing authority, their school and classes, and of the profession at large. In order to address this question and the ones posed earlier, the next few stages of the discussion are grouped under three by no means mutually exclusive headings. These stages deal with (a) provisions for beginning teachers during the during the early phases of their entry to the profession, (b) provisions made for them by their schools (ie school-based induction activities), and (c) the provisions by local or regional educational authorities during the first year of teaching (ie system-based activities). Clearly in a short account it is neither possible nor appropriate to describe all the facets of professional support that can be provided. More detail is provided elsewhere (Bolam, 1973; Bolam and Baker, 1975; Tisher, Fyfield and Taylor, 1978, 1979). However, the next three sections seek to identify key induction activities.

Induction activities: provisions for new teachers on entry to teaching

Provision of information

Beginning teachers can receive important professional support when they first encounter an educational employing authority, whether this be represented by a school principal, a local school selection committee, a state authority panel or personnel officer. During the encounter the new teachers gain some impressions about the authority's views of their worth and status in the profession, so these meetings can be quite significant. At this time most employing authorities provide printed information about schools and districts, and about conditions of appointment. These and other matters are usually discussed as well in associated interviews. The quality and nature of printed materials and interviews vary greatly between authorities and *prima facie* it seems their value and significance as professional support are greatly under-rated. At times, then, if

Australian experiences are any guide, smaller local education authorities as well as monolithic state authorities do not provide adequate information about their schools to facilitate applicants' choices. Furthermore, larger education authorities often delay the confirmation of new teachers' appointments, thereby generating anxiety and feelings that they may be of small worth. In a country such as Australia, where the majority of new teachers enter one of the geographically extensive state or territory systems, the nature of their first encounter with a state employing authority can be quite important in shaping professional attitudes.

It is appropriate here to note that the administrative pattern in Australian education is complex. Government schools (the majority) are administered under six separate State education departments and two Territory authorities: within these there is a clear separation of primary, secondary and, in one case, technical divisions. To cater more adequately for localized needs and to reduce the high degree of centralization of authority in the capital cities most government systems have introduced a moderate degree of regionalization by creating regional educational offices. In addition to the government systems, there is a well-developed Catholic system of schooling and a large number of independent schools, both Catholic and non-Catholic. This complexity is to be found in a country which equals the United States in area but has only one sixteenth of its population. Furthermore, some State education departments, though only responsible for a staff and pupil population comparable in number to staff and pupils in the Chicago education district, are spread over a geographical area almost one thousand times the size. It is difficult therefore to make brief general statements about educational practices in Australia, but, at the risk of over-simplification, some of the flavour of existing procedures set up to assist people entering the profession will be incorporated in the ensuing descriptions of induction practices. Where appropriate, comparisons will be made with other countries.

In Australia, once an application for appointment is accepted appointees are generally notified by letter, although about one in seven are contacted by telephone: only about one in seventeen are informed at interview. New teachers entering the State and Territory systems and some Catholic school systems undertake to serve in any one of the authority's schools, whereas for independent schools new applicants can expect to teach in the particular school to which they apply. The various State, Territory and Catholic school system authorities do invite applicants to specify preferences for teaching positions but the final assignment to a school for most of the nation's new teachers is done by a Senior Officer in a head office in one of the capital cities. It is intriguing, therefore, to note that 82 per cent of beginning teachers throughout Australia believe they are able to exercise a preference for appointment and about the same proportion were satisfied with their school when asked a few months after taking up the appointment (Tisher, Fyfield and Taylor, 1979). These figures are comparable to ones reported in the UK eight years earlier. Taylor and Dale (1971) observed that 89 per cent of the new teachers they surveyed were reasonably satisfied with the process of their appointment and their placement.

In the event of a teacher being employed by an Australian State Education Department, contact with his employers is often brief. Probably for this reason, as noted earlier, some employing authorities rely on printed materials to help new teachers bridge the gap between professional training and taking up a particular teaching position. Certainly, on appointment, a beginning teacher's need for information escalates dramatically. Beginning teachers seem to want printed handbooks issued at this stage; in a survey conducted by one Australian State Education Department, the teachers requested information on such matters as leave, legal position, transfers, retirement funds, resource materials, clerical duties and availability of consultants. Some states take account of new teachers' needs by producing this information. A few also produce 'profiles' of their schools. Generally, the only brochures available from non-government schools are those geared to the needs of prospective parents rather than teachers.

Although it is generally accepted beginning teachers require a great deal of information on entry to teaching, it is surprising that quite a number maintain they did not receive any. Whether they actually did, or did not, is not clearly known; what is significant is their perception. For example, when asked towards the end of their first year of teaching, 51 per cent of Australia's beginning teachers maintained they had not received written materials on their conditions of appointment. A higher proportion (78 per cent) admitted, however, that it was readily obtainable. Towards the end of their first year about one-third were still worrying about receiving information regarding specialist services available to their school and about the availability of curriculum materials. These findings imply that, despite the claims from employing authorities that printed information is readily available, beginning teachers are not as well served as might be expected. Furthermore, it is highly likely that this situation applies in other nations as well as Australia.

Prior visits to schools: orientation programmes

For some beginning teachers, the lack of readily available information can be compensated for, to some extent, by a visit to their school before the first term starts. In 1977 in Australia about 69 per cent of beginning teachers made these visits, half of which were initiated by the teachers themselves. For the remainder the initiation and organization came from the system authority or individual school. The visits were generally of short duration but are regarded as having several benefits, including the reduction of the new teachers' anxieties about entering an unfamiliar environment. The brief visits allow teachers to become familiar with the lay-out of the school, its educational philosophy, the courses offered and the likely levels they will be teaching.

In the UK, while there was a firm government intention to foster induction programmes, a number of Local Education Authorities placed great weight on paid pre-service orientation visits by new teachers to their school. The visits range from a few days to three weeks. According to some UK observers these 'orientation programmes', though varied, are much more comprehensive than ever before, and indicate that the principle of a professional orientation is now generally accepted. Financial pressures have meant that some LEAs have not been able to initiate many induction activities including orientation visits. In December 1978 it was reported in the Statistical Bulletin of the Department of Education and Science that about 33 per cent of LEAs had arranged prior visits and only a further 20 per cent were planning to do so.

This notion of an orientation programme has also been implemented in the Northern Territory in Australia. However, since many new teachers in the Territory enter remote aboriginal and pastoral schools, the programme lasting about two weeks, is organized by the Northern Territory Education Department in Darwin. The programme, in addition to covering certain methodological topics such as 'teaching English as a second language', provides beginning teachers with some basic anthropological concepts, information about the Departments of Health and Aboriginal Affairs, Technical and Further Education (TAFE) services and the Northern Territory Schools' Branch.

Reduced work load

On entry to teaching, professional support other than that through printed materials or prior visits is provided by employing authorities in several countries by reducing the beginning teachers' work load. In the UK the reduction of a new teacher's teaching load was an element of the funded schemes in the national Teacher Induction Pilot Scheme (TIPS) 1974-78. The attitude that has developed now is such that, despite the costs involved, a reduced teaching load is regarded as essential. According to the 1978 December issue of the Statistical Bulletin, about one quarter of LEAs were allowing a lightened load and about the same proportion planned to do so in the future. The amount of time allotted varies, but is most usually within the range of five to ten per cent of a normal teaching load. In Australia, where a number of the State and Territory authorities have a policy that beginning teachers will receive a reduced work load (eg a reduction in their teaching load of 20 per cent compared with that of a teacher in his second year), only about half of the nation's new teachers receive any concessions. About a quarter receive a reduced teaching load, and a comparable proportion have either classes of small size, several parallel classes (in secondary schools), or fewer administrative, supervisory or clerical duties.

School-based induction activities

Meetings within the school

Teaching is a profession that makes heavy emotional demands on the conscientious person, and it is a positive developmental approach to induction processes that will ultimately help establish the new teacher's credibility as a full professional person with pupils, fellow teachers, parents and other members of the community. Because induction is so closely concerned with the particulars of teaching in a real life setting, most of the special arrangements made for it are probably best based in the school where the teacher is a staff member. Certainly this was one of the definite viewpoints derived from a detailed study of Australian practices (Tisher, Fyfield and Taylor, 1979: 69). Many schools in the UK, USA and Australia for example, organize special activities for their new teachers. These may take the form of meetings for staff and special consultations throughout the year for beginning teachers. In Australia in 1977 42 per cent of the nation's new teachers had professional activities organized especially for them, and the majority (87 per cent) were briefed on the first day, albeit along with other staff. 56 per cent of those for whom professional activities were organized saw much value in them. In some parts of the USA, eg in Houston, the first week of school is usually a work week for teachers with no pupils in the building. During this period teachers are allowed planning time for the first week of school, as well as learning what materials and resources are available to them. The first day of the week is generally dedicated solely to all new teachers (new, that is, either to the local district or to the profession) when they are given information on policies for discipline, attendance, sick days, personal days, health insurance, etc. Essentially, this first day fulfills a function similar to that of the orientation visits described earlier. Also during this first week days may be set aside for in-service workshops on various topics, for example, current innovations in teaching methods, drug use and abuse.

Personal tutoring or consulting

One key feature of school-based induction policies in several countries or in local educational regions is the appointment of a person to be responsible for the induction of new teachers and/or for the professional development of all teachers. Some USA authorities maintain that their schools delegate one teacher to be a 'buddy' to help a new teacher, but just how prevalent or effective this buddy support is is not accurately known. Some USA observers believe that most first year teachers find their induction, including buddy support, to be a matter of trial and error. One North American research study (Newbury, 1978) indicates that there is a reluctance on the part of experienced teachers to help their colleagues. They felt that beginning teachers ought to be able to cope on their own. Even when beginning teachers came for help, the experienced ones were very wary of pushing their opinions too strongly, or else deliberately remained as uninvolved as possible.

In Australia a prevalent practice is to assign responsibility for beginning teachers' school-based induction to the deputy-principal or principal, who then meets with them on a regular basis to discuss a variety of teaching issues. Judging from the responses to a national principals' questionnaire (Tisher, Fyfield and Taylor, 1979: 29), the majority of principals stated that those responsible for new teachers in schools should definitely help them with their teaching, for example by observing and helping them in classrooms and by helping them with their programmes of work. Figure 1 summarizes the information obtained relating to the perceived responsibilities. What were seen to be the responsibilities of the beginning teachers' mentors differed somewhat from the views the new teachers had of the help they ought to have received when they reflected on this towards the end of their first year. As Table 2 shows, a significant proportion (82 per cent) of Australia's beginning teachers believe they should be given a greater opportunity to observe other teachers' methods of teaching.

The opportunity for beginning teachers to observe other teachers occurred in the Teacher Induction Pilot Scheme in the UK where trained teacher-tutors were appointed in schools, with some released time to counsel beginning teachers, to observe them teaching and to be observed. These teacher-tutors, rated as effective by a majority of the new teachers, performed a crucial role in guiding the teachers — so much so that the appointment and training of teacher-tutors is an element of induction that is receiving a great deal of attention at present. Funds have been made available to facilitate the development and dissemination of training materials for teacher-tutors, and some local colleges and universities. It seems that more will still be done to facilitate teacher-tutor development in the UK; it is also interesting to note that increased attention is being paid to the idea that support for new teachers should be part of the job of senior management in the school, perhaps the responsibility of a designated teacher, as part of a general staff development responsibility. Of course, there can be difficulties when senior school personnel who have certain evaluative responsibilities also assume counselling roles in induction. The interplay of personal and institutional factors makes the induction process a complex one. The complexity means that not all experienced and competent teachers are *ipso facto* well suited or well prepared to assist in the induction of newcomers. There is no doubt that

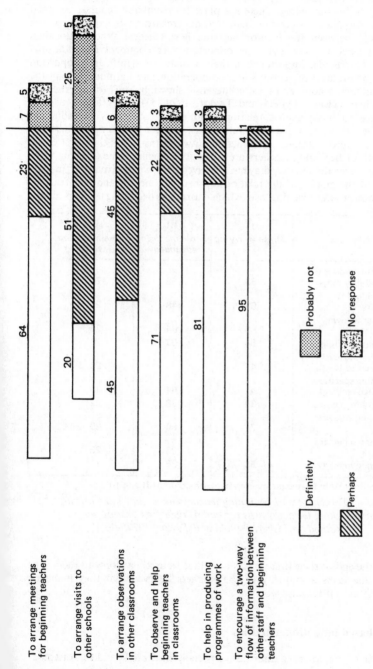

Figure 1 *Activities which should be promoted by person responsible for beginning teachers: responses to principals' questionnaire (percentages) (from Tisher, Fyfield and Taylor, 1979: 33)*

training courses are required, but what is probably equally, if not more, important, is that those responsible for helping beginning teachers should acquire skills in counselling. There is a place for counselling courses designed especially for them — courses that give due regard to the quality of the relationship between the mentor and the new teacher. When Australian beginning teachers were given the opportunity to comment on additional features of particular importance in their induction a significant proportion cited the helpfulness of school staff, co-operation and harmony among the teachers in their school, and the consideration shown by staff toward the first year teachers (Tisher, Fyfield and Taylor, 1979: 53). They attached great importance to interpersonal relations and the effectiveness of induction activities was dependent upon the mutual trust between beginning teachers and more experienced colleagues. The fact that towards the end of their first year a proportion of beginning teachers are still not managing some teaching tasks adequately, even though they may have received help, can be explained, in part, in terms of the quality of the relationship between mentor and new teacher. Table 1 shows the ten teaching tasks which Australia's beginning teachers named

I Teaching task	II Those worrying	III Those managing adequately	IV* Those managing and worrying
Teaching groups with wide ability range	63	55	26
Teaching slow learners	62	48	22
Evaluating own teaching	55	64	25
Motivating pupils	54	67	26
Discovering level at which to teach	47	73	25
Teaching specific skills (eg reading)	41	64	23
Controlling classes	39	78	22
Assessing students' work	37	80	20
Devising schemes of work	35	86	25
Teaching immigrants	30	36	11

*   Column IV indicates the overlap between columns II and III

Table 1 *Percentages of beginning teachers managing and worrying about teaching tasks towards the end of their first year of teaching (based on Tisher, Fyfield and Taylor, 1979: 49)*

towards the end of their first year as ones that were still a worry to them. For most of the tasks a majority of the teachers believed that they managed adequately even if they did worry.

System based induction activities

A number of employing authorities, especially in the UK and in Australia, provide professional support for beginning teachers by granting them time to attend short conferences of two to three days duration in their local region to learn about new curriculum materials, media resources, conditions of employment, teaching strategies and social background of pupils. Generally experienced colleagues, who have received a brief training prior to participating, act as tutor-advisers. Whereas regional conferences are by no means a prevalent induction activity in Australia, some very successful ones have been held and have included reviews of elements of pre-service programmes, for example lesson planning, managing small groups, evaluation procedures, classroom management and control, tricks of the trade and the examination of critical incidents in teaching. From all reports beginning teachers reacted favourably to all features of the conferences.

In addition to providing useful information, one distinct value of regional conferences is the opportunity given to beginning teachers to meet together to share perspectives and to learn that they are experiencing similar successes, frustrations, satisfactions and worries. Experiences from the UK and Australia also indicate that the following were some of the factors associated with the more successful conferences:

1 Conference advisers/tutors were well briefed and trained for their tasks.
2. School principals actively supported the conferences and encouraged beginning teachers to attend (often new teachers are reluctant to go since they believe they are neglecting their school responsibilities).
3. Provisions were made for relief staff to take beginning teachers' classes, and beginning teachers received financial support to attend.
4. Local schools received information on the beginning teachers' perceptions of how they were being inducted by the schools.

One disadvantage of the regional conferences is that the new ideas and help which beginning teachers receive are not visible to their experienced colleagues who remain at the schools. At times new teachers cannot implement conference suggestions because they do not receive their colleagues' support.

Perhaps the most prevalent system-based induction activity within the UK and Australia is the half or one-day meeting organized within a local region. The format of these meetings varies from workshops to group discussions and talks by guest lecturers. Other released time provisions include visits to resource centres or other schools, or unsupervised 'free' time. Bradley and Eggleston (1978) have documented the benefits which can accrue from different patterns of released time, and they certainly support the case for one day release.

Recommendations for induction

Recommendations from beginning teachers

From information gathered in several countries, including data contained in published reports on induction, it is not possible to argue for the superiority of any one induction practice. In fact, beginning teachers find something of value in all the provisions made for them and, as Table 2 shows for Australian teachers, believe that other new teachers should continue to receive similar opportunities. Column 2 of Table 2 shows the proportion of Australia's beginning teachers for whom various opportunities were created or provisions made (with the exception of reduced work load). Column 3 shows the proportion who recommended that the provision be continued for other new teachers. In all cases, apart from the opportunities to attend meetings, about three quarters of those who received the opportunity recommended it. The table shows that 80 per cent and more of beginning teachers believed that other new teachers should continue to receive written materials on school matters and conditions of appointment, be given advice on classroom management or help in producing programmes of work, and be allowed to observe other teachers' methods of teaching. About three quarters favoured opportunities to look at local education resources and to have their own teaching evaluated. Although only 62 per cent recommended visits to other schools, this is quite a high proportion and is all the more significant when it is noted that only 20 per cent of the nation's new teachers received the opportunity to visit.

Opportunity or provision	Percentage of beginning teachers who:	
	were given the opportunity	recommended the opportunity
Receiving written materials on conditions of employment	51	80
Receiving written materials on school matters	74	86
Accepting advice in classroom management or help in producing programmes of work	74	86
Accepting evaluation of own teaching	55	73
Participation in organized consultation with experienced school personnel	53	68
Attending group meetings for beginning teachers at school	42	65
Attending group meetings for beginning teachers elsewhere	45	56
Observing other teachers' methods of teaching	44	82
Visiting other schools for observation/consultation	20	62
Conferring informally with beginning teachers from other schools	59	65
Looking at local educational resources	48	74

Table 2 *Recommendations on provisions to be made or opportunities to be created for beginning teachers (based on Tisher, Fyfield and Taylor, 1979: 49)*

In actual fact the characteristics of what ought to be done in induction will be governed to a great extent by current local practices and historical antecedents. In some situations the fostering orientation visits might be more appropriate, in others the appointment of experienced teachers as school-based counsellors. While no general rules can be established for the superiority of one procedure over another, there are, nevertheless, several directions that might be explored with profit by schools and education employing authorities. The following pointers proffered for consideration are derived from the author's experiences with induction in Australia and interactions with UK, USA and Canadian educationists who are concerned with induction. It is appropriate throughout the ensuing discussion to bear in mind that, because induction is so closely concerned with the particulars of teaching in a real life setting, most of the special arrangements made to improve the process are probably best based in the school where the new teacher is a staff member. Here trained, experienced, trusted colleagues can counsel the less experienced teachers as well as capitalize on their creative potential.

Extending the purposes of induction

The purposes of induction are an important consideration. These, as presently conceived, can be inferred from the nature of the provisions for beginning teachers, printed statements on induction (eg Australian State Education Departments' policy booklets and induction manuals), and responses to national questionnaires (eg Tisher, Fyfield and Taylor, 1979). By and large, the aims appear to overlap several of the purposes identified by Eraut (1972) as objectives for in-service education, namely:

1. to extend the teachers' knowledge about the school and the education system and how both function;
2. to increase the teachers' awareness and comprehension of the complexities of teaching situations and to suggest alternative ways of coping with these complexities;
3. to acquaint the teachers with support services and resources within the school and the region;
4. to help the teachers (generally through counselling activities) to apply knowledge they already possess, or could obtain for themselves, to the daily tasks or problems which confront them.

Whether by intention, design or oversight these presently conceived purposes direct attention to provisions for beginning teachers and, as a consequence, cast experienced colleagues and organizers of induction opportunities in the role more of providers than of facilitators of problem-solving. The creative, problem-solving potential of beginning teachers is rarely emphasized. The situation mirrors the stance of many theoretical explanations of the socialization of teachers, which place a greater emphasis on the constraining rather than the creative, features in the process (eg the formative role of prior experiences; potent influences of colleagues in authority. Now, as Lacey (1977) and Fenstermacher (1979) indicate, induction and socialization are more complex than most early explanations allow. They agree that these are interactive, negotiated and provisional processes involving a continual re-shaping of teachers' perspectives and behaviours as they confront various situations. Beginning teachers face up to a constant flow of choices during their first months of teaching and are invariably required to propose practical alternatives for many problems they encounter (eg which of several strategies to follow in order to assist slow learners; what particular learning conditions to create in order to cater for the wide ability range in class). It seems most appropriate, therefore, that induction provisions should foster teachers' creative and problem-solving potential and that the purposes of induction should be extended to include, as Tisher, Fyfield and Taylor (1979: 112) suggest, fostering the resolution and implementation of practical alternatives to teaching issues, and engaging in the evaluation of the implemented alternatives. (Presumably if they are judged inadequate a cycle of activities will be initiated to resolve, implement and evaluate other alternatives.)

Improving the quality of education

Extending the aims of induction, basing induction in the schools, and training experienced teachers who have special responsibilities for induction in counselling skills are recommendations aimed at improving the quality of induction. In addition, some consideration must also be given to the quality of changes likely to occur if there were changes in (a) expectations regarding induction on the part of schools, training institutions and beginning teachers, (b) pre-service teacher education and (c) the teaching conditions under which beginning teachers start their career. Those concerned with induction could well explore these three directions with some profit. It is the case, for example, that schools (and particularly principals) do not believe that the training beginning teachers have received matches their eagerness to cope with the realities of the job (Tisher, Fyfield and Taylor, 1979: 43). Perhaps this perspective arises from the fact that principals have unrealistic expectations of what pre-service programmes can accomplish. Furthermore, their perspective can affect their approach to induction, which may then be structured and viewed as a repair job for pre-service education rather than as a further stage in the personal and professional growth of a teacher. On the other hand it may be that training institutions and beginning teachers have unrealistic or mistaken expectations of what may be accomplished during induction. Perhaps changes in their expectations can definitely alter the quality of induction. These questions, rarely included in the published literature on induction, need to be explored by all who are involved with induction programmes and policies.

In addition, it seems that employing authorities and schools should assess what effects alterations in the complexity of the beginning teachers' job would have on induction. Now job complexity can be reduced in a variety of ways. For example, in secondary schools beginning teachers could be assigned several parallel classes, like three year-nine English classes. On the other hand, they may be allocated smaller, less disruptive classes. In primary schools it may be profitable to place new teachers in teaching teams including teachers who have particular skills in teaching subjects about which the beginning teachers are unsure. If the new teachers felt competent in teaching mathematics, English and social science they could be responsible for these in their class and then observe and co-operate with other teachers when these taught drawing, music and science. The preceding suggestions are presented as illustrations of the directions which might be explored in attempts to enhance the quality of new teachers' entry to the profession. But there is one caveat. It is imperative to regard induction as only one part in the overall process of professional and personal development, and not to stay too long in an induction mode.

Another matter for careful consideration is that of selection criteria. This, however, ought not to result in employing authorities adopting the view that selection might accomplish quickly what a good induction programme should set out to achieve. The danger would lie in supposing that the teaching profession was best served by selecting teachers from a narrow range of personality types, eg the more emotionally robust recruits. Teaching, being the very personal profession that it is, calls for a variety of personality types within its ranks, not the least important in this variety being people of fine sensitivity. Likewise, an important goal for the induction process is to ensure that the profession does not operate to screen out sensitivity either by forcing its less emotionally robust recruits to an early resignation when they find they are not coping, or by inducing them to harden their manner in a way that may ultimately suppress or distort the very qualities it should be cultivating.

It is very difficult, as several researchers on induction have noted (eg Tisher, 1979; Tisher, Fyfield and Taylor, 1979: 65), to make a clear distinction for teachers between professional and personal development, and any proposals for the better induction of teachers need to take cognizance of this dual aspect of teacher development. This view has been neatly encapsulated by Guy Claxton (1978), who writes: 'Learning to be a teacher is not just learning a job — it is learning a new way of being yourself.'

References

Bolam, R (1973) *Induction Programmes for Probationary Teachers* A report on an action research project, School of Education, Research Unit: University of Bristol

Bolam, R and Baker, K (eds) (1975) *The Teacher Induction Pilot Schemes* (TIPS) Project, 1975 National Conference Report, School of Education: University of Bristol

Bradley, H W and Eggleston, J F (1978) An induction year experiment *Educational Research* **20**: 89-98

Claxton, G (1978) *The Little Ed Book* Routledge and Kegan Paul: London

Department of Education and Science (1972) *Teacher Education and Training* (The James Report) HMSO: London

Department of Education and Science (1978) *Statistics Bulletin 78: Induction and In-Service Training of Teachers: 1978 Survey* DES: London

Eraut, M (1972) *In-Service Education for Innovation* National Council for Educational Technology: London

Fenstermacher, G D (1979) *What needs to be known about what teachers need to know?* Paper presented at the national invitational conference *Exploring Issues in Teacher Education: Questions for Future Research* Research and Development Center for Teacher Education: University of Texas, Austin, Texas, January, 1979

Lacey, C (1977) *The Socialization of Teachers* Methuen: London

Lortie, D C (1975) *Schoolteacher: A Sociological Study* University of Chicago Press: Chicago

Murdoch, R P (1978) *Professional Development: The Induction and Education of Beginning Teachers* Research Report, Christchurch Teachers' College: Christchurch, New Zealand

Newbury, J Mc (1978) The barrier between beginning and experienced teachers *Journal of Educational Administration* **16** 1:46-56

Taylor, J K and Dale, J R (1971) *A Survey of Teachers in their First Year of Service* School of Education: University of Bristol

Tisher, R (1979) *Teacher induction: an aspect of the education and professional development of teachers* Paper presented at the national invitational conference *Exploring Issues in Teacher Education: Questions for Future Research* Research and Development Center for Teacher Education; University of Texas, Austin, Texas, January, 1979

Tisher, R, Fyfield, J and Taylor, S (1978) *Beginning to Teach Vol I The Induction of Teachers: A Bibliography and Description of Activities in Australia and the UK. Report on Stage I of the Teacher Induction Project* ERDC Report No 15, Australian Government Publishing Service: Canberra

Tisher, R, Fyfield, J and Taylor, S (1979) *Beginning to Teach Vol II The Induction of Beginning Teachers in Australia. Research Report on Stage II of the Teacher Induction Project* ERDC Report No 20, Australian Government Publishing Service: Canberra

Zeichner, K M (1979) *Teacher induction practices in the United States and Great Britain* A paper presented at the annual meeting of the American Educational Research Association: San Francisco, April, 1979

Note

The author is indebted to a number of people who responded to personal requests to provide perspectives on induction and professional support for new teachers in their country. In particular he wishes to acknowledge contributions from Dr Ray Bolam, University of Bristol; Dr Robert Crocker, Memorial University, Newfoundland; Professor Jim Eggleston, University of Nottingham; Dr Madeline Hunter, University of California, Los Angeles; Peggy Landgraf, Bammel Middle School, Houston; Dr Richard Miller, Elkhart Community Schools, California; Mary Parslow, South Australian Education Department; Ian Thurstans, Tasmanian Education Department; Dr Ronald Townsend, Evanston Township High School, Illinois, and Dr Kenneth Zeichner, University of Wisconsin.

5. In-service education and training

Ray Bolam

Summary: This chapter presents some of the key findings and issues arising from an OECD review of recent developments and innovations in the in-service education and training of teachers (INSET). The needs of beginning teachers in their first year of service have been reasonably well established but the concept of a longer term career profile for teachers has proved to be more controversial. Recent work on needs is focusing upon teachers as adult learners. INSET is provided by a wide variety of agencies but increasing attention is being paid to the role of the school as an initiator and provider. Internal roles like the professional tutor are being introduced. The training of INSET trainers is itself being recognized as an important aspect for future work. Great difficulty has been encountered in trying to cost INSET but the problems are being clarified. Rather better progress has been made with the evaluation of INSET, where a significant shift towards an illuminative style is evident, although political pressures for accountability may lead to a renewed emphasis on the collection of outcome data. Although the research base is weak, there is some consensus about what constitutes effective in-service and here too the school-focused approach is highly valued. This emphasis reflects a growing commitment to the role of in-service education as a deliberate instrument of system improvement. However, it is far from clear what proportion of the teaching force should receive INSET in any one year. The personal and career development needs of individual teachers are not yet receiving adequate attention.

Introduction

Since 1975, a group of member countries of the Organization for Economic Cooperation and Development (OECD) have contributed to an international review of recent developments and innovations in the in-service education and training (INSET) of teachers. The purpose of this chapter is to present some of the key findings and issues arising from that review. The project has produced numerous case studies, reports and conference summaries, only some of which are mentioned here. Nevertheless, it is hoped that even an incomplete selection from work which is not easily accessible will result in some of the more innovative practices and thinking in the developed countries of the world being made available to the WYBE readership.

The interim report on the first phase of the project concluded that there were three main reasons for the recent growth in commitment of national governments to INSET:

First, it is inherently important that teachers, of all people, should continue with their personal and professional education; second, the rapid, extensive and fundamental nature of present-day change — technological, economic, cultural, social, political — makes it imperative for the education system in general and teachers in particular to review and modify teaching methods and curricula; third, for widely prevalent demographic reasons, the demand for new teachers is dropping sharply and the INSET needs of a stable teaching force become especially important. (Bolam, 1978: 11)

The same report also concluded that there was broad agreement in OECD member countries that INSET could and should make an important contribution to the resolution of problems associated with several contemporary major task areas in education:

1. the curricular problems associated with the extension of compulsory schooling, especially the needs of the 13-16 age group;
2. the needs of special school populations, such as immigrant groups, multi-ethnic communities and disadvantaged rural communities;
3. the needs associated with particular subjects, notably science and mathematics, and student groups, notably those with special educational needs (ie variants on the mainstreaming problem);
4. the new demands on teachers caused by the radically changing nature of school-community relationships, eg relations between education and working life, and renewed community demands for accountability related to educational standards and assessment;
5. the curricular and organizational consequences of declining enrolments;
6. the strategic need to provide adequate INSET for those with internal school management responsibilities. (Bolam, 1978: 46)

Notwithstanding this broad agreement about its importance, there were some significant differences in the way member countries defined INSET and its aims. Some countries excluded courses leading to advanced university degrees; others excluded courses which aimed to equip teachers for promotion to a headship. Space does not permit a full exposition of these differences or their implications, but it will be obvious that comparisons between countries about, for example, the costs of INSET must be preceded by careful definition of terms.

In this chapter a broad and all-encompassing definition will be used: INSET will be regarded as those education and training activities engaged in by teachers following their initial certification. It therefore includes training in the induction year, short courses, school-based training and university award-bearing courses. Naturally, this definition begs many questions, some of which will arise in the course of this chapter.

Following its first phase, the OECD project concentrated on seven main aspects of INSET:

☐ teachers as adult learners
☐ school-focused INSET and teachers' centres
☐ evaluation
☐ INSET materials
☐ training the trainers
☐ costs and resources
☐ teacher participation.

The rest of the chapter draws on the work carried out during this second phase.

What INSET do teachers need?

Surveys of teachers' INSET needs have been carried out in many countries at all levels — national, state, local authority and school. These provide useful information about self-reported needs in relation, for instance, to the teaching of particular subjects and to the management of schools. Such common-sense categorizations are one important way of looking at teachers' needs but in recent years other approaches have also been adopted.

For example, a series of research and development studies into the induction and training needs of beginning teachers in England and Wales has led to a six-stage framework, which can best be understood within the chronology of the school year:

Pre-service	1	Appointment and placement
	2a	Orientation
Autumn term	2b	Orientation
	3	Adaptation
	4a	Assessment
Spring term	5a	Development
Summer term	5b	Development
	4b	Assessment
	6	Overview

The probationers' needs begin at the time of appointment. Following this, orientation to the routines and procedures of the school and Local Education Authority (LEA) can take place during a pre-service visit or during the first days and weeks of the autumn term. The adaptation period is one in which the probationer is coming to terms with and reconciling the frequently conflicting demands of the school, the pupils, his own inclinations and the advice given to him in initial training. In short, he is formulating his own teaching style in a particular context. Towards the end of the autumn term, most LEAs ask the head to complete a progress assessment form so that probationers at risk can be identified. From about Christmas onwards, the majority of probationers have settled in and are ready for more sustained training activities to meet their professional development needs. The final assessment form is usually completed towards the end of the summer term and can be used to stimulate an overview both of the past year's experience and of career and in-service education and training opportunities during the second year and beyond. (See DES, 1976, 1977.)

A more generally relevant attempt was made by a national committee for INSET in England and Wales to devise a needs framework based upon the likely career patterns of teachers. The concept of a career profile included the following key stages:

1. the induction year;
2. a consolidation period of four to six years during which teachers would attend short, specific courses;
3. a reorientation period, after six to eight years experience, which could involve a secondment for a one-term course and a change in career development;
4. a period of further studies, in advanced seminars, to develop specialist

expertise;
5. at about mid-career (after about 12 to 15 years) some teachers would benefit from advanced studies programmes of one year or more in length, possible to equip them for leadership roles;
6. after mid-career, a minority would need preparation for top management roles while the majority would need regular opportunities for refreshment.

Somewhat predictably, the 'career profile' met with considerable opposition because it was thought to be too prescriptive, so it has not been widely used as a basis for identifying needs.

A new departure is evident in an American study which treats teachers as adult learners. Corrigan *et al* (1979) argue that INSET has neither been regarded as adult education nor has it drawn on theories of adult learning. Most learning theories have been developed instead in relation to animals and children and, in any case, INSET has some important distinctive features. They derive seven theoretical orientations from the literature on adult education.

First, psychometric research on adults, with some qualifications, is said to have found negative correlations between age and tests of intelligence, achievement, memory and creativity. On the other hand, a second theoretical orientation stresses the positive potential of the ageing process because older people have accumulated more knowledge and experience; however, there is a shortage of research data to support this approach. Mastery learning theory suggests that the content or skills to be mastered must be organized sequentially and logically. School learning theory generates propositions about motivation, feedback, readiness, etc, which, though sometimes contradictory, of variable importance and not equally research-based, appear to have direct relevance to adult learning. Personal development theory contends that adult development is a continuation of early (ie child) internal development and involves a series of stages or phases in which different life tasks and needs arise. Organization theory indicates that the situational pressures upon individuals have to be taken into account, and perhaps changed, if meaningful learning is to occur. Finally, group learning theory stresses the significant influence of peer groups on individual learning.

This summary does scant justice to a comprehensive review and analysis. Corrigan *et al* go on to explore some implications of these theoretical orientations for INSET and provide three illustrative case studies. This should be a major and fruitful area for research and development with implications not just for INSET but for recurrent education in general.

Who are the providers?

INSET is provided by a wide variety of agencies including universities, teacher education colleges, teachers' centres, curriculum centres, professional associations and television and radio broadcasting agencies. The people involved are equally varied and include lecturers, advisers, consultants, principals and teachers. In the USA, it has been estimated, a quarter of a million people are actual or potential providers (Rubin and Howey, 1976).

It is notable that the providers differ significantly from country to country. For example, teachers' centres in Australia, unlike their British counterparts, often involve non-professional participants (Skilbeck *et al*, 1976: 42) while those in Italy are still at the planning stage (Vincente-Missoni, 1978). Similarly, distance teaching methods of providing INSET range from the extensive programmes broadcast throughout the UK by the Open University (Bolam and Porter, 1976; see also Chapters 16 and 18) to more specific approaches like the Dutch TELEAC project to facilitate the introduction of the 'flexible' school (Deen and Boeder-Rijdes, 1976: 21) and the Canadian PERMAMA project for secondary school mathematics teachers in Quebec (Bélanger, 1976: 16).

Perhaps the most significant recent development, however, has been the increasing attention paid to the role of the school in INSET. To a large extent this has arisen from dissatisfaction with traditional approaches to INSET whereby individual teachers attend an externally-planned and provided course and either find it too theoretical and general or are unable to implement its recommendations in their schools because of the particular circumstances which prevail there. The response to this dissatisfaction in many countries has been to provide INSET which is more directly focused upon the needs, tasks and problems of particular schools and of sub-groups within them. In many cases this has involved the development of new roles and procedures within schools and of changed roles and methods for external providers.

In Denmark, for example, a school-based INSET programme was mounted in a primary school by researchers from the Royal Danish School of Educational Studies. Olsen reports that the three-year action-research study aimed 'to meet the needs of teachers with regard to content in a realistic setting where they work with colleagues on a team and can draw upon expertise and information from outside geared to their needs and wishes' (Olsen, 1978: 13). Olsen concludes that it took far more time than anticipated to develop fruitful working relationships and for the crucial task of needs definition; that the researchers must be prepared to adopt an active consultancy role; and, finally, that it was important for the researchers to work collaboratively with teachers in their classrooms.

Similar initiatives have occurred in other countries like Australia (Skilbeck *et al*, 1979), Sweden (Larsson, 1978), and England (Chapter 13). A related development is also occurring in several countries — the introduction of a professional tutor role within schools. In England, for instance, a number of LEAs have encouraged their secondary schools to develop their own in-service policies and programmes and to appoint professional tutors with so-called triple-I responsibilities (Initial, Induction, and In-service). The in-service training aspect of one such tutor's job specification includes the following responsibilities:

1. Organize meetings for induction of new staff to the school.
2. Acquaint them with relevant topics on probationary teachers' in-service course and invite them to meetings.
3. With the Head's authority, co-ordinate all further professional studies courses, eg ensure information on course reaches interested/involved staff, control INSET notice board, monitor staff absence from school on courses, etc.
4. Encourage staff to be aware of internal/external promotion, eg departmental staff may not have thought of involvement in careers department, examination entries, outdoor activities group, etc.
5. Observe and analyse lessons of certain staff as requested, eg by ex-probationer, supply teachers, fixed-term contract staff.
6. Assist in the writing of references for staff.
7. Encourage staff to keep the Head fully aware of their 'extra' activities, eg attendance at courses, running of clubs/societies etc.
8. Where possible identify/prepare those staff ready for promotion.

9.Encourage staff to consider their own in-service requirements and to involve them in the planning of such courses.

10.Seek the expertise of outside agencies, eg adviser, external tutors, etc, to act as sources of information for specialist speakers, resources, literature, etc. (Bolam, forthcoming)

This tutor has 'triple-I' reponsibilities but in many schools these are split between two or more experienced staff. In one secondary school, for example, a deputy head co-ordinates the professional development programme and concentrates on that aspect aimed at experienced teachers. He is assisted by a tutor who looks after probationers and student teachers. The school's professional development committee is chaired by the deputy head, with the tutor acting as secretary, and the membership is made up of teacher representatives, the LEA's general adviser for the school, and the liaison tutor from the college of education.

The tutor role and its analogues is potentially a crucial one both for the provision of INSET and for integrating it into the overall school improvement policies of schools. There will not, of course, be a single model for the role. It will vary according to the size of the school, whether it is primary or secondary, and how the job is defined, ie for initial and/or induction as well as for in-service.

Who trains the trainers?

It is widely acknowledged that those who provide INSET could themselves benefit from some form of training. For example, in a study of 14 English local authorities (Bolam *et al*, 1979), some attention was given to the training needs of local authority advisers, most of whom spend a great deal of their time providing INSET. Less than 15 per cent had received any specific training yet almost 70 per cent recommended that advisers should receive specific training.

A particular study was also made of the training needs of teacher tutors with responsibilities for providing school-based INSET for beginning teachers during pilot schemes in the UK. Whereas, at the outset of the project, there were uncertainties about both the need for and content of tutor training, by the end, the case for training teacher tutors was made most forcibly: 71 per cent of all respondents agreed that tutors needed some form of training. Tutors themselves were most convinced of this, especially those from secondary schools (94 per cent). However, only 53 per cent of tutors considered that the training they had received had been adequate: 87 per cent said that the LEA should also produce written guidelines for tutors and 69 per cent thought that continuing and not simply preparatory training was necessary (Bolam, Baker and McMahon, 1979).

These two national studies find wider support in a review carried out by Mulford (1979) who analysed 18 case studies in nine OECD countries. These included experience in Portugal, where a centre has been established to define training needs and which has run experimental seminars on group dynamics and pedagogical evaluation; in France, where integrated centres for training adult trainers have been set up; and in Japan, where school-based research co-ordinators have been trained. Mulford concludes that:

> Most of the material here tended to emphasize the general factors that training should take into consideration rather than specific methodologies. These general factors were synthesized into eight points: the need to be aware of schools as organizations, the nature of teachers and teaching, the school's context, the

trainer input dilemma, adult learning theory and emphasis on participatory approaches, experiential learning and educational administrator training. (Mulford, 1979: 110-11)

Several general practical conclusions are worth drawing out from experience and research in this field. First, the training of INSET trainers should be continual: initial or preparatory training is not sufficient.

Second, although the particular roles occupied by trainers are extremely diverse (eg principals, advisers or college lecturers), the INSET components have enough in common for us to be able to identify core tasks and the knowledge and skills needed to carry them out. Third, these core skills include clinical supervision, teaching analysis, organization development and interpersonal communication. Fourth, the training can be made more effective by including a substantial clinical or on-the-job emphasis.

What does INSET cost?

One of the most important yet intractably problematic aspects of INSET is that of obtaining reliable information about costs. According to Henricson,

> Even in a centralized system like the Swedish one, it is, for many reasons, not possible to reach an exact overall calculation of the cost of INSET. In some cases where the total costs can be determined it is not possible to allocate the expenditure to specific types of costs. (Henricson, 1979: 24)

Of course, this is even more true in decentralized systems like those of the UK and the USA. Yet, if existing INSET resources are to be used sensibly, some reasonably clear account of the relative costs of different methods and approaches is essential.

A start is certainly being made. In England and Wales, for instance, the Department of Education and Science recently surveyed expenditure on INSET in all local education authorities for the first time (DES, 1978). Perhaps the most important findings were that the information was difficult to collect but that certain categories of costs could be identified. It appears to be the case that several countries have reached the stage of clarifying the major components in the total costs; this in itself represents a great step forward.

This is well illustrated in Australia where, according to Cameron (1978), the injection of Commonwealth funds has led to a massive increase in INSET at the state and regional levels and to a consequent concern over costs. Cameron (1978: 21) distinguishes between four major types of recurrent costs: assembly costs which include accommodation and travel costs; replacement costs, which are for providing replacement or substitute teachers for participating teachers; clerical staff and the costs of general office supplies and postage; and organization costs, which cover lecturers' fees, materials and equipment for specific courses. Cameron estimates that the average distribution of these costs for short courses and workshops is:

Assembly	—	20-25%
Replacement	—	60-65%
Administration	—	10-12%
Organization	—	8-12%

Many questions remain unresolved. For example, what proportion of the salaries of advisers, who often have inspectorial and administrative as well as

INSET responsibilities, should be counted? What proportion of the captial costs of teachers' centres, which provide INSET alongside curriculum development and other system renewal activities, should count against the INSET budget? Even more fundamentally, what kind of arrangements for financing and funding INSET are effective? For instance, should schools have their own INSET budgets to encourage school-focused INSET, and is it the case that 'all INSET activities should take place in school time' as is claimed by Swedish teachers' unions (Henricson, 1979: 19), with all that such a policy implies for costs? And how can the various providing agency resources be used to maximize their potential? For instance, should a proportion of staff time in initial training institutions be allocated for INSET duties, as in the UK?

How is it evaluated?

With the growth in commitment to INSET has come a series of questions about evaluation which usually stem from one or both of two issues. First, there is a desire that INSET should offer value for money, which we may call the concern for programme accountability. Second, there is a desire to improve the quality of INSET, which we may call the concern for programme improvement. Both have direct implications for the purposes, nature and methodology of evaluation.

Quite understandably, the principal and fundamental concern of those who have to provide the resources for INSET is whether it brings value for money. In England for instance, local authority advisers need to be able to convince local politicians that it is worth spending money on INSET rather than on reducing the size of classes or on some other social service like housing. Ideally, they would like 'hard' information about the effects of a particular INSET programme on teacher performance and, even better, on pupil or student performance if possible. In practice it has not proved easy to provide this type of product or outcome information. Most evaluations have asked teachers to make a follow-up judgement, say a month afterwards, about the impact of the course. When these self-reports have been checked independently, however, their reliability is shown to be questionable. For example, Henderson (1978) found little evidence to support the self-reported change in teachers' behaviour following a distance teaching course on reading improvement.

It is technically possible to obtain convincing 'product' data about effectiveness if some form of competency measurement approach is adopted. Writing from an American perspective, Borich (1978) outlines three evaluation models based upon a definition of competency which is tied to a validated and confirmed 'relationship between a teaching behaviour and a pupil outcome'. Experience in Europe indicates that it is rarely feasible to use such sophisticated instruments and evaluation designs because they are expensive, because the course being evaluated is usually not amenable to a behavioural approach and because programme improvement data are both easier to obtain by other methods and more highly valued.

The issues are posed very clearly in the Swedish study. For example, it refers to

> a shift towards what could be called a *participatory INSET evaluation* model. This change is qualitative in nature and can be seen as a reflection of a general trend discernible in a great many fields. Characteristic features of the model are, among

other things:

☐ the broadening of the field of evaluation so that product evaluation is just one of the components

☐ INSET and INSET evaluation as an integrated part of the total school development programme

☐ evaluation programmes as decentralized, group-focused and field-centred activities

☐ INSET evaluation as an information service to the participants about the characteristics of the school's whole development programme and thus a basis for participatory planning and decision-making. (Eklund, 1978: 3)

The study goes on to argue, with respect to data collection methods, that

If you know — and have been able to control — relevant background and situation variables (frames, processes, etc), the products of a training period provide an excellent basis for evaluation — you need no more. You have a kind of *one-dimensional evaluation* situation (summative and product-centred). On the other hand, if you are uncertain which variables are the relevant ones (which variables you have been able to hold constant), the mere study of results becomes somewhat pointless. In this case you also need information that makes it possible to estimate the congruence between aims and the didactical model and between the didactical model and the actual behaviour. You get a *multi-dimensional evaluation* situation (formative and process-centred). (Eklund, 1978: 36-7)

Essentially then, the argument turns upon the importance attached on the one hand to obtaining formative process evaluation information about the ways in which a programme was implemented to inform decisions about programme improvement and, on the other hand, to obtaining summative product information about the effectiveness and outcomes of a programme to inform decisions about whether or not to continue with it.

Process data and 'soft' product data (eg follow-up studies) are technically easy to obtain, relatively cheap and tend to satisfy the 'professionals' but not the 'politicians'; 'hard' product data are technically difficult to obtain, are more expensive and tend to satisfy the politicians but threaten the professionals. Borich is, therefore, right to stress that

the 'best' evaluation methodology is dictated by context and dependent upon resources at hand, time and commitment of those conducting the study, requirements and policies shaping the evaluation, and, of course, the objectives of the training institution. (Borich, 1978: 32)

It is worth noting, incidentally, that neither these issues nor the technical problems of evaluation are peculiar to INSET; they have already been confronted in the evaluation of curriculum development and social action programmes where they have given rise to similar debates and rival solutions (see Stake, 1976 and Jenkins, 1978).

What works best?

A recent paper by a Canadian to a British audience gave a sombre warning about the lack of impact made by research, theory and, by extension, training, upon the behaviour of education administrators (Greenfield, 1979): he might equally well have been talking about the impact of INSET in general. Most of the research and evaluation work on INSET has been done in the USA and it is salutary to note Rubin and Howey's remark that 'there has been little rigorous review of the research on in-service' (Rubin and Howey, 1976: 149). Similarly, in his study of the costs and efficient use of INSET resources in the UK, Bradley says:

> There is almost no evidence of the effect of INSET for teachers on schools or children. It would be useful to have data about the comparative effectiveness of courses run within a school for its staff and outside schools for groups involving teachers from many schools. Information about the effectiveness of different learning techniques in relation to different course objectives would also be helpful. (Bradley, 1978: 35)

Some progress is, however, being made. In the USA, Lawrence (1974) reviewed 97 studies of INSET and came to some tentative conclusions about their effectiveness. He concluded that school-based INSET was more effective in influencing complex behaviour changes and teacher attitudes; that the collaborative involvement of teachers in course planning led to greater success; that it was easier to achieve success in improving teacher rather than pupil performance, in changing teacher behaviour rather than attitudes and, finally, in improving teachers' knowledge rather than behaviour (see also Rubin and Howey, 1976: 32-4, 149-50).

In a report on an extensive evaluation of the Australian School Commission's Development Programme, Batten concludes that 'no one model has emerged to demonstrate the best way to achieve effective professional development' (Batten, 1979: 286). She, too, stresses the importance of teacher involvement in course planning and follow-up work and says that 'no single aspect of the Programme has been received with such universal acclaim as the trends towards school-centred professional development' (Batten, 1979: 287).

Evidence about effective INSET is also being collected in related fields. A notable and influential example is the series of studies into the process of change at the school level carried out by the Rand Corporation. McLaughlin and Marsh (1978) summarize the implications of the Rand Studies for staff development as follows:

> In summary, the Rand study suggests that effective staff development activities should incorporate five general assumptions about professional learning:
>
> ☐ Teachers possess important clinical expertise.
> ☐ Professional learning is an adaptive and heuristic process.
> ☐ Professional learning is a long-term, non-linear process.
> ☐ Professional learning must be tied to school-site programme-building efforts.
> ☐ Professional learning is critically influenced by organizational factors in the school site and in the district.
>
> These assumptions support a view of staff development emphasizing learning for professionals as part of programme-building in an organizational context. (McLaughlin and Marsh, 1978: 90-91)

Given that importance is being attached to school-focused INSET, it is surprising that more use has not been made of organization development as a strategy for improving the school as a problem-solving system (see Schmuck, 1974; Mulford, 1979). One explanation is that it requires a high degree of specific technical experience and competence on the part of the trainers. Nevertheless, in a comprehensive and critical review of organization development practices in the USA and Canada, Fullan, Miles and Taylor (1978) conclude that

> it appears to be a good way to increase institutional innovation, increase

participation by all levels of personnel and to improve various aspects of task and socio-emotional functioning, if it is done *right*!

Conclusions: some policy issues

The follow-up phase of the OECD project has certainly confirmed that there is a great deal of interest and activity in INSET among member countries. Moreover certain broad policy issues are emerging, of which the following are a selection.

First, there is the issue of participation and governance. There is widespread agreement that more effective INSET can be achieved if the participating teachers can contribute collaboratively to decisions about INSET policies and programmes at all stages — planning, implementation and follow-up. Thus procedures are needed at several levels:

1. the individual teacher, in consultation with a professional tutor and within a school policy framework;
2. the department or functional group, in consultation with a professional tutor and the school's professional development committee;
3. the school, in consultation with the local authority's advisers and its consultative group on INSET, on which teachers and providers are represented;
4. area groups of schools, in consultation with advisers and consultative groups;
5. the local authority, in consultation with its own consultative group;
6. at national level, the government in consultation with its national consultative group;
7. the providing agency, in consultation with a consultative group;
8. the programme and course organizers, in consultation with the participants.

A key policy issue is whether non-professionals are represented at any of these levels and stages. What of non-teaching staff, parents and other community representatives for example?

Secondly, it is clear that this burgeoning interest and activity in INSET is, to a worrying extent, built upon an act of faith. Expenditure on research into INSET has been minimal, so it is hardly surprising that we have so little systematic and reliable information about costs, resource use, and effectiveness, both of particular approaches and overall investment. Undoubtedly the position has improved, but a great deal of research must be funded and carried out in individual countries if this situation is to be fully rectified. Moreover, the feasibility of sharing international experience (see Davis, 1979) and research deserves closer attention and appropriate funding.

Thirdly, we may reasonably conclude that the ways in which INSET can meet the needs of the system, whether at school, local or national levels, are being very actively considered. Teachers, principals, advisers, administrators and researchers are all agreed that school-focused INSET is better received and more effective than the traditional course-based model. Indeed, other *WYBE 1980* authors provide evidence that in Sweden (Chapter 14) and California (Chapter 8) INSET is being used consciously and deliberately as an instrument of social policy. Other evidence to support this comes from the Netherlands where INSET is being seen as a major part of a proposed strategy for increasing the relative autonomy and problem-solving capacity of secondary schools (van

Velzen, 1979). In all three settings, and elsewhere, great strategic importance is being attached to the provision of INSET in administration for principals and senior staff in schools.

This shift in emphasis raises several policy issues. In considering plans and priorities, organizers need to be realistic in their publicly stated expectations and goals for INSET, not least because the wider community and its politicians are frequently unrealistic about such matters. INSET is no panacea. It cannot make much impact on those fundamental social, cultural, political and economic constraints within which schools and teachers have to operate. Goals have to be formulated with caution. Moreover, desirable as it certainly is to meet the needs of schools and the wider needs of society, the needs of individual teachers must be kept very clearly in mind. A balance has to be struck which ensures that the legitimate aspirations of individual teachers for career development and further personal education are met (see Belbenoit, 1976). Hence, appropriate funding for advanced studies at universities and for sabbatical periods must be maintained and extended.

Finally, a number of basic policy questions have yet to be formulated properly, let alone answered. The fundamental one concerns the quantity and nature of INSET which any education system needs in order to maintain and renew its teaching force and its schools. It has taken many years for the developed countries to answer a similar question in relation to initial teacher training and to find the necessary resources to finance the capital and recurrent costs of the initial training system. Many OECD countries are now moving uncertainly towards answering key questions about INSET such as: how much reliance should be placed upon voluntary teacher involvement? What percentage of the teaching force should be engaged on longer courses at any one time? Is the British suggestion of 3 per cent generally acceptable (and, if so, why?) or is the figure arbitrary and culture-bound? What answers have industry and other professions given to these questions? How should INSET relate to initial training?

There are no easy answers to these broad policy questions and, no doubt, the position will in any case vary from country to country. The OECD study demonstrates, however, that such questions, and those subsidiary questions which relate to them, are likely to recur throughout the 1980s.

References

Batten, M (1979) *National Evaluation of the Development Program* Schools Commission: Canberra

Bélanger, M (1976) *Innovation in INSET: Canada* OECD: Paris

Belbenoit, G (1976) *Innovation in INSET: France* OECD: Paris

Bolam, R (1978) *Innovations in the In-Service Education and Training of Teachers* OECD: Paris

Bolam, R (ed) (forthcoming) *School-Focused INSET* Heinemann Educational Books: London

Bolam, R, Baker, K and McMahon, A (1979) *Teacher Induction Pilot Schemes: Final National Evaluation Report* School of Education: University of Bristol

Bolam R and Porter, J (1976) *Innovation in INSET: the United Kingdom* OECD: Paris

Bolam R, Smith, G and Canter, H (1979) *LEA Advisers and the Mechanisms of Innovation* National Foundation for Education Research: Slough

Borich, G (1978) *The Evaluation of INSET for Teachers in the United States* OECD: Paris

Bradley, H W (1978) *Cost and Efficient Utilisation of INSET Resources in England and Wales* OECD: Paris

Cameron, P (1978) *Cost and Efficient Utilisation of Resources in Australia* OECD: Paris

Corrigan, D, Haberman, M and Howey, K (1979) *Adult Learning and Development: Implications for In-Service Teacher Education: An American Viewpoint* OECD: Paris

Davis, J (1979) The Educational Policy Information Centre (EPIC): an introduction and a review of the background of European co-operation *Educational Administration* 7 1: 107-22

Deen, N and Boeder-Rijdes, E S (1976) *Innovation in INSET: The Netherlands* OECD: Paris

Department of Education and Science (1976) *Helping New Teachers: The Induction Year* (Report on Education 84) DES: London

Department of Education and Science (1977) *Teacher Induction: Pilot Schemes Progress* (Report on Education 89) DES: London

Department of Education and Science (1978) *Statistics Bulletin 78: Induction and In-Service Training of Teachers: 1978 Survey* DES: London

Eklund, H (1978) *The Evaluation of INSET for Teachers in Sweden* OECD: Paris

Fullan, M, Miles, M and Taylor, G (1978) *OD in Schools: the State of the Art: Volume 1* (available from M Fullan, Dept of Sociology, Ontario Institute for Studies in Education, Toronto, Canada)

Greenfield, T B (1979) *Research in Educational Administration in the United States and Canada: An Overview and Critique* Paper presented to a research seminar of the British Educational Administration Society, University of Birmingham

Gregersen, J (1978) *The Evaluation of INSET for Teachers in Denmark* OECD: Paris

Henderson, E (1980) The evaluation of an Open University course *in* McCabe (1980)

Henricson, S E (1979) *Cost and Efficient Utilisation of INSET Resources in Sweden* OECD: Paris

Jenkins, W I (1978) *Policy Analysis* Martin Robertson: London

Larsson, T (1978) The 'Local School Development Planning and Evaluation' Project *in* Eklund (1978)

Lawrence, G (1974) *Patterns of Effective In-Service Education* Department of Education: Tallahassee, Florida

McCabe, C M (ed) (1980) *Evaluating INSET* National Foundation for Educational Research: Slough

McLaughlin, M W and Marsh, D (1978) Staff development and school change *Teachers College Record* **80** 1: 69-94

Mulford, W (1979) *The Role and Training of INSET Trainers: An Interim Report* OECD: Paris

Olsen, T P (1978) The Lundebjerg Project: a study of school-based INSET *in* Gregersen (1978)

Rubin, L and Howey, K (1976) *Innovation in INSET: United States* OECD: Paris

Schmuck, R A (1974) Interventions for strengthening the school's creativity *in* Nisbet, J (ed) *Creativity of the School* OECD: Paris

Skilbeck, M, Evans, G and Harvey, J (1976) *Innovation in INSET: Australia* OECD: Paris

Skilbeck, M, Ingvarson, L, Edgar, W, Merrill, P and Beacham, J (1979) *School-focused and School-based INSET in Australia* OECD: Paris

Stake, R (1976) *Evaluating Educational Programmes* OECD: Paris

van Velzen, W (ed) (1979) *Developing an Autonomous School* Dutch Catholic School Council: The Hague

Vincente-Missoni, M (ed) (1978) *Teachers' Centres in Italy* OECD: Paris

6. Careers in teaching

Geoffrey Lyons and Lloyd McCleary

Summary: 'Careers in teaching' represents an attempt to apply certain conceptions of career to careers in teaching. Hughes' conception of a career as a set of interrelated compartments and Roth's time blocks for structuring of career maps are employed to obtain a description and explanation of how careers in teaching are shaped. The extent to which teachers deliberately construct career maps, set career goals, read the organization and play the 'career game' are examined in terms of data about teaching in British, US, and Third World countries. Certain myths and misconceptions arise from the matches and mismatches between bureaucratic career structuring and individuals' attempts to make a career and find professional fulfillment. The concept of career proposed and the analysis offered permit proposals about how teaching as a career might be made more rewarding and in turn contribute to organizational effectiveness.

To think of teachers as representing a homogeneous body of professionals pursuing relatively standardized careers within relatively standardized organizations is a myth which represents a widely held perception of teaching. In a discussion of teaching as a career one colleague reflected this oversimplified view by saying, quite seriously, *à la* Gertrude Stein, 'a teacher is a teacher, is a teacher.' Teaching has been studied from the view of the sociology of work, the socialization processes involved in becoming a teacher and serving in a particular school, and as a set of roles from which preparation programmes are considered. Teaching, and the administrative, supervisory, and education development roles which teachers assume has not been, until recently, the subject of deliberate examination as a career configuration which is evolving, and which provides purpose and direction to those who pursue it. As important are the conditions which shape a career in teaching, and their effects. When a teaching career of 30 to 40 years is normal, the examination of what constitutes such a career, and of its effects upon the individual and upon the profession of teaching, takes on importance.

Educational organizations have career structures and do attempt to 'manage' careers in their interest. Likewise, individuals have career plans which may, or may not, be compatible with the system. The career policies of school systems are largely implicit, vague and changing. The ability of the individual to construct realistic career plans, cope with family needs and personal conditions, 'read' the organization, and prepare adequately to achieve professional goals, leads to ambiguities and distortions. Out of these conditons grow the myths and realities by which the individual shapes and pursues a career.

A conception of career

A career is an imprecise concept, particularly in the case of teaching, but involves at least these considerations: 1) the nature of the work or job, 2) occupational activity implied by such phrases as 'having a career' or 'being a professional' which provide status or recognition, 3) a definition of success which includes opportunities to increase responsibility, financial reward, and recognition, 4) a defined and recognized vocational content to which dedication or a sense of mission is necessary. In addition, as with teaching, there exists a protracted formal training linked with induction into a society of peers through academic credentials and legal licensing procedures. This latter condition is characterized by postponement of short-term gains for the attainment of long-term rewards, a process of socialization or apprenticeship, and a progression through job roles in which increasing responsibility and autonomy are acquired.

A perspective of careers in education, the configuration of roles and statuses which we refer to as teaching, is the collective of perceptions of how the individual views, constructs and conducts his movement through working life. Since teaching is institutionalized within schools and school systems, consideration must be given to the limitations and opportunities afforded careers within the institutional context in terms of career events and perceptions of them.

A career in education, it turns out, is not as standardized and simplistic as might at first be assumed. In terms of motives, aspirations, satisfactions, career steps and strategies, to say nothing of institutional demands and opportunities, wider social conditions or specific individual and family conditions, teachers are as individualistic as we know pupils to be. There is in all this, which will be treated more explicitly, what will be referred to as the 'career game'. However, it is possible to group and classify individuals and make generalizations about these variables, including changes which typically occur over time. In this way, through study and refinement, conditions of career development and professional growth can be better understood and facilitated to improve educational effectiveness and to benefit those who serve the profession.

To continue the development of the concept of what constitutes a career in teaching, the central trunk from which subsequent career tracks are pursued is classroom teaching — the daily conduct of instruction with groups of learners. As individuals move along a given track, defined by subjects taught and the maturity level of learners, the degree of prediction of moves, or lack of them, increases. Early in a career movement between tracks is feasible. As a teacher career unfolds, age, experience and specialization restrict the possibilities of transfer to other branches or even of backtracking. Often, external conditions which limit movement are more restricting — these include general economic and social factors or even personal considerations of family, health and community interests, which may outweigh any forces for change. Within all this, the individual pursues a career in terms of his perceptions of 'success', and this is cast against the system's opportunities and arrangements to fill its personnel needs. It is important to determine how teachers perceive their career, and how they attempt to fulfil themselves in it. Thus, how the individual comes to terms with the organization and uses it is central.

The matter of what constitutes success is an important consideration in a conception of career. The organization, an educational bureaucracy, projects an image, which has been changing rather dramatically over the past two decades. Educational systems, at least in Britain and the United States, have moved to an economic model of rewards. This model includes a negotiated, open salary schedule which clearly signals to teachers that 'upward is better'. Some teachers reject the criteria of success which are basic to this model and, by their actions, indicate a desire to be judged on other grounds. Some feel that a career is essentially a private concern which is not to be examined with colleagues. Some, because of non-job circumstances or by disposition, cannot play the career game. Some never recognize, or refuse to admit, that their careers are a game to be played out with many implicit and relatively few explicit rules. Some decide how they want their careers to develop, study the 'rules' as best they can, and go about the career game quite deliberately.

The degree of success attained in any career is determined by the statuses and rewards associated with positions occupied along the particular career route. These statuses and rewards are highly visible signs which form the basis upon which the individual and others judge the degree of success attained and the possibilities for future movement. The visible, tangible rewards and the often not so visible personal gratifications provided by positions along a career chain are essential to the building and maintenance of one's concept of self. Therefore, the individual's perception of a career, expectations for it, and satisfactions derived are highly personal, but also crucial to whether or not success is achieved.

Routinization and bureaucratization of careers in teaching

During the 1960s fundamental changes in the character, structure, and organization of secondary education occurred in Great Britain, the United States and, to a somewhat different degree, in Third World countries. In Britain the selective secondary system was largely replaced by the comprehensive school. Teachers who had worked in selective grammar schools with the top ranges of ability preparing young minds for college and university, where school and community loyalties were of importance, frequently returned to the school where they had been pupils and remained there throughout their careers. Those who did not elect to attempt to obtain a head teacher post perceived themselves as having joined a select group of colleagues in a college of peers. High status was accorded by the school and community, and the title of 'senior master' was conferred, through seniority and good service, as the ultimate accolade. As with US and Third World schools, the British comprehensive school reflected wider social changes. Larger size and diversity of programme brought on an inevitable bureaucratization. Uniform salary schedules were one means by which career routes became defined and regulated by the bureaucracy. A career structure was established, apparent to those who had the drive to set about achieving promotion, in which no one could move from class teacher to head teacher without going through the prescribed stages. In effect, a career game was created, and the rewards of the system would go to those who could match individual career plans and preparation with an institutionally established career structure.

In the United States a parallel and simultaneous development was occurring. Massive growth in school enrolments, coupled with consolidation of schools into large diversified, comprehensive high schools, truncated the organizational structure so that administration became quite separated from teaching. Administration was established as a separate career chain, with some advocating that principals of schools need not have teaching experience as a qualification. Unionization of teachers forced fixed salary schedules, with experience and preparation as the only explicit criteria for job placement and movement. Within the teaching ranks the only movement besides leaving teaching altogether was into a department chairmanship. Statuses and rewards, beyond those which could be provided through the salary schedule, could be provided only by movement into administration or into ancillary developmental project work. Alan Peshkin (1978) refers to these changes as a shift to a large city model of education, and he treats the changes and effects in some detail.

Third World countries have uniformly adopted national salary schedules, sometimes set by a ministry of education in negotiation with a national teachers' union. Ministries typically assign and transfer teachers and control promotions. Here all the attributes of a career game are present and easily identified. A major exception in certain of these countries of Latin America and the Middle East is the high status still accorded the teacher and principal (or director) within the community. Here positions and even salary adjustments can be negotiated by the able teacher, but these, again, are determined in relation to an established, institutionalized procedure.

Teaching experience and competence provide the initial gatekeeping device for the career track. A career structure has been established. The career game as it functions in education has not been the subject of widespread examination. Van Maanan (1980) has examined this phenomenon in other settings and uses the game metaphor to emphasize that there are winners and losers over the span of a career, the outcome being determined by certain rules of play. With the plurality of individual orientations and needs, educational bureaucracies have not generated the capability to offset the negative impacts of low job-career satisfaction. They have, it seems, enforced impersonal approaches to career development which have brought about career abandonment, unionization, retaliation and lowered effort, without making a serious effort to achieve long-term career productivity.

Career maps and perceptions of career

Two perspectives offer assistance in an examination of conditions relative to the organization and pursuit of a career in education. Hughes (1958) employs the concept of a career as a set of sequentially arranged compartments. Entrance to and exit from each compartment requires certain qualifications and preparations as well as a 'fit' with organization needs and opportunities. Graves, Dalton and Thompson (1980), examining careers of scientists and engineers, found four distinct career compartments over a long-term work history, each with different functions and performance requirements.

Hughes' conception, applied to careers in teaching, permits the posing of questions around the two perspectives of the individual and the organization. One can ask if careers in teaching can be structured to provide options across a long-term work history that will match the needs of the individual teacher. Does the system establish identifiable career compartments? If so, what are the established entry and exit requirements for these compartments? What are the characteristics of teachers who are allowed to progress or who are retained? At what rate and time frame do teachers typically progress through the career chain? How and when is information made available, and of what should it consist? What assistance is provided to help teachers engage in meaningful goal setting? Answers to such questions could permit educational organizations to design career paths that correspond to the abilities and needs of costly human resources.

From the point of view of the individual, a series of questions arise. Is the teacher aware of the established career structure and of the requirements for movement from one compartment to another? How is this set of requirements accepted as a philosophy of a career in teaching? How does the teacher learn while in a given career compartment that other compartments exist? How does the teacher determine the requirements, both explicit and implicit, for entry into other compartments? How much distortion occurs between perceptions and reality? Do myths and misconceptions arise that guide teacher thinking and planning? From the individual's perspective, it is important to become informed and to understand the implications of implicit, vague and changing rules in order to manage career planning more rationally.

An approach to conceptualizing what occurs in the mapping of a career is provided by Roth (1963). He suggests the idea of a timetable stretching into the future, divided into blocks of varying time lengths. An individual's progress through time blocks can be measured against the rate established by observation of a specified reference group. Thus, a norm or standard rate of progression can be used against which to compare an individual's movement through a career. Certain periods have more importance than others and prove to be crucial to a judgement on the part of an individual concerning rate of success and timing of moves. For example, a frequent response to these writers was 'I must be a head (principal, director) by 40 or I will have failed.'

Each of us constantly attempts to structure uncertainty and, according to Roth, in terms of career structuring one does this by observation of the careers of members of a reference group. In this way judgements are made about one's own progress, goals, standards of performance, actions to take, etc. These judgments are tempered in terms of wider circumstances of health, family, etc, and form the basis of individual career planning. They also provide the measures by which success is judged, and this, in turn, shapes one's self-concept and feelings of self-worth.

This kind of conceptualizing indicates that an individual observes a reference group and learns, in more or less rational fashion, the conditions and rules of the career game. In the process one clarifies career purposes and possibilities, sets expectations, and plans career moves. In effect, the individual maps a career and attempts to fulfil it — a career is something one plans and at which one works. To be satisfying, individual goals must be fulfillable; each career compartment, from the individual's point of view, must supply the appropriate rewards in terms of expectations provided by the career map. A large part of the satisfaction comes in seeing that a career compartment provides the requirements needed for entry into the next and future compartments. Additionally, the alert and mobile teacher seeks career compartments that contain alternatives and which insure that one does not become blocked or held too long — age being one important factor in career movement in education.

Lyons, in an unpublished study based upon the Roth and Hughes formulations, investigated career perceptions of British teachers. Some of his data are used to illustrate how teachers view their careers. Lyons surmised that teachers would have formulated some sort of career map and that this map could be described for various age groups and teaching specialities. For instance, those with more experience could be expected to show a better formulated and more realistic perception than those just entering teaching. It was noted that students in training as physical education teachers are made aware of the need to be able to switch to other specializations or to teach a subsidiary subject as they become older and less physically agile. It was also noted that young women entering teaching deliberately plan to leave in order to rear children, and they consciously explore the problems of returning to teaching after raising a family.

To investigate the nature of teachers' perceptions, an interview schedule was prepared containing the following questions: Is there a time when a teacher clearly sees the career opportunities in education? If yes, when did you see this? Replies were classified as shown in Table 1.

Number		Map always		Map never		Map acquired	
		N	%	N	%	N	%
Males	70	22	31.0	30	43.0	18	26.0
Females	51	10	20.0	29	57.0	12	23.0
Total	121	32	26.4	59	48.8	30	24.8

Table 1 *Career mapping by teachers*

Less than half of the teachers sampled had no clear perception of their career goal and the method whereby they might attain one. Over one-quarter held a clear perception of the route they wished to follow from the time they began teaching; and just under one-quarter began teaching without a career map, but organized one at some subsequent time.

Differences due to age did not turn out to be statistically significant. Yet it was apparent that the proportion of those who were 'map acquired' increased markedly with age, as would be expected, while the proportion of those who were 'map never' decreased with age. Likewise, the difference between teachers of different statuses was not statistically significant, but the proportion of 'map never' was highest for assistant and lowest for top post teachers.

The career perceptions and strategies for arriving at desired goals by different teachers can be oversimplified. However, regardless of the variety of factors, both intrinsic and extrinsic to the teaching situation, family and wider social events were found to constrain and affect the career patterns chosen. Also, the same perceptions and strategies appeared widely different according to the time scale in which they were perceived — the leisurely rise of an individual with his sights set on an ultimate headship before retirement appeared very different from the meteoric career of the teacher who feels that a headship must be attained by the age of 35 . Two of the teachers in the study sample who achieved senior positions in large comprehensive schools in their early thirties saw their career possibilities from the start, and their subsequent experience confirmed the original perception of their career map. Clearly, the teacher who sees from the start the moves needed over a long span of his career to best fulfil career goals is in a position of advantage over one who does not.

Statements descriptive of careers are surprisingly similar across cultures. Whether in Britain, the United States, the Middle East, or Latin America, similar terms and similar perceptions are expressed. Instances in which a clear career orientation was held, and which occur repeatedly regardless of culture, might be paraphrased as follows: 'I saw clearly the possibilities of the position, and I expect to use this school as a springboard to a better job.' 'I'm not ambitious; I know the career opportunities. I married young so I'm not concerned with promotion. I take jobs that are available where my husband moves — any local school will suit me.'

The most common means by which career maps are acquired appears to be a gradual recognition of possibilities which become structured over limited time spans. In Hughes' terms careers unfold compartment by compartment. As one attains experience with, and success in, one career compartment, one begins to investigate the possibilities of movement to other compartments. A common expression is, 'You have to feel your way a step at a time,' or 'I master one job and then see where it might take me.'

One consequence of the piecemeal view of a career is that the desire for a particular post may be acquired when there is no longer the opportunity to satisfy the conditions of attaining it. One statement exemplified this all-too-common condition: 'I didn't think about it. The change of head made me look around. I discovered I had stayed too long and could have got further if I had moved. I regret now that it didn't occur to me.'

The gradual fashion in which a career viewpoint is acquired can function either to provide a mature and reasoned approach to career fulfilment or to engender a sense of failure. Additional paraphrases of actual statements serve to illustrate this point: 'Young teachers have little idea about how anyone gets ahead; they haven't been told and don't think about it themselves.' 'After three years as department head I saw that I could make a go of it, and I felt I could do as well in other things.' 'After 20 years I became aware of colleagues who moved ahead or left teaching sometimes even for skilled jobs with larger incomes and more leisure than I have — it's a prostitution of professional ability.' 'Used to have ambitions 20 years ago, but they're all gone now, the dreams.'

The conception of career employed here can be used to assess how realistic career goals might be for a given group of teachers. In Table 2, data are presented showing percentages of a sample of teachers in terms of their stated ultimate career goal. More than one-fifth of this sample of teachers indicated that they were aiming for a top career post. However, in the schools which contributed to the sample, junior and top posts combined totalled slightly more than 5 per cent. These data are from Britain, but checks of a set of school districts in the US and data from one Latin American ministry (Bolivia) indicated even higher ratios of individuals who had acquired certificates for administration to actual posts.

As shown in the table, just under one-fifth (18.9 per cent) of the teachers of this sample indicated their ambitions as being multi-goal. They held two or more clearly visualized goals by stating, for example, 'I could become a headmaster or I might go into a college as a lecturer.' Because of the need to classify, the table tends to present an oversimplified picture. There are teachers who do not have a clear career goal or who may see how a career might be planned in terms of realistic goal setting but reject the idea of doing it themselves. To illustrate, a department head said, 'A cut-and-dried future and goal moves are not for me.' Another said, 'It's a pity you have to leave a school to further your career. I wouldn't. It's not worth the extra pennies.'

In terms of a conception of a career in teaching one can, at this point, draw a general picture with the very limited data available. The young teacher at the beginning of a career is generally quite uncertain as to the goals to which he or she may reasonably aspire. The individual may have some general idea of ultimate posts but is unable to select among those that are possible. If the person

Goal	%
Top posts (headmaster)	21.3
Multi-goal	18.9
Other educational work	17.2
Terminal	15.6
Don't know	10.7
Mid-posts (in the school)	9.0
Non-educational	5.7
Assistant graded posts (in the school)	1.6

Table 2 *Teachers' ultimate goals*

does choose, it is usually a low or intermediate career goal. After the first promotion, or with experience, the career path becomes clearer and the career map becomes more or less apparent. The career path immediately ahead and perhaps an 'ultimate' goal may be reasonably clearly perceived, but the branching possibilities, the dead ends and the intermediate steps are likely to be quite unclear. When one reaches the post to which one has always aspired, other possibilities may become apparent or, alternatively, one may find one cannot backtrack to begin another path.

Characteristics of the top post (successful) teacher

Obviously, the 'successful' teacher may be in the classroom in an intermediate post such as department chairman or assistant; however, for an examination of career as the concept applies to teaching, the authors choose to focus upon the head of the school; headmaster, principal or director. This perspective permits one to observe a series of career posts or steps. The US author directed the research team of the National High School Principal Study in the United States which was completed in 1979 (NASSP, 1979), and data from this study were compared to the British data to which reference has already been made. In addition, data from Turkey, Jordan, and Bolivia were available to the authors in the preparation of this commentary.

Uniformly, top post individuals from all the countries noted above appeared to have clear, strongly held career maps and a determination to acquire the experience necessary to progress through career compartments to an ultimate post. One characteristic evident from the data is the ability of these individuals to mesh organizational and individual career requirements. They perceive what steps to take and, just as important, what steps not to take in the career game. They do not run out of organizational space, or, if they do, they move. They use the organization and make it work for them. In terms of the British sample, where quotations will again be used by way of illustration, each had consciously developed a career map, virtually from the entry to the first post. With the exception of one individual, they were able to keep from being blocked and retained in one compartment. They clearly perceived the need to gain entry to successive career compartments and the need to insure that each compartment offers alternative exits.

British top post individuals compare closely with those from Middle Eastern and Latin American schools. They are graduates of 'mainline', academic subjects. Many are completing, or already hold, a master's degree in education. They have achieved their various levels of promotion more quickly than their age/experience cohort and have maintained that promotion rate over a length of time. Those who are obtaining top posts are doing so at the comparatively early age of 35-40. They have characteristically used in-service training to equip themselves for their next career move prior to that move, and they use such training as much for visibility as for the content it offers.

Compared with others of comparable age and experience, they have made more moves between schools and between geographical areas. They also show greater satisfaction with the administrative content of the job than do their peers. They realized the possibilities of promotion early: 'My grammar head expected staff to be young, to stay two or three years and then be promoted away', or 'I picked up the possibility of promotion early. My first post gave me sixth form experience, and then I talked my way onward.' The aim is to reach a chairmanship or headship of a department: 'The ambitious want to be head of department within five years.' After the post of department head different routes are followed. Some move to a larger department, to a larger school, to other intermediate posts, or to a lectureship. As one said, 'Length of service is irrelevant. Those who get promoted are those who move quickly from job to job. You must be willing to move.' Top post teachers made significantly more promotion moves between schools than other sampled teachers of the same age and experience.

In the US study cited above, principals could be characterized as having a master's degree plus substantial formal training; they have an undergraduate major in the social sciences, sciences, or humanities (in that order of frequency); they achieve appointment as high school principals between the ages of 30 and 40 with 50 per cent of all principals achieving that appointment by the age of 35; and more than 40 per cent aspire to move now to positions other than the principalship. Principals in the United States average six years of teaching before moving to an intermediate post as department head, dean, director of guidance, or an assistant principalship. Over 80 per cent achieved the principalship from an assistant principalship, and 85 per cent achieved the principalship in the same school district in which they took their first teaching post, although they averaged moves to three different schools.

As with the US counterparts, achieving a top post in any country presents the incumbent with the difficulty of finding branching alternatives. Having reached the goal of a top post at the age of perhaps 35, most find a problem of deciding future moves, and they seem unsure of what they might do for the rest of their working lives. From a sample of 60 US principals who were identified as 'effective' in their jobs, over half said that they would not remain long as principals. One-third had subsequently left the principalship within a two year period, and half of that number had left education. Here, as with the reports of British teachers' perceptions of career noted earlier, the educational bureaucracy needs to become conscious of the wastage which is promulgated when career planning and career enhancement are not deliberately undertaken by the organization.

Sponsorship

As has been pointed out, organizations 'manage' the careers of their members in order to guarantee their own survival. The organization not only needs talent, it needs stability; and it needs loyalty to its goals and programmes. In almost all countries, heads may promote staff internally with a minimum of clearance with superior authority, and seldom would an appointment to a school be made if a head objected to it. The question, then, is how teachers attract the attention of those who influence promotion. Somehow they must do this and yet stay within the rules of the career game; in effect, how do teachers achieve creditable visibility?

Teaching is a relatively isolated and insulating occupation. In an excellent sociological study of teaching, Lortie (1975:232) analyses this condition and its effects. One of his observations is that 'the current organization of teaching tasks fosters conservation of outlook. Change is impeded by mutual isolation, vague yet demanding goals, dilemmas of outcome assessment, restricted in-service training, rigidities in assignment and working conditions which produce a more-of-the-same syndrome among classroom teachers.' Restricted though it is, teachers favour in-service training as a means of obtaining sponsorship. The content of such training must be seen as preparation for a career move, but equally important is the opportunity afforded to gain association with figures who can influence promotion. Along with opportunities afforded by in-service, those who are concerned with promotability actively seek person-to-person contacts. Lyons (1976:153), in a related research activity, collected data relative to person-to-person communications from the sample used in the British data reported here. When the career ambitions of sub-groups of the total sample were studied, it was apparent that those with high communication scores were more likely than any other group of teachers (significance at the .01 level) to have a clear idea of the senior position for which they were ultimately heading. This sub-group was displaying one attribute of becoming promotable, that of achieving visibility as one avenue to sponsorship.

One can speculate about means by which teachers might get the attention of potential sponsors, how and what kinds of sponsorship develop and exist, and what effects are derived from the activities associated with sponsorship. Too little is known about these specifics as they relate to education, although we know that they exist and that they are important to career development. Clawson (1980), in examining what he refers to as 'mentoring', differentiates between life mentors, career mentors, coaches, and bosses. He finds that each can either help or hinder and that the effects depend upon characteristics of the relationship. There are, especially in education, those who have an internal need for, and feel an obligation to develop, their junior associates. The dynamics of helpful sponsorship in education is a topic which needs investigation.

Terminal posts and perceptions of success and failure

One condition which dominates the complex topic of career success and failure is that the individual is constantly, often painfully, coming to terms with himself — that is, taking stock of ambitions, opportunities and achievements, and, in the process, reconstructing his own self-concept. This process usually centres upon one's career, as movement within or between career compartments is considered.

Data tend to indicate that some teachers are quite unhappy about what has happened to them in the course of their career — they judge themselves, and others judge them, as being unsuccessful. Some are unhappy with themselves because of their career moves, but are judged by others to be successful and satisfied. The mix of motives and derived satisfactions appears to be the primary determinant of feelings of success or failure.

It is almost certainly true to say that the simplistic notion of a single, stable, inherently satisfying career in teaching does not exist. There are many careers and career orientations, most quite different from the hierarchically structured career pattern projected by the bureaucracy. For some teachers, teaching was never their primary commitment, and they pursued it as a means of satisfying a deep interest (for example, in the arts or in the content of a specific subject). Some find rewards, often monetary ones, which can be pursued more or less at leisure while occupying a teaching post. We have labelled these as alternative careers within a teaching career.

The end of a career in teaching need not necessarily imply the fulfillment of the hopes with which the beginning teacher set out, nor may it adequately reflect the post the teacher wishes to obtain or the post for which he was most suited; most, at some stage in their career, will have compromised, and this may have been done with varying degrees of frustration or resignation, or it may, more simply, be a coming to terms with themselves. As one teacher observed, 'when you get older, you come to terms with your limitations. When you're younger, you dream of getting to grips with them.' Even those who have achieved the highest post in a school may have sensed their limitations, and have wished to redefine further goals for themselves; or they may have been frustrated in an original ambition. For example, one head said, 'I look back with regret that I never used my higher degree to follow up academic work, for when I entered teaching I thought industry was the only other available alternative.'

For many, the ultimate goal at which they aim is constantly being redefined. With greater experience and the knowledge that accrues from this, the expectation would be for the average teacher to redefine more fulfillable goals based upon the accumulation of experience.

It is anticipated that, with the exception of those who leave the profession early, those holding self-perceived terminal goals will fall into three main categories: those who feel themselves frustrated in their ambitions; those who have redefined their ambitions to suit their circumstances; and those who have succeeded in achieving the goals of their ambitions. Not all of those in the latter category will necessarily aspire to the most senior positions in a school: 'Some colleagues devote their lives to making the right move at the right time, are in it for the money, etc — cut-and-dried moves, that's not for me. I'm not ambitious because I have to limit my time. I've decided I'm happy to take a back seat.'

Although the possibility exists for teachers to reach what they consider to be their terminal goal in a comparatively short time, this may in fact prove to be a relatively junior post. Those who claim to be in a terminal position fall into the older range of teachers and are more likely to be occupying mid posts or top posts in a school. Table 3 provides data from the British sample.

It seems somewhat self-evident that there should be a sub-group of age 26 + females who regarded themselves as occupying terminal posts, since this is an age when women will often leave teaching to have their families, and will be restricted in employment opportunities by the need to look after young children. Four of the teachers who fell into this age group were of this category. They were

Present post	Male	Female		Age	Male	Female
Assistant teacher	3	2		21 +	0	0
Graded post	1	1		26 +	0	5
Mid post	10	7		36 +	2	1
Top post	5	3		46 +	17	7
Total	19	13		Total	19	13

Table 3 *Those who state that their present posts are terminal*

in their late twenties and early thirties, generally having between seven and ten years' teaching experience behind them. They turned to teaching because it 'looked like a good career to combine with marriage'. They appear to be 'satisfied with (their) present post — its responsibility and financial rewards are adequate for what (they) want'. 'Hoping for a family and am now trying for one, now we can afford it. I hope it will be very soon, and then I will leave. Otherwise I will leave in five years' time, when my husband will be better off — we're now still paying off furniture and things.'

It seemed that, in this sample of interviewed teachers, few were really frustrated by their inability to achieve an aspired-for post, and there may be many reasons to explain this. Coming to terms with apparent failure manifests itself in a number of ways. The following examples may be typical. One teacher, after a successful career elsewhere, entered teaching to be in the classroom and to have contact with children. He is most frustrated to find that other teachers are concerned with promotion and that 'promotion takes you out of the classroom'. Two others expressed considerable bitterness and frustration because the world had changed around them, leaving them stranded doing a different job in an entirely different type of school from the one they had originally joined. They wait somewhat impatiently for retirement. Another, a craft teacher, has gone as far as his qualifications will allow. Promotion within his subject, he feels, 'depends on dead men's shoes'.

Most, in fact, have come to terms with themselves and rationalized their apparent lack of success. They expect to be in their present post up to retirement. Perhaps if things had gone more their way, perhaps if opportunities of promotion had been greater when they started teaching, perhaps if more grants had been available when they were students, the situation could have been changed. They have had their dreams, and 'not everyone can be a headmaster, a college lecturer or LEA adviser'; the job is rewarding, they like the craft of teaching, and, after all, promotion is out of the classroom.

Terminal posts and alternative careers

A school, from its point of view as an organization, has a need to have loyalty, commitment, and stability from its staff. It has a need to have all the posts filled by teachers who perform competently, and therefore its own requirements could lead to a judgement of successful performance of its staff different from the views they hold of themselves. A succinct way of expressing this is encapsulated in the notion of alternative careers. Clearly, from an examination of the data revealed by this sample of teachers, there are two major types of alternative careers. (1) The first is where a teacher frustrated in the original career goal turns to other activities which will give some satisfaction of those motives and aspirations currently held. (2) The second type is where a teacher has always had at most a shared commitment to teaching and to an alternative career, or perhaps the alternative career has always been that giving the larger share of personal satisfaction and reward.

Factors relating to the first condition noted above are likely to be age-related and most easily illustrated from data relating to retirement plans or late career choices. Indeed teachers may choose, with the recognition that the end of their career is in sight, to abandon whatever other ambitions may still remain unfulfilled and to take whatever post offers itself that will allow them to achieve other satisfactions. The following statement from one of the interviewed teachers illustrates this:'One came to the stage when one was too old to get a bigger allowance in a bigger school, so I came to this authority because it's a nice part of the country and the biggest allowance I could get.'

The above condition permits us to raise the idea developed by Howard Becker (1971) of the accumulation of advantages/valuables. Becker refers to the investment in the job, family, and community and its surroundings, such that the forces against a career change far outweigh any force likely to induce change. The cost of housing, the moving of children at a critical stage in schooling, elderly parents, or a host of other factors represent advantages/valuables. These, along with the acquired statuses and the life-style of being in a particular school for a long period of time and the accumulations that have come to mean a comfortable life, deter teachers from moves which might otherwise be career enhancing.

We can now examine, somewhat briefly, the second type of alternative career, where teaching has never necessarily been the major commitment. The teaching profession, more, perhaps, than any other profession, lends itself to different types of alternative careers.

Clearly, the young woman whose expectations were always that she would leave the profession as soon as marriage and child rearing made demands, is merely using teaching as an interim step. However, many married women have always intended to return to teaching after child rearing is completed, and they must plan re-entry carefully. However, the demands and commitments that a family give an alternative career are such that, although loyal to the school, they are unlikely for a number of years to be interested in seeking promotion and additional responsibility. From the sample, it appears that, once child rearing was comfortably contained, many of these women were interested in coming out of their mainline academic subjects and taking on pastoral/welfare posts. Certain categories of teachers, musicians, dance specialists, potters, artists, etc can use teaching as an avenue to the practice of their craft. Teaching provides financial security but allows the individual to continue work at his or her more consuming interests.

Another category of teachers comprises those for whom teaching provides a second career. Craftsmen who have worked in industry and those who have been in the armed services (from which they will already have a pension) are cases in point. All of these may enter teaching, fully qualified, after having had a satisfactory career elsewhere. However, because of the way in which (as we have seen) careers are conducted in sequential stages, and where the movements between stages must be accomplished according to the appropriate timetable,such teachers are never likely to be able to progress beyond the level of mid posts in school. Experience gained elsewhere is likely to have demonstrated this to them fairly early.

Concluding statement

Although much of what has been presented is based upon limited data, such data consistently confirm the conceptualization of careers as described. Experience leads us to suggest that the career game, as it is played in educational institutions, may not be as idealistic and fulfilling to teachers and administrators as is generally believed. We have presented primarily the view of the individual in a struggle over a length of time to achieve success in a career — success being defined by the individual's goals and work satisfactions. There yet remains the organization's side of the career equation. Educational organizations should, at least in the interest of the long-term productivity of their members, keep teachers informed about options and assist them in goal setting, attempt to provide options that match teacher needs at various career stages, and provide an adequate, flexible staff development programme. There is at present a lack of evidence about educational organizations' efforts in terms of career development practices. Our evidence and experience indicates that serious mismatches occur between career options provided and personal/career goals of individuals. There is a widespread scepticism about the adequacy of in-service development programmes, a scepticism particularly centred upon uniformity of treatment and lack of quality. Concern also exists about the routinization of teaching and about the time demands of the job. Clearly the time has come to engage in serious inquiry about the nature of careers in education.

References

Becker, H (1971) *Personal Change in Adult Life* Routledge and Kegan Paul: London

Clawson, J (1980) Mentoring in managerial careers *in* Derr (1980)

Derr, C (ed) (1980) *Work, Family and Career: New Frontiers in Theory and Research* Praeger: New York

Graves, J *et al* (1980) Career stages *in* Derr (1980)

Hughes, E (1958) *Men and Their Work* Free Press: Glencoe, Ill

Lortie, D (1975) *Schoolteacher: A Sociological Study* University of Chicago Press: Chicago

Lyons, G (1976) *Heads' Tasks: A Handbook of Secondary School Administration* National Foundation for Educational Research: Slough

Lyons, G (1980) *Teacher Careers and Career Perceptions* National Foundation for Educational Research: Slough

National Association of Secondary-School Principals (1979) *The Senior High School Principal* (3 volumes) The Association: Reston, Virginia

Peshkin, A (1978) *Growing Up America: Schooling and the Survival of the Community* University of Chicago Press: Chicago

Roth, J (1963) *Timetables: Structuring the Passage of Time in Hospital, Treatment and Other Careers* Bobbs-Merrill: Indianapolis

Van Maanan, J (1980) The career game: organizational rules of play *in* Derr (1980)

Part 3: National Case Studies

7. The role of central government in educational development in Sweden

Sixten Marklund

Summary: This chapter discusses the role of central government and local government in educational development and how this development is influenced by the nature of the balance between these two agencies.

Educational policy-making in Sweden is usually made by governmental commissions who investigate special questions of policy on behalf of the central government, and specify goals and measures for the improvement of education. An example (the 1960 Commission on Teacher Training) is described. Implementation of these decisions is effected by independent national authorities, one of which is the National Board of Education (NBE). Swedish experiences suggest that a change of education in schools has to be co-ordinated with a parallel change in the central administration. A special part of the reform machinery is educational research and development (R and D). Funds for R and D are allocated to NBE for the purpose of furthering policy goals determined by the government; R and D is therefore specifically decision-oriented. Another important part is the system of in-service training of teachers; this is centrally organized by the NBE as a means for the implementation of education policy.

Countries with a centralized school system seem to strive for decentralization, while countries with a decentralized system seem to look for a strengthening of central planning. These trends are, however, not simple and clear. In international studies by the Organization for Economic Co-operation and Development (OECD) no simple relationships between decentralization and local autonomy were found. The hypothesis that central funding of education should result in a homogeneous school system was, on the whole, not verified when schools were studied on a national level. Nevertheless, it was found in a Swedish analysis of data from an international project that Swedish schools were more like one another in terms of student knowledge of science than schools in a group of other comparable countries. The conclusion is offered that centralization of educational policy and administration is necessary but not sufficient for equality of school standards.

Central and local government

Who is responsible for the development of education — the central government or local government? Or is it neither of these two agencies but rather individuals, groups of individuals, teachers and laymen outside school?

In this chapter I will discuss the role of central government as promoter of educational development. Some examples will be taken from Sweden, and, in spite of the national characteristics, it is hoped that these will be of interest for other educational systems.

Historically, the school has mainly been a local governmental concern.

Central government has normally not been very much involved with issues of education. This is especially true for elementary education, but it also applied to so-called higher education. For example, the colleges that prepared for service to church and state were for a long time predominantly a local concern. In some countries, especially Protestant ones, higher education became a central governmental concern when the church changed from being an international Catholic institution to a national church, subordinate to a central national government. This made higher education a concern for national government, while primary education for people in general remained the responsibility of local communities. The fact that these local communities as a rule consisted simply of local clergymen and parishes is beside the point.

What has happened during the last century is that not only primary education but also part of secondary education have become common to the majority of students, and this has made the distinction between primary and secondary education less relevant than before. In some countries and school systems both primary and secondary education have become a local responsibility, while in other countries and systems both have become a central responsibility.

To this distinction between primary and secondary education can be added another one, namely that between church and state, which for a long time constituted an extremely important dividing line of responsibility. In general, during the sixteenth and seventeenth centuries, the primary as well as the secondary school was seen as a responsibility of the church. During the eighteenth century, with its philosophy of enlightenment and utilitarianism, the role played by the state grew. Education was no longer just a spiritual and moral matter. It became a worldly and economic matter to be taken care of by the state. Later, during the nineteenth and twentieth centuries, the educational system grew strongly and became secularized, which reduced the leading role of the church even more.

Thus, the boundary between primary and secondary education, which was earlier an important demarcation line, is nowadays less important. The same thing happened with the boundary between responsibilities of the church and the state. The third boundary, however, that between central and local government, has become more important today. This brings us back to the question with which we started this chapter. Should education be predominantly a responsibility for central government or for local government? Or, if it is the responsibility of both, which mostly seems to be the case today, how should this responsibility be shared between the two?

The Swedish school system is usually conceived of as a centralized one, as are those in France and Italy, for example. A centralized system also exists in the Netherlands, although it is divided into three separate systems, a Protestant, a Catholic and a state system. Federal countries sometimes have a 'centralized decentralization', such as that in Australia, where every state has its own fully centralized system. Another is the Federal Republic of Germany, where each 'land' has its own school system.

Decentralized systems, where the development and administration of education predominantly rest with local agencies, are found in England, Scotland, Denmark, and Norway. The schools in the USA also usually belong to this group, even if there are states with a fairly strongly centralized school administration. The socialist countries not only have centralized systems but also decentralized ones — Yugoslavia belongs to the latter group. Yet, as a rule, school systems cannot be simply classified as either centralized or decentralized. Mostly they are both, but with different distributions of responsibility between the two levels. Moreover, in many countries there are also regional and provincial authorities intermediate between these two.

A centralized school system is often equated with an authoritarian system. This is not entirely correct. A decentralized system can be seen as authoritarian by single individuals. A group of teachers can find themselves strongly governed by a local school board, as well as by a central government and its administration. Since World War II the Swedish school system has been subject to almost total change. One of the important outcomes of this change is that all compulsory schooling has become integrated, meaning that academic, general and technical vocational education are given in the same kind of school. The already strong centralization became even stronger during this reform period. The reform strategies and mechanisms have therefore sometimes been seen as authoritarian and hierarchical, with changes having been initiated at national level and then spreading, first to regionally and then to locally responsible educational bodies.

Still, this is not an entirely fair picture. In fact it can be claimed that during the post-war period, educational issues in Sweden have been more clearly rooted in public opinion and public policy than was previously the case. Evidence of this is seen in the annual Parliamentary debates during 1950-62 on the results of the experimental programmes undertaken to develop a nine-year comprehensive school. Characteristic of Sweden is the strong position enjoyed by popular movements over the past century. The blue-collar and white-collar labour movements have grown strong and now include most private and public employees. Educational issues have been widely discussed within these movements as well as within the free churches, the sports movement, the temperance organizations, the consumer co-operative movement, the women's movement, the parent-teacher movement, and in various kinds of adult education organizations. The role of these popular movements and organizations as institutionalized moulders of opinion can hardly be overestimated. They have influenced the political parties, which in turn are behind the political decisions made by Parliament and the central government.

Here I want to turn to two kinds of issues in the development of education in Sweden, namely (1) the role of central governmental commissions as originators of educational policy, and (2) the role of central administrative bodies as executors of political decisions in educational development.

Educational policy-making

The pathway to political decisions about education ordinarily runs via government-appointed commissions. These commissions have in fact become a crucible for the creation of Swedish reform policy. They represent an essential ingredient.of the central government system, which hence operates somewhat differently from its counterparts in other countries.

The initial stage in this committee system is that the appropriate minister (in this case the Minister of Education and Cultural Affairs), writes instructions for its work and receives the authorization of the government to appoint its members and secretariat.

Educational commissions are ordinarily composed of: (1) parliamentary or other political party representatives, (2) representatives of interest groups within the educational system, usually teachers and school administrators, and (3) special experts in educational research and development work.

After investigation work usually lasting two to five years, the commission publishes its final report which includes recommendations for action. This customarily includes both a timetable for putting into effect the proposed reforms and a cost estimate for these measures. The series of reports published by a commission often incorporates scientific and statistical studies of the issues covered. In Sweden, during the reform period since 1950, a number of doctoral dissertations in education have actually been written as parts of commission reports on educational matters.

The commission presents its work to the Minister of Education and Cultural Affairs, who is normally expected to send the final report and attached special studies to all public agencies affected by the work of the commission, as well as to organizations representing teachers, parents and pupils, and to special-mentioned popular movements, as well as to municipal authorities, colleges and universities affected by the commission's recommendations.

The organizations to which these publications are circulated often put in a large amount of work studying the commission's report, the background material on which it is based, the recommendations it leads to, the timetable proposed for these changes, and the finance the reform is supposed to require.

As a rule, the central government presents to Parliament a bill based on the recommendations made by the commission and the viewpoints on them which it has gathered. It happens only rarely that a commission report does not result in a government bill being submitted to Parliament. It is thus characteristic of Swedish reform strategy that an issue which has been raised finally ends up in one form or another before Parliament. Another characteristic is that the lag between the presentation of a commission report and the subsequent Parliamentary decision on the same issue is comparatively short.

Table 1 gives some examples of how this system has functioned during the post-war period.

An additional characteristic of Swedish policy-making is the division of the decision-making process into various stages. It has thus often happened that Parliament has first approved a decision *in principle* on a reform (the best known is the decision taken in 1950 on the principles governing the future development of the school system), and then, later, has come back to make decisions on the *details* of this development.

To illustrate how a committee works, the 1960 Committee on Teacher Training may be taken as an example. This committee comprised 11 members, mainly representatives of teacher training, school administration and educational research. One of the members acted as head of the secretariat, where there were usually ten or so persons engaged full-time. Experts were attached to the committee — and especially to the secretariat for various purposes — 153 altogether. These experts, most of them subject-specialists, had limited tasks. When dealing with peripheral problems, the committee was divided into a number of sub-groups. During the period 1960-65, the complete committee held 68 meetings, lasting a total of 101 days, to which can be added individual work and meetings of sub-groups — work which was, naturally, much more demanding. On special problems, the committee conferred with other committees and with the authorities; opinions were also expressed on a large number of reports from other committees. Altogether, seventeen reports were published. As can be seen in Table 1, the report of this committee gradually resulted in a new national system for teacher training from 1968.

Commission	Worked during years	Parliamentary decision in year	Local implementation in years	Effects on regular school activities
1946 School Commission	1946 - 1952	1950 and 1954	1950 - 1962	Experimental activities
1951 School Board Commission	1946 - 1955	1956	1958	New local and regional school administration
1957 School Commission	1957 - 1961	1962	1962 - 1972	Transition from the old 'parallel' school system to the comprehensive school system
1960 Upper Secondary School Commission	1960 - 1963	1964	1967 onwards	Reformed 3-year upper secondary school. Introduction of 2-year upper secondary school
1960 Teacher Training Commission	1960 - 1965	1967	1968 onwards	Replacement of special teacher training institutes for primary and secondary teachers by 'Schools of Education'
1963 Vocational Training Commission	1963 - 1967	1968	1970 onwards	Integration of vocational education and general academic upper secondary education
1968 Education Commission	1968 - 1973	1975	1975	New structure of tertiary education with new admission rules
1970 Commission on the Internal Working of the School	1972 - 1975	1976 and 1977	1978	New rules for state support. Decentralization of detailed curriculum-making

Table 1

Educational administration

1. Central administration

All countries possess an administrative machinery for schools and education. There is a central administration, and as a rule also a local administration. The former is usually part of the Ministry or Department of Education, which has both a political and an administrative side. In some countries the administrative side is entirely dependent on changes on the political side; when a new policy and a new Minister or Secretary for Education take over, the Ministry also changes the administrative heads. In other countries, the administrative heads are more independent of political changes and it is assumed that they will loyally follow the political decisions taken, even when those involve a new thrust in educational policy. This administrative independence can be more or less marked. In Sweden, the heads of central administration enjoy a strong position. The reason for this is mainly that the administration is run essentially by agencies (authorities) that are independent of the ministerial departments. They serve not under any specific department, but under the Government as a whole.

The central agencies are mainly charged with carrying out decisions by Parliament and Government. During the lively reform work of the post-war period, these agencies have had to assume responsibility for giving more exact, concrete definitions to educational policy objectives. Besides legal and economic experts, they have made increasing use of professional experts on educational, organizational and informational matters.

The directors of the central administration agencies, their divisions and bureaux are civil servants and thus, in principle, independent of changes in Government. Each agency has its own board, which includes representatives of various national interest groups on the labour market, in the social welfare field and in education.

The educational system is administered at national level by the National Board of Education (NBE). Primary and secondary education, including most vocational education, is under NBE jurisdiction. Municipal and state adult education, in-service training for teachers, and educational research and development work also come under NBE jurisdiction at national level.

2. Local administration

Each municipal authority has its own local board of education, which is politically elected. The local school administration is headed by one or more chief education officers. The latter are responsible for primary and secondary education in the municipality, and also adult education. Previously, there were separate chief education officers for the compulsory and secondary schools. The former schools were always municipal, the latter could be either state or municipal. An important aspect of the comprehensive school reform was a decision by Parliament to place all primary and secondary schools under local administration as from 1958. The teachers and heads who had previously been part of the state system and thus served directly under the NBE, now became municipal employees. Prior to that time, the local educational administration had been very imperfectly developed, particularly in the small rural districts. The fusion of primary and secondary school administration in 1958 to make a uniform educational administration was one of the many necessary conditions for 'comprehensivization' of the schools.

3. Reforms in the administration of the schools

The comprehensive school reform, started in 1950, presupposed a reorganization of the central school administration, ie the NBE. Already in 1949, the NBE had acquired a special Experimental Division. This was expanded, and it acquired, from 1952, three bureaux for the administration of experimental activities in the country at large. The previous Primary School and Grammar School Divisions were abolished, their places being taken by an Organization Division, a Curriculum Division, and a Planning and Building Division.

Questions previously relating to the primary and secondary schools were co-ordinated with questions relating to experimental activities, and grouped under the headings 'organization', 'curriculum', 'building and construction', etc. The fact that the previous school system no longer had a coherent central administration of its own was of great importance for the emergence of the new school. This change proved to be a kind of silent revolution in the central administration, for without it the NBE would hardly have been able to lead the nationwide experimental activities with the new comprehensive schools. This, then, is one example of how it is necessary first to reform the central school administration in order to obtain a corresponding reform in the school system itself. This way the new schools obtained a clearly designed and strong centre in the administration and also, significantly, the old schools were deprived of their previous compact central administration.

Another example of the same sequence in educational change is to be found 12 years later in teacher training. The NBE at first had no teacher training division. Administrative issues of teacher training were taken care of by the primary school division, the secondary school division, and later on by the division of school organization. Not until 1964 did the NBE obtain a special division for teacher training, which was discouragingly late, as the new schools at the time had already come a long way. Indeed, the new teacher training with both primary and secondary teachers in the same kind of institutions did not begin on a full-scale basis until 1968. With the wisdom of hindsight we can now say that the NBE should have had a teacher training division from the beginning of the 1950s, which might have given a better teacher supply for the new schools and improved support for the implementation of the reform.

I have mainly discussed the change of central administration as a prerequisite for changing the schools system in general. Clearly, the local school authorities and the local school administration also experienced corresponding changes. The most important of these was the creation of bigger and stronger municipal authorities. Before 1952, Sweden had nearly 3000 local school districts, most of which were too small to organize the new schools. Through a series of reforms, which will not be described here, these were merged into fewer but stronger units; at the moment only 278 exist.

Educational research and development

In taking over the aggregate responsibility for implementing the political decisions, the NBE has resorted with increasing frequency to professional experts in education. These experts include researchers, teachers and school managers. In this way the educational research and development work (R and D) performed has been given a clear linkage with reform activity. This linkage can here be seen as a component of the Swedish school reform strategy.

Educational R and D in present-day Sweden is for the most part decision-orientated. This kind of activity had its origin, first, in the research programme that the governmental commissions had been pursuing since the 1940s and 1950s, and second, in the experiments with the nine-year comprehensive school that the NBE conducted between 1950 and 1962.

Since 1962, the National Board of Education has received a special R and D grant, of which about half is spent to pay for research pursued at different kinds of university and college departments. From 1962 to 1978 the annual grant has grown from two million kronor to 36 million kronor (US$ 8.5m), which is equivalent to about 60 per cent of all the specially earmarked funds for educational R and D in Sweden.

By international standards the size of this appropriation is fairly large. It constitutes a 'variable' resource in addition to the 'fixed' resources allocated to research posts and research departments. As the latter are limited, it is generally true to say of this R and D strategy that the variable resources are relatively large and the fixed resources relatively small. This strategy makes it possible to link R and D to school reform activities. The greater part of the variable resources are put at the disposal of the NBE, which decides orders of priority for R and D projects. The 'steering' exercised by NBE is of three kinds; (1) delimitation of R and D problems, (2) choice of research departments, and (3) determination of time and money frameworks for the projects. The *intrascientific* issues on research methods and procedures are entirely left to the researchers themselves.

This kind of decision-oriented or reform-oriented educational R and D has four attributes which distinguish it from what is termed discipline-oriented research or basic educational research:

1. It is conducted in accordance with a *plan*, whose budget covers one five-year period, and which, as regards detailed planning, spans one year. The majority of large-scale R and D projects run for two to five years. The plan is officially adopted by NBE after consulting a group of educational researchers.

2. The sub-programmes within this plan are based on *co-ordination of R and D*. In other words, the measures taken to use and apply the knowledge which research provides are often built into the activity. Hence a great deal of R and D is not educational research in the traditional sense. The development segments often pertain to curriculum building, development of teaching aids, and development of evaluation instruments.

3. R and D is designed so as to facilitate, in particular, the *diffusion of results*. Means for the transfer of information to the in-service training of teachers are built in from the start of the project. This is not so much intended as a means of identifying solutions to educational problems, but as a way of vitalizing the educational debate on a broad front. As noted above, this debate is of great importance for decision-makers on educational policy and in the administration of the educational system.

4. R and D of this kind should be examined and evaluated against the goals set up for educational policy. Such examinations and evaluations have been made in Sweden a number of times. First, the project activity has been analysed by educational researchers; second, it has been rated by educational politicians and educational administrators. An Educational Advisory Council attached to the NBE, which includes representatives of the political parties, the municipalities, educational research, and teachers and students, then passes judgement on the R and D, taking

account especially of the evaluation issues, and this committee submits an annual report to the Ministry of Education.

One of the big difficulties with this reform-oriented and decision-oriented educational R and D has been to diffuse the results gained and disseminate information about them. A considerable portion of R and D funds has been spent on measures which aim at linking R and D with the in-service training of teachers and other school personnel.

For the most part, the NBE has carried on its R and D within two main organizational structures. About half the resources were used for projects pursued in research departments at the universities. The responsibility for, and supervision of, these projects rested with the research department in question. The other half of the resources was used for development work under the direction of NBE personnel, but most of the time through personnel *outside* NBE, ie teachers, teacher training staff, school managers and experts. The problems at issue may have had to do with developing a data base for classroom instruction, changing the course content, modifying study routes and time schedules. Also in the latter category of development work have been projects which were carried on in partnership between the NBE and individual municipalities ('municipal educational development blocks').

The importance of R and D for educational reform work in Sweden has often been discussed. It has sometimes been contended that the reform decisions under educational policy were based on scientifically established results. This is not entirely true. Reform decisions were based on positions in educational policy. These positions, however, have been more or less influenced by research. Besides, several problems of educational policy cannot be solved through research. They are more in the nature of value judgements than topics for research. However, one should not underestimate the importance of the fact that the Swedish community has succeeded in bringing about a dialogue between politicians, administrators and researchers. The latter have been able, by virtue of their independent status, to shed further light on how the educational issues interrelate with social, economic and cultural problems. Research projects have also contributed information about developmental psychology and educational psychology — valuable facts in an often value-laden debate.

In-service teacher training

In the 1962 Parliamentary decision on measures to introduce the new nine-year comprehensive school as compulsory throughout Sweden, two measures were singled out as particularly urgent. Both were based on the results of the pilot scheme of experiments which ran from 1950 to 1962. The first measure was the need for an intensified development of teaching aids. The decision also implied that funds would be set aside to operate a national centre and a number of regional centres for the development of educational aids in support of the new school.

The second measure had to do with the strengthening of the in-service training of teachers. It was mainly through such training that these aids, together with the new modes of work recommended in the curricula, were intended to be put into practice. In 1962 the first steps were taken to form an in-service training organization. Sweden was divided into six in-service training regions, each with its own department for this purpose. Resources for in-service training were also assigned to the country's 24 County School Boards. Each county was given a training officer, some ten training consultants employed on a half-time basis, and funds to carry on and pay for regional in-service training activity. Another significant factor was that the schools were given, as from 1962, the opportunity to use one of the school year's 40 weeks for the in-service training of teachers. This compulsory week-long programme concentrated on the question of how the new nine-year comprehensive school was to be realized in the local school system.

The initiatives on how to conduct this in-service training of teachers came from two sources; the local school managements and the regional and central organs.

There was a great diversity of in-service training programmes during the 1960s, when Sweden changed over from the old to the new educational system. Space does not permit the mention of more than two of these programmes. One ensured that all of Sweden's primary school teachers and secondary school mathematic teachers were informed about the 'New Mathematics' during the years 1967-70. Two means were used to convey this information: first, the five study days *per annum* mentioned above; and second, a series of week-end courses or holiday courses. Use was made of centrally produced teaching aids and publications giving information about the New Mathematics. Unfortunately, this information could not be passed on in specific training programmes about the New Mathematics. However, such programmes were operated in varying degrees within individual schools and municipalities.

Another further-training programme was designed to let primary school teachers assume responsibility for the teaching of English. This project, known as JET (Junior English Teaching), ran from 1968 to 1972. It absorbed a comparatively high proportion of the state funds set aside for the in-service training of teachers.

English was introduced as a compulsory subject in primary education as from 1962. By that time, the majority of teachers at the class teacher stage had acquired, either from their formal education or from their enrolment in in-service training programmes, the competence to teach English at the primary level. However, a great many teachers, about 12,000, had not been able to acquire this competence through their own efforts. Through efforts made by the NBE and regional training units, as well as a number of municipalities, numerous in-service training courses were arranged in English teaching. To take part in such training the individual primary teacher was given leave of absence from his or her classroom duties.

The broadcasting media, radio and television, mounted special courses in English, for which special extension course material was also produced. A special testing procedure was organized through the NBE. By the end of the in-service training period, all but about 2000 teachers had acquired the competence that these courses were meant to provide.

In-service efforts of this kind were widespread during the implementation period of the 1960s. Sometimes, on the strength of agreements reached between the teachers' unions and the central educational authorities, they took on the character of so-called educational supplementation, ie a programme of necessary training for duty in the new school that can be taken in paid working time.

In the 1970s, special nationwide in-service programmes aimed at personnel training within the school were started. These contain two ingredients which form integral parts of a rolling reform activity. The one is *staff-team training* for the compulsory school; the other is *school manager training*. (The school manager training is described in Chapter 14 by Mats Ekholm.)

Central evaluation

Planning and implementation of broad schemes or programmes for educational development is thus the main obligation of the NBE. Part of this work consists of central evaluation carried out *via* certain specific projects which look at the *'effects'* of decisions taken, and the *effectiveness* of the educational system.

Traditional assessments of outcomes on single individuals in single grades, subjects or courses are not the focus of interest for the NBE. This type of assessment is at one end of a dimension on which evaluation of school systems is at the other extreme. Between these two poles there are many intermediate and mixed types of evaluation. Two types of more complex evaluation have been seen by the NBE as especially relevant. One is a *'total curriculum'* evaluation, where knowledge, skills and attitudes of the individual student, seen as a unit, make up a composite picture. Another type is the effect (product) on a *total group of students* judged on one or more evaluation criteria. In this second type of evaluation, differences between schools and regions become important subjects of analysis.

In its attempts to evaluate the school system, the NBE has found the *variability* of achievement as important as the mean of achievement. The former indicates how many students fall *under* an acceptable minimum standard (and therefore might need extra support), and how many are *extra high* (and therefore perhaps should be observed and treated in a special way). Here it is important to have not only traditional achievement test scores but also estimations of different kinds of non-cognitive results of education.

Considerations of this kind, emerging from the over-riding egalitarian goals, underline the need for different analyses of variance, such as:

  inter-individual variance
  intra-institutional variance (classes, groups)
  inter-institutional variance (schools)
  intra-system variance (regions, districts)

A study of differential student achievement within Sweden was made in 1975 by the NBE. Standardized achievement tests were applied to all students in grade 6, the end of primary education (student age 12), in seven of the total of 24 Swedish counties. These counties had 91 municipalities with 1950 schools altogether. The total number of students was nearly 48,000. They were all given three test batteries: Swedish, Mathematics and English. Evaluation was made on a five point scale with 3 as the national mean and 1 as the unit of standard deviation (NBE, 1977).

As expected, the variance in student knowledge between municipalities was greater than the variance between counties, just as the between-school variance was greater than that either for counties or municipalities. The general rule that the variance between units increases when the size of the units decreases, can be deduced from Table 2.

Studies of this kind have shown that high-achieving and low-achieving students were found in all schools and nearly all classes, but the proportions of these two groups vary. Special concern has been directed toward the low-achieving group. A restricted study was made in the Swedish city of Linköping on student achievement in reading and writing at the end of compulsory

	Counties	Standard deviation between Municipalities	Schools	Students
Swedish	0.04	0.17	0.28	1.03
Mathematics	0.12	0.24	0.36	1.05
English	0.04	0.18	0.31	1.02
Swedish Mathematics and English	0.06	0.18	0.30	0.91

Table 2 *Standard deviation of achievement in three subjects (Swedish, Mathematics and English) in grade 6*

education, ie grade 9 (Grundin, 1975). According to this study, 15 per cent of the students at the end of their compulsory education had a reading and writing score which was lower than the mean score in grade 6, which was defined as the 'minimum level of competence'. The 15 per cent of students with results lower than this were in the study classified as 'functionally illiterate'. The school was criticized in the ensuing public debate as responsible for creating functionally illiterate citizens every year. On the other hand, there were people who felt that the mean level of achievement for grade 6 students was too high a minimum to set.

This and corresponding results from system evaluations have created an increasing awareness of how the school works. They have made people start thinking about how available resources might be better used. A law enacted by the Swedish Parliament in 1977 now gives the local education authorities increased opportunities to use state grants the way they decide themselves, in that 25 per cent of state grants are not earmarked in advance by state authorities. Spending of this 'free quarter' forces system evaluations on a broader scale at the municipal level as well as at regional and national levels.

Quite clearly, a system evaluation of this kind presupposes a careful analysis of evaluation criteria, instruments and processes. It is also important to relate 'effectiveness' not only to traditional subject knowledge but also to non-cognitive and non-traditional procedures.

Centralization or decentralization

In many countries a discussion is now going on of how a good balance between central government and local government should be achieved in order to promote educational development. Countries with relatively strong centralization seem to strive for a more decentralized system, while traditionally decentralized countries seem to be looking for stronger central planning and co-ordination of development activities.

Two interesting international studies have recently ben made by the Organization for Economic Co-operation and Development (OECD). One of them dealt with *Educational Financing* (OECD, 1977), and drew on primary education data from ten OECD member countries. Its aim was to analyse the variety of contexts in which educational policy and educational goals are set and in which financial instruments operate. It presented a brief description of revenue production, sources of funds and financial instruments. It also discussed disparities of resource allocations, disparities of prevailing systems of financing related to various objectives and an analysis of the inter-relations between these objectives and the financial instruments.

It was somewhat surprising to find that the balance between central and local financing seemed to be of minor importance for the degree of local autonomy and local variations, when comparisons were made between the countries in this study. Studies within the separate countries seemed to be necessary to explain the reasons for local disparities. Another surprising conclusion was that central funds often proved to have emerged from local pressure and local needs which had not necessarily been recognized and stressed in the central policy-making.

The hypothesis that central payment of education should result in a homogeneous school system was on the whole not supported by this study. The degree of homogeneity, or absence of local disparities, was less related to the amount or proportion of central funding of the school system, or even to the degree of central earmarking of state grants, but more related to the amount and kind of control of the way in which central regulations for funding were followed by the local authorities.

According to the study team, it was found necessary to have central rules and central funds to satisfy the needs of special groups in education. Yet while these central rules and funds were a prerequisite, they were no guarantee that the students in greatest need of support were helped. A combination of central and local decision-making was recommended as a means of properly using central funds.

The second OECD project of interest to the question of centralization or decentralization was *Education in Regional Development Policies* (OECD, 1978). An analysis was made of some attempts to regionalize education in 15 OECD member countries. It dealt with three aspects; (1) the function of education at regional level, paticularly its relation to employment and migration, (2) regional inequalities in education, and (3) planning and regionalization of educational policies.

On the whole, education was found to play a subordinate role as a means for social, economic and cultural development of special regions. There were both advantages and disadvantages of regionalization in terms of decentralization of decision-making in educational matters from central level to regional level. Advantages such as increased scope for using resources optimally (which could raise the general standard of the region) had to be weighed against the risks of a narrow provincialism and too strong a linkage of vocational education to special local needs. In the countries studied, no general trend towards either decentralization or centralization could be found. The solutions looked for seemed rather to be in terms of an increased co-operation between central and regional organs and in an improved two-way communication between these two levels.

In none of these OECD studies were there any estimates of how centralization *versus* decentralization of education was related to educational outcomes in schools. Such a study was made in Sweden (NBE, 1978) through an analysis of some data from the big international IEA project (IEA stands for 'International Association for the Evaluation of Educational Achievement'). One of the IEA studies was concerned with knowledge of science among students ten and 14 years old in nine countries (Husén, 1973). Some results of this analysis are reproduced in Table 3.

IEA data have mostly been discussed in terms of national differences of mean student level of knowledge. As can be seen from the Table, the level in

1	2	3	4	5	6	7	8	9
Country	Individual results				Between-school variance		Between-school variance in % of individual variance	
	Mean		Variance					
	age 10	age 14	age 10	age 14	age 10	age 14	age 10	age 14
England	15.7	21.3	72.2	198.8	13.7	65.6	19	33
Finland	17.5	20.5	67.2	112.4	18.8	22.5	28	20
Germany (FRG)	14.9	23.7	54.8	132.3	14.8	39.7	27	30
Hungary	16.7	29.1	64.0	161.2	25.6	54.8	40	34
Japan	21.7	31.2	59.3	213.0	10.7	42.6	18	20
Netherlands	15.3	17.8	57.8	100.0	13.3	40.0	23	40
Scotland	14.0	21.4	68.9	201.6	20.0	86.7	29	43
Sweden	18.3	21.7	53.3	136.9	8.0	16.4	15	12
USA	17.7	21.6	86.4	134.6	27.6	37.7	32	28

Table 3 Results of IEA achievement tests in science in nine countries in 1979 (Husén, 1973: 123-6; NBE, 1978:17)

Japan is slightly higher than that in the other eight countries (columns 2 and 3). The national differences, however, are small, if we consider the large individual variances (columns 4 and 5). The interesting thing here is the *between-school variance* given in columns 6 and 7. Here Sweden emerges with the lowest figures. In the two right-hand columns (8 and 9) the between-school variance is related to the total variance. Here too Sweden has the lowest figures, which indicates that schools in Sweden are more like one another than schools in the other eight countries.

Sweden thus has the highest national homogeneity of schools, when student achievement is used as the criterion. In one of the special IEA studies (Passow *et al*, 1976) Sweden appeared as the only one of these nine countries to have a fully implemented national non-selective comprehensive education for students of these ages. And — as already noted — this school structure is both a consequence of and a condition for the strong centralization of educational policy-making and of the educational administration.

It is debatable whether this is good or bad for Sweden. Official Swedish policy says that students should have the same opportunity to get a good education, regardless of socio-economic status and geographical location. Judged by this goal, the result must be seen as good. Sweden has roughly the same proportion of 'good' and 'bad' students, but they are not concentrated in specific schools to as great an extent as in the other eight countries.

The Swedish homogeneity of schools is evidently not paralleled by homogeneity of students. The total student variance (columns 4 and 5) is roughly the same in Sweden as in the other eight countries. What can be done to support the low-achieving group, which obviously exists in Sweden as in the other countries? Here Sweden clearly follows the trend towards decentralization in decision-making and towards the allocation of the responsibility of provision for these student categories to the local level.

Conclusion

This chapter has examined the role of central government and local government in educational development, and how this development is influenced by the balance between these agencies. Educational policy-making and educational administration are two important sides of government. Sweden, a country with a relatively strongly centralized school system, was taken as a case study.

A special instrument for educational policy-making in Sweden is the system of governmental commissions. These can have politicians, school-managers, teachers and researchers as members. On behalf of the central government they investigate special questions of policy, and in their reports they specify goals and measures for the improvement of education. As a rule these proposals one way or another end up before Parliament, where a specific policy is decided upon. Usually the time between the start of the committee work and the political decision is relatively short.

Implementation of these decisions centrally is taken care of by independent national authorities, one of which is the NBE. According to Swedish experiences, a change of education in schools has to be co-ordinated with a parallel change in the central administration.

A special part of the reform machinery is educational research and development (R and D). This has to a large extent become decision-oriented in that the R and D funds are given to NBE as a resource for implementation of the over-riding educational policy goals. Another important part of the reform machinery is the system of in-service training of teachers. This is centrally organized by the NBE as a means for implementing educational policy.

Central policy-making and administration also has to include certain efforts at central evaluation. As far as student achievement is concerned, the NBE has concentrated its evaluation on finding out how different regions, districts and schools vary, rather than how individual results vary.

Countries with a centralized school system seem to strive for decentralization, while countries with a decentralized system seem to look for a strengthening of central planning. However, these trends are not simple and clear. In international studies by OECD, no simple relationships were found between decentralization and local autonomy. The hypothesis that central funding of education should result in a homogeneous school system was, on the whole, not verified when schools were studied on a national level. Nevertheless, a Swedish analysis of data from the IEA project found that Swedish schools were more like one another in terms of student knowledge of science than schools in a group of other comparable countries. Thus it seems that there should be a correlation between centralization and equality of school standards. A plausible conclusion is that centralization of educational policy and administration is necessary, but not sufficient in itself for this kind of equality.

References

Beckne, R (1975) *The Working Environment in School: A Summary of the SIA Report* National Board of Education: Stockholm

Grundin, H (1975) *Läs-och Skrivförmågans Utveckling genom Skolåren* (Development of Reading and Writing in School) SO/FOU **20** 1975: Stockholm

Husén, T *et al* (1973) *Svensk Skola i Internationell Belysning: Naturvetenskapliga Ämnen*. (Swedish School in International Comparisons: Science) Stockholm

Marklund, S and Bergendal, G (1979) *Trends in Swedish Educational Policy* The Swedish Institute: Stockholm

Marklund, S and Eklund, H (1976) *Innovation in In-Service Education and Training of Teachers. Sweden* OECD/CERI: Paris

Marklund, S and Söderberg, P (1967) *The Swedish Comprehensive School* Longman: London

National Board of Education (1976) *Educational Research and Development at the NBE* Stockholm

National Board of Education (1977) *Standardprovsresultat i Arskurs 6 i Sju Län* (Results of Standardized Achievement Tests in Grade 6 in Seven Countries) Pedagogiska Nämndens Verksamhets-Berättelse för 1976/77, Skolöverstyrelsen: Stockholm

National Board of Education (1978) *Enhetlig Skolstruktur och Likvärdig Utbildningsstandard* (Unified School Structure and Equal Educational Standard) Anslagäskanden for budgetåret 1979/80 i sammanfattning, Skolöverstyrelsen: Stockholm

OECD (1977) *Educational Financing* OECD/CERI 77 5, Paris, April 27 1977 (mimeo)

OECD (1978) *The Place of Education in Regional Development Policies* Education Committee, Paris, April 18 1978 (mimeo)

Passow, A H *et al* (1976) *The National Case Study: An Empirical Comparative Study of Twenty-One Educational Systems* International Studies in Evaluation, International Association for the Evaluation of Educational Achievement: Stockholm/New York

Vinde, P (1967) *The Swedish Civil Service. An Introduction Published by the Ministry of Finance* Stockholm

8. State government role in staff development: the Californian experience

David Marsh

Summary: Staff development policy and practice in California are examined in several ways designed to be helpful to an international audience. First, it is shown that the broader educational context in California is having considerable influence on staff development policy and programmes; some of these external factors or forces are identified and discussed. State-funded programmes in staff development and the state government organization related to these programmes are described and analysed. To illustrate significant programme features, several of the more innovative staff development efforts are described. Government strategies for assisting the implementation of state-funded staff development programmes are discussed along with views about the relative effectiveness of these strategies. Several recent studies are discussed which shed light upon the results of the state of staff development policy and practices. The chapter concludes with a review of some unresolved issues which are related to the policy and practices discussed earlier in the chapter. The implications of this review for an international readership are also discussed.

Staff development in California is influenced by demographic conditions and other external forces. As the most populated state in the Union and one of the most geographically and ethnically diverse, it has been clear that a single model of staff development would certainly be neither appropriate nor effective. California schools serve just over three million students in grades K-12 within 1000 school districts. While pupil enrollments have not declined, on a state-wide basis, as much as in some eastern states, Kirst comments:

> ... the school population has declined drastically in many of the suburbs and cities of California. For example, it is not unusual for a suburb in the San Francisco Peninsula area to have lost half of its enrollment within the decade 1970 to 1980. This has eliminated slack resources in the system, led to a change in the teacher force towards senior teachers, and generally made people unenthusiastic about entering the profession of education. (Kirst, 1979: 28)

At the same time, the proportion of students from minority ethnic groups has increased dramatically, especially Hispanic-surnamed students who currently constitute 23 per cent of the pupil population. Many of these students require some type of bilingual educational programme which teachers are frequently unprepared to provide.

Currently, approximately 180,000 teachers are employed in public schools within the state. With each new school year, the average number of years of teaching experience for all teachers in the state increases because few new teachers are being hired into regular teaching positions. At the same time, several emergency teacher preparation programmes are being carried out to provide teachers with special skills in working with minority populations. These patterns in teacher employment when linked with trends in pupil enrollment and demography have created a number of important staff development needs.

Another relevant aspect of the educational context is the nature of the State Department of Education (SDE) itself. With the election of a new State Superintendent of Public Instruction, Dr Wilson Riles, in the early 1970s, several shifts were made within the SDE. These shifts include a greater commitment to: (a) quality education for minority children; (b) the creation of locally-directed change processes in individual schools; (c) increased involvement of parents as decision-makers in local change efforts; and (d) an activist role for the SDE as a facilitator of local change and staff development efforts. The implications of this new SDE role for staff development will be discussed later in the chapter.

Finally, Kirst (1979) has characterized the overall context of California's public schools in the 1970s as 'organizations in shock and overload'. He reports:

> The California Public School System has been or will be buffeted by nine major external forces. Each of these forces will cause some adaptation in organizational structure and function. These forces are not the same as the 'reform by addition' of the past. Moreover, they are coming with such rapidity and depth that the organization will probably be thrown off balance. Organizational shock, overload, and paralysis are all possible. The question becomes how much change can an organization take yet continue to deal effectively with its clients. (p27)

These external forces include:

1. At least 50 'reform' initiatives, including the continued impact of pre-1970 mandates by federal and state legislatures. The latest reforms are minimum competency tests, special education, and school site councils.
2. A complete reversal from growth in enrollment to declining enrollment with the loss of the growth psychology. As part of this, there is a dramatic increase in the Hispanic population from 11 per cent of total school enrollment in 1967 to 23 per cent of total enrollment in 1978.
3. Declining public esteem and support for public education.
4. The *Serrano* decision from the California Supreme Court that has caused four different financial systems within a decade.
5. The imposition of collective bargaining that includes 90 per cent of the teachers in unions.
6. The passage of Proposition 13.(This is a constitutional amendment approved by voters which severely limits property taxes. This form of taxation was the major source of school funding; the funding base has now shifted dramatically to the state level.)
7. State Court-ordered (racial) integration of the largest school systems in the state with a major issue concerning metropolitan integration across district lines in the Los Angeles area.
8. The likelihood of a 1980 ballot measure requiring funding through educational vouchers. The state would make payments for schooling directly to parents and not to public school systems.
9. A state constitutional amendment (which requires) a statewide spending limit. This (is) in addition to fiscal restraints caused by Proposition 13. (pp27-8)

Each of these external forces could have a dramatic effect on teacher morale and performance as well as on staff development needs and practices within the state.

Staff development programmes in California and the related state government organizational structures

There are a large number of state funded, or federally-funded yet state-co-ordinated staff development programmes in California. Joyce *et al* (1979a) examined these programmes to determine their history, purposes, implementation strategies, clients, and funding levels. Expanding this information, Birdsall (1979) prepared a list of staff development programmes and their funding levels, which is summarized in Table 1.

Programme Category/ Source/Type-title	Estimated funding level in $ millions (rounded)	Estimated staff development expenditure
Programmes for pupils with special needs		
California state-funded:		
Educationally disadvantaged youth	113	little to none
Special education master plan	102	little
Education for exceptional children	224	little to none
Bilingual-bicultural	11.1	unknown
Mentally-gifted minors	13.4	little to none
Child care services	81.5	none
Pre-school	24.5	little to none
General aid to districts (low income)	44.1	little to none
Native American Indian education	0.3	little to none
American Indian education centres	0.6	none
Federally-funded:		
Title 1 (low income children basic grants, low income children special grants, migratory children, handicapped children, neglected and delinquent children)	3336	little
Education for handicapped	977	6%
Bilingual education	159	33%
Indian education	72	7%
Follow-through	59	2%
Adult education	100	unknown
Specific programmatic support		
California state-funded:		
Reading and math demonstration	3	unknown
Elementary reading instruction	14	unknown
Environmental protection	0.3	unknown
Driver training	19.8	unknown
Career guidance centres	0.3	unknown
Federally-funded:		
Basic skills improvement Right to read	28	20%
Metric education	1.8	20%
Arts in education	2.0	25%
Consumer education	3.6	15%
Community schools	3.2	14%
Vocational education	682	4%
Career education	10.1	10%
Alcohol and drug abuse education	2.0	2%

Programme Category/ Source/Type-title	Estimated funding level in $ millions (rounded)	Estimated staff development expenditure
Capacity-building programmes		
California state-funded:		
School improvement programme	123	low
Professional development and programme improvement centres	0.7	100%
School site staff development programme	0.5	100%
School resource centres	0.5	100%
Bilingual Teacher Corps	1.1	100%
County school service fund	108	moderate to little
Instructional materials	28	little to none
Instructional television	0.8	unknown
Assistance to Public Libraries	4.8	none
Federally-funded:		
Teacher Corps	37.5	100%
Teacher centres	12.6	100%
Instructional materials and school library resources	162	unknown
Improvement in local educational practices (Title IV-C)	190	unknown
Emergency school aid	332	20%
Civil Rights Act, Title IV	41.4	33%
National Institute of Education	96.8	unknown
Dissemination of information/ national diffusion network	14	30%
Other selected general support funds		
California state-funded:		
Block grants	4206	little to none

Table 1 *State and federal school improvement and staff development programmes (taken from Birdsall, 1979)*

Several observations related to Table 1 are important. There are over 70 state-funded or state-co-ordinated programmes which have staff development components. These staff development programmes can be divided into three distinct categories:

1. *Capacity-building programmes (also called agency-building and strengthening efforts).* For example, both state and federal programmes are used to *create* new agencies called 'Teacher Centres'. Legislation such as AB 65 is designed to *strengthen* the ability of schools to improve educational programmes partly or primarily through in-service activities.
2. *Specific programmatic support.* State and/or federal funds are authorized to bring attention to specific curriculum areas. Examples include initiatives from the Women's Equity Act at the federal level. Under this Act, programmes are designed to increase consideration of creating sex-fair curricula where neither women nor men are advantaged or disadvantaged by what is taught, how it is taught or access to any kind of general or vocational training. Another example is in mathematics education where authorizations at the federal level have provided funds to

develop procedures for increasing teacher's and, hence, student's understanding of the metric system and ability to use metric measurement.

3. *Programmes for pupils with special needs.* The third category consists of authorization to use funds to provide certain kinds of educational services to children with the provision that a proportion of the authorized funds may be used to educate teachers in the area of concern. The exact proportion of funds may or may not be stated in the legislation. Wide latitude is generally left to state and local administrators (Joyce *et al*, 1979a: 2-3).

Each of these categories of staff development programmes has a different pattern of funding, policy generation, and state government administrative organization. For example, staff development within programmes for pupils with special needs tends to be a neglected although often mandated component of the programme. Even in those special need programmes where the percentage of all funds to be spent on staff development is prescribed, the actual levels of expenditures within these programmes for staff development is less than the required amount. In addition, staff development sometimes has little relationship to other aspects of these important programmes.

The funding level for staff development within specific programmatic support efforts has a different pattern. For these programmes, the state government monitors have usually established technical assistance efforts which serve local programmes receiving state funds in these curriculum areas. The technical assistance is provided directly by state government officials, or indirectly through regional technical assistance centres or consultants housed either at the district county level. For relatively small amounts of funding, extensive technical assistance is often provided. Each of the many programmes tends to have its own separate network.

Expenditures for staff development within capacity-built programmes vary extensively. The School Improvement Programme is the major SDE strategy for bringing about programme improvement in local schools. Within the School Improvement Programme, staff development is a required component yet few resources are in fact used for staff development within local programmes. In the capacity-building programmes where nearly 100 per cent of funds are spent on staff development, local efforts typically generate extensive staff development activities, especially on an activity-per-dollar basis.

Joyce *et al* (1979a) report that policy origins for staff development programmes are more complex than previously appreciated. The study negated the simplistic impression that policy for state-funded programmes is created in the state legislature, administered at the state level by the SDE and implemented at local sites. Instead, many of the staff development programmes represent interactions of state and federal policy. A sampling of such policy arrangements for staff development programmes is as follows:

1. *Teacher Centres and School Resource Centres.* The federal Teacher Centre legislation provides funding to local teacher centres. A fixed proportion of these funds is given to the appropriate unit within the SDE to provide technical assistance and monitoring to local proposals before they are transmitted to the federal agency. In California, another staff development programme, the State School Resource Centres, was designed with guidelines very similar to the federal Teacher Centres so that a common network of centres could be established across the state.

2. *Special education*. The State Special Education Master Plan and the Federal Education for the Handicapped programmes are closely intertwined. The State Master Plan must include state and local staff development components which are in compliance with federal regulations, and the state plan must be approved by the federal government.

3. *Mentally-gifted minors*. State funds provide the support for special programmes offered to mentally-gifted minors within local school districts. In competition with other states, California's SDE was able to win funds from the federal government which supports state technical assistance and staff development efforts given to staff within local districts who operate these special programmes.

Many of the other staff development efforts 'funded by the state' result from interactions of state and federal policy, and this arrangement influences the design and operation of the staff development programmes.

Organizational structure for staff development at the state level

There are three types of state government agency that have a direct relationship to staff development programmes in the public schools in California. The State Department of Education is the largest state agency directly concerned with elementary and secondary education. This agency has 3000 employees and has several organizational features salient to staff development policy and programmes. Most of these staff development programmes, listed in Table 1, are administered by the Programmes Branch of the SDE. Within the Programmes Branch is the Office of Staff Development which is directly responsible for the capacity-building programmes with 100 per cent of programme expenditure for staff development. The Office provides technical assistance and programme co-ordination within a limited budget and with only a few professional staff.

The other state-funded staff development programmes are housed within different administrative units of the Programmes Branch, a very large organization. To co-ordinate these staff development efforts and to link the Programmes Branch with evaluation and research branch (known as the Office of Programme Evaluation and Research) the SDE has recently established a Staff Development Policy Council chaired by Deputy Superintendent Davis Campbell. The Policy Council discusses ways to improve administrative policy at the state level for staff development programmes and ways to increase the effectiveness of these programmes in the field.

A second state agency, the Commission for Teacher Preparation and Licensing, is primarily responsible for the approval of teacher preparation programmes and the awarding of appropriate licenses to teachers and specialists within local school districts. The Commission has an interest in staff development as part of its mission for teacher preparation and development. The Commission, in conjunction with a federal agency, conducted a study of teacher effectiveness which was designed to have implications for the preparation, credentialing, and development of teachers in California. This study, the Beginning Teacher Evaluation Study, has led to a set of mini-grants which have been awarded to individual teachers, and/or districts, who wish to use the findings of the BTES study within staff development efforts. However, in general, the staff development activities of the Commission have been quite limited, especially in comparison with the SDE.

The state college and university system, and the major public university system in California, are each administered by separate state agencies. Not surprisingly, it has been difficult to involve universities and colleges in staff development programmes for public school staff. Marsh and Carey (1979) discuss the myriad of economic, political, sociological, and programmatic dilemmas which greater involvement in staff development creates for universities and colleges.

Programme design

Many of the state staff development programmes do have noteworthy features. While it is not possible to summarize each programme or each feature in this chapter, there are several programme design elements that will be discussed. The heart of the staff development programme design for California is a two-level design characterized as follows:

School level: Schools rather than school districts or individual state-funded programmes emphasizing: (a) parent/teacher/principal (and secondary student) collaborative decision-making, (b) a three-year development plan based upon a comprehensive needs assessment, (c) a requirement that the plan should address curriculum areas such as reading, math, writing, and career education. The state guidelines also require that attention be given to instructional processes such as individualized instruction.

Within these programmes, staff development is a required component designed to help the school staff implement the broad new programme features described above, to help each school solve persistent yet sometimes unique problems, and to strengthen the capacity of schools as problem-solving and programme improvement-oriented organizations.

District, regional and county levels: Districts, regional centres and County Offices are designed to play a training/technical assistance/resource linkage function which will help individual schools carry out their current programme improvement efforts.

Districts are asked to monitor school-level development efforts, select new schools for inclusion in state programmes, and provide technical assistance to school sites. Several types of regional centres have been established to assist schools in their staff development and programme improvement efforts. One type of centre is the set of Professional Development/Programme Improvement Centres which have been established to provide skill-oriented training to teachers within a region.

A second type includes School Resource Centres and federal Teacher Centres which have several possible functions. They can provide in-service teacher education directly to teachers and developmental assistance to school sites, they can serve as resource-linking facilitators within a region, and/or they can develop training materials. Under the direction of a governance board controlled by teachers, these centres across the state have taken on different configurations tailored to local and regional needs. Finally, County Offices continue to provide extensive assistance in curriculum content areas, staff development training approaches, programme development approaches, and evaluation services to districts and local schools.

Another critical feature of the staff development design in California is the emphasis on providing staff development for school principals. Two years ago, a task force chaired by Assemblyman Dennis Mangers examined the staff development needs of school principals. The task force found that the following conditions prevailed:

> Although principal leadership is essential to effective schooling, research shows that many principals are neither prepared nor encouraged to be educational leaders. According to principals, administrator training does not always match responsibilities of the job, the role and tasks of the principal are seldom clearly defined, systems for evaluating principal performance are often ineffective, and opportunities for continued development are inadequate. (Mangers *et al*, 1978:2)

The task force proposed a number of far-reaching recommendations for the staff development of principals concerning instructional skills, management skills, human relations abilities, political and cultural awareness, leadership skills and self-understanding. Subsequent state efforts have led to the identification and refinement of training materials and resources, and the funding of seven pilot projects to provide innovative staff development to principals.

State-led developmental assistance to local staff development efforts

Over the last decade, an important shift has taken place in the way the State Department of Education provides developmental assistance to local staff development and programme improvement efforts. Ten years ago, developmental assistance was characterized by curriculum guides for 'model' programmes, assistance given primarily to district rather than school-level personnel, and extensive workshop/training held outside the school setting with insufficient attention given to applying these ideas at school sites. While some excellent guides were developed and excellent training carried out, this approach to developmental assistance was discarded because state officials believed it was having insufficient impact upon local school programmes.

Currently, many of the state-funded staff development and programme improvement efforts use state-level task forces to design and improve the original legislation and plan developmental assistance. Many of the programmes also use networking or trainer-of-trainer approaches to deliver developmental assistance and prepare school, district or regional staff to help others in their regions in implementing programmes. Working with representatives of local role groups, SDE staff have also developed a variety of manuals designed to assist local schools in planning and carrying out their staff development and programme improvement efforts. The SDE staff have also run regional conferences where regional, district and local school staff present ideas to their peers.

At the same time, a peer review process has been established to evaluate the progress of a local school carrying out its staff development and programme implementation effort. Using a collaboratively developed programme review instrument, trained teams of school and school district staff spent two days at a local site in order to observe instruction, interview relevant role groups, and review programme documents. At the end of the visit, the programme review team meets with parents, the school staff, and the principal in a joint meeting where results of the programme review are presented and discussed. An extension of the programme review process is the formation of consortia of local schools and school districts formed to provide mutual technical assistance and programme review.

An analysis of the SDE developmental assistance efforts reveals that much greater attention is now being given to the process of helping local schools to solve problems relevant to their local settings. Perceptive leaders within the SDE now have a more sophisticated idea of how change can be encouraged in local settings. However, not all staff within the SDE are capable of translating these insights into productive developmental assistance.

The numerous task force and trainer-of-trainer efforts have led to the identification and employment of the extensive talents of regional and local staff. These staff are typically experienced in bringing about change within their local settings, yet some lack the ability to help other staff in other settings solve curriculum and staff development problems. Moreover, while potentially useful planning guides and resources have been developed, these often have not penetrated the local school's organizational structure. Frequently these materials are not known or used by the wide variety of role groups involved in local decision-making and programme development. At the same time, many local staff still have not grasped the *gestalt* of programme improvement, nor how to use staff development to enhance programme change.

Developmental assistance focuses on assisting schools where staff are experiencing extensive stress and the organization itself is reflecting shock and overload. In many cases, developmental assistance does not include strategies (assuming that these exist) to assist staff under these conditions. While these external factors would make even the best developmental assistance unlikely to solve some of the most critical problems in local schools, there are some other factors which limit the effectiveness of the assistance as well. For example, the developmental assistance often appears to lack co-ordination even within one state programme. Moreover, the staff development models and procedures proposed within the developmental assistance are often insufficiently powerful to bring about real changes in schools. At the same time, providers of developmental assistance often present inadequate techniques for linking staff development to broader school change. Finally, providers of developmental assistance, especially SDE staff, must often address (or choose to address) concerns about compliance with state regulations rather than the solution of local problems. Many SDE staffs still communicate the message that state-funded local improvement efforts must be carried out with the primary purpose of pleasing the state, even though this is explicitly not the intention of policymakers and senior administrators at the state level.

Recent research related to staff development in California

Several recent studies shed light on the effectiveness of state-funded or state-co-ordinated staff development policy and practices in California. Yarger, Howey and Joyce conducted a survey in 1977 of staff development practice in California, Michigan, and Georgia (Yarger *et al*, forthcoming). Table 2 presents the amount of assistance which teachers currently receive through in-service teacher education in the three states included in the study. While California fares slightly better than the other two states in the amount of assistance which teachers receive, over 40 per cent of teachers in California report they receive very little or no assistance. The study also reports that fewer than 5 per cent of teachers have ever experienced video-tape feedback of their teaching, intensive clinical supervision, or some of the more rigorous training technologies. Finally, schools in California which are funded through what is now referred to as the School Improvement Programme are not providing greater amounts of staff development for their teachers than are other schools in the state. In general, one can conclude from the study that the numerous staff development initiatives at the state level still have not been able to provide extensive amounts of assistance for most teachers in the state.

Assistance	California	Michigan	Georgia
More than I can use	8.3	3.7	5.2
All I can use	13.2	7.1	13.4
Good amount	34.6	27.2	45.4
Very little	36.1	53.8	30.7
None	7.8	8.2	5.3

Note: all figures in this table are percentages

Table 2 *Amount of assistance currently received by teachers (teachers were asked: In performing your present job, how much in-service help do you receive?)*

Joyce *et al* (1979a) and Joyce *et al* (1979b), in a series of studies known collectively as the California Staff Development Study, examined the impact of state staff development initiatives through a set of case studies of local teachers and schools. The case studies were developed around the construct of the ecology of staff development. Joyce *et al* (1979b) report:

> The ecology of staff development emphasizes the personal and organizational contexts in which staff development occurs. The concept of ecology steers the inquiry toward an examination of the formal and informal systems in which staff development occurs, and towards the interaction of events, individuals, and environments.

From the case studies, Joyce *et al* (1979a) report:

> There is at present no ongoing, flowing, smoothly operating staff development organization in place in the state. As a result, many teachers are presently engaged in almost no formal staff development activities. Because there is no 'staff development organization' as such, in-service activities are generally planned on an *ad hoc* basis. Teachers are rarely visited by administrators, consultants or other teachers who work near them and could help them in their teaching. There are many barriers between staff development centres at any level (the state, universities and colleges, counties, districts and local teacher centres) and the lives of teachers. Thus, initiatives do not fall on fertile ground.

Consequently, innovative state initiatives and the proposed two-tier staff development organizational structure with regional and district resources assisting local schools has not led to the creation of a comprehensive staff development system in local settings. At the same time, it is important to point out that many fruitful staff development activities have been carried out by means of state initiatives. The problem identified in the California Staff Development Study is that such activities have not been co-ordinated within an integrated and properly functioning staff development system.

The Evaluation of the California Early Childhood Education Programme (Centre for the Study of Evaluation, 1977) sheds light on the effectiveness of staff development within the major state-funded school reform initiative currently known as the School Improvement Programme. Elementary school teachers were asked to describe and rate aspects of the in-service training programme provided for them. Questions relating to the quality of in-service, its relevance, its helpfulness to them directly, and its general organization were posed. The authors report, 'In summary, in-service training was judged to be relatively positive on all four of these dimensions, with little variation as a function of programme differences' (CSE, 1977:127).

Informal studies conducted by the SDE also reflect the theme that staff development components have been implemented within state-funded staff development initiatives. For example, the review process within the School Improvement Programme reveals that most schools are at least moderately successful in implementing their staff development components of the School Improvement Programme. Similarly, Joyce et al (1979a), in developing abstracts of the state-funded staff development initiatives, were able to document numerous staff development activities which had taken place.

Persistent staff development issues in California and their implications for policy and practice in other settings

In this chapter, a number of persistent staff development problems have been discussed. These include:

— the substantial impact which the broader educational context is having on staff development policy and practice, and how staff development can help resolve or at least ameliorate the negative effects of these external forces.

— a plethora of government initiatives in staff development and how these can be better co-ordinated at the government level.

— the low level of actual expenditures for staff development and how direct or in-kind resources can be used more effectively.

— the inability of technical assistance sufficiently to penetrate the school organization, and how technical assistance can be improved.

— the lack of comprehensive staff development models and the lack of a co-ordinating mechanism for staff development in local schools.

— the still inadequate linkage of staff development to broader school change.

These issues are substantial, and are probably faced by staff development policymakers around the world.

There appear to be several lessons to be drawn from what has been the generally very positive and progressive experience in California. First, it has been very helpful to have a progressive State Department of Education which has created major school reform efforts in local settings. Second, the various technical assistance strategies used by the State Department have been very helpful in assisting local schools to implement school reform efforts, even though these technical assistance efforts have not been able fully to penetrate static local school organizations. Third, the two-tier structure of staff development has been exceedingly important. Schools have made great strides in developing school reform efforts where staff development plays at least some role in implementing school change. Regional and district resources have been helpful to schools although, as indicated earlier, better linkages between regional resources and local school efforts are needed. It is clear that regional staff development training centres would not be nearly as effective as they are if schools themselves were not also undergoing school reform efforts.

Finally, the broad approach to school reform itself has been helpful. With varying degrees of success, schools have been able to broaden their programmatic response to student needs such as the development of basic skills, career goals, and social growth. Local staff development efforts with a problem-solving orientation have made important contributions to the implementation of these school reform efforts. Finally, it has been exceedingly helpful to provide staff development for all relevant local role groups. Staff development has been provided to role groups on an individual basis as well as to cross-role group teams, including parents, students, teachers, aides, and principals, which are carrying out broader school reform efforts. These lessons are an important contribution to our international understanding of staff development policy and practice.

References

Birdsall, L (1979) *Network: A Schedule of Activities for Spring-Summer 1979* California Staff Development Network: Sacramento, Ca

Center for the Study of Evaluation (1977) *Evaluation of the California Early Childhood Education Programme* (Vol 1) UCLA Graduate School of Education: Los Angeles, Ca

Collins, J F, Porter, K, Beam, A, and Moss, D (1979) *Sources and Resources: An Annotated Bibliography on Inservice Education* National Council of States on Inservice Education: Syracuse, NY

Joyce, B, Bush, R, Marsh, D Meyers, H and Birdsall, L (1979a) *Recommendations for the Evaluation of Staff Development in California: Report of a Preparatory Study* Office of Programme Evaluation and Research, California State Department of Education: Sacramento, Ca

Joyce, B, Bush, R, Marsh, D and McKibbin, M (1979b) *The California Staff Development Study: Instruments and Guidelines for Implementation in Schools* Booksend Laboratory: Palo Alto, Ca

Kirst, M (1979) Organizations in shock and overload: the California public schools 1970-1980 *Educational Evaluation and Policy Analysis* 1 4:27-30

Mangers, D *et al* (1978) *The School Principal: Recommendations for Effective Leadership* Assembly Education Committee: Sacramento, Ca

Marsh, D and Carey, L (1979) *The Involvement of Universities in Inservice Education* American Association of Colleges for Teacher Education: Washington, DC

Yarger, S, Howey, K and Joyce B (forthcoming) *Inservice Teacher Education* Booksend Laboratory: Palo Alto, Ca

9. Professional development: the Inspectorate in England and Wales

Pauline Perry

Summary: HM Inspectorate's role is primarily to give professional advice to the Secretary of State and the Department of Education and Science. This advice is based on first-hand observation of, and judgement about, what goes on in educational institutions throughout the country. Equally, in its various activities HM Inspectorate helps to promote good practice at local and institutional level, not least through the exercise of inspection, which in itself makes an important contribution to the professional development of teachers.

Recent years have made it clear that successful professional development involves the partnership of teachers and providers. In particular, it involves a creative self-assessment of needs within schools, and an appropriate high-quality response from the providers, building on their specialist strengths.

Three research projects currently in progress are helping to provide a satisfactory theoretical framework for professional development, incorporating the elements of partnership. These projects have established international links through the OECD/CERI project on school focused in-service training.

'Professional' is a word with many meanings, conveying different values to different people, and indeed without any parallel in some languages. At its most neutral, the phrase 'professional development of teachers' implies the growth of individual teachers in their working lives, the strengthening of their confidence, the sharpening of their skills, the continuous updating, widening and deepening of their knowledge of what they teach, and a heightened awareness of why they are doing whatever it is they do in the classroom. But at its most positive, the phrase means even more. It implies a growth into that intangible area of performance which goes beyond skill and becomes virtuosity: into an area which lifts a job into a vocation, and which transforms expertise into authority. I use the phrase 'professional development' in this latter sense, recognizing that teaching is not a 'professional activity' at that level for more than a minority of teachers, but I am convinced that professional development must always attempt to move in that direction, and to lift and maintain each individual teacher as far along the path of professionalism as he or she can go.

It is dangerously easy to speak of professional development as if it were an end in itself. Society wants good teachers because it wants and needs a well-educated population; ultimately the test of professionalism must always be the quality of education which pupils and students receive. Although it is not easy to demonstrate, I am sure we are right to believe that this quality is related to all of the elements of professionalism which are defined above. This is why the professional development of teachers is an inescapable concern of the national

Inspectorate in our country.

The role of Her Majesty's Inspectorate has gradually, in the past few years, become better understood. Primarily, the Inspectorate exists to give professional advice to the Secretary of State and the Department of Education and Science, and so to help in the formation of policy. Its advice is not, as in the case of professional advisers to some other national governments, derived from academic theory alone. It rests always on first-hand observation of and professional judgement about the day-to-day activities and developments in schools and colleges throughout the country. HMI's duty is to 'inspect' (ie to observe and judge) and to report on what he sees. HMI is inevitably and daily concerned with quality and with standards, for these are the concerns of the members of our society and their elected representatives in parliament. Equally important, the task of judging and advising at the centre must be balanced by advice and help to those who implement policies and are responsible for quality at local level. In so far as the Secretary of State's function to 'promote' education is a part of HMI's responsibility, so the Inspectorate's concern and activities spread wider than those of the administrators of the Department of Education and Science. The Senior Chief Inspector has said that 'by right and by obligation' HMI explores with his professional clients not only matters related to curriculum, but also the interrelationship of curriculum with standards and with teaching methods.

This exploration takes several forms and all are based on the fundamental process of inspection, that is of observation and judgement. HM Inspectors in routine visits will explore with individual teachers and individual institutions the implications of the work they have seen. More formally, a full inspection of an institution or group of institutions will result in the issue of a report to the Secretary of State, the local education authority and the institutions inspected.

This report, and the discussions which precede its issue, provide a focus for institutions and teachers to review, evaluate and perhaps improve their standards of performance. Regional and national survey reports, and the HMI publication series *Matters for Discussion* are of course based on the experience and judgement derived from visits to many individual institutions. These publications are intended to provide material for professional debate, and to help in establishing national standards of good practice. In a very real way, therefore, inspection is itself a contributor to professional development. For those teachers and institutions inspected, the process of inspection itself contributes to a continuing professional debate; the wider educational population have access to this debate through the reports and conclusions of such inspections.

The arithmetic dictates less than one HMI to every 1000 teachers; this means that despite an extensive programme of visits and inspections, many individual teachers do not see HMIs in their classrooms. Several thousand teachers do meet HM Inspectors each year on the nationally advertised programmes of DES short courses, which are directed by members of the Inspectorate. Each year, the content of this programme is decided by the internal processes of Inspectorate discussion at various levels, in the light of priorities identified either by national policy concern or by developments HM Inspectorate has encountered in daily contact with the educational system. Many of these courses are on broad general areas of interest, such as curriculum planning, school organization or educational disadvantage, while others are concerned with specific subjects in the curriculum. In recent years, the national programme has reflected the emphasis of central publications such as the Bullock Report *A Language for Life* (DES, 1975) or the Warnock Report *Special Educational Needs* (DES, 1978c). Outside the formal programme, HMI has initiated various courses and conferences to stimulate professional debate, for example on the Green Paper on education *Education in Schools: A Consultative Document* (DES, 1977b) the discussion document *Higher Education into the 1990s* (DES, 1978a) as well as HMI publications such as the reports of the national primary and secondary surveys (DES, 1978b, 1979a), the survey of BEd degrees (DES, 1979b) and some surveys of subject provision. In its partnership relationship with regional and local initiatives, the Inspectorate is involved in varying degrees with the DES/Regional programme of courses, and with many LEA courses and conferences. These specific in-service training activities represent as much as 10 per cent of the total time available for all HMI activities, including formal and informal inspections, links with local authorities and institutions, correspondence and formal writing; in all of which activities, elements of teacher support and professional development are to be found.

The Inspectorate has probably exercised its most important influence on the nature and emphasis of professional development in its central partnership with the policy-making functions of the DES, and with bodies like the Advisory Council on the Supply and Training of Teachers (ACSTT). In this country, the past few years have been eventful and awesomely decisive in the history of teacher education, and the shape of professional development has changed in ways which may affect the next several decades.

One major challenge of recent years has been to define and co-ordinate the role of initial training colleges and departments in the further professional development of teachers. The Government White Paper *Education: A Framework for Expansion* (DES, 1972) laid on initial training institutions the task of knitting together into what it called a 'seamless garment' the entire professional development of teachers, from pre-service to retirement. This implied an expansion of the institutional commitment to in-service training and to the induction of new teachers in such a way as to enrich and strengthen the contact between teachers and training institutions. As a falling birth-rate caused school rolls to shrink, so a cut-back in initial teacher education was necessary. Amongst the many painful options available to them, ministers of the time chose the closure of as few institutions as possible, and a reduction in the unit size of all remaining colleges and departments of education in the non-university sector. It became possible to cushion the effect on staffing of the cut-back, by retaining substantial numbers (two-ninths of the total) of the staff in teacher education to make an expansion of in-service provision possible. At the same time, the additional staffing allowance helped to diminish the danger of a qualitative cut in BEd provision. From 1975, staff, premises and equipment from initial training institutions began to be available on an annually increasing scale for the further professional development of teachers.

Inspectors were all too aware of the practical difficulties of successfully implementing the full intentions of this policy. Local authority advisers, teachers' centre wardens and teachers themselves were at some times and in some places sceptical of the value and relevance of the colleges' contribution. Many colleges were still suffering from the rapid expansion of the late sixties, had barely absorbed the shock of large reductions, and had never had more than minimal involvement with serving teachers. Such institutions badly needed help if their resources were to be properly and effectively used. An Inspectorate survey was mounted in 1976 to look in some depth at a number of institutions where in-service training was already developed and to report on the elements of good practice. The DES report *In-Service Training: The Role of Colleges and Departments* (DES, 1977a) gave wide circulation to the findings of the survey. The salient features of good provision were constant, and the lesson to be learned was vital; the teaching profession had grown past the days when it was prepared to sit patiently receiving the wisdom which others had planned. If in-service training was really to be concerned with the professional development of teachers, then both planning and provision must reflect the partnership of professionals. The experience of teachers could be used to enrich the preparation of the pre-service student, while the expertise of the academic tutor could be a consultancy resource for the practising teacher.

One even more important lesson was coming through, not just from the survey of in-service training, but from contacts with schools and teachers in other contexts, and it was this: the planning of in-service training, that is to say, the identification of professional needs, is to a large extent most effectively undertaken at school level. Good schools conduct their own internal dialogue about their philosophy, aims and objectives, review their individual and corporate needs, including those for in-service training, and then make articulate and highly professional demands upon the sources of training available to them. Reciprocally, good colleges and departments welcome this kind of approach and the partnership it represents, and plan their own resources so as to meet this demand.

It is a rare school which has reached this level internally without some stimulus from outside, although examples do exist. The challenge to advisers, teacher educators, heads and senior staff, is to find ways of stimulating the right kind of professional self-assessment in all schools. As one colleague from the USA has commented (Thurber, 1976), 'the school is the living cell of the body educational': we must look to the health of the individual cell if the body as a whole is to flourish. While there are many sources of professional stimulus towards self-assessment, it is the Inspectorate's experience that inspection itself is an important element in heightening self-awareness and encouraging self-assessment, both for the individual teacher and for the school as a whole.

The quality of professional life in the school is, however, only half of the equation. When needs are identified, the provision available to meet them must be of high quality both academically and professionally. DES Report 88 said clearly that provision must be 'firmly rooted in the existing strength and expertise of the providing institution' (DES, 1977a). The high standards in teaching to which we are committed can only be achieved if extremely high standards are maintained in all the stages of professional training. In the longer term, all providers must be prepared to seek and maintain their own academic and professional excellence, and shun the temptation to offer to teachers anything less than such excellence.

In order to clarify a satisfactory theoretical framework for professional development, and to identify long-term strategies, the Inspectorate joined in discussions with the research community about possible long-term investigations. Two large-scale projects currently in progress are intended to illuminate the educational debate. The first is at Bristol University, in co-operation with Avon, Wiltshire, Northampton and Ealing Local Education Authorities. This Schools and In-Service Teacher Education (SITE) project is an attempt to describe and evaluate intensive school-focused professional development activities. (*See also Chapter 13.*) Teachers are encouraged to identify their own training needs, as individuals as well as in the context of the needs of their school. Resources from institutions of initial training, the local educational authority and the university are made available, and teachers from the project schools are given priority on courses for which they apply. From this project we hope to be able to identify some of the processes whereby a school becomes a 'thinking school', self-aware in a creative sense, and the processes which allow this to translate into real, institutional change within the schools. At the same time, we are learning how initial training institutions can respond most effectively to the 'thinking schools' who turn to them.

The second project, Initial and In-Service Education and Training for Teachers (IT-INSET), co-directed from the Open University and a polytechnic, is an attempt to monitor and evaluate pilot projects linking most closely the curriculum of initial training with in-service activities. Moving close to central questions about the nature of professional development at both pre-service and in-service stages, the project weaves together the school experience and professional studies elements of the pre-service students' course, with in-service experience for the teachers with whom the students are placed. A tripartite professional partnership of tutor, student and teacher is formed, in which the practical experiences of the classroom become the source material for mutual exploration of theoretical understanding.

In each of these projects, as in all DES-funded research, the Inspectorate is closely involved, not only at the research level itself, in close communication with the research team, but also at the level of action in schools and colleges, where the effect of project development can be independently monitored.

There is currently a third study entitled The Preliminary Evaluation of In-Service BEd Degrees, based at the Cambridge Institute of Education, which is a small-scale investigation of the in-service opportunities for teachers to acquire a BEd degree. The project is examining in detail the ways in which an academically demanding course can build upon and contribute to the classroom performance of the teacher.

Each of these studies has been enriched by international links with similar projects overseas, arranged through a project on school-focused in-service training in OECD/CERI, which has been running since 1976, and in which the UK has played a leading part. In consultation with HMI, the National Association of Teachers in Further and Higher Education and the Committee for Research in Teacher Education have held conferences to disseminate the experience from the research projects to institutions of higher education and the research company. The DES, in co-operation with OECD/CERI organized a conference in September 1979 to inform local education authorities about the projects' findings and the experience from their international links. In this way, the nature, timing and dissemination of the work of the projects should enable carefully controlled and monitored experiments to illuminate and guide the decision-makers at national, regional, local and institutional levels.

It is tempting, in conclusion, to speculate about the long-term nature of the national Inspectorate's role in the further professional development of teachers. Certainly, anybody whose concern is with standards in education cannot avoid a close and continuing concern with teachers' professional growth. HM Inspectorate's role as adviser to policy-makers must remain paramount, and this advice must continue to rest on the Inspectorate's corporate judgement of the needs of schools, and of the measures currently being taken at all levels to meet those needs. The Inspectorate's role as provider has been slightly reduced in recent years by the practice of stern self-discipline to confine its provision to only those kinds of course which could not, for one reason or another, be equally well done by other agencies, and by a resolution not to overstrain the scarce financial resources of local education authorities, who support teachers on HMI courses. It is, perhaps, a strength of our country's system that policy decisions at national level can be immediately reinforced by the professional activities of a national Inspectorate, just as policy decisions at LEA level can be reinforced by the work of local advisers and inspectors. (*See also Chapter 10.*)

The danger for all providers of in-service teacher training is to try to do too much. The challenge is to identify those areas which are best left to others, to perform one's own part well, and so to produce a network of provision in which universities, colleges, local authorities, teachers' centres and industry all contribute their appropriate piece of the pattern. Above all, each agency must increasingly work in full partnership with teachers, if the ideals of professionalism are to be realized.

References

Department of Education and Science (1972) *Education: A Framework for Expansion* (Cmnd 5174) HMSO: London

Department of Education and Science (1975) *A Language for Life: Report of the Committee of Enquiry appointed by the Secretary of State for Education and Science under the Chairmanship of Sir Alan Bullock* (The Bullock Report) HMSO: London

Department of Education and Science (1977a) *In-Service Training: The Role of Colleges and Departments* (Report on Education No 88) HMSO: London

Department of Education and Science (1977b) *Education in Schools: A Consultative Document* (Cmnd 6869) HMSO: London

Department of Education and Science (1978a) *Higher Education into the 1990s: A Discussion Document* DES: London and SED: Edinburgh

Department of Education and Science (1978b) *Primary Education in England: A Survey by HM Inspectors of Schools* HMSO: London

Department of Education and Science (1978c) *Special Educational Needs: Report of the Committee of Enquiry into the Education of Handicapped Children and Young People under the Chairmanship of Mary Warnock* (The Warnock Report) HMSO: London

Department of Education and Science (1979a) *Aspects of Secondary Education in England: A Survey by HM Inspectors of Schools* HMSO: London

Department of Education and Science (1979b) *Developments in the BEd Course: A Study Based on Fifteen Institutions* (HMI Series Matters for Discussion 8) HMSO: London

Perry, P (1977) Keynote address on school-focused INSET given at OECD/CERI International Workshop: Palm Beach, Florida

Perry, P (1977) In-service training: a national perspective *Trends* Autumn 1977

Thurber, J (1976) Paper given at OECD/CERI International Workshop on School focused INSET: Stockholm

10. Professional development: advisory services in England and Wales

Joan Dean

Summary: The education service in Britain is locally administered through a committee of selected councillors advised by a chief education officer, who maintains an overview of the effectiveness of the service through his advisory service.

Members of an advisory service may be called inspectors or advisers and most have both functions. The details of their work may vary in different local authorities but most are concerned with advising the chief officer and councillors on the provision and maintenance of standards of education in the schools and other establishments; the appointment, deployment and promotion of teachers; curriculum development and in-service education, and the design and equipping of school and other educational buildings. The advisory service is also a source of advice to teachers and head teachers on the organization and managements of schools, the curriculum, the appointment and deployment of teachers and day-to-day problems.

Advisory teams attempt to meet these demands in various ways. It is usual for a team to include experts in different aspects of curriculum and different stages of education and also for each member to have a pastoral responsibility for a group of schools. The team will be expected to have a good knowledge of individual schools and to know the state of aspects of education across the authority. This involves regular visiting of schools and some team studies.

Advisory teams are usually led by a chief adviser and may have other senior members with a co-ordinating role. To be effective and credible to teachers, members of an advisory team need to have had substantial and successful teaching experience.

The education service in the United Kingdom is provided by local government with some central and some local funding and some central controls. Each local authority must have an education committee of locally elected councillors which co-opts some professional educators. The education committee is advised by a chief education officer and his staff, and he is responsible for implementing the policies of the education committee and for the administration of the service which must cater for the needs of the population of the area which the council serves.

If the education committee and its chief education officer are to carry out their responsibilities effectively, they need an overall view of what is happening in the schools and colleges for which they are responsible. The overall view is needed first as a background to decision and policy-making and then as a means of assessing the effectiveness of what has been agreed and carried out. The provision of this overall view is usually a function of a local authority advisory service.

But there is more to running a successful education service than making and implementing central decisions. It is part of our tradition to act in the belief that teachers and head teachers are more likely to function effectively if they have opportunities for decision-making within their schools and we therefore give them very considerable opportunities for this; in particular, curriculum decisions are seen as the responsibility of the school. If this choice is to work satisfactorily, teachers and head teachers need support and advice of many kinds. The provision of this support and advice is the other major aspect of the work of the advisory services.

Local government in Britain was reorganized in 1974 and since then virtually every local authority has developed an advisory service for its schools and colleges. Patterns vary from one authority to another, but there are usually four main services:

— Educational advisers
— School psychological service
— Youth (or youth and community) service
— Careers service.

These four services may be co-ordinated in some way or each service may work separately linking with the others as appropriate. Educational advisers have probably the most wide ranging of the advisory functions and it is with this group that the rest of this paper is concerned.

Local authority inspectors of schools have existed from the early years of this century. London established its inspectorate very early on and was joined by some other large authorities. By 1918, local authority inspectors were sufficiently numerous to form an association which is now known as the National Association of Inspectors of schools and Educational Advisers. The early duties of local authority inspectors appear to have been fairly similar to those of today's advisers. An early NAIEA statement said that 'they advise their committees on every department of school activity and on the development of educational policy...upon the inspector falls a large part of the training which the teacher receives after having commenced his professional work'. These functions are very similar to those described earlier.

Services gradually developed through the years and by 1960 some authorities had built up teams representing many aspects of the curriculum. Others only had advisers for physical education, music, craft, drama and home economics because historically some of these were taught to groups of children at centres serving a number of schools and in some cases there were safety risks involved.

Often the various specialists worked in some isolation, especially where there were no advisers with more general responsibilities and no chief adviser. Appointments of advisers with general responsibility for a group of schools or a stage of education, primary or secondary schools, became increasingly common during the 1960s and in particular, many authorities began to appoint advisers for primary education.

The 1960s also saw a gradual change of emphasis from inspection to advice, and the term 'adviser' began to become more common. This is now changing again as public demands for accountability have led to a number of LEAs returning to the title 'inspector'. The titles 'adviser/inspector' tend to be used interchangeably to designate officers with similar functions, although in some authorities the more senior advisers are called inspectors. Most have inspectorial and advisory functions.

In 1968, a select committee of the House of Commons met to consider inspection of schools. One result of this was a gradual reduction in the number of HMIs and a gradually changing role for them, which increased the importance of local advisory teams. Local government reorganization in 1974 saw much needed improvements in advisory services as the new authorities planned more co-ordinated services to provide advice on all aspects of education. Unfortunately inflation has overtaken this development and much planned development has been shelved for the time being.

We have seen that local authority advisers have functions relating partly to teachers and schools and partly to the administrative officers of the authority and through them to the councillors. The need for this service is suggested in the 1944 Education Act, section 77, subsection 3, which says:

> Any local education authority may cause an inspection to be made of any educational establishment maintained by (ie in receipt of grant from) the authority and such inspection shall be made by officers appointed by the local education authority.

The detail of work undertaken by advisers varies from one authority to another, but the following functions are fairly common:

1. Advising the chief officer and councillors and carrying out work connected with the following:

   (a) Provision and maintenance of adequate standards of education in the schools and other educational establishments of the authority.
   (b) The organization of education within the authority.
   (c) The appointment, deployment and promotion of teachers. This may involve:
      (i) advising on staffing establishments for each school;
      (ii) organizing the entry of first appointment teachers to the service of the authority and advising on the completion of a probationary period for each teacher;
      (iii) advising managing and governing bodies on the appointment of head teachers, senior staff and teachers and taking part in interviewing for these posts; and
      (iv) reporting on the work of teachers who are candidates for promotion.
   (d) The design of school buildings and selection of furniture and equipment for schools.
   (e) Curriculum development and the in-service education of teachers including:
      (i) planning, running and taking part in in-service courses, and supporting the professional development of teachers;
      (ii) the secondment of teachers to long and short courses; and
      (iii) the authority's involvement with national projects.

2. The local adviser is also the chief source of advice to heads and teachers on all matters within the school or college. He may be asked to advise on the following:

   (a) The internal organization and management of the school. An adviser should be able to make available to a head or head of department, from his experience of a number of schools, information about ways of organizing and deploying staff.

(b) The curriculum. The adviser should provide for the school a source of advice and information about current curriculum development, research findings, methods, new books and materials. He should also be able to advise on ways of improving existing work and on developments within the curriculum, and should evaluate with the school what has been attempted.

(c) The staff. The adviser should be able to advise a head or head of department on the appointment and deployment of teachers. He should visit schools in order to look at the work of individual teachers and advise them, particularly those in their first year of service. He may also be involved in providing career advice for some teachers.

Advisory teams try to meet these needs in various ways. Most try to provide specialist expertise in each aspect of curriculum, so that it is very usual to find an authority with advisers for English, mathematics, science and so on. It is also usual to find advisers with responsibility for phases of education particularly at the lower end of the primary school and in further education. Many teams meet the demand for close knowledge of each school by allocating to each adviser a number of schools for which he has pastoral responsibility. It is very usual for him to have specialist responsibilities in addition.

General pastoral responsibility involves knowing the school and its teachers well enough to provide information about it when necessary and to be able to offer useful advice to the head on running the school. This means visiting it as frequently as possible, talking with pupils and teachers, studying the curriculum and timetable and looking at how these work out in practice. It may involve being concerned with staff selection and development and helping to tackle problems such as the weak or failing teacher. It may also mean advising the authority when a teacher has satisfactorily completed his probationary year and providing reports on any who are candidates for promotion. It may mean talking through with the head and senior staff patterns of organization, alternative approaches to work, deployment of staff, and a range of more specific problems. It is very usual too for a general adviser to alert his specialist colleagues to any situation in which specialist help is needed. Where this system is fully operational, it usually works well; trusting relationships are built up which enable the adviser to offer support and guidance unobtrusively and to interpret the policies of the authority to the school and the school to the authority. It gives the authority an immediate and personal method of communicating with each school's staff, an immediate source of information and someone who knows the school and can act as a trouble-shooter.

The specialist adviser cannot know each school as well as its general adviser, but he must aim to have an overall picture of work in his specialism throughout the service and offer support and guidance to teachers covered by it. Like the general inspector he will be concerned with curriculum, teaching approaches and standards achieved. He may also be involved with the appointment and promotion of teachers and with staff development depending upon the distribution of tasks in the particular authority. He will be expected to know the state of his particular specialism across the schools of the authority and help to form and implement policy for the development of this aspect of work and deal with problems where specialist help is needed.

We have already seen that the public demand for accountability which has been fairly universal in recent years has tended to lead to a greater emphasis on the inspectorial function of advisory services. It is now fairly usual for teams of advisers to study aspects of the service in some depth from time to time. This may be a matter of studying an individual school or college very thoroughly or of looking at such matters as the state of a particular subject in the authority's schools, or the effects of a particular policy. This has made new demands on advisory services.

Local government reorganization in 1974 led to a good deal of rethinking about advisory staff structures. There was encouragement for a team approach, and this led to the appointment of chief advisers in many places, while in the larger authorities other senior posts were also established, most commonly for the leadership of a team dealing with one stage of education, eg primary schools, or for dealing with schools in one geographical area, or for work in a subject or group of subjects. The chief adviser and team leaders are responsible for the organization of the work of the team and for the support and training of its members, and they are also the spokesmen for the service.

An advisory service needs to be acceptable to the schools it serves as well as to the officers and councillors of the authority. This means that its members must bring an adequate level of experience and judgement to their tasks. Heads and senior teachers find advice acceptable and indeed welcome when they recognize that the adviser is genuinely speaking from wider experience than their own and has taken the trouble to get to know their particular situation in some detail.

The early advisory services fought a hard battle to establish the need for well qualified advisers with substantial teaching experience and the majority of advisory teams contain people offering a wide range of relevant experience and qualifications. Many advisers in the primary field will have been heads themselves. This is less usual in the secondary sector because the salary and career structure in the two sectors do not encourage it, but most advisers in secondary work have held senior posts in schools.

Specialists are usually graduates and the majority of advisers are likely to have, in addition to their initial training, qualifications gained after teaching experience. A recent study by Bolam, Smith and Canter (1979) shows that advisers are generally better qualified and have had wider experience than the teaching profession as a whole. Until very recently, the training needs of advisers for advisory work had been little considered. People joined the service and picked up skills as best they could, sometimes learning from colleagues but often simply working by trial and error. This situation has tended to change following local government reorganization. In many authorities there were new groupings of advisers and some for the first time were given a structure which gave some advisers responsibility for the work of groups of others. The effect of this has been to have some training on the job built in and there is an increasing interest in the provision of other training.

One of the results of the close connection between the teaching and advisory services is that after a long series of struggles, the salary structure for advisers is similar to that of heads of schools, although conditions of service are usually somewhat tougher. There is still a great deal of local discretion about the levels of salary, as there is about the size and structure of the service within a particular authority. This is not entirely satisfactory since it means that a teacher in one authority may be far better supported with advisory help than a teacher in another, but it is consistent with our strong belief in local autonomy.

If one thinks of educational advisers in terms of their inspectorial role and of monitoring standards and maintaining an overview, it would be easy to receive the impression that the role is essentially a conservative and possibly a dominating one offering few opportunities to work creatively. The tradition of the service and the preferred style of most advisers is otherwise. Advisers see themselves mainly as working with teachers to improve and develop the work of the schools, even though they may play a different part in some situations. They expect to work by helping heads and teachers to think through their ideas, not by telling them what to do. Success in advisory work depends upon the relationship an individual adviser is able to form with others. He will be successful in schools if teachers have confidence in his knowledge and skill and are stimulated by his thinking. In a similar way administrative officers and councillors need to feel that he knows what he is talking about. He will work more effectively with all these groups if they feel that he is a sympathetic and thoughtful person who is mature and well balanced, and able to see a problem from many points of view. There will be occasions when he will be asking teachers to face unpalatable truths or offering to administrative colleagues and members views which are administratively inconvenient or politically difficult. His success in such situations depends upon the relationships he has built up.

Advisory services have a particualr importance at the present time, when all local government spending is being questioned. Good advice on spending is needed both centrally in the education office and in the schools. It is also important to monitor the less measurable aspects of the service. If we cut spending on building maintenance the results are soon there for everyone to see. If we place a timid five-year-old in a class of 40 in a classroom which is inadequately equipped, we have no easy means of assessing the damage we may be doing. Possibly the most effective way of assessing the less measurable effects of policies on the individual child in the classroom is to use skilled and experienced observers to monitor what is happening over the area of authority.

But perhaps the real importance of having a good advisory service, the aspect which has a long term effect, is the extent to which an adviser can provide vision and inspiration. Vision may of course come from any part of the service — from administrators, councillors and above all from teachers, but the adviser is uniquely placed to make vision become reality and it is perhaps vision above all that we need at the present moment.

Reference

Bolam, R, Smith, G and Canter, H (1979) *LEA Advisers and the Mechanisms of Innovation* National Foundation for Educational Research: Slough

11. Teachers' unions in the USA: an aggressive striving for professionalism

Eugenia Kemble

Summary: The growth of teacher unionism in the United States closely parallels the new concern among teachers for their professionalization. Historically, the American Federation of Teachers has been committed to the linkage between the growth of power through teacher unionism and the development of excellence in professional practice. Within the past decade, the National Education Association, the second major teacher organization in the United States, took on union-style tactics and stopped trying to distinguish between professionalism and unionism.

Educational problems facing teachers in the 1980s lend themselves to at least partial solutions through the collective bargaining process. A number of new ideas emerging from unionized teachers contribute markedly to their professionalization. Among the most promising are teacher centres, internships and entry tests for beginning teachers. If these programmes are to work, they will have to involve co-operation between sectors within education. If any teachers' organization attempts to claim complete control or works to eliminate colleges and local school boards from the operation of the programmes, the whole effort could backfire. While teachers deserve a greater say in their own professionalization — perhaps the controlling voice — theirs cannot be the only voice to be heard.

If handled co-operatively and carefully, what could emerge from the new ideas supported by teacher unions is a common understanding among teachers of the basis of their professional knowledge and skill and how their shared experience can unify teachers and increase their professional self-respect. Teachers have not enjoyed this common understanding before the present decade. With the power that unionism gives them they could obtain the kind of professional control that now exists for other professions.

Advocates of teacher unionism in the United States believe that it is impossible for teachers to become true professionals unless they have the power to influence strongly both the conditions under which they work and the definition of what constitutes sound educational practice. Historically, the American Federation of Teachers (AFT) has been committed to a linkage between the growth of power through teacher unionism and the development of excellence in professional practice. It is only recently that others in the educational community have come to agree. Unfortunately much of their agreement comes more from their new-found perception of necessity than from intellectual choice.

Today a variety of groups will at least pay lip-service to a belief that unionism and professionalism go hand in hand. Within the last decade, for example, the National Education Association, the second major teacher organization in the

United States, has shifted its stance dramatically. Formerly it made its appeal to teachers by attempting to draw a distinction between professionalism and unionism. As a 'professional association', it claimed, only the NEA could truly represent teachers. A union like the AFT, on the other hand, was seen as beneath professionalism by the NEA leadership because of its alliance with other workers within the American Federation of Labor and Congress of Industrial Organizations (AFL-CIO), and because it engaged in 'disruptive' tactics like strikes. It was not until the AFT became a competitive threat to the NEA in the late 1960s that the NEA embraced union-style tactics, began to call itself a union and stopped trying to draw lines between professionalism and unionism.

The American Association of Colleges of Teacher Education (AACTE) is another group that has begun to acknowledge that powerful teacher unionism and professionalism are not mutually exclusive. While many of its 784 institutional members resent the strength of teacher organizations, they now realize they will have to cope with it. The result has been a continuous attempt on the part of the AACTE to consult with teacher organizations and take their recommendations seriously. Many of AACTE's institutional leaders would be aghast at the prospect of having their own colleges unionized, but at the same time acknowledge their own vulnerability to the power of both national teacher organizations.

To the American Federation of Teachers, professionalism is not possible without unionism. A degree of self-control, the ability to help set professional standards , mastery of a specific body of knowledge and the authority to define conditions of work are essential elements in the AFT's definition of professionalism. Since none of these can be gained without the kind of collective assertion of power that unionism makes possible, the AFT maintains that without unionism, teaching can never become truly professional.

I

A number of educational trends emerging in the 1970s have contributed to a new concern for the professionalization of teachers in the United States. Many of them are related to a combination of forces outside education itself. The declining birth-rate behind declining student enrolments is perhaps the most influential of these. Because of the drop in the number of students, fewer teaching jobs are available. High unemployment throughout the economy has combined with low enrolments to mean not only fewer teaching jobs, but fewer jobs for those who might want to move out of teaching. Together these developments contributed to low turnover among teachers, fewer beginning teacher positions and a more stable, older teaching force (Dearman and Plisko, 1979).

Other pressures, many felt to be negative by teachers themselves, have fed the new concern for the professionalization of teachers. Educational opportunity expanded in America in the 1960s and 1970s — more students were completing high school than ever before, and about half the high school graduates were going on to higher education of some kind. While this by itself was a very positive development, many failed to realize that broadening the base of graduates and post-secondary school students inevitably meant that standards at the higher educational levels would fall. More students began to take Scholastic Aptitude Tests (SATs), which are required by most colleges as part of their entry requirements. With more students taking the tests, the averages began to fall (Wirtz, 1977) and, as high school completion became more widespread, those who failed to graduate became the focus of more distress and attention. The irony was, and is, that as American education has become democratized and opportunity has extended, there has been an accompanying outcry over declining standards. The first and last to be blamed for this effect are America's teachers.

Whatever dissatisfaction the public began to feel about education in the 1970s was exacerbated by at least two related developments. Inflation began eating away at the dollar's buying power at ever increasing rates. By the second half of the decade annual rates of 7 per cent and 8 per cent were becoming a matter of course. The public began giving closer scrutiny to the expenditure of its tax dollars, and while schools managed to maintain wide support, national polls showed nearly a quarter of the American public wondering if too much was not being spent on education. The fact that fewer adults had children in the schools meant that this particular public service did not touch as many homes as it once had (Eisenberger, 1979). While public school parents continued to support their public schools (Gallup, 1978), other adults were more swayed by what they read in the papers or heard on television about declining performance. Teachers were the obvious focus for their discontent.

Concurrent with the growth in suspicion about schools and their teachers was, surprisingly, a growth in expectations about what schools should be able to do, and what they were responsible for. Rising concern over student discipline once again brought attention to the abilities of teachers to cope. New programmes for the handicapped, the non-English-speaking, and for school districts with high concentrations of students from low income families, all carried the implicit assumption that the school system was expected to handle all kinds of burdens students brought to school with them and, in doing this, to create equal opportunity. Naturally, the more the system was asked to do, the greater became its potential for failure. As a result, choice has become a *cause célèbre* for private school advocates. They want public money to offer parents an opportunity to escape the overburdened public schools — for the ease of coping with selective education away from problem students and exhausted teachers (Coons and Sugarman, 1978).

II

This general discussion, by way of an introduction, is intended to show that the subject of professionalism is a highly problematic one for American teachers. Today's environment is a negative one in which to be approaching the topic, and yet, that negativity is also making the need to address it increasingly compelling. The response of the two teachers' organizations has differed. Teacher educators, who have had little power on their own to do anything about the situation, have largely followed the lead of teachers, sometimes willingly, but more often because they have been pressurized into doing so.

Unfortunately, much of the discussion about teacher preparation and in-service professionalization has suffered from the parochial, narrow tendencies of some educators. The National Education Association has responded to the negative atmosphere surrounding the subject by assuming an extremely defensive posture and by muscle-flexing over every proposal that is not exclusively its own. It has reacted to the concentration on test performance — whether by students or teachers — by calling for a moratorium on the use of all standardized, norm-referenced tests (NEA Convention, 1973). It has attempted to minimize the governance role of higher education and local school boards through new proposals creating in-service support for teachers. The NEA has attacked existing programmes when these programmes involve shared governance (NEA Convention, 1978). In advocating that existing support be shifted from the federally funded Teacher Corps (a programme jointly administered by teacher education schools and local education agencies — *See Chapter 15*) into the teacher-run teacher centres programme, the NEA posture undoubtedly contributed to the recent cut of $7.5 million from the Teacher Corps budget for 1979.

While pushing for a greater teacher voice, the American Federation of Teachers, on the other hand, has pursued a more co-operative approach that considers the problems and viewpoints of other education constituencies. The AFT, for example, has defended the key role of teacher preparation schools in defining good pre-service as well as in-service education. It has maintained that local education agencies are the legitimate fiscal agencies for administering publically funded programmes, and has defended this principle against NEA claims that teacher centre policy boards should be the direct recipients of federal teacher centre funds (Kemble, 1977). The AFT recently took a position in favour of the administration of pre-service tests for teachers as an aid to eliminating those lacking minimum literacy skills and with the hope of upgrading entry standards for the profession (AFT Convention, 1979). And, while critical of the misuses of standardized tests, the AFT has maintained that their continued appropriate use is necessary in order to obtain some sense of the comparative achievement of students, so that educators and public officials can learn which school systems are denying their students equal educational opportunity (AFT Convention, 1978).

What has really happened to teaching in the midst of all of this? Unfortunately, so far, very little. Day-to-day classroom life has not changed very much; teachers have not yet succeeded in redefining their own professionalism at a higher level and in a way that has gained public recognition. However, the stage has been set and the potential is there. Because the political and social atmosphere is loaded with possible problems and criticisms, this opportunity could be lost if not handled carefully. Divisions within the profession and the weak posture of the teacher education schools could be real barriers to the fulfilment of this potential.

III

There are a number of new ideas emerging from unionized teachers which, if they do not become destroyed in the midst of wars over programme governance, could contribute markedly to their professionalization. Before discussing them, it makes sense to look at the problems they are attempting to address — both at the pre-service and in-service levels.

Lack of integration and breadth characterizes many aspects of pre-service teacher training. Teachers may have to take courses which supposedly teach them how to teach reading, for example, and be given simple exposure to a few commercially developed programmes or a limited range of techniques, without ever confronting the whole scope of approaches known or the variety of educational philosophies which back them up. Connected with this lack of exposure is the fact that few states have demanding certification mechanisms which might help ensure that all teachers experience preparation of range and scope. For the most part graduation from an approved education school or programme constitutes certification (Koerner, 1963).

In the end, most teachers never receive rigorous pre-service training. Compounding this is the fact that many education students are part-timers, who experience a highly fragmented training programme. This tends to produce what Robert Dreeben calls a lack of 'collegiality' among teachers. Because endurance and struggle are not as much a part of teacher preparation as they are of law or medical training, teachers tend not to hang together as much or have as great a feeling of professional solidarity (Dreeben, 1970).

If these are the conditions — and there are many more which could be included here — then what are the teaching styles and states of mind that they tend to produce? How 'professional' are they? Most teachers tend to approach beginning teaching with the feeling that they are inadequately prepared to perform well. Since they know very well that getting into teaching is less arduous than getting into any other profession, their first year of work experience is often characterized by feelings of insecurity and fear.

Since most teachers come from the fragmented experience of the education school into the isolating experience of classroom teaching, they may tend to 'go it alone' in trying to teach (Dreeben, op cit). Consequently, many new teachers are afraid to ask their colleagues for help. The result is self-perpetuated isolation, and learning to teach through trial and error. While this may be understandable, it hardly contributes to professionalism.

As teachers move into teaching for a longer period, they begin to modify their teaching styles to meet the demands of the school, but professional isolation continues. For the most part the teacher's school day is spent within the confines of a single classroom in the company of children. Working with children all day is a highly intensive, exhausting experience. Those breaks which do come are hardly viewed as a time for professional consultation since they are needed for simply reviving one's energy. Intensity also contributes to the desire on the part of teachers to get out of the school building, as soon as their day is over. All this means that teachers rarely have an opportunity to consult professionally with one another (Dreeben, op cit).

Lack of collegial support is exacerbated by lack of administrative support. It is a rare principal who will spend time giving educational advice to teachers. Administration is viewed in the United States as primarily a function of rating and evaluation (in Great Britain, in contrast, the administrative role is more educationally supportive). Teachers see administrators as punitive people rather than as helpers, a perception that is encouraged even further by the inadequacies of most existing in-service education.

There are other aspects of teaching itself — as distinct from the type of school administration and the degree of teacher responsibility — which have the effect of deprofessionalizing teachers. One has to do with the intellectual aridness of the school day. It has already been noted that teachers function in isolation. All of their emotional and mental energy is focused on clusters of children who are sequestered in individual classrooms. Another factor is the number of children a teacher must deal with. In the elementary school this is important simply in terms of class size, whereas in secondary schools it must also take into account the total number of different classes, and hence different children, a teacher must work with.

It must also be noted that much of what teachers have to do has little to do with the professional role of teaching. It is common practice in school systems throughout the country to have teachers do as much paper work, lavatory duty, playground duty, lunch duty, bus duty, etc, as possible (Smith, 1969). Such practices are bound to influence teachers' professional self-concept and hence their classroom practice.

The continuing isolation of teachers from one another during the period in which they are adjusting to the hard realities of school life probably feeds such tendencies as they already may have toward a self-reliance marred peculiarly by helplessness and insecurity. Some may see the lack of institutionalized teacher sharing as a clear indication that they must succeed either on their own or not at all. It may also encourage them to view teaching as a highly individualized style of operating which cannot, and therefore need not, be touched by the experience of others. Naturally such opinions may result in a tendency among teachers to stick to approaches they know well, to avoid experimentation, and to reach for the advice of others with scepticism and resentment.

The punitive, as opposed to supportive, role of the principal, reinforces the initial inclination of teachers to make their own decisions about classroom practices. If they dare to admit ignorance or uncertainty, this could easily be used by the administration as supportive evidence in negative rating procedures. The cumulative effect of isolation and this punitive definition of administration is to increase the fears teachers have of admitting their own failings, of seeking help, and of trying new techniques — in other words, to make them less open to professional growth (Smith, op cit).

Lack of available resources and limited choice in their use cause intense resentment and frustration among teachers. Teachers are well aware of the injustice of being held responsible for classroom performance when they have little to say about choice of texts, materials to be used in supplementing texts, and the like (Broudy, 1972; Dreeben, op cit). In many systems, teachers may see the need for a particular teaching aid but be unable to convince the administration of its value; or, teachers may judge the materials they are using to be worthless and resent the fact that they are unable to select others. Such frustrations ultimately affect their own enthusiasm for teaching since they have little control over what they do. Negative attitudes are magnified when teachers realize how unimportant are many of the things for which they do have responsibility. All of the various 'administrative' duties like bus and hall duty, etc which many teachers must face, serve only to diminish further professional self-esteem and morale.

Test pressures, combined with parental and public pressures on teachers to raise them, no matter what, must inevitably have a rigidifying effect, making experimentation with new styles or enthusiasm about new approaches risky at best. The weight of parental opinion, in situations like these, suggests to the teacher that his knowledge about teaching is not really respected very highly. Since it is outside forces, not professional judgement, which determine what goes on in his classroom, his confidence, drive, and sense of professional control are likely to be seriously shaken. Undoubtedly these will take their toll when it comes to classroom behaviour and pupil-teacher interaction.

While the political atmosphere and the scope of what needs to be done may seem to pose impossible obstacles to further professionalizing teaching at present, there are also a number of strengths that must be considered. A number of the problems discussed lend themselves to at least partial solutions through the collective bargaining process. For example, over the selection of materials, determining of class size, adoption of evaluation procedures used by administration, the degree of parental oversight and the status that comes with high salaries, teachers have, and will continue to bargain for, conditions that will enhance their professionalism. These are examples of where union strength and professional growth go hand in hand.

The American Federation of Teachers has also proposed a number of other ideas aimed at upgrading teaching and increasing its professional status. As long ago as 1971, AFT President Albert Shanker wrote in his *New York Times* column that teacher centres modelled on their British counterparts could greatly enrich the professional lives of teachers by enabling them to share skills and experiences with one another. New research works have added to the thrust of analyses like that of Robert Dreeben's in pointing once again to teacher isolation and in focusing on the need for teacher support and co-operation if new educational programmes are to take root successfully in the schools. In one study called *Schoolteacher*, Dan Lortie pictures the individual classroom as an isolated 'cell' (Lortie, 1977). Another, *Federal Programs Supporting Educational Change*, found that innovations became institutionalized and actually worked only in school districts where teachers were thoroughly involved in their development and implementation (Berman and McLaughlin, 1978). Together, the push from teacher leaders like Shanker and the recognition from researchers of both teacher problems and teacher potential, give both political and intellectual support to the teacher centre movement.

Behind the AFT's push for teacher centres was the union's belief that centres could focus on diminishing teacher isolation by providing a place where teachers could go to share ideas and consult with each other. It could be a place to relax; a place to get away from the pressures of school; a place to find materials that might be helpful in the classroom. A good teacher centre could provide teachers with a choice of resources and a consultative service on how to use them. It might give high level in-service training in the form of mini-courses or in-depth consultations. It might provide a supportive link between the preparatory education school and the public school experience of teachers, since there is no reason why colleges and public school systems could not co-operate in both the development and use of a teacher centre.

A decision was made by the AFT and the NEA to focus on the passage of federal legislation since a major breakthrough was needed, and because the states, who traditionally are responsible for professional teaching standards in the United States, were bemoaning their lack of funds and generally dragging their feet on the subject. Finally, in autumn 1976 the work that the AFT and the NEA had done to press for a federal teacher centre bill won success. As part of the Education Amendments of 1976, Congress authorized a new teacher centre law that provided up to $60 million in federal funds for centres run by policy boards composed of a majority of teachers. While funds would go to local education agencies, teacher centre policy boards in which teachers had a majority voice would have the main say in deciding how it should be spent.

So far the programme is really too new to have had tremendous impact. Congress has appropriated only between $10 and $12 million for the programme and the two teacher organizations have been warring over the distribution of funds. Inept administration by the Federal Office of Education has failed to keep teacher politics out of funding decisions, and this failure is undoubtedly hurting the programme somewhat in the eyes of Congress. But teacher centres are developing and the programme's growing pains will probably soon be overshadowed by the successful service the centres give to teachers.

The AFT also believes that now would be a good time to begin experimenting with special support for beginning teachers — the introduction of an internship, or induction, phase to teacher preparation. With the number of new recruits entering teaching so low, experimentation of this kind would be more inexpensive now than ever before. An internship programme for teachers could be designed in such a way as to effect changes in attitudes which arise from the present failings of teacher preparation. Essentially an internship programme might provide that all prospective teachers spend at least one year, or possibly more, carrying a partial load of teaching combined with part-day consultative and/or class work. Such interns, unlike student teachers, would be paid for their work. An internship programme could go far to help establish 'collegiality' among teachers, and to develop a sense among prospective teachers that teaching must be learned through rigorous long-term training which combines academic background with on-the-job experience supervised by professionals (AFT Convention, 1975).

In advocating teacher centres, internships and entry tests for beginning teachers, the American Federation of Teachers has taken on the issue of teacher professionalism in a comprehensive and direct way. These three elements link pre-service and in-service education for teachers and, if done well, they will have to involve not only teachers, but local education agencies and colleges of teacher education. While it will be difficult to implement these ideas in a period of economic scarcity when public services are being eyed suspiciously, the fact that they represent an aggressive attempt by teachers themselves to improve the profession should give them some credibility. The very act of proposing programmes like these is an admission from teachers that their professional role is not what it should be.

While the possibilities are great, there is also a delicate balance that could easily be upset. If these programmes are to work they will have to involve co-operation between sectors within education. If any teachers' organization attempts to claim complete control, or works to eliminate colleges and local school boards from the operation of the programmes, the whole effort could backfire. Power grabs will not be accepted by either of these groups, or by the general public. While teachers deserve a greater voice in their own professionalization — even *the* controlling voice — they cannot be the only influence, and if they try to exclude others, support for any new ideas they might try to project is bound to erode very quickly.

If handled co-operatively and carefully, what could emerge from the implementation of these ideas is a common understanding among teachers of what the knowledge and skill base for their profession really is — that thread of shared experience that can unify teachers and instil pride in teaching. Teachers have never had either the freedom or the opportunity to do this before. With the power that unionism gives them they will now have a chance. Their success could give them the kind of professional control that now exists for other professions, and the self-respect that goes with it. If these ideas succeed, teaching may no longer be an isolated and anxiety-ridden career. Teachers will be more open to new ideas — to professional growth — since it will be well known that these new ideas incorporate the needs and thinking of the teachers who will make them work.

References

AFT Convention (1975) *Resolution on Lifelong Learning III: Teacher Internships* American Federation of Teachers: Washington, DC

AFT Convention (1978) *Resolution on Minimum Competency Testing* American Federation of Teachers: Washington, DC

AFT Convention (1979) *Resolution on Entrance Examinations* American Federation of Teachers: Washington, DC

Berman, P and McLaughlin, M W (1978) *Federal Programs Supporting Educational Change* The Rand Corporation: Santa Monica, Ca

Broudy, H S (1972) *The Real World of the Public Schools* Harcourt, Brace, Jovanovich: New York

Conant, J B (1963) *The Education of American Teachers* McGraw-Hill: New York, Toronto, London

Coons, J E and Sugarman, S D (1978) *Education by Choice: The Case for Family Control* University of California Press: California

Dearman, N D and Plisko, V W (1979) *The Condition of Education* US Government Printing Office: Washington, D C

Dreeben, R (1970) *The Nature of Teaching* Scott, Foresman and Company: Glenview, Ill

Eisenberger, K W (1979) *Demographic Change: The Cost of Decline* Washington, D C

Gallup, G H (1978) *Tenth Annual Gallup Poll of the Public's Attitudes Toward the Public Schools* Phi Delta Kappa: Indiana

Kemble, E (1977) *At Last: Teachers' Centres that are Really for Teachers* American Federation of Teachers: Washington, DC

Koerner, J D (1963) *The Miseducation of American Teachers* Penguin Books: Baltimore, Maryland

Lortie, D (1977) *Schoolteacher: A Sociological Study* University of Chicago Press: Chicago, Ill

NEA Convention (1973) *Resolution on Standardized Testing*

NEA Convention (1978) *Resolution on Teacher Corps*

Smith, B O (1969) *Teachers for the Real World* American Association of Colleges for Teacher Education: Washington, D C

Wirtz, W (1977) *On Further Examination* College Board: New Jersey

12. The role of Australian colleges and universities

Glen Evans

Summary: The 1970s in Australia have seen the adoption of longer periods of pre-service teacher education and a surge of development in in-service education. These changes coincide with a dramatic increase in the complexity of the teacher's role in curriculum decision-making, increased and sometimes conflicting public pressures on the content and style of teaching, and the need to cater for a wider diversity of students. Universities and colleges have responded with courses for serving teachers that may be seen as having a variety of functions — upgrading, reconceptualizing and extending initial training in the light of teaching experience, developing specializations, and training for research and development. They have also been involved in other forms of in-service education, eg short courses and consultancies, but on a relatively small scale, reflecting uncertainty about this kind of role for tertiary institutions and lack of funding for it. On the other hand, the institutions are working hard to overcome a mythology that courses leading to qualifications are carried on apart from the concerns, and without the participation of, schools and educational systems and that they do not effectively address the real problems of practice. The problems of articulation between various forms of in-service teacher education and of the relationship between theory and practice are examined in this paper, and a number of examples of progress described.

Introduction

The last 15 years have seen dramatic changes both in the tasks required of Australian teachers and in their level of professional education and training. In that time the minimum qualification required for teachers has increased from two years post-secondary training to three, and in some cases four, years of tertiary education, including at least one year of specific professional training. These minimum requirements are enforced by registration laws in four states and by conditions of employment in the others. There is now talk of an all-graduate profession at pre-school, primary, and secondary levels. A recent report on teacher education in Queensland, for example, recommends that: 'Teachers whose initial qualification for employment is a three year diploma should be required to complete a degree in education by a further period of formal study after an induction period of teaching of at least one year' (Bassett, 1978:48).

Apart from trends to credentialism, these changes are, in part, a response to the increasing complexity of the teacher's task. For example, schools have gained much greater autonomy in curriculum planning and student assessment, and this alone has meant greater pressures on teachers in terms of the need for skills and knowledge. Over half of the 1600 teachers from all states questioned by Campbell (1975) in his survey in 1973 expressed this concern by rating as of moderate to very great concern the item: 'I feel overwhelmed by the new teaching demands that are made upon me'. More than one third of those teachers rated similarly the item: 'I feel that I am not fully qualified to handle my job'. Such a state of affairs has meant an increasing need for in-service or post-experience teacher education.

Schooling in Australia

Educational provisions in Australia are constitutionally the responsibilities of state government rather than federal. For this reason, there are differences both in school organization and curriculum management from state to state. However, the minimum school leaving age is generally 15 years, and most students (88 per cent in 1977) continue at school at least until Year 10, by which time they will have experienced three or four years of secondary schooling and six or seven of primary, preceded by pre-school and kindergarten in many cases. In 1977, 52 per cent went on to Year 11 and 35 per cent of the age group finished the final year of secondary schooling (Year 12). The state educational systems account for the majority of students, but there is a significant Catholic system in each state and territory, together with independent schools, often with religious affiliations.

Three broad issues could be said to dominate educational decision-making in Australia. First, as mentioned earlier, the focus of educational decision-making has, in recent years, tended to move from central system authorities to the school. This devolution of responsibility has been most pronounced in the area of curriculum planning.

The second issue is that of curriculum style, both in the content and in the procedures that are used in classrooms. This issue has been heightened by the recent report of the committee appointed by the federal government to enquire into education and training, chaired by Professor B R Williams (1979).

Many submissions to the enquiry contrasted practical pre-vocational goals and emphasis on basic skills, on the one hand, with the development of personal growth and social awareness on the other. Yet recent studies (eg Collins and Hughes, 1979; Campbell and Robinson, 1979) suggest that parents, students, teachers, and the general community value all of these.

Even among teachers, there is no consensus on style of teaching. In a survey by Evans (1978) of a national sample of teachers, it was apparent that the most pervasive difference among teachers was the extent of their belief in, and use of, teaching practices granting a fair measure of pupil autonomy and choice. While the overall use of such practices is, on the evidence, low in Australian schools, there is a marked desire among teachers, on the average, to make more use of them, although there is a large variation in how much more.

The third issue in schooling is that of how to provide for those children who are either disadvantaged or exceptional in the extent to which they can benefit from schooling. This has been a major concern of the Schools Commission, which was established in 1974, and is the agency through which the federal government makes about 14 per cent of the total educational expenditure as earmarked grants to the states. For the classroom teacher, this concern is reflected in the increasing numbers of handicapped children being absorbed into mainstream classes and school programmes aimed at overcoming particular disadvantage. Apart from this, there is now much greater awareness of the educational needs of an increasingly multi-cultural society, with its attendant problems of values in education and expectations of schooling.

Many of the problems of beginning teachers are centred on classroom management and control, and the motivation of pupils (eg Otto *et al,* 1979). Tisher *et al* (1978) in their study of teacher induction in Australia, listed 'teaching groups with wide ability range', 'teaching slow learners', 'discovering the level at which to teach', 'devising schemes of work', 'controlling classes', 'motivating pupils', and 'teaching specific skills' as the most worrisome aspects for beginning teachers, as seen by both themselves and their principals. Campbell *et al* (1977) found a sharp change in the attitudes of primary teachers after six months teaching experience, from more child-centred to less child-centred, and a widespread concern with their teaching skills.

It is unlikely that these concerns entirely disappear with experience, but the priorities of longer-serving teachers appear to shift towards the tasks of curriculum planning, diversity of approach, and personalization of teaching, referred to above. Class size, time available for dealing with particular topics, the nature of the student group, the nature of the subject matter, and availability of resources appear to be ubiquitous constraints recognized by teachers (Evans, 1978; Perrott, 1979). Most Australian teachers could fairly be categorized as highly directive, according to several studies, but there is considerable evidence of their interest in becoming less so.

Teacher education courses and teacher career patterns

Pre-service teacher education in Australia is provided either in colleges of advanced education (CAEs) or universities. Both sectors are funded from the federal government's Tertiary Education Commission (TEC) through a state grants procedure. Within each sector, there are two main patterns of initial training — 'consecutive' or 'end-on', and 'concurrent'. The end-on pattern generally offers a year of professional studies in teaching to graduates in various fields other than education. In the concurrent pattern, educational studies and teacher training are undertaken throughout the course, or at least during the last two years, along with studies in arts, science, or other fields.

The typical college course for primary teacher preparation is concurrent over three years, leading to the Diploma of Teaching (DipTeach). Its essential components are general liberal studies, specialization in one or two disciplines or content areas, educational foundation studies, curriculum studies including media, and teaching practice in schools, together with microteaching. The college pattern for secondary teachers is varied. It is usually concurrent, but may span either three or four years, in the latter case usually leading to the Bachelor of Education (BEd) Award. A minority of college courses adopt the end-on pattern, leading to a Graduate Diploma (GradDipTeach).

A majority of universities follow the end-on pattern leading, for example, to the BA/DipEd degree, but a considerable number offer a four year concurrent course for a combined first degree in arts or science and diploma in education or BEd qualification.

One of the few salary differentials attached to qualifications depends on whether a teacher is three year or four year trained. There is consequently some motivation to convert from a three year (Diploma of Teaching) to a four year (BEd) qualification by extra formal in-service study. Further, as required qualifications have strengthened, there has been a need for courses to allow many teachers to upgrade their qualifications to the minimum three year level. These courses, however, in the nature of things, have a limited life, and the need for them is now dwindling, at least as far as the Diploma of Teaching qualification is concerned.

Tertiary institutions have also provided a variety of opportunities for the specialization and deepening of knowledge about teaching and education through graduate diploma courses in such fields as early childhood education and special education, of the equivalent of one year duration. The universities offer higher degree studies, either in educational foundation disciplines or in specializations such as educational administration, counselling, and curriculum studies. A small number of colleges also offer masters programmes. Finally, a considerable number of teachers are engaged in formal studies other than education that bear on their professional development, eg undergraduate and masters programmes in science, arts, commerce, or economics. The majority of teachers involved in further studies are pursuing them part-time in the evening, while a number of universities and colleges offer external study facilities.

It is easy to associate all of this activity with merely helping teachers to upgrade and obtain promotion. However, there are many teachers who undertake further formal courses in order to improve their competence in their present jobs. This motivation more closely matches some conceptions of the developing professional in an increasingly complex vocation. It is the underlying rationale of all forms of in-service education and training (INSET), to which we now turn.

Patterns of in-service education

The recent review of teacher education in Queensland (Bassett, 1978) takes in-service education to mean 'all the planned activities undertaken by teachers to improve their effectiveness, both in the conduct of regular duties and of new duties occasioned by promotion or transfer to new positions'. If this definition is accepted, approaches to INSET practised in Australia include the following: upgrading courses, award courses, non-award courses of various length, seminars, conferences, meetings, workshops, visits, use of libraries, resource centres, school-based conferences and seminars, school-based problem-solving and curriculum development, participation in curriculum development projects, personal reading, and informal discussions. These activities are carried out through a variety of agents: universities and colleges, professional associations concerned with teaching in particular subject areas or at particular levels, teachers' unions, inspectors, advisory teachers, consultants, regional education directorates, state education department curriculum, research, and media branches and resource centres, education centres and teacher centres, publishers, and schools.

Most of the *non-award* bearing activities have increased considerably since 1973, particularly following the establishment of the Australian Schools Commission. There are several Schools Commission programmes which bear on teacher development, but the main one is the Teacher Development

Programme, administered in each state by a state development committee, which broadly represents the main teacher associations and school systems. State departments of education also independently conduct in-service activities and are the other major source of funding. Other sources include non-government school systems, colleges, and universities. By way of example, in the two years 1975 and 1976, teachers in Victoria attended an average of 1.7 in-service courses or activities per year, compared with an average of 1.0 per year in the previous three years (Batten, 1979). A fuller description is given by Skilbeck *et al* (1977).

A recent evaluation of the Teacher Development Programme (Batten, 1979) draws a number of conclusions based on findings from several studies concerned with the conduct and effects of the programme up to 1977. Batten concludes *inter alia* that:

— there has been increasing recognition of the value of in-service education
— teachers need to learn to use a particular form of in-service education before they can obtain much benefit from it
— teachers have become most involved where they have also contributed to course planning and follow-up
— individual teachers need continued support from courses and school personnel in order to implement methods and reinforce attitudes resulting from courses
— schools need to plan a continuing programme of development, making use of the contribution of those teachers who have taken in-service courses
— there is a need to establish links between pre-service and in-service education of teachers
— peer group influence is of major importance in teacher development
— school-centred professional development has been received with universal acclaim.

Roles of universities and colleges

Batten's conclusions confirm the developing professionalization of teaching; teachers as a group are learning to draw on their own resources in order to solve problems of schooling and develop their professional competence. There is a problem for tertiary institutions in that much of the explosion of INSET has proceeded without specific reference to them as institutions. In-service education is sometimes seen not only as a thing apart from pre-service education but also as largely independent of the award courses provided for serving teachers (Batten, 1979: 54; Cameron, 1978: 16).

As Cove (1975) pointed out, the original report of the Interim Committee of the Schools Commission ignored upgrading and other courses being undertaken by thousands of teachers, as if nothing could be done through formal studies which would assist in bringing about change. Yet, Cove argues, 'short courses lasting a few days cannot be a substitute for intensive study designed to meet the special needs of mature, practising teachers' (Cove, 1975: 57-8).

Assertions about the remoteness of the formal award courses and the tensions they reflect raise a number of important questions of fact and principle. It is to these questions that the remainder of this paper is devoted. Some of the information reported was summarized from responses to a brief questionnaire sent to each of the 16 universities and 48 colleges with teacher education programmes. Other information is drawn from published reports.

1. Participation of teachers in award-bearing courses

Participation rates have been variously estimated. The figures given by the recent Queensland enquiry (Bassett, 1978) may not be typical for all states: about one in four Queensland teachers were, in 1978, undertaking courses for further qualifications ranging from the Diploma of Teaching to higher degrees, either in educational studies or in arts, science, commerce, economics, and other faculties. Overall, about one in eight teachers are taking educational studies courses in Australia.

The proportion of tertiary education resources devoted to this task is also considerable. Faculties, schools, or departments of education are frequently among the largest on university campuses, and most colleges of advanced education either have large schools of education or are single-purpose teachers'colleges. Some appreciation of the investment in teacher education can be gained by studying the statistics and estimates given in Tables 1 and 2 which show the numbers of students commencing and participating in pre-service courses and participating in in-service courses in 1978. Nearly one quarter of all tertiary enrolments are in teacher education courses (more, if those intending teachers taking first degrees not in education are counted) and over 35 per cent of the teacher education enrolments are in formal courses provided mainly for serving teachers. Again, teachers make up a large proportion of students undertaking courses part-time or by external studies.

Table 1 shows that the major component of teacher education, both pre-service and in-service, is undertaken by the colleges, but the universities attract a proportionately large number of in-service students. The future trend will no doubt be that the colleges, which have come relatively recently to offer bachelor degrees and graduate diplomas, will attract increasingly more in-service students.

It is difficult to tell from published figures what proportion of those teachers enrolled in award-bearing in-service courses are undertaking the Diploma of Teaching for upgrading purposes. However, from the responses received from 30 colleges which have responded to the questionnaire at the time of writing, 4360 teachers out of 11,224 enrolled in their in-service courses are in this category, ie 39 per cent. The remaining 61 per cent are enrolled mainly in BEd and graduate diploma programmes.

2. The nature and utility of the award-bearing courses

The courses available to serving teachers offer a wide variety of options which are frequently tailored to emerging social and educational needs within the community and the local educational system. There is thus increasing emphasis on courses in educational administration, curriculum, special education, the teaching of reading, language learning, multi-cultural education, English as a second language, technical and further education, and continuing education. Graduate diploma courses tend to be built around one or another of such themes; bachelors and coursework masters programmes adopt them as specialist areas, but also emphasize foundation studies in such disciplines as educational psychology and the philosophy, sociology and history of education. A number

Sector	Total tertiary enrollments	Pre-service teacher education	In-service teacher education	DipTeach	BEd graduate diploma	Total teacher education
Universities[1]	159,506[2]	4000[3] (2.5)[4]	5800[5] (3.6)			9,800 (6.1)
CAEs	149,747[2]	41,400[6] (27.6)	19,200 (12.8)	40,752[2]	19,867[2]	60,619[2] (40.4)
Total	309,253	45,400 (14.7)	25,000 (8.0)	40,752	19,867	70,400 (22.6)

Table 1 *Enrollments in teacher education courses 1978*

(1) These figures do not include those intending or serving teachers taking courses in universities in other than education studies. However, CAE figures include all intending teachers.
(2) Figures from Tertiary Education Commission (TEC) Report for 1979-81 triennium (Vol 2).
(3) Estimated number of equivalent full-time students actually undertaking DipEd or education studies component of BEd and B/DipEd courses (see Table 2).
(4) Percentages shown in brackets in terms of particular sector total.
(5) Estimated from TEC figures for enrollments in various courses.
(6) Estimated from TEC figures for students commencing and completing pre-service teacher education courses.

	Universities DipEd	4 yr concurrent	Universities total	CAEs DipTeach	Total
Primary	250	538	788	7722	8510
Secondary	2340	939	3279	6251	9530
Total	2590	1477	4067	13973	18040

Source: Report of the Tertiary Education Commission for 1979-81 triennium (Vol 2)

Table 2 *Numbers of students commencing pre-service teacher education courses in 1978*

of masters programmes in other fields have been designed, at least in part, with teachers in mind, eg in music, mathematics, English literature, and the like. Further, within some of the programmes offered to teachers in education and teacher education, a proportion of the course may be devoted to studies other than education. The formal courses thus provide opportunities to improve and extend subject matter knowledge in teaching areas as well as take further professional studies. It is an unfortunate side-effect that these improved qualifications are often likely also to make teachers attractive candidates for jobs which take them out of the classroom.

3. Accessibility to formal courses

The network of colleges and universities in Australia is largely confined to the large capital cities and provincial cities. While they thus cater for the main areas of population, many teachers are still too remote from tertiary institutions to attend classes, or are transferred away from the centre in which they began a course of study. For this reason, many institutions offer external studies programmes with some vacation school requirements. Several universities have large distance teaching programmes, while over a dozen other colleges and universities make substantial provisions for it. Distance teaching in these universities entails correspondence, visits by tutors, and compulsory short residential schools held during school vacations.

A different problem of access has to do with the entry requirements for the formal courses. While many of the experiences offered in the graduate diploma and degree courses might be considered of value by all teachers, they are open only to suitably qualified teachers prepared to enrol for the complete course (see Table 2 for prerequisites). Further, a particular subject may have defined prerequisites within the programme that put it out of reach of students who may be prepared to enrol for only a single course.

4. Links with other agencies

One of the criticisms of the formal course structure is that it is remote from other agencies and that the planning of courses does not involve the rest of the profession sufficiently. There are signs that this remoteness is breaking down and that, increasingly, teachers and state education department representatives are being involved in planning. A striking example of this kind of co-operation is the Centre for Continuing Education of Teachers in Tasmania (CCET). This centre is a consortium of the Tasmanian State Education Department, the Tasmanian College of Advanced Education and the University of Tasmania's Faculty of Education. This centre co-ordinates part-time and external studies for teachers undertaking award-bearing courses within the College and the University, but at the same time it offers some of the advantages of a teacher centre. Its general approach to teaching makes extensive use of students' experience in planning, and its activities act as a focus for research and a forum for discussion of educational issues.

5. Utility of the award-bearing courses

While formal courses are recognized as the major means of gaining general and specialist qualifications, it remains necessary to test their value against other forms of in-service education. It is difficult to obtain data bearing on such a question, but two kinds of evidence can be reported.

First, there is the perception of teachers. Between 1974 and 1977, an extensive evaluation was made of in-service education programmes in Victoria (Batten, 1979: 63; Ingvarson, 1977) using a stratified random sample of teachers — 626 teachers in the 1977 study. While the questionnaires were aimed principally at eliciting reactions to non-award activities, one question concerned original teacher training and another 'formal study, research, and professional reading'. The results showed that, as far as their professional development was concerned, teachers considered these two formal sources, together with 'meetings within the school to discuss educational topics', to be of most importance — markedly more important than 'in-service courses', 'meetings of teacher groups outside the school' and 'assistance from visiting consultants'.

A second approach to the question of utility is to analyse the extent to which formal courses meet the criteria which are beginning to emerge from evaluation studies of INSET generally, for example those listed by Batten (1979) and mentioned earlier. In this regard several points need to be raised.

1. On most campuses, 'evening' students are still brief visitors. Much more needs to be done to help the part-time student who is a full-time teacher, to contribute to and use his association with a lively academic community to test and expand his ideas about education and teaching. Several institutions have developed such an ethos, but the 'teacher centre' opportunities have barely been tapped.

2. College courses face a stiff process of state and national accreditation, which, while safeguarding standards, tends to decrease flexibility. There is presently little tradition, and less established policy, of involving students in the planning of courses they themselves are pursuing.

3. At the conclusion of any particular course, finding opportunities to apply new approaches or working through the consequences of new viewpoints is usually left to the teacher, who, faced with unaltered contextual constraints, tends progressively to separate 'theoretical ideals' and 'practical reality'. While this is a common failing of all INSET, the need to develop implementation strategies is well recognized as far as the teachings of qualificatory courses are concerned.

4. Allied with the last point is the current enthusiasm for school-based or

school-focused study. While arguments can be made for distancing some of the material of courses from the particular context of the teacher (eg Skilbeck *et al*, 1977), the applicability of formal studies to the practice of teaching is an explicit concern in much material that is presently emanating from tertiary institutions. There are, however, important organizational difficulties in this, which have been tackled in various ways.

As part of its Bachelor of Education programme, LaTrobe University, for example, offers the opportunity for students to become members of one of several task forces, which work with teams of teachers in specific schools on particular problems, developing particular programmes in the school in liaison with the principal, district inspector, and school staff concerned. The function of the course is thus to equip its teacher-students with the necessary theoretical perspectives and methodological skills to carry out the tasks, while the university staff maintain close liaison with the school over the two year period involved.

In a similar way, the University of Queensland has introduced curriculum workshops at bachelors and masters levels which require the teachers taking the course to carry out actual curriculum projects within their own schools. The emphasis is again on providing the conceptual and methodological background to the development tasks.

Deakin University uses an open systems approach to secure school-focused studies. In its large distance teaching programme, it uses a wide variety of resources for external students. A number of schools have in turn contributed to the development of these resources, particularly the preparation of case studies. These activities have included a widening net of teachers, often not participating formally in the degree programme, contributing to and drawing from the resource pool. In 'high activity' schools particularly, student teachers, teachers, principal, school council, parents, and the community generally may all be involved in development, research, or dissemination.

Similar examples are to be found in many colleges and universities, and there is probably some school-focused work in most programmes, but it could not be claimed that such experiences are yet the norm.

6. Links with pre-service teacher education

The much advocated linkage between pre-service and in-service education (eg Batten, 1979; Department of Education and Science, 1977) can be conceptualized at least four ways: through links with induction programmes for beginning teachers, by continuity between pre-service and in-service award courses, by systematic involvement of those offering pre-service courses in recurrent education programmes, and by using pre-service courses to inform and provide a setting for in-service education.

In recent years a variety of school-based approaches to induction have been attempted, including forward information on the school of first appointment, organized consultations with more experienced teachers, group meetings for beginning teachers, and observing experienced teachers. However, beginning teachers frequently experience unsettled arrangements about their teaching assignments and only about a quarter of them receive concessions in teaching load (see Tisher *et al*, 1979). The tightening of the economy will in fact make such concessions, including school release for systematic course work, even less likely. However, a number of colleges and universities have arranged seminars and short courses for first-year teachers on a less formal, voluntary basis and, in some cases, an attempt has been made to encourage continuing contact between lecturing staff and their past students through correspondence, associations, and visits to schools by staff members.

The essence of the induction process is the striving of the new teacher to make his ideas and intentions fit the reality of classroom experience. There is, in this process, a danger that the teacher will see himself 'starting again', denying so much of his pre-service training as to be virtually 'untrained' and relying almost totally on intuitive interpretations of experience and advice from other teachers. If the teacher is eventually to bring to his task a professional understanding of alternatives in teaching, as they relate to the context of this work and the students he teaches, the initial period of development is critical, and there need to be close, frequent interchanges between practice and its conceptualization. One route is the kind of internship used by Flinders University in its four year BEd programme for primary teachers.

In this case, the first three pre-service years involve full-time study. In the fourth 'internship' year, the student is, ideally, employed in a South Australian school on the salary of a three-year trained teacher. Students unable to find employment undertake an extended period of teaching practice for one semester. In addition to satisfactory teaching, the student is required to attend three in-service conferences and submit written assignments. The conference seminars are concerned with two areas — applications of educational theory and primary school methods. This course is unique in Australia in a variety of respects, not least in the co-operation between the University and the school system.

A more usual approach is the provision of in-service award courses which the teacher may take in the early years of his teaching, for example, after one year's experience. Many see the fourth year of the BEd degree, taken in-service, as fulfilling this purpose. In this sense, it can be seen not as upgrading but as genuine in-service development which would be necessary irrespective of the length of the pre-service course. As noted earlier, at least one state inquiry has recommended mandatory adoption of this practice for all beginning teachers.

The articulation of non-award INSET with pre-service teacher education has posed many difficulties and there clearly needs to be more collaboration between those making general in-service provisions and the tertiary pre-service education staff, at least in attempting to understand the purpose of each and the needs of the beginning teacher.

The opportunity for a somewhat different kind of link between INSET and pre-service training arises through the universal teaching practice requirements of the latter. It has always been realized that the supervising teachers in co-operating schools can, under the right conditions, benefit from participation in the *practicum*. Similarly, the *practicum* has served to keep tertiary staff alive to emerging issues in schools. Some institutions are now attempting to gain more from these opportunities, although less formally than in the UK project undertaken by Henderson *et al* (1978). Deakin University's 'high activity schools' provide an example of the generalization of this approach.

Involvement in non-award INSET

So far the emphasis has been placed on award-bearing courses as a means of INSET. Responses to the questionnaire mentioned above show that colleges and universities use both internal and external funding to provide a variety of short courses ranging from one day to several weeks. One or two such courses span a year or more. The number of teachers involved in a particular activity also varies considerably, from as few as ten to several hundred. Generally only a small number of staff are involved in any single activity — usually one or two, but, in some cases, up to ten. The kinds of activity reported were extremely varied — helping schools organize school-based curriculum development, training in supervision of student teachers, courses in curriculum studies in special areas, eg science, and workshops on the implementation of curriculum guides, to mention just a few.

A number of institutions have formalized these activities through the establishment of a teacher centre on campus and/or a department of continuing education. The former not only provide for in-service activities but have established links with, and encouraged use by, the local community.

Not only do institutions take responsibility for a wide range of shorter in-service activities, but very many individual members of staff also participate in activities arranged by other bodies, for example, teacher centres, professional associations, schools, state education departments, and the like. These activities run the gamut from consultancies to teaching in short courses. College and university staff are frequently closely involved with the organization of these in-service activities, influence their direction, and play a key role in evaluation studies of them. Their unofficial contribution is thus considerable.

Conclusion

Many of the non-award activities undertaken in colleges and universities are in part externally funded through state development committees or from the state department of education. However, in submissions to the National Inquiry into Teacher Education presently being conducted, a common theme has been that, while institutions recognize the importance of these modes of teacher education, they are simply not receiving funds from the Tertiary Education Commission to carry them out. For example, the submission from one college, which has contributed considerably to such activities, stated: 'The college faces increasing problems in meeting requests to provide services on a partially funded or totally unfunded basis. It seems totally unrealistic to expect it to do so'.

Two points can be made about this situation. First, Australian colleges and universities rely almost totally on government funding and recurrent expenses, and very little on endowments or benefactions — the colleges hardly at all. Given the extent to which business and industry in Australia rely on schools and tertiary institutions for the trained workforce, and their current interest in the pre-vocational purposes of education, this is surprising.

Secondly, the funding arrangement is evidence of the assumption that the role of colleges and universities is primarily to provide formal courses for qualifications. Indeed the report of the Queensland inquiry makes this explicit. 'Recommendation 21: The main role of tertiary institutions in in-service education should be that of providing formal courses...' (Bassett, 1978: 94). However, this assumption, which derives from a particular view of the nature of colleges and universities, is not universally shared. Many institutions are striving for funding to widen their range of activities in more general forms of INSET, and are already devoting a significant proportion of their resources to these activities.

There has been a very large increase in the number and variety of formal award-bearing courses available to teachers as a means of in-service education. These courses are gradually striking a balance between the needs for intellectual refreshment, conceptualizations of schooling and the teaching-learning process, and the demands of practice. There has been a corresponding increase in the provision of a variety of non-award INSET activities. There is some evidence that colleges and universities in Australia are increasingly sharing the former task with the rest of the profession and also coming themselves to be associated more fully with the latter.

There has yet to be any more intimate coupling of the two forms, in which more general INSET activities can be used to gain credit towards professional qualifications.

References

Allwood, L M (1975) *Australian Schools: The Impact of the Australian Schools Commission* Australian International Press and Publications: Melbourne

Bassett, G W (1978) *1978 Review of Teacher Education in Queensland* Report of the Committee appointed by the Board of Advanced Education and the Board of Teacher Education to advise on desirable developments in teacher education in Queensland: Brisbane

Batten, M (1979) *Report of a National Evaluation of the Development Program* (Schools Commission Evaluation Studies) Schools Commission: Canberra

Cameron, P (1978) *The Cost and Use of Resources for In-Service Education* Schools Commission Services and Development Program, Discussion/Review Paper No 2, Schools Commission: Canberra

Campbell, W J (1975) *Being a Teacher in Australian State Government Schools* Australian Advisory Committee on Research and Development in Education Report No 5, Australian Government Publishing Service: Canberra

Campbell, W J, Evans, G T, Philp, HWS and Levis, D S (1977) *The STEP Project: A Study of Three-year Primary Teacher Education Programmes* Report to the Commission on Advanced Education: Canberra

Campbell, W J and Robinson, N M (1979) *What Australian Society Expects of its Schools, Teachers and Teaching* Department of Education, University of Queensland: Brisbane

Collins, C W and Hughes, P W (1979) Expectations of secondary schools: a study of the views of students, teachers and parents *in* Williams (1979)

Cove, M (1975) Implications of the Australian Schools Commission for teacher development *in* Allwood (1975)

Department of Education and Science (1977) *Education in Schools: A Consultative Document* HMSO: London

Evans, G T (1978) *Teacher Decision Making* Paper delivered to the Conference of the Queensland Chapter of the Australian College of Education, September 1978

Henderson, E, Merritt, J and Mortimer, D (1978) *The Development of a School-focused Pattern of INSET* Paper presented to the International Workshop on School-focused In-service Education of Teachers in Bournemouth, England, March 1978

Ingvarson, L (1977) *Some Effects of the Teacher Development Program in Victoria* Monash University: Melbourne

Otto, E P, Gasson, I S H and Jordan E (1979) Perceived problems of beginning teachers *South Pacific Journal of Teacher Education* 7 1/2: 28-33

Perrott, C (1979) *The Context of the Operational Curriculum in the Primary School and its Impingements* Unpublished MEd thesis, University of New England: Armidale

Skilbeck, M, Evans, G T and Harvey, J (1977) *In-service Education and Training — Australian Innovations* Curriculum Development Centre: Canberra

Tisher, R P, Fyfield, J A and Taylor, S M (1979) *Beginning to Teach Vol II* Education Research and Development Committee Report No 20, Australian Government Publishing Service: Canberra

Williams, B R (1979) *Education, Training and Employment* Report of the Committee of Inquiry into Education and Training, Volume 1, Australian Government Publishing Service: Canberra

Part 4: Case Studies of Innovations

13. Planning school policies for INSET: the SITE Project

Keith Baker

Summary: The SITE Project is studying the problems and issues involved as school staff, with the help of the employers and outside support agencies (eg colleges), attempt to develop and implement school-focused in-service education and training (INSET) programmes. Schools have responded to an external project stimulus, requesting them to identify their in-service needs, and then support agencies have attempted to meet their school-formulated INSET programmes. The programmes frequently involve an increase in school-based activities, eg classroom consultancy, work with visiting experts, talks to staff at the school by a visitor, and the formation of teacher co-operative work groups supported by an outsider. Some, but not all, project schools have moved towards planned INSET programmes. Staff motivation towards and participation in INSET has been increased and various change effects have been identified. Despite school difficulties in conducting a needs analysis and certain logistic difficulties of the approach for support agencies, the school-focused approach appears to have considerable potential for the development of schools and for more effective teacher involvement with INSET.

Project rationale and focus

The Schools and In-Service Teacher Education (SITE) Evaluation Project is funded by the Department of Education and Science and the research team is centred at the University of Bristol School of Education Research Unit. SITE is primarily concerned with the development of planned approaches by schools towards the use of in-service education and training (INSET) for teachers. This approch involves a fundamental shift in the focus and reasons for involvement in INSET away from the present generalized and individualistic approach to a specific and more collegial basis. The approach rests upon staff consideration of the needs of a particular school and definition of the areas in which INSET may help as the basis for the formulation of a programme of INSET activities. The programme is clearly focused upon the INSET requirements of a particular school and the activities may therefore be designated as *school-focused INSET*.

The project team adopted the view that 'the distinguishing characteristic of school-focused INSET is that it is targeted on the needs of a particular school or group within a school. The actual activity may take place on-site or off-site and equally importantly may be internally provided by certain school staff or externally provided by an outside agency like a college or a university' (Bolam and Baker, 1978).

Some of the principal components in a school-focused approach to INSET were set out in an early paper in this field by Hoyle (1972) who suggested that:

1. INSET should be linked to specific school innovations.
2. INSET should focus on functioning groups (a departmental team or a whole primary school staff).
3. Schools should establish their own staff development programmes.
4. Schools should receive external support including consultancy services.

The theoretical bases of the project were derived partly from the above, partly from the work of Havelock (1969, 1973) on problem-solving schools and change agent roles (catalyst, resource-linker, solution giver and process helper); and partly from studies on the implementation of change. We have viewed schools as open social systems of a potentially problem-solving kind, but taken as problematic both the extent to which they did or could engage in systematic problem-solving and the extent to which they did or could make systematic and effective use of outside resource agencies. These problems are being studied in the context of the SITE project as attempts are being made to initiate a school-focused INSET policy for the school as a whole, functional groups (department, age-range or task groups) and individual teachers.

The evaluation activities were primarily focused upon:

1. the practical problems for all involved in providing a concentrated programme of in-service activities in response to school-formulated statements of needs;
2. the effects, implications and generalizability of this approach for the individual teachers, departments, schools, INSET providing agencies and Local Education Authorities (LEAs);
3. the development and utility of on-site INSET activities.

Project outline and structure

The project is spread across four Local Education Authorities (LEAs) in England with a total of 49 schools and just over 1000 teachers involved. There are certain differences in the bases of the project in the LEAs involved, which are indicated in Table 1.

The central principles of the project in the four LEAs involved were:

1. that the schools should engage in a needs analysis to determine the INSET requirements of staff by whatever means they considered appropriate;
2. that these requirements should be put in order of priority and formulated into a programme of suggestions for INSET activities, but that teacher involvement was to be on a voluntary basis:
3. that the programme was to be given to a Project Co-ordinator, or external 'linkage agent', who would commence negotiations to find a suitable provider and facilitate contact between the provider and school;
4. that the providers were to respond supportively, and by prior agreement, giving some degree of priority to the teachers in the project schools for admission to the normal INSET courses which they provided; also, if possible without undue cost, they were to service requests for experts to go on 'consultancy' work to the schools or provide courses at the schools with a rather smaller membership than might normally be the case.

Features	LEAs A and B	LEAs C and D
1. Initiative for project	University research team	The LEAs
2. Criteria for deciding no. and type of schools	University research team	The LEAs
3. Size of project	A — 2 schools — rural B — 2 schools — urban	C — 18 schools — urban D — 27 schools — part urban/part rural
4. Length of action programme	One year	Two years
5. Project funds	For evaluation only	For evaluation (½ time appointment) plus Action Co-ordinator and secretarial services
6. Co-ordination work	a. DES Steering Committee for A and B b. LEA Adviser doing this in addition to normal workload c. School co-ordinator in each school d. No project committees in A or B	a. DES Steering Committee for C and D b. Special appointment on half-time basis — Project Co-ordinator c. School co-ordinator in each school d. D had two area committees at which school co-ordinators met C had occasional meetings for school co-ordinators
7. Teacher release	A and B promised some 'extra' release in addition to normal LEA policy. Clear understanding that LEA resource inputs be limited.	C and D undertook to allow teacher release between the 1-2% level to facilitate involvement in INSET during school time.

Table 1 *Differences in project bases between the LEAs involved*

The schools therefore were to have control of the formulation of an INSET programme focusing on their own defined areas of needs, which could include on-site activities (eg at the school) with resources provided from a variety of external sources. They were, in effect, to have 'favoured' status with some degree of extra resources to support an intensive programme of school-focused INSET which was particularly aimed at group or whole staff requirements.

Project implementation

We may now consider how this idea worked out in practice when the schools, providers and co-ordinators began to implement the project.

Needs analysis

In two LEAs (A and B) schools began their needs analysis during the summer term and before the end of term in July had devised outline programmes or submitted lists of needs to their external 'linkage agent' for negotiation with providing agencies. All the schools in these LEAs were well into their action programmes by October 1978. As two LEAs (C and D) had joined the project at a later date, their preliminary meetings with the teachers did not occur until the summer term. Many schools delayed the needs analysis process until the autumn term and their action programmes were commenced at various times, but most had begun by January 1979.

It must be stressed that this project was in the hands of the teachers and no directives had been given about how to conduct a needs analysis. Indeed, the evaluation team were particularly concerned to ascertain just how schools would go about determining a programme. A variety of procedures were used by the schools, eg:

1. some primary schools held full staff meetings and open discussions resulting in the formulation of programmes;
2. some collected individual staff opinions which were simply collated and then presented as school 'needs';
3. some devised and used their own questionnaires to ascertain staff views and/or used rating schedules to establish views about priorities;
4. some secondary schools set up INSET committees to discuss issues and formulate programme suggestions;
5. some held no formal meetings and did not collect views in any formal way but took some informal soundings of staff views.

Some overlap of these methods did occur, eg one school used a combination of (3) and (5). There are questions relating to the extent of head teachers' input into the discussions or into lists presented as a result of methods (2) and (5) particularly. Some of the above methods fall far short of staff jointly deciding a programme and this may relate to the degree of staff motivation to participate in proposed action. In schools where full meetings were held, it was reported that the group agreement, together with the realization of involvement in a project, did constitute some sort of pressure on staff to participate in activities. Thus an important aspect of participatory discussion and joint identification of needs is its role in increasing awareness and in motivating staff to participate in the subsequent activities designed to meet the needs.

The methods used in most cases lacked sophistication; no formal models of needs analysis technique were used (cf Houston *et al*, 1978). From questionnaire and interview responses the evaluators concluded that the needs analysis was conducted in a superficial way in many schools and the validity of the 'needs' was questionable. This may be seen in the nature of the requests made to the Project Co-ordinators which often merely indicated broad areas (eg mathematics or language) with no attempt to specify detail.

Many schools had difficulties with the needs analysis process, which requires not only a degree of openness and co-operation but also the commitment of time, usually after school. Primary schools with their smaller staff numbers and less complex organizational structures, seemed to find method (1) a much easier and more 'natural' approach than did secondary schools, which usually felt a need to gather information and put INSET as an agenda item for Departmental meetings, Heads of Department meetings, etc. Several set up committees to plan

INSET for the school (Hider, 1978). If these continue to function effectively after the project ends, they will constitute a clear innovation institutionalized within the school management structure for INSET, and the attendant processes will then, of course, be open to further development and sophistication.

School INSET programmes

Response to the project in terms of INSET activity has also varied widely. One or two schools virtually rejected the approach and mounted no special school-focused activities. Some staffs have responded by engaging in more INSET activity but are doing so as individuals without any clear relationship to group or whole staff needs. More INSET activity by a school staff should not be confused with the planned school-focused approach to INSET which many of the schools are beginning to develop.

A school-focused approach can, of course, include some individual teachers engaging in particular activities related to particular school needs. Frequently it is reflected in a growth of school-based activities, such as bringing in visiting experts as consultants, or having group discussion sessions or talks at school. An example of a primary school programme is given in Table 2 to illustrate the range of activities undertaken and how most of these relate to the previous discussion of needs at the school.

In this programme, a particularly active one, there was a mixture of activities. These include visiting experts and teachers themselves giving talks and leading discussions, demonstration lessons, classroom work with teachers and non-classroom activities, series of talks on a need identified by the school and, lastly, off-site activities. The programme essentially related to the preliminary identification of needs which was achieved by whole staff discussions with some participation in normal courses by individual staff. Some of these were clearly tied to identified needs; eg a unit for educationally sub-normal children had recently been established in the school and both the specialist teacher appointed and the head teacher attended a course on teaching in such a unit. This school made extensive use of outside experts to visit the school and work in a variety of curriculum areas. This was a departure from previous practice and it was seen as beneficial by the teachers; staff felt that they had not always prepared adequately for such visits and had not made the best possible use of them, but the general opinion was that they had learned a good deal about how to organize future visits to obtain more benefit. In this school the project has now ended but visits of this type are being continued.

Another primary school placed particular emphasis upon the need to visit other schools or educational institutions to observe or discuss matters which were relevant to their previous INSET activities. The school was allocated ten days of supply teacher time and after consultations with staff the head teacher made the necessary arrangements for the visits. In fact, most of these visits were to other schools but they also included a Language Development Unit and a Reading Centre. Many other teachers in the project schools opted for such visits but not to the same extent nor with such clear links to their whole INSET programme.

Teacher time for INSET

Some of the activities took place in school time, some in the teachers' own time;

Term and level	INSET subject	Type of activity	Number of teachers involved
Autumn 1978 Personal/group	Drama with 6-7 year old children	Visiting expert took lessons and held after school discussion with staff	4
	Music for beginners	Normal county course	2
	Language development	Normal county course	3
	Language and writing in primary school	Normal county course	2
Whole staff N = 11	Pottery and glazing techniques*	Demonstrations by one member	11
	Mathematics*	Visits to other schools	11
Spring 1979 Personal/group	Creative writing	Visiting expert to classrooms	variable weekly
	Children's literature	Normal county course	2
	Children's literature	Normal county course	2
Whole staff	Diagnostic testing*	Visiting expert lecture and discussion	11
	Language and reading	Visiting expert lecture and discussion	11
	Mathematics*	Visited other schools	11
Summer 1979 Personal/group	Creative writing continued	Visiting expert in classrooms	variable
	Gymnastics	Visiting expert demonstration	4
	Teaching ESN children	Normal county course	2
Long courses	BEd first degree	Normal courses	1
	Diploma in Advanced Studies in Education		1
	Mathematics for leaders		1

* The LEA allocates three days per calendar year (January to December) as INSET days for teachers during which no children attend. This school was able to have 4 days within this particular *school* year (September to July).

Table 2 *Primary school INSET programmes for one year*

the overall amounts involved in the previous programme are summarized in Table 3.

All the teachers agreed that such a programme could only be done as a 'one-shot' venture. They would not want such a high level of INSET activity as a permanent feature of school life, but thought this level of INSET investment could only be attempted, say, every four or five years.

INSET days are not allocated by all LEAs, and their classification as school time is frequently a matter of negotiation with teacher associations. The large amount of private time (345 hours) spent on INSET by the teachers in this school is impressive. Less than half of this time related to gaining further qualifications

	School time		After school
	Teacher release from classes (hours)	No release — consultant visits (hours)	Teacher time (hours)
Term 1	50	24	127
Term 2	10	12	78
Term 3	35	50	0
INSET days	—	220	—
Long courses	75	—	140
Totals	170	Consultancy — 86 INSET days — 220	345
Grand total of teacher time	170 + 306 + 345	=	821 hours

Table 3 *Teacher time for the INSET programme*

and most was accounted for by attendance at short courses. The school's use of visiting experts for 86 hours in school time (plus a further 10 hours after school not included in the table) was usually within classroom situations and no release was given to teachers for this. Indeed, 79 per cent of the total time required no release of teachers from classes and only 7 per cent was actually covered by specially allocated substitute teachers as the head teacher took some classes himself when staff were out for INSET activities. Thus the cost of this programme to the employing LEA was very small, with only ten days of substitute teacher time plus travel and other payments for visiting experts. Some of these were, in any case, within the LEA's own employ and did not figure as actual costs, but naturally if the exercise were to be costed fully they would have to be included.

The total use of paid substitute teacher time by the project schools in LEAs C and D for the school year 1978-9 is shown in Table 4. It must be stressed that the figures relate only to the use made of LEA-financed substitution and do not reflect the full amount of INSET activity during school hours.

Some primary schools wished to increase their liaison with secondary schools with which they were associated (and vice versa); much of this was done by visits arranged during the teachers' allocated non-teaching time. This use of non-teaching time and the use of internal staff to substitute for absent colleagues avoids the use of the LEA-financed substitute staff and disguises the actual extent of INSET activity during school time. Despite these reservations, the actual cost of the INSET activity in the first year of the project to the LEAs was relatively small, eg only three-quarters of a substitute teacher in one LEA (D), and less than one and a half in the other (C). It is possible that there was some lack of familiarity with the procedure for obtaining substitute teachers and that the delayed start of the scheme in these LEAs limited the use of them. This may increase during 1979-80. The full extent of teacher involvement in INSET and the range of activities that appear to have INSET benefits for teachers is difficult to establish through superficial investigations. Only in schools in which we conducted intensive case studies were we able to collect sufficient data to give a complete picture.

One concern about the principle of extending INSET activity during school time, which teachers often expressed to the evaluation team, was that harmful effects for children might result from frequent absence of the regular class teacher. The team therefore collected information about teacher absence in the case-study schools and the results for one secondary school are given in Table 5. This shows the number of 40-minute lessons missed by the 82 full-time teachers of one secondary school during the academic year 1978-9 together with the reasons given for absence.

These lessons were not actually 'lost' but the classes involved did not have their normal teacher at the time and had to be covered by someone else. The total number of lessons missed (5981) was 6.4 per cent of all timetabled periods and absence caused by involvement in INSET activities was 1 per cent of all timetabled lessons. Absence through illness was the major reason for missed lessons, as both the teachers and researchers expected, but the relatively small amount missed because of INSET, the extent of absence for 'other' reasons and the variety of reasons that entailed substantial absence caused surprise (Baker and Sikora, 1979). The problem is one of concern to teachers with implications for issues such as staffing ratios, continuity of pupil learning and school record keeping. In general, there is a lack of detailed work on the extent of teacher absence, the reasons for it and its effects upon pupils, colleagues and school efficiency.

LEA	Substitution time in LEA (in days)	Number of schools making use of the substitute teacher arrangements	Number of schools in the project
C	287	16	18
D	154	24	27

Table 4 *Use of substitute teacher time in LEAs C and D*

Project effects

The effects of such projects are difficult to evaluate, both in the short and long term, not only on the school generally, but also on particular teachers' attitudes and behaviour towards their colleagues or pupils, and especially on the ultimate goal of pupil learning.

Some of the specific results brought about by the INSET programme referred to earlier included:

— the adoption of a different approach by some teachers to the discussion of mathematical concepts, particularly the use of mathematical terms and language with children;
— the adoption of a different style of work presentation as a stimulus to the children's creative story writing resulting, in the teachers' view, in increased motivation, especially amongst the more able pupils;
— greater use being made of certain materials and equipment in the school (eg clay and kiln) thereby widening the learning opportunities for children;
— adoption of particular books recommended and not previously known;
— adoption of a different technique of teaching mathematics (eg through gaming strategies);
— experimentation in drama methods with children.

Reason	Year group*						Total for each reason	Percentage of lessons missed
	1*	2	3	4	5	6		
1 INSET activity	158	162	202	156	147	80	905	15
2 Illness	346	446	254	338	371	171	1926	32
3 Others consisting of:								
a personal	127	150	110	144	125	70	726	
b trips	70	104	74	62	47	49	406	
c drama/music	56	74	85	76	37	59	387	
d meetings/visits	158	90	61	86	70	71	536	
e exams/tests	32	64	51	45	106	38	336	
f sports	20	33	37	24	48	15	177	
g dept. business	20	32	22	68	74	28	244	
h unspecified	50	61	38	77	82	30	338	
'Other' total:	533	608	478	582	589	360	3150	53
Total periods missed (categories 1 + 2 + 3)	1037	1216	934	1076	1107	611	5981	100%
Periods missed as % of total missed (5981)	17.3	20.3	15.6	18.0	18.5	10.2	99.9%	

* Year group 1 = 11-12 year olds, etc.

Table 5 Lessons missed during one academic year in one secondary school

The staff believed that there may have been other effects, some of which they found difficult to identify precisely and others they thought were of a longer term nature and could only be detected by a later investigation.

Earlier I noted that one school had engaged in a series of visits. Some resultant effects were that most of the teachers brought back notes or worksheets from other schools; a library cataloguing system was established; a speaker was invited to address staff about a reading scheme they had seen operating; and a new reference book was brought into use. The teachers were enthusiastic about the visits and all of them referred to their generally stimulating and broadening effect. Some specifically indicated that the visits had helped them to overcome feelings of isolation. All staff referred to the positive value of the reinforcing effect or reassurance that they had derived from seeing things they did also being done elsewhere (and this effect of visits has been remarked upon by many other teachers). No measurements were made of these suggested gains in self-confidence but this could prove to be a worthwhile concern for future research.

Similar effects are reported to have occurred in many of the project schools, with clear supporting evidence that teachers have changed their views or attitudes or teaching methods as a result of particular INSET activities. This is not to say that all the activities provided have been successful. Some have had no effect other than to confirm negative views about INSET. Nevertheless, we have concluded that, in terms of practical classroom and everyday school problems of concern to a school staff, much of the short-term INSET provided in response to school definitions of need appears to have given satisfaction to teachers, to have been perceived as valuable, and to have produced change.

Towards school planning for INSET

Whatever the value of long-term release may be, the fact is that most teachers never experience it. In a questionnaire at the beginning of the project, only 6.2 per cent of our sample of 990 respondents said they had had such release. For most teachers, INSET is typically experienced through traditional courses mounted by providing agencies which themselves determine the content and run them at central venues such as colleges. Only 27 per cent of our sample said they had been involved in any INSET provided at their own school and only 26 per cent had been involved in INSET away from school together with several or all of their colleagues. But 65 per cent of our respondents said they would attend more INSET if it focused on their school's particular requirements, 70 per cent thought there were general school problems for which INSET for the whole staff was appropriate and 73 per cent thought that head teachers and their deputies should take action to use INSET for staff development. Although 82 per cent thought that their type of school *should* formulate a clear INSET policy, only 13 per cent agreed that their schools already had one.

School planning of a policy for INSET does not seem widespread at present, and deciding a policy through a needs analysis process appears to present some difficulties for schools. Yet the SITE project evidence strongly suggests that staff motivation is high for involvement with INSET defined by them as relevant to their needs, and that change results quite quickly from such INSET.

School-focused and school-based INSET poses several problems. One concerns the costs and logistics of provision for the employers and INSET providing agencies. Another is that teachers' hopes of quick solutions to almost any problem may be unduly raised if school-focused projects are not presented with caution. A third problem is that once schools have submitted their programmes they usually want a quick and positive response which providing agencies may not find easy to make. From our experience in the SITE project we consider that the benefits to both the providing agencies and schools appear to justify efforts to increase this type of INSET activity. Naturally the implementation of complex innovations such as school-focused INSET planning for several schools within an LEA can be expected to encounter problems. The following suggestions based on experience in the SITE project may help others to meet some of the problems.

1. Consideration should be given to what appropriate 'catalytic agents' are available which could be used to encourage schools to engage in planning a school-focused INSET policy.
2. A preliminary period of at least six-nine months should be allowed for school needs analysis and planning.
3. Schools should be offered the opportunity to involve outsiders (eg advisers or persons from providing agencies) in their planning discussions, but there must be due regard to the sensitivity of such work and it may help if those involved have credibility as practitioners in the eyes of the teachers. They must have an overview of possible INSET strategies and be familiar with locally available INSET opportunities.
4. Some additional resource allocations for the schools involved is required. *For both items 3 and 4, steady and constant support is advised rather than preliminary efforts which are left to fizzle out.*
5. School programmes should be limited in scope and framed as specifically as possible. Providers should consult with the schools about programme suggestions before going ahead.
6. Providers should be alerted to the likelihood of demand so that some preliminary allocation of staff can be made to the project schools. At least one fairly swift response to a specific item should be made once the INSET programme is submitted.
7. A school-focused approach usually results in requests for school-based activities and as much care as possible should be taken to ensure that the first major school-based activity is successful.

When schools are invited to engage in planning their involvement with INSET through a school-focused approach, it should be stressed that the programme must be balanced. The complexity of teacher requirements for professional support requires a variety of provision of and approaches to INSET. Between them these must supply support for realizing specific school goals, for helping the teachers' classroom practice and for ensuring the professional development of teachers with a breadth of vision and open attitudes in this period of rapid social and technological change. A school INSET policy needs to avoid excessive introversion and it must balance school, group and individual needs to attain these results.

References

Baker, K and Sikora, J (1979) *SITE Project Evaluation Report No 3 (AW) Covering for Staff Release and Absence: A Secondary School Case Study* (mimeo) SITE

Project, School of Education Research Unit: University of Bristol

Bolam, R and Baker, K (1978) *The Schools and In-Service Teacher Education (SITE) Evaluation Project* Paper presented at the DES/OECD/CERI International Workshop Conference at Bournemouth, England on School-Focused In-Service Education and Training (INSET) of Teachers

Havelock, R G (1969) *Planning for Innovation through Dissemination and Utilization of Knowledge* Centre for Research on Utilization of Scientific Knowledge, Institute for Social Research: Ann Arbor, Michigan

Havelock, R G and Havelock, M C (1973) *Training for Change Agents: A Guide to the Design of Training Programs in Education and Other Fields* Centre for Research on Utilization of Scientific Knowledge, Institute for Social Research: Ann Arbor, Michigan

Hider, A T (1978) *Evaluation Report No 2E: Determining INSET Requirements in Secondary Schools* (mimeo) SITE Project, School of Education Research Unit: University of Bristol

Houston, W R *et al* (1978) *Assessing School/College/Community Needs* Centre for Urban Education: University of Nebraska, Omaha

Hoyle, E (1972) *Innovation and the Social Organization of the School (Creativity of the School: Technical Report No 1)* OECD/CERI: Paris

14. The impact of research on an educational programme for school leaders in Sweden

Mats Ekholm

Summary: A compulsory educational programme for school leaders (heads/principals and deputy heads/principals) in Sweden is discussed in the light of educational research on change and development. The educational programme is two years long and consists of three components — courses, home periods and 'socially aimed practice' whose purposes are described. The origin and the methods of the educational programme are illuminated through a discussion of the research experiences and commission work which had an impact on the programme. This discussion is conducted in the light of the three main targets for the educational programme — the development of the school, the development of the school leader role and the personal development of the school leader who takes part in the programme.

The aims and planning of school leader training

By the end of the 1980s all Swedish school leaders* will have been through a compulsory training programme which started to run on a regular basis in 1976. In all essentials, this training is based on the recommendations of the report of the PLUS Commission (PLUS = Plan for the Training of School Leaders). In its comment on the Swedish Inner Workings of School Reform (SIA) Commission report, the National Board of Education suggested that the training should be of the type that has now been introduced. Thus, the Government, in the SIA bill, combined the training plans proposed by the PLUS Commission and the National Board of Education, and Parliament voted in favour of the Bill in the Spring of 1976.

The school leader training is carried out by ten instructional teams, consisting not only of instructors but also of school inspectors, chief education officers, local politicians and trade union representatives. The goals of the school leader training can be summarized briefly in the following three points. It should contribute to:

1. the development of the activities of the school unit;
2. the development of the role of the school leader;
3. the personal development of the individual participant.

School leader training is a part of the development of the school as a social unit, which is aimed at making school activities more meaningful for the pupils,

---

*Throughout, I use the term 'school leader' to include head teachers, deputy heads and also education officers.

increasing internal democracy and openness, and creating a better balance between those activities of the school which aim at developing pupil performance and good personal relationships.

Concentration on the development of the role of the school leader, together with associated personal development, is largely concerned with changing his way of working. In the training plans, a schedule for the school leader's way of working is drawn up. This schedule is usually summarized in four stages, all of which interact in a perpetual cycle, namely: observation, preparation, decision-making and taking action. Each is seen as being concerned with developing democratic leadership within the school and in society generally. Fulfilling such a leadership role in an organization such as the school demands self-knowledge, emotional maturity and the capacity for self-renewal. It also involves the ability to understand and improve personal relationships within the organization.

The components of the training programme

Each individual participant undergoes training over a period of two years. The programme consists of three different elements: course periods, home periods, and 'socially aimed practice'.

Altogether, the course occupies 25 days over the two years in periods of two to four days. The purpose of these concentrated course periods is partly to give the school leaders an opportunity to prepare their work during the home periods, and partly to deepen their understanding of the school and its way of working. This understanding is built up through a consideration of the school's work process and the personal role of the school leader. Patterns of study are largely based on the assumptions of group psychology. During the main part of the course, the participants work in small groups on tasks concerning the function of the school: relationships within the group itself are also discussed. Course membership is around 30, with small groups consisting of from five to seven participants differing in background and experience.

The training programme is based on the concept of a steering process taking place in the interaction between the participants and the instructors. The longer a course proceeds, the more the participants are expected to take part in this steering process. The work during the home periods is also drawn up according to an agreement between the participant and the instructor. The initiative here, however, lies more with the school leader and his colleagues at school. Work during the home periods mainly involves scrutinizing the work process at school itself and the attempts made to initiate new developments. The course instructors require the school leaders to formulate their own 'home-work' tasks. They then make several visits during the home periods to those schools where the school leaders work in order to discuss the development of the individual school and the specific situation of the school leader. During these home periods participants work with other school leaders in the same community. (Sweden has 277 'Kommuner', here called communities.)

They have study groups on subjects they choose themselves, eg the financial situation of the community, pedagogical theories, or environmental planning. The chief education officer usually functions as group leader during these community meetings and local politicians may also sometimes participate. The meetings are not included in the 25 training days.

The agreement between the government and the union organizations for school leaders specifies how much time may be used by the school leaders for their work during the home periods, with the result that approximately one-tenth of the school leaders' working hours have been set aside for the home period work.

In the spring of 1976 Parliament decided that Swedish school leaders should carry out 'socially aimed practice' in connection with their basic training. This practice extends over two periods, each of a fortnight. During one of these periods, the school leader involves himself in one of the industries of his locality. The main purpose of this experience is to familiarize the school leader with knowlege of the working conditions experienced by parents, and which may face the pupils themselves on leaving school. During the other two-week period the school leader works with some part of the child and youth welfare programme of the local council. The purpose of this period is to facilitate co-operation between different community agencies.

To summarize: the training programme for the school leaders consists of about 85 days of study (25 course days, 20 days of 'socially aimed practice' and 40 days of home periods) spread out over a period of two years.

The PLUS Commission

The drawing up of the aims and organization of school leader training extended over several years, involving a committee of about 85 members (mainly school leaders) for almost two years. The number participating in these preparations was so large that it is impossible to determine the source of the ideas which contributed towards the basic plan. There is no doubt, however, that within the committee there were a number of groups which made key contributions to the final synthesis. Ideas on how the training could and should be carried out have subsequently been developed within the instructional teams and within the standing group which has been responsible for implementing the training programme.

The following section will discuss some of the central ideas of school leader training. An attempt is made to trace the origin of these ideas, and the ideological background to the current school leader training will be discussed in relation to the three broad goals of the training previously mentioned. The discussion on each goal follows the same pattern. Firstly, there is a short description of the characteristics of the training activities with a view to the goal in question. This is followed by a discussion of how these ideas were turned into action in the light of four different kinds of influence: experience from research and development work, relevant literature on pedagogy, personal contacts, and the work of the PLUS Commission.

Development of the school

Each school and its management area should ideally be organized in such a way that its activities correspond to the curriculum. Very few schools manage to achieve in their activities a quality as high as that demanded by political objectives as expressed in the curriculum and in the SIA bill. Patterns of work, contacts between the teachers and pupils, and the distribution of power rarely match expectations; traditional approaches remain strong. Thus most schools are in need of support for their innovative activities.

School leader training, and broader forms of staff development, are based on the view that school development is possible despite the existence of conservative forces within the structure of the school and within society generally. This optimism is based on the belief that development *can* be initiated by forces within the school unit, providing that appropriate external support is available.

Initiating processes of development

This fundamental view permeated the entire PLUS Commission. Various assumptions and theories on the process of development were discussed in the leading groups of the Commission. According to one of these theories, development occurs when there has been some disturbance in the equilibrium of that which is to be developed. A state of absolute and lasting equilibrium is hardly ever achieved. Instead, the process of development perpetually gives rise to new states of disequilibrium, which, in their turn, can form points of departure for a further process of development. According to this idea of development, interaction with the environment leads to disequilibrium. In this manner, the conditions as well as the necessity for development are created. However, need for development is not always obvious to those who live at the centre of events. What needs to be developed cannot in many cases be experienced until a general view of what is taking place has been grasped. Thus, where a state of disequilibrium is experienced within a system, the alternative ways of functioning which emerge precede the potential for development. When a part of the whole has changed, it often follows that the whole must be changed. Then the process of development has been initiated. Important parts of school leader training are the efforts to clarify the necessity of development and to describe the disequilibrium of the local school structure. This is mainly brought about by the participants making 'observational reports' in which they try to describe the pattern of management in their school and their daily experience. Ideally, the school leaders present the observations to colleagues in their own schools. The discrepancy between the observations of the school leader and those of others active in the school creates a fruitful synthesis of perceptions of the school held by different groups.

These ideas on how to initiate the process of development in the school are largely based on the experience gained from a research project at the Department of Educational Research at Göteberg University. The project, which was carried out during the first half of the 1970s, was called the SOS (Studies on School Socialization) project. This project studied the school and the potential social development of pupils during their years at comprehensive school. The research group chose to attempt to clarify their questions by using a research strategy directed at change. They intended to bring about actual changes in everyday school routines and limit their studies to a few experiments, but in order to instigate these changes in normal school routines they tried a number of different methods of initiating the process of development within the local school unit. Three particular methods were tried: 'curriculum ideology discussions', the presentation of suggestions for activities, and the presentation of concrete descriptions of reality. The experience of working with these three methods showed that the third strategy — concrete descriptions of reality — proved to be the most effective. Thus, in current programmes for the training of school leaders, efforts are being made to equip school personnel with the competence to give accounts of these results so that they can·be used to help initiate change.

School development and time

The school leaders participate in a basic training programme extending over two years. During this period, the intention is to initiate the process of school development. The PLUS Commission had the somewhat higher ambition of ensuring that the process became well-established during the period. This optimism has been somewhat dampened since the training began on a regular basis and routines were established. Gradually, attention has been increasingly paid to the extension of school leader training and to the establishment of a support organization for the development of schools throughout the country. Training programmes are now based on the recognition that significant developments in the school take a good deal of time. Changing the forms of work and the relationships between individuals in the school — something which is often required for the school to meet the requirement for a meaningful period of learning for the pupils — seems to require a period of approximately five to seven years. Only a change process over that length of time has a realistic chance of achieving tangible effects. During the current training programmes, instructors and participants pay considerable attention to the rate at which and and the way in which demands for taking initiatives in schools are made. Instructors find it essential throughout to stress to school leaders the fact that the two years of training are only the beginning. In that time, participants can only create the initial conditions for the development of their own schools.

This stress on the length of time required has come from several directions. Naturally members of the PLUS Commission have been aware of how slowly the development of local schools has proceeded, in spite of the relatively rapid rate of organizational reforms. Experience from many years of further training in Sweden has also shown that changes in the local school do not take place very rapidly. The few systematic follow-up studies that have been made on adults who have participated in further training in Sweden also show that the effects of further training are neither particularly obvious nor lasting (eg Carlberg, 1978; Lander, 1978). Experience from various research and development projects within the field of education has also shown how slowly development within the individual school unit takes place. This applies not least to the experience gained from the SOS project previously mentioned.

International literature points to the length of time necessary for developing organizations such as schools, and account has been taken of this evaluation in the school leader training project. Rogers and Shoemaker (1971), for example, distinguish five crucial stages in the adjustment process which is a prerequisite for a successful innovation: 'awareness, interest, trial, evaluation, adoption'. Rogers' model has been used in educational research (Miles, 1964) but it has also been subjected to criticism (Gross et al, 1971). It cannot be directly applied to innovations within schools since one of the basic assumptions of the model is that at any given moment in the process of innovation, each individual has the possibility of making a personal decision as to whether or not to try the innovation: within schools, this is rarely the case. The individual teacher, for example, is constrained by current educational policy. His freedom to take initiatives is limited and he cannot entirely reject that role which is allocated by his superiors in the social system. The distribution of roles within the educational system means that individual pupils have even less chance of initiating new notions of work, for example, since these are imposed by the teacher.

However, the fact that the individual's freedom of action is limited by the educational system does not mean that he is prevented from resisting, or must be slow in adopting changes. Gross *et al* (1971) are of the opinion that the organizational structure of the school results in the innovation process taking a different form there from other fields in which innovation studies have been carried out, eg agriculture, technical industry and medical work. Three basic stages of the innovation process can be distinguished in the attempt to change the work patterns within an organization ('planned organizational change'). These stages are:

1. the period of initiation of an organizational innovation;
2. the period of its attempted implementation;
3. the period during which an innovation is incorporated into the organization.

What distinguishes Gross and his research team from other researchers who have dealt with problems of innovation is the fact that they have studied only one attempt at innovation and have concentrated on understanding the implementation stage of the innovation process.

The research team is of the opinion that this stage is too often ignored and they call for more studies to follow the actual innovation process over time. The study carried out by Gross and his colleagues is *quasi* social anthropological in approach. Smith and Keith (1971) spent two years studying the change process in a newly established elementary school, and Schmuck *et al* (1972) reported on a number of attempts at change over a period of two years in elementary schools in Oregon.

Gross *et al* identified five conditions which they believe must be fulfilled in order to facilitate reforms in patterns of working and studying in a regular school. Those who participate in the attempt at change must understand the new form of work in their own terms. They must also be able to acquire the competence to work in a new way, and there must be material accessible which makes it possible to work in this way. The organization in itself must be open to changes in parts other than those which are directly affected by attempts at change, so that the latter are not hampered by relics of a previous system, and those who participate in the attempt at change must do so voluntarily.

Before one can know how the school can be organized to maximize the conditions for development, it is necessary to increase one's knowledge of the innovation process itself and its different phases. If the innovation is in patterns of work and relationships, as in the case of school leader training, it is possible to distinguish four phases in the process of development: preparatory, accommodation, application and dissemination phases.

The development of the school leader role — a development of the roles at school

The role of the school leader is a component of the social structure of the school and changing this role involves bringing about simultaneous changes in related roles. Experience from the SOS project (Ekholm, 1976) suggests that one of the most effective ways of bringing about desirable social development in the pupils is to create a pupil role which demands that the pupil acts in a way that coincides with the goals of the curriculum, ie an active, responsible, independent and co-operative role. However, there is little scope for this role in the ordinary school since the teacher dominates most of the collective relationships. Just as the roles of the teacher and of the pupil are interdependent, the teacher role is dependent on adjacent roles. In order to change the role of the school leader, it is necessary to work with these other roles.

Observations as a basis for role development

In the work to change the relationship between teachers and their pupils, the SOS project found it important to strengthen the role of the pupil. One way the need for this was found was through systematic observation of the everyday interaction between teachers and pupils. Methods for carrying out such observations were developed within the project. The intention was that the teachers should be able to use these methods to observe interaction within the school class, and in some instances teachers observed one another. These observations were followed by open and comradely discussion about the role situation. Some of these systematic classroom observations were presented to the teachers in order to initiate discussion about how the work-context of the classroom might be improved. The experience of role development gained from the SOS project led to the production of observation instruments which the school leaders were expected to use; it has also formed a basis for the school leader's systematic observations of his own behaviour. Self-observations have been made by some participants of the way in which they behave as school leaders and almost all the participants in the training programme have watched video-tapes of themselves role-playing typical school leader situations.

The roles of the change agent

Discussions in the PLUS Commission and later within the different instruction teams of the school leader training project have used the experience gained from the SOS project. During the SOS project the research group tried out various roles for the change agent (Havelock, 1973). The experience gained by the research group suggests that the most effective approach was to adopt a combination of different roles. The least effective role was that of the solution-giver. It is easy for the person who is expected to take the initiative also to present solutions to the problems experienced, but few others take notice of these suggested solutions. It is likely to prove far more effective for the change agent to act as a catalyst or as a process-helper while also aiding this development by the provision of resources.

In the contemporary school, the school leader has plenty of opportunity to function in the role of organizer of resources. He is the person in the school who normally deals with the financial authorities of the local council. But it is less natural for him to act as a catalyst in the development process. In school leader training, therefore, both aspects of the role are dealt with. Since the instructors meet the participants both during the concentrated course periods and in their schools, it is possible for the school leaders to take the instructors as role models, and they are encouraged to develop both aspects of the role themselves. The catalytic component is encouraged in the course of preparing the 'observational report' and when presenting these observations to the school staff.

Personal development

In one way or another, education aims to affect the personal development of the participant. This may involve encouraging the individual to increase his knowledge or it may be concerned with changing his attitudes. Thus this approach to the training of school leaders often aims at raising the individual participant's consciousness of his interaction with others. School leaders are expected to interact with other adults and with children in a democratic manner. The democratic climate of the school should be of such a quality that pupils will be encouraged to act democratically in various future contexts.

A democratic approach is quite demanding for the school leaders, particularly in terms of self-knowledge, emotional maturity and a capacity for self-renewal. It takes a long time to develop, and one could hardly expect it to emerge during a relatively short period of training. It requires close and recurring contact with other interested people who are capable of offering honest reactions. Within the project, the instructors and the participants themselves attempt to feed back to each other their reactions and also try to transfer these practices from the training programme to their own school situation.

The most important outcomes of the research work within the SOS project concern the work patterns of pupils. In co-operation with investigators from another project, the so called UKU ('experience learning and cognitive development') project based at the University of Göteberg, ways of influencing children's moral concepts were developed. These were based on developmental, psychological and educational assumptions. In order to make children aware of the patterns of interaction in which they were involved in their own schools, situations were created in which children had powerful experiences. Initially a large amount of time was set aside in which pupils gained experience through pre-planned situations. But eventually it became possible to deal with more spontaneous events. This ensured that the pupils reacted to real-life everyday situations.

Attempts to develop a more systematic way of handling experience in natural situations showed the necessity of putting this programme into practice in the normal educational environment. It appeared to work for young people in their interaction with one or two adults. In the school leader training, only adults who have relatively high professional status participate. Furthermore, in the training it has become essential to deal with experiences in a frank and open fashion. Some of the instructors have also embarked upon trying out this form of work in their own activities. Others still feel alienated from forms of work such as have been outlined above. The observations that have been made of the effects of this type of work on school leader training show that the participants are affected as individuals. Course participants have reported that these discussions, concerned with real experiences and having a critical/self-critical element, often led them to reflect on their own actions. Some participants claim this to be the element in the course from which they profited the most and report that it made them more confident in some ways and less so in others.

Participants initially try to pose their own questions about what they wish to learn. They then try to design or construct the ways in which they think they may find information which may clarify these questions. Then follows a phase of independent reflection on the information. This analysis takes place both from emotional and rational stances. The attitudes adopted by an individual in this phase then lead either to his finding confirmation that his previous ideas about the world around him were correct or else to his being forced to reconstitute these conceptions.

Concluding observations

School leader training is directed towards people who are at the very centre of school activities. Their everyday life is full of opportunities to learn about their own context. However, merely to experience a situation rarely generates a readiness to act in the future. It is also necessary to work on and process one's experiences. The school leader training project attempts to provide its participants with 'instruments' for carrying out this work. The pedagogics of school leader training are based on the assumption that knowledge is synonymous with readiness to act. This knowledge or readiness to act is built up by the individual learning to master the existing 'instruments' for understanding and action within the field to which this knowledge applies. He must also master the 'agreements' or 'conventions' that exist within this field of knowledge and know the background of the instruments and conventions. It is also essential that he has a knowledge of how the instruments and conventions are actually used. The last, and perhaps most important point, is that knowledge does not itself precipitate genuine readiness to act until the individual has taken a stance towards his knowledge. Not until such a position has been taken is it possible to attempt the application of the knowledge developed.

When the school leader training project was being planned there was a lively debate in the PLUS Commission on how the interaction between theory and practice should be organized within the training programme. Initially, there were two approaches. The first used as a point of departure the experience that had been gained from the research and development project that had been carried out at the Teacher Training College in Malmo in the beginning of the 1970s. This project essentially concentrated on analyses of professional positions including analyses of school leader roles. The results of the project provided an essential basis for the organization of school leader training, ie a common training for all school leaders. It was also a part of the work of the project to develop training programmes for school leaders, among others. An important component of these training programmes were the simulations of the school leader's work situation. By working through a number of simulated situations the school leaders were expected to increase their readiness to act in future situations. (*See also Chapter 18.*) Advocates of this approach maintained that future school leader training should use the simulation techniques extensively.

Another line of argument maintained that the point of departure should be the concrete and immediate experiences and problems that each participant brought with him from his own situation, since it should be possible to use the real world as a resource for learning. This approach would also motivate participants highly by making the purpose of their training more clearly relevant.

These two ways of creating readiness to act resulted in very different suggestions as to how the school leader training should be organized. Both ways had been tried out during experimental training which took place prior to and during the work of the PLUS Commission.

There were also sources of support for these developments. The simulation approach was supported by programmes of school leader training carried out in other parts of the world, above all in the United States. However, simulation was rejected by those who advocated direct and personal practice as the basis of training; they argued that simulation was less effective in preparing participants directly for the school leader profession.

The simulation approach was regarded as less appropriate when training people who had already had direct experience and were, in fact, actually in the situation with which they were being trained to cope. Eventually, it was decided to dispense with simulation approaches to training but the debate brought out more clearly views which had not previously been openly expressed.

School leader training and future R and D work

It remains to be seen whether the school leader training will be capable of successfully implementing the ideas on which it is based. The programme is being scrutinized not only by internal interest groups such as teachers' unions, instructors and participants, but also by educational politicians and other external agencies. The programme as a whole is being evaluated by a special research project which is based at the University of Linköping. There are also other research projects which may evaluate the programme more indirectly in connection with studies of the process of change in individual schools. Various R and D projects have had a considerable impact on the present school leader programme. An activity with as wide a scope as the school leader training needs much R and D support. In taking the trainee's description of reality as a point of departure for further development, the approach assumes the availability of expertise to help with the description and evaluation of the school context. It is also essential that the programme should be scrutinized by researchers and it may be necessary to draw upon the expertise of people from other countries who are experienced in the field of school development. Such contributions from people who are not directly involved with the work of the training often provide valuable insights into the development of the activities.

School leader training is constantly developing. This process must thus be supported by various forms of R and D work which aim at raising the quality of school leader training. It also seems important that training for R and D work is made available in order to carry out studies of the effects of training on local school development. Moreover, the results of such R and D projects would not only be of benefit to the school leader training, but would also be valuable for local development in general.

References

Carlberg, T (1978) *En Studie av Fortbiidning i Lag (A Study of Further Training in Teams)* Unpublished manuscript, Department of Educational Research: University of Linköping

Ekholm, M (1976) *Social Development in School: Summary and Excerpts* Reports from the Institute of Education, University of Göteberg **48:** 13

Gross, N, Giacquinta, J and Bernstein, M (1971) *Implementing Organizational Innovations* Harper and Row: New York

Havelock, R G (1973) *The Change Agent's Guide to Innovation in Education* Educational Technology Publications: Englewood Cliffs, NJ

Lander, R (1978) *Profeter i Egen Skola (Prophets in Your Own School)* Report No 168, Institute of Education, University of Göteberg

Miles, M B (ed) (1964) *Innovation in Education* Columbia University Teachers' College: New York

Rogers, E M and Shoemaker, F F (1971) *Communication of Innovations: A Cross Cultural Approach* Collier-Macmillan: London

Schmuck, R A, Runkel, P, Saturen, S, Martell, R and Derr, C B (1972) *Handbook of Organization Development in Schools* National Press Books: Palo Alto, Ca

Smith, L M and Keith, P M (1971) *Anatomy of Educational Innovation* John Wiley and Sons: New York

15. The American Teacher Corps Programme

William Smith

Summary: The goal of the American Teacher Corps programme is threefold: to strengthen the educational opportunities available to children in areas having concentrations of low-income families; to encourage colleges and universities to broaden their programme of teacher education; and to encourage institutions of higher education and local educational agencies to improve programmes of training and retraining for teachers, teacher aides and other educational personnel. This chapter discusses the following in detail: the project's historical development; the role of the federal government concerning Teacher Corps; the programme's temporary systems approach; the programme's components and its delineators; action toward the future; and a summary of the *status quo*.

The Teacher Corps is a federal discretionary grant programme authorized as amended in the Higher Education Act of 1965 by the Congress of the United States of America with the following mandate:

to strengthen the educational opportunities available to children in areas having concentrations of low-income families; to encourage colleges and universities to broaden their programme of teacher preparation; and to encourage institutions of higher education and local educational agencies to improve programmes of training and retraining for teachers, teacher aides and other educational personnel.

The Teacher Corps' mission: an introduction

Teacher Corps exists in recognition of the continuing need to improve the educational experiences provided in schools for the children of low-income families. At its initiation in 1965, Teacher Corps was authorized to create a corps of teachers prepared to teach low-income children and to define a teacher preparation programme which would train such teachers effectively. Teacher Corps still exists to achieve those same purposes, but the years of experience have shown the mission of Teacher Corps to be an extremely complex and demanding task. Teacher Corps today aims, more than ever, at the roots of the public school system and, at the same time, at the heart of teacher training institutions of higher education. The programme centres on making changes at the local level — changes identified by local personnel, administered by local leaders, and supported by the local community.

1980 is the fifteenth year of Teacher Corps' existence. As needs have changed and understanding of problems and their potential solutions has been developed, the mission of Teacher Corps has continually altered in ways which define the means of accomplishing the mission more effectively. The individual local project and its activities and efforts are the total mission of Teacher Corps. The programme holds as its primary responsibility the facilitation of local project efforts to identify, practise, institutionalize and disseminate those programmes, policies, and procedures which will eventually result in permanent improvements in educational personnel development and in the educational opportunities available in the nation's public schools in general, and in schools serving low-income families in particular.

The Teacher Corps' mission: a historical review

A historical review of the Teacher Corps' mission can best be accomplished by identifying three major phases. From its inception in 1965 to 1973, Teacher Corps projects were essentially pre-service efforts, aimed at producing a cadre of teachers to serve in schools having predominantly low-income populations. In 1974, as the teacher shortage eased and the need for in-service training and institutional change became more apparent, Teacher Corps began to fund Demonstration Projects — projects designed to demonstrate strategies for integrating the training of teacher-interns (pre-service teachers) with experienced teachers and aides.

1978 began the present phase of programme operations within the five-year projects. The five-year project phase may well be termed the institutionalization phase of Teacher Corps. A primary mission is to ensure that the Teacher Corps' products, practices, processes, and values become institutionalized throughout existing educational agencies.

1965-73

Teacher Corps began by legislative mandate in 1965 in response to the tremendous need for teachers in schools serving low-income families. Designed specifically to address the needs of low-income children, the legislative mandate included two of the three mandates existing today. Teacher Corps was to:

1. strengthen the educational opportunities available to children in areas having concentrations of low-income families;
2. encourage colleges and universities to broaden their programme of teacher preparation.

Teacher Corps began the joint involvement of schools, the communities they serve, and institutions of higher education to plan and carry out collaborative field-based teacher education programmes. At that time, projects funded under this legislation produced a cadre of multi-ethnic teachers, interns, and team leaders, 70 per cent of whom have remained in education, building careers serving low-income families.

In 1969 a legislative amendment expanded the Teacher Corps' mission to provide trained personnel to serve what has been termed 'troubled youth' — juvenile delinquents, youth offenders, and adult criminal offenders. This thrust remains in Teacher Corps today in specific local projects, labelled 'Youth Advocacy Projects'.

In 1970 a legislative amendment again expanded the Teacher Corps' mission,this time by allowing Teacher Corps projects to attract volunteers to serve as tutors and/or instructional assistants in schools. This move was indicative of Teacher Corps' growing concern for increasing community involvement in schools.

1974-7

As the teacher shortage eased and the needs for training and retraining for existing teachers and school system personnel emerged, the emphasis of Teacher Corps began to shift in the direction of school-based change efforts and towards in-service and staff development for teachers and teacher aides.

Following legislative amendment in 1974, Teacher Corps began to focus on demonstration programmes for training and retraining experienced teachers and teacher aides. Each two-year project in the tenth, eleventh, and twelfth cycles of Teacher Corps was built around a demonstration strategy which integrated the training of teacher interns with that of experienced teachers and teacher aides. Demonstration project designs operationalized one of five different training frameworks, documenting their approach for the purpose of adopting successful elements and making the approach available to other institutions. The five training frameworks demonstrated from the tenth through the twelfth cycle projects included:

1. training complexes;
2. competency-based teacher education;
3. training for alternative school designs;
4. systematic adaptation of research;
5. interdisciplinary training approaches.

Such projects focused on selected 'site' schools with the retraining programme encompassing the entire teaching faculty. Institutions of higher education committed major efforts to the new retraining/in-service function, forging greater collaboration with the school and the local education agency.

Six programmatic themes predominated through the second phase of Teacher Corps which were and are seen as major components of the Teacher Corps' mission. These include collaboration, community-based education, field-based instruction, instructional team programming, multicultural education and strategies to identify, diagnose and prescribe activities for children with learning and behavioural problems in the regular classroom.

Also during the demonstration project phase, the concept of multicultural education was redefined. The term changed from 'multicultural education' to 'education that is multicultural'. The rationale behind the change was the recognition of the need to provide educational programmes which reflect perspectives from a variety of cultures. The change was instituted to ensure that the concept of multicultural education was treated not as a subject to be taught in single training sessions, but as an approach to education which reflected the fundamental values and perspectives evident in all aspects of a pluralistic society.

1978 to the present

The demonstration projects and the evaluative data which resulted from them led to the third phase, and the redefinitions of mission found in Programme '78 and '79. It was in these projects and in the knowledge and experiences gained from them that the fundamental programmatic thrusts and operational principles were articulated for the five-year institutionalization projects.

After 12 years of existence, Teacher Corps legislation was amended and regulations were approved which established five year Teacher Corps projects. The first 79 projects funded under current legislation began in July 1978 — known as Programme '78 projects. In 1979 an additional 53 were funded, and are known as Programme '79 projects.

Each Programme '78 and '79 project is authorized for five years and is funded for one year, to be followed by four non-competitive continuation proposals/grants. Each project must be carried out jointly by one or more institution of higher education, one or more local educational agency and an elected community council. Each project must include enough schools (usually two to four) so that grades one through 12 are included and so that the selected schools constitute a feeder system.

Each project is to be funded for three distinct phases of activity:

— initial development
— implementation
— institutionalization and adaptation.

It is assumed that the first will take a year and the second and third two years each, although some activities from each phase will take place each year. During the first year of a project it must be developed and organized, the community council must be elected and trained, the team leader must be hired, the interns must be recruited, and activities must be planned and developed to the point that they are ready for implementation.

All project activities are governed by a policy board which must include as members the dean of the school of education, the superintendent of the local education agency, and the chairperson of the community council. These three individuals may decide to increase membership on the policy board. Each project must be designed to achieve outcomes which:

— improve school climate
— improve the educational personnel development system
— continue project improvement after funding ends
— cause the adoption/adaptation of those improvements by other agencies.

The role of the federal government concerning the Teacher Corps

Education in the United States is decentralized, with the prime responsibility entrusted to the states. The American constitution restricts the role of the federal government to that of encouraging and helping authorities in the over 16,000 independent school districts, over 1400 teacher training institutions of higher education and over 50 state education agencies in the states, the District of Columbia and in the Trust and Commonwealth Territories. The Teacher Corps programme is presented at the project level as far as possible in the schools themselves, not in university classrooms. This way of working also reflects a conviction that the unit of change in education is the individual school. Training must be designed to serve the needs of the educational personnel, who must meet the particular needs of those children in a specific school.

This kind of retraining for educational personnel already in service must be integrated with the training of the four new teacher-interns. Interns with a baccalaureate degree and no teaching experience are a required part of each of the 132 projects in the Teacher Corps programme. These four interns must rotate as a team through the three levels of schools in each project (elementary, middle and senior high) during the two years of the internship regardless of the areas of concentration and certification desired. The intent is both to provide varied experiences with children of all ages and to allow the interns an opportunity to observe teaching techniques and work with educational personnel at all levels.

A licence to teach is really a learner's permit. Professional development is a process that extends without interruption from the first day when the individual is involved with children as a volunteer or assistant or intern teacher, to the day of retirement from service as an academically qualified, licensed and experienced teacher. Accordingly, a Teacher Corps project has one continuous and graduated programme for trainers, helpers and experienced teachers.

The programme of training is 'performance-based'. It does not ignore the need for teachers — pre-service or in-service — to read books and hear lectures, but it insists that the only way to learn to teach is to deal with living children, and the only credential that counts is a visible effect on those children. Teacher trainers are not only university professors, but teachers and principals in the school itself whom other teachers as well as interns and aides can benefit from seeing in action.

The levels of training presented to all educational personnel in a Teacher Corps school show two distinctive features: the use of human dynamics, and a new kind of professional training. The training programme is designed to enhance the wise use of the human dynamics generated by experience in working with children. The retraining programmes rarely suggest a neat and harmonious master plan. The shape is usually odd and unsymmetrical because it responds to the requests and needs of teachers who have varied experiences and different responsibilities in each and every school; but teachers have enough professional responsibility to be regarded as the most competent judges of their own needs. Many of their training experiences are found to be no less useful for those who are not yet licensed to teach. Other experiences needed by the project's four interns include whatever is required for a master's degree certificate in the state where the school and university are located. The Teacher Corps regards a graduate degree as the appropriate entry to the teaching profession.

Since the Teachers Corps' main concern is for educationally different and disadvantaged children, all levels of training show two peculiar features designed to respond to their distinctive needs. It is the poor child who is most likely to have problems in learning or even in relating to others. Accordingly, teachers are trained to deal with this learning and behavioural problem in the classroom, consulting with specialists when this is needed, but not automatically sending each exceptional child to an expert.

Because poverty in the United States has so often been linked with membership of an ethnic or racial minority, every Teacher Corps training programme includes experiences designed to sensitize teachers to the particular characteristics and values of people whose cultural background may be quite different from their own. In bilingual neighbourhoods, including Indian reservations, this can include training in teaching children who speak another language at home. All Teacher Corps interns are required to spend 20 per cent of their internship time in the community itself.

Most of the pupils for whom the Teacher Corps was specifically designed are found in the great cities throughout the country; in rural areas of the South where traditionally schools had long been racially and legally separated; in remote mountain areas and on Native American (Indian) reservations; and among disadvantaged minority ethnic groups. So the students in Teacher Corps schools are mainly Blacks, poor Whites, Indians, children of Hispanic and Asian origin, migrants, and members of other minority groups relegated to low-class social status, and long-term victims of adverse discrimination and racism. Within this framework, a major effort of every one of the Teacher Corps schools in 132 sites is to improve the school climate by building personal relationships and creating a physical, cognitive and affective environment conducive to teaching and learning. In every case this goal implies making instruction individual and personal; this applies to the activities of the Youth Advocacy Programme which is designed to meet the educational needs of children within the compulsory school age whose behaviour has been so anti-social as to constitute a major problem.

Findings from studies of the Teacher Corps projects as instruments of change provide the educational community with a theoretical and organizational basis which may be used in exploring the whole range of educational personnel development. This is a matter which transcends the Teacher Corps and which relates to broader issues of American education.

Because of the great variation among project sites and hence among project requirements, it was obvious at the outset that innovative and practical means had to be found to define the problems in these localities and to attack them. It was also obvious that this would require school administrators, teachers and supportive people who were geared to undertake the task of working co-operatively. Most school systems had long believed failure to be inevitable, as a result of past inequities. They were in need of incentives which would stimulate them to seek and find new approaches to both pre-service and in-service teacher education, and to risk the failures, the controversy and the difficulties that must accompany the new and the different, the untried and untested. Many schools hesitated to take the chances entailed in making real and radical changes. Many school systems lacked resources for taking risks in new programmes. Many lacked the requisite imagination and leadership. In every project, all available resources had to be marshalled toward the attainment of the Teacher Corps' goal, and everywhere collaboration was required for the attack on intransigent realities.

In the Teacher Corps, collaboration entails deliberate, co-operative, mutual decision-making on the part of those giving service and those receiving service. Many times this is as much a political process as it is a programmatic one and it is essential to building trust and to achieving goals. It has application from the university staff to the school staff; from the principal to the teachers; from the teachers to the children; and from the school staff to parents and community members, or any combination that gives and receives services.

Teacher Corps' temporary systems approach

Perhaps the most useful way to define the operations of today's Teacher Corps projects is to review their status as temporary systems functioning simultaneously within and among several permanent systems. Permanent (non-time-based) systems have fixed locations and memberships, possess a 'difficult to change' set of purposes, easily recognized characteristics and, typically, a clearly defined organizational hierarchy. Temporary systems, by contrast, have definite starting and ending times, variable memberships or members representing a variety of permanent systems, and emerging characteristics, purposes, and organizational relationships. The local Teacher Corps project is a temporary system attempting to affect several large and extremely powerful permanent systems, ie the local education agency, up to four schools, and the institution of higher education, while simultaneously attempting to organize another informal system, the community, into a more influential, formal system. Such a task cannot be undertaken without a full understanding of the difficulties and complexities involved.

Temporary systems require that those involved in them have a knowledge of social systems and organizational behaviour applied to the planning and conduct of short-term educational programmes and project management. A temporary system — a Teacher Corps project in this instance — consists of five major phases, each of which contains different tasks and may involve different staff members. The five major phases include: planning, building, operating, closing, and follow-up. Planning and operating, the two most important phases, include pre-planning, securing resources, phasing out, providing for re-entry into permanent systems, and evaluating.

The programme components

The goals of Teacher Corps impinge upon economic, social and political issues that affect their attainment. In putting the programme into action, it was clear that it would be necessary to move beyond the conventional boundaries of the school, and to link all available resources in order to achieve the desired results.

The 'Nine Dot' design (Figure 1) illustrates a plan which was adopted for Teacher Corps' purposes in achieving these results. It will be noted that two of the components are represented by diagrams which extend beyond the original boundaries of the nine-dot square. This reflects the relationship of the community components to the programme's central plan for action.

The multicultural component

With reference to the multicultural component, the heterogeneity of the school population poses a major issue. In some schools, as many as 50 nationalities are represented by the pupils enrolled. Children of the poor and the wealthy, the illiterate and the highly educated are sometimes found in the same school. But in the largest of the inner cities, Black Americans, Americans of Hispanic origin and to a lesser extent certain other minority groups are forced by circumstance to live in distinct neighbourhoods. Consequently, their children attend schools in which there is less variation of cultural background and economic level. In fact, too many of them are still completely isolated racially and economically. The same observation may be made about rural children who live in remote and mainly depressed areas, as in the Appalachian mountain region, or on Indian reservations.

Because of the close connection between poverty and minority group

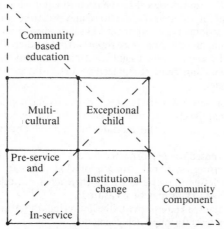

Figure 1 *The 'Nine Dot' design*

membership, Teacher Corps early in its history called to attention the fact that respect for diversity is fundamental; without it all those who are 'different' are excluded from full participation in our society. It follows that it was felt imperative to use this programme to help build respect for human diversity in the nation's schools.

Meanwhile, in Teacher Corps, as in the country at large, it was clear that the issue was not that of a specific minority group alone, but rather concerned the whole country. Dominant groups as well as minority groups must believe in the value of diversity if there is to be both self-respect and respect for others so that all citizens can enjoy their constitutional rights.

Until recently, Americans have viewed society as monocultural (or unicultural), and this perspective has created insensitivity to the many cultures which have built the nation and which still have so much to offer. The contributions of many minorities have been disregarded and records of their achievements have been excluded from most history and other textbooks. Cultural differences have been played down in the name of nationalism. The potential that springs from diversity might have been used as a stronger bond than spurious uniformity. Failure to recognize this has resulted in our schools in an absence of an understanding of cultural pluralism and of the values that may be derived from it, and there is a dearth of materials for use by both teachers and students to build the necessary understanding.

Our goal must be to develop commitment to the principle that to be 'different' is not, *per se*, to be inferior; each individual is unique, and each should have an opportunity to develop to his or her own highest potential. In working toward that goal, Teacher Corps gives special recognition to proposals that address their programmes to the poorest group of children and their problems; it encourages such proposals, and requires that education that is multicultural must be part of any programme it funds.

The exceptional child component

'Exceptional' child refers not only to those with learning and behaviour problems but also to gifted children. This component, which was added to the programme in 1973, was addressed to the need to equip all regular classroom teachers with the ability to identify, diagnose and prescribe for all exceptional children in the classroom. The component was established in response to several factors. Outstanding among these were reports from studies which had shown that in many regular classrooms, a significant number of exceptional children had needs which were not being recognized or met. Strategies for coping with this problem include:

1. collaboration between special education experts and regular teachers at all organizational levels, ie institutions of higher education and local education agencies, at the administrative level and also in regular classrooms;
2. competency-based (or performance-based) teacher training and teacher assessment, using a systematic analysis of what makes an effective teacher in order to define the criteria by which teacher attitudes, behaviours, information and skills may be measured;
3. pupil assessment, an alternative to the limitations of norm-referenced and standardized tests for pupil achievement;
4. parent education, beginning with the training of special and regular teachers to talk with the parents of exceptional children;
5. a Youth Advocacy Programme which is concerned with compulsory school-age children who have been identified as delinquent or disruptive. This programme is a dynamic, challenging and forward-looking activity. It is among the first programmes in the United States which is developing strategies for educating delinquent youths.

Figure 2 illustrates how Teacher Corps teams and parents work together, in one exemplary project, to translate ideas into reality, starting with shared decision-making, by creating the educational environment and the flexibility of experience which improves learning opportunities for exceptional children both in and outside the classroom.

The pre-service and in-service education component

The language of the law is explicit in its requirement that the local school and the university come together in a collaborative effort to demonstrate ways of broadening the preparation and professional development of educational personnel. This whole phenomenon is unique. Through the Teacher Corps programmes, for the first time, partnership between local schools and institutions of higher education has a legislative base. The mandate is for a national effort to integrate pre-service, in-service and continuing education. It requires the university to be involved in retraining teachers as groups and not as individuals. The chief ultimate objective is to improve the quality of education for children. Evidence shows that each school has its own training needs based on the needs of the children it serves.

For the Teacher Corps, this mandate highlights the importance of power sharing at the school system level as well as at the college or university level. At the university, the person with real power in teacher education is the dean of the school of education. It is the dean who must assume the decision-making role to determine how Teacher Corps resources can be used to effect changes that will be consistent with institutional and organizational goals. History has shown that, because of the early emphasis on pre-service education, it was enthusiastic

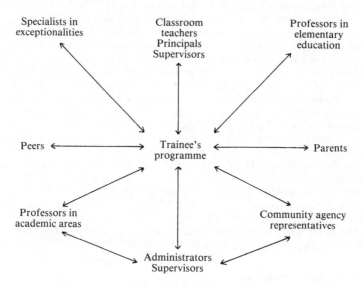

Figure 2 *Shared decision-making*

professors who were usually responsible for the development of a Teacher Corps proposal. They negotiated for the use of the school where the interns would be placed, with only superficial accountability to the co-operating teachers to whom interns were apprenticed. With new legislation, this can no longer happen. The Teacher Corps is now dealing with the total school staff and with the power of the school staff to make decisions about the kind of educational service they feel is needed from the university. Furthermore, the role of the university in the training, development and continuing education of teachers at a Teacher Corps site is now linked to educational development and continuing education.

The fact that in-service teacher education must be related to, and is often dependent upon, pre-service education makes it necessary to look at both at the same time. It is an issue that has caused problems, both fiscal and programmatic in the institutions of higher learning. But the Teacher Corps experience has shown that this problem can be resolved by working closely, from the very inception of a project, with those who have the decision-making power — the deans or equivalent administrators.

The pre-service component of each project has decreased, from an average of 28 interns per project in 1966 when Teacher Corps was primarily a pre-service programme, to the current assignment of four per project in order to integrate it closely with aspects of the in-service programme, and to enable all interns to work with pupils of all ages. The pre-service programme is now used as a vehicle for innovative pilot activities in the associated colleges and universities. The training programme conducted by each project during its second and third year must provide training experiences in all project schools, meet state certification requirements, and lead to a master's degree for successful interns. In each project, the activities of the four interns are co-ordinated by a team leader, usually a successful experienced teacher from one of the project schools. The degree programme for the interns may be one that already exists, one created especially for them, or an existing one with new features added.

The in-service programme usually functions in direct relation to the goals of the school learning climate. Typically, the in-service activities involve parents, paraprofessionals, counsellors, administrators and pupils, as well as teachers and interns. School principals are seen as a critical component of the educational change process and therefore are always included. Training for paraprofessionals and volunteers may also be included. The range and scope of in-service activities is extensive, particularly as specific inclusions vary from project to project. Planning activities for the in-service component are the responsibility of a collaborative group with representatives from both the local school system and the institution of higher education, and are based on the needs of the children in each school. Special attention is given to planned integration between the formal in-service and the pre-service programmes. The in-service component is primarily the responsibility of both the local school system and the higher education institution. These collaborative relationships result in the definition of new roles in the local school system. Usually, activities performed as part of the in-service component relate to the solution of particular problems or the development of products to aid 'on the job' efforts.

The community components

Since its origins in 1966, Teacher Corps has emphasized the involvement of the community. Community-based education, from the Teacher Corps' point of view, reflects the assumption that the school belongs to the community; that the education provided in the school is based upon the needs of the children in the school community, and is in conformity with the wishes and desires of the community; that it is derived from and is enhanced by the use of the human, social, cultural and organizational resources found in the local community; and that education is available to all residents in the community regardless of race, creed, colour, ethnicity, religion, age or sex.

Teacher Corps projects involve teacher interns in community affairs as part of their teacher education programme, and the community representatives of the projects in the decision-making processes. Also the projects provide learning experiences designed to improve the leadership and collaboration skills of community, school, and university people who work together to improve learning opportunities for low-income students.

In 1978, Teacher Corps began to intensify its assessment of objectives. Local projects were charged with showing which of their key elements improved the learning climate for low-income pupils; improved the staff development system for educational personnel; worked to ensure that effective practices were continued in schools, universities and communities after federal funding ended; and helped others outside the project site to adapt and adopt successful practices.

Community-based education is evolving as a dynamic and realistic approach to education. It placed the community and its interests in a central position in relation to schools and institutions of higher education. Although the community collaborates with the school and the university in decision-making, each of the three partners has primacy in some areas:

— As the primary formal education institution of the community, *the school* uses the people and agencies of the community to assess school needs, implement learning programmes, and co-operate in the decision-making processes.

— As the primary personnel training agency for the schools and the community, *the university* is most effective when it uses the people and agencies of the community in the planning, implementation, and evaluation of its training programmes.

— As the primary elected representative of the community served by the project, the *Teacher Corps community council* is effective when it articulates the community's wishes and desires for the project to the schools and the university, keeps the community informed about the resources, activities and results of the project and uses the community as an intrinsically viable educational resource.

Bringing the programme into focus

By 1975, it was evident that Teacher Corps interns needed to develop a stronger *esprit de corps* — a sense of personal identification with the national programme effort. It seemed to the project directors, and this was confirmed by the evaluators, that a common training session could be an extremely realistic and profound cross-cultural learning and living experience. As an outcome of this conclusion, the new interns and project team leaders were participants in the first national training institute which was held at the University of Richmond in 1975. The same kind of experience, known as the *Corps Members' Training Institute* (CMTI), has been repeated for other corps members in the following years.

The institutes have three goals:

1. to develop an *esprit de corps* among the newest Teacher Corps members;
2. to provide them with a rich multicultural living-learning experience;
3. to involve them and their experienced teachers/team-leaders in an academic experience designed to open their minds to theories of organization, in both structure and behaviour, and to the many styles of learning and teaching that provide a variety of options.

Programme evaluations by third parties have pointed to the need for interns to understand the organizational features of schools. Outstanding among these was the first programme evaluation, a two year study funded through the National Education Association and the Ford Foundation (Corwin, 1973). The report of the study emphasized the crucial need for the Teacher Corps teams, and particularly for the interns, to realize that schools are social systems and to understand the implications of organizational characteristics. The following year, a second study, performed under contract to the Office of Education's Office of Planning, Budgeting and Evaluation, reinforced this point.

A major study of Teacher Corps over at least a five year period (1979-83) conducted by SRI International is now underway. It is to be a policy-oriented study for Teacher Corps/Washington, a study responsive to the local projects, describing the actual practices taken by the project and programme participants and illuminating the problems and difficulties and the degree of success and failure, as well as the impact of implementing the Teacher Corps' rules and regulations in field practice. In addition, the study is expected to provide a learning experience for evaluating similar dynamic federal programmes whose impact has, so far, been difficult to define and evaluate.

Through research on the management of change, we know now that Teacher Corps interns are not, and should not attempt to be, change agents. We do expect that they will be the best and most highly qualified teachers available to the profession, not in the traditional sense as dispensers of knowledge but as facilitators in the learning process. This new role requires more and different theories and training than has been the case typically in teacher education. It starts with the assumption that facilitating means managing. Teachers must manage processes, products, and young people in an organized way if they want and expect positive growth and change to occur in the learning and behaviour of their students. This seems easier to accomplish when the school is viewed as a formal organization, a social system, and when the classrooms in that school are viewed as subsystems. This systematic approach treats the classroom as an organization within a larger organization — the school.

Previous teacher training programmes, which focused on the individual teacher-learner, tended to provide new knowledge or skills to that teacher-learner but did not make an impact for change on the school to which the teacher returned. In many cases, the teacher's new knowledge was seen as a threat to teaching peers who had not themselves benefited from such training. Administrators often felt threatened when the teacher attempted to implement new knowledge and skills acquired during the training programme. Now we know how these problems can be avoided. Many have come to believe that for institutionalized growth and development of educational personnel, and for impact on the school, the school as an organization is the smallest unit of change.

Systems theory and organizational behaviour theory have an important place in the conceptualization of pre-service and in-service education. Many good and talented teachers feel unable to use their talents effectively because they believe that the hierarchical structure of administrators and supervisors, and the environmental field force known as 'the community' have placed unwarranted constraints upon them. This sense of alienation and powerlessness in the finest teachers often proves to be contagious. Not even all idealistic beginners are immune. The fact is reiterated that Teacher Corps has been persuaded that if schools as social systems are to be changed for the better, everyone with a role or an investment in the education and/or schooling of children must be collaboratively involved in the change process. Because both new and experienced teachers have an opportunity to study the nature of organizations in general, and the various ways in which members of organizations interact, they learn to view objectively certain behaviour characteristics they observe in the schools. And, as the next step, they learn to understand the behaviours in question and to deal with them successfully.

Action toward the future

Now, in 1980, the task at hand is to re-examine the Teacher Corps programme and to assess the extent of its success in actively involving the community in its efforts to reduce alienation in our schools. It has been suggested that this assessment should be in terms of rediscovering traditions and values, reviving life in the cities, reaffirming communal relationships, returning public property to the people, reducing bureaucratic complexity, and recognizing collaboration as the preferred use of power.

Focus on the single school

At a time when schools are being consolidated in rural communities and in communities where school populations are shrinking, or when they are being decentralized into new artificial units where school districts have become massive and unwieldy, a question has been raised: 'Wouldn't smaller be better?' Teacher Corps has continued to focus on the single school building and on a single feeder system (all grades located in one, two, or three buildings) as the unit of change. This philosophy assumes that school improvement comes from the bottom up — that the grass roots level of the organization is the level from which change is initiated. Teacher Corps belongs to that school of thought and has reason to believe that small is better and more beautiful.

Conclusion

Teacher Corps reflects society's growing recognition that the major problems facing schools serving children from low-income families are national problems. In this society, no single organization nor segment has the answer to those problems. But certainly Teacher Corps has demonstrated that a meaningful partnership must be formed to mediate the conflicts and remove the main obstacle to co-ordination. These partnerships are necessary for the improvement of education on any scale — school, district, state or national. Teacher Corps' mission over the next decade will be to encourage and support successful efforts which attack at least one major national problem through the improvement of the quality and performance of educational personnel — especially the teachers — in schools in low-income areas.

Approximately fifty million children and their parents are clients of the Teacher Corps enterprise which continues to address its complex undertaking and its multitude of clients by performing three outstanding functions:

1. It responds to the need to sustain and publicize the conviction that the alleviation of major problems by educational personnel development is both necessary and possible.
2. It provides a vehicle and a resource which enables communities, schools and universities to experiment advisedly, evaluate innovations, test some hypotheses, and try out ideas of potential value in the search for answers to relevant questions.
3. It provides demonstration models which support the national goal and which may be adopted by local projects which, in turn, must share the results of their hypothesis-testing activities with the whole education community. In this way, the programme subscribes to the demonstration mandate: to record and share the wisdom and products from local sites with others across the nation — sites which may not be part of the Teacher Corps.

Such a mode of conduct — the local project working in terms of the national mandate — creates an apparent need to foster and maintain a balance between the local and national levels. National concerns are global, general and holistic. Project concerns are related to specific sites and situations. The result is the ever-present struggle which characterizes the process of allocating resources to meet competing demands. For example, there are the traditional demands for resources for research in the social sciences versus the demands for direct social service programmes. Teacher Corps, as a school improvement programme focusing upon development and dissemination, must referee this competition within its own narrower sphere.

Operationally, Teacher Corps is on a continuum between *research,* eg the National Institute of Education (NIE), on one extreme, and on the other *support* or *installation*, such as the Programme for the Education of the Disadvantaged (Title I of the Elementary and Secondary Education Act of 1965). Teacher Corps sees its demonstration strategy as relying upon past research to build a solid theoretical base for eventual installation in target area schools.

The identification of the broader market, local, regional or national, the use of appropriate evaluation devices, and the use of available dissemination activities for sharing the wisdom and knowledge gained from a variety of Teacher Corps experiences will determine the programme's eventual and critical residual impact. It is the nature and extent of that residue for which Teacher Corps must eventually be held accountable.

Reference

Corwin, R G (1973) *Reform and Organizational Survival: The Teacher Corps as an Instrument of Educational Change* John Wiley and Sons: New York, London, Toronto

16. The role of the Open University

John Raynor

Summary: This article provides an assessment of the contribution made by the Open University to the professional education of teachers since its foundation in 1969. Noticeable from the beginning has been the fact that, when analysed by occupation, 'teachers and lecturers' have formed the most significant group of students reading for an Open University degree, though there has been a steady decline in the number of applicants from this occupational group over the ten year period. Possible reasons for this decline are explored.

The contribution of the Open University to *professional* teacher education is examined through an account of the work of (i) the Faculty of Educational Studies and (ii) the INSET section of continuing education. Its contribution to the *general* education of teachers is assessed by examining the part played by all other faculties of the University in providing courses which assist in updating knowledge in subject areas. The University also provides learning materials which support and complement the teaching of educational studies in colleges and universities, and this indirect influence is described.

Finally, a number of questions are asked about the continuing part the Open University can play in the professional education of teachers in the current economic climate.

In 1979, the Open University celebrated its tenth anniversary. In a relatively short period the University has come to be seen as making a significant contribution to the professional development of teachers. It is appropriate, therefore, at the end of its first decade to review the part that it has played.

It might, at first, have seemed unlikely that an institution established to provide a 'second chance' for those adults who had been denied the opportunity of higher education would become a major agency for the further professional development and retraining of teachers, a group which had already received some kind of higher education. Nevertheless, that is what has happened. The University's contribution has been both direct and indirect. Directly, it has made a major contribution through the courses in its undergraduate and associated student programmes. Indirectly, it has had important consequences for other institutions in the development of their own courses for teachers.

Basic University statistics

The size and scope of the University can be seen from the following basic data.

Students. There are currently over 71,000 students in the University, of whom 61,000 are in the undergraduate programme, 9000 in the associate student programme and 500 registered for a higher degree.

Courses. * Since 1971 when teaching began, 136 courses have been presented: 117 are in the undergraduate programme and 19 in the associated student programme.

Graduates. In 1972-8 32,700 students graduated, some 3300 with honours.

Staff. There are currently 2900 full-time staff of the University working at the University campus in Milton Keynes and in the 13 regions of the country, and 6000 part-time staff working in the regions.

Teachers as students

It has been noticeable from the beginning that, when student applications were analysed by occupation, 'teachers and lecturers' have formed the largest group of applicants. The reasons for this are not difficult to discover.

In 1969, there were known to be more than 250,000 certificated teachers in England and Wales who were non-graduates. It was clear that here was a possible source of student recruitment to the University. In 1967 the University's Planning Committee estimated that 10 per cent of that figure, or some 25,000 non-graduate teachers, would apply to take an Open University degree to achieve graduate status. This figure proved to be a considerable underestimate. Of 41,000 applicants in 1970 35.9 per cent were classified as 'teachers and lecturers'. The attractiveness of the Open University to teachers was enhanced by the limited opportunities at that time for them to take an in-service BEd degree at one of their local polytechnics or colleges, and by the fact that the Open University was prepared to exempt three credits from their degree by virtue of their possession of a professional diploma including a teacher's certificate. The consequence of this was that teachers qualified for a degree in a shorter period of time than non-qualified entrants and success brought immediate returns for the student in the form of improved salary and increased promotion chances.

Since the first year, the proportion of teachers has declined, as Table 1 shows.

This decline can be viewed in two ways. Clearly, for the University as a whole the trend is not unsatisfactory. In the early years the high proportion of middle-class applicants (of whom teachers made up a considerable part) produced adverse criticism that the original objectives of the Open University were being distorted (Perry, 1970). On the other hand, for those working directly on the preparation of courses in educational studies there is cause for some anxiety, and the reasons for the decline are by no means clear. It may be that the University (along with other institutions) is draining the 'pool' of non-graduate teachers who wish to achieve graduate status, or that the kinds of courses on offer are not the ones that teachers are looking for. Alternatively, rising fees and limited financial support for students may discourage applicants in times of economic hardship.

Though there has been a decline of teachers in percentage terms, in 1978 there

*An Open University course is generally of a full-credit or half-credit type. A full-credit course consists of some 320 hours of study through printed texts, television, radio, course readers and 'set books'. Half-credit courses are designed for 160 hours of work.

	1970	1971	1972	1973	1974	1975	1976	1977	1978
Total applicants	40,817	34,222	30,414	33,220	49,550	50,340	45,834	44,839	41,321
Teachers and lecturers	14,633	10,335	9002	9634	11,892	11,628	11,190	9519	8779
Percentage of total	35.9	30.2	29.6	29.0	24.0	23.1	23.2	21.2	21.2

Table 1 *Number of applicants in year of application by occupation*

were still nearly 9000 teachers applying for admission (or over one fifth of all applicants), and teachers continue to be the most significant occupational category of students. When one compares that figure with the 5000 students on postgraduate certificate of education courses in all the universities of England and Wales in 1978, or, more appropriately, the 4500 teachers on in-service release in 1977, the figures can still be considered relatively buoyant.

The contribution of faculties

Let us leave aside for the moment the work of the Faculty of Educational Studies and the In-service Education of Teachers Unit of the post-experience area, whose courses are specifically professionally oriented, and look at the work of the five other faculties (arts, social science, science, mathematics and technology). Here we can see how through their course offerings they are making a major contribution to the general education of teachers, as Table 2 indicates.

Faculty		'Teachers and lecturers' in total enrolment (%)
A101	(Arts)	30
D101	(Social science)	28
M101	(Mathematics)	29
S101	(Science)	22
T101	(Technology)	15

Table 2 *Percentage of 'teachers and lecturers' on foundation courses in 1978*

A selection of second and third level courses from each faculty shows that teachers form a significant percentage of students taking these non-educational courses (see Table 3).

Subject	'Teachers and lecturers' in total enrolment (%)
Twentieth-century poetry (A306)	38
Fundamentals of human geography (D204)	32
Differential geometry (M334)	42
Comparative physiology and environment (S233)	27
Food production systems (T273)	19

Table 3 *Percentage of teachers and lecturers on a selection of courses at second and third level in 1978*

Thus the general education of teacher students is being catered for by all faculties; up to 1978 there have been some 87,000 registrations for their course offerings.

But to describe the contribution of the five faculties as being of a 'general' nature is too limiting, for they offer courses which are directly relevant to the subject specialisms found in schools. Through these courses the teacher of physical science, mathematics, design and technology, and humanities will be receiving up-to-date knowledge which will have major consequences for the teacher's own curriculum development in his subject specialism.

The courses offered by the five faculties have not been designed especially with teachers' needs in mind. Nevertheless, with suitable adaptation, they could be usefully adopted for retraining in specific areas of the school curriculum. For example, *Science: A Foundation Course* (S101) could be adapted to retrain non-specialist science teachers who have to teach a combined science curriculum in their schools. Similarly, *Living with Technology* (T101) could be adapted to help improve the presentation of technology to the school pupil. The mathematics faculty has gone furthest in this direction by producing a course entitled *Mathematics across the Curriculum*(PME233), which, together with the educational studies course *Developing Mathematical Thinking* (EM 235), will eventually form part of a university diploma in mathematics education.

Faculty of Educational Studies

The Faculty of Educational Studies presented its first courses in 1972 and has since introduced 21 courses with another eight in production. Its courses have been taken by over 75,000 students, the majority of whom (between 80 and 90 per cent depending on the course) have been teachers (57 per cent by age distribution male and 43 per cent female). The breakdown by age distribution is shown in Table 4.

	(%)
Post-1950	10
1946-50	28
1936-45	35
1926-35	19
1916-25	9
Pre-1916	1

Table 4 *Year of birth of students on educational studies courses (1978)*

As these figures show, well over half of the students reached the 'age for minimum entry' to initial teacher training when all that was available to them were two and later three year non-graduate courses.

The Faculty is organized into four discipline areas: psychology, sociology, curriculum studies, and administration and management. The courses offered by the Faculty are broadly of three kinds each aimed at a specific target audience:

Level 2   Foundation and general studies in education
Level 3a   Non-professional studies in educational sciences
Level 3b   Professional studies in education.

The current courses on offer or in production can be seen from the following list:

Level 2

Contemporary issues in education (E200)
Personality and learning (E201)
Schooling and society (E202)
Curriculum design and development (E203)
The control of education in Britain (E222)
Developing mathematical thinking (EM235)
Language in use (E263)
The handicapped child in school (E241)

Level 3a

Methods of educational enquiry (E341)
Society, education and the state (E353)
Cognitive development: birth to adolescence (E362)

Level 3b

Management and the school (E323)
Curriculum evaluation and assessment in educational
institutions (E364)
Ethnic minorities and community relations: an educational
perspective (E354)

Further professional studies are planned for the management of tertiary education and in continuing education.

The following courses which have been developed jointly by the Faculty of Educational Studies and the Faculty of Social Science, or the post-experience area, are also on offer.

Research methods in education and the social sciences (DE304)
Economics of education (ED322)
People and work (DE351)
Mass communication and society (DE353)
Reading development (PE231)
Language development (PE232)

In addition to its undergraduate programme, the Faculty also has a higher degree programme. Over 100 students are currently registered as part-time students conducting research on a range of topics within the field of education. Additionally, a collaborative scheme has been established with a college of higher education whereby the local education authority nominates a number of students to take the Open University's BPhil degree with the tutorial support being given by staff of the college. The students' research focuses on areas, such as problems of transfer, the 16+ age group, and the movement of secondary pupils to further education, which the school or local authority identifies as important. Finally, the Faculty plans to develop structured higher degrees when finance becomes available.

Indirect influence

Apart from the direct involvement of the Faculty with its own undergraduate students there are unquantifiable but substantial indirect effects as well. By virtue of the Open University's system of teaching, it has become something of a national resource centre for teacher education. This process takes place in several ways.

First, it is open to all course teams preparing Open University courses to appoint external consultants to prepare written materials for each course. This allows the course team to draw on a very wide range of expertise and permits a more accelerated dissemination of current research and thinking than would be possible by normal means, such as the consultant directly teaching a handful of students each year in his university or college classroom, or through writing his research papers or books which are likely to be read by a minority anyway.

The second indirect effect is through the availability of the course unit texts and readers in bookshops and libraries. The extent to which these are available to full and part-time students studying elsewhere has never been quantified but sales of Educational Studies course units totalled 250,000 in the years 1972 to 1978. Coupled with the publication of the teaching materials is the very considerable output of BBC/Open University productions. To date, the BBC has produced over 222 television and 306 radio programmes on current work in education, both at home and abroad, and these too find their way into the teaching of educational studies in more conventional institutions of higher education.

Finally, there is the critical part played by the part-time tutors whose task is to give tutorials to the undergraduate student. There are between 500 and 600 part-time tutors teaching educational studies for the Open University. The majority of these also have full-time jobs in universities, polytechnics and colleges of education and there is almost certainly a two-way sharing of experience and knowledge, with the ideas and content present in the OU courses being incorporated into the teaching of their regular full-time students.

Continuing education

A further and significant contribution the Open University is making to the professional development of teachers can be found in that part of its activities known as continuing education (see also Venables, 1979). An associate student programme was established in 1973, and one of the first courses that was specially produced within the then post-experience unit by staff in the Faculty of Educational Studies and funded by the Department of Education and Science was *Reading Development* (PE261). It was a course which proved to be of considerable importance in the development of the teaching of reading in this country. That success undoubtedly led to the creation of an in-service education of teachers (INSET) 'line of development' within the Delegacy of Continuing Education which the University has established. The INSET area has its own Academic Co-ordinator — Professor John Merritt. Continuing education programmes are all self-financing and have to rely, therefore, on outside sources for the money for course development.

Courses within the INSET area are designed to meet specific in-service needs. The first of these courses, *Reading Development* (PE261) was, over a three year period, taken by more than 5000 students — predominantly teachers. Its successor, *Reading Development* (PE231) has been taken in the two years 1977-8 by 1800 students. The latter course is now part of a low-cost Diploma in Reading which has two modules based on extensive practical work in classrooms. An indication of the potential contribution that could be made to the in-service education of teachers in this country can be seen from the fact that the reading development course (PE231) has provided the full-time equivalent of some 600 teacher study years, which in itself is equivalent to just over 13 per cent of the total annual provision. And, as an example of the size of the potential market, in 1977 some 170,000 teachers were undertaking in-service education which involved no absence from normal classroom activities (DES, 1978).

The principle followed by the INSET area is that of making courses both school-focused and classroom-based, as far as is possible with distance teaching methods. To that extent, the Open University's offerings can be seen as part of that spectrum of INSET provision in the country which ranges from school-based group work, LEA short-courses, the work of teachers' centres and courses produced by other institutions. It is therefore essential that the Open University provides courses and learning materials which are complementary to those produced by other agencies. To that extent, the INSET area of continuing education is collaborating closely with local education authorities. An example of institutional collaboration is that three Scottish colleges are offering their own approved version of one of the modules in the reading development diploma.

There is an extensive development plan for INSET courses to be produced by the Open University. Currently, a course funded by the Schools Council on *Curriculum Evaluation and Pupil Assessment* is in production, and diplomas in professional studies and special education are at the planning stage. The difficulty lies in uncertainty about the willingness of the funding bodies outside the Open University adequately to fund development at a time of economic stringency.

Despite these misgivings, it can hardly be disputed that the Open University could become a major contributor to in-service work, particularly as the cost per student is less than that incurred by other higher educational institutions (Wagner, 1976). Moreover, the scope for initiatives by the University in this area is hard to deny. The current level of in-service provision works out at little more than two days per teacher per year, and the proposal for a fourfold increase by 1981 will still only produce the equivalent of eight days per teacher per year.

Conclusion

It is incontrovertible that within the short period of ten years the Open University has had a major effect on the retraining and further professional development of the teaching profession, both directly on its own students and indirectly through the influence of its teaching methods. It has made a contribution to retraining in subject specialisms through existing courses in mathematics, science, technology and in the humanities, and in the area of professional specialisation through studies in education. It is currently enhancing in-service provision through its reading diploma and the work of the INSET area of continuing education. The Open University could substantially develop teachers' capabilities and satisfy their growing demands for advanced qualifications through its higher degree programme, particularly through a taught higher degree. However, at present, the future is as uncertain as in teacher education at large. The most appropriate conclusion to this chapter is a series of questions:

1 . Will the number of teachers applying to take OU courses be drastically reduced in the future as money becomes scarcer, and as teaching moves towards becoming an exclusively graduate profession? And will the pool of non-graduate teachers anxious for graduate status eventually dry up altogether?

2 . To what extent will there be funds available to expand the developments made so far? In times of economic stringency, will the potential for development of the INSET area of continuing education be fully realized if the providers of funds have to cut back? How serious is the Department of Education and Science about OU developments in this area?

3 . To what extent will individuals or local education authorities meet the rising fee levels that have to be paid to take an OU course?

4 . To what extent can the OU identify new areas in education, such as industrial training and work in adult education, that will become relevant to teachers?

5 . How quickly can the OU's machinery be improved in order to make for a faster production of courses to meet identified needs?

6 . Under present circumstances, how quickly can the OU's educational staff develop their own research and generate their own knowledge as opposed to disseminating that of others?

The last ten years have shown that the unique methods of the Open University can be a potent force for the further education of teachers. It is to be hoped that the OU will be allowed to capitalize on its considerable achievements to date.

References

Department of Education and Science (1978) *Statistical Bulletin* (Issue 8/78) HMSO: London

Perry, W (1970) *Open University: A Personal Account* Open University Press: Milton Keynes

Schuller, T and Megarry, J (eds) (1979) *World Yearbook of Education 1979: Recurrent Education and Lifelong Learning* Kogan Page: London

Venables, P (1979) The Open University and the future of continuing education pp 271-84 *in* Schuller and Megarry (1979)

Wagner, L (1976) *Economic Implications of the Open University* OECD/INHE Third General Conference: Paris

17. The Mobile Teacher Training Programme in Nigeria

David Kolawole

Summary: The programme of training Mobile Teacher Trainers (MTTs) was designed to upgrade the professional competence of primary school teachers in northern Nigeria. It is part of the Primary Education Improvement Project (PEIP) which is also a part of the Network of Educational Innovations for Development in Africa. The MTT Programme was launched in 1971 to improve primary education through training of teachers on the job. It was hoped such a training programme would supplement teacher production through teacher training institutions, since there was a continued trend of increasing demand for education and a shortfall of competent teachers.

This article outlines the training, role, skills and handicaps of hundreds of Mobile Teacher Trainers in Nigeria. The teachers carry curriculum innovations to other teachers working in their normal classrooms. After a short training course, carried out in the Ahmadu Bello University or in their own Ministry of Education, MTTs are competent to organize workshops in science, social studies, cultural and creative activities, etc. As a result of the lack of incentives, transport and materials, some of them become discouraged. Nevertheless, the Programme has been a contributory factor to the amount of success achieved in the implementation of the Universal Primary Education scheme in northern Nigeria. The chapter summarizes reports on the evaluation of the Programme, which illustrates what developing countries can achieve through the co-operation of different agencies such as UNESCO and UNICEF in a determined effort to upgrade the professional competence of teachers by using the traditional African pedagogy — 'the apprentice system'.

Background

Between 1955 and 1976 Nigeria experienced phenomenal expansion of primary schools under its policy of Universal Primary Education (UPE). This started in the south as a surging desire for the corollaries of independence — desire for agricultural expansion, development of transportation, improved health education schemes — while in the north it was meant to bridge the gap between the south and the north where education of the Western European and North American pattern had lagged behind.

In the south, as a result of inefficient planning, there was a shortage of teachers (Abernethy, 1969: 156). In the north, even in 1968, there were only 16,113 teachers in the primary schools; 83 per cent of these were men of whom only 39 per cent held a Grade II teachers' certificate. The remaining teachers in northern state primary schools had lower qualifications. By January 1970, the number of teachers had increased to 20,101 in northern Nigerian primary schools, 86.5 per cent of whom were men. 5 per cent of the total number of teachers had a Grade III certificate or better qualifications. The remainder were either uncertificated or had a Grade I certificate (Federal Ministry of Education Statistics, 1970: 53). When the Nigerian Federal Government launched the UPE scheme in 1976, the number of pupils and teachers increased many times over, but with a proportionately greater increase in the number of trained teachers. Reports from Benue and Anambra States show this general trend both in the northern and southern states of Nigeria. Out of a teaching force of 15,746, only 4021 were qualified in Benue State (Benue State Report, Joint Consultative Reference Committee, 1977). In the southern States where western education had taken root for many years, Anambra state recorded 25,647 primary school teachers in April 1977, of whom only 45 per cent were trained.

In an effort to arrest the falling standards of work described above through in-service training, a teacher education project was designed and supervised by the Institute of Education at Ahmadu Bello University. The programme, known as the Primary Education Improvement Project (PEIP), was to produce Mobile Teacher Trainers (popularly known as MTTs) for the mass of untrained and under-trained teachers of Nigeria. It was funded by UNESCO/UNICEF for six years (1970-6) through material aid and finance. In-service training is not a new idea but the apprenticeship method of the MTT makes it unique. The central idea is that the master teacher educates the classroom teacher *on the job*. The teacher therefore learns by doing; he is not taken away from his pupils as is the case when untrained teachers go away to normal teacher training colleges. This Programme — in which the key person (or MTT) observes his apprentices, teaches them how to teach, and watches their professional growth — will be referred to as the Mobile Teacher Training Programme (MTTP).

The MTTP is meant to provide constant professional support for teachers in the classroom not only by helping them to interpret the materials produced by the Institute but also in providing Institute staff with feedback on the effectiveness and viability of these materials. Since 1971, the MTT's main channels of interaction with the Institute have been in two major areas: (a) through training courses and (b) through feedback sessions.

The purpose of this chapter is to discuss the Programme with particular reference to the Mobile Teacher Trainers' appointment and role, the professional skill and problems involved in the Programme, and also the evaluation of the Programme to date.

Mobile Teacher Trainers' appointment and role

The MTT is first and foremost a Ministry employee. He is appointed by the Ministry and in most states he is responsible to the Ministry Official in charge of the project (called the State Co-ordinator). His success, therefore, depends to a large extent on the understanding and co-operation he receives from the Ministry in the execution of his job. He hopes for some measure of identification with the avowed aims and methods of the project by the Inspectorate. He is sensitive to the on-the-spot problems of teachers involved in the Programme. Though MTTs are employees of the Ministries of Education, project schools are under the direct control of local education authorities who appoint and transfer classroom staff, provide classroom buildings and facilities and are therefore directly responsible for ensuring an overall environment in which worthwhile learning can take place.

Between 1970 and 1976, when primary education became the sole responsibility of the local government authorities, a number of experienced staff of the Ministries of Education were recruited in the six former northern states of Nigeria to serve as MTTs. Though still appointed by the Ministry of Education, they are attached to the local government education authorities. In 1970 there were 11 MTTs in the Programme; they worked in 11 centres, and visited 66 schools to help 132 teachers and 5280 children in 132 classes. By 1974 the numbers had increased to 30 MTTs in 12 centres visiting 500 teachers with 2000 children; in 1978 there were 123 MTTs in 69 centres, who visited 4182 teachers with 175,718 children.

The duties of a Mobile Teacher Trainer are as follows:

1. providing close supervision, giving professional help to classroom teachers, supplying them with materials, and explaining difficulties and misconceptions that arise;
2. running short courses for Project teachers for orientation purposes;
3. recently, training new MTTs and assistants to assist in the expansion phase of the Project.

Close supervision

The MTT goes into a classroom and sits where he is of least disturbance to the class teacher. He listens carefully to the teaching and observes learning experiences during a lesson. If he notes a professional error or problem he uses his discretion whether to stop the teacher at that particular point or wait till the end of the lesson. If he decides that it is more prudent to stop the lesson, he corrects the mistake, which might be the incorrect pronunciation of a word, a misleading explanation of a problem, or misinformation. Sometimes the MTT waits till the end of a lesson to discuss other approaches with the teacher if this will not lead to difficulties in resolving the confusion later. For instance, he may wish to supply the teacher with additional information, or to provide the teacher with alternative ways of doing the same thing for variety and for greater interest. During such visits he may supply the teacher with new materials if available. He visits all the classes in a school, then goes to the next school according to his plan. Schools visited by the MTT in villages and towns are sometimes only a few yards apart, but they can also be 15-40 miles away (Kolawole, 1978a: 18).

Training courses for teachers

Initially, Mobile Teacher Trainers were trained by the Institute subject specialists, ie curriculum developers in such primary school curriculum areas as science, mathematics and languages. Short orientation courses were provided, lasting from two to three days to a week or two. During such courses, new materials were introduced and distributed to MTTs for use in schools. In the training programme, MTTs were provided with information on how to train others and how to organize courses for experienced teachers in the Project or for new MTTs. Later, courses were organized for tutors in teacher training colleges by Mobile Teacher Trainers trained by the Institute to upgrade their methodology courses. In addition, the Institute provides longer courses lasting a whole school session for potential Mobile Teacher Trainers, classroom teachers and head teachers. The major focus of the course (known as the Infant Method Diploma Course) is the training in new methods of education at the primary level and the exposure of students to new materials developed in the PEIP.

Training other MTTs

Once or twice annually during 1972-6, Mobile Teacher Trainers' conferences were convened by the Institute to gather feedback on materials already tried out in schools. These conferences gave greater understanding of problems in the field not only to Institute staff but also to Ministry officials. Discussion showed that the problems were not purely professional but also administrative. During such conferences (which last for about a week) workshop sessions were arranged by the Institute's subject specialists to train old and new Mobile Teacher Trainers and Ministry officials who, in turn, were to organize workshops to train other new Mobile Teacher Trainers and teachers in their respective states. New and revised materials were discussed in detail at such workshops.

Professional skills of the Mobile Teacher Trainer

The Mobile Teacher Trainer is expected to possess skills in the following: (a) activity methods, (b) classroom organization and grouping, (c) primary science, (d) discussion, (e) display.

(a) Activity methods. In the Mobile Teacher Training Programme, activity methods are emphasized in all subjects. This is in strong contrast to the traditional chalk-and-talk method. Though the idea that young children should learn through activities is known to most Nigerian educators, often they seem to neglect this basic principle in primary schools in practice. It is not uncommon to see children neatly arranged in rows in classrooms learning by rote. Once in a while, one comes across a sincere effort by some teachers to adopt the activity approach but it seems to be difficult. It appears that their attempts lack structure while the general direction of growth appears unclear. The greater difficulty suggested by Aleyideino was the absence of good resource materials which the teacher can consult to crystallize his own ideas (Aleyideino, 1973: 4). To tackle this problem, the Institute of Education prepared a teacher's guide to activities for primary school classes. The content of the book *Activities for Primary Classes* was prepared by experienced Mobile Teacher Trainers and it was edited by the Institute ·staff. The resource book does not assume any previous knowledge of how to conduct activity lessons. This is also true of other teacher's guides being used by Mobile Teacher Trainers. Usually the guides explicitly tell the teacher the philosophy behind activity lessons in a particular subject. This is well illustrated in the teacher's guides prepared for primary science lessons.

Another feature of the resource material is that it guides teachers in rural areas in the use of local materials to teach effective lessons. The book *Activities for Primary Classes* was designed for teachers who have never tried activity methods, but it is also useful for anyone with more experience who is looking for fresh ideas.

(b) Classroom organization and grouping skills. Creative activities lessons demand other skills mentioned above. The Mobile Teacher Trainee's class may look like this:

Several children are outside the classroom. Some are building a river and a village out of wet sand and others are collecting seeds. A steady noise fills the classroom, and the visitor cannot see the teacher. The children are working in small groups, some on desks and others on the floor which is dotted with newspaper pieces and cornstalks. Girls and boys are talking excitedly to one another. A few children are walking around the classroom, collecting tins or paper and admiring their friends' work...Eventually the teacher appears from behind the screen of the home corner. She explains that she has been listening to a small girl whose doll is sick. (Young, 1977: 3)

In the above description, Young picks up three characteristics of activity methods quite commonly observed in PEIP. First, the children are happy and interested in their play. Second, the classroom is very messy and busy. Third, the teacher has put in a lot of work before the lesson. Initially, teachers often wonder why they should bother to do this hard work just for the children to 'play' in school. Sooner or later they discover that such play is a necessary preparation for understanding basic knowledge, strengthening literacy and enhancing the acquisition of basic skills.

(c) Primary science. Important features of the approach include a positive attitude towards primary science teaching, the 'process' approach and an emphasis on scientific method, appropriate language for instruction, 'learning by doing', and skills in arranging the classroom environment.

Since primary science is one of the unique features of the MTTP, it is emphasized here to illustrate what is needed by the MTT as a transmitter of knowledge and skills and as an agent of change.

1. The MTT should convince the teacher (the apprentice) that he does not have to be a qualified science teacher in order to teach primary science successfully.

2. The teacher should know that PEIP primary science follows the process approach (Young, 1977: 13). The traditionally separate components of science are integrated through this approach. Before primary science was introduced, the primary school timetable had nature study, hygiene, sanitation, agriculture and domestic science each as a distinct subject and each allotted a number of minutes per week. These have now given way to primary science.

3. In the first three years, children are expected to learn to observe, to classify, to measure, to infer, and to make intelligent predictions. In the last three years children are expected in addition to broaden and deepen their experience and understanding of themselves and the world around them (Institute of Education, 1975: 19).

4. In order to grasp the teaching of primary science well, materials written in English should be taught in the vernacular by the class teacher. Even when English is used, it may be necessary at times to translate or adjust the level of language in the book so that children can understand the ideas. Children grasp scientific ideas more readily when they are expressed in the mother tongue (Fafunwa, 1976: 7).

5. The Mobile Teacher Trainer should ensure that the teacher is aware of the fundamental basis of science — as a way of looking at the world, how science asks questions about things, what things are made of, properties of things, how things are alike or different, how things work and how things can be changed.

6. It is emphasized by the MTT during workshops that when teachers teach primary science, children should be encouraged to think and look at old things in a new way, and to develop a spirit of enquiry.

7. Children are encouraged to work in small groups or individually.

8. Children should learn to understand science by doing. In PEIP, primary

science children go outside the classroom to collect leaves and seeds, for identification, sorting, matching, leaf-prints, etc. Children do simple experiments, both inside and outside the classroom. They are allowed to play games, to talk to their teacher and each other, to make models and to tell stories.

9. The Mobile Teacher Training Programme encourages curriculum integration through the teaching of science. The science programme is related to other subjects, especially language and mathematics. Language is essential for the communication of ideas; in science, terms must often be invented to describe observed situations. Mathematics constantly appears in science lessons; for example, we can ask 'How much air can be blown into a can?' or 'What is the weight of a box of matches in grams?' The MTT is taught how scientific problems can be expressed in mathematical terms. Science is also integrated with creative activities.

10. The MTTs teach their teachers how to set up the classroom in such a way that the environment is a stimulus to learning in science. A Project class is quite often distinguished from a traditional class through the wealth, or poverty, of environmental stimulation. In a typical Project class, children's graphs, charts, drawings, writing, paper-cuttings, etc are displayed on the walls, sometimes on strings across the room. One notices a nature table for science where materials are changed every two or three weeks to sustain interest.

What has been said about science activities applies generally to the other subjects in the Project. These are cultural activities, mathematics, physical education, health education, social studies and language arts in English and Hausa. The Mobile Teacher Trainer learns the skills of story-telling, dramatization and discussions in all subjects, but they are of most use in cultural activities.

The MTT and his handicaps

As may be expected, the Mobile Teacher Trainer is not without his problems. These are both administrative and professional. These problems will be considered under eight headings.

(a) Material production

The main problem here is that once it has been decided to introduce new materials then it becomes crucial to keep the flow of material production moving steadily. If for some reason the flow of materials were suddenly to stop, the whole Programme would be placed in jeopardy. In such cases, it is the pupils who will suffer the consequences. So one of the problems is how to keep the wheels of curriculum development turning. Again, if for some reason certain subjects are allowed to lag behind, the concurrent consultations necessary for co-ordinated planning and interdisciplinary approaches become difficult or impossible. In the face of both shortages and frequent changes of staff, it is not easy to maintain an even flow of materials. Other problems in this area can be attributed to the inadequacy of logistic support for materials production. Lack of paper and ink and frequent breakdown of machines are examples of apparently minor problems that slow down curriculum development considerably.

(b) Materials distribution

With large quantities of materials, distribution becomes a problem. For proper distribution of such materials, an effective packaging machinery is needed. There are few organizations which specialize in collecting and packaging educational materials. Producers of materials such as the Institute of Education are not really suitable for carrying out this work, but in the absence of alternatives, the Institute has no choice. Distribution of materials is also affected by the long supply line of such materials. For some time to come, Europe will continue to be the main source of supply. Because of possible interference with this long supply line it is sometimes difficult to predict when ordered materials will be available in schools. This constitutes a major handicap in advance planning in a project of this kind.

(c) Use of materials

Before the materials are used, they have to be protected from theft or damage. This is difficult, partly because most schools have no proper storage places. Again, in general, doors and windows are not secure against heavy damage from wind. There is also a need to have groundsmen to watch over the school property.

The greatest problem of the MTT is, in fact, that of ensuring the appropriate use of materials by teachers. Undoubtedly, this is partly due to the limited training provided, but there is also a more fundamental problem of lack of motivation. There are plans for mounting more in-service courses to increase their competence in using materials, but the motivation problem is more difficult to overcome.

(d) Lack of continuity of staff and incentives for teachers

1. *Incentives:* Project teachers and Mobile Teacher Trainers often complain of excessive time spent on the Project without compensation either in the form of further training or payment.

2. *Transfer of teachers:* Mobile Teacher Trainers are often unhappy when trained or experienced teachers in PEIP are transferred from a Project school to a non-Project school.

3. *Lack of PEIP state coordinators:* New states need full-time PEIP co-ordinators for the Project. As a result of manpower constraints it is not possible to appoint anyone to this post; consequently the Programme suffers.

(e) Poor physical facilities

There was feedback on materials from MTTs during workshops and conferences, but it was difficult to collect feedback regularly from centres. The Institute is now embarking on summative evaluation of the Project; changes in personnel have been the greatest handicap in this endeavour.

The problems of inadequate classroom space and facilities are often mentioned. Overcrowding in classrooms is not uncommon; it hampers good teaching and inhibits fair trial of the materials. There are times when furniture is insufficient or inappropriate for the type of work to be done. Lack of proper storage facilities (eg lockable classrooms and cupboards) leads to loss of materials through stealing and exposure to the weather and insects. A constant problem is that of remuneration for classroom teachers involved in the Project. They feel that, because of the extra effort they invest, not only in attending courses but also in preparing for their classes, they are entitled to some extra reward. This is a perpetual Nigerian problem stemming from the fact that the teacher feels he is underpaid as compared with his counterpart in the civil service and elsewhere.

For example, the teacher may say that if civil servants and factory workers can claim an overtime bonus for work done outside office hours, his extra efforts in serving the nation should also be recognized. Events may, however, overtake this claim since states are now planning to expand the project into other schools faster than has hitherto been anticipated. The special place of the teacher in UNICEF schools will then no longer be justified. As a result of UPE and financial constraints, there are a number of schools and classrooms without essential physical facilities. These include classroom furniture, classroom shutters and secure doors. PEIP teachers need tables for display and various activities; when they are not available, they turn to the MTT for substitutes and alternative ideas.

(f) Evaluation techniques

Most Mobile Teacher Trainers depend on the Institute for instruments needed in evaluating their programmes. It has been difficult to collect feedback regularly through questionnaires by post because of the slow postal system and distance from central postal facilities in some cases. Another problem, and probably a more serious one, is the defensive attitude of teachers who think that instruments sent to them from the Institute reflect on the quality of their work and consequently might affect their records, promotions or progress in their teaching service.

(g) Extra demands

The claim that the Project makes extra demands on the teacher is not surprising, since its purpose is to improve the quality of education through the development and introduction of new materials. Such a programme is bound to force the teacher to rethink his methods, practise the use of new materials and prepare new apparatus to replace old. He may even, in extreme cases, find himself teaching one or two subjects that are entirely new to him. The pressure on him for the first year or two of his involvement in the Project is therefore great, but as he gains experience on the job his confidence in handling the materials increases and its demands on his energy and time also decrease.

(h) Medium of instruction

This is a very serious educational problem at the primary level. Youngsters are best taught in their own language but unfortunately, despite the existence of many local languages, the majority of materials have been written in Hausa. Their impact is therefore seriously reduced. Teachers face the extra burden of translating materials into their local language as best they can in order to communicate properly with pupils. Since we cannot expect teachers to be professionals in every aspect of the curriculum there is no doubt that what is transmitted to the children will only be second best.

Project evaluation

The MTT efforts would have been fruitless and wasted if the teaching in primary schools had not responded favourably to the injection of carefully screened materials and efforts to improve methods of teaching. Fortunately, however, the three million dollars spent by UNICEF, the strong moral and financial support of the government of Nigeria, the untold hardship and sacrifices made by Institute of Education staff in terms of long journeys on bad roads and frequent meetings to improve materials, and the contributions of UNESCO have not been in vain. There are strong indications, supported by evaluation results, that MTTP is a successful in-service innovation for teachers in the northern states of Nigeria today. Some of the evidence gathered through formative and summative evaluation of the project is summarized below.

Formative evaluation

This was mainly collected through feedback from Mobile Teacher Trainers during their annual conference workshops, 1971-6. Curriculum developers from the Institute were told the problems of teaching in different subject areas topic by topic. These problems were discussed fully and the content of the curriculum modified to facilitate more effective learning. (Details of these evaluations are contained in Mobile Teacher Trainers' Conference Reports.) In the early stages, evaluation programme panels were too ambitious. To illustrate, an English Workshop organized in January 1974 aimed to consider 'existing materials for primaries 1, 2 and 3 in terms of their (a) suitability (b) adequacy, and to make concrete suggestions for their improvement'. Further, the workshop wanted to identify the nature and scope of the language needs of the rest of the primary course, that is primaries 4, 5 and 6, to identify which language needs in primaries 4-6 could be satisfied using existing published course books and other materials, and which would require extra material production. In the same workshop, attempts were to be made to produce materials from primary 3 'if the existing ones are judged inadequate and also to produce primary 4 material for the school year beginning in September 1974' (Omojuwa, 1974: 3).

No sooner had they embarked on these objectives than the participants discovered their mistake. 'It became clear after the workshop had started that the aims set were too ambitious to be accomplished within the timetable' (Omojuwa, 1974: 3). This awareness prompted a modification of the workshop's aims. The following were recorded as glaring defects in one of the Readers: '(a) inefficient method of teaching reading (b) poor grading of vocabulary and structures' (Omojuwa, 1974: 5). They detected 14 new reading words and structures in the first six lines of a reading passage in a book meant for a child in the second year of schooling. They also realized that frequently completely new words were presented in the body of the text as distinct from instructions for the exercises, and that the summaries of new vocabulary in the Reader were defective: eg unnecessary and inaccurate naming of parts of speech. In sum, the materials finally presented must go through careful screening through formative evaluation prior to their use in schools.

Summative evaluation

1. In 1975 and 1978 attempts were made at the Institute of Education to gather data on PEIP structure and general administration during MTT

workshops. Major findings from these studies showed (a) that PEIP schools were much livelier as reported by all respondents (b) that children learned more easily in PEIP schools and (c) that the methods were more effective. As a result of these observations, parents preferred to send their children to PEIP schools (Kolawole, 1978: 29).

2. Though it is not yet possible to evaluate all the subject areas of the Programme, a study carried out at Maiduguri Centre confirmed the hypothesis that PEIP classes were doing better than non-PEIP classes in mathematics, oral English and English reading (Hopkins and Lassa, 1977: 27). Teachers indicated the following factors as the most positive aspect of PEIP:

(a) children were happier and learned more easily;
(b) there was greater emphasis upon individual progress;
(c) more practical than traditional methods were employed;
(d) teacher/supervisor relationships improved;
(e) the quality of materials and methods was higher.

3. National Common Entrance Examination results showed higher scores for PEIP schools in Sokoto State and Kano State, Nigeria (Wilder and Fodeke, 1977: 2).

Other observations

Like Frazier, Kolawole studied 600 children in PEIP and non-PEIP classes. According to Frazier 'the schools must offer the stimulation, the time, the spaces, the materials, and the guidance that enable the child to pursue an interest intensively. The child who spends time developing an interest under such favourable circumstances is likely to come out with the breadth and depth of understanding, the high level of skills and the intensity of commitment that we often define as talent' (Frazier, 1960: 88-92). Kolawole's study supports the idea that the environmental stimulation provided in the Project affected cognitive learning (Kolawole, 1978: 30). Furthermore, the experimental group could express themselves better than the control group irrespective of geographical location (Kolawole, 1978). Also, Brown (1975) shows that in spite of all the constraints on the teaching of primary science in Project classes, the aims of PEIP were generally achieved.

Conclusion

This chapter has presented the Mobile Teacher Training Programme as a means to an end. Its objective was to portray the efforts of the Nigerian government to raise the standard of professional competence of primary school teachers through the PEIP. The success of the Programme co-ordinated by the Ahmadu Bello University Institute of Education has been made possible mainly through the dedication of Mobile Teacher Trainers who are Ministry of Education officials in the ten northern states of Nigeria.

It is difficult to imagine what would have been the fate of the Universal Primary Education scheme in the northern states of Nigeria since its launching in 1976 without the professional competence of the Mobile Teacher Trainers. The urgent need for developing nations to devise ways of overcoming the dearth of competent teachers at all levels of education is well known. If the MTT programme has generated some thinking about new ways of improving teacher competence in primary schools in other countries, the three million dollar cost will have yielded dividends which justify every dollar spent.

References

Abernethy, D (1969) *The Political Dilemma of Popular Education — An African Case* Stanford University Press: California

Aleyideino, S (1973) Primary Education Improvement Programme: the production and installation of new curricula materials in the northern states of Nigeria *Institute of Education Bulletin* **8** 2:12-16

Benue State Ministry of Education (1977) *Joint Consultative Reference Committee on Primary Education Report* Ministry of Education: Makurdi

Brown, G (1975) *Microteaching: A Programme of Teaching Skills* Methuen: London

Castle, E (1970) *The Teacher* Oxford University Press: London

Emmer, E (1972-4) Direct observation of classroom behaviour *International Review of Education* **18** Special No:473-90

Fafunwa, B (1976) *The Six Year Project Report (I)* University of Ife: Nigeria

Fafunwa, B (1977) The problem of recruitment retention, promotion, transfer and discipline of teachers *in* Bamijoke (ed) (1977) *Proceedings of the Seminar on Teacher Education in Nigeria* Institute of Education: Zaria

Federal Ministry of Education (1970) *Educational Statistics* Government Printer: Lagos

Frazier, E (1960) Talent and the school environment *Elementary School Journal* 60:88-92

Hanson, J (1964) The spirit of the teacher *in* Hanson *et al* (1964) *Nigerian Education* Longman: Nigeria

Hanson, J and Brembeck, C (1966) *Education and the Development of Nations* Holt, Rinehart and Winston: New York

Hicks, S (1969) *Northern Nigeria Primary Education Development* (UNESCO/UNICEF) Programme *Institute of Education Director's Annual Report* 1969/70: 8-9 and *Director's Report* 1970/71:7

Hopkins, D and Lassa, P (1977) An evaluation of the Primary Education Improvement Project in Maiduguri Centre *ABU Institute of Education Bulletin* **12** 1:27

Institute of Education (1975) *Primary School Syllabuses* Institute of Education: Zaria

Kolawole, D (1975) Primary Education Improvement Project: activities *Institute of Education Bulletin* **10**

Kolawole, D (ed) (1975-78a) *Mobile Teacher Trainers' Reports* Institute of Education: Zaria

Kolawole, D (1976) *General Information on Primary Education Improvement Project* Institute of Education: Zaria

Kolawole, D (ed) 1977) *Proceedings of the State Co-ordinators' Conference* Institute of Education: Zaria

Kolawole, D (1978) *The Effects of Environmental Stimulation on Cognitive Learning in Creative Activities* Ahmadu Bello University Research Board: Zaria

Lauwerys, J (ed) (1969) *Teachers and Training* Evans: London

Nduka, O (1964) *Western Education and the Nigerian Cultural Background* Oxford University Press: Ibadan

Omojuwa, R (1974) *MTT Conference Report* Institute of Education: Zaria

Solary, T (1964) *Teacher Training in Nigeria 1840-1960* Africana: New York

UNESCO (1970) *Practical Guide to In-Service Teacher Training in Africa* UNESCO: Paris

UNESCO (1978) *Educational Reforms and Innovations in Africa* UNESCO: Paris

Wilder and Fodeke (1977) *PEIP Coordinators' Report* Ministry of Education: Sokoto

Young, E (1977) *Activities for Primary Classes* Oxford University Press: Nigeria

Part 5: Methods

18. Selected innovations in methods of teacher education

Jacquetta Megarry

Summary: This chapter identifies two significant recent developments in educational methods — simulation/gaming and distance learning — and examines their implications for teacher education. It is argued that these innovations must be demonstrated and used *with* teachers if they are ever to be used *by* teachers; teacher educators must practise what they preach. If innovations in method are perceived to threaten employment or conditions of service they are likely to be resisted.

Simulations, games and role play embrace a whole spectrum of participatory techniques, ranging widely from structured to open-ended student responses. Examples of ten such techniques are given from recent experience in the USA, the UK and Australia. Distance learning is an increasingly popular organizational arrangement with far-reaching implications for methodology in the structuring of learning experiences, use of print and audio-visual media, and course planning and evaluation. Examples are drawn from the Open University and from a distance learning educational technology course for teachers.

The speed of technological progress and the social changes it causes are together creating a major challenge for education at large as well as offering scope for new techniques. Recent developments in telecommunications and microelectronics may enhance the learning potential of simulation/gaming and distance learning, both separately and in combination. But they will also provide teacher education with its greatest challenge to date.

A great deal has been said in other chapters about the nature of professional development, about strategies for promoting it among teachers and about its implications for the organization of teacher education at pre-service, induction and in-service stages. The task of this chapter is both modest and concrete. It is concerned with *methods*. It is an essential requirement for professional teachers that they should have a wide repertoire of methods at their disposal and the competence to select the most appropriate methods for the task. It is axiomatic that the same applies to the teacher educator. To promote genuine changes in classroom practice, teacher educators must alter their methods, not just their rhetoric.

The development of new methods of teaching and learning in schools and higher education has been rapid. The last decade in particular has seen an explosion in the literature on a wide variety of methodological innovations: resource-based learning and resource centres; simulations, games and role play; independent and distance learning; education based on computers and microprocessors. These developments are significant not only for the content of teacher education, but also for its methods. In other words, there is no point in 'telling teachers' about innovative methods; it is far more effective to use them. To paraphrase McLuhan, the method is the message.

Teacher trainers have been severely and rightly criticized for neglecting this rather obvious point and their credibility has thus been undermined. As a student teacher, I was lectured at for 50 minutes at a time, including instruction on how to plan lessons in view of students' limited attention span. Lecturers in physics, chemistry and biology all separately told us with heartfelt conviction that integrated science was a 'Good Thing' — on separate occasions, in separate rooms and to separately sceptical audiences. We were lectured on the value of independent study. We had seminars on the evils of streaming — in our carefully insulated groups divided according to type of degree (honours, ordinary or none).

It is easy to produce special pleading to justify some, at least, of these ironies, but quite beside the point. The way to convince teachers that new methods work is not to tell them so; it is to let them discover it for themselves. This applies as strongly to in-service as pre-service training: 'It is generally agreed, both in and out of the teaching profession, that conventional lecture-oriented courses in teaching methods are of little value' (Borg, 1971:14). Let me illustrate with an example of good practice. The establishment of a staff tutor service in 1965 by Jordanhill College, Glasgow, undoubtedly did more to change methods employed by primary teachers than any amount of traditional exhortatory pre-service or in-service courses. Their valuable contribution to the implementation of the Primary Memorandum (SED, 1965) has been made through school-focused in-service work in which they go into schools and classrooms, and *use* the methods advocated with the pupils and their teachers. School-based work is also used as a means of testing out ideas for themes, organization and materials which are then worked out with teachers on short courses mounted either in college or at teachers' centres. Good relations with the education authorities have been an important feature of the staff tutors' work from the start (Archer *et al*, 1977).

The present relevance of these courses is not their location but their methodology. Suppose the subject is a topic study, in which a changing story-line includes incidents, problems and a variety of thinking and expressive activities (Rendell and Bell, 1980). The course begins, not with a lecture, but with the problem-solving, discussion, writing, acting out or art and craft activities themselves. While the teachers clearly produce a very different *standard* of work from primary age pupils, the *nature* of their activity is closely similar; in a real but unselfconscious sense, the teachers take on the roles of pupils. The quality of their reflective discussion afterwards testifies to the value of the experience; it can be likened to the debriefing discussion which is a necessary follow-up to a simulation exercise if participants are to analyse the experience and explore its implications. Follow-up visits and evidence of transfer to other teachers and topics demonstrate that the staff tutor service has been successful in securing real change in schools as opposed to superficial conformity with whatever innovation is currently fashionable.

This is an important distinction. Scotland has a highly centralized education system and teachers have usually found it politic to pay at least lip-service to official thinking. As Bloomer explains (p 365) the apparent pace of change is misleading. Large numbers of primary schools who claim to be 'doing the Memorandum' are actually doing no such thing. In the aftermath of publication of an official document, the language in which teachers describe their activities tends to change far more than their classroom practice. Bloomer describes the role of teachers' unions as a fifth column in promoting this innovation without change.

The professional associations' role in relation to innovation may not always, however, be so benign. Any significant change in methods of teaching requires a change in the teacher's role and skills; the traditional role of the teacher as the source of knowledge and centre of attention may no longer be appropriate. He may more appropriately be a designer of distance learning materials, a manager of individualized learning resources, a facilitator/referee in a simulation game, a computer programmer or handbook writer. These roles demand new skills and experience, and have clear implications for pre-service and in-service training. As long as innovations are perceived as strengthening the case for more in-service release or higher salaries (Bloomer, p 368), they may be tolerated or even welcomed by the professional associations; but as soon as they appear to threaten employment prospects, such innovations may be publicly denounced, quietly subverted or simply sabotaged.

A major recent attempt at promoting individualized learning in teacher education has foundered partly because of problems related to conditions of service and redundancy fears. Drastic cuts in student numbers, coupled with persistent rumours of college closure, have made lecturers understandably reluctant to replace even, say, 20 per cent of their student contact time by packaged learning resources. Why should lecturers who receive no extra financial reward or compensatory release from teaching contact voluntarily create materials which could — in principle, at least — be used with other student teachers, in future years and, perhaps, in other colleges, thus reducing still further the number of college lecturers needed? However, perhaps fortunately, most innovations have so far proved expensive, rather than economical, of teachers' time. Whether this will remain true once the microelectronic revolution is under way is a problem to which I return at the end of the chapter.

Two recent innovations in methods of teaching and learning seem to me particularly significant: simulation, games and role play; and distance education. They illustrate well the need for new skills and roles for the teacher, and also for teacher educators to use such approaches and not merely to advocate them. These two innovations might seem quite unrelated, or even in tension. Most people probably visualize games (whether educational or entertaining) being played by players who are in the same room if not in close proximity. Simulation/gaming does not sound like a promising medium for distance learning. However, requirements of privacy (for example by teams representing competing business companies or players of DIPLOMACY) may dictate the use of separate rooms or locations; games and tournaments have often been organized by post and more recently the telephone and computer have allowed simulation gaming at a distance to be truly interactive (Megarry, 1979:157).

The two main sections of this chapter consist of a closer examination of simulation, games and role play and, in the following section, of distance education. A brief final section further explores the relationship between them in the light of future developments. It is argued that technological advance in computers and telecommunications could combine and enhance the strengths of each.

Simulation, games and role play

'The idea that play and games have value in education and training has a long and distinguished pedigree. It can be traced back through the writings of eminent theorists like Bruner, Piaget, Mead, Moreno, Dewey and Rousseau all the way to Plato' (Megarry, 1978a). However, published work on simulation and gaming in education dates only from the 1960s and the recent rapid growth in books, journals and societies all over the world has been a feature of the 1970s. It was marked in the UK by the foundation in 1970 of the Society for Academic Gaming and Simulation in Education and Training (SAGSET) whose journal *Simulation/Games for Learning* is a major resource and communication channel. Its first 36 issues demonstrate and document the applicability of the technique to almost all subjects and levels, and in primary and secondary education as well as higher and adult education. The process by which education imported the technique from business and management education, which in turn derived it from military training, has been documented elsewhere (Megarry, 1978b). The first published account of simulation in teacher education was probably the JEFFERSON TOWNSHIP SCHOOL DISTRICT simulation (Hemphill *et al*, 1962) but diversity and proliferation have since been a feature of simulation in teacher education not only in the US but worldwide.

Terminology in any rapidly expanding field is a battleground, as authors try to negotiate ascendancy for their own connotations of disputed terms. Here I shall merely stake out my territory in the context of teacher education, having taken and defended a more general position elsewhere (see Megarry, 1978a for definitions and references). In a *simulation*, aspects of the educational world are replicated or recreated and run through over a period of time. The school, classroom or social system is usually fictitious and often greatly simplified; events may be slowed down, classes and teaching staffs scaled down, difficulties reduced. But for the duration of the simulation, fiction replaces reality and participants are held responsible for decisions, sometimes within the constraints of specific roles adopted for the purpose. In a *game*, there are essential and explicit boundaries to acceptable behaviour codified as rules (which, if broken, disrupt the game); generally there are also definite objectives or pay-offs for which participants compete and/or cooperate. Although the notions of *simulation* and *game* are distinct, then, they are not incompatible: a *simulation game* is thus a learning experience in which participants recreate a competitive reality by acting in some rule-bound way.

Role play occurs when participants take on differentiated roles in a simulation. These may be highly prescribed, including biographical details, and even personality, attitudes and beliefs; or loosely indicated by an outline of the function or task. If participants are not differentiated but all have the *same* function or task, the simulation is usually described as *situation play*, not role play.

These techniques have already demonstrated their applicability to a wide range of learners, subjects and levels. There is impressive evidence that they can be extremely effective educationally, though the evaluation issue is complex (see Megarry, 1978b). Moreover, there is a clear consensus that they are highly motivating techniques and offer a unique approach to affecting attitudes. This section concentrates on their use for teacher education, where they have been used both to promote and practise teaching skills and for a broad range of more general aspects of the preparation and in-service education of teachers.

Preparation for teaching certainly seems to offer obvious scope for simulation. Teachers have to make large numbers of decisions, usually on their own and often under time pressure, many of them in front of a classroom audience. Mistakes can have serious consequences for the teacher's future relationship with the class and his colleagues: they may affect his career, his peace of mind, and, no less important, his pupils' learning and attitudes. There are strong arguments for practising and rehearsing such decisions in circumstances where the consequences of errors are limited and the advantages and pitfalls of the various courses of action can be discussed openly with peers. The analogy between training teachers and aircraft pilots was put convincingly by Bishop and Whitfield (1972); it is developed in Figure 1.

Stage		Trainee pilot		Trainee teacher
1	(a)	Theoretical study and exercises in background disciplines (eg aerodynamics, meterology)	(A)	College-based theoretical studies in teaching subjects and professional studies
2	(b)	Practical training and exercises in basic skills (eg navigation, calculating flight times and fuel consumption)	(B)	College-based practical exercises (eg in audio-visual media production and handling, construction of tests and appraisal instruments
3	(c)	Flight simulator experience to practise co-ordination, decision-taking, emergency action	(C)	Simulation
4	(d)	Actual flight experience in a dual-control aircraft with progressive transfer of control to the trainee	(D)	Teaching practice, induction, probation
5	(e)	Solo flight with full responsibility	(E)	Teaching career
6	(f)	Retraining and refresher courses	(F)	In-service training
		This column is a modified version of Bishop and Whitfield's five-stage summary (1972:8)		This column represents tentative ideas about what are or should be analogous processes in teacher training

This column is a modified version of Bishop and Whitfield's five-stage summary (1972:8)

This column represents tentative ideas about what are or should be analogous processes in teacher training.

Figure 1 *A partial analogy between the training of aircraft pilots and teachers*

The analogy between training teachers and airline pilots must not be pressed too far, of course. There is far less consensus about the qualities needed by a good teacher than those required by a good pilot, and the fact that teachers are primarily concerned with human beings, and pilots mainly with machines, has important implications. Nevertheless, for the aspects of teacher training which depend on identifiable skills, it is a very fruitful one and it is the training analogy which is developed in Figure 1. Obviously the professional preparation of teachers involves more than mere transmission of classroom skills; even more clearly, the aims and scope of in-service education are much wider than the component indicated under 6F.

Note also that the right-hand column is sometimes more prescriptive than descriptive; to change the analogy from flying to swimming, many student teachers' experience of teaching practice (4D) represents a plunge into the deep end, rather than the gradual progression from the shallow end of the pool which 4d suggests. Again, most teachers who have survived their training courses have experienced an abrupt transition from student status to that of fully-fledged teacher without benefit of an induction scheme and after a probationary status which has been a one or two year formality. This would be analogous to a pilot moving from stage 2 or 3 straight to stage 5. The casualties caused by teachers skipping stage 4 may be less visible and spectacular than plane crashes, but the human cost and waste is nonetheless real. (See also chapters by Tisher and Bolam.)

It is clear from the diagram that simulation could make a major contribution to teacher training, especially at stage 3C, but also at stages 2B and 6F. Although there has undoubtedly been a rapid growth in publication about the use of simulation in teacher education over the last decade, it is impossible to quantify reliably because the term embraces such a wide spectrum of activities (see Figure 2). Not all users of these techniques would label themselves simulation users even if asked, and the majority never publish their work. Nevertheless, a recent ERIC bibliography of nearly 2000 publications on educational simulations and games (Cruickshank and Telfer, 1979) lists 99 in the teacher education category alone, and most of the remainder are of potential relevance to teachers.

Three surveys of percentage use of innovative techniques in pre-service teacher education in the USA conducted in 1968, 1973 and 1976 are reported by Cruickshank (1979). It is very difficult to interpret these figures outside the context in which they were gathered, however; not only do methodological problems vitiate comparison between their results, but there are also acute problems of interpretation and definition. For example, Sherwin's study reports that 61 per cent of the institutions surveyed used simulation 'moderately' or 'a great deal' (Sherwin, 1974), whereas Joyce's figures indicated a much lower level of usage — between 15.1 and 27 per cent depending on the interpretation of non-responses (Cruickshank, 1979; Joyce et al, 1977). Whether this reflects a change over time, different interpretations of the response category, different perceptions of practice, or different desires to portray it, by those who filled in the questionnaires, is a matter for speculation.

The main purpose of this part of this section is to illustrate the tremendous variety in the nature, scope and aims of the simulations which have been developed for teacher education by a brief outline of a number of examples with references to more detailed descriptions and evaluation results. To this end, ten of the more common varieties have been arranged along a dimension in Figure 2. Since different writers use the terms with bewildering meanings, and some blithely use several interchangeably, their arrangement is not intended to be definitive or prescriptive. Although, for example, in-basket exercises are usually more highly structured than case studies, the existence of counter-instances does not invalidate the usefulness of the structure dimension as a row of pegs on

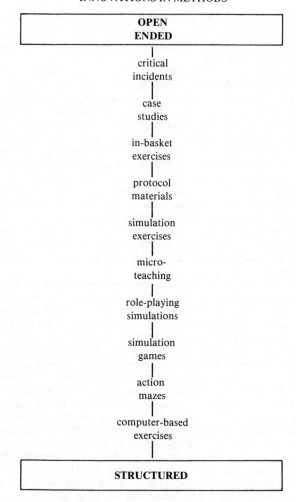

Figure 2 *The structure dimension in simulation*

which to hang the descriptions which follow.

At the open-ended extreme of the spectrum is the use of *critical incidents*; these are usually presented on paper, often in one or two sentences, perhaps a paragraph or a page. Student teachers decide what action they would take in the hypothetical situations put forward, working perhaps first as individuals, certainly discussing solutions afterwards as a group. The decisions would have to be taken 'on-the-spot' in real life. Bishop and Whitfield (1972) introduce their collection with the observation that experienced teachers' reactions differ from those of inexperienced students in that the former have developed a framework into which they fit such situations and from which they decide how to react, whereas student teachers are frequently nonplussed by each fresh situation. They argue for helping students to rehearse their reactions and develop their decision-making frameworks in the safety and privacy of initial training. No general background information is presented on the school or the teacher (though some of the incidents betray an automatic assumption that a secondary science teacher will be male).

A greater richness of background information is implicit in the term *case studies*; a useful collection was published by Perry and Perry (1969). Like Bishop and Whitfield, they stress the advantages of the method for linking theory and practice and also its potential for developing 'casemindedness', that is, the habit of seeing all sides of a question and thinking clearly about complexities. They quote Pigors and Pigors' (1961) assertion that case studies 'narrow the gap between hindsight and foresight', and increase understanding of human problems. They advocate that students first study the cases individually, and then proceed to discussion in sub-groups of three to five students before a larger seminar group takes over. Their case studies give much more background colour than the critical incidents; principal characters are sketched, the accounts extend to half a dozen printed pages, and are followed by discussion questions. They cover a wider range of issues and the decisions required are usually less immediate, requiring deeper thought. More recently, case study material has been published in audio cassette form, containing an extended recording from a staff meeting (CET, 1975).

Published *in-basket exercises* date from the late sixties in Britain, inspired perhaps by early American examples (Hemphill *et al*, 1962). The usual format is a scenario describing the background: the school building, history and catchment area, a list of classes and teachers, perhaps with brief sketches, a series of in-basket items in the form of letters from staff and parents, memos, notice-board items and reports of telephone calls. The technique was developed particularly for management courses, especially in in-service education, but materials have also been used with pre-service students. Participants are expected to decide how to respond to these items, usually as if they were in a particular role, eg headteacher. In an early Scottish example, participants have to identify with the newly-appointed young headmaster of a comprehensive school whose only experience is of selective schooling (Bone, 1968). Sometimes printed in-basket material is complemented by the use of audio-visual media, supplementary readings and discussion questions. For example, the trio of simulations which Bill Taylor built around the fictional SEVERNSIDE SECONDARY SCHOOL, contains in-basket items incorporated into a printed workbook to be used by groups of teachers viewing the series of associated television programmes (Taylor, 1969 and 1973; Taylor and Moore, 1970; Taylor, 1972). In all three, the participant is expected to react from the viewpoint of the headmaster, details of whose background, family and biography are given.

Although film and video-tape may complement the presentation of in-basket exercises, they are an *inherent* part of the *protocol materials* discussed by Orlosky (see Chapter 19). The 'slice of reality' is captured, like a fly in amber, to illustrate a particular concept to which students have been sensitized by background reading and to which they respond during and/or after the filmed episode. It would be difficult to draw a sharp distinction between these and the type of media-based simulation exercises pioneered by Kersh in Oregon as a direct result of his experience of the effectiveness of simulation in a military context. It is interesting to recall his starting point: 'the shortage of qualified teachers, limited training facilities, and too few expert supervisors dictate that new methods be found to provide systematic training practice teaching opportunities for beginning teachers' (Kersh, 1962:109). The origins and development of Kersh's simulated classroom (MR LAND'S SIXTH GRADE) are described by Twelker (1971), who directed the project. Student teachers were given background information on the school and community and cumulative record files on each of the 22 pupils; they were to imagine that they were attached to Mr Land's class for observation and teaching practice. The 20 short filmed episodes presented classroom incidents spaced throughout one day; each faded out with a cue to the student to make an immediate acted-out response. The supervisor coded and recorded the response in one of several predetermined categories, and accordingly selected one of several filmed feedback sequences to replay, supposedly representing the consequences of the student's action. Kersh's approach was explicitly based on behaviourist psychology; he used an operant conditioning model and tried to 'shape' appropriate student response by differential reward through the feedback sequences. The theoretical difficulties inherent in this prescriptive approach, combined with the expense and technical difficulties, make its value questionable. Ideally only one student could be trained at a time; four film projectors and a sophisticated electronic control system were needed simultaneously and also an educational supervisor and technical support.

Cruickshank (1971: 192) notes other criticisms of Kersh's technique, and describes an alternative approach which he and Broadbent developed. The TEACHING PROBLEMS LABORATORY (1967) cast the student as a new fifth grade teacher, Pat Taylor, at Long Acre Elementary School and presented critical incidents from the teacher's viewpoint both literally and metaphorically. The incidents were designed to cover the 31 problems most often mentioned in a survey of 163 first year teachers they conducted. Unlike Kersh's CLASSROOM SIMULATOR, they expected participants to suggest alternative strategies for coping with these incidents and to predict their consequences; feedback and evaluation were provided by a peer group. Role play, group discussion and background readings helped students to examine their values and assumptions. Cruickshank was clearly uncomfortable about the absence of criteria and models in his own work. He speaks of providing 'no rules of the game' and resorting to 'pooled ignorance' (Cruickshank, 1971:198). He later gave a stronger role to the 'instructor', making the simulation less open-ended than it appears. Science Research Associates published INNER CITY TEACHING PROBLEMS LABORATORY in 1967; this was a major revision in which problems are located in an inner-city environment.

By 1970, over 300 universities and public school districts in the US were reported to be using the TEACHING PROBLEMS LABORATORY (Cruickshank, 1971:200), and they have been sold worldwide. This is surprising, as an important limitation of these media-based simulations is that they are very difficult to transplant and use in a different context, let alone a different country or continent. However general the problems and issues raised, teachers find it hard to relate to 'pupils' with unfamiliar accents, from different ethnic groups, of different ages, and in a school system which employs a different vocabulary and method of organization and reflects culturally inappropriate assumptions. Although the adaptation of print-based materials for another context or country might be relatively straightforward, the editing task would be impossible for filmed material — a total re-make is the only solution. For example, Turney and Ryan of Sydney University have developed INNER CITY TEACHING , a close

Australian parallel (Diehl, 1979:271); Lesley Vivian, a young teacher, and her pupils and colleagues are recreated in the Australian community of Parish Point. Apart from the greater accessibility of this material to Australian teacher trainers, its acceptability to their students must be incomparably greater than that of the American inner-city context.

Even when ҭhe cultural context *is* appropriate, however, this type of simulation still presents considerable problems of credibility which make it difficult for students to achieve 'that willing suspension of disbelief'. They are supposed to *identify* with the hypothetical unseen teacher; the usual tactic is to give the teacher a sexually neutral name and to shoot scenes as if from the teacher's angle so he/she does not appear on the film; the teacher's supposed statements are conveyed by slow-moving captions. However, there may be more important barriers to identification than gender; for example, if the simulated teacher is supposedly presented with major problems of class control and the viewers believe (rightly or wrongly) that they would never have got into that position in the first place, they may reject the simulation and discussion will be abortive. Moreover, there are theoretical difficulties inherent in the claim to portray a teacher's view of the classroom. Teachers perceive the world with their brains, not their eyes; different teachers perceive the same classroom differently. A camera lens is passive, whereas an experienced teacher's perception is selective and active. Viewers could justifiably argue that they need control over editing and shooting in order to identify with the teacher's predicament and perceptions.

It has also been assumed that a crucial feature of simulations of this type is to enable participants to 'step into the shoes' of the hypothetical teacher. In this they are very different from the in-basket/case study approach in which discussion is generally at one remove. However, such empirical evidence as has been published on these simulations does not convincingly demonstrate the need for such identification (Twelker, 1967). Moreover, for educational simulations in general, 'the optimum degree of realism is an empirical, not an armchair, question... The cardinal sin committed by designers of early simulations was to build models of overpowering complexity...' (Megarry, 1978b:199). In an account of a different style of simulation designed for Australian pre-service teachers, Marsh criticizes the Kersh/Cruickshank models not only for excessive detail and paraphernalia, but also for concentrating exclusively on classroom problems and confrontations to the neglect of broader aspects of the teacher's role and for portraying the art of teaching as a fragmented collection of techniques and strategies for containing classroom problems (Marsh, 1979). However, even if the simulation has limited credibility this does not *necessarily* vitiate its effectiveness; it may still act as a useful stimulus for discussion, for example.

The place of the next category in Figure 2 is arguable. *Microteaching* lies on the boundary between simulation and reality. Regarded by some as a form of simulated teaching practice in which duration and numbers are scaled down, a key feature is that a particular teaching skill is identified and practised (see Orlosky's chapter for an extended treatment and references). It has been included in Figure 2 for convenience, and because Orlosky clearly sees it as a form of simulation (p 277). However, there is no consensus in the literature or among WYBE contributors as to whether it forms a separate category. Both terms appear, as if distinct, in the three American surveys reported by Cruickshank (1979); and Dennis and Gaede (1977)(who also discuss the pilot training analogy referred to earlier) would clearly place microteaching in Stage 2 of Figure 1. Part of the problem in locating microteaching is that a number of different styles and schools have evolved; within Britain, for example, it is practised differently in Ulster, Stirling and Lancaster (Brown, 1975; McIntyre *et al*, 1977; Perrott, 1977). Worldwide, the Haifa model is different from the Sydney one, Zambia from California. These variations include crucial issues such as the use of peers (fellow student teachers) in place of 'genuine' pupils, and the nature of the feedback provided. In Zambia, for example, Garvey reports that 'where peers are used for learning there is not a great advantage in using a videocamera' (Garvey, 1978:147). High among the criticisms which have been levelled at microteaching is that of artificiality. A highly-prepared five-minute lesson to 'teach' fellow-students some isolated piece of knowledge which they already possess scarcely resembles the task facing a beginning teacher, any more than the questions and difficulties posed by student teachers when role-playing pupils will be realistic, even if they are sincerely trying to be. Critics could argue that this variety is so far removed from the reality of a teacher's world that it is quite misleading to call it simulation. You could place microteaching under 2B or 3C in Figure 1, according to your conception of it.

An interesting simulation has been devised at the Tokyo Institute of Technology which aims to improve lesson planning and teaching skills of pre-service and in-service teachers but uses paper puppets in place of live pupils. As in many microteaching applications, feedback is provided by peer responses as well as videorecording replay. Preliminary evaluation results, in which the same instruments were used as in their evaluation of microteaching, show promising improvements between sessions (Sakamoto, 1980).

Role-playing simulations have been developed for a variety of purposes which do not require elaborate media. A few British examples should suffice; at Liverpool University, trainee secondary teachers played out specific roles in Ferguson's TORESIDE COMPREHENSIVE SCHOOL simulation (Ferguson, 1977). The purpose was to encourage students to think about the relationship between subject disciplines and to allow them to explore the social and psychological tensions within a teaching staff. They therefore not only had the opportunity to engage in conflict and experience the non-rational factors which influence decision-making in schools, but also, in the subsequent debriefing, they could distance themselves from and analyse that conflict. Student reaction was very favourable (Ferguson, 1977:157); a notable feature of his approach was the use of deliberately incomplete role *pro formas*, in which minimal details are prescribed well in advance and the participants are asked to supply the rest of the role biography, character and attitudes (Ferguson 1977:150-1). This is a most useful way of helping participants to embrace their roles and reduces the danger of rejection and stereotyping. Other examples have demonstrated that simple low-cost materials can form powerful learning experiences. Cross (1978) used a similar structure to involve 70 third year college of education students at Exeter in a curriculum development exercise; playing roles as the newly-qualified staff of a comprehensive school, they were to plan a humanities curriculum. The only resources needed were time, paper and the co-operation of ten briefed students in key roles, though tape-recording was used in the debriefing (Cross, 1979).

A variety of other simple role-playing simulations and games for enabling student teachers to explore communication and other issues are described by Adelman and Walker (1975). One powerful and subtle example they reprint is the TOTALITARIAN CLASSROOM GAME whose origins and fascination are explained by Glandon (1978). It is almost impossible to convey the flavour of this game in a brief mention; the teacher allocates to three of the students explicit roles as *Yes Person, No Person* and *Scribe,* but the rules and roles of the game establish and protect the teacher's power. Participants are prompted to comment and reflect on their own and each others' performances and many reach a perplexing stage of not knowing whether they are *playing at* or *being* the 'good student'. There is little connection between projecting oneself as a 'good student' and being a good learner. The game's title evokes its designers' belief in the 'soft fascism' of the classroom; it provokes a painful consciousness of the teacher's belief in his own knowledge and right to control — painful often for teacher and students alike. It is highly appropriate to use a simulation to explore the issue of the source and limits of the authority of the teacher. For, contrary to popular belief, simulations 'offer extremely powerful and sometimes subtle procedures to enable authoritative teachers to manipulate their students and project their ideas and personalities' (Megarry, 1978b:196).

Another example in which the authority of the 'teacher' is deliberately enhanced and manipulated for a specific purpose is a simulation of imposed dialect change designed at Jordanhill College, Glasgow, to help student teachers to appreciate the problems of dialect speakers and their difficulties (Casciani and Megarry, 1978). Here the 'teacher' played the role of an authoritarian teacher who was imposing his dialect, one spoken by the working classes of Dundee, on his 'pupils', whose Standard English grammar was thus defined as 'incorrect'.

A parallel can be drawn with the use of arbitrary discrimination in a family of simulation games called the ABZ GAMES, devised by Christiansen at Defiance, Ohio. These have been used to give student teachers and others experiential knowledge from the receiving end of prejudice by a teacher who arbitrarily oppresses and discriminates against those whose surnames fall in the second half of the alphabet, idealizing and favouring the A-J group (Christiansen, 1979). With only slightly more elaborate resources, a simulation game can be used to establish two artificial sub-cultures in two different rooms and afterwards have participants inter-visit and attempt to integrate (Bloomer, 1975). The game OUTSIDER has been used especially in pre-service education to help participants realize the difficulties and dangers of relying on 'travellers' tales' about a sub-culture, and to alert them to the likelihood of misunderstanding and being misunderstood when operating in an unfamiliar culture.

Action mazes were first popularized as a format in management education (Zoll, 1969) but have been adapted to in-service training. A problem is posed (usually in print for individual use but possibly on overhead projector transparency for group use) and the participant has to select which of four to six courses of action would be most appropriate. In the HARRY SCOTT ACTION MAZE (Bloomer, 1973) the problem is experienced by a head of department who is worried by persistent Monday absences of one of his/her teachers. According to the choice made, a different feedback frame is given; for example a different impression of Harry Scott's personality and family circumstances is created according to whether the participant decides to discuss him with his previous head of department, the headteacher or the assistant headteacher. Subsequent frames pose additional questions, the maze branching out at each choice point. Depending on how the situation is handled, there can be escalation and industrial action in the school, compulsory transfer for Harry Scott or an exchange of confidences and amicable resolution of the problem. An action maze closely resembles a branching programme, except that there is not usually an 'ideal' path through it, nor an absolute 'right answer'.

One of the difficulties that emerges when designing action mazes is that of making the range of possible courses of action sufficiently wide and realistic for participants to be willing to adopt one of them. Another is that of devising and managing the feedback frames so that they are genuinely adaptable to the choice made — ideally they should take into account the previous history of decisions. However, keeping track of all these complexities becomes extremely difficult to manage without the assistance of a computer — which is the ideal medium for an action maze.

One *computer-based exercise* which demonstrates this effortless adaptability is TENURE, which was developed for pre-service students at the University of Illinois on the PLATO IV computer-assisted instruction system (Dennis and Gaede, 1977). The student is faced with the task of making a series of about 50 decisions concerning the handling of incidents which supposedly occur in his or her first year of teaching. This is compressed into about an hour at the computer terminal. Early decisions include seating arrangements, teaching methodology and the weighting of various forms of assessment; these partly influence the choice of problems to be presented later. Examples include a student observed cheating on a test, a colleague persistently keeping students late, a parent complaint, etc. The student's objective is to obtain tenure; depending on performance, the outcome may range from being fired to promotion to departmental chairman. Although success partly depends on (simulated) pupil achievement and opinions and reactions from parents, teachers and administrators, the greatest weight is given to the school principal's opinion, so a strategy of trying to discover and conform to the principal's educational philosophy is rewarded. (One of four basic types of principal is randomly generated at the outset so students can use the simulation more than once.) The simulation had been run for over 10,000 simulated 'years' in its first year of availability (Dennis and Gaede, 1977:8) and the authors believe it has been effective in making pre-service teachers aware of the conflicts and compromises which first-year teachers may face. However, there is a real danger that what they will actually learn is cynicism and conformity. One of the disadvantages of computer-based simulation is the difficulty of arranging a post-simulation discussion soon enough after the student completes the simulation or even perhaps at all. After completing a simulation like TENURE, students should surely be gathered in groups to discuss the experience, to question the model and its built-in assumptions and values, and to discuss the ethical and professional implications. 'The computer' nowadays has, if anything, a more spurious authority than the printed word.

Another computer-based exercise provides participants with a simulated classroom of 30 students for whom they have to plan lessons (Mitchell, 1978). It was devised at Concordia University, Montreal, in an attempt to overcome limitations in the Kersh-Cruickshank models of simulations described earlier. Mitchell makes three criticisms of these: they confuse the role of teacher as classroom manager with that of instructor and initiator; they rely upon the teacher trainer or peer group to provide reactions to the trainees' decisions, and they emphasize extemporaneous classroom decisions and interactions to the neglect of instructional planning (Mitchell, 1978:192). EDSIM presents the trainee with data on the students' capabilities and predicts the effects of his or her instructional planning decisions according to a mastery learning model in which all *mathemata* (things to be learned) are either learned completely or not at all ('1' or '0' in the capability matrix). Examples of instructional decisions offered and their assumed consequences reveal some interesting assumptions:

> 16. *Introduce humour.* A decision to introduce humour, whether or not it is related to the instructional objectives, will increase general motivation of the student slightly. (*time 1 min.*)
> 19. *Counsel student(s) after class.* If it is ever desired to discuss (a) student(s)' progress after class, it is assumed that his rate of learning with respect to the mathemata specified will increase as a result. (*time 15 min.*) (Mitchell, 1978: 195)

Clearly the likelihood of learning from EDSIM being translated into classroom behaviour is limited by its extreme artificiality and the simplified quantitative learning model it embodies. Mitchell himself suggests the need to supplement it with other varieties of simulation and, of course, teaching practice. Preliminary evaluation data suggested that students enjoyed EDSIM and were motivated to additional study by it; but although the intellectual flexibility it generated was thought to be worthwhile and generalizable, they thought it unlikely that the particular strategies which were successful in EDSIM would be useful with a real class of pupils (Mitchell, 1978:202).

This review has tried to illustrate the range and variety of simulations which have been used for a variety of purposes in teacher education. No attempt has been made to cover the use of games and simulations in schools *by* teachers. Over the past ten years, my experience of introducing practising teachers to the use of games and simulations supports the argument at the outset of this chapter: *using* games and simulations *with* teachers is the best way to present their potential. Not only do the advantages then become obvious (teachers who are reluctant to stop talking about a simulation do not need to be *told* that simulations can be involving and motivating); but also the management problems they present, and the organizational skills they require, can be identified, demonstrated and discussed in the light of a shared experience. The use of simulation techniques *with* teachers is a prerequisite to credibility in advocating their use *by* teachers.

Distance education

It has usually been taken for granted that the teacher and the taught must be gathered together in one place — frequently in a special building dedicated to learning. This, after all, is the basis on which schools and colleges have been built, and it is why a high proportion of their floor areas consist of spaces in which face-to-face teaching takes place. Universities have traditionally expected rather more independent study of their students and formal tuition has occupied a lower proportion of the students' time, and lower still of the teachers'. Until recently, however, at least in the western world, they have not seriously questioned the need for physical proximity, and the concept of a residential university education has occupied a special place in the ideals of teachers and students alike. However, the past ten years have seen a rapid growth of interest in techniques and arrangements for mature students to learn at a distance. This section briefly reviews the development of distance education, looks at its implications for the professional development of teachers, and then reports an example in more detail.

Definition, development and rationale

By distance education I mean education provided by any organization at any level to cater for learners and teachers who are physically separate. Learning may be by means of print or other media, separately or in combination, and distance learning is often complemented by face-to-face teaching, group work or tutorials. The students are generally, but not necessarily, adult or mature. Materials designed for distance education are sometimes used by institution-based students in addition; when students who *need not* be physically distant from their teachers learn directly from packaged resource materials, they are generally described as engaging in 'resource-based learning' rather than 'distance learning' — but there is no sharp division *in principle*. In practice, however, distance learning materials are designed for students whose circumstances demand self-reliance; since they may have no access to tutorial support, they require materials which are both explicit and well-tested in the field.

It is important to clarify what (apart from coinage of the new term) is new and distinctive about the modern concept of distance education. Obviously the notion that learning can take place without face-to-face contact is far from new; the most important educational implication of the spread of the printed word was the emancipation of would-be learners from dependence on the physical presence of a teacher. But from Caxton to the twentieth century, this emancipation remained more theoretical than actual. Few were, like Samuel Taylor Coleridge, sufficiently literate, motivated and equipped to pursue studies to advanced levels from books alone, unsupported by personal tuition. Those who did — *amateur* learners in the noblest sense, and formidable polymaths some of them were — had no means available whereby their learning could be recognized by any sort of qualification or degree (unless, of course, they became) sufficiently eminent to receive honorary degrees).

Apart from this élite group, then, any real prospect of home-based learning for everyman waited on the development techniques of structuring print to make it more self-instructional than conventional books. 'Teach yourself' books and correspondence texts can be traced back to the mid-nineteenth century self-improvement trend popularized by Samuel Smiles, but their serious academic development, like that of programmed learning, occurred in the twentieth century. The last hundred years have also seen the growth of commercial and charitable correspondence schools and extension colleges like Pitman's, Hermods, the National Extension College and the International Extension College. These have remained education's Cinderellas, low in prestige as institutions, their qualifications mostly below degree status and of limited currency, their existence insufficiently acknowledged in the literature. Drop-out rates were high, and it is perhaps surprising they were not higher. For people who were frequently working long hours and a six-day week, finding enough time and energy to pursue studies from correspondence texts without human support or contact was a hard grind up a steep hill. Gritty determination was necessary to sustain the effort to complete the course and the common assumption was that the arrangements were at best a poor substitute for the 'real thing'. 'Distance education (in the form of "pure" correspondence study) was created to give those a chance to study who could not go to an ordinary school or university for financial, social, geographical or medical reasons' (Holmberg, 1977:17).

This 'second-best' mentality affected morale and recruitment, of both students and teachers, and prevailed until quite recently. It had inevitable effects on standards, drop-out rates and the status of qualifications available.

Recent developments in Britain and abroad

A dramatic transformation of this situation has now taken place; over the last decade, distance education has become an accepted term and its positive features have come to be valued (see Holmberg, 1977 and 1979). This rise in prestige and popularity is in large measure a direct result of the trail blazed by a British institution which recently celebrated its tenth birthday, the Open University. The OU's direct contribution has been to demonstrate that degree-level standards *can* be achieved by learners at a distance; degrees awarded by the OU unquestionably command respect. Although it was conceived as a university of the second chance, it has proved that, for the many adults who *prefer* to study while continuing to work (McIntosh and Woodley, 1978), learning at a distance need *not* be second-best. The OU's development in its first ten years has been well-documented (Venables, 1979:273; Perry, 1976); its impact since courses were first offered (January 1971) has been considerable, both in Britain and overseas. As John Raynor comments (see Chapter 16) its indirect effects should not be underestimated; the correspondence texts and readers which are the core of OU courses have had wide sales and even wider influence on teachers and courses in higher education generally.

The OU's house journal *Teaching at a Distance* broke new ground when it was started in 1975. It will soon be complemented by an international and more general periodical called *Distance Education*, to be edited from Australia (Keegan and Mitchell, forthcoming). The existence of learned journals on distance education surely sets the seal of academic respectability on the technique.

There has been a rapid development of distance teaching universities elsewhere in Europe, too — for instance the well-known Fernuniversität at Hagen, West Germany, and the Universidad National de Educacion a Distancia in Spain (Garcia, 1976). Examples abound in other continents. In Australia, for example, three universities pioneered external university-level courses — the University of Queensland as early as 1911, the University of New England from 1955 and Macquarie University from 1967; Murdoch University (1975) and Deakin University (1975) followed and external enrolments in all five total nearly 12,000 students (Smith, 1979). The University of Wisconsin was a notable pioneer in the US; Athabasca University in Canada and the National Open University, Venezuela, further exemplify the concept in the Americas, as do Everyman's University, Israel and the Free University of Iran in the Middle East. The Far East includes other examples, like the Allama Iqbal Open University of Pakistan. Some of the recent examples have been directly influenced by their consultancy links with the Open University Centre for International Co-operation and Services (OUCICS) whose closure (announced for Spring 1980) is a casualty of recent expenditure cutbacks. Distance teaching universities are discussed in a forthcoming book by OUCICS staff (Kaye and Rumble).

Teachers as consumers of distance education

What is the relationship between the rise of distance education and the professional development of teachers? To begin with, teachers have been avid *consumers* of distance education, for both their personal and professional development. As Raynor illustrates (in Chapter 16) teachers and lecturers are still the largest occupational group among OU students, though their proportion has shrunk from 36 per cent to 21 per cent over the past eight years. The decline partly reflects progressive satisfaction of the ulterior motivation of some (eg attainment and upgrading of degrees). More strikingly, Smith (1979:20) in his review of external studies at the University of New England, reports a decline in the proportion of teachers and lecturers among external students from 85 per cent to 41 per cent over the past 25 years. However, although teachers' motives for distance education may be mixed and changing, distance learning methods should have positive advantages for practising teachers at least in courses of direct professional relevance. Of all the criticisms which have traditionally been made of teacher education, the most persistent is that of a yawning gap between theory and practice. If the students are teachers who are in post, the courses have not only an opportunity but an obligation to draw on the teachers' wealth of classroom experience as a proving-ground for theory. Examples could be given from the OU's INSET unit; Raynor refers (p 226) to their attempts to make their courses school-focused and classroom-based. However, to give flesh to this section, I want to present in some detail a different example of a vocational course for teachers involving distance education (one in which I am personally involved) and to compare its features with the larger-scale and better-known OU formula.

Teaching educational technology at a distance: the Jordanhill example

DEVELOPMENT AND RATIONALE. Jordanhill College of Education pioneered the teaching of educational technology at a distance through its Diploma in Educational Technology, a two year part-time course for teachers who are in-service in schools and higher education. Materials are produced and distributed from Jordanhill and residential sessions are held there periodically (one week-end per month throughout the first year, less frequently in the second). Students work on a 'module' — our basic distance learning unit — for five or more hours each week at their home bases. The course was designed by David Butts (who became its first Course Director in 1975) partly in response to a market survey of training needs and likely uptake of various combinations. Although it emerged that economic constraints would preclude the long-term release necessary for a purely college-based course, the format has positive advantages for facilitating application of ideas, experimentation with innovative techniques and evaluation of learning materials (Butts and Megarry, 1977:268).

STAFFING AND STUDENTS. In terms of numbers, our course is on a very modest scale compared with the OU. We adapted their concept of a course team to suit our own needs. At present, we have the equivalent of two and a half full-time lecturers, distributed among five members of the Audio-Visual Media Department; one full-time lecturer (who also acts as Course Director) and four others with varying levels of part-time commitment up to 50 per cent. We all have other departmental or college teaching commitments. In addition, we are assisted by colleagues from other departments (notably Psychology and Education) who write some of the modules and teach occasional college sessions. Members of the course team, usually as individuals, though occasionally jointly, both design and revise most of the modules, teach nearly all the college sessions, set and mark all the exercises and assignments and provide tutorial back-up service to students by post and telephone, and by individual visits and meetings. This is in contrast to the OU pattern of multiple and joint authorship of course units by a central team supported by part-time staff who conduct tutorials face-to-face and by telephone, mark assignments and undertake counselling, but do not write units. We can and must combine roles because of our small numbers. This assists coherence and minimizes confusion from indirect communications (Smith, 1979: 33-54).

To date, we have had 95 enrolments in five intakes and only half a dozen withdrawals (Megarry, 1979a). We are obliged to limit numbers to a ceiling of 20 or so largely because of pressure on accommodation and practical facilities. The remarkably low drop-out figure perhaps reflects the degree of personal involvement by staff and the tutorial support they provide. The fact that students are 'paced' through the course by a regular rhythm of residential week-ends, assessment exercises and the like may also be relevant.

Students have included schoolteachers in primary and secondary schools, including schools for the handicapped, maladjusted and young offenders; college lecturers, mostly in further education, but also in universities, colleges of education, polytechnics and central institutions; and a handful of others from libraries, curriculum development agencies, and training establishments. The geographical scatter has been wide, including students from England and Eire, as well as from all over Scotland.

ROLE OF COLLEGE SESSIONS. Although some aspects of the course's design and mode of operation have profited from the Open University experience several of its features are distinctive. For example, we place a greater emphasis on face-to-face teaching in combination with distance learning than does the OU, which only *requires* attendance at an annual summer school and that only for some of its courses. More frequent tutorials are available to OU students, especially in more populous areas, but attendance is optional and variable. In the Jordanhill course, by contrast, distance learning notionally accounts for only about one-third of the official total of formal study time: 175 hours out of a theoretical total of 475 hours (though evaluation data suggests that course members spontaneously spend much longer than this, see Megarry, 1979a). Nearly all the theoretical work, embracing management studies as well as theoretical aspects of educational technology, is covered by modules. These are followed up by seminars and participative learning techniques in college sessions. For example, a theoretical module on *Computers and Educational Technology* (Megarry, 1979c) is complemented by 'hands-on' experience of computer-assisted learning and discussion of wider implications in the college sessions. Again, theoretical studies of the management of innovation are backed up by written exercises and role-playing simulations which help the student to practise decision-making and handle personal relationships in a realistic situation (Kirkland, 1978). A major component of the college sessions, however, is the acquisition of practical skills — like making audio-visual materials and handling equipment — which are less suited to distance education and which require the equipment and facilities of a central institution. Miscellaneous purposes are also served by college sessions — including, for example, access to the book and audio-visual libraries, occasional guest speakers, visits and tutorial group meetings.

MODULES: USE OF PRINT. A typical module consists of a printed A4 spiral-bound booklet of 40 to 100 pages; most also contain audio-visual material. The booklet is not a mini-textbook, but nor is it as highly structured and prescribed as a programmed learning text. The text is broken up and signposted, open-ended questions are posed, audio-visual material is often interspersed and written activities are built in. The latter are printed on self-copying paper; students (mostly, not invariably) post completed response sheets back to the course team, who use them mainly for evaluation and revision of the modules and activities. Feedback on the activities, including suggested answers where appropriate, is provided at the end of the module. We originally intended each module to have a lifespan of three years before major revision but the course has changed so rapidly and continuously since the start that this is probably an overestimate. Changes have affected the duration, content, methods, assessment, evaluation, organization, materials and status of the course (Megarry, 1979a). In general, our use of print is similar to the OU's, though our modules tend to be shorter, to include fewer and shorter unbroken stretches of straight reading, to emphasize immediate feedback on activities, to be less glossily produced (they do not, for example, include photographs) and to be revised more frequently. Rather than rewriting the whole course simultaneously, we try to update and revise only where necessary.

MODULES: AUDIO-VISUAL COMPONENTS. Our use of audio-visual materials for distance learning is simpler than the OU's, but we also incorporate them into the materials more centrally. We standardized on audio cassettes and filmstrips, and most modules include either or both, separately or in combination, *as an integral part* of the learning material. For example, in a module on accountability, an audio cassette presents material on the payment by results scheme, including a dramatized reconstruction of its parliamentary presentation by Sir Robert Lowe (Butts, 1979). Again, filmstrip frames provide a cheap and effective way of presenting sample 'hands' and circuits made in CIRCUITRON, an instructional game on electric circuits covered by the module on *Simulation and Games* (Megarry, 1979b). It is complemented by an audio cassette which paints a verbal picture of a classroom in which the game was played, and includes 'overhead' conversation between teacher and pupils and pupil interviews. Synchronized tape/filmstrip presentation is used to give various examples of computer-assisted learning sequences for analysis (Megarry, 1979c) and to present case studies of school resource centres (Kirkland, 1977). In most cases, the audio-visual material is followed up by an activity with written responses which cannot be completed unless the student has used the audio-visual materials.

Although the OU has diverted a significant proportion of its funds to producing radio and television broadcasts, and though it was originally billed as a University of the Air by Harold Wilson in his Glasgow speech in 1963, the status of broadcasts in OU courses is both variable and controversial. In some courses, the course units do not even refer to the broadcasts associated with them, much less do they depend on them, whereas in other courses, assignments are sometimes set on them. The differing role and status of broadcasting in the various courses is reflected by student viewing figures, whose averages range from less than 50 per cent to nearly 80 per cent for television and below 30 per cent to nearly 75 per cent for radio (Bates, 1975). In any case, broadcasting schedules are inflexible, and reception in some remote areas is poor or non-existent; postal distribution is at present only a feasible alternative for audio, not for video cassettes, because of cost and availability of replay machines. In any event, broadcasting is inherently identified with one-way communication at a fixed pace; cassettes and filmstrips are more easily brought under student control and it seems likely that the future of sophisticated audio-visual material which is an integral part of distance learning courses lies in developments like CYCLOPS (described later). At present, then, though the OU commands the use of more sophisticated media like colour television, Jordanhill's mixture may be more cost-effective. On the rare occasions when moving, as opposed to still, visuals are required — for example, in the study of characteristics of such media themselves, or where examples of different styles of teaching are to be presented for analysis — we replay films or video-tapes in college sessions. In the current climate of severe cuts in public expenditure, OU student opinion is strongly in favour of reducing the OU's broadcasting budget and a minority would 'scrap it altogether' (*Sesame*, December 1979:8).

Our use of telephone communication has been largely for pastoral and tutorial support; we have not used it as a teaching medium. This is in contrast to the OU, who are currently considering extending their use of telephone tutoring and setting up a teleconference network of dedicated telephone lines both for teaching and administration (*Open Line*, December 1979). Although this would be based on the University of Wisconsin model, there are already over 40 such educational networks in North America.

ASSESSMENT AND EVALUATION. Our assessment arrangements are radical but, we believe, appropriate. Contrary to OU practice, traditional examinations have had no place in our course from the start. Award of the Diploma is based entirely on course work completed by students, mostly in their own time at their home bases; in the first year they complete various theoretical exercises on objectives, methods and evaluation among others and practical exercises in production skills like graphics, tape recording and photography. In their second year they complete two major assignments and a project. Assessment of the last three is moderated by our two external examiners, and the whole Diploma has been validated by the Council for National Academic Awards since 1977.

Like the OU, we have always attached importance to evaluation as part of our commitment to a systematic and self-regulating model of course improvement. Originally we had a lecturer whose principal Dip Ed Tech role was to evaluate, though her role became progressively more mixed. As evaluation has now been added to my remit, I am acutely conscious of the difficulties and dangers of trying to combine the roles of teacher, author, tutor and evaluator. Nevertheless, we draw on a variety of evidence for the evaluation (Butts and Megarry, 1977). The principal means of collecting information, on both base modules and college sessions, are evaluation questionnaires, assessment exercises and assignments, and feedback sessions held in college. In addition, evaluation of college sessions is sometimes supplemented by observation; and of base modules, by analysis of the copy sheets, follow-up seminars in college and, experimentally, by cassettes on which students 'talk through' their reactions to a module (Megarry, 1977b).

INDIRECT INFLUENCE. Like the OU, we know that our materials find a much wider audience than the small numbers who actually take our course. More than three-quarters of the students reported showing modules to family, friends and colleagues (Megarry, 1979a). On visits to our students' institutions we note a variety of signs that the course is having wider effects, including the circulation of modules and involvement by their colleagues in the course members' curriculum project — for example in an evaluator role. Also, in response to a large and growing number of requests for our materials, we made most of them available for outside sale in 1977. During the first two years, over 2000 of the printed booklets alone were bought by institutions and individuals all over Britain and overseas. Moreover, there are strong indications that our modules have affected non-distance learning within Jordanhill; not only are the materials themselves often used to support face-to-face teaching on other courses, but there are signs of their influence on the packaged learning materials used to support seminars and tuition in the college at large.

However, the Jordanhill Diplomates are nearly all involved in conventional institutions, most of which employ face-to-face methods. It will be interesting to see whether their experience of the course leads them to make greater use of the methods through which we have taught them. Will they become *providers* of distance education as well as *consumers*?

Meanwhile, as distance learning courses proliferate around the world, one need is clear and urgent — for research to identify, and training to promote, the distinctive skills and practices for designing and structuring effective distance learning materials. There is even a scarcity of books in this area. Notable exceptions are publications from the two Cambridge non-profitmaking establishments, the International Extension College and the National Extension College, who give practical guidance on writing and editing distance learning materials; see Perraton (1973) and IEC (1979) for examples. There are some general suggestions in *A Handbook on Distance Education* (Harris and Williams, 1977) and the Council for Educational Technology has sponsored support materials on independent learning in connection with the Technician Education Council programme (Manchester Polytechnic, undated). CET's Open Learning Systems project teams are also producing a training pack to assist with the design of distance learning materials for further education (CET, forthcoming). This should be a useful complement to the training manual based on OU experience (Rowntree and Connors, 1979).

Valuable though the published advice of experienced practitioners may be, however, empirical testing of the strategies and techniques used in distance teaching materials is in its infancy, even at the OU (Nathenson, 1979). The suggestions Nathenson offers may or may not be applicable to other material and authors, but they contribute to a literature which is in its infancy. As he remarks, particular conventions and practices tend to become institutionalized without any evidence to support their effectiveness. Like the OU, we at Jordanhill have evolved something of a house style; but we could defend its features only by reference to theory, not with hard empirical evidence. Both research and further publication of the advice and examples of experienced practitioners are now needed as input to recognized training in the production of materials for distance education. The fact that many distance learning tutors are unconvinced of the need for training (Harris, 1975:46) is beside the point. It is widely accepted that teachers should have formal training before teaching face-to-face; their need for training of a different kind for distance teaching is no less real.

Interaction and future developments

It was argued at the outset that the apparent contradiction between simulation gaming and distance education is an illusion. Future developments seem likely to reconcile them more closely. There are signs that rapid progress in computer technology and telecommunications is about to revolutionize the nature and potency of distance learning and perhaps, indeed, our whole lives. Gosling has written elegantly and convincingly of 'the quite incredible discontinuity in the nature of our society which is just beginning' (Gosling, 1978:11). The microelectronic revolution has been widely hailed as potentially at least as fundamental as the industrial revolution.

In a previous *World Yearbook*, the educational implications of the emerging post-industrial economy and information revolution have been spelled out (Stonier, 1979) and Hubbard argues for future diversity of educational provision in response to the challenge and needs of lifelong education (Hubbard, 1979). Advances in automation are already progressively replacing manpower by machines for unskilled work in industry, with dramatic effects on the employment market. If human beings are relieved — or deprived, depending on one's point of view — of the need to perform routine and repetitive tasks for a significant proportion of each day, they will be faced with the problem of how to spend their time profitably. If the employment of leisure, or the leisure of unemployment, is the next major 'problem' to be faced, it also presents a challenge and an opportunity to which our educational system must rise. 'Education will eventually become the principal industry, but what sort of education do we want?' (Stonier, 1979:34).

Just as the new technology undermines the role of mechanical and repetitive human labour in the employment sector, so in education 'the computer is peculiarly suited to reducing the amount of inauthentic student labour' (Hooper, 1977:41). Our reaction to the replacement of human labour by computer labour for tedious and boring tasks is as ambivalent in education as in employment; gratitude for the release from drudgery is tempered, if not overwhelmed, by perplexity about the question of 'release for what?'. Writing about the role of computer-based games and simulations in geography, Walker makes the point that many students (and their teachers) clearly miss the 'hard work' of repetitive calculations and feel at a loss. 'The computer... takes away the time-consuming but mentally undemanding activities so that the pupil is faced with the much more demanding tasks of drawing conclusions about results with a much higher frequency. This is good educationally, but it can destroy some cosy educational customs' (Walker, 1978:183).

Education by computer, like the other innovations discussed, demands new skills and new roles from the teacher. Howe and du Boulay (1979) identify some of the difficulties which arise if computers are used as surrogate teachers, and the benefits which accrue when computers and teachers form a partnership, each specializing in what they do best. Teachers must be educated to adopt these new roles and to develop these new skills if they are to react more positively to the new technology than have some other groups of workers. The personal and creative aspects of the task of education should ensure that teachers will never be simply replaced by computers; but if teachers feel that their jobs are under attack, they cannot be blamed for resisting the threat. It is critical, therefore, that the teachers' organizations should be involved in constructive discussion of these developments at an early stage. It is also essential that teacher education should recognize these new roles and skills, and start training teachers to develop and welcome a partnership with the computer rather than reject it through fear of its effect on teacher employment.

The microelectronic revolution thus changes the methods of education, as well as its aims. Some models of computer use in education and training were explored by the National Development Programme in Computer Assisted Learning (NDPCAL) — both as a direct learning resource and as a flexible device for managing the learning paths and assessment of students' progress as individuals (Hooper, 1977). One of its projects was directly concerned with the use of computer-managed learning in teacher training at the New University of Ulster (McMahon *et al*, 1977). Most of the others had at least indirect implications for teacher education and development in general. In the wake of a suddenly dawning awareness of the microelectronic revolution, triggered partly by the screening of a BBC television *Horizon* programme called 'Now the chips are down' in 1977, the colleges and institutes of education in Britain are currently and belatedly considering their response. To date, the role of computers in the teacher education curriculum has been all too marginal, with the possible exception of that for intending secondary mathematics and science teachers. Dennis has argued the need for such education to be initiated during the prolonged and intensive training experiences which are only possible at pre-service level (Dennis, 1979).

The impact of the new technology is not confined to the aims and methods of education; there are widespread predictions that its organization will also be fundamentally affected. The continued existence of schools and other educational institutions has been questioned:

> ...might not colleges and universities be up for sale by the end of the century as plentifully as churches are today? Might not the great majority of the population find what passes for eduation at the end of a phone or over the television screen in their own homes? ... Will the vast data-banks of information that will become available provide the 'distant' teacher with the comprehensive detailed profile of the student's education? (Wilson, 1979:49-50)

Lest this seem like a flight of fancy or speculative journalism, and neither is a common feature of university professors writing in academic journals, it is imperative that we recognize the *accelerating* speed of change. Fact frequently overtakes fiction, and writing on this subject probably has a shorter half-life than on any other. At a conference in 1977, I indulged in speculation which, if not particularly well-informed, was thought slightly daring, about the possible effects of television/telephone/computer link-ups on the development of education through simulation and gaming (Megarry, 1978b:202). Only a year later, I had *used* Prestel, the Post Office viewdata system which is now publicly available in Britain. This not only allows users access to a huge range of information stored in a central computer through a telephone link to a modified television receiver, but it has also begun to offer education in a way that capitalizes on its *interactive* nature. Fedida (1978) gives a concise description of the Post Office system. In June 1979 the OU started developing its own viewdata system called Optel which is designed to be compatible with existing OU systems and Prestel.

Other sophisticated OU systems are already transforming the speed and nature of feedback in distance education. For example, CICERO is a computer-assisted scheme which conducts diagnostic testing, offers feedback (both of correct answers and of reasons for mistakes) and can also provide tutorial help. It has only recently been available on some courses and uptake by students is currently limited by access to study centres and the need to book terminals as well as by psychological barriers. Should systems like this become available in students' homes, they will become dramatically more useful and acceptable.

Another promising development, which will capitalize on widespread television ownership, is the CYCLOPS system. This uses an ordinary audio cassette to store audio-visual information which can then be replayed on an equally ordinary television set; what is extraordinary is the microelectronic computer (not unlike a videogame control box) which analyses and synthesizes a television picture from the information stored on the tape. When the description was published, the system produced black-and-white pictures not colour, animation was slow and resolution limited (the array of dots is 256 x 256) but a future price was predicted to be perhaps as low as £40 (Read, 1978). Further development work can only lead to lower prices and higher quality, and audio cassette tape is already cheap and widely available. It can be used for audio-visual replay under student control, for telephone communication with 'electronic blackboard' between users, and for direct communications with a central computer giving access to data-banks. The use of a light pen or similar response device enables users to 'draw' as well as to respond to questions and instructions. The real educational potential of CYCLOPS, then, lies in its computer 'compatibility'.

At present, the educational applications of viewdata and similar systems are comparatively primitive. The push-button control in Prestel is used merely as a page-turner in an encyclopaedia or programmed text; similarly, software development for CYCLOPS is still at an early stage. If, however, the quality of the educational software can match that of the hardware, systems like these could revolutionize the nature and potential of education at a distance. Simulation and gaming has already proved itself a major application area for computers in education (Megarry, 1978d; Walker and Graham, 1979). There is every likelihood that distance education will include simulation and gaming as a major strategy. This is not to say, of course, that no place will remain for face-to-face simulation and gaming; there will still need to be places where discussion, demonstration and, perhaps, traditional teaching take place, whether or not they resemble schools as we now know them.

Learning and teaching have different characteristics face-to-face from at a distance; human beings learn from the experience of talking, listening, touching, moving and laughing together in a way which will never be replaced by the impersonal, static isolation of a screen and keyboard. Unlike Evans (1979:228) I do not envisage 'a complete shift from group to personalized teaching'. But in the future, people will only need to travel for educational purposes when there is a genuine reason to meet, such as participating in a live human simulation. Many of the conventional preoccupations of schools at present could be covered more effectively and conveniently at a distance using these new media, given adequate student motivation. This proviso reminds us that the whole issue of compulsion in education would be called into question. What would be the role and justification of compelling attendance *per se*?

Concepts of distance education have received fresh life from the new technology. Recall the history of media for distance learning since the advent of print. An efficient postal service, which in Britain dates back nearly 150 years, was the basis of correspondence education. The telephone, which is gaining popularity as a supplementary form of communication both for academic and pastoral purposes, is about half as old. Radio is a phenomenon of the last half-century and television is a decade or so younger. Neither of the 'broadcasting' media readily provides any feedback to the learner; interaction requires the use of 'phone-ins' or postal responses. This severely limits the instructional capabilities of these more recent — and perhaps more glamorous — media. A system comprising computer and telephone or other links to television-type terminals in people's homes can combine all these options, and is not confined to the traditional pattern of teacher-student communication. Links *between* 'students', as well as with the teacher *via* the central computer, could be organized, enabling students to form peer learning self-help groups, or even to reverse the traditional pattern by devising 'instruction' for their 'teachers'. Optel will explore the possibilities of a personal message service between and among OU students as well as from authors to students ('electronic publishing').

Moreover, the age of the cheap, portable personal computer is already dawning. In a chapter entitled 'The decline of the professions', Evans (1979) describes a prototype device recently developed at the National Physical Laboratory. MINNIE (its provisional title) is outwardly similar to a pocket calculator, but has a full alphabetic keyboard and display, and a range of learning programmes ('software'); for example, it can test and teach French vocabulary. Already in the shops are other portable devices which use microprocessors to produce a *synthesized* voice which teaches spelling, provides feedback and also tests. The commercial pressures to market and sell such devices ensure that they will be bought by an increasing proportion of the population as prices tumble further; witness the spread of pocket calculators — already commonplace among schoolchildren of the western world — and videogames, which are rapidly spreading. It is too soon yet to know whether the major thrust of development in computer-based learning will come through home-based terminals linked to central computers or through widespread possession of portable personalized computers, perhaps with plug-in software. At present, only the former can easily provide graphics, colour and animation, though this could change. As paper 'hard copy' of computer and student output may still be useful, access to a printing device (possibly home-based) will be needed on occasion, at least.

Whether the home-based system or portable device predominates, or whether they develop complementary roles, the challenge posed for the professional development of teachers is considerable. Unless teachers respond to this challenge by embracing the new technology, the decline in the teaching profession which Evans predicts will occur. Teachers must develop and capitalize on those skills which are *not* easily replaced by microelectronic devices — human and personal skills of communication, motivation and counselling, design skills for producing computer-based software and learning systems, and evaluation and research skills to assess the impact of the new media and methods. These are different from the skills currently possessed and valued by the teaching profession, and they may be distributed differently among the population from which it draws. Education in the future will demand a highly skilled teaching profession, but of a different character and perhaps reduced in size.

All this will require not only a massive increase in microelectronic awareness by those who train teachers, but also a change of heart. Until recently, the teacher education world tended to regard those few of its members who were computer-literate with suspicion or amused superiority, if indeed they recognized them as distinct from the mathematics department(!) This attitude must change drastically and sincerely; awareness of the potential and limitations of the computer *for* education and its impact *on* education must be given a central place in the education of teachers. Otherwise tomorrow's teachers will be as handicapped as yesterday's illiterates.

References

Adelman, C and Walker, R (1975) *A Guide to Classroom Observation* Methuen: London
Archer, E G *et al* (1977) In-service training and primary schools: some Scottish experiences *The European Teacher* **15** 2:14-20
Bates, T (1975) Survey of student use of broadcasting *Teaching at a Distance* **5** 45-52
Bishop, A J and Whitfield, R C (1972) *Situations in Teaching* McGraw-Hill: London
Bloomer, J (1973) What have simulation and gaming got to do with programmed learning and educational technology? *Programmed Learning and Educational Technology* **10** 4:224-34
Bloomer, J (1975) OUTSIDER: pitfalls and payoffs of simulation gaming *in* Gibbs, G I and Howe, A (eds) *Academic Gaming and Simulation in Education and Training* Kogan Page: London
Bone, T R (1968) HAWKHEAD HIGH SCHOOL Jordanhill College of Education: Glasgow (mimeo)
Borg, W R (1971) The minicourse — a milestone on the road to better teaching *British Journal of Educational Technology* **2** 1:14-23
Brown, G (1975) *Microteaching. A Programme of Teaching Skills* Methuen: London
Butts, D C (1979) *Management of Innovation: Accountability within a Systems Approach* (B203A) comprising booklet and cassette. Jordanhill College of Education: Glasgow
Butts, D C and Megarry, J (1977) Teaching educational technology at a distance *in* Hills, P and Gilbert, J (1977) *Aspects of Educational Technology XI* Kogan Page: London
Casciani, J and Megarry, J (1978) First steps toward a simulation of dialect change pp 101-9 *in* Megarry(1978c)
CET (1975) *The Staff Meeting* Evaluation Case Study No 2. User's Manual and two cassettes. Council for Educational Technology: London
CET (forthcoming) *Writing Materials for Distance Learning* (A training pack produced by a team co-ordinated by Roger Lewis) Council for Educational Technology: London
Christiansen, K (1979) How the ABZ GAMES work *Simulation/Games for Learning* **9** 3:107-16
Cross, D (1978) A little Bullock goes a long way: a college of education simulation exercise *British Journal of Educational Technology* **9** 3:193-200
Cross, D (1979) Talking past one another's ears: a simulation debriefing dialogue pp 24-30 *in* Megarry (1979d)
Cruickshank, D R (1971) Teacher education looks at simulation: a review of selected uses and research results pp 185-203 *in* Tansey (1971)
Cruickshank, D R *et al* (1979) The state of the art of simulation in teacher education *Simulation/Games for Learning* **9** 2:72-82
Cruickshank, D R and Telfer, R A (1979) *Simulation and Games: An ERIC Bibliography* (Bibliographies on Education Topics No 11) ERIC Clearinghouse on Teacher Education: Washington, DC
Dennis, J R (1979) Undergraduate programs to increase instructional computing in school *Association for Educational Data Systems Monitor* Jan/Feb/Mar: 8-11
Dennis, J R and Gaede, O R (1977) Simulation gaming in the teacher education curriculum *Illinois Series on Educational Applications of Computers Number 18:* Urbana, Illinois
Diehl, B (1979) Current simulation gaming in Australia *Simulation and Games* **10** 3:265-74
Evans, C (1979) *The Mighty Micro* Victor Gollancz: London
Fedida, S (1978) Viewdata in education pp 78-86 *in* Howe and Romiszowski (1978)
Ferguson, S (1977) TORESIDE COMPREHENSIVE SCHOOL: a simulation game for teachers in training pp 148-59 *in* Megarry (1977a)
Garcia, G M J (1976) *La Universidad Nacional de Educacion a Distancia, Su Implantacion y Dessarrollo Inicial* Ediciones CEAC, SA: Barcelona

Garvey, B (1978) Microteaching: developing the concept for practical training *British Journal of Educational Technology* **9** 2:142-8

Glandon, N (1978) The TOTALITARIAN CLASSROOM GAME: reflections on authority *SAGSET Journal* **8** 1:24-9

Gosling, W (1978) *Microcircuits, Society and Education* (CET Occasional Paper No 8) Council for Educational Technology: London

Grugeon, D (ed) *Teaching at a Distance* Quarterly journal published by the Open University: Milton Keynes

Harris, W J A (1975) *The Distance Tutor* (Manchester Monographs Number 3) University of Manchester

Harris, W J A and Williams, J D S (1977) *A Handbook on Distance Education* (Manchester Monographs Number 7) University of Manchester

Hemphill, J K *et al* (1962) *Administrative Performance and Personality* Bureau of Publications, Columbia University: New York

Holmberg, B (1977) *Distance Education: A Survey and Bibliography* Kogan Page: London

Holmberg, B (1979) Distance study in educational theory and practice *in* Page and Whitlock (1979)

Hooper, R (1977) *National Development Programme in Computer Assisted Learning: Final Report of the Director* Council for Educational Technology: London

Howe, A and Romiszowski, A J (1978) *International Yearbook of Educational and Instructional Technology 1978/79* Kogan Page: London

Howe, J A M and du Boulay, B (1979) Microprocessor assisted learning: turning the clock back? *Programmed Learning and Educational Technology* **16** 3:240-6

Hubbard, G (1979) The need for diversity of provision pp 80-85 *in* Schuller and Megarry (1979)

IEC (1979) *Writing for Distance Education, Manual* and *Samples* International Extension College, 18 Brooklands Avenue, Cambridge CB2 2HN, England

Joyce, B *et al* (1977) *Preservice teacher education* Center for Educational Research and Development: Palo Alto, Ca

Kaye, A R and Rumble, G (eds) (forthcoming) *The Distance Teaching Universities: Lessons from a Decade of Innovation Across the World* (provisional title)

Keegan, D J and Mitchell, I McD (forthcoming) *Distance Education* A quarterly periodical scheduled to commence publication in March 1980. Publishers: School of External Studies, Royal Melbourne Institute of Technology, 167 Franklin Street, Melbourne 3000, Australia

Kersh, B Y (1962) The Classroom Simulator *Journal of Teacher Education* **13**:110-11

Kirkland, G H K (1977) *Resource Centres: Justification and Role* (B210) comprising booklet, filmstrip and four cassettes. Jordanhill College of Education: Glasgow

Kirkland, G H K (1978) Managing innovation: simulations for potential innovators pp 116-24 *in* McAleese (1978)

McAleese, R (1978) *Perspectives on Academic Gaming & Simulation 3* Kogan Page: London

McIntosh, N E and Woodley, A (1978) *Combining Education with Working Life or The Working Student* Paper presented at the 4th International Conference on Higher Education, University of Lancaster, September 1978

McIntyre, D *et al* (1977) *Investigations of Microteaching* Croom Helm: London

McMahon, H F *et al* (1977) Student response to differentiated learning tasks in CML *Programmed Learning and Educational Technology* **14** 2:168-75

Manchester Polytechnic (undated) *Designs for Teaching: Independent Learning* Self-study unit designed by the Staff Development and Educational Methods Unit, Manchester Polytechnic, and sponsored by the Council for Educational Technology

Marsh, C J (1979) Teacher education simulations: THE CHALLENGE OF CHANGE example *British Journal of Teacher Education* **5** 1:63-71

Megarry, J (ed) *Simulation/Games for Learning* Quarterly journal published by Kogan Page: London

Megarry, J (ed) (1977a) *Aspects of Simulation and Gaming* Kogan Page: London

Megarry, J (1977b) Teaching at a distance: the long arm of Jordanhill *Times Educational Supplement (Scotland)* 22.4.77

Megarry, J (1978a) Developments in simulation and gaming pp 22-33 *in* Howe and Romiszowski (1978)

Megarry, J (1978b) Retrospect and prospect pp 187-207 *in* McAleese (1978)

Megarry, J (ed) (1978c) *Perspectives on Academic Gaming & Simulation 1 & 2* Kogan Page: London

Megarry, J (1978d) Computer-based educational games and simulations in schools: a feasibility study pp169-78 *in* Megarry (1978c)

Megarry, J (1979a) Home environment and learning: educational technology at a distance pp 77-87 *in* Page and Whitlock (1979)

Megarry, J (1979b) *Simulation and Games* (B222) comprising booklet, cassette and filmstrip. Jordanhill College of Education: Glasgow

Megarry, J (1979c) *Computers and Educational Technology* (B223) comprising booklet, cassette and filmstrip. Jordanhill College of Education: Glasgow

Megarry, J (ed) (1979d) *Perspectives on Academic Gaming & Simulation 4* Kogan Page: London

Mitchell, P D (1978) EDSIM: a classroom in a computer for lesson planning practice pp 191-204 *in* Megarry (1978c)

Nathenson, M B (1979) Bridging the gap between teaching and learning at a distance *British Journal of Educational Technology* 10 2: 100-9

Page, G T and Whitlock, Q (1979) *Aspects of Educational Technology XIII: Educational Technology Twenty Years On* Kogan Page: London

Perraton, H D (1973) *The Techniques of Writing Correspondence Courses* International Extension College/National Extension College: Cambridge

Perrott, E (1977) *Microteaching in Higher Education: Research, Development and Practice* Society for Research into Higher Education, The University of Surrey: Guildford

Perry, G and Perry, P (1969) *Case-Studies in Teaching* Pitman: London

Perry, W (1976) *The Open University: A Personal Account by the First Vice-Chancellor* Open University Press: Milton Keynes

Pigors, P and Pigors, F (1961) *Case Method in Human Relations: The Incident Process* McGraw-Hill: New York

Read, G A (1978) *CYCLOPS — An Audio Visual System. A Brief Description* Open University Press: Milton Keynes

Rendell, F and Bell, H S (1980) Why topic studies? *in* Tymister (1980)

Rowntree, D and Connors, B (1979) *Developing Self-instructional Teaching* Open University Press: Milton Keynes

Sakamoto, T (1980) Development and use of DESK TOP TEACHING SIMULATION GAME *in* Race, P and Brooks, D (1980) *Perspectives on Academic Gaming & Simulation 5* Kogan Page: London

Schuller, T and Megarry, J (1979) *World Yearbook of Education 1979: Recurrent Education and Lifelong Learning* Kogan Page: London

Scottish Education Department (1965) *Primary Education in Scotland* HMSO: Edinburgh

Sherwin, S (1974) *Teacher Education: A Status Report* Educational Testing Service: Princeton, NJ

Smith, K C (1979) *External Studies at New England: A Silver Jubilee Review 1955-1979* University of New England: Armidale, NSW

Stonier, T (1979) Changes in western society: educational implications pp 31-44 *in* Schuller and Megarry (1979)

Tansey, P J (ed) (1971) *Educational Aspects of Simulation* McGraw-Hill: London

Taylor, W (1969 and 1973) *Heading for Change* Routledge and Kegan Paul: London

Taylor, W (1972) *Theory into Practice* Harlech Television Publications: Bristol

Taylor, W and Moore, S (1970) *...And Gladly Teach* Harlech Television Publications: Bristol

Twelker, P A (1967) Classroom simulation and teacher preparation *School Review* **75**:197-203

Twelker, P A (1971) Simulation and media pp 131-84 *in* Tansey (1971)

Tymister, H J (ed) (1980) *Deutschunterricht im 5 bis 10 Schuljahr: Praxis und Theorie des Unterrichtens* (German Education from the Fifth to the Tenth School Year: Theory and Practice) Urban und Schwarzenberg: Munich

Venables, P (1979) The Open University and the future of continuing education pp 271-84 *in* Schuller and Megarry (1979)

Walker, D R F (1978) Computer-based games and simulations in geography: a problem in innovation and diffusion pp 180-5 *in* McAleese (1978)

Walker, D and Graham, L (1979) Simulation games and the microcomputer *Simulation/ Games for Learning* **9** 4:151-8

Wilson, R (1979) Looking towards the 1990s *British Journal of Educational Technology* **10** 1:45-51

Zoll, A A (1969) *Dynamic Management Education* Addison-Wesley: London

19. Skill training for teachers

Donald Orlosky

Summary: Teacher preparation includes provision for teachers to acquire skills to interpret classroom events, and skills to act on those events. These two kinds of skills require conceptual knowledge to diagnose events, and performance ability to promote appropriate pupil behaviour. Conceptual skills can be acquired in the vicarious learning of teacher training programmes traditionally offered in college classrooms. These skills can be developed further through exposure to classrooms by observing teachers and pupils. Both approaches have commonly been used, but the transition from the theory of the classroom to the application with pupils is difficult. Another approach to supplement this training is through the study of filmed episodes that portray concepts. These films make the theory more understandable without necessitating the inconvenience and uncertainty of actual events in elementary and secondary classrooms. These filmed episodes and their accompanying printed materials of student guides, instructors' manuals, and research reports are called protocol materials. Protocol materials bridge the gap between theory and practice, and strengthen the diagnostic skills of the teacher. The second kind of skill required for teaching is actual performance to act on classroom events. The theory of methods courses and the application of those methods in classrooms include transitions similar to those faced in conceptual acquisitions. An approach that provides for an effective transition in these skills is called microteaching. Microteaching provides for safe practice under controlled supervision to improve these skills. Both protocol materials and microteaching offer productive approaches to teacher preparation in the area of skill development.

Background

From Plato to the present, the question of how to train teachers and what they should be expected to do has been an issue of pedagogical debate. Past developments include the establishment of professional schools of education, certification standards to license teachers, accreditation criteria, and research to determine the body of knowledge and skills required for effective classroom teaching. But final decisions have not been made within the profession on these matters. As a consequence, teacher training programmes vary according to the institutions and locations where training is provided. Nevertheless, there are common elements that characterize most teacher education programmes as regards the skill development of teachers. These common elements can be explained within the organizational framework in which teacher training takes place.

Teacher training programmes are divided into two major components. One component is 'pre-service' training, which is completed prior to provisional certification. Initial certification is temporary and becomes permanent after successful teaching and additional training. The second component is 'in-service' training, which refers to training acquired after completing the pre-service phase and occurs concurrently with or following full-time classroom teaching.

This general approach for training teachers is different from the format for training in other professions and presents some special considerations. One major factor is that pre-service preparation is provided simultaneously with the undergraduate programme as contrasted with most professions in which professional schools at the postgraduate level provide preparation. This procedure for teacher preparation limits the time available to prepare students to become licensed teachers. As a result, the pre-service programme contains (1) an introduction to educational theory and foundations, (2) a minimum of instruction about teaching methods, and (3) some exposure to real classrooms as student teachers in a *practicum* assignment. Efforts to strengthen the pre-service programme are devoted to the proper blend of these three components, the relationships between them, and the content of each. But there is far more to be learned than time permits, and each of these elements is reduced more than is desired.

The in-service training of teachers introduces several additional concerns. In-service training contrasts most sharply with pre-service in the opportunity offered in advanced study for teachers to train as supervisors, administrators, guidance counsellors, and so forth. Despite these contrasts, the similarities between pre-service and in-service training of teacher skills are greater than the differences. Skills require practice for their development and the perfection and refinement of skills can be promoted at both levels of teacher training. Experienced teachers can draw on a backlog of encounters enabling them to relate to training better than can the inexperienced teachers. But the methods of learning skills for pre-service teachers can be effectively used in in-service situations. Both levels face similar needs as regards skill attainment. Some adaptations for experienced teachers should be made, to capitalize on their experiences and avoid 'talking down' to them, but the essential characteristics of good training apply to both pre-service and in-service programmes.

This brief conception of the organization of teacher preparation programmes is clarified by examining the role of four major factors. These factors are (1) the conceptual knowledge required, (2) the skills to be developed, (3) the philosophical position of schools and their purposes, and (4) ideas as to the best learning situation. The latter two factors will be discussed briefly next and the first two factors about conceptual and skill training will constitute the dominant theme in the remainder of this article.

The philosophical position taken by those who provide training introduces questions about the schools such as: What should be taught? Who should be expected to learn? What knowledge is of most worth? Is teaching an art or a science? Are schools leaders or followers of society? The history of schools is rich with stories of educational leaders who have wrestled with questions such as these. Among the early theorists and practitioners were Jean-Jacques Rousseau (1712-78), Johann Pestalozzi (1746-1827), John Dewey (1859-1952), Edward Thorndike (1874-1949), J E Herbart (1776-1841), George Counts (1889-1974), and Alfred Binet (1857-1911). The views of these educational leaders (and numerous significant others) cannot be elaborated here. However, the viewpoints they expressed and their contributions can be studied in the history of education and through the analysis of such philosophical positions as pragmatism, essentialism, idealism, social reconstructionism, existentialism, realism, and the educators who describe philosophical positions in their writings (Brubacher, 1962; Brameld, 1955; Ozmon, 1972; and Morris, 1961). The philosophical positions offered can be interpreted to indicate a rigid, non-elective, and no-nonsense approach to curriculum and instruction, rather than an open-ended, discovery, and unstructured approach to learning. The point of view accepted by a teacher training institution will determine the skills and concepts they consider important for their students to acquire.

The learning situation envisaged by educators is closely related to their philosophical position but relates more to the 'means' of instruction than the 'ends' for which schools educate. Advocates of different instructional methods range from authoritative to non-directive methods of teaching. A student enrolled in a teacher training programme that favours the directive approach will learn skills such as lecturing, structuring student learning, and rigid classroom organization as the desired methods for effective teaching. Schools that favour a more permissive approach will emphasize skills to help pupils nurture their learning in a minimally structured classroom situation. During the peak of the Performance Based Teacher Education (PBTE) movement in the United States one of the major catalogues of teaching skills provided a classification of classroom management skills according to such diverse approaches as authoritative, behaviour modification, cognitive developmental, and non-directive (Turner, 1973).

Despite the unsolved issues of the preferred philosophical position or the ideal setting and circumstances for learning to occur, the practical matter of establishing appropriate skills and providing for their acquisition is a task for teacher training institutions to complete. The basis for decisions about training is a combination of theory, research findings, and conventional wisdom. The rationale for teacher preparation includes the expectation that a teacher should possess (1) general knowledge as provided in liberal arts studies, (2) specific knowledge of his major fields of study such as mathematics or history, and (3) pedagogical knowledge. The conception of teacher preparation espoused here supports this rationale and further states that in the pedagogical domain teachers must acquire (1) interpretative skills to be able to diagnose learning situations and (2) performance skills to be able to act on the situations they have diagnosed. Interpretative ability is increased through the acquisition and use of concepts; performance skills are acquired through practising and perfecting the actions required to instruct effectively. This conception of teacher preparation calls for the establishment of a valid body of conceptual and performance knowledge. It also calls for procedures to enable the conceptual knowledge to be learned in a useful, applicable form, and for skill development that includes safe ways of developing skills without doing harm to pupils during the learning process.

Body of pedagogical knowledge

A concerted effort in recent times to establish the knowledge base for teacher preparation is found in the Performance (or sometimes Competency) Based Teacher Education (PBTE) movement. The major thrust of this movement occurred in the United States, but high interest and some activities can be found in other countries. The idea behind PBTE is deceptively simple. Before the advent of PBTE, the pre-service programme was primarily a traditional pattern of lectures, reading assignments, completion of projects, and discussion, capped by an assignment in a school as a student teacher. Upon completion of this programme and fulfillment of the requirements for an undergraduate degree, teachers were provisionally licensed to begin teaching. Initial certification was based on completion of courses and a bachelor's degree, demanding little evidence of the ability of the practitioner to perform in the classroom. The PBTE movement was designed to convert teacher education courses from their verbal and vicarious learning to a performance approach. Most conversions called for institutions to designate the objectives of their training programme and to establish learning experiences, often organized into individual learning units called modules, which the student would complete. Completion of the module typically required the student to actually 'do' something rather than merely read about it or discuss it. The modules set forth the task to be completed, the standard that represented satisfactory completion, and the conditions under which the student would perform the skill. For example, a student might be asked to demonstrate ability to lead a class discussion and involve most of the pupils. The student would complete activities which might lead to the development of this skill. These activities might include visiting classrooms to observe discussion techniques, studying the literature about how to create an atmosphere conducive to discussions, and learning about the terminology, body language, and voice inflections that promote pupil participation. Eventually, the proof of the student's ability to lead discussions would be displayed in a real situation rather than by the completion of a written examination about conducting discussions. The 'real' situation might require a meeting with a group of pupils, perhaps ten or 12, and to be assigned a topic on which he should initiate a discussion. Within a given period of time, perhaps five or ten minutes, the student would be expected to elicit comments from a certain percentage of the pupils, usually 70 or 80 per cent. The student who met the requirements for the module would receive credit for that task. After completing the prescribed number of modules, the performance of the student could be attested and recommendations for certification would be issued from the training institution. Only the student's pedagogical training was performance-based in most instances. A few scattered attempts were made to incorporate PBTE into the non-pedagogical areas of teacher training but, for the most part, the liberal arts studies and specialized fields of study remained intact as traditionally taught.

The PBTE movement triggered a flurry of activity to create lists of teacher competencies and prepare modules for their attainment, and research to establish the validity and reliability of the teacher competencies that were established. The American Association of Colleges for Teacher Education (AACTE) was funded by the United States Office of Education (USOE) to establish a Commission on PBTE. The Commission sponsored the publication of 16 papers which explored the pros and cons of the movement between 1971 and 1974. The Commission was established as a neutral agency but it commissioned articles from opponents, proponents, and neutral writers whose views formed an influential basis for the direction of the movement. In the first paper published by AACTE (Elam, 1971), the implied characteristics of PBTE were listed. This list stated that: (1) instruction is individualized and personalized; (2) learning is guided by feedback; (3) the overall programme is systematic; (4) emphasis is on exit, not on entrance, requirements; (5) instruction is modularized; and (6) the student is held accountable for performance. A year later the fourth paper under AACTE sponsorship was published (Broudy, 1972) in which the underlying assumptions and implications of PBTE were challenged. This challenge included the statements:

> According to PBTE the teaching act is the sum of the performances into which it is analysed.
> This is a notoriously inadequate description of any human action, let alone one so complex as teaching. (Broudy, 1972:3)

Additional criticism arose about the validity of the competencies selected, the standards established to judge their completion, the lack of unanimity as to the kinds of learning that teaching ought to achieve, and the methods for achieving them.

PBTE continued to develop as a popular topic and the notion of holding experienced or newly-qualified teachers accountable for their performances had high appeal to state legislatures and state boards of education. This interest led to some state mandates that future teacher education programmes should become performance-based and that state approval of programmes would depend on their conversion to PBTE. The AACTE Commission felt compelled to issue a statement of caution in its 16th monograph in 1974:

> Because the present level of knowledge about performance-based teacher education is limited, states are advised to avoid legislation which prescribes or proscribes PBTE. State education agencies are encouraged to maintain a flexible and open position regarding performance-based education and performance-based teacher certification until sufficient knowledge about PBTE has been generated through experience and research. (AACTE, 1974:25)

The PBTE movement brought into sharp focus the realization that the body of knowledge on which teacher training is based contains controversial and subjective elements. It became clear that teacher training programmes were based on limited research evidence, conventional wisdom, and the logical analysis of appropriate content for training teachers. The content of teacher training as presently practised is not necessarily deficient or wrong because of this. It simply does not include the substantial validating evidence desired to proceed confidently with 'the' training programme that will promote teacher effectiveness.

The foregoing discussion provides a brief explanation of the factors that complicate the mission of institutions undertaking teacher training. Skill training for teachers entails far more than the procedures in the programme. It also requires elaborate and difficult decisions about the content to be learned. However, the profession cannot afford to be paralysed by the problems uncovered by the analysis of its content. Programmes are in operation and better ways to provide training are continually being developed through experimentation and innovative practices. These new programmes undergo the scrutiny of the profession by its practitioners and researchers.

Two developments have been created which focus on the two major aspects of training cited earlier, namely conceptual training to improve the teacher's ability to diagnose classroom events and skill development to improve the performance of teachers. Other programmes could be cited but these two typify practices which make use of technology, provide non-traditional approaches, have survived sufficiently to be found in teacher training programmes, and offer students an opportunity to practise their skills in controlled settings whereby improvement can develop under supervision. The approach for conceptual development is provided through the use of *protocol materials* and the performance skills approach described here is found in *microteaching*.

Protocol materials

One type of skill required by teachers is to interpret events accurately in order to apply the proper action to them. The ability to diagnose school episodes depends on objective and accurate observation, the ability to distinguish between important and irrelevant cues, and the conceptual knowledge with which to classify the observed phenomena. These conceptual skills have traditionally been taught in theoretical courses in which concepts are named and explanations of the characteristics of those concepts are described. For example, the concept of 'questioning' may be contrasted with the concept of 'probing'. The major distinction is that questioning entails teachers asking different students to answer questions without persisting with any one student. Probing is teacher behaviour in which a student who responds to a teacher's question is asked to explain his answer, to provide supporting reasons or information for the answer, to consider other possible answers, and so forth. This verbal explanation provides helpful information and students might correctly answer a written test on the differences between probing and questioning. However, there is little assurance that these same students will recognize whether probing or questioning is being used in a regular classroom, or that they will be conscious of their own use of these two different approaches. The reason for this uncertainty is partly because the form in which the students learn the concept (verbally) and the form in which they experience it (in classrooms) are two different circumstances and transferability is difficult. The traditional solution attempted to this problem has been to assign students to classrooms in real settings to observe events that they have studied. This approach has benefits but it also has a number of drawbacks. The drawbacks include (1) high administrative and supervisory costs to arrange for visits, (2) uncertainty of what will occur in the classrooms — which reduces learning to a 'chance' experience, (3) the complexity of a typical classroom which makes it difficult for the untrained observer to isolate significant events and study them, and lastly, (4) as soon as an event occurs, it is over, and is not available for study and analysis.

A solution to these problems was advocated (Smith, 1969) in which filmed clips of real classroom events could be shown to give students a means to study behaviour that exemplified concepts. These materials were called protocol materials, defined as an unedited account of an event, episode, or transaction, because the idea was to record 'slices of reality' from classrooms for study. A programme was launched in the summer of 1970 with support from the United States Office of Education to develop protocol materials. Between 1970 and 1974, funding was continued which enabled over 150 protocol packages to be developed at 16 different sites throughout the United States.

The developers of protocol materials completed a sequence of planning and production tasks that led to the development of these materials. Each developer selected concepts by drawing from literature, research, or conventional wisdom. Furthermore, the concepts chosen were organized according to a master plan (Smith *et al*, 1973) that included variables such as age of pupils to be shown, setting of the episode, source of behaviour, type of knowledge to be illustrated, and content in educational methods where the protocol would be used. After selecting concepts for the protocol, the developer was required to provide a definition of the concept and justify the selection of the concepts on the basis of their importance and validity. It was also found that protocol films needed to be staged, to some extent, to avoid high expenditures of time and financial resources. After the developer recorded the desired behaviour, manuals for teachers and students were developed on the basis of the cues emitted in the film and field testing evidence obtained during the production and experimental work conducted during the production of the films.

To assist students in learning concepts through protocol materials, they included a minimum of three components. Printed materials, usually in the form of a student guide, were produced to define the concepts displayed in the film and to guide the student to the significance and research support for the concept to be learned. A second phase included observation of the filmed episode, to help students to become familiar with the behaviour that illustrated the abstract concept which had been recorded. The third phase included student response and feedback as they interpreted the film. This third phase ranged from a checklist that was completed while viewing the film to a discussion or written reaction to the episode.

The developers of protocols provided formative and summative data on their materials. The formative data was information obtained during the production phase to determine the initial effectiveness of their materials and to identify modifications that would be needed before final production. The summative data was collected to assess the effectiveness of the materials. Effectiveness was judged on the basis of how accurately students were able to identify and classify behavioural cues emitted in the protocol film. The paramount concern of developers was to create the protocol product and, therefore, the quality of the research evidence sometimes suffered from lack of time and resources. However, the evidence supported the protocol approach to concept learning and significant differences were found in favour of the protocol approach in projects where data was obtained. Student reaction to learning through protocols was also positive and evidence that pupils in the classrooms benefited from teachers who had learned through protocols was also found (Borg and Stone, 1974; Borg, 1975; Gliessman et al, 1974; Woodley and Driscoll, 1975; Zidonis and Fox, 1975; Lanier, 1975).

A number of contributions to education emerged from the protocol programme. The protocol projects introduced an improved method for skill development of conceptual learning.

A catalogue of concepts was developed (Hudgins, 1974) which served to organize concepts according to rigid, definitional forms (Orlosky, 1974). The clarity of concept definitions turned out to be one of the fortunate by-products of the protocol programme since ambiguous language about pedagogical concepts has been one of the barriers to communication within the profession. A beginning was made in standardizing some of the critical terms. Furthermore, it was learned how to use technology to strengthen conceptual learning and help bridge the gap between theory taught verbally in traditional classrooms and the actual practice of teaching in regular elementary and secondary schools. However, funds diminished for teacher education because of the teacher surplus and support for the protocol materials project ended in 1975.

The use of protocol materials continued and between 1975 and 1979 over 3000 institutions in the United States and in 18 other countries obtained protocol materials from the National Resource and Dissemination Center at the

University of South Florida. Furthermore, individual developers continued to use their own materials and about half of the developers maintained a separate dissemination programme for distributing their materials.

Microteaching

Another innovative and non-traditional approach to skill development of teachers is microteaching. Microteaching is similar to protocols because it affords an opportunity for the student to learn outside the traditional lecture-discussion approach, but does not entail practising skills in the regular classroom. It is also a selective simulation or modification of reality that focuses on the specific skills to be acquired. Unlike protocols, which are designed to improve conceptual and interpretative skills, microteaching helps students improve performance skills and the application of their knowledge to the improvement of pupil learning.

Microteaching is a procedure in which a student practises teaching with a reduced number of pupils in a reduced period of time with emphasis on a narrow and specific teaching skill. In a microteaching approach, the student practises a specific skill by teaching a group of four or five students in a lesson that may require no more than three or four minutes. During the shortened lesson, a supervisor observes the lesson, and ideally, a video-recording is also made of the lesson. After the lesson has been completed, the student and supervisor discuss the lesson and observe the video-recording to study the teaching behaviour and criticize the lesson. As a consequence of this discussion, the student can identify ways to improve the performance. After analysing the performance, the lesson can be taught again with different students. The microteaching approach offers an opportunity for immediate reteaching of the lesson to practise the improvements that have been identified during the discussion with the supervisor.

Microteaching provides a 'safe' practice opportunity. In teaching it is not uncommon for much of the development of skills to occur at the expense of the pupils who are taught by an inexperienced teacher. Most professions have their safe practice procedures to allow students to become proficient before working with their clients. The medical student has a cadaver and law students have their mock trials. But teachers often make the transition from the verbal learning in the college classroom to student teaching and/or actual teaching without a transition phase that protects the pupils and is realistic. Microteaching offers help in this direction because the pupils are exposed to an inexperienced teacher for a limited time and the application of specific skills is controlled and supervised.

Microteaching evolved at Stanford University with support from the United States Office of Education and the Kettering Foundation. The developers were looking for a way to make the methods of teaching more meaningful and substantive. Through a series of trials and innovative efforts involving technology, observation schedules, and selection of appropriate skills, microteaching was developed sufficiently to be used effectively in teacher training. The story of microteaching and its early development (Allen and Ryan, 1969) describes the procedure which is currently employed in microteaching. This procedure includes (1) selection of a skill to be practised, (2) preparation of a mini-lesson to practise the skill with a small group of pupils (peers can be used), (3) provision for supervision and feedback — preferably with a video-recorder for playback analysis — and (4) reteaching after receiving suggestions and identifying specific changes to be made to improve the skill.

Some of the skills listed as appropriate for the early work in microteaching included effective use of lecturing, divergent questioning, planned repetition, stimulus variation, set induction, closure, silence and non-verbal cues, reinforcement of student participation, fluency in asking questions, probing questions, higher order questions, recognizing attending behaviour, illustrating and using examples, and completeness of communication.

Students' performance during the reteach portion significantly improved, but additional advantages to microteaching have been listed which have far-reaching effects on the kinds of problems listed in conjunction with the PBTE movement. These advantages include the fact that microteaching helps to: (1) identify categories in which additional research is needed, (2) improve methods of criticizing student performance, (3) determine the length of training time required to master certain skills, (4) improve ways of analysing pupil learning, and (5) make distinctions between general teaching skills, specific teaching skills, and teaching styles and their impact.

Microteaching does not replace the existing and important traditional elements in the teacher training programmes. Microteaching does afford an approach that enables students to practise techniques of teaching under controlled conditions.

Conclusion

Pedagogical training calls for three elements to be provided. One is identification of the body of knowledge and skills which teachers need to acquire. Progress is being made in establishing this knowledge but it will probably always be subject to revision. This body of knowledge may never stabilize. It may not stabilize because different philosophical views will always prevail about the role and purpose of schools, and agreement will not be reached on conditions that optimize learning. The variables that promote learning include such factors as student motivation, parental influence, maturity, social conditions, and other factors that cannot be isolated and conclusively measured through research. The complexity of solving these issues was expressed by a task force on PBTE (Rosner, 1972) although support to continue working at this task remains, for it is through this effort that the quality of teacher training programmes will be strengthened.

A second element to be provided is conceptual skill to improve the accuracy of diagnoses of school events. This element calls for a progression from awareness of concepts, principles, theories, and so forth to the use of this knowledge in classrooms. Protocol materials help to bridge this gap and have proved their usefulness. However, the protocol programme has only scratched the surface of its potential and the quality of these materials will undoubtedly be viewed as a primitive beginning if more effort is made in the future to produce protocol materials.

The third element is the actual skill of performing. The knowledge about teaching provided in methods classes and the trial-and-error learning of student teaching has been mediated and enhanced through microteaching and its variations. Microteaching capitalizes on the basic principle of skill development by providing controlled practice under supervision with feedback.

Critics of teacher training programmes may consider the lack of certainty about the best skills and the most effective methods of learning these skills to be an inherent weakness of the profession. The profession would be the first to admit that improvement is needed and that the difficult and arduous task of improving this important aspect of schooling is worth the effort. However, two necessary preconditions for the solution of such a problem are present within the profession. The first is the admission that improvement is needed, and there is little reluctance to recognize that this is the case. The second element is the willingness to work at solutions through a systematic and effective approach. Microteaching and protocol materials are two excellent examples of productive efforts aimed at solving some of the problems of training teachers.

References

AACTE (1974) *Achieving the Potential of Performance-Based Teacher Education* (Recommendations by the Committee on Performance-Based Teacher Education) American Association of Colleges for Teacher Education: Washington, DC

Allen, D and Ryan, K (1969) *Microteaching* Addison-Wesley: Reading, Mass

Borg, W R (1975) Protocol materials as related to teacher performance and pupil achievement *Journal of Educational Research* **69** 1:23-30

Borg, W R and Stone, D R (1974) Protocol materials as a tool for changing teacher behaviour *Journal of Experimental Education* **43** 1:34-9

Brameld, T B (1955) *Philosophies of Education in Cultural Perspective* Holt, Rinehart and Winston: New York

Broudy, H S (1972) *A Critique of Performance-Based Teacher Education* PBTE Series, American Association of Colleges for Teacher Education: Washington, DC

Brubacher, J S (1962) *Modern Philosophies of Education* McGraw-Hill: New York

Elam, S (1971) *What is the State of the Art?* PBTE Series, American Association of Colleges for Teacher Education: Washington, DC

Gliessman, D, Pugh, R C and Perry, F L (1974) *Effects of a Protocol Film Series in Terms of Learning Outcomes and Reactions of Users* National Center for the Development of Training Materials in Teacher Education, Indiana University: Bloomington

Hudgins, B B (1974) *A Catalog of Concepts in the Pedagogical Domain of Teacher Education* State Education Department: Albany, NY

Lanier, J E H (1975) Ruminations of a wiser but more skeptical Protocol Materials Director *in Development of Protocol Materials in Teacher Education: A Case Study in Relating Theory and Practice.* (ERIC Report) US Department of H E W National Institute of Education: Washington, DC

Morris, Van Cleve (1961) *Philosophy and the American School, an Introduction to the Philosophy of Education* Houghton Mifflin: Boston, Mass

Orlosky, D E (1974) The Protocol Materials Program *Journal of Teacher Education* **25** 4:291-7

Ozmon, H (1972) *Dialogue in the Philosophy of Education* Charles E Merrill: Columbus, Ohio

Rosner, B (1972) *The Power of Competency-Based Teacher Education: A Report* Allyn and Bacon: Boston, Mass

Smith, B O (1969) *Teachers for the Real World* American Association of Colleges for Teacher Education: Washington, DC

Smith, B O, Orlosky, D E and Borg, J (1973) *Handbook on the Development and Use of Protocol Materials for Teacher Education* Panhandle Area Educational Cooperative: Chipley, Florida

Turner, R L (1973) *A General Catalog of Teaching Skills* State Education Department: Albany, NY

Woodley, C P and Driscoll, L A (1975) The University of Colorado Protocol Project: a case study *Journal of Teacher Education* **25** 4:314-22

Zidonis, F and Fox, S (1975) Protocols of children's language *Theory Into Practice* **14** 5:312-17

Part 6: Research Issues

20. A matrix for research on teacher education

Lilian Katz

Summary: Teacher education is defined as a set of activities deliberately intended to prepare candidates for the occupation of teaching. Nine broad categories of variables, referred to as the parameters of teacher education, are proposed and defined. These include: 1) the goals, 2) characteristics of the candidates, 3) characteristics of the staff, 4) content of the programme, 5) time and its allocation, 6) the ethos of the programme, 7) location and setting, 8) regulations, and 9) financial resources and restraints. These parameters are then displayed in a nine-by-nine matrix generating nine diagonal within-parameter cells, and 72 intersecting cells which can 'contain' summaries, analyses and syntheses of the available research on the variables within the parameters. In addition, some examples of how the matrix can be used to generate new research questions are presented.

It comes as no surprise to note that we begin the 1980s with a large literature on teacher education. A simple scan of the ERIC document holdings, for example, indicates that we enter the new decade with 8000 document and almost 6000 journal citations from this one source alone. (The acronym ERIC stands for Educational Resources Information Center, a national network of centres funded by the National Institute of Education of the United States Department of Health, Education and Welfare, holding more than 160,000 documents on microfiche, with computer-based bibliographic searching capability.)

The purpose of this chapter is to present a definition of teacher education and its parameters from which a matrix can be developed. Some examples are presented of how the matrix can be used to organize, analyse and synthesize the available literature and to generate new research questions.

Definition of teacher education

Common-sense tells us that teacher education is whatever happens in programmes and on courses in institutes, colleges and universities engaged in teacher training. A little more common-sense, some would argue, reveals that if we knew more, and furthermore tried harder, great teachers would emerge from these institutions. This error of oversimplification made by 'outsiders' is compounded by the tendency of 'insiders' to confuse the study of teacher education with the study of teaching. Discussions among the latter quickly turn to the correlations between teacher behaviour and pupil achievement. While such correlations are of interest to teacher educators, they tend to detract from examination of the determinants of teacher education, and the complex ways in which those determinants interact.

For the purposes of this chapter, teacher education is taken to be a special case of the more general case of professional or occupational socialization. As Moore defines it, professional socialization 'involves acquiring the requisite knowledge and also the sense of occupational norms typical of the fully qualified practitioner' (Moore, 1970:71). It can be assumed, then, that the function of a teacher education programme is to provide those experiences which can be expected to facilitate the acquisition of the skills, knowledge, etc of the group into which candidates are to be socialized. This function yields the following definition of teacher education:

> Teacher education consists of sets of events and activities which are deliberately intended to help candidates to acquire the skills, dispositions, knowledge, habits, attitudes, values, norms, etc, which enable them to enter the occupation of teaching.

The potential sets of events and activities which could constitute teacher education programmes or courses are numerous and varied. They may include, for example, lecture classes, excursions and field trips, a vareity of *practica*, modules on specific topics, microteaching, observations of children and teachers, workshops in arts and crafts, independent reading, tutoring of individual children, and so forth.

Parameters of teacher education

For the purpose of this discussion, the term *parameter* is used to describe a broad category of variables of which every teacher education programme or course can be said to have a case, or an entry, and which remains relatively constant throughout a given candidate's participation in the programme.

Although the parameters are enumerated below as a list of distinct classes of variables, experience suggests that they represent complex interacting and confounding forces, separated here so as to facilitate ordering of the literature and to encourage discussion and enquiry. Neither the order of importance of these parameters, nor their relative impacts on the activities or outcomes of teacher education is known at present. The nine parameters are defined as follows:

I Goals. This includes the aims, goals and objectives which the events and activities of teacher education are intended to achieve. Included also are the methods used to assess the extent to which the goals are reached.

II Candidates. This includes such characteristics of the candidates as age, sex, socio-economic status, motivation, intellectual ability, creativity, ethnicity, and any other characteristics which can be thought to be related to the nature and outcome of the teacher education programme.

III Staff. This includes such characteristics of the staff as age, experience, skill, ideological commitment, ethnicity, specialization, and so forth. Staff members are all those whose assignments include activities deliberately intended to help the candidates' induction into the occupation. Among them are senior professors, lecturers, graduate teaching assistants, adjunct professors, co-operating teachers, counsellors, advisers, principals, heads, teachers' centre wardens, etc.

IV Content. This includes the facts, information, skills, competencies, ideas, techniques, philosophical principles, academic disciplines, etc transmitted to the candidates by the activities and events constituting the teacher education programme.

V Time. This includes the duration of the programme ie one, two or three or more years; it includes also timing and sequencing as well as simultaneity of the events and activities constituting the teacher education programme.

VI Ethos. This refers to the intellectual and social climate or atmosphere of the programme; the ethos of the setting is reflected in the affective tone and content of the personal relationships between and among the candidates and staff members.

VII Location. The location of a teacher education programme may be a conventional college campus site, an urban commuter campus, a teachers' centre, community college, polytechnic or monotechnic, demonstration school or campus laboratory school, etc.

VIII Regulations. This covers the laws, regulations, legal restrictions and stipulations related to teacher education and certification, as well as the requirements of labour or trade unions, school districts, local educational authorities, regional and national regulations, edicts of boards of trustees, and governors or other authorizing bodies who have power over the activities and events constituting teacher education.

IX Finances. This includes variables related to the costs of teacher education, including capital and personnel costs, candidates' tuition fees and living expenses and anticipated financial rewards of teaching, etc.

It is assumed here that every instance of a teacher education programme has entries in the variables within each of the nine parameters defined above. The ways in which the variable values in each of them contributes to the ultimate kinds of experiences available to candidates remains to be ascertained.

A matrix showing how these parameters can be used to organize the existing relevant literature and to generate questions for further research is shown in Figure 1.

A matrix for teacher education

In Figure 1, the nine parameters that affect and determine teacher education are presented as a matrix. The shaded cells in the diagonal created by the matrix indicate potential summaries of the literature and research on within-parameter variables. For example, the first cell in the upper left-hand corner of the matrix marked I, would 'contain' a summary of all that is known about the aims, goals and objectives of teacher education. It could also 'contain' summaries of the available knowledge on specific sub-topics within the parameter. Much of the data summarized in the diagonal cells can be expected to come from surveys, as well as from experimental research. In this way, each cell in the diagonal represents a state-of-the-art report on the particular parameter or on any of the sub-topics within it. Some examples of the types of topics and questions to be

Parameters	I Goals	II Candidates	III Staff	IV Content	V Time	VI Ethos	VII Location	VIII Regulations	IX Finances
I Goals	I	II x III							
II Candidates		II	III x II	II x IV					
III Staff			III						
IV Content				IV	IV x V				
V Time		V x II			V				
VI Ethos		VI x II				VI			
VII Location			VII x III				VII		
VIII Regulations				VIII x IV				VIII	
IX Finances	IX x I	IX x II							IX

Figure 1 *A schematic representation of a matrix for teacher education*

addressed in each diagonal cell and a few of the intersecting cells are presented below.

Research on goals

Cell I on the diagonal, designates summary, analysis and synthesis of the literature pertaining to goals and objectives as well as their assessments. The data might be derived from surveys, for example, and could be analysed in terms of their explicitness, coherence, ideological assumptions, changes over time, within-programme consistency or compatibility, etc. In addition, the potential relationships between goals and objectives and the methods of assessment used can be summarized in this cell. The number of potential sub-topics in this parameter is large.

One illustrative example of a topic which falls into this cell is performance or competency-based teacher education. An interesting problem is the extent to which competency-based teacher education leads to a reductionist conception of the nature of teaching, and hence of teacher education (Merrow, 1975). Pressure to specify 'demonstrable' skills as the desired outcomes of training could result, although not necessarily, in the formulation of long lists of distinct skills. These would be small units of action, each of which could be observed and evaluated separately, involving the assessor in very minimal inference as to the presence or absence of the skill of interest. This approach to both the goals and the assessment of candidates in teacher education implies that teaching consists of an aggregate of separable skills, an implication also embedded in much of the available research on training as well.

While teaching certainly includes skills and other small units of action, it is more useful to think of teaching in terms of larger patterns of behaviour, including the ability to decide which skills to use and when to use them. It may be that the effects a teacher creates derive not from his or her behaviour *per se*, but from the total or overall pattern of which a given learner perceives that behaviour to be a part. Episodes of teacher behaviour can be compared to words in sentences: it is the sentence that gives the word its meaning. If teachers or candidates are evaluated on the basis of checklists of separate demonstrable skills, there is a danger that the really powerful aspect of teaching, namely the meaning individual learners assign to teachers' behaviours, will be neglected. It may be that individual children assign meanings to teacher behaviour that observers may either define differently, or do not even recognize. Isolated or quick judgements can be made about the presence or absence of a given behaviour, but not about the probable meaning individual children might attach to that behaviour. While the goals of competency-based teacher education programmes might be to equip candidates with a repertoire of 'beginner's' skills, they may inadvertently overlook some of the larger concerns of socialization into the profession.

The potential risks of competency-based assessment (as well as goal orientation) in teacher education must be weighed against the risks of alternative approaches. One of the most common practices in assessment of teacher education is reliance on grades obtained in classes and examinations. Combinations of class grades, state or national examinations are used in some institutions and some countries. These assessment techniques tend to make the error of inducting into the profession those who are good at being 'students' in the narrowest sense. The extent to which the latter is associated with success at teaching is not clear.

Some institutions place great reliance on the evaluations of the supervisors of the *practica* and internships. While the bases upon which such assessments are made are likely to have greater 'content' validity than grades or examinations, they are susceptible to the vicissitudes of candidate-co-operating teacher relations and other aspects of the *practicum* or internship site.

It is very likely that every assessment technique employed produces errors. Combinations of assessment procedures (eg performance criteria, plus class grades, plus personal interviews, plus supervisors' ratings) may help to counterbalance the errors inherent in each technique, or may compound them. Even if multiple assessments could be shown to counterbalance the errors, their costs (Parameter IX: Finances) would make such combinations impractical.

Assessing the outcomes of teacher education seems to be a question of which errors we prefer to make. An error-free strategy is not likely to be found. Summaries of research on the stability, reliabilities or predictive validity of each of many assessment techniques used in teacher education programmes would belong in this cell.

Research on candidates

In cell II on the diagonal, summaries of studies of candidates' characteristics would be placed. Of all the potential characteristics of interest, socio-economic status and attitudes have probably received the greatest proportion of researchers' attention (Turner, 1975). Summaries of research on such other candidate characteristics as intelligence, creativity, and role-taking ability might also be useful in understanding the nature of teacher education programmes.

If we now go across row II (Candidates), to the cell under column III (Staff), we arrive at the cell (II x III) in which we summarize available data concerning interactions and/or effects of selected candidate characteristics upon selected characteristics of the staff. Questions concerning candidates' evaluations of their instructors, and how the publication of the results affects the staff and the content (Parameter IV) offered in the teacher education programme would be the type of questions belonging to this cell.

Research on staff

The number of potential questions concerning characteristics of the staffs of teacher education programmes is very large, and it is difficult to know which of them might contribute most powerfully to the constituent activities of the programme.

A popular view in need of empirical testing is that teacher educators' effectiveness is related to the amount of their own first-hand school teaching experience as well as to how recent it was. The relationship between success as a classroom teacher of children and as a teacher of teachers is not known at present. Similarly there is some feeling to the effect that staff members who are interested in research and theory are less effective in their roles as teacher educators than those who are more fully devoted to their teaching responsibilities. Data bearing upon these 'myths' could be very useful.

General impressions suggest that staff members themselves suffer from low morale, and generalized cynicism towards their own role in the improvement of the teaching profession.

Career patterns of teacher education staffs might also be of value in accounting for the nature of teacher education. It would be of some interest to know, for example, whether there are obvious attributes of teacher educators which distinguish them from the school teaching colleagues they leave behind. It may be that those who left classroom teaching are more energetic or intellectually curious than their former colleagues. How such distinguishing characteristics might impinge upon the nature of teacher education and its effectiveness is open to speculation.

If we now go across the row labelled III (Staff) to the cell in column II (Candidates) — cell (III x II) — we can ask questions concerning the ways staff characteristics impinge on or interact with selected candidate characteristics.

It would be of interest to know, for example, in what ways staff members can and/or actually do serve as models for the candidates. Let us suppose, for example, that members were asked to enumerate a list of 'professional' attributes which they wish to foster in candidates. To what extent would candidates perceive the same attributes in staff members? General impressions suggest that candidates perceive professorial staff members, for instance, to be impractical and too removed from the realities of day-to-day work in schoolrooms. Another question concerns how candidates perceive their teacher education instructors' intellectual competence compared to their instructors in classes outside education (eg psychology, English literature, natural science, etc). What might be the effects of the relative standings of teacher educators and non-education instructors on the processes of occupational socialization?

Research on content

A survey of teacher education programmes is likely to indicate agreement concerning appropriate content. With slight variations, most programmes provide candidates with a mixture of foundations (philosophy and history of education, educational psychology, etc), child development, teaching methods classes, field experiences, observation of children and teachers, and so forth. The relative contributions of all or each of these types of content to the outcome of the programme are not clear.

There appears to be general agreement on the usefulness of *practica*, but they are not without problems. In many communities opportunities to observe 'good' practices, and in fact to practise or rehearse them, are in short supply. Sometimes candidates complain of having to engage in teaching practices that their teacher educators reject or deplore.

It is not really clear what candidates learn from such experiences. Often their responses to 'bad' placements can be broadly typed as excessive idealism or excessive realism (Katz, 1974). The truism that 'practice makes perfect' overlooks the fact that only 'good' practice is related to 'good' learning. If candidates can indeed learn what is desired from rehearsing 'bad' practices in 'bad' field settings, then there need be no undue concern about the quality of teaching observed.

At the junction of row IV (Content), with column V (Time) questions concerning which types of content might be provided for candidates at which particular points in the period of preparation are suggested. For example, there are currently strong pressures for *practica* to be offered earlier rather than later in the sequence of activities of a programme. One strong argument in favour of early *practica* is that they provide candidates with opportunities to 'try out' the teacher role and to make an informed career choice prior to the completion of a large portion of their required work. Another argument is that simultaneous as well as subsequent course work acquires greater relevance when such 'trying out' of the teacher role has occurred in addition to the exercise of teaching techniques. No evidence to support these arguments has been found so far.

Research on time

The activities that constitute a teacher education programme vary as to the total period of time in which they occur and with respect to when during that period they occur. In addition, there may also be variations as to the order, sequence and simultaneity of the events and activities.

In academic institutions, the concept of 'residency' implies that candidates acquire valuable assets from the continuous and intensive contact with the staff and other candidates in the setting. Obviously the duration of both residency and candidacy affects the number of opportunities to engage in given activities.

If we now follow the row marked V (Time) to the cell in column II (Candidates) — cell (V x II) — we can examine the research now accumulating concerning the developmental stages of candidates as well as teachers. This research (eg Fuller and Brown, 1975; Heath, undated) suggests that developmental tasks and concerns vary as candidates progress through the activities and experiences provided by the programme. Among the many attributes of candidates which may be developed are those related to the candidate's *understanding* or conception of teaching. It seems reasonable that their understanding develops as experience, knowledge and practice accrue. Early in candidacy, the understanding of teaching may consist largely of perceptions of what activities occur in classrooms, and simple stereotypes of children and teaching situations. It seems reasonable to predict that candidates' understanding of what teaching involves would be less finely and fully differentiated earlier in their careers than it becomes later on. The differentiation could be expected to increase in such attributes as the number of levels of analysis, the conception or construction of teaching situations, attributions of the causes of children's behaviour, etc.

Research on ethos

Ethos, somewhat like social climate, may be defined as the affective tone which characterizes the feelings generated by the total sets of relationships within a given socialization setting (Wheeler, 1966). Thus the ethos of a given teacher education programme might be characterized as 'warm, friendly, relaxed and humanistic', or 'cold, unfriendly, and efficient', etc.

Questions about how the ethos of a setting might affect candidates are suggested by the junction between row VI (Ethos) and column II (Candidates).

To the extent that the relationships within the social setting of a teacher education programme are intellectual and professional, the ethos is likely to be a serious as well as a stimulating one. When the content of relationships tends to consist of personal and mundane matters, the ethos is unlikely to strengthen or support intellectual vitality in either the candidates or the staff.

One of the factors affecting the ethos of a socialization setting is its size. As the numbers of candidates and staff increase, the ability of the staff to create and maintain a given ethos may decrease and regimentation or bureaucratization may increase. Of course, there may be an optimum size such that too small a programme yields problems of over-intimacy, insufficient variety of participants at candidate and staff levels, and deficiencies in resources. On the other hand, general impressions suggest that the larger a teacher education setting is, the more the ethos resembles (by analogy) a 'cafeteria' rather than a 'dining room'. In the 'cafeteria', the ethos is apt to be flat or lacking in either social or intellectual vitality. 'Cafeterias' seem to be low on both affective and aesthetic considerations, whereas 'dining rooms' maximize both these qualities.

The risks of such 'cafeteria' atmospheres can be seen more clearly when compared with small charismatic institutions identified with particular leaders and/or ideologies. The small institution can be called charismatic when it has a clear ideological commitment and/or when it relies heavily on the attractiveness or persuasiveness of a charismatic leader or leadership group. Aside from the effects of ideological commitments on the ethos of the programme, ideologies seem to help the staff to organize their priorities, activities and ideas, and to help candidates interpret their experiences and develop their understandings of what their future occupation will be like. Research would be useful on the ways in which the ethos of programmes and their relative effects vary.

Research on location

Teacher education occurs in a wide variety of settings and locations within countries and around the world. This is a variable whose relevance is likely to be clearer in interaction with other variables than on its own account.

For example, in cell (VII x III), created by the intersection of row VII (Location) and column III (Staff), questions concerning the impact of different settings upon staff members can be posed. How does the pressure upon staff members in universities to 'publish or perish' affect the content (Parameter IV) or the ethos (Parameter VI) of the teacher education programme? It may be that a larger proportion of candidates' experience in universities is provided by instructors with less training and experience (ie teaching assistants) than is the case for candidates in institutes and small colleges. This suggests that universities might provide less vigorous intellectual training than the smaller institutions. On the other hand, the wider intellectual community surrounding the teacher education programme in a large university might supply an ethos which more than compensates for the differences in staff qualifications.

Research on regulations

The number and scope of regulations governing teacher education in a variety of settings appear to increase steadily. The regulations may determine the number and characteristics of candidates, qualifications of staff members, allocation of time to various types of content, and so forth. In the US, teachers' unions are actively engaged in sponsoring legislation at various governmental levels which will affect teacher education programmes both directly and indirectly. The recent passage of federal legislation concerning the 'least restrictive environment' for the education of handicapped individuals (Public Law 92-142) is already having important impact upon the content of teacher education programmes (cell VIII x IV).

Research on finances

Although this is last on the list, finance is probably of primary importance to most of the other variables. The pervasiveness of financial considerations is illustrated by the first cell in the row marked IX (Finances). This cell draws attention to the relationship between the assessment procedures used in teacher education programmes and the cost they might involve. For example, both interviewing and classroom observations of candidates are likely to be better predictors of professional competence than course or test grades. But the costs of such procedures militate against their use.

In the next cell (IX x II), we might ask questions about how the anticipated incomes of teacher education candidates determine their level of motivation, socio-economic background and/or their intellectual qualifications. How much higher would anticipated earnings have to be to change the composition of the candidate pool? Just how those characteristics impinge upon the quality of the overall teacher education programme is not known.

Similarly, in each of the cells in row IX, questions arise concerning the ways in which financial resources affect the other eight parameters.

Summary

It has been proposed in this chapter that teacher education consists of sets of activities intended to socialize candidates into the occupation of teaching. Furthermore, it has been asserted that the determinants of teacher education can be thought of as nine interacting classes of variables called parameters. The parameters have been arrayed in a matrix to show how the available literature could be summarized, analysed and synthesized, as well as how new research questions can be generated.

The number of potential variables that can be generated in each parameter is almost limitless. The next problem is to select those which are most likely to improve our understanding of teacher education, and to guide the kind of subsequent research and development which may serve to improve it. In order to select from among this vast potential set of variables, some persuasive theories as to which variables might be related to which other ones are required. It is hoped that the ordering of available literature and the generation of new questions facilitated by the matrix will be followed by the identification of useful theories for the next steps in the development of the field.

References

Fuller, F and Brown, O (1975) Becoming a teacher pp 25-52 *in* Ryan (1975)

Heath, D (undated) *Toward Teaching as a Self-Renewing Calling* (personal communication)

Katz, L G (1974) Issues and problems in teacher education *in* Spodek, B (1974) *Teacher Education* National Association for the Education of Young Children: Washington, DC

Merrow, J M (1975) *Politics of Competence: A Review of Competency-Based Teacher Education* National Institute of Education, Department of Health, Education and Welfare: Washington, DC

Moore, W E (1970) *The Professions: Roles and Rules* Russell Sage Foundation: New York

Ryan, K (1975) *Teacher Education* 74th Yearbook of the National Society for the Study of Education, Part II. University of Chicago Press: Chicago

Turner, R L (1975) An overview of research in teacher education pp 87-110 *in* Ryan (1975)

Wheeler, S (1966) Structure of formally organized socialization settings pp 51-107 *in* Brim, O and Wheeler, S (1966) *Socialization after Childhood: Two Essays* John Wiley and Sons: New York

21. The contribution of research to quality in teacher education

Donald McIntyre

Summary: This paper discusses the contribution which research, especially research on teaching, has made and could make to teacher education. It is argued that research on teaching has demonstrated the complexity of classroom processes and provided a rich store of concepts and information which can help one to reflect on these processes; but that any generalizations emerging from this research must be viewed as tentative, value-laden, not in a form which provides recipes for action, yet highly consistent with much of teachers' common-sense experience-based knowledge. A conception is outlined of teacher education based on dialogue between teachers and researchers and on students' formulation and testing of their own hypotheses, and it is suggested that such teacher education could be best facilitated by interpretive and action research designed to elucidate, examine, explain and extend teachers' working knowledge. Research showing a similar concern for the perspectives and strategies of student teachers is advocated and exemplified for teacher education itself. Finally, a plea is made for research into the professional ideologies and activities of different groups of teacher educators, and into the various institutional pressures and constraints to which these are related.

How research can contribute to quality in teacher education must depend on one's view of teacher education. It is also the case, however, that one's ideas about what teacher education should be concerned with may be radically altered by the findings of research. Thus, research may contribute both to our ideas of what would be desirable in teacher education and to our efforts to realize these ideas in practice.

What I shall attempt to do, therefore, is to indicate how my ideas of what we should be trying to do in teacher education have been influenced by one or two areas of research, and to consider also how research in these areas might be developed so as to facilitate the realization of these ideas. The areas of research with which I shall be concerned will be, first and most fully, research on teaching within the positivist tradition, second, research on the socialization of teachers, and third, research on the institutions and people involved in teacher education. I shall be concerned predominantly with pre-service teacher education.

Research on teaching

It is from research on teaching that we might hope to learn most to help us reflect on the criteria which should direct our efforts in teacher education. Almost by definition, teacher education is concerned with helping student teachers to come to terms with the opportunities and problems with which they may be confronted as professional teachers. Research on teaching should not only help us to understand the nature of these opportunities and problems, and perhaps enable us to identify the skills and strategies which teachers need, but it should also help us to reflect on more general questions, such as whether it is possible to formulate generalizations about classroom teaching and learning as valid as the laws of natural science.

The contribution to our knowledge of research on classroom teaching was well assessed by Dunkin and Biddle (1974) and in most respects their assessment remains valid in relation to what has been achieved since. At the most general level, they conclude that 'at long last we are beginning to know what is actually going on in classrooms' (page 408). Research has provided an extensive information base which allows the teacher educator and the student teacher to reflect very much more intelligently on why things happen as they do. In addition, Dunkin and Biddle concluded that research had generated a wide range and variety of concepts for thinking about teaching, but that any positive generalizations emerging from research would have to be considered as tentative. On the other hand, a major contribution had been the debunking of naive all-purpose solutions to the problems of teaching.

This debunking value of research is, I believe, of major significance for teacher education. There has, in the past, been too much enthusiastic propagation of facile single solutions to the multiple problems of education. Inquiry learning, computer-based instruction, rational curriculum planning and mastery learning, for example, all have much to commend them, but not as solutions to every problem. But the debunking value of research on teaching goes further: the complex findings of classroom research have by now clearly demonstrated the hopelessness of attempting to make direct application of social science theories developed in other contexts to the task of teaching. Various reasonable arguments can be advanced for social science courses within teacher education programmes, but it is now clear that the claim of direct relevance or applicability to teaching is not valid for any such course not based firmly on the findings of classroom research. This is a lesson which many of us, at least in Britain, have still to learn.

For those of us who sought from classroom research a new basis for generalization about effective teaching, reviews such as Dunkin and Biddle's were disappointing. It may, however, be argued that the 1970s have produced more encouraging evidence from this point of view. Thus, in a recent article, Good (1979) suggests that it is now possible to make fairly confident generalizations about the contribution to teaching effectiveness of both teachers' managerial abilities and also their use of 'direct instruction', ie teaching which is explicit in its goals, task-oriented, highly structured, and seeks high levels of teacher and pupil involvement.

These developments are extremely interesting. I believe that we must accept Good's verdict on the evidence for the generality and strength of these relationships; but we should also note several points about them.

First, they are not conclusions which will surprise the majority of teachers who, despite changing fashions, have tended to maintain over the years a commitment to such maxims as 'stopping trouble before it starts', 'having eyes in the back of ones's head', 'getting them settled down quickly', 'getting on with the work', 'covering the work', and other practical ideas which are paralleled by

THE CONTRIBUTION OF RESEARCH TO QUALITY

the recent findings. Furthermore, those components of direct instruction which correlate most highly with pupil achievement also tend to be the components which teachers use most readily. Research seems to be catching up with teachers' craft knowledge.

Second, we might note the strong ideological commitment implicit in the ideas of managerial skills and direct instruction, which is reflected in the narrow range of dependent variables to which the impressive research findings are limited. And we may remember that even Flanders' (1970) conceptually untidy variable of teacher indirectness, which carried a very different ideological commitment, was consistently found to be related to pupils' initiation of ideas and commonly found to be related to various measures of pupils' affective responses. This contrast exemplifies a commonsense generalization that I would offer: patterns of teaching are commonly successful in attaining the goals towards which they are most obviously directed, but rarely successful in attaining other goals. In teaching, one has to choose what one considers important bcause one cannot have everything. I fear that in teacher education we often appear to suggest the opposite, that it is possible for a skilled teacher to attain a wide variety of goals; perhaps we should place more emphasis on the need for thoughtful choice of one's priorities.

The third point is that both managerial skills and direct instruction are defined only in terms of high-inference variables, ie ones which involve relatively subjective observer judgements; this appears to confirm a trend noted by Rosenshine and Furst (1971) for high-inference variables to show stronger and more consistent relationships. If this is generally the case, its implication for teacher educators is that we cannot hope to *train* student teachers: whatever one's criteria of effectiveness, the components of effective teaching cannot be spelt out in operational terms, but are crucially dependent on the teacher's qualities.

In considering the potential contribution of research on teaching to teacher education, it is of some value to look not only at the findings of the research but also at researchers' comments on how their research might be improved. It appears to me that there is a measure of consensus among researchers about three types of problems, those of finding clear and less arbitrary ways of describing phenomena, of taking account of aspects of teaching which have been neglected, and of generalization.

The problems of describing phenomena may be exemplified by the difficulty of deciding the units in terms of which classroom events should be described. Researchers have developed a wide variety of units, for example segments, transactions, episodes, ventures and moves, but have concentrated, in justifying these units, on demonstrating the reliability of the resulting descriptions. In general, we do not know how to set about assessing whether the use of any given units is a sensible way of describing classroom events; we cannot validate our descriptions.

The second problem, of neglected aspects of teaching, is one which has received increasing attention in recent years. It is clear that one is providing only a very limited account of classroom events by simply categorizing them, by counting their frequency or even by examining sequences. However one classifies events, similarly classified events obviously vary considerably in their significance as a result of the specific context in which they occur, their specific characteristics, and the intentions of the teachers or pupils responsible for them. In particular, what is necessarily ignored by systematic observation of classrooms is the information-processing and decision-making skills of teachers. Recognition of this limitation has led to a growing tendency to complement classroom observation evidence with evidence of other kinds, especially on teachers' perceptions of pupils. For example, Calderhead (1980) has combined the use of direct observation, repertory grid and stimulated recall by teachers of their lessons and has shown that teachers' observed behaviour can be better understood through each teacher's individual repertoire of routine procedures, which depend on the distinctive ways in which he or she conceptualizes differences among pupils. Thus there has already been a substantial shift in patterns of research in this respect; but there are still considerable problems in studying the ways in which teachers adapt their behaviour to specific situations.

The third type of problem about which researchers on teaching have become more and more aware is that of generalization. There are many sides to this problem, but all relate to the fact that few research findings have been consistent over several investigations and that as the number of demonstrably relevant variables increases, the likelihood of attaining such consistent findings seems to diminish. Cronbach (1975) has pointed to the immensity of the problem by demonstrating the need to take account not only of first-order interactions between variables, for example between teaching strategies and pupil characteristics, but also of higher-order interactions, for example between these two interacting variables and subject matter. Furthermore, as he points out, contexts change with time, and the desire to establish generalizations, together with the range of situations and populations to which they apply, will therefore be defeated by continual changes in the nature of situations and populations. His conclusion is that the generalizations which we must seek can never be anything other than tentative, and therefore that the exception must be taken as seriously as the rule; in research, therefore, we should concentrate on attaining maximum understanding of why things happen as they do in specific situations, not only testing our hypotheses but also being sensitive to unexpected influences.

In considering the implications which research on teaching might have for our concept of quality in teacher education, it is this impossibility of attaining firm and lasting generalizations which I would take as my starting point.

Implications for the conceptualization of teacher education

As recently as 1970 some of us, for example those associated with microteaching, thought that the findings of research on teaching could form the basis of a body of theoretical knowledge which would, more adequately than general social science theories, generate prescriptive principles which could form the core of a theoretical/practical teacher education programme. We were wrong. Not only has research on teaching so far failed to produce any such body of knowledge; but further, reflection on this research, especially along the lines indicated by Cronbach, leads to the conclusion that it will not be possible to produce such a body of knowledge. My conclusion, therefore, is that there is not, nor could there be, *any* systematic corpus of theoretical knowledge from which prescriptive principles for teaching can be generated.

This conclusion will, I believe, be disappointing to many student teachers who are anxious to find secure principles on which they can base their practice. It will also be disappointing to many of us as teacher educators; it is the most obvious and easy, as well as the traditional, rationale for theoretical courses in teacher education programmes. Furthermore, it is the rationale on which more prestigious professional education programmes, such as those for medicine and engineering, are based, and therefore, the most obvious way to establish the academic respectability of our programmes. However, *secure* academic respectability will depend on our rejection of this kind of rationale, on the firm assertion that 'teaching is not like that', and the development of alternative ways of approaching our task.

What alternatives are there? The obvious one is that we should rely on the practical knowledge of experienced teachers. Certainly my argument seems to lead in that direction. I have suggested that the strongest process-process and process-product relationships which have been established by researchers are very similar to some of the working maxims by which large numbers of teachers have guided their efforts for many years. Furthermore, researchers have not been able to put these generalizations into action in ways which are much more specific than those used by teachers. In addition, I have argued that progress in the study of teaching is dependent on relating teachers' behaviour to their intentions, perceptions and ways of making decisions. Does this not imply that experienced teachers are in practical possession of the knowledge which we seek to formalize, and that they could therefore pass it on to student teachers directly?

There are severe limitations to such a solution. Teachers, not having any need in normal circumstances to make their working knowledge explicit, tend to do so in highly selective and idiosyncratic ways; and observation of teachers' practices, unguided by appropriate cueing, is demonstrably inadequate as a means of acquiring the knowledge they are using. Without the confirmation of research, one does not know which of a teacher's working rules are valid, even in a specific context, especially for people other than himself. Furthermore, teachers vary in the quality of their working knowledge. As Dunkin and Biddle suggest, although Kounin's findings correspond to what is known by many teachers, 'We have the disturbing feeling that considerable improvement in classroom teaching could be wrought by alerting teachers to Kounin's major concepts and findings' (Dunkin and Biddle, 1974:377). The other important argument against total reliance on teachers' practical knowledge is that it is an inherently conservative approach to teacher education. However rich teachers' knowledge might be, no professional education could be defended which did not subject current classroom practices to critical examination.

McNamara and Desforges (1978) therefore, seem to me to be much closer to a satisfactory conception of teacher education when they place their emphasis on 'the objectification of craft knowledge'. The ways in which experienced teachers think and act should, they suggest, be taken as the starting point for initial teacher education:

> The source of data for the envisaged enterprise is the classroom, its artefacts, and teachers' accounts of the use of artefacts and diagnostic and intervention skills. These data are to be treated as sources of hypotheses for the direct development of improved materials and for the longer term development of general theories of instruction. (McNamara and Desforges, 1978:27)

The enterprise they envisage is one involving the collaboration of teachers, college lecturers and student teachers in exercises conceived as both research and self-education. I believe that it is not a realistic plan, largely because teachers have to commit too much of their energy to the task of teaching, but I believe that the goal is right: the core of teacher education should involve students' gradual introduction to effective and detailed debate between currently practising teachers and those engaged in research on teaching from various perspectives. It is not enough that students should learn the concepts and findings of research and be exposed to the practices and ways of thinking of experienced teachers: what is important is that they should be helped to use each to illuminate and test the other, and such help can only be provided through the collaboration of the teacher and the theorist.

My conception of what teacher education should be about has been influenced in three further ways by reflecting on research on teaching. First, and most obviously, since generalizations about teaching are necessarily tentative, learning to teach must be a process of continual hypothesis-testing in one's own teaching. It is too easy, however, to say that every practical principle of teaching must, for the student teacher (if not for the experienced teacher) be treated as a hypothesis to be tested in relation to each new context; viewed either in terms of research design or in terms of the cognitive and emotional load upon the teacher, that is grossly unrealistic. One of the demanding tasks for the teacher educator is therefore to guide the student teacher in the choice of hypotheses which he then tests for himself at different stages and in different contexts; part of this guidance must be the planning of helpful contexts and procedures for hypothesis-testing.

Secondly, one cannot escape the fact that teaching entails making ideological choices. Certainly, ideological commitments are inadequate bases either for analysing teaching or for teaching itself, but they are nonetheless inescapable. Consciously or not, one selects goals and other criteria at the expense of alternatives. I do not think, then, that we can sustain such notions as 'technical' skills; and if this is so, we have either to ask students to accept without examination the values implicit in the concepts and hypotheses for teaching which we offer them, or to encourage them to identify and examine these values and to select hypotheses for testing on the grounds not only of their plausibility, but also of their ideological implications. This, in turn, has consequences for our own roles, for our relationships with schools, and for our assessment of students' teaching.

The danger in initial teacher education of emphasizing the ideological implications of strategies of teaching is that students will commit themselves to styles of teaching which they later find to be impractical in schools; they will then be disillusioned and lacking in any alternative repertoire of skills. This relates to the final implication I would draw for teacher education from research on teaching: implicit in many of the findings of this research — the patterns of similarity among teachers, the emphasis on lower order cognitive activity and on teacher initiation, and especially the evidence on teachers' differentiation between pupils — are indications of the powerful constraints under which teachers work. I know of little research, however, which has been directed towards clarifying the nature of these constraints. The result is, I believe, that we know that there are powerful constraints and can guess what, in general terms, they are, but we know very little about how they operate. It is this theoretical incoherence about the constraints on what teachers can do and achieve in classrooms which I judge to be one of the major weaknesses of teacher education. Student teachers could be forgiven for concluding that judgements about what it would be rational to attempt in any specific context must depend solely on personal preference and on experience. This being so, it is not surprising that many commit themselves to unworkable ideals and are later disillusioned, and that the majority, having once found approaches that do work, never explore the limits of the possible.

In summary, the findings and problems of research on teaching suggest a conception of teacher education in which

1. no body of theoretical knowledge is presented as having prescriptive implications for practice;
2. the curriculum has at its core the knowledge of practising teachers matched closely against researchers' analyses of teaching, each type of knowledge being used explicitly to explore the strengths and weaknesses of the other;
3. students are encouraged to approach their own teaching practice with the purpose of testing hypothetical principles drawn from the considerations of these two types of knowledge;
4. the ideological implications of the hypothetical principles of teaching are emphasized;
5. among the hypothetical principles which students are encouraged to test, emphasis is placed on those relating to constraints on what it is possible for teachers to do.

Research on teaching to facilitate such teacher education

Before making any suggestions, I would emphasize the value of the research which has been done in the last 20 years. The information, concepts and hypotheses which have been developed offer a very rich field which any student teacher or teacher educator could profitably spend a great deal of time exploring. In suggesting developments, I am seeking ways of going beyond this achievement, not questioning its value.

The major change which I believe to be necessary is in the perspective of researchers: to be more useful, we should identify much more with educational practitioners, most obviously with teachers. Whether the assumption that one can stand aloof from social reality and attain the position of an uncommitted observer can be justified in any circumstances has been very seriously questioned in recent years. It seems to me that research concerned with effective teaching cannot *but* be committed; values and goals are clearly implicit in any idea of effectiveness and therefore, also in any rational hypothesis about the patterns of teaching which might attain such goals. Yet most of our research has been conducted within a framework which implies that the researcher is a neutral onlooker. Our first step must be, I believe, to develop a perspective on research which is not logically flawed in this way.

There are good practical reasons also for doing this. One is the need for research which is conducive to the formulation of useful hypotheses for student teachers to test in the development of their teaching competence. A statement of the kind: 'The more the teacher does X, the more likely pupils are to do Y', the kind of conclusion which the onlooker researcher might make, is only of limited value to the aspiring teacher. He or she needs to make judgements about when to do X, what particular X to do, how to lead up to X and how to follow on from it, and so on; these are issues of which the researcher who takes the perspective of the teacher must necessarily take account. Like the observer, the actor has to be selective in focusing on a limited number of aspects of the situation in which he is involved; but the actor cannot afford to be as *arbitrarily* selective as the observer. We have tended to think that our selectivity as researchers has enabled us to look rigorously at aspects of teaching which receive only superficial attention from teachers. That is no doubt so, but the consequence has been that we have neglected things that teachers logically cannot neglect, and in so doing have made our research less helpful for teacher education.

A second reason for taking the perspective of teachers is the need which I have suggested for teacher education to be based on a dialogue between practising teachers and researchers. The problems of achieving such a dialogue are considerable. One of these problems is the difficulty which teachers experience in making explicit the routine and taken-for-granted patterns of thinking and decision-making on which their classroom fluency depends. This difficulty can only be overcome if the concerns and concepts of researchers are sufficiently closely related to those of teachers to help teachers to articulate their agreements, disagreements, qualifications, questions and alternatives to the ideas advanced by researchers. A necessary starting-point for dialogue is that the researcher should submit himself to the discipline of using concepts which make sense, given the constraints experienced in the classroom.

This does not mean that researchers' ideas must be limited by those of teachers. What is necessary is that the researcher should be sufficiently in empathy with the teacher to understand and articulate the latter's interests, concerns, perceptions, intentions, choices and actions. Equally necessary, however, is the researcher's capacity to stand back from the teacher's position, in order to examine the assumptions and values implicit in the teacher's perspective and to explore the implications of these. Identification with the teacher's perspective and critical questioning of teacher's constructs and strategies are both essential.

The knowledge towards which this proposed kind of research would be directed is knowledge to understand and to guide action. It is knowledge which, in its emphasis on action rather than on observed behaviour, goes beyond the kind of knowledge we have mainly been seeking to acquire over the last 20 years, but which, I believe, can build on that already acquired knowledge.

Two main categories of knowledge and two corresponding research strategies may be distinguished: interpretive knowledge and research, and action knowledge and research. In interpretive research, the purpose is to understand existing patterns of activity. An excellent example of such research is Hargreaves' (1975) investigation of teachers' rules for classroom behaviour, of the procedures they used for identifying what they conceived to be deviant acts, of the processes through which they came over a period of time to label certain pupils as troublemakers, and of their ways of coping with these perceived troublemakers. His study was in what has come to be known as the phenomenological tradition, which tries to describe and interpret surface features of reality *as perceived by the participants*, including the discrepancies between their perceptions; phenomenologists caution against the easy assumption that a single 'reality' exists. In its use of participant observation, its detailed analysis of events, with interpretations rigorously checked against the accounts of these events given by teachers and by pupils, this study seems to me a model for the production of interpretive knowledge, and a valuable basis both for student teachers' formulation of hypotheses for their own teaching and for dialogue among them, their college tutors and their supervising teachers.

Studies in which observers seek to describe behaviour and apparent social structures in classrooms much as an anthropologist would study an unfamiliar culture have come to be known as 'ethnographic'. These are not, however, the only appropriate ways of seeking interpretive knowledge of classrooms and indeed they have some serious limitations. As Hargreaves himself points out:

> Within the phenomenological paradigm... there is no widespread consensus about the nature of social scientific theory, or methodology — at least at the present time. There is, however, consensus among the phenomenologists concerning the inappropriateness of the positivistic paradigm to the study of man. They are united in what they are against, but they are much less clear in the details of what they are for. (Hargreaves *et al*, 1975:25)

In their critique of positivistic research, as well as in their exploration of alternative approaches to research, ethnographers have done the rest of us great service, and we must learn from them. I have yet to be convinced, however, of the necessity or the value of maintaining that there must be a mutual exclusiveness between ethnographic and more traditional approaches. Thus two of the unresolved problems in ethnographic research are those of how to deal with the necessarily quantitative basis of many of the generalizations made, and of how to justify adequately, rather than merely to exemplify, generalized conclusions. These are problems which more traditional research has been accustomed to handling. The kind of interpretive research which I should therefore like to see developing would be one which recognized in large measure the validity of the phenomenological critique, but which drew on both traditions, accepting for example the heuristic value of correlational statistics and the value of systematic classroom observation for testing the validity of generalizations about individuals' teaching (cf McIntyre and Macleod, 1978). Work such as Calderhead's (1980) study seems to me to provide the basis for such a synthesis from the more traditional perspective.

Interpretive research is not, however, sufficient. On the one hand, it fails to provide its audience, and especially student teachers, with any information about the implications of attempting to seek goals or to adopt teaching strategies which are not found to occur 'naturally'. On the other hand, and equally important, it does not allow us to test our conjectures about the constraints which lead teachers to adopt particular teaching strategies. For these purposes, action research is necessary.

In action research on teaching, the researcher can adopt any one of several positions: he may himself be the teacher, attempting to test hypothetical principles, and more generally to explore the consequences of acting in specified ways; he may be an outsider testing principles for, and exploring the consequences of, attempting to persuade teachers to adopt new approaches; or he may engage in collaborative research, one researcher being the teacher and another the observer gathering evidence to test hypotheses implicit in the teacher's intentions and actions. Whichever of these is the case, the research will be concerned with formulating and testing principles about the nature and effects of the researcher-teacher's actions.

Some action research can be very similar to traditional experiments. Thus Good (1979) reviews three projects in which teachers were asked to implement various components of a direct instruction approach to teaching, their subsequent teaching behaviour and the attainments of their pupils being compared with those of control groups. More commonly, however, the significant questions of action research would be concerned with the difficulties involved in following new approaches and with the distinctive consequences of attempting these approaches, questions for which control groups would be of little value. Probably the best example of this kind of action research is that of the Ford Teaching Project in England, described by Elliott (1976). (*See also Chapter 22.*) This research involved collaboration between teachers who were attempting to implement inquiry/discovery approaches to teaching and two outside researchers. The purpose of the research was to develop some general rules about the nature of the problems encountered in attempting this type of teaching and to develop and test practical hypotheses about how these problems might be resolved. Its outcome again seems to be just the kind of material which is ideally suited to provide the basis for dialogue between teacher educators and practising teachers to which student teachers should be introduced, and also the basis from which student teachers could choose or develop hypothetical principles for testing in their own teaching. This approach also provides an excellent model for in-service teacher education.

I have dwelt at some length on research into teaching because I think it contains the core of any useful research contribution to teacher education. I have attempted to show, first, that the contribution to teacher education of research on teaching has up to now been substantial and valuable, but subject to certain important limitations; second, that this research has influenced my conception of what we should be trying to do in teacher education in some significant ways; and third, that there are opportunities for research on teaching to contribute to teacher education in the future in new and, I believe, more fundamental ways.

Now I want to comment briefly on the contribution of research in two other areas, both more directly concerned with teacher education: research on the socialization of student teachers and on teacher educators themselves.

Research on the socialization of student teachers

If research on teaching is the most fundamental area of research which can make a contribution to teacher education, it is research on teacher education itself which can make the most immediate and obvious contribution, and which has indeed already done so.

This contribution has been many sided. It is worth noting, however, that it has been limited largely to components of teacher education programmes which have been innovative and based on a fairly clear rationale, such as microteaching. It is unfortunate that the more traditional components of our programmes have not received their share of research attention. What we do out of convention is as important, and merits as much questioning, as what we do as a result of conscious planning.

Microteaching typifies the direct contribution which research can make to teacher education. (*See also Chapter 19.*) The provision of materials for microteaching has increasingly been based on surveys of existing practices, problems and experienced needs (eg Turney *et al*, 1973). Microteaching has been subject to continuing questioning which has led to clearer ideas about what can profitably be attempted and has identified crucial problems still to be resolved. Thus research recently completed at Stirling (Batten, 1979) confirms clearly some apparent trends from earlier research, such as the overwhelming importance of the quality of preparatory materials and study before microteaching practice, the lack of detectable effects from using expensive video-tape feedback, and the fact that mastery of teaching skills in a microteaching context is no guarantee that these skills will be transferred to the school classroom. The scale, variety and value of research on microteaching, then, may be taken as an example of the useful research that can potentially be done on teacher education; it may be noted, however, that the use made of the research findings on microteaching is very uneven.

I want, however, to focus more generally on research on the professional socialization of student teachers, on the ways in which they develop those patterns of thinking and activity which will characterize them as teachers. It was not until recently, I believe, that we began to ask some of the right questions in this area. Previously, researchers tended to ask whether students' knowledge, skills or attitudes changed in the ways teacher educators wanted them to change, or changed on other preconceived dimensions. Not surprisingly, perhaps, it was found that most students changed, at least to a limited degree, in ways of which most teacher educators approved. Less satisfying, however, the fairly consistent findings were that in many respects beginning teachers, once they left us, tended to change in the opposite direction: our influence seemed to be short-lived. If that made us think twice about what we were doing, then it was of some value; but it did not give us much guidance as to how we might change our practices to make them more fruitful. This research had the same limitation as much of our research on teaching has had: it ignored the perspectives of those with whom we claimed to be concerned, the student teachers. Some recent research, however, has begun to correct this oversight.

Much of this more recent research has been concerned with the strategies which students use, more or less effectively, to 'get by', especially when faced with the demands of school practice. Lacey (1977), for example, talks of the situationally specific social strategies which students use to cope with their problems. He describes the 'collectivizing' strategies which students tend to use in the university context, sharing their teaching problems with peers and tutors, gaining support from the knowledge that these problems are not unique to them, and gaining recognition from tutors for their ability to conceptualize classroom realities. He contrasts these strategies with the 'privatizing' strategies which students tend to use in the school context, keeping their problems as much as possible to themselves lest they should be judged inadequate or should generate conflict.

It is of the greatest importance that we should understand more fully such aspects of students' coping strategies, especially in order that our institutional arrangements should take realistic account of students' likely subjective experiences and reactions. If we do not, then, to pursue the example from Lacey, we are likely unknowingly to socialize students into undesirable conceptions of a theory-practice dichotomy and into isolationist roles as teachers. Nonetheless, it would be unfortunate if such research were focused too exclusively on student teachers' ways of coping with the temporary problems they face as students; there are more fundamental aspects of their thinking, relating to their orientations to teaching, about which we also need to learn.

For example, another of Lacey's findings is that, when faced with teaching problems, students cope by displacing the blame for their apparent failures either downward on to the stupidity or laziness of pupils or upward on to the inadequacies of the education system. He also produces evidence which indicates that those who adopt the downward displacement strategy tend to be consistently more conservative in their attitudes, more committed to a teaching career, and in practice more likely to persist therein: it is difficult to commit oneself to a teaching career when one believes that the system will not allow one to do what is worth doing. Such findings as these seem to me of immense value in helping us to clarify further our purposes in teacher education and to face up to the problems of fulfilling these purposes.

There are, however, equally fundamental and more specific aspects of students' thinking which we need to understand: in what terms and with what kinds of strategies do they think about the task of teaching itself, about the subjects they are to teach, and about their pupils? Of course, teacher educators know a good deal about their students' thinking, through seminars, assignments, examinations and more informal contact; but what we know is necessarily very much in terms of our own preferred frameworks, and about the extent to which these are assimilated and mastered by our students. I wonder how much we know about how students construe teaching when they are thinking about it for themselves, rather than relating to us, or about how their thinking about teaching changes as a result of their various experiences in teacher education programmes, or about how it informs their developing classroom practices. It is in providing some answers to these questions that I believe research can make one of its most vital contributions to quality in teacher education.

One of the very few examples of such research is Macleod's study of students' constructions of their microteaching lessons (reported in McIntyre, Macleod and Griffiths, 1977). Macleod followed students through a semester's work on microteaching, asking them after each of several of their microteaching lessons to write down their reactions to these lessons, and exploring relationships between these comments and the characteristics of these and subsequent lessons. He found that students initially made relatively little use of the concepts in terms of which the skills were defined, but their use of these concepts gradually increased during the course of the semester. They evaluated lessons primarily in terms of pupils' behaviour, and they evaluated their own behaviour less in terms of the prescribed skills than of their generally accurate perceptions of which aspects of their behaviour influenced pupils. They formulated hypotheses based on their experience of one lesson, which guided their behaviour in their next lesson; focusing on their own behaviour, negative self-evaluation, and confidence in their ability to improve were conducive to success in the subsequent lesson.

These and other findings have led us radically to reappraise and refine our conception of what happens in microteaching and to see its value very much more in terms of its contribution to the gradual development of students' cognitive schemata for teaching than in terms of their acquisition of specified behaviour patterns. My concern here, however, is not with microteaching in particular but with the value of research such as this in relation to every aspect of teacher education programmes. For example, one of the findings of our research on microteaching has been that students' conceptualization and practice of teaching depends critically on their beliefs about their subjects: according to their subjects, students appear to use different constructs for thinking about teaching and to impose different types of limitations on the range of teaching strategies they consider. It would be valuable to know the nature of these subject ideologies of teaching and how they are acquired. Again, questions similar to those asked by Macleod could usefully be asked about the development of students' ideas and practices in teaching on school practice and about how concepts and suggestions from various sources are assimilated and used in this context.

I suggested earlier a conception of teacher education which had at its core student teachers' gradual introduction to an effective dialogue between practising teachers and researchers on teaching, together with the provision of opportunities and support for students to test for themselves hypotheses which they generate or select from such dialogue. The kinds of research which I have been exemplifying on the socialization of student teachers can and should enable one to modify and elaborate upon this conception and, together with research on teaching, provide the information and ideas through which it can be operationalized as a coherent curriculum.

Research on teacher educators

The final way I would highlight in which research can contribute to quality in teacher education is its potential for making us as teacher educators more aware of our own concerns, assumptions and ideologies and of how these relate to our positions within distinctive types of organizations. It is a plausible hypothesis that the status of people within education is inversely proportional to the frequency with which they are the subjects of research; if this is so, then teacher educators are a very high status group, since very little attempt has been made to understand us and the ways we work. I suggest, however, that this is an area of research which would be very valuable. Like everyone else, we are subject to social and institutional pressures and constraints which make us inclined to hold distinctive attitudes and values. The more aware we are of such pressures and of how they tend to influence us, the more able we should be to transcend our distinctive positions and to approach teacher education with a sensitivity to what is in the interest of those in other positions, such as teachers and pupils in schools.

Of major importance in this respect is the difference between the perspectives of college-based teacher educators and of practising teachers who supervise our students in the schools. We have a good deal of evidence from studies like that of Cope (1971) about the strengths and weaknesses which students perceive in the kind of help they are offered by these two groups, and about the problems which arise for students in attempting to relate to both groups. I believe, however, that we do not yet have a sufficient theoretical understanding of how the different social positions of people in these two groups encourage them to perceive teaching in systematically different ways and to have systematically different concerns in their dealing with students; and, largely because of this, we are still very far from attaining the kind of detailed and continuous dialogue between practising teachers and people with research perspectives which I have suggested to be critical to quality in teacher education.

Our understanding of the position and perspectives of supervising teachers is a good deal better than our understanding of college-based teacher educators, and has grown considerably in recent years. Nonetheless, the relationship between those pressures which encourage teachers to adopt the perspective of alienated workers bargaining through their unions in terms of conditions and rewards external to their activities as teachers, and those other pressures which encourage them to adopt a professional service perspective, and the consequences of these interacting pressures, are, I believe, inadequately understood and also crucial to their involvement in teacher education.

Similar issues, which have been studied even less, arise when we consider college-based teacher educators as a group, or rather as a collection of several rather different groups. One of the more obvious pressures on people in tertiary institutions is the pressure to demonstrate one's academic expertise through research and publication. Yet this would seem to be a pressure experienced only by some teacher educators, while others experience quite different pressures which appear often to encourage attitudes of opposition to research. No doubt a partial explanation of this lies in college-based teacher educators' continuing identification with classroom teachers in emphasizing the importance of craft knowledge rather than abstract academic knowledge of teaching; but this *is* only a partial explanation, and there must be other pressures at work. For example, it seems to me that when able schoolteachers are appointed to posts as full-time teacher educators, they experience considerable pressure, not to articulate the knowledge which made them able teachers, but rather to develop new ideas which did not inform their practice as teachers at all, and which they have therefore not submitted to the tests which teachers working full-time in schools would generally apply.

These are speculative ideas. My general point is that we need to attain a much greater understanding of the social and institutional pressures which influence each of us involved in teacher education, of the nature of the ideologies which we are inclined to adopt as a result of these pressures, and of the social strategies we use to deal with them. Only through attaining such an understanding will we be able to plan realistically in order to realize our conceptions of quality in teacher education. For me, three key people are necessarily involved in teacher education: the practising teacher; the researcher on teaching; and the full-time 'teacher educator' who is also an experienced teacher, and can mediate and facilitate the dialogue between the first two and the student teacher. I might, however, change my conception of the roles which need to be fulfilled if I understood better the social realities of teacher education institutions. Such a greater understanding would certainly be necessary in order to make fruitful proposals about how teacher education institutions should be developed to attain greater quality in teacher education.

Research can neither provide us with specifications for quality in teacher education nor tell us how to meet specifications derived from elsewhere. What it can do is to sensitize us to the realities and the possibilities, in the schools, in our students and in ourselves, of which we shall have to take account in formulating conceptions of quality, and in working to realize them.

References

Batten, H D (1979) *Factors Influencing the Effectiveness of Microteaching in a Teacher Education Programme* Unpublished PhD thesis submitted to the Department of Education, University of Stirling

Calderhead, J (1980) *Teachers' Classroom Decision-making: its Relationship to Teachers' Perceptions of Pupils and to Classroom Interaction* Unpublished PhD thesis submitted to the Department of Education, University of Stirling

Cope, E (1971) *School Experience in Teacher Education* Bristol University: Bristol

Cronbach, L J (1975) Beyond the two disciplines of scientific psychology *American Psychologist* **15**: 116-27

Dunkin, M J and Biddle, B J (1974) *The Study of Teaching* Holt, Rinehart and Winston: New York

Elliott, J (1976) *Developing Hypotheses about Classrooms from Teachers' Practical Constructs* North Dakota Study Group on Evaluation: University of North Dakota

Flanders, N A (1970) *Analyzing Teacher Behaviour* Addison-Wesley: Reading, Mass

Good, T L (1979) Teacher effectiveness in the elementary school *Journal of Teacher Education* **30** 2:52-64

Hargreaves, D H, Hester, S K and Mellor, F J (1975) *Deviance in Classrooms* Routledge and Kegan Paul: London

Lacey, C (1977) *The Socialization of Teachers* Methuen: London

McIntyre, D and Macleod, G (1978) The characteristics and uses of systematic classroom observation, *in* McAleese, R and Hamilton, D (eds) *Understanding Classroom Life* NFER: Slough

McIntyre, D, Macleod, G and Griffiths, R (1977) *Investigations of Microteaching* Croom Helm: London

Macleod, G and McIntyre, D (1977) Towards a model for microteaching *in* McIntyre *et al* (1977)

McNamara, D and Desforges, C (1978) The social sciences, teacher education and the objectification of craft knowledge *British Journal of Teacher Education* **4** 1:17-36

Rosenshine, B and Furst, N (1971) Research on teacher performance criteria *in* Smith, B O (ed) *Research in Teacher Education: A Symposium*, Prentice-Hall: Englewood Cliffs, NJ

Turney, C, Clift, J C, Dunkin, M J and Traill, R D (1973) *Microteaching: Research, Theory and Practice* Sydney University Press: Sydney

Acknowledgement
This chapter is based on material originally presented as an invited address at the annual conference of the South Pacific Association in Teachers Education, Sydney, August 1979, and subsequently published in the South Pacific Journal of Teacher Education **81** (1980). *It is reprinted with the editor's kind permission.*

22. Implications of classroom research for professional development

John Elliott

Summary: The author argues that the process-product paradigm involves an acceptance of a radically different view of the nature of teaching and learning from the action research paradigm. These underlying assumptions imply different methodological approaches to the study of teaching and learning. Process-product methodology treats the teacher exclusively as an object of research and assumes his professional development to be a quite independent activity. By contrast, action research necessitates dialogue with the teacher and thereby involves him as a participant in the research process itself. Such involvement itself constitutes a mode of professional development. Therefore action research is not only a research process but also a process of teacher education.

Introduction

During the last decade the study of classroom events has become a major growth area for educational research. In this chapter, I shall not be reviewing specific research findings in order to discuss their relevance for teacher education. Rather I shall interpret my task as that of answering the general question, 'How can the study of classroom events contribute to the professional development of teachers?' I shall contrast two distinct approaches to classroom research in terms of their underlying assumptions about the relationship between teaching and learning, and in the light of these assess their potential for influencing professional development. It will be my contention that not every way of influencing the practice of teachers in classrooms contributes to their professional development. Such development is an educational process, and in order to influence this process, classroom research must possess educative potential.

Process-product studies

The 'triple-play'

To date, the dominant approach to classroom research has been that of the process-product study; these studies have been reviewed by Berliner and Rosenshine (1977) and Dunkin and Biddle (1974). Studies of this type attempt to describe observable regularities in teaching performance, and then to discover whether any causal relationships exist between such performances and learning outcomes as measured by achievement tests. In discovering these relationships, process-product researchers would claim to have identified certain elements of effective teaching, which can be formulated as technical rules to be applied in teacher education. Fenstermacher (1978) suggests that the motive to furnish 'imperatives for teacher training' is so strong that process-product researchers tend to engage in a kind of 'triple-play'. He argues that research findings are usually based on statistical correlations which answer the general question 'What relationships obtain, if any, between teacher performances Pl, P2, P3...Pn and success at learning tasks K1, K2, K3...Kn by students assigned to complete these tasks?' Having isolated a positive correlation, say 'P1 and P2 are significantly correlated with success at task K1 by students assigned this task', researchers tend to conclude that teachers should do P1 and P2 in answer to the question 'What should teachers do in order to be effective in getting students to succeed at K1 and tasks like it?'

Now Fenstermacher claims that this leap from correlational findings to prescriptions for teacher training begs two important questions; first, the causal question 'Do teacher performances P1 and P2 *result* in success at task K1 by students assigned this task?' A correlational relationship does not necessarily imply a causal one. From the fact that a correlation exists between P1-P2 and K1, one cannot logically infer that a causal relationship exists between them. It could be that the causal relationship exists between both these correlated variables and a third. In order to establish where the cause lies, a researcher would have to embark on a series of experimental studies. Fenstermacher argues that the standard procedure in process-product research is to assume that the correlational question answers the causal question, 'Why do P1 and P2 result in student success at K1?' Thus process-product research rarely provides us with a theoretical explanation as to why the correlations or causal relationships it discovers obtain in the context of the study. Having ignored this question, the third and final move is to translate the assumed cause-effect relationships between teaching and learning into rules for teacher training.

I have dealt extensively with Fenstermacher's account of how process-product classroom researchers reason from theory to practice, because it enables me to spell out the implications of some key assumptions which underly their approach.

The assumption of teachers' causality

The first key assumption is that teaching *causes* learning. On the basis of this assumption the process-product researcher tends to focus on the performances of the teacher rather than those of students in the classroom, and to interpret correlations between these performances and learning outcomes as evidence that the former caused the latter.

This assumption also has implications for educational accountability. It suggests that teachers alone can be held accountable for student learning, rather than, say, the students themselves or educational managers and administrators. In the absence of the assumption of teacher causality the discovery of correlations between classroom events and learning outcomes might be a stimulus for entertaining the possibility that, rather than being causally linked with each other, these variables are caused by factors originating beyond the classroom in its institutional and administrative context. The assumption of teacher causality is bureaucratically and politically convenient since it suggests that deficiencies in educational provision can only be rectified by doing something about the way teachers perform in classrooms rather than by doing something about the way schools as institutions are organized, or the provision of educational resources administered.

The causal knowledge generated by process-product researchers can easily be formulated as sets of technical means-ends rules intended to govern teacher performance. One might argue that the researcher's knowledge is based on the view that teaching is a technology or form of instrumental action (see Habermas, 1972). Such action involves the agent (teacher) administering certain treatments (teaching methods) to passive objects (students) in order to produce preconceived outputs (objectives). In the field of social relations, instrumental action influences people's behaviour by securing compliance, and this involves the employment of power expressed in the use of positive and negative sanctions (rewards and punishments). Thus teaching conceived as instrumental action is power-coercive and its object, learning, is power-dependent.

When teaching is conceived as instrumental action, learning is conceived as passive behaviour directed by the teacher rather than self-directed by students. Presupposed in the process-product approach is a bias against the ideas of 'self-directed', 'discovery', 'inquiry' learning. If effective teaching is a set of causally efficacious performances then by definition it cannot result in learning conceived in these ways. It should hardly be surprising, then, that process-product correlations fail to demonstrate 'the effectiveness' of informal teaching methods when employed by teachers who construe learning in the terms cited above. Yet the failure to establish causal relationships here is interpreted by the researchers as an outcome of their research, rather than being an inevitable implication of their research design. There is no way in which progressive methods of teaching can 'look good' from the perspective of process-product research.

Finally, the assumption of teacher causality implies a division of labour between researchers who produce causal knowledge and teachers who apply it in practice. The causal statements produced by process-product researchers refer to publicly observable acts rather than the subjective states of teachers. They can be tested independently of any reference to the beliefs, intentions, and meanings teachers express in their actions. Thus the production of knowledge about teaching does not have to be validated against teachers' understanding of their own actions, and does not require their participation: their role is to apply the knowledge researchers produce. The process of professional development involves the application of research knowledge but not its production.

Generalizability

Let me now turn to the second key assumption underlying process-product research. Power (1976) sums it up neatly when he argues that for this kind of research, 'situations and events are not regarded as unique. This means actions can be repeated and probability statements linking situations and actions made...Generalizations across classrooms about classroom phenomena, their antecedents and consequences are believed to be both possible and useful.' This is the assumption of *formal generalizability*, that there are general laws governing the relationship between classroom events to be discovered. This assumption explains the process-product researcher's apparent failure to explain why the causal relationships he infers from his correlations obtain. Such an explanation would be given only if the researcher thought that it might not be possible to generalize across all classroom contexts.

It is my view that process-product generalizations are applicable only to some learning contexts. Doyle (1979) argues that process-product research has tended to assume a homogeneity in the quality of learning tasks given to students, leading to the use of a single criterion for assessing outcomes. The result is a general focus on the quantifiable aspects of teaching and learning. Thus *how much* is learned becomes more significant than the type of learning involved, and in an attempt to discover correlations, quantifiable aspects of teaching, such as pacing of content and the amount covered, have priority over qualitative aspects.

Three types of learning task

Doyle distinguishes three types of learning task. First, there are 'understanding' tasks, requiring students to apply cognitive operations, such as classification, inference, deduction and analysis, to instances not previously encountered, or to comprehend information by reproducing it in transformed or paraphrased form. Secondly, there are 'memory' tasks, requiring recognition or recall of facts, principles, or solutions the student has previously been acquainted with. Thirdly, there are 'routine problem-solving' tasks, such as dividing fractions or squaring numbers, which require students to learn a standard and reliable formula or principle. Doyle goes on to argue that different types of learning tasks can be compared in the light of the degrees of ambiguity and risk inherent in them. Ambiguity inheres in a learning task, not because of the teacher's lack of clarity, but because it does not tell the student the exact performance that will be required and how to produce it. Risk refers to the likelihood of students being able to cope with the demands of a task. According to Doyle 'understanding' tasks score high on both ambiguity and risk. 'Memory' and 'routine problem-solving' tasks on the other hand are low on ambiguity and when the amount of content to be covered is small or the routines to be mastered simple, low on risk.

In the light of these qualitative differences between learning tasks, Doyle suggests that one can expect greater variance in learning outcomes, and therefore lower mean achievement, on 'understanding' tasks than on 'memory' or 'routine problem-solving' ones. This implies that it is easier for teachers to control mean achievement when the learning tasks are of the latter rather than the former kind. It follows that one is more likely to discover general rules for maximizing learning outcomes when the learning tasks are of the 'memory' or 'routine problem-solving' kind than of the 'understanding' kind. If this is correct, then we have a possible explanation for the causal generalizations established by process-product research. It is that they only apply to classroom contexts where students are performing on 'memory' or 'routine problem-solving' tasks. The fact that the criteria employed by process-product research tend to measure outcomes of these kinds of tasks reinforces this point.

The qualities of ambiguity and risk, intrinsic to 'understanding' tasks, indicate why process-product methodology is quite inappropriate for the study of classrooms where students are performing them. Such qualities imply that learning is contingent on the personal characteristics of individual students and thereby introduce an element of unpredictability into teaching. In 'understanding' contexts one can no longer assume that the relationship between teaching performance and learning outcomes is a causal one, let alone generalizable across students and classrooms. A new paradigm of classroom research is required, but before sketching it, I want briefly to return to the implications of process-product research for teacher education.

Teacher training and teacher education

Most educational theorists would view education as a process of 'teaching for understanding'. Process-product research therefore masks and distorts education. This is why I have elsewhere described such research as 'research on education' rather than 'educational research' (Elliott, 1978b). The outcomes of education cannot be detected by its methods, and *educational* methods are bound to show up rather poorly in its research findings. If these findings are then translated into prescriptions for competency-based teacher education and implemented on a large scale, the teachers of the future will certainly not be equipped to be educators of children. Moreover, the process of teacher training will also not be an *educational* one. All process-product research can do is to furnish rules governing teaching performance in typical situations. These rules are learned by applying them uncritically in such situations. In other words the process of teacher training will involve teachers performing 'routine problem-solving' rather than 'understanding' tasks. In my view the professional development of teachers is an educational process which involves developing understanding of the particular classroom situations in which they work. The application of general rules pre-empts such understanding.

Educational action research

Curriculum development as a context for research

It is no coincidence that action research in classrooms tended to emerge in association with the curriculum development movement in the 1960s and early 1970s. Many of the projects which constituted this movement were concerned with shifting the learning context in classrooms from 'memory' and 'routine problem-solving' to 'understanding' tasks. Such innovations tended to articulate this shift in terms of ideas like 'self-directed', 'discovery', and 'inquiry' learning. As I suggested earlier these ideas embody a more active and personal conception of the learning process than the one presupposed by process-product research. Each of the above terms picks out a particular aspect of this process. 'Self-directed' implies that learning outcomes are the result of the student's own autonomous activity and not of teaching. 'Inquiry' provides a general description of the kind of activity involved, constituted by the cognitive operations cited by Doyle in his account of 'understanding' tasks. 'Discovery' refers to the quality of the intellectual experience which results from this kind of activity, indicating both its personal and impersonal aspects. In its impersonal aspect an objective reality which exists independently of the student's own thinking is disclosed. In its personal aspect this reality can only be personally appropriated by the student as he brings his own cognitive structures to bear on the problems defined by the task. These orienting ideas, employed in the curriculum development movement, simply pick out different dimensions of performance on 'understanding' tasks in terms of its agency, the operations involved, and the quality of the intellectual experience which results.

The problems teachers experienced in initiating and sustaining student performance on 'understanding' tasks generated a whole movement of classroom research conducted largely by people attached to the development teams of national projects in collaboration with participating teachers. (See Barnes, 1976; Elliott and MacDonald, 1972; Elliott and Adelman, 1976; Jenkins, 1977; Parlett and Hamilton, 1973; Smith and Schumacher, 1972; Walker and Adelman, 1972; Wild, 1973.) Interestingly, this research conceptualized the problems of teaching in a radically different way from process-product research. In place of technical problems of selecting causally effective means for bringing about certain pre-specified learning outcomes, the problems were seen as ones of achieving a certain quality of communication with students about the problems and issues posed by learning tasks. Teaching was viewed as a mode of communicative rather than instrumental action (see Habermas, 1972).

In viewing teaching in this way classroom researchers were simply adopting the same perspective as the curriculum developers. Indeed, many of them, like myself, played the dual roles of developer and researcher. The reason I have called this alternative mode of research action research is simply because it adopts the action perspective of curriculum developers (Elliott, 1978a). I will now attempt to give a more detailed account of this perspective.

The action perspective of curriculum development

Many curriculum development projects neglected to spell out the pedagogical implications of 'teaching for understanding' in the content areas they were concerned with. Perhaps naively it was assumed that they would be tacitly understood by teachers. Stenhouse's *Humanities Curriculum Project* (1971) and Bruner's *Man: a course of study* (1970) were notable exceptions. Both formulated pedagogic principles which specified conditions of teaching and learning to be realized in classrooms rather than learning objectives. Stenhouse called them 'principles of procedure', while Bruner used the phrase 'pedagogical aims'. Such principles or aims specified intrinsically, rather than instrumentally, valuable qualities of teaching and learning tasks. Although some curriculum development projects attempted to fit their ideas to a behavioural objectives model of curriculum design, Stenhouse (1975) claimed that such a model was inconsistent with teaching for understanding and education. He argued that the Humanities Project's aim of 'developing an understanding of controversial issues' could not be broken down into specific learning objectives without distorting its nature. This is entirely consistent with Doyle's account of 'understanding' tasks as high in ambiguity, in the sense that there are no absolute rules for producing correct answers, and therefore no ways of predicting in advance exactly what constitutes successful performance.

Stenhouse posed the 'process model' of curriculum design as an alternative to 'behavioural objectives'. He claimed that the general aim of 'understanding' could be logically analysed into principles governing the process of teaching and learning in classrooms. For example, he argued that the teacher who used his position of authority in the classroom to promote his own views would necessarily impose constraints on the development of an understanding of controversial issues. The actions involved would be logically inconsistent with such development. From this consideration Stenhouse formulated the principle of procedural neutrality, ie the obligation to refrain from taking sides on a controversial issue *qua* teacher. Similarly, he argued that students would necessarily lack opportunities to develop their understanding of issues if the teacher denied them access to some views rather than others. Thus failure to protect divergence in classroom discussion was logically inconsistent with the project's aim. Only the teacher whose actions realized the principle 'protect the expression of divergent views' would be acting consistently. Stenhouse's 'procedural principles' functioned as criteria for selecting teaching acts which were logically consistent with the development of understanding on learning tasks. Acts which realized these criteria constituted a worthwhile form of teaching regardless of their outcomes. His inspiration for the 'process model' of curriculum design came from R.S. Peters' seminal paper entitled 'Must an educator have an aim?' (1968). In this paper Peters argued that *educational* aims specify what is to count as a worthwhile educational process rather than its extrinsic outcomes.

The process model embodies a radically different set of assumptions about the relationship between teaching and learning from the behavioural objectives model and the process-product research which matches it. The aim of teaching is viewed as 'enabling', 'facilitating' or 'providing opportunities for' the development of understanding. Such aim descriptions specify conditions to be realized by the teacher rather than his students. A teacher can *enable* pupils to perform certain learning tasks successfully without them then actually doing so. The student's task performance is ultimately his or her responsibility. The teaching aim of 'enabling the development of understanding' must be distinguished from the learners' aim of 'developing an understanding'. The teaching aim is concerned with establishing conditions in the classroom which enable students to develop their own understanding of the subject matter. The process model, inasmuch as it specifies enabling conditions, embodies an active conception of learning and does not assume that it is caused by teaching.

I will now examine more closely the nature of the enabling conditions specified by the principles of educational procedure which govern 'teaching for understanding'. I have argued that understanding is developed by the student from 'within', through the exercise of his own rational capacities, and therefore cannot be caused from 'without'. However, a student could hardly be described as exercising his rational capacities if he were closed to the reasons and arguments put forward by others. Intellectual development necessarily involves being open to discussion. The fact that it is not causally effected does not imply that it cannot be effected in other ways. This kind of learning, although inconsistent with the employment of power strategies aimed at securing quasi-causal compliance from the student, can be rationally influenced by teaching which involves the student in discussion or discourse about the learning task. In discourse, the teacher seeks to influence a student's task performance by citing evidence, reasons, and arguments.

According to Habermas (1974) pure discourse constitutes 'the ideal speech situation' presupposed in all interpersonal communication. It is characterized by an absence of all constraints on people's thinking, save that of 'the force of the better argument'. For Habermas, the influence exerted through this ideal form of human communication is quite distinct from the power influence exerted in instrumental action upon another. The consensus which results beween the participants in discourse is a justified or warranted one. But this raises the problem of how one distinguishes a warranted from an unwarranted consensus, a rational acceptance of another's argument from a non-rational one. Applied to 'teaching for understanding' the issue becomes one of how to distinguish the rational from the non-rational influences a teacher might exert. Habermas attempts to resolve this problem in terms of the formal properties of discourse. He argues that participants must have an equal opportunity to adopt dialogue roles, and in particular equal freedom 'to put forward, call into question, and give reasons for and against statements, explanations, interpretations and justifications'. Thus the conditions of discourse correspond with the liberal-democratic values of 'equality', 'freedom' and 'justice' and constitute the conditions which enable people to develop their understanding through communication with others. In educational contexts, where students encounter 'understanding' tasks, the provision of such discourse conditions is the *educational* responsibility of teachers.

Inasmuch as it is discourse which enables, rather than causes, the development of understanding, then teachers enable this development when they realize discourse values in their communications with students. The relationship between means and ends here is not a technical or instrumental relation. Discourse values are not extrinsic outcomes of communicative acts but intrinsic norms which ideal acts of this kind ought to satisfy. They are not so much realized *by* as *in* acts of teaching.

Stenhouse's 'principles of procedure' and Bruner's 'pedagogical aims' can both be interpreted as attempts to explain the implications of discourse values for teaching in their respective subject areas.

I described the classroom research generated by the curriculum development movement as action research because it conceptualized problems of teaching from the same action perspective as those involved in developing and implementing new curricula. This perspective defines *the educational perspective* on teaching and learning and can be summarized in terms of:

1. a focus on the quality of the teacher's discourse with students about learning tasks;
2. construing learning as a student-directed rather than teacher-directed activity;
3. construing teaching as a mode of exerting rational rather than causal influence on student learning.

It might be argued that classroom action research does not necessarily adopt an educational perspective. In some classroom research contexts the action perspectives of teachers may be very different. I would agree that classroom action perspectives may differ. However, it is not merely a contingent fact that research from an educational perspective appears to be the only mode of action research currently existing in classrooms. There are some kinds of human action which can only be described from a phenomenological perspective, ie by adopting the point of view of the agent. Other kinds of action can be described without any reference to the agent's point of view. Let us compare instrumental with communicative action in this respect. An instrumental action is one which is viewed by its agent as a means to an extrinsic end. But it can be described quite independently of the instrumental meaning ascribed to it by the agent, perhaps on the basis of observational criteria alone. A communicative action on the other hand is an action defined by rules which are logically presupposed by its occurrence. For example, an assertion is an action *in* which the agent places himself under an obligation to speak the truth. Thus one cannot describe the act independently of the agent's perspective in performing it.

It is only when the teaching acts to be described are defined by the teacher's action perspective that research needs to adopt it. Inasmuch as teaching for understanding involves communicative actions defined by the teacher's obligation to realize discourse values, research can only identify them by adopting the same perspective. But inasmuch as teaching for 'routine problem-solving' or 'memory' learning is a form of instrumental action, the activities involved can be identified and described quite independently of the teacher's point of view. It is only in the discourse context of teaching for understanding that classroom research must adopt the teacher's perspective if it is to produce valid accounts of such teaching. Process-product studies, by construing teaching as a form of instrumental action, assume that it can be described quite independently of the teacher's action perspective. Such studies therefore cannot be described as educational action research.

I now want to sketch out the main features of educational action research and explore its implications for the role of teachers in research, and their professional development.

Clarifying action perspectives

The first task of educational action research is the explication and clarification of the educational perspectives from which teachers identify and diagnose problems in their teaching. For classroom researchers working with teachers attempting to implement the Humanities Project, the action perspective of the project had already been clarified, through discussions between the project team and teachers prior to implementation. But for many classroom researchers the action perspective of the teachers they work with is not explicitly formulated. It is in this situation that the first stage of the research must involve an explication of action perspectives.

A good example here is the Ford Teaching Project (Elliott and Adelman, 1976), which was sponsored by the Ford Foundation. In this project we involved 40 British teachers in an investigation of the problems of implementing inquiry/discovery approaches to teaching, in a variety of curriculum areas. All the teachers claimed to be actively involved in curriculum developments which employed these approaches, and to be interested in monitoring the problems of implementing them.

Initial discussions with participating teachers were concerned to elicit their understandings of the aims of inquiry or discovery teaching. They revealed that the majority saw the main aim as 'enabling independent reasoning'. We then studied tape-recordings of our teachers discussing transcripts and video-recordings of classroom situations with a view to extracting the main terms they employed in talking about them. The meaning of these terms was then clarified through further discussions and interviews with teachers. We finally produced three sets of categories which together defined the main features of the action perspective shared by our teachers. They were those of informal/formal, unstructured/structured, open-ended/guided-directed. The first set picked out the degree of intellectual independence the teacher allowed to students working on learning tasks. The second set picked out the extent to which teachers worked with preconceived task outcomes in mind, and the third the manner in which their intervention influenced students' thinking on tasks. It is obvious that all three sets of categories pick out dimensions which are pedagogically significant for teachers who aspire to enable independent reasoning.

Parallel to this elicitation exercise we analysed the idea of 'independent reasoning' into four constituent student freedoms:

1. to initiate and identify their own problems for inquiry;
2. to express and develop their own ideas;
3. to test ideas against relevant and sufficient evidence;
4. to discuss ideas with others.

From this analysis some pedagogical principles governing the selection of teaching acts were derived. We argued that teaching acts could only constitute an enabling influence on the development of students' powers for independent reasoning, if in performing them the teacher *refrained from*:

I. preventing them from initiating and identifying problems;
II. preventing them from expressing and developing their own ideas;
III. restricting their access to relevant and sufficient evidence;
IV. restricting their access to discussion.

We found that the above principles closely corresponded to the tacit criteria our teachers employed in distinguishing 'formal' from 'informal' teaching situations, and describing teaching strategies within them. For example, 'open-ended' questions were seen to constitute an informal situation, and 'leading' questions a formal one. It is obvious that 'open-ended' implies that the student is free to express his own ideas while 'leading' implies the presence of constraints on such expression. Thus principle II is tacitly employed in distinguishing formal from informal teaching situations.

The price which process-product research pays for neglecting teachers' perspectives is that it so often appears to them to be irrelevant to their practical concerns. This 'irrelevance' stems from the fact that the process-product perspective on the phenomena of teaching and learning differs radically from that of teachers themselves. When both parties talk about these phenomena, they find themselves talking about different things. This makes it impossible for process-product studies to appeal to a teacher's 'understanding' as a mode of influencing his practices, and explains the tendency for teacher education based on such studies to take the form of behaviour modification programmes in which the teacher's behaviour is manipulated in a quasi-causal manner.

Explicating and clarifying the action perspectives of teachers ensures that the phenomena of teaching and learning are understood from their point of view. Thus researcher and teacher are now able to speak the same language and engage in discourse with each other about classroom events. This enables classroom research to exert rational, as opposed to causal, influence on teachers' practices. Through discourse, the researcher can appeal to a teacher's 'understanding'. Such a solution to the familiar communication problem between teachers and researchers has two very important implications. First, in engaging teachers in dialogue and appealing to their 'understanding', action research submits itself to their judgement. There is an important sense in which classroom action research can only be validated in dialogue with teachers. It therefore involves them as active participants in the generation of research knowledge. Secondly, in making dialogue possible, action research enables teachers to use it as a tool for developing awareness and understanding of what they do in classrooms. Such self-knowledge is, in my view, at the heart of the professional development process. By involving teachers in dialogue, classroom action research itself constitutes an educational process.

Teacher education looks very different when examined from the point of view of action research rather than that of process-product research. From the former point of view it is a matter of rationally influencing the teacher's understanding of his classroom situation by engaging him in dialogue about it. From the latter point of view it is a matter of getting him to perform in accordance with certain technical rules.

Identifying problems in teaching

These rather abstractly formulated points about the collaborative and educative nature of classroom action research will be illustrated in a more concrete form later. After explicating and clarifying action prespectives, the second task is that of identifying and describing the problems teachers have in enabling the development of their students' understanding. This is a matter of identifying acts which constrain students' thinking in certain respects, eg the constraints cited in principles I - IV above. From the point of view of its power to influence rationally changes in teachers' classroom practices, it is obviously more important for action research to identify cases of failure to realize principles than cases of success, ie constraining acts rather than enabling acts. As Karl Popper claims, we make progress by reflecting about our errors rather than basking in our strengths. However, the identification of enabling acts may have the pragmatic merit of giving a teacher sufficient confidence in his strengths to face up to his weaknesses.

Criteria for identifying constraining acts will differ in one important respect from criteria for identifying enabling ones. Compare each statement in the following pairs:

1. (a) By performing X the teacher prevented students from developing their own ideas.
   (b) In performing Y the teacher gave students an opportunity to develop their own ideas.
2. (a) By performing Z the teacher prevented students from discussing divergent views.
   (b) In performing E the teacher protected the discussion of divergent views.

Statements 1(a) and 2(a) imply infringements, while 1(b) and 2(b) imply realizations of principles II and IV respectively. Whereas enabling influences — acts 1(b) and 2(b) — entail an absence of causal influence on students' thinking, constraining influences — acts 1(a) and 2(a) — entail its presence. In imposing a certain kind of constraint on students' thinking, a teacher must perform a separate act which has the constraining effect. Action research is concerned with identifying those teaching acts, which by virtue of their effects, constitute negative cases of the principles to be realized. For example, in the Ford Project, we discovered that when teachers initiated 'changes in topic' they often prevented students from developing their own ideas, and when they said 'Do you all agree with that?' following the expression of a student view, they often prevented students from continuing to discuss alternative views. Both these acts, cited above, can be identified on the basis of observable evidence alone, and the evidence extracted from recordings as well as direct observation.

I will now describe the methods action research employs for describing the effects of teaching behaviours on students' thinking. It should be clear that the effects to be described are on students' thought processes rather than directly on their behaviour. However, these subjective effects may be observably indicated by students' overt responses. Overt responses, like the acts which cause them, can be both directly observed and extracted from recordings. Participant observation, assisted by audio and audio-visual recordings, plays an important role in action research. Neither teachers nor their pupils, engaged as they are in interaction, are in a good position to isolate the observable elements of their interaction. The 'outside' observer has an epistemological advantage in this respect.

However, in order to describe the constraining effects of a teacher's acts, observation alone is not enough. Both the observable behaviour of the teacher and the observable responses of his students require interpretation. I will deal with the interpretation of students' responses first. An observed response may be susceptible to a variety of interpretations. In the Ford Project I often observed students responding to 'Do you all agree with that?' with silence. The teacher would then fix each student in turn with his eyes until someone said 'yeh' or 'mm, yes', before proceeding. Were the students silent because they felt unsure about whether they agreed or not, or because they were indifferent to the view expressed, or because they were reluctant for some reason to express any felt disagreement? The observer will tend to form his own judgement based on inference from observable evidence. But these judgements can be cross-checked against other evidence, namely students' accounts of their own subjective states. The best way of checking out an interpretation is to 'ask the students'. They are in the best position to know their own subjective states of mind. The observer can only infer them from behaviour, but the students have direct access to them through introspection. When I asked students how the 'Do you all agree?' behaviour influenced their responses they often said it made them reluctant to express any disagreement. If they are honest, then their reply is evidence that the behaviour is a constraining influence. But it does not explain how it influences their thinking in this way. In addition we need to elicit students' interpretations of what their teachers mean when they say 'Do you all agree?'. In my experience students frequently interpret their teachers to mean 'You had better agree', or words to that effect.

In communicative interaction the relationship between cause and effect is mediated by the hearer's interpretation of the meaning the speaker is trying to convey in his behaviour. Therefore, descriptions of the ways teachers constrain students' thinking should cite the latter's interpretations of the former's meaning in addition to effects. Interviews with students about the ways they interpret and subjectively respond to the behaviour of their teachers is a key action research method for cross-checking observers' interpretations.

In describing the constraints exerted by teaching behaviour on students' thinking we also need to know whether they were intended or unintended. To return to my 'Do you all agree?' example once again, the fact that students often interpret the meaning of this question as 'You had better agree' is not sufficient to warrant the conclusion that the teacher did mean that. An observer will interpret the meaning of teaching acts on the basis of inference from observed behaviour. But his interpretations need checking out. 'Do you all agree?' *may* mean 'You had better agree' but it may *also* mean 'I would like you to tell me whether you agree or disagree'. Since the observer is concerned here with the subjective meanings conveyed by a teacher through his observable behaviour, the person in the best position to know what they are is the teacher himself. The observer is methodologically obliged to cross-check his interpretations of teaching behaviour by interviewing the teacher concerned.

In order to understand the exact nature of the problems teachers have in enabling the development of understanding, the distinction between intended and unintended constraints is crucial. If in saying 'Do you all agree?' a teacher does not mean 'You had better agree' but his students take him to, then the constraining effect of this behaviour can be simply removed by the teacher clarifying what he really does mean. In other words, the problem is one of communication, of misunderstanding on the part of students. But if the teacher means what his students take him to mean then we have a different kind of problem, which requires the teacher to change his behaviour radically in order to solve it.

I am now in a position to define the main features of an action research account of teacher-imposed constraints on the development of students' understanding. They are:

1. A descriptive account of observed teaching behaviour and student response.
2. An interpretative account of the effects of teaching behaviour on student thinking.
3. An interpretative account of student interpretations of teaching behaviour.
4. An interpretative account of the meaning conveyed by teaching behaviour.

The observer's descriptive account (1) is cross-checked against recordings, but his interpretative accounts (2-4) can only be cross-checked against accounts provided by the teacher and his students. The production of an action research account involves the collection of accounts from three points of view: those of an observer, the teacher, and his students. In this way teachers and students are involved in the research process.

A question of procedure arises when either teacher or students disagree with the observer's, or each others' interpretation of their behaviour. The procedure we tended to adopt on the Ford Project was to allow all three parties access to the three accounts, and after a period for reflection bring them together to discuss inconsistencies. Inevitably, limitations of time may prevent issues from being resolved in dialogue. In this situation the dialogue must simply be reported, and the main areas of disagreement cited. The process of collecting accounts from three different points of view, and then contrasting them in a discussion involving all three parties, is called *triangulation* (Adelman, 1978).

Even when disagreements remain unresolved there are ways of assessing the degrees of confidence one might have in the accuracy of accounts. For example, if the observer and students agree in their accounts of constraints, but the teacher's account disagrees with theirs, one would be justified in suspecting the teacher's account to be an idealization of his practice. Again, if students support their teacher in denying that constraints cited by the observer obtain, then one would be justified in suspecting the observer's account.

This outline of the structure of action research accounts, and the methods employed in cross-checking and validating them, illustrates in concrete form the points I made previously about the collaborative and educative nature of action research. In involving the teacher in a triangulation procedure for cross-checking and validating his observer's interpretations, he is provided with opportunities for developing self-awareness and understanding.

Case study

The kind of accounts described are produced through case rather than sample study. Action research does not assume that its findings are generalizable. Which teaching acts constitute a particular form of constraint may vary from classroom to classroom. However, through the comparative study of cases it is possible to identify similar cases, and therefore teaching problems shared by different teachers.

The identification of common problems was one of the aims of the Ford Project, and was the reason it involved 40 teachers drawn from different curriculum areas and age levels of students. We wanted to discover the extent to which similar problems arose in apparently very different teaching contexts. At the end of the project we were able to describe some of the problems our teachers shared. They were stated in the form of 'general hypotheses' to indicate a contrast between the status we claimed for our findings and that claimed for the generalizations of process-product research. We wanted to encourage other teachers to test the extent to which the cases of constraining influence cited by the hypotheses could be generalized to their situation. The hypotheses expressed anticipations of classroom possibilities, derived from the common experience of a particular group of teachers. They provided an orientation for teachers wanting to examine their own classrooms.

In action research, generalization is an unstructured process of proceeding from case to case. In process-product research, it is a formal process based on theoretical sampling methods. Unlike the generalizations of process-product research, those of action research can only be validated in the self-knowledge of teachers working in particular classrooms. Action research does not prescribe rules governing the ways teachers enable the development of understanding in students. But it can give general guidance in the form of hypotheses, to teachers who wish to develop their understanding of the particular situations in which they teach.

The two tasks described so far locate classroom action research firmly in the 'interpretative', 'phenomenological' or 'hermeneutic' tradition of social inquiry. This tradition can be contrasted with the 'empiricist' tradition in which process-product research belongs. However, if classroom action research merely restricts itself to explicating teachers' perspectives and studying teacher-student interaction in the classroom, its educative power to influence the self-awareness and practice of teachers may be weakened.

Action research and critical theory

Such a restriction assumes that once a teacher becomes aware of the acts which constrain students' thinking, he is in a position to refrain from them. But in the Ford Project some of our teachers became increasingly aware of the gaps between their aspirations and practice, while at the same time claiming they lacked the freedom to do much about it. They cited various constraints originating in the institutional, social, and political contexts in which they taught. If such teachers are to increase their freedom of action at all, they need not only to understand what it is they are doing in their classrooms, but how their actions are influenced and shaped by institutional, social, and political structures.

The understanding involved in professional development transcends the boundaries of the classroom. Classroom action research therefore also has the task of developing what Habermas and other members of the Frankfurt school of social science might call a *critical theory* of the teaching situation. Such a theory would explain the ways in which teaching is constrained by factors operating outside the classroom in its institutional, social and political context. It would inevitably be conditioned by political beliefs and values. But this kind of bias, like the educational bias of classroom action research, need not imply a lack of objectivity.

If the practical interest served by process-product research is one of technical control over student behaviour, and that served by the interpretative tasks of action research is one of increasing the educational quality of teacher-student discourse, then the interest served by a critical theory of teaching is one of increasing the professional autonomy of teachers (see Habermas, 1974, on knowledge-constitutive interests). To my knowledge, few classroom action research programmes have, up to the present time, incorporated a highly developed critical perspective. They have tended to stop short at classroom-bound interpretative or phenomenological description, perhaps for prudential reasons. Power (1976) in his review of classroom research in science education, cites three research paradigms which roughly correspond to the empirical, interpretative, and critical traditions of social inquiry. He cites no examples of the latter, and names the Ford Project as an example of classroom research in the interpretative tradition. Certainly, we did not systematically provide critical explanations for the feelings of powerlessness which accompanied the development of self-awareness amongst some of our teachers, although such explanations were often subjects for discussion at meetings and conferences. However, a critical science of teaching should not merely be concerned with explaining why teachers act inconsistently with their educational values.

In the Ford Project, we tended to be rather preoccupied with teachers who resisted opportunities to develop their understanding and awareness through reflecting on the alternative 'understanding' held by students and observers. We eventually developed in a fairly systematic way a set of hypotheses about the conditions which enabled and constrained the development of self-awareness in teachers (see Elliott and Adelman, 1976). Here is one of the 43 hypotheses we generated:

The less financial and status rewards in schools are primarily related to administrative and pastoral roles, the more teachers are able to tolerate losses of self-esteem brought about through increased self-awareness.

This cites an institutional constraint on the development of self-awareness and understanding. In order to participate fully in classroom action research at the level of describing problems in his teaching, a teacher must be open to having his understanding of problems rationally influenced through dialogue with observers and students. But we discovered a tendency, varying in its strength, for teachers to resist being so influenced, and sought explanations for such resistence in the institutional, social, and political settings of their classrooms.

How is this critical task of elucidating the structures constraining teachers' classroom practices, and their thinking about them, accomplished? First, like the task of describing constraining influences of teaching in the classroom, it will involve case study. The structures which constrain teachers' thoughts and actions may vary from one institutional, social or political context to another. General critical theorems must depend for their development on comparing similarities and differences between cases. The generalizability beyond the context of the research must be hypothetical and dependent on further grounding in case study. Secondly, the critical theorems of action research must be validated in dialogue with teachers; they are in the unique position to test critical hypotheses by negating them in action. But their participation in the validation of critical theorems also enables teachers to develop an understanding of the wider influences which impinge on their freedom of thought about, and action within, the classroom. Again, teacher participation in action research is potentially an educative one.

The professional development of teachers can be seen as possessing three aspects. The development of self-awareness in the classroom is one. But this assumes that the teacher is free to develop his self-awareness. In this respect an understanding of the institutional, social and political structures which constrain such development is a first step in his professional development. Finally, the development of self-awareness may not be sufficient for bringing about the improvements in his practice which he has come to desire. He may discover that he does not enjoy the freedom of action he once assumed he did. In order to implement the desired changes he must first understand the structures which constrain his freedom of action in the classroom. If action research is to contribute to all three aspects of professional development, it must go beyond the study of teacher-student interaction in classrooms to focus on the structures which distort its educational function.

References

Adelman, C (1978) On first hearing *in* Adelman, C (ed) (1978) *Uttering, Muttering* CARE: University of East Anglia, Norwich

Barnes, D (1976) *From Communication to Curriculum* Penguin Books: Harmondsworth

Berliner, D C and Rosenshine, B (1977) The acquisition of knowledge in the classroom *in* Anderson, R, Spiro, R and Montague, W (eds) (1977) *Schooling and the Acquisition of Knowledge* Lawrence Erlbaum Associates: Hillsdale, NJ

Bruner, J S (1970) Man: a course of study *in* Bruner (1970) *Evaluation Strategies* Educational Development Center: Cambridge, Mass

Doyle, W (1979) *The Tasks of Teaching and Learning* Invited address at the Annual Meeting of the American Educational Research Association, San Francisco, April 1979

Dunkin, M J and Biddle, B J (1974) *The Study of Teaching* Holt, Rinehart and Winston: New York

Elliott, J (1978a) What is action research in schools? *Journal of Curriculum Studies* **10** 4:355-7

Elliott, J (1978b) Classroom research: science or common sense *in* McAleese, R and Hamilton, D (eds) (1978) *Understanding Classroom Life* National Foundation for Educational Research: Slough

Elliott, J and Adelman, C (1976) *Innovation at the Classroom Level* Course E203 Unit 28, Open University Press: Milton Keynes

Elliott, J and MacDonald, B (1972) *People in Classrooms* CARE Occasional Publications No 1: University of East Anglia, Norwich

Fenstermacher, G D (1978) A philosophical consideration of recent research on teacher effectiveness *Review of Research in Education* **6**

Habermas, J (1972) Technology and science as 'ideology' *in* Habermas (1972) *Towards a Rational Society* Heinemann: London

Habermas, J (1974) *Introduction to Theory and Practice* Heinemann: London

Jenkins, D (1977) Saved by the bell *and* Saved by the army *in* Hamilton, D *et al* (1977) *Beyond the Numbers Game* Macmillan Education: London

Parlett, M and Hamilton, D (1973) Evalution as illumination *in* Tawney, D (ed) (1973) *Evaluation in Curriculum Development: Twelve Case Studies* Schools Council Research Studies, Macmillan Education: London

Peters, R S (1968) Must an educator have an aim? *in* Macmillan and Nelson (eds) (1968) *Concepts of Teaching* Rand MacNally: Chicago

Power, C (1976) *A critical review of science classroom interaction studies* mimeo, School of Education, University of Queensland: Australia

Smith, L and Schumacher, S (1972) *Extended Pilot Trials of the Aesthetic Education Program: A Qualitative Description, Analysis and Evaluation* CEMREL Inc: USA

Stenhouse, L (1971) The Humanities Curriculum Project: the rationale *Theory into Practice* **10**:154-62

Stenhouse, L (1975) *An Introduction to Curriculum Research and Development* Heinemann: London

Walker, R and Adelman, C (1972) *Towards a Sociography of Classrooms* Final report, Social Science Research Council (Grant HR996-1): London

Wild, R D (1973) *Teacher participation in research* Unpublished conference paper, SSRC and Gulbenkian Project on Problems and Effects of Teaching about Race Relations, CARE: University of East Anglia, Norwich

Part 7: Viewpoints

23. Professional development or personal development?

William Taylor

Summary: Some of the literature of teacher education contains an implicit or explicit assumption that 'professional development' and 'personal development' are distinguishable processes. It is the argument of this chapter that they are one and the same, and that responsibility rests with the individual teacher rather than the national system, the employing authority, or the school. Furthermore, if this is not recognized, programmes of professional development are likely to be ineffective and to encourage forms of organization and control that are very *un*professional in their character and consequences.

The reasons are examined for the upsurge of interest in how the quality of education might be improved through the post-experience education and training of teachers. Some weaknesses are identified in the knowledge base of this concern and of the programmes that it has spawned, and some steps are suggested to overcome these weaknesses. Professional development is best conceptualized in relation to a multi-stage process of teacher education, the elements of which are outlined. Finally, *desiderata* are stated that programmes of professional development should satisfy if they are to recognize and respect individual teachers' responsibility for their own growth.

Why the current interest?

The improvement of in-service education and training and the pursuit of the professional development of teachers are currently high on educational agendas. In untangling the many reasons for this, we have to weave a path between the cynicism of the disbeliever — 'professional development? More free periods and a chance to get away from the kids for a bit'; the unctiousness of the missionary — 'professional development? A deep personal commitment on the part of responsible individual practitioners to the continuous ongoing improvement of classroom *praxis*'; — and the thinly-veiled authoritarianism of the systematizer — 'professional development? An operational and enforceable requirement that teachers equip themselves to satisfy stringent performance criteria and are held accountable for the outcome of their efforts'.

These are several reasons for the current concern with professional development in all its forms:

1. There is dissatisfaction with existing pre-service provision, coupled with a recognition that however good they are, by their very nature such programmes cannot equip intending teachers with all they need for a lifetime of work in the classroom.

2. There is increasing awareness of the impact of social, political and technological change in the schools and of the need for teachers to be conscious of and responsive to such change.

3. There are clear indications in many countries that teachers are members of an under-educated profession, whose working conditions do not encourage the kinds of peer interaction which would improve performance.

4. There is disenchantment with the systematized models of curriculum change that featured so prominently in educational — and non-educational — discourse of the 1960s and early 1970s. Hope is now invested in the capacities of individual teachers to reform their own practice. Curriculum development, it is argued, means nothing unless it is happening 'at the sharp end', in the daily routine of classrooms.

5. The minority of teachers who are already well qualified are concerned to maintain and enhance their competitive advantage in an occupation where opportunities for preferment, especially outside the classroom, are likely to diminish rather than increase in the years ahead.

6. Education authorities want to find answers to some of the criticisms of teacher quality posed by the accountability and 'back-to-the-basics' movements, especially in an occupation where the absence of generally accepted performance criteria and a high degree of organized unionism make it difficult to identify and dislodge inadequate performers.

7. A stress upon continuing education, recurrent education and *éducation permanente*, has been strongly encouraged by the activities of international and inter-governmental organizations.

8. The over-supply of teachers in some parts of the developed world, due to a combination of demographic factors and restrictions on public expenditure, has released teacher education plant, resources and staff for other purposes.

9. The larger numbers of administrative and supervisory staff now employed by local, regional and national authorities are in the process of seeking a new role for themselves, in which more fashionable, active and prestigious academic, professional and developmental tasks feature more prominently than less popular and more contested allocative, inspectorial and assessment functions.

If the level of in-service activity generated by these pressures is new, their form and content is not. Post-experience refreshment and training has been part of the teacher education scene for a very long time, and can be traced back to the first systematic efforts to institutionalize the professional preparation of teachers at the end of the eighteenth century (Taylor, 1974). But the scale and coverage of this work has been relatively small, most of its manifestations have been highly diverse, and its importance has not been part of the educational *zeitgeist*. Hence it has hitherto failed to attract the descriptive, classificatory and analytical attentions of the academic, and the systematizing and co-ordinating hand of the central administrator. These omissions (if such they are) are now rapidly being made good. Conferences, seminars and workshops on professional development have proliferated. To serve the needs of such gatherings, specialists in the field are devising categories and conceptual systems with which they hope to tease out the pattern of current activity and impose some order upon a relatively under-developed area of enquiry.

What do we need to know about professional development?

In relation to this upsurge of activity, it is important that we remind ourselves of some of the limitations of our knowledge about professional development, and some of the factors that militate against its rapid institutionalization.

We know little at present about the types of experience best calculated to result in professional growth, and the relationship between such growth and student learning in the classroom. The imperatives of professional development and accountability may not coincide. The kind of teacher growth through professional development that results, for example, in a more child-centred, flexible, problem-orientated and individualized teaching style may cut no ice at all with the basics-besotted politician. Some find it convenient to believe that higher standards in reading and mathematics and other 'basics' can be achieved without cost to other areas of learning. It happens not to be true. Of course, the costs may be well worth paying; but that is not a decision dealt with simply by jacking up the level of resources devoted to courses, conferences and school-based in-service work.

We are also ignorant of the effects of different kinds of professional development experience on individual careers. Experiences which promote growth for some may wither others. And we do not know much about the ages at which professional development interventions are likely to be most effective, especially in relation to their costs.

While today there are in nearly all systems incentives and informal sanctions which favour teacher participation in professional development activities, there are also informal pressures, arising from the peer group, from pupils, from school level administrators, from shortages of money to pay for replacement teachers and from the constraints of working conditions, that militate against the more widespread institutionalization of professional development.

Our knowledge about what goes on is limited by the fact that in nearly every education system, systematic and organized post-experience education and training for teachers is essentially (and in my view, desirably) a voluntary activity. There are two major exceptions. In some systems, participation in some form of induction training during the first year after graduation and/or certification is required if such certification or registration is to be confirmed. In a few systems, teachers are required to be present in the school premises or in attendance elsewhere for more days in the year than pupils are in classrooms.

Whilst in most countries, pre-service teacher education is the responsibility of a limited number of types of institution (universities, teachers' colleges, polytechnics) there is much greater diversity in provision of post-experience opportunities. In addition to the more or less publicly supported agencies, such as universities, teachers' centres, supervisory services and the media, there are numerous private and commercial interests active in the field, and a vast array of voluntary associations, from teachers' trade unions to specialist subject groups.

This diversity of provision — a *desirable* diversity from many points of view — makes for difficulties in articulating the structure, organization and content of the experiences that the intending teacher obtains during his or her pre-service education and training and those offered on a post-experience basis.

It follows from all this that we are largely ignorant of the amount of time and effort that teachers devote to activities that contribute to their professional development. The wider we cast our net, to include more than mere attendance at courses and conferences and participation in school-focused and school-based activities, the greater our ignorance.

Although there have been few attempts to calculate the true costs of a full-blown professional development effort for national systems, local employers and individual institutions, it is likely that these will be high. The greater the dependence on institutionalized means of provision, the more likely it is that programmes will be disrupted by changes in the economic climate. In the United Kingdom at the beginning of the 1970s, an official committee (Department of Education and Science, 1972) recommended a level of in-service provision that would entail 3 per cent of the total of serving teachers being released for further study at any one time. Although governments have subsequently committed themselves to this level, and to the release of beginning teachers for a part or full day each week, financial stringency has made it impracticable to implement this policy fully. Restrictions on public expenditure are likely to be experienced in many countries during the 1980s, and models of professional development that require substantial increases in educational resources are unlikely to find favour or be implemented.

Recent years have seen efforts to reconceptualize post-experience education and training for teachers as professional development, and to widen its terms of reference to include all the experiences available to or provided for teachers that promote personal, intellectual and professional growth and enhance the possibility of favourable learning outcomes. However, despite all this, there is a continuing tendency for attendance at courses, conferences and workshops, other than between 9.00 and 4.00 on term-time week-days, and usually away from one's own school, to be seen as the basic model of professional development. Whilst it has its uses, it is by no means clear that this type of provision is most likely to embody the principles that should characterise properly thought-through professional development programmes.

Strategies for professional development

An effective strategy for professional development encompasses several levels of action, including the following:

— deciding the level of resources likely to be available in support of professional development activities, and how these might most effectively be deployed in improving the level of student learning and satisfaction;
— ensuring that the content and organization of both pre-service and in-service programmes for intending teachers are such as to encourage a personal commitment to improving knowledge and skills, and to identify and seek out those kinds of experience likely best to contribute to the development of an 'educated person';
— conceptualizing the different levels or stages through which individuals pass in the course of a typical career in education;
— determining the knowledge, skills and attitudes which it is desirable and appropriate to encourage at each stage, taking into account what is known about individual and group learning;
— providing suitable institutional arrangements that will strengthen the commitment to personal growth, remove obstacles to its fulfilment and facilitate learning appropriate to each stage;
— devising means for such measure of articulation and co-ordination of the various activities involved as is consistent with maintaining a plural basis

of provision, enhancing individual choice and making most effective use of resources;
— undertaking multi-level evaluation, the results of which can be used not only to improve the quality of provision at each stage, but also to facilitate appropriate kinds of co-ordination.

Some elements of this strategy require more detailed comment.

Teacher education as a multi-stage process

In terms of the argument of this chapter, professional development describes a process in which forms of provision that are administratively, organizationally, conceptually and sequentially discrete must achieve coherence in the careers of individual teachers. The elements of this provision are described below.

Selection is the means by which applicants for training who possess the statutory minimum academic and personal qualifications are chosen or rejected in accordance with more or less explicit criteria and predictions of ability, potentiality, and subsequent classroom success.

In countries that have suffered chronic teacher shortages, especially of primary and lower secondary teachers, there has been little real selection for some considerable time. Practically all those with basic minimum qualifications have been able to obtain a place at a college or university. This has not, however, precluded selection *within* the total range of applicants by the more prestigious and better placed institutions, which have often been able to pick and choose amongst first-choice candidates.

In many countries the supply of classroom non-specialist teachers now exceeds the demand. Where the number of training places has been trimmed to match employment opportunities, and demand from potential students has been maintained, institutions lower down the pecking order have better opportunities to be selective in filling their places.

In some countries, such selection is strictly in accordance with academic criteria, with the cut-off point on the performance scale being determined by the ratio of applications to vacancies. Elsewhere, there is an effort to employ criteria based upon personality and character, on interest, non-academic activities, commitment to teaching and other non-cognitive factors.

A strong identification by psychologists with the mental testing movement during the first half of this century encouraged research on student selection (Taylor, 1969; Lomax, 1969). A realization that in fact little real selection was taking place led to a decline in such work in the 1960s. If pressure on places for teacher training grows during the next few years, we can expect renewed interest in the development, testing and validation of selection criteria. Such interest may remain small in countries which already have clear-cut criteria of acceptability, usually related to high school graduation. Elsewhere, if selection criteria are problematic, and/or a proportion of 'mature' candidates are accepted, the findings of such research may have a larger part to play.

About the next stage, *pre-service education and training*, a large literature already exists. Debates have been conducted about the organization and content of such education and whether it should be brought more firmly into the university or higher education sphere, with longer courses characterized by a higher degree of academic and practical rigour. Arguments about the relative merits of concurrent and consecutive education and training continue, as does the endemic dispute about the relation of 'theory' to 'practice' and the organization of educational studies. The distribution of power in respect of pre-service training between ministries of education, local and regional authorities, universities, and other higher education institutions and teachers' organizations, varies somewhat from system to system. On the whole, there seems to have been a shift of authority and influence in recent years from the training institutions to the providing agencies and future employers.

Pressures on the curriculum of pre-service education and training have been numerous. Demands that teachers should know more about the subjects they are teaching, and give due emphasis to common elements of language and number, have combined with demands from disciplinary pressure groups and minority interests that more time be given to child development, moral education, equalizing opportunities and multi-cultural education, to name but a few of the contenders. The result has sometimes been to create excessive fragmentation and loss of programme coherence.

One of the ways out of this dilemma has been the realization that if opportunities exist for later systematic study, geared to the gradual enrichment of the teacher's experience, some of the course content, both traditional and new, can safely and beneficially be left until later. Indeed, some have gone so far as to suggest that the main purpose of pre-service professional training is to meet the needs of the student's first post. To see the pre-service stage as part of 'recurrent', 'permanent', or 'continuing' teacher education is to argue for a clearer identification of those forms of knowledge and skill appropriate to each part of the teacher's career. Thus perceived, there is no longer a compulsion to crowd everything into initial training.

The stage of *certification* involves the conferment of recognized or qualified teacher status by the national, state or other teacher employing authorities. In some countries, this has traditionally been by means of a state examination, in which the academic and professional staff of the university or training institution have played only a minor role. Elsewhere, employing authorities accept the award of a university or college diploma or degree as constituting a sufficient claim to qualified status, although there is sometimes the requirement that the recommendation by the institution on behalf of the student shall include a statement about his 'personal', as distinct from academic, suitability for teaching.

Where the qualifying examination is set by employing authorities, it inevitably has a backwash effect on the syllabuses and methods of instruction employed in the training institution. This has sometimes had the effect of laying stress on arguably 'inappropriate' approaches to learning and teaching, and efforts are now being made to encourage styles in training institutions more relevant to the approach the students might use in contact with children.

Initial certification is commonly on a probationary basis. The former probationary period of a year or two during which a beginning teacher had to provide further evidence of suitability, and on the successful completion of which long-term certification was granted, has now in some places been re-conceptualized as part of an *induction* sequence, with a stress on positive training and learning rather than on assessment.

During their induction year(s), teachers have a lighter timetable and are either required or encouraged to take part in classes and discussion groups under the auspices of the employing authority, the training institution or both, with a view to maximizing the learning potential of this critical period and minimizing the disciplinary, curricular and personal problems that young teachers commonly encounter.

In some places, stress is being put on the role of a professional tutor, a senior teacher with special responsibility for the guidance of newly joined members of staff. In the United Kingdom the preparation and training, function and role of these professional tutors has generated a literature of its own since the idea was formally mooted in the James Report (DES, 1972).

On the basis of evaluation of existing induction programmes, Bolam (1977) has argued that good programmes are likely to contain two main elements. First, an internal/school aspect, including a clearly formulated and prepared policy for induction, discussed with staff and made known to all; visits to other schools; a reduced teaching load for probationers, and designated individuals responsible for helping them. Second, an external programme, to provide release time for probationers; help from advisory teachers, inspectors and advisers; workshop sessions; individual consultations and other kinds of provision within a clearly formulated induction policy.

The next element of provision, which I shall label *post-experience study*, encompasses or runs parallel to some of the other elements that remain to be identified.

There is a tendency to limit the consideration of post-experience study opportunities for the teacher to such courses, conferences and other events as are provided by universities, colleges, employing authorities, specialist associations, teachers' unions and other bodies active in the in-service field. This is a mistake. Teachers are in fact among the most frequent participants in general and non-vocational adult and continuing education of all kinds. As Raynor documents (Chapter 16), teachers account for a high proportion of Open University registrations, not just for professional courses and those in education, but for the full range of subjects offered. Many adult and continuing education classes that take place in the evening and week-ends, on a wide diversity of subjects, include large numbers of teachers among their members.

Any properly conceived definition of professional development must reckon with the fact that almost any experience that gives the teacher fresh information about himself or the world he lives in, that increases his understanding and enhances his judgement, has a potential for contributing to the improvement of teaching and learning in schools.

Elite schools in many countries have traditionally sought as teachers the graduates of high status colleges and universities, with extensive knowledge in particular subject fields, a highly developed sensibility and understanding (or at least the potential for its development), but *without* professional training. It has been assumed that such people have a commitment to the improvement of their own education, which is not necessarily the same thing as a willingness to attend courses and meetings arranged especially for teachers. The man or woman who is widely read, has informed tastes and discriminating judgement in art, music and literature, and who cultivates a civilized life-style, brings qualities to the classroom which advanced professional training may focus and enhance, but for which it can never substitute.

The nurture of a commitment to self-improvement needs attention at every stage of the training sequence. Teachers trained to make proper use of print materials and with access to a good general and professional library, need never lack for ideas and inspiration. The aim of any national system of post-experience provision should not be simply to make available courses, conferences and other professional study opportunities, but also to develop teachers' own responsibility for learning and to encourage such self-educative efforts as teachers are able to make on their own behalves.

Experience in itself can be educative, but it is not always so (Wilson, 1975). There must be opportunities for teachers to reflect upon their experience, to make use of the feedback received from colleagues, pupils and other professionals, and to find their proper place within a community of fellow teachers in department, subject group, division or school.

There is growing interest in many countries in the responsibilities that administrators and heads of institutions have for ensuring that the school is an environment in which not only children, but also teachers, can grow and mature. The need for counselling and guidance facilities does not end with the successful completion of the induction stage, but is needed at many points in the teacher's career, especially when a change of employment or career direction is contemplated or planned.

With the diminution in the range of promotion opportunities that accompanies the increasing size of units and the declining birth rate in many countries, it is important that individual institutions should give as many staff as possible a chance to exercise personal initiative in the development of their own work. With promotion at a premium, opportunities to assume responsibility for particular areas of the school's activity, if not on a long-term career footing, at least in the short term and on a rotating basis, may be a useful antidote to that combination of bitterness and boredom that can follow the frustration of promotion expectations.

Preparation for specialized roles constitutes a further element in the provision of professional development opportunities. Over the past two decades, teaching as a profession has experienced a marked division of labour. This has been most evident in larger schools and school systems, but its effects are apparent even in primary and elementary schools of quite limited size.

A useful example is provided by the categories the Department of Education and Science recently set out as the basis for recording staff responsibilities. These include head of faculty; deputy head of faculty; head of department; deputy head of department; general administration and timetabling; responsibility for curriculum (eg director of studies, curriculum co-ordinator, etc); responsibility for external examinations; teacher tutor; head of block; head of year; deputy head of year; head of house; deputy head of house; counsellor; careers teacher; library/resources; audio-visual aids; extra-curricular activities; outdoor pursuits; and the inevitable 'other'.

The effective performance of many of these tasks requires specialized training, and involves the exercise of leadership skills and judgement of a high order. 'Administration' no longer describes a function limited to the head and one or two senior staff. A great number of teachers are engaged in activities that demand administrative expertise, and this is being recognized in the programmes of university schools of education. But here, as in respect of other skills, there is a danger in the technological approach to instilling management techniques. The teacher as administrator is much more likely to gain from a programme of advanced studies based on critical and liberal principles and designed to deepen understanding rather than one which tries to train for specific performance. This contention would not command universal assent. Some recent discussions of in-service provision have stressed the significance of *relevant* studies, and it seems clear that in their use of limited resources for the secondment of serving staff, employers are tending to favour those applicants who wish to enrol for courses and programmes of study that offer a more or less direct pay-off for their own subsequent tasks. Such courses are often offered in institutions with a local or regional rather than national or international reputation. The alleged gains of greater 'relevance' need to be off-set, however, against the fact that some 'advanced' courses are now being taught by people who not only make no personal claim to scholarship or research experience, but have not themselves been taught by scholars.

Advanced studies of good quality are expensive in both direct and opportunity costs. In some countries, opportunities for advanced study in education are now so widespread and so easily available that doubts are being expressed within the academic community about the quality and rigour of the work involved. Elsewhere, teaching is still a very under-educated profession, with only a small number of higher awards in education, most of which go to people whose jobs are either already outside teaching altogether, or become so as a consequence of obtaining the award. (*See also Chapter 26.*)

The purpose of advanced study in education seems to me to include the following:

1. To advance, by means of both empirical research and reflection, knowledge about the process of education.
2. To bring the fruits of research and experience in the humanities and physical and social sciences to bear on educational problems.
3. To improve and extend the awareness, professional understanding and competence of individual practitioners in the field of education.
4. To provide initial preparation and training and appropriate further professional study opportunities for an increasing variety of specialist educational roles.
5. To stimulate a critical dialogue with the profession on matters affecting the structure and organization of the school system, the values and beliefs embodied in teaching procedures and practices and the continuous evolution of curriculum, pedagogy and evaluation.
6. To elaborate and sustain among colleagues, professionals and the public an awareness of the universities' and colleges' responsibility towards and involvement in the work of educational institutions at all levels.

There is an aspect of the professional sequence that is often forgotten or neglected, and for which little explicit provision yet exists in any developing country, namely *preparation for retirement*.

This, one of the most significant watersheds in anyone's life, is traditionally little regarded, and only recently has begun to receive attention from social scientists and those concerned with personal growth and development. While recent years have seen no great increase in life expectancy of either males or females, there are indications of a trend towards early retirement, especially in countries moving towards teacher surplus and wishing to encourage older teachers to leave the profession and create opportunities for their younger counterparts.

The fact that resources devoted to preparation for retirement produce no demonstrable pay-off for the educational system or for society may help to explain the neglect of this topic. Equally, such neglect may have something to do with the denial of ageing that characterizes the ethos of modern Western society, and the cult of youth evident in advertising and the mass media. In any event a shift in population balance towards older age groups, and the tendency for the period of post-retirement life to be prolonged, all indicate a need for schools and educational authorities to make appropriate provision for those who are about to give up full-time work (See also the *WYBE 1979*).

In a few countries it is possible, without loss of salary or status, and while remaining in employment, to step down from more responsible and demanding positions some years before retirement is due, and to develop interests and activities essential to a satisfying post-retirement life, often inhibited or denied by the insistent demands of every-day activity in school, college or university. No sequence of elements in the provision of opportunities for professional development is complete without attention being given to education for retirement.

Conclusion: professional development as personal growth

I referred earlier to the way in which some administrators, systems managers and others of a tidy frame of mind, disappointed with the results of Rational Curriculum Planning as it was practised during the 1960s, have now turned their attention to the subject of professional development. I have tried in subsequent sections to make clear why, given the retention of a voluntary basis for in-service attendance, and a continuing variety in providing agencies, there are severe limits to the extent to which such systematization and co-ordination can be effective. Indeed, these limits are so severe that it is best to conceive of professional development not as a coherent pattern or programme offered within a co-ordinated framework of institutions, but as an individual process, facilitated or inhibited by the kinds of organization and content that characterize the various stages of teacher education: these range from selection through pre-service education and training, certification, induction, post-experience study, preparation for specialized roles to education for retirement.

If all this is conceded, it follows that the single most important feature of teacher education is to encourage and construct a commitment on the part of the individual to professional growth that will enable available resources to be used, or gaps and deficiencies in such resources to be overcome in ways that have favourable outcomes for student learning in the classroom. With such commitment, the rather slow pace at which opportunities for in-service study have been growing, and current limitations on provision, become less important. Without such commitment, the most carefully organized school-focused and school-based training, the most generous provision of post-experience study opportunities, the most thorough induction sequence, will all be of little avail.

With the allocation of a larger proportion of educational resources to various kinds of in-service provision, there is the likelihood that the imperatives of accountability and answerability will lead ministries and employing authorities to take a more direct and prescriptive hand in the direction of professional development activities. To some extent, this is an inevitable price that must be paid for the investment of interest and money. Efforts to systematize provision, to co-ordinate and articulate stages, and to relate contents to the needs of classroom and school must, however, be undertaken in ways that will retain and enhance the professional core of the teacher's identity.

Professionalism has become somewhat unfashionable. Tired old clichés about the professions being organized conspiracies against the public are trotted out as if they are new revelations. The long-standing argument continues between those teachers, on the one hand, who wish to move towards a closer identification with the established professions and, on the other, those who support closer ties with organized labour. The first group is more likely to support the establishment of a General Teaching Council which controls access to the profession, and to refrain from industrial action and other forms of working class militancy. The others would use their bargaining power to obtain higher salaries and would eschew the middle class values that the notion of a self-governing profession is seen to imply. Most of the recent victories seem to have been won by the proponents of organized unionism. Yet in some respects, the terms of this debate have failed to keep up with changes in the nature of work and the implications of these changes for the relations of different occupational groups to each other, to the economy and to society.

Recent efforts to increase industrial democracy in the workplace have much in common with what in the present context I would call a professional model of in-service provision. Such a model assumes that people are happier and are likely to work better when they have control over as wide an area of their activities as the technology they are employing makes possible, and can exercise maximum opportunities for personal discretion in the pacing, distribution and structuring of their activities. In a complex technological world characterized by a high degree of mutual interdependence, there are many jobs where such opportunities are necessarily limited. Teaching is not one of them.

It might be argued that many people are happy without such opportunities for individual discretion and self-pacing, that they positively prefer to be told what to do either by a person or by a machine, and that they reject any kind of responsibility for the conduct of their working lives. It is difficult to believe that anyone who teaches could be in these categories.

Close supervision, detailed day-to-day accountability, the absence of discretion to vary content and method are all inimical to effective teaching. To acknowledge that the teacher has a responsibility to his students and to the community that employs him is one thing. To put it in terms of job descriptions and accountability procedures that reduce him to the level of a technician is another.

The balance of power between political authorities, employers, training institutions, teachers' organizations and school administrations is hardly ever static. The shifting balance demands the critical study and attention of all within the education service, lest by negligence or an ill-judged stress upon short-term benefits, the essential conditions of effective professional development be sacrificed.

I have argued that professional development is *not* just a matter of arranging courses and conferences, designing school-focused and school-based activities, making induction work, using simulation and microteaching and mini-courses and all the other paraphernalia of contemporary teacher education at the right time and in appropriate contexts. All these things are important enough. But more important than any of them is the recognition that the prime responsibility of the teacher is not to the employer, or even to the students, but to him or herself, and that a comprehensive overview of professional development opportunities needs to reckon with *all* the means available for the teacher to become a better-educated person, to develop judgements and skills, and to keep in touch with ideas and innovations in his or her own and cognate fields. What we need, therefore, is professional development that is not simply based on more courses and conferences, but which takes into account the contributions to improved teaching that can be made by library and information services, newspapers and broadcasts, teacher-centre and school-based programmes, and all those other self-improving activities in which teachers participate as individuals or in groups.

Given the voluntary and pluralistic character of professional development activities, there needs to be an opportunity for genuine participation by the teacher, not only in the work of study groups or conferences, but in the selection and organization of what is to be listened to, read, discussed, or written about. The methods used should reflect the teacher's own concerns and require him or her to participate actively in the planning and design of what is offered. One of the attractions of what is now fashionably called school-focused and school-based in-service work is that such participation is easier to organize than where the programme is designed by one group of people to meet what they imagine to be the needs of another.

To identify professional development with personal growth does not make the effective organization and provision of opportunities for professional development less significant or important, nor does it diminish the gains that have been made in recent years in the scope and breadth of such provision. But it does serve to emphasize that one of the essential purposes of every kind of organized provision must be to establish, maintain and enhance the teacher's own commitment to his own education. Every teacher who makes excessive sacrifices in the time and attention needed for his own personal growth to the demands of the organization within which he works or its students is ultimately denying to that organization and those students the very knowledge, understanding and skill which it is his professional responsibility to offer. It is easier and less contentious to talk about professional development in terms of structures, frameworks, resources and methods, rather than in relation to desirable forms of personal knowledge and understanding. Thus the new interest in professional development — reflected in the theme of this *WYBE* — runs the risk of stressing form at the expense of substance. The purpose of this chapter has been to help to ward off this danger.

References

Bolam, R (1977) *Innovation in the In-Service Education and Training of Teachers: Towards a Conceptual Framework*. OECD/US National Institute of Education: Philadelphia, Pa

Department of Education and Science (1972) *Teacher Education and Training* (The James Report) HMSO: London

Lomax, D (1969) A review of British research in teacher education *Review of Educational Research* **42** 3

Taylor, W (1969) Recent research on the education of teachers: an overview *in* Taylor, W (ed) *Towards a Policy for the Education of Teachers* Butterworth: London

Taylor, W (1974) Teacher education *in Encyclopaedia Brittanica*

Wilson, J B (1975) *Educational Theory and the Education of Teachers* National Foundation for Educational Research: Slough

Acknowledgement
Parts of this chapter are based on sections from the author's Research and Reform in

Teacher Education *and are reproduced by permission of the copyright holders, the Centre for Cultural Co-operation of the Council of Europe.*

24. Teaching and professionalization: an essay in ambiguity

Harry Judge

Summary: Teachers, and those who observe them, remain unclear about whether they do or do not belong to a 'profession'. The reasons for these persistent doubts are analysed and assessed here in two very different contexts: England and the United States. Teachers do not compose a tightly-knit group, do not earn fees and do not control entry to their own ranks.

Two conflicting versions of the attempts by teachers to become acceptably 'professional' are then explored. One of these has stressed the acquisition of marketable skills and of competency, and has done so by elevating the importance of severely practical experience in schools. The other — both in England and the United States — has striven to confer professional acceptability upon teaching by associating it with the prestige and with the values of a university. This has tended to distance both teacher preparation and educational research from what are perceived as the needs of 'the real world'. It is an urgent task of university schools of education to reconcile these tensions and ambiguities.

I

The teaching profession remains, in most parts of the world, unsure of its own position and status and unclear about whether it is a profession in any public and precise sense of that term (Etzioni, 1969). It is, therefore, hardly surprising if narrower questions about teacher training or about its institutional settings mirror these uncertainties and imprecisions. I should like to reflect upon some of the structural and historical explanations of these contemporary doubts and, more tentatively, upon possible resolutions of them.

This attempt will be made against a double background, although it may well be that many of the observations will prove (within the context of this Yearbook) to have a wider reference. The first and more fully developed background is English, and the second American. My own working experience has been exclusively in an English framework: as a teacher and headmaster in secondary schools, a full-time member of the James Committee of Enquiry into Teacher Education and Training (Department of Education and Science, 1972), and most recently within the Department of Educational Studies at Oxford University. These bare facts may assist the reader in discounting certain prejudices — for example, on the relationship of experience and expertise in primary and secondary schools to the tasks of teacher preparation, and on the role of the university in relating teacher training to educational research and development of a high order. The second, and more obviously slender background, is American. During 1979 I was enabled by a grant from the Ford

Foundation to visit a number of the most distinguished universities in the United States in order to explore certain general questions about the place within them of the schools of education. Such questions touched upon the relationship between those same schools and the public educational system which they were created to sustain and improve. That study is in no sense completed, but has already evoked a number of comparisons with and contrasts to the English scene — contrasts that will interweave the argument of this paper.

That argument is developed from the axiom that, in England and the United States and also elsewhere, teachers have never enjoyed that degree of professional confidence and autonomy which marks the practice of medicine or of law. The reasons for that deprivation are not hard to find. In the first place the activity of 'teaching' is much less exact and narrow than those other practices with which it is most often wistfully compared (Judge, 1974). No one, not even the most ferocious defender of the arcane dignity of the teaching profession, has claimed that teaching can be effectively performed only by teachers. It is, of course, true that laymen cure and in that sense practise medicine, but the sense is a trivial one. It is not difficult to recognize and describe tasks which can and should be performed only by a qualified doctor. Where are the analogous tasks for teachers? Every conversation, every parental direction, every newspaper or TV programme, every sermon can properly be represented as a contribution to teaching (Cremin, 1976). Teachers, unlike doctors and lawyers (but not, significantly, social workers) occupy no sharply delimited territory (Langford, 1978).

The vagueness and the difficulty do not disappear even when a crudely functional definition of 'the teacher' is imported into the argument, as it now must be (Hoyle, 1969). Let us agree that a teacher is someone who is paid to instruct according to some programme, pupils choosing or being compelled by law to follow that programme within a formally defined institution (Musgrove and Taylor, 1969). This, after all, is what we generally mean by the word 'teacher' even if the explicit definition does sound bizarre. The difficulties are then reduced, but do not disappear entirely. This is because the tasks being performed by these teachers vary greatly along a number of dimensions. The scholarly university professor, grounding his life and its values in research and the uninhibited pursuit of truth, finds little in common with the hard-pressed teacher in an inner-city school. Nor does the teacher of 17-year-olds in an academically selective private school feel very much professional affinity with a craft-based instructor dealing with members of the same age group in a college of further education. This is not to say that there are no gaps within the 'classical' professions — between the highly-paid metropolitan consultant and the rural general practitioner, or between an internationally famous judge and the city lawyer specializing in meeting the needs of dubious clients. But among teachers, the gaps become chasms and, certainly until very recent times, have been clearly visible in the institutional patterns of teacher training.

Before those institutional patterns can usefully be explored, one further cluster of contrasts suggests itself. A profession can defend its frontiers most successfully when it is economically based upon fees rather than salaries or wages, when it dispenses for those fees a marketable skill which can be acquired only with considerable intellectual effort, when it controls access to and training for the carefully defined profession, and when it is small (Schein, 1972). Each of these generalizations is historically true of medicine; none applies to teaching (Waller, 1932). A more extended treatment of this harsh contrast would demonstrate how, even within the framework of a nationalized helath service in the United Kingdom, doctors have accepted public money without, in most cases, becoming employees and have even more clearly continued to control the terms of access to the profession.

Teaching, on the other hand, is a mass profession. If all children are to be taught in schools, many teachers will be needed and not all of them can be expected to achieve or to need comparable qualifications. They will, for the most part, be paid from the public purse; that is to say, given the massive demand for teachers, they are unlikely to be paid adequately. Their training, were it to be prolonged at the public expense for more than a minimal period, would be cripplingly expensive. Yet it would be undertaken at the expense of the student himself, or of his family, only if the social and economic rewards were comparable with those in the established professions. They never have been, and so the steel circle snaps closed (Tropp, 1957).

Teaching, unlike surgery, is an activity with loosely defined frontiers. Those who are actually paid to do it include an embarrassingly wide range of practitioners approaching the task with different assumptions, intentions, intellectual equipment and qualifications. Some of the most distinguished of those practitioners, for example within the universities, will have had no training at all. For the rest, and even within one country, no universally recognized pattern of education and training has ever existed. Still less has there been agreement on what the necessary content of that training might be (Taylor, 1969).

Why should such gloomy and unhelpful facts be catalogued here? Simply in order that their repetition may preserve the reader from unwarranted pessimism in recalling the recent history of brave attempts to professionalize teacher training, or unjustified optimism in contemplating what might be achieved in the 1980s. These two themes — the attempt to make teaching respectable and possible objectives for the next decade — will therefore be developed in the two succeeding sections.

II

Talk about 'attempts to professionalize teacher training' conceals an ambiguity. There are two very different senses in which teacher training might in principle be rendered more professional, and the tension between those two senses and the policies in which they issue has become painfully obvious in the recent past. The first, and simpler, interpretation is that teacher training should be de-emphasized, that 'competence' should be stressed, and that the schools themselves (and/or the teachers in them) should become the most influential agents in the business of training (Houston, 1972). Unsurprisingly, the opponents of such tendencies complain that all this conspires to canonize an apprenticeship model, to sweep aside the importance of a knowledge-base, to condemn education to a repetitive conservatism, and to eliminate the possibility of teaching ever becoming a 'profession' (Peters, 1977). They point out, and it is here that the second and contradictory sense of 'professionalizing' is tellingly introduced, that the 'other' or 'real' professions have not advanced themselves in this way. On the contrary: they have embedded themselves within the universities, establishing professional schools there, and thus identified themselves with the proposition that entry to their ranks requires the prior mastery of a body of knowledge dispensed within an institution devoted primarily to the pursuit of truth. This model, and not that of competency or the imitative acquisition of practical skills, is the one which teachers should follow.

How have these rival interpretations of 'professionalizing' worked themselves out in England and Wales? (Scotland is, of course, very different; given the close structural similarities, 'England' should, for the rest of this chapter and in the interests of brevity, be taken to embrace Wales). One clue to the historical peculiarities of the English system — not without its parallels elsewhere in Europe, however — lies in the sharp divisiveness of the system of elementary and secondary schooling for which the intending teachers were being prepared (Judge, 1977). That divisiveness made explicit assumptions about the school curriculum and about the academic and social destinations of pupils. There was, on the one hand, a nineteenth century tradition of popular and public education, provided by rates and taxes for the great majority of the nation's pupils, dedicated to producing minimum standards of literacy and numeracy as efficiently and cheaply as possible. Alongside that elementary tradition, and skilfully connected with it only by slender threads, lay a different tradition of schooling. This, deeply embedded in Victorian assumptions about middle-class responsibility and leadership sprang from the 'public' (that is, private) schools, with which were associated in growing numbers grammar schools, provided or supported by public funds. The products of this tradition were destined for the professions and for the universities.

This dual system of curriculum and schooling, by no means unfamiliar in the rest of Europe, led naturally to a double system of 'training' for the teaching profession (Dent, 1977). Grammar (and public) school teachers nearly always received their general education at the universities and, if they needed any training at all, thereafter followed a one-year course of graduate training in a university education department, the activities of which were rarely viewed with very much respect by the parent university. Teachers for the 'other' schools — the vast majority, that is — were recruited at the earliest possible age and given the shortest possible course of basic training, in institutions outside the universities (training colleges, later re-named colleges of education).

This, in the barest outline, was still the situation 20 years ago. It served, of course, to divide teachers into (at least) two categories, to consolidate a pattern of rival trade unions or professional associations, and to strengthen the barriers lying across the path to professional and academic respectability already identified in Section I. The slow transition, by no means yet complete, from a divided to a unitary system of national schooling weakened the rationale for a dual system of teacher training. More important for the purposes of the present analysis, however, is some discussion of how various pressure groups sought to raise the status of the teaching profession by lengthening and intellectualizing the process of training.

Certain key changes can readily be identified, notably the lengthening of the standard course in the training colleges (outside the universities) from two years to three and the symbolic redesignation of those establishments as colleges of education. The efforts to incorporate the colleges within the universities were frustrated, and the apostles of integration were forced to remain content with relatively weak if generally polite forms of association (Niblett, Fairhurst and Humphreys, 1975). These made possible the development of a new degree, the BEd (Bachelor of Education) — taught for the most part within the colleges themselves, but awarded (or 'validated') by the academically prestigious universities. This development, curiously unlike what was happening at the same time during the 1960s in the United States, represented the main thrust within England towards academic and therefore professional respectability.

Efforts to achieve other gains in professional status — for example, control over entry to and discipline of the profession — were comparatively weak (Gosden, 1972). The academic form of professional respectability did, at the same time, assume some curious shapes. The surface changes were relatively simple and harmless: the validation of the degree of BEd by the universities and the consequent lengthening of the course for at least the more able students in the colleges of education from three years to four. Two problems — one of motive, and the other of intellect — lay, however, just below the surface, and were rarely discussed at the time of expansion and development. The problem of motive affected the 18-year-olds leaving the secondary schools and making a choice of courses within the field of higher education. It was an act of common-sense justice to seek to guarantee that those who chose colleges of education should, if they succeeded there, receive the same award as their cousins in universities or polytechnics: that is, a degree. But why should those who had the choice — that is in effect, the more able — not go first to a university, secure a degree with currency on the general market (which the BEd was always unlikely to acquire) and then take a one-year course of teacher training? A pattern of higher education within which a disproportionate number of entrants to courses of professional education as teachers would be women and relatively less able men is hardly an appealing formula for raising the professional status of teaching.

The other problem, lying below the surface of apparently benign changes, is a more strictly intellectual one. Lawyers and doctors express little doubt, outside their closed ranks at least, about what should be the content of a long pre-service course. If they do argue about the content of such courses in terms of modernization or competing priorities, they do not seriously doubt their own capacity to resolve such fruitful disagreements. This has never been the case with teachers in England — nor, as I shall wish to suggest — in the United States. It is for this reason that the development of the BEd proves a sufficiently interesting case study to justify its inclusion in this chapter.

To put it another way, there existed no confident and autonomous tradition within higher education or within the teaching profession to allow a definition of the proper content of 'a degree in education' (Wilson, 1975). In those promising circumstances — so unlike the prevailing conditions in engineering or dentistry — other disciplines and subject areas had to be raided briskly. What was also, of course, lacking was any ready-made principle of coherence which could in some sense unify the contributions now made, under often remote university auspices, to the blushing new degree. The rest of the story is familiar enough. Given that this was to be a 'concurrent' degree, study for which would both extend the higher education of the student himself and impart to him professional knowledge and skills, it is surprising that an even more unsatisfactory package was not produced.

The general component — in history, mathematics, literature, biology or whatever — was adapted to meet what were, or were perceived to be, the requirements of a university course in those subjects. Little attention was, or within these terms of reference could have been, given to such questions as the direct relevance of such knowledge to the needs of the teacher or the cultivation of practical skills. Unhappily, similar pressures tended to distort that part of the degree which was concerned with 'Education'. There was, and is, no agreement on what the knowledge base of such a subject might be. But, since this was to be a degree validated by universities, it could plausibly be argued that such disciplines as philosophy, psychology, sociology, history or comparative education must have information, methods and insights to contribute. How could the colleges of education avoid the trap of developing a degree which represented an uneasy amalgam of fragmented disciplines, lacking any clear focus or rationale? The universities generally, however polite their public comments, had little confidence in the degree over which they uneasily presided, and for which they did not teach (Hencke, 1978).

For this uncertain gain in professional status — an undergraduate degree effectively limited to intending teachers, marked by deference to powerful academic prejudices, combining disparate elements — a heavy price was paid. That price, paradoxically but unsurprisingly, was the relative devaluation of professional skills and practical experience. And so the cry was again heard: the needs of schools and pupils in them were being neglected; theorists, often drawn from other subjects and inexperienced in the world of teaching, were gaining credit at the expense of the most gifted practitioners. These discomforts were a significant part of the background to the James Report (Department of Education and Science, 1972).

It would be presumptuous, from one side of the Atlantic and within a reassuringly small system, to trace in comparable detail similar developments in the United States. The composition and sociology of the teaching profession there are markedly different. The differences between the States are probably as great as those among the various countries of western Europe. The variety of institutions providing teacher education in its various forms is such as to defy description or even fair categorization. There is no neat relationship between patterns of schooling and those of teacher training. Teacher preparation has always been, for good or ill, entangled in undergraduate education in the States. The pace of change has been rapid, and is so still.

Such cautionary notes should discourage glib comparisons. Nevertheless, I believe that some useful transatlantic discussions can be initiated provided that the following apparently arbitrary rules for that discussion can be accepted:

1. A key to the search for professionalization by the teaching profession lies in its relationship to the universities.
2. There is tension between that form of the search and what is perceived, often by teachers themselves, as the severely practical needs of the teacher in the school.
3. That tension can best be illustrated in the United States by concentrating on those schools of education which have the strongest reputation and which are housed in universities of international renown.

Here I offer simply what I believe to be an uncontroversial view of the recent development of those university schools of education which have the strongest reputation and which are housed in universities of international renown. Four general characteristics stand out in that development over the past 20 years.

First, although most universities have traditionally had a strong commitment to providing courses in 'Education' for undergraduates who may subsequently wish to become teachers, those schools of education which have now the freedom to do so have withdrawn, whether completely or not, from the undergraduate field. Secondly, they have won that freedom by developing successful graduate courses and research programmes, nearly all of which have depended on winning research contracts and grants. Thirdly, given the concentration on graduate studies, many of the most 'successful' schools have as a matter of emergency policy reduced or eliminated teacher and practitioner training at any level, graduate as well as undergraduate, post-experience as well as pre-service. Fourthly, within universities which value scholarship and match publications with tenure, the reputation of the schools has been built in large measure upon the work and reputation of able people drawn into the schools from other disciplines — psychology, history, sociology, economics and so on (Mayhew, 1970:5).

It is, given these governing factors, not surprising that there should now be an uneasy sense that the schools of education, in pursuing the goal of comparability with other graduate schools, have steadily drawn away from direct encounters with schools, teachers, the world of practice and even the world of policy. That uneasiness is naturally exaggerated at a time of contraction, in finance as well as in the size of the school population; when numbers fall, euphoria evaporates, and some of the schools are addressing the question of what their mission should now be. The tension is increased when forces outside the universities, outside the whole teacher training world, or even outside the educational establishment itself, call for a return to basics, emphasize the importance of competency in some practical and measurable sense, show clear signs of anti-intellectualism, and seek to impart a sharp note of accountability into the training as into the employment or promotion of teachers (Goble and Porter, 1977). At the same time, professional associations of teachers claim that they — and not the universities — know how to specify the knowledge and skills required by teachers, and moreover that they know how to impart them in a context of school-based training (Atkin, 1978).

Professionalism, perceived as the pursuit of academic respectability, has come close to open conflict with professionalism interpreted as the promotion of sound practical skills at the expense of irrelevant theory taught by non-practitioners. This conflict is, at least in its intensity and audibility, peculiar to the teaching profession. How, if at all, might it be resolved?

III

It might seem idiosyncratic thus to compare two such different case studies: the development of the BEd outside the English universities and the evolution of the schools of education inside a handful of the greatest American universities. But it has, I hope, been established that these two histories exemplify the same principle and illustrate the same tension. When the teaching profession, and those institutionally associated with it, seeks to raise its professional status by making its initiatory programmes more central in a university and more responsive to its key values, a problem is created by success. The pursuit of scholarship, rigour and academic respectability as conventionally defined, deflects those programmes from a concern with such *desiderata* as professional competence, practical skill and on-the-job training. Meanwhile, it must be recalled, the English universities themselves continue to offer the PGCE (Postgraduate Certificate in Education) as a one year course of professional preparation for those who have completed their undergraduate studies. Not only has it survived, but it has been and is still being subjected to a good deal of critical revision and is likely to remain, alongside the BEd, a main route into the teaching profession (Taylor, 1979) and fundamental to the work of most university departments of education. The key question therefore is: what ought to be the attitudes and policies of university departments or schools of education towards the teaching profession *and* towards their parent university?

It might, of course, be argued that the attitude should simply be one of peaceful and remote coexistence. Let the schools of education strive to become research institutes, modelling themselves on the methodologies of the social sciences, distancing themselves from the messy world of practice, shunning the tasks of training and happily relinquishing such work to other institutions. Let the teaching profession, on the other hand, pursue professional status away from the universities, leaving to them their proper but remote tasks. Such a policy is, however, unlikely to have many whole-hearted advocates. The teaching profession will not lightly abandon the status-rich universities. The schools and departments of education might face decline and extinction if they based their case for survival on so pure and slight a platform.

What, in that case, might be some of the guiding principles to which schools and departments should have regard in forming their policies for the next decade? Two points of preliminary explanation must be made. First, 'schools of education' refers for the rest of this chapter to the schools or departments in (a) most — perhaps all — of the English and Welsh universities *and* (b) a small number of the leading 'research universities' in the United States (see editorial on the Cartter Report in *Change* 9 2:44-8, 1977). Second, it will immediately become clear that not all the guiding principles have equal force or relevance in each of the schools and that, moreover, the principles themselves are in a state of some conflict. With these reservations in mind, an attempt must now be made to state the principles.

Schools of education should seek, rather than fear, smallness. Since they cannot plausibly claim to dominate in some numerical sense the worlds of educational studies and teacher training, they should choose a commanding place within them with particular care and discrimination. Otherwise they will lack distinctiveness and credibility. They ought, wherever this is practicable, to retreat tactically from the arena of undergraduate studies. Such a retreat is required on grounds of expediency and of principle. It is expedient because schools of education, which must exist within the texture of university life and politics, never have endeared themselves, and probably never will, to other 'liberal' departments specializing in undergraduate work. It is right in principle because, in my judgement at least, 'Education' as a subject for study has not developed sufficiently, and probably never will, to be a worthy peer of literature or mathematics. Moreover, the first commitment of a university to its undergraduates is to educate them and, if they thereafter become teachers, to offer them a mastery of the subject matter to be taught (Koerner, 1963).

It follows that schools of education should be, at least predominantly, graduate institutions and — if they remain in the business of teacher training at all — committed to a consecutive rather than a concurrent pattern of teacher education (Judge, 1975). As graduate institutions they should of course give a high priority to research and to the training of research workers. They should, finally, seek urgently and continually for ways to demonstrate that they take seriously the practice of education and respect the practitioner (Harvard, 1966). These last two principles remain in conflict: if English universities have tended (often through no fault of their own) to ignore the first, American schools of education have more recently been tempted to neglect the second.

Respect for the practitioner will take different forms in different settings. It may well include a strong version of graduate teacher training — a version which should not be simply a replica of courses which could equally well be offered elsewhere, and which should itself incorporate research interests and innovative strategies. Equally, the schools of education should develop post-experience courses which move beyond the frontiers of a training programme and yet achieve the objective of improving practice. Any school of education can demonstrate the sincerity of its respect for the practitioner by committing major tasks of training to him and, in making its own appointments, by according credit to a decade or two of successful experience as well as to a dozen or so scholarly articles.

Schools of education will not assist the professionalization of teachers and teaching if they sacrifice a healthy respect for practice to a single-minded pursuit of scholarship for its own sake. Nor, ironically, will they purchase with that sacrifice the respect of their peers — a favour they have sought for so long and with no great success. They will flourish by being scholarly, to be sure, but their scholarship must be related to the improvement of practice in schools. Even if it is sometimes for selfish and narrow reasons, this is precisely what their university colleagues (who teach students coming from those schools) expect and require of them. It is also the means, and especially when associated with the education and improvement of teachers, of linking the work of teachers with the university and contributing to the elevation of their professional status as of their professional competence. The schools of education therefore have it in their power, as no-one else has, to contribute to the resolution of that ambiguity which this chapter has attempted to explore.

References

Atkin, J M (1978) Institutional self-evaluation versus national professional evaluation *Educational Researcher* **7** 10:3-7

Cremin, L C (1976) *Public Education* Basic Books: New York

Dent, H C (1977) *The Training of Teachers in England and Wales: 1800-1975* Hodder and Stoughton: London

Department of Education and Science (1972) *Teacher Education and Training* (The James Report) HMSO: London

Etzioni, A (1969) *The Semi-Professions and their Organisation* Free Press: New York

Goble, N M and Porter, J F (1977) *The Changing Role of the Teacher* UNESCO: Paris

Gosden, P H J H (1972) *The Evolution of a Profession* Basil Blackwell: Oxford

Harvard (1966) *The Graduate School of Education: Report of the Harvard Committee* Harvard University Press: Cambridge, Mass

Hencke, D (1978) *Colleges of Crisis* Penguin Books: Harmondsworth

Houston, W R (1972) *Performance Education: Strategies and Resources for Developing a Competency-based Teacher Education Programme* New York State Education Department: Albany, NY

Hoyle, E (1969) *The Role of the Teacher* Routledge and Kegan Paul: London

Judge, H G (1974) *School is Not Yet Dead* Longman: London

Judge, H G (1975) How are we to get better teachers? *Higher Education Review* **8** 1:3-16

Judge, H G (1977) American history and schooling: an English view *Oxford Review of Education* **3** 1:3-16

Koerner, J D (1963) *The Miseducation of American Teachers* Houghton Mifflin Co: Boston

Langford, G (1978) *Teaching as a Profession* Manchester University Press: Manchester

Mayhew, L B (1970) *Graduate and Professional Education, 1980* McGraw-Hill: New York

Musgrove, F and Taylor, P H (1969) *Society and the Teacher's Role* Routledge and Kegan Paul: London

Niblett, W R , Fairhurst, J and Humphreys, D W (1975) *The University Connection* National Foundation for Educational Research: Slough

Peters, R S (1977) *Education and the Education of Teachers* Routledge and Kegan Paul: London

Schein, E H (1972) *Professional Education: Some New Directions* McGraw-Hill: New York

Taylor, W (1969) *Society and the Education of Teachers* Faber and Faber: London

Taylor, W (1979) Universities and the education of teachers *Oxford Review of Education* **5** 1:3-11

Tropp, A (1957) *The School Teachers* Heinemann: London

Waller, W (1932) *The Sociology of Teaching* John Wiley and Sons: New York

Wilson, J (1975) *Educational Theory and the Preparation of Teachers* National Foundation for Educational Research: Slough

25. The beginning years of teaching: attention, focus and collaboration in teacher education

Robert Bush

Summary: The beginning years of teaching are a problem for the education profession. Beginning teachers who come to their first position from the collegiate training institutions are generally not well treated. Senior teachers have first choice of assignments, newcomers take what is left over. New teachers develop a survival mentality that takes its toll in many ways, not the least of which is in reducing their freedom to consult more experienced colleagues and supervisors concerning weaknesses and failures.

At a time when attention is focusing less on pre-service and more on in-service education, the viewpoint here expressed recommends that the attenion of the profession be directed at these beginning years; by so doing, new sources of energy could be unlocked for the energy-impoverished field of teacher education. A specific plan is advanced for adding these beginning years to the initial preparatory period, thus substantially lengthening the period of training of teachers, enabling newcomers and 'old-timers' to collaborate as colleagues in school improvement. It invites others too to join in the process: the colleges and universities, the state accreditation and licensing officials, the trainees, the students in the schools, and members of the community. The proposition advanced is that this is an opportune time in educational history to increase sharply the amount of energy — time, money and other resources — devoted to teacher education. The new sources of energy that can be tapped lie in the community, the schools, the institutions of higher education, the local, state, and national governments, and in the redirection of some of our present energies. The central idea is that this new force should focus upon reforming the beginning years of teaching in such a way that the whole of teacher education would be influenced. Strong leadership will be required. The effort would not be without risks. But the result might be a renaissance in teacher education that would reverberate throughout the education system.

The argument of this chapter is that the beginning years of teaching are a problem for the education profession. If we could focus our attention on this period and bring about a collaboration of all who are concerned and have a role to play, then this trouble spot could be turned into a new source of energy for the reformation of teacher education. Even though this viewpoint is stated with the United States context foremost in mind, the problem and my suggested approach to its solution are international in scope.

Let me begin with an analogy to the energy question which is ever present in the world today. Since the situation in teacher education reflects what is happening in schools, and since conditions in schools mirror what is taking place in society, it follows that teacher education may have 'energy problems'. I believe that it does, but that they are of a somewhat different character from those now confronting society and being discussed worldwide. The energy problems in society seem to be those of using too much, a matter of wastage, resulting partly from there having been an abundance that now threatens to dry up and/or become prohibitively costly. In teacher education, it is quite otherwise. We have never had enough energy to serve our needs. Teacher education is an 'energy-impoverished' enterprise. We need far more if we are to solve the problems now confronting us.

Before becoming hopelessly entangled in this analogy, let me state my thesis concerning the central problems in teacher education on which we should concentrate our attention. Teacher education is grossly 'under-energized'. As a result of demographic forces in the United States and a number of other countries, the pendulum is now swinging from an earlier preoccupation with pre-service to one with in-service education. But this is to 'rob Peter to pay Paul'. Admittedly, in-service teacher education needs all possible attention. But should less effort go into pre-service teacher education, already long under-funded? We need much more energy that is better directed, in both fields. My argument is that it may be possible to improve both, if we collaborate and jointly concentrate our energies at critical points, thus multiplying our power.

The central proposition to which I invite attention is the possible advantage if *all* parties would collaborate and focus our attention not on pre-service or in-service teacher education, but on the transition period between the two, especially the first three to five years when new teachers begin their practice — a highly impressionable period. The strategy that I propose for consideration is that we would substantially increase the effectiveness of our efforts in teacher education by a decade of focus on the beginning years in the profession. By 'we' I mean *all* the interested parties: those in the institutions of higher education; the experienced teachers and administrators in the schools; the licensing and accreditation officials; the research and development agencies; the professional organizations and associations; teacher trainees; students in the schools, and members of the community. If these eight groups could enter into active collaboration, we could significantly increase the efficiency with which the teacher education dollar is spent; this is essential, given the forces of inflation and the increasing competition among all social services for a share of the tax dollar. One of the reasons that I propose and am optimistic about the possibilities of collaboration grows out of my experience during the past six years with the National Urban/Rural School Development Programme. In our final report (Joyce, 1978), we documented the fact that school community councils made up of one or two community members and one or two educators and which had real power to make decisions on programmes, personnel and budget, can work effectively. The greater the degree of parity between the two groups, the better the programme of in-service education — sharing power increases power.

Concentrating attention on the beginning teacher may not be a new idea. I know that increased attention to the beginning teacher has been advised for years, and some attention has been devoted to it. Some promising beginnings have been reported in England (Bolam and Baker, 1976, 1977). But little has actually been accomplished. The time is now ripe to achieve something substantial and far-reaching.

Beginning teachers who come to their first positions from the collegiate training institutions are generally not well treated. Senior teachers have been given first choice of teaching in the 'better' schools, and are assigned to the 'preferable' classes, subjects, pupils and hours in the day. The newcomers take what is left over. After a short orientation, they are left to fend for themselves. New teachers develop a survival mentality and do not feel free to consult more experienced colleagues about what they may consider some of their weaknesses and failures. They do not have lighter loads for the first year or two, which would be preferable, given their lack of experience and the amount they have to learn in those beginning years. However excellent their initial preparation, there is much that cannot be learned until a teacher is in a natural classroom situation with full responsibility. The socialization of the newcomer into the profession is handled poorly, often because of sheer neglect. A more detailed description of the conditions and the problems surrounding them will be discussed below.

I shall organize the argument in support of my thesis around three questions: (1) What current problems in teacher education would such an approach address? (2) What are some of the difficulties and problems that might be encountered and how realistic is it to think that they could be overcome? (3) What conditions are requisite for an effective mounting of such an effort?

Before tackling these questions, I shall describe in some detail what this strategy would look like in practice so that what I am advocating can be better understood. If we are to mount a genuinely collaborative effort in teacher education and to engage in research on it, the first order of business is to initiate meaningful collaboration. For that reason, I offer a specific proposal that gives shape and substance to the idea of collaboration.

Description of the strategy

There would be three phases:

Phase I: The pre-professional work

The first phase consists of a strong liberal arts background which in the United States culminates in an AB degree. This contains little or no pedagogical theory or practice (Bush, 1977), and concludes typically at the end of the period when a person has been engaged full-time in a higher educational institution. It could be less or more than four years, depending upon the individual.

Phase II: the training

To enter this training would not be easy. Those who wished to undertake training would take the initiative and be responsible for applying and being accepted for an internship/externship/residency sequence of positions that would then last from two to five years, perhaps in one or two different locations, 2-3 years in one place and 2-3 years in another. These positions would be in training complexes and in individual schools within them. The complexes would consist of consortia of teacher trainers from the institutions of higher education, personnel of the local education agencies, and community representatives (Bush, 1975). This is our first collaborative step.

Upon acceptance into a training complex, the candidate would be given a limited credential, good only for the duration of the internship. These complexes would be located in neighbourhoods of different socio-economic and ethnic composition in both urban and rural areas. A large attrition or drop-out rate between those who completed an AB degree in pre-professional education and those successfully achieving admission into training would be anticipated. This is a strong feature of the plan. This large attrition would not be a loss to the social system. It represents to some extent a selection process, leaving only those with above-average motivation to enter teaching. Those who chose to enter other fields would still have a good liberal background, which would serve them well not only as workers in other fields but also as citizens and parents. And the cost is not high in comparison with professional training. The programme in these training complexes may, for purposes of discussion, be divided into two strands — although they should operate so as to be almost indistinguishable: strand 1 — *school improvement* and strand 2 — *training*.

The dominating and permeating idea of the plan is contained in strand 1 — *school improvement*. The model of this collaborative venture is a problem-solving one, in which the regular teachers and administrators in the school, teacher training representatives from the co-operating institutions of higher education in the region, the beginning teachers, interns, pupils in the school, and community members would be engaged in a comprehensive effort to improve the school so that a better education would be provided for the pupils. Accompanying this problem-solving effort would be the training effort of strand 2. The heart of this would be extensive practice by the intern over a period of several years, in classrooms and in non-formal educational settings, in learning how to work with students individually and in small groups, and with parents and community members. There would be extensive observation of this practice, by different groups — peers, school and higher educational personnel. Time would be provided for critical, thoughtful discussion about practice, and then the opportunity to try again and to perfect that practice. There would be timely feedback, opportunity for discussion, and correction. Sufficient practice of this kind over an extended period of time would be provided so that attention could be given not only to the perfection of a wide array of technical skills, but also to the professional decision-making side of teacher preparation which is so often now neglected and left to chance. Trainees would thus be given a chance to develop their own unique styles of teaching and learn how to make wise professional decisions as to which of the repertoire of skills to draw upon in a given situation.

In a school or group of schools where both of these strands, school improvement and training, were underway, there would emerge new roles in which both higher education professors and school staff would become colleagues in the role of clinical instructor, conducting continuing seminars that would be organized and offered for the interns, sometimes in the school and sometimes at the university. This training would operate on a 12-month basis, with regular time and finance budgeted for it.

Phase III: assessment and licensing

Sometime after four or five years of teaching, the individual would say 'I am ready to take my examination for admission to practice'. This could be a joint decision with his adviser or main seminar leader. It would not be a hurried affair, but would take place over a period of several months, interspersed with or even as an integral part of the trainee's regular work in the school. It would consist of at least these parts, perhaps with new ones to be developed: *demonstration* of a variety of basic skills in specific situations; *observation* by experienced clinical instructors from schools and colleges; *written examinations* on pedagogy and subject matter; and possibly an *oral examination*, and/or *a written project* which would demonstrate the trainee's problem-solving (research) capacity. New parties in the collaboration enter at this point, namely those responsible for licensing and accrediting standards. The examination would be jointly set, given, and scored by the state and the profession, and would, when successfully passed, result in the issue of a basic licence to practise. It might be desirable to design into the system a higher, more 'specialized' licence that would be achieved later. It would be assumed that the state licensing and accreditation system, as well as the colleges, schools and professional organizations, would set standards and in other ways encourage the development of such a system.

The problems in teacher education that this scheme addresses

What important porblem of teacher education would be addressed if all groups were to collaborate and concentrate attention for a decade upon the beginning years as I have just sketched? There are at least four, which will be briefly touched on: time, practice, inter-relationship of the various parts of the system, and inquiry (research and development) about the system.

Time. One of the main lessons that we have learned over the past decade or two is that the proper training of a teacher takes time (Bush, 1977). We are forever trying to crowd too much into too short a period. As a consequence, we do too little thoroughly, skip shoddily over many parts, and miss others altogether. Ideas about teaching need time to mature. Skills require repeated and criticized practice. Time is required for a unique teaching style to emerge in a manner that is suited to an individual's talents. Under current conditions, that transition from neophyte to socialized professional is crowded into such a brief period under such unfavourable circumstances that this aspect constitutes one of the weakest parts of the system, with consequent extremely high costs in morale and professional self-esteem. The provision of a period of several years in which to perfect skills and competence in decision-making and to begin a positive socialization into the profession would be a major improvement in teacher education. This was brought home forcefully to me over the past several years as I watched the difference between our regular trainees at Stanford, who had one year of post-baccalaureate training in the regular intern programme, and the Teacher Corps interns of our tenth cycle project in co-operation with the San Jose City Schools, who had two years to complete their programme. *(See also Chapter 15.)* There was a marked advantage in the degree of confidence felt by the two-year trainees, when they entered their first regular positions; in the breadth and degree of skill represented, including the capacity to handle discipline, provide individualized instruction, relate to the community, and make mature plans about their own future professional development; and in their favourable attitude towards being in the profession.

Practice. Even though practice has long been considered by many to be the most useful part of the training programme, it has been so little and so late, that it has not been possible to take full advantage of it. Both the need for, and the positive consequences of, providing trainees with much more, varied practice, observed and criticized at a variety of grade levels and under different conditions, have been proven again and again. It is clear that practice needs to take place under relatively 'safe' conditions, where mistakes and weaknesses are expected and shared, so that these conditions can become rooted in normal expectations for a lifelong period. Under the present short period of practice, there is only one chance. It must be right the first time. This is the sole source of judgement as to whether the candidate passes or fails. Under the plan outlined, critical summative evaluation does not take place until after several years of practice. There is no immediate threat of passing or failing 'student teaching' or of jeopardising tenure. Not only would much of the threat typically surrounding beginning practice be reduced, but also the deep satisfaction that derives from perfecting practice and overcoming errors in skill performance would be enjoyed and shared. The psychological relief at not having to 'hide' shortcomings would have a salutary effect upon the mental health of the profession.

Interrelationship of various parts of the system. Teacher education has always been rife with dysfunctional dichotomies: between theory and practice, beginners and 'old-timers', schools and universities, subject matter and method, to mention a few. They constitute serious obstacles that need attention if the profession is to grow to full maturity. The traditional conflicts, misunderstandings and differences in points of view about teacher education that abound between those in the schools and those in the colleges have many harmful effects on newcomers to the profession. Just as they begin their careers and are in process of becoming socialized into the profession, they are subjected to disharmony between those who have just trained them and those who are now their seniors in the schools. What are they to believe about a profession that is so badly split? The 'old-timers' tell them, 'Forget those theoretical and impractical ideas that you learned at the university, and we will help you learn to teach here in the real world.' That teachers in the schools convey this message is disturbing enough to the neophyte, but that they then also typically fail to deliver the help only compounds the mischief. It is probably one of the most debilitating matters that confronts the newcomers. It makes them unnecessarily wary and impels them even further than is natural to keep their own counsel. It surely contributes — as do many other factors — to the erection of the classroom 'castle' concept, with high barrier walls built between classrooms.

It is our contention and hope that in the scheme proposed, the newcomer's first few years would be under much more favourable circumstances than those just alluded to. With experienced teachers and university trainers working together in the school site, over a period of several years on a regular basis, in which the university personnel are immersed in real school problems, sharing the difficulties and contributing something to their solution, attitudes toward one another would probably alter. We have some evidence that under such circumstances they indeed do. This would have a positive effect upon the trainees. The manner of working in a school problem-solving situation with continuous seminars taught on site both by the college and the school clinical instructors should make the traditional gap between theory and practice much easier to bridge. The manner of training and the work in which the trainees would be engaged, would emphasize a collegial, team approach to tasks much more than now prevails in the schools or in typical student teaching programmes. The new model would bring teaching much more into the open and begin to overcome the paucity of teacher-teacher dialogue that prevails in schools today. For too long, teachers have lived mainly within their classroom walls, so that most of their relationships are with younger, immature persons. More than most professionals, teachers have suffered from too little interaction with their colleagues and other mature adults. The more stimulating environment of sustained dialogue with colleagues on important matters of teaching which this model provides would be salutary.

Inquiry. Until fairly recently, the colleges were considered to be the producers of research, and the schools its consumers. Teachers claimed little understanding of or interest in research. Researchers were interested mainly in gaining access to classrooms to gather their data as easily and as quickly as possible. No questions were asked on either side, and there the matter ended. Little wonder that the researcher's findings were seldom consequential and that there was little demand for them or interest expressed by the practitioners. Happily, things are beginning to change. The roles of practitioner, researcher, and policy-maker are beginning to merge as the educational research and development process matures. As we approach a problem-solving, collegial attitude in the study, improvement, and practice of teaching, many new and interesting things may begin to happen. For example, we know very little about the 'curve' of learning to teach or about how it might be shaped in a more favourable way. This is a principal research question on which we might concentrate in the period ahead. It would be particularly useful if an international team from several countries co-operatively undertook such an inquiry. Under the circumstances outlined in this proposal, it would be possible to tackle this problem. It is our hypothesis that the curve of learning to teach might change significantly under the new model (see Figure 1).

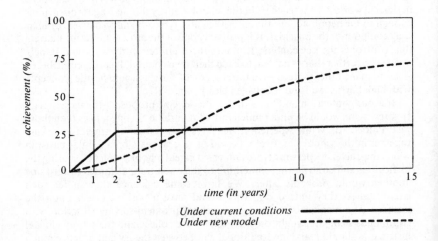

Figure 1 *Curve of learning to teach*

Under current conditions, the newcomers have to learn to swim very quickly, or they will sink. Consequently, the stress is upon learning how to survive the moment, not necessarily upon how to develop a powerful performance that will be sustained and will improve over time. This early crisis mentality of quickly learning successful survival techniques, which often becomes frozen into the teacher's basic repertoire and style, results in a potential far below that which could be achieved if a more gradual approach were taken in which there was ample time, in a safe atmosphere, to practise potentially more powerful strategies that take longer to perfect. Under better-designed early years, a long-term, sustained growth in teaching power would be more likely to result. This is mere hypothesis at present. But it would be possible to test the proposition under the model proposed. It would be no small achievement if in training we could promote the long-term sustained growth of teaching skill, professional competence in decision-making, and the development of a wide repertoire of skills and unique teaching styles. Co-operation in team teaching would under this system be given a better chance to work than before. This again would be a significant outcome.

These four problem areas of time, practice, inter-relationships of the parts of the system, and attitudes toward inquiry that the new system tackles are illustrative, not exhaustive; but they do, however, deal with some of the more serious problems that have long confronted teacher education.

Why will it not work?

What are the obstacles? How serious are they? Here are some problems that should be thoroughly explored.

1. It would be too costly. The system would cost more money; the teachers' loads would have to be lighter; there would need to be adjustments to make time for clinical instruction, and this new training load could not be assumed without added compensation. The answer to this objection is, perhaps, 'yes'; but it might not need too much extra money, rather the spending of present resources differently. If so, what would be cut? A universal answer for all places is difficult, but such an alternative is not impossible to contemplate.

2. Teachers are entitled to their seniority rights and are not going to give them up to newcomers. True. But there will be plenty of routine and lesser tasks that the trainees can properly assume which can relieve senior teachers. Also, with more total staff available to help in the school, the experienced teacher load might be less and the total accomplishment more, hence teacher satisfaction might be greater. In addition, the new system will not require the elimination of all seniority rights such as preferred classes and periods of teaching.

3. Applicants desiring to enter teaching would be unwilling to spend this longer time in preparation. It is true that many who apply to enter teaching have always wanted a career that was easy to enter without extensive preparation. This system would help to weed out many of those who were not strongly motivated. This would be desirable. In the present time of surplus, it becomes much more possible. Moreover, subsidy through payments to interns will be attractive in helping to alleviate their difficulty, as for example, has been the case in the Teacher Corps programme. (*See also Chapter 15.*)

4. The incentives have been low both for the university teacher to go into the field and for the schoolteacher to take on the added load of teacher training. This is an old problem, but it is not exacerbated by the new approach. We have been making progress on this problem over the past few years in our increased emphasis on field-based teacher education. As decreasing demands are being made on college faculties for pre-service education, they are being freed for field assignments. College faculties derive substantial satisfactions from good field assignments.

5. Colleges and universities do not have a very good track record in collaborating with one another in teacher education projects, hence establishing training complexes would not be easy. This is undoubtedly true. However, if there were financial incentives connected with the complexes, as there would need to be, and if there were a prospect of having graduates from the college or university practice in a good training complex, in whose design it may be presumed that the colleges would have had something to say, some important barriers to collaboration would be lowered.

6. *This proposal represents a complex, comprehensive change and as such has little likelihood of being brought off.* True as this may be, the end to piecemeal and patchwork attempts to save the system may be at hand. New forces are at work today. Funds for pre-service education are dwindling and large sums are beginning to be directed towards in-service teacher education. In California, even in the face of Proposition 13, which recently substantially cut back property taxes on which school support relies so heavily, Assembly Bill 65, the comprehensive new school finance law, contains a major school improvement provision, which will pump almost $150 million per year for the next several years into the schools for their improvement, a substantial part of which will be devoted to staff development. This is over ten times the amount appropriate this year for the new United States federal teacher centres. Further, elements of the new proposal have already been experimented with in different places. Now may be the propitious moment to begin to bring all of the different pieces together into a new design.

This is not an exhaustive list of problems, but it is a beginning. Further consideration should bring out more. We can then assess the situation, to see if the obstacles outweigh the potential advantages, or whether the potential is worth an effort.

Requirements to make such a proposed system work

The following four requirements at least seem essential:

1. *Master planning.* The different segments of the system and agencies therein would need to work together. Collaboration of the many different parties is essential. No institution of higher education or local school district could accomplish the task alone. A sub-geographical region of a state or, preferably, a whole state plan would need to be developed. In California, after World War II, a statewide master plan for higher education was developed that has not only had a phenomenal success but has been a model for other places in this country and abroad. I have been working with the California Commission for Teacher Preparation and Licensing about the possibility of building a master plan for teacher education in California. Perhaps another state or two in the United States and some places abroad might join in a collaborative effort. If the idea began to succeed in several places, we might well be on the way toward making a national and even an international impact on problems in teacher education. I believe that nothing short of this magnitude of effort will be required to make a fundamental improvement in teacher education at this juncture.

2. *Necessity for those in the field of teacher education to change ways of thinking about teacher education.* Teacher education should not be something that we do mainly or solely in the colleges, and which then requires a refresher course several years later. It should be a continuous process, that begins with a modest effort, and gradually assumes greater concentration and attention as the training proceeds, in regular school settings. It should be a genuinely joint effort

of school, college, trainee, the state and the community. This has not been our traditional way of thinking about the problem. But this shift in thinking is beginning to take place as many of us face the future realistically.

3. Change in the way in which teacher educators spend their time. For the college personnel, the amount of time spent in a series of separate and formally organized single teacher-taught classes with textbook, assignments and written examinations, will probably decrease. The amount of time spent on the university campus in relation to that spent out in the schools will decrease. Lecturing may decrease and the amount of small group discussion and tutorials will increase. Demonstration and modelling, now largely absent, may appear in increasing amounts. Experienced school personnel will spend less time in the classroom with students and more time with their younger colleagues who are just beginning. They will spend less time teaching, more in observation of teaching and in discussing the results; more time in working in groups with colleagues (peers, trainees and administrators) in planning and in solving school problems; more time in homes and in working with community members as partners in the life and work of the school; more time in thinking and talking about teaching and of ways to determine how effective it has been.

4. An absolute increase in resources now devoted to teacher education — not just by taking them from other parts of the system. The most likely sources of new funds in the United States will be the state and the national governments. This is a long overdue necessity, and there is some suggestion that it is not an unrealistic expectation. Both national and state levels of government are already beginning to realize, as suggested by results from research, that resources put into *effective* and *well-aimed* teacher education, both pre- and in-service, are among the most useful dollars that can be spent in improving schools.

Conclusion

To sum up, our proposition is that at this time in educational history, we need to increase sharply the amount of energy — time, money, and other resources — devoted to teacher education. The new sources of energy that can be tapped for teacher education lie in the community, the schools, the institutions of higher education, the local, state and national governments, and in the redirection of some of our present energies. In directing new energy to teacher education, there ought to be a shift in where and how we use our augmented power. The central idea is that this new force should focus upon the beginning years of teaching. This will call for strong leadership and will not be without risks. But the result might be a renaissance in teacher education that would reverberate throughout the educational system to its enduring benefit.

References

Bolam, R and Baker, K (1976) *Helping New Teachers: The Induction Year* DES Report on Education No 84 (Marsh 1976) Department of Education and Science: London

Bolam, R and Baker, K (1977) *Teacher Induction Pilot Schemes: Progress Report* DES Report on Education No 89 (May 1977) Department of Education and Science: London

Bush, Robert N (1975) Teacher education in the future: focus upon an entire school *Journal of Teacher Education* **26** 2:148-9

Bush, Robert N (1977) We know how to train teachers: why not do so! *Journal of Teacher Education* **28** 6:5-9

Joyce, B (ed) (1978) *Involvement: A Study of Shared Governance in Teacher Education* National Dissemination Center: Syracuse University, NY

26. The teacher as professional and trade unionist

Keir Bloomer

Summary: This chapter looks at the role of teachers' unions in promoting the professional development of their members. A working definition of the term 'professional' is offered and the status of teachers is measured against it. To protect the interests of their members, it is argued, teachers' unions have a duty to enhance this status.

The task of teachers' unions is to improve the professionalism of teachers. The regard in which they are held is examined with particular reference to three areas of policy: education, conditions of service and salaries.

The effects of delegating educational decision-making to possibly unrepresentative activists are examined; there are inherent dangers in unions facilitating changes for which the profession as a whole is not ready. The unions must have educational policies but they must take care that the views they express are representative of the profession.

Teachers' unions are under pressure to demand better working conditions, smaller classes and hence more teachers. This has implications for salary levels and hence for the quality of recruitment. Within foreseeable financial circumstances, only limited improvements in the conditions of service are seen to be possible.

The chapter considers the use of the salaries structure as a tool for encouraging professional development; a clear need is seen for rewarding successful classroom practitioners rather than administrators.

Teachers' unions exist in order to protect and advance the interests of their members as perceived by those members. Teachers tend to assume that because the existence of a well-qualified and well-motivated teaching force of sufficient strength is an absolute prerequisite of a successful education system, a major conflict of interest between teachers and the service is impossible. The extent to which this is true — and it would certainly be disputed by education authorities — is a subject of considerable interest (which must, however, lie outside the scope of this chapter).

Both employers and teachers have felt that an increase in professionalism, whether measured in terms of expertise, commitment, or financial reward, would be substantially to the advantage of teachers and education system alike. Teachers' unions have the power to influence considerably the attitudes and work habits of their members and alter the policies and priorities of the education authorities. They have an important, if as yet largely unconsidered, role to play in any programme designed to further the professional development of teachers.

This chapter considers this role within the context of a single education system: that of Scotland. Conditions in Scotland may be taken as broadly similar to those throughout the United Kingdom but there is no intention to imply that they are in any way typical of conditions elsewhere. However, the problem of reconciling an effective defence of their own interests by teachers with the long-term interests of the education system as a whole is a universal one.

Over the past ten years, union organization in the Scottish teaching profession has become steadily stronger. About 95 per cent of Scottish teachers now belong to a union. By far the largest of these is the Educational Institute of Scotland (EIS) with 48,000 members (nearly 80 per cent of the total) distributed among all sectors of education. The remainder are divided among half a dozen organizations, most of them concerned only with a single sector and several of them very small. It is thus to the EIS that the profession as a whole looks, and it is with the policies of the EIS that this article is mainly concerned.

The past ten years have seen a considerable change in the attitude of teachers towards their unions. Educational issues have become less prominent while salaries and conditions of service have been hotly disputed. Resort to industrial action has been relatively frequent and is no longer the subject of deep moral debate. Indeed, it is probably no exaggeration to say that industrial relations have steadily deteriorated, for complex reasons, and are now as bad as any in the public sector. There has been much discussion of the way in which the role of the teacher can best evolve in the coming years.

Any discussion of the role of teachers almost inevitably involves the use of words like 'professional' and 'professionalism'. They are weapons freely employed both by teachers' unions and education authorities in debates over teachers' salaries and conditions. As used by teachers and their representatives, the words contain an implied wage claim; an implicit comparison is made with other better-paid professions. The employers also use them to establish a comparison, but one based upon level of commitment and flexibility of job description rather than upon financial reward. Both sides, however, share the assumption that teachers are or should be 'professionals', and that it is desirable to increase as far as possible the level of their professionalism.

In fact, the words 'profession', 'professional' etc are seldom defined: they are used for their implications rather than their precise meaning. Nor will a watertight definition be offered here, but rather a general description whose edges are somewhat blurred. Professionalism is primarily an attitude of mind: the connection with money is indirect. A large salary does not establish a *prima facie* case for professional status, although it is possible that high financial rewards are an indispensable inducement to adopt professional attitudes. The essence of professionalism is an acceptance of responsibility.

A person is not a professional, however well he may perform his job, if he feels no deep involvement with it, is indifferent to, and accepts no responsibility for, his level of success or failure, and can with unmixed feelngs abandon his task at any time. A professional is employed to carry out his work with a high degree of competence and with reasonable diligence. This will tend to necessitate a flexible approach to working hours and job definitions. A professional is called upon to exercise responsible personal judgement based on specialized knowledge. He is independent of immediate supervision and detailed control; he has full charge over the discharge of his immediate area of professional responsibility. This autonomy extends from the individual to the group. Professions in large measure control their own standards. They establish criteria governing qualifications and entry: they enforce codes of discipline and retain the power of expulsion. To a large extent, they are also self-governing.

On this loose definition, teaching undoubtedly exhibits some of the characterisitics of a profession. Most teachers are deeply involved in their work. They think and talk about it whenever a group of them are gathered together. A substantial, arguably excessive, degree of responsibility is accepted for the development of their pupils. Work extends far beyond school hours and school terms; indeed for many teachers the boundary between work and leisure is often ill-defined. Collectively also teachers often behave as a profession. They are closely involved in the control and development of the service. Entry and professional standards are controlled by an elected body (the General Teaching Council, set up in 1965) on which practising teachers form a majority. The activities of teachers' unions have frequently been restrained by professional considerations.

Teachers themselves are virtually unanimous in claiming professional status: any other suggestion is widely resented. They frequently and perhaps self-consciously use the term 'the profession' as a description of themselves. Indeed it is not so long since the majority insisted on referring to their unions as professional associations. The general public, however, is less inclined to grant teachers the status they covet. In the public mind they are not grouped together with lawyers and doctors in the way teachers feel appropriate: at best they are seen as second-class professionals, in a category perhaps with social workers and nurses.

In part this is unavoidable. Education has little mystique. Everyone has been exposed to it and many would claim to have benefited little from it. All too often it is seen as consisting merely of the conveyance of knowledge or information. Apart from a knowledge of his subject matter, it is not immediately apparent what expertise a teacher possesses to set him apart from others. The readily expressed contempt of so many teachers for their own professional training does little to enhance their standing. The man in the street believes that he who knows a subject can therefore teach it: every qualified teacher who denies the value of his college training confirms this view.

In recent years the credibility of the profession has suffered from the manifest uncertainty which has surrounded the education system. So long as teachers remained confident that multiplication tables, general analysis and Latin grammar were universally beneficial, most people were prepared to accept this on trust. Once teachers began to question openly the usefulness of what they taught, the effectiveness of the way they taught it and the justification for the way in which their schools were organized, much of that easy acceptance was lost — perhaps not before time.

In place of apparently simple, limited, and widely (if unthinkingly) accepted aims, the education system has adopted more grandiose, less universally shared goals. During the 1960s, economic and social purposes came to be seen as of at least equal importance to the acquisition of academic learning. The success of the national economy, it was argued, required a high general standard of education and, in particular, a vigorous expansion of higher and further education. Changes in the organization of the school system were seen as an essential prerequisite of egalitarian social change. It is clear that large numbers of teachers neither fully accepted these new aims nor believed in their capacity to achieve them. However, the increased emphasis which governments were placing on education helped to make greater resources available and was therefore widely welcomed even by teachers who were deeply sceptical about the new directions.

Today, as reformers become less convinced that the changes they seek can be achieved through education, and the economic miracle has yet to be accomplished, the service suffers as a result of its failure to achieve aims which in large part were foisted upon it, were incapable of fulfillment and were widely known by teachers to be so.

However, even if the successes of the changed educational system had been greater and more widely publicized than they were, it is doubtful whether they could have sustained the esteem in which the system was held. Changed objectives reflected a widening gap between the purposes of education as viewed by practitioners, theorists and politicians and those purposes as viewed by consumers and the public at large. 'Basic skills', 'academic standards' and 'effective discipline' remain the top priorities of the public, and to the extent that they are perceived, however inaccurately, as having been displaced in the minds of the educational establishment, the prestige of the system has fallen. Teachers are now often seen as pursuing less accepted aims less successfully; they have in consequence fallen in popular esteem.

Most important of all, however, is the poor level of material reward. Perceived status is almost always a direct function of income, and on this criterion, teaching compares unfavourably with almost every other self-styled profession. Inevitably a low level of salary has sometimes bought only a low level of commitment, with consequent further loss of professional standing. Such measures as teachers have taken to improve their financial position have tended to involve trade union action which is perceived as being at variance with the traditional professional stereotype.

The consequence of this lowered esteem should not be underestimated. The recruitment of an adequate supply of well-qualified and well-motivated young teachers has always been a major problem. The post-war period has in general been one of overall shortage. Even when, as at present, this is not the case, shortages in some subjects remain serious and the long-term prospects for balancing supply and demand remain poor. In large part, of course, this is caused by fluctuations in the balance of advantage in terms of salary, career prospects and the security of a job in teaching compared with other potential careers. Even if the recurring cycle of decline in the relative position of teachers' earnings could be broken, changes in circumstances in the economy as a whole would perpetuate this problem. Nevertheless the constant ability of the profession to secure recruits of quality, if not in sufficient quantity, even at the low points in the cycle indicates the existence of features attractive to potential recruits and not related to financial reward. Amongst these may be numbered the independence enjoyed by the teacher in his own classroom, the assumed importance of the educational process and the attractions of belonging to an occupational group to which some, at least, of the coveted status of the professional attaches. But as the esteem in which teachers are popularly held declines, the capacity of these factors to maintain even a limited level of recruitment must also decline.

Any reduction in the public standing of the service will also be reflected in a reduction in the resources made available by local and national government. In part, demographic trends make it almost inevitable that educational spending will decline at least in relative terms during the 1980s. Combined with a loss of confidence in the service this could lead to an absolute decline in spending levels and a severe crisis for both teachers and schools.

Perhaps most important of all, the effects of low public esteem upon the attitudes of pupils is profound. For many pupils, the teacher is the only academically successful person of their acquaintance. He therefore symbolizes the merits, rewards and life-style to be associated with success at school. If the teacher is discontented, unmotivated and badly paid, obvious conclusions will be drawn. Success at school, entry to further education and acceptance of the values of the school will be seen as pointless. The teacher is an educational salesman but he is also a sample of the product. He will be judged as such, and the whole education system with him. It is for this reason above all that the rewards and attitudes of the teaching profession must be maintained at a truly professional level.

Teachers' unions have thus been faced with a decline in the public regard for both teachers and education, and made aware of potential ill-effects upon the interests of their members. How have they responded? Have they evolved and pursued policies calculated to improve the professionalism of teachers and the respect with which that professionalism is treated by the public?

The remainder of this chapter considers three major areas of union policy in the light of these questions: education, conditions of service and salaries.

Education

If a union is to protect and advance its members' interests it must first identify them. This is relatively easy in salary matters, more difficult where conditions of service and staffing levels are involved, and deeply problematic in educational issues.

Traditionally, teachers' unions have adopted policies rooted in educational principles on all the major issues of the time and have sought to advance these policies by representations to government departments and education authorities. The method of formulation of these policies has normally been very different from those on so-called 'professional matters' (ie salaries and working conditions). General meetings of members both at national and branch levels are dominated by professional concerns: educational policies are determined within the committee structure of the national body. This is not because of a greater desire on the part of the union establishment to control educational policy than salaries policy; it reflects the attitude of the membership of the union. For a variety of reasons — lack of belief in their union's effectiveness in the purely educational field, availability of other channels of influence, and simple apathy — teachers do not clamour to influence the educational policies of the unions. It is significant, for example, that the publication in Scotland in 1977 of two major reports on the curriculum and examination system of secondary schools (Scottish Education Department, 1977a, 1977b) did not produce a demand for a general meeting in any single branch of the EIS, whereas each spring the salaries campaign unfailingly leads to many such meetings.

The result of the membership's indifference is that educational policy is made almost exclusively by activists. In a literal sense, these activists are quite irresponsible. They owe their places on major national union committees to popular elections where the issues influencing the voters are almost invariably concerned with salaries and conditions. Their educational views play no part in their election and they may be reasonably sure that any educational policies they produce are unlikely to lead to a loss of office. They are thus at liberty to commit the union to such views as they may choose to hold. They do not necessarily reflect the views of the membership as a whole and can claim no real mandate for their policies.

The recent record of the larger unions has mainly been one of support for officially proposed educational changes. For example, the EIS was quick to declare itself in favour of comprehensive schooling, the raising of the school leaving age, and mixed-ability grouping. It is unlikely that these policies carried the support of the majority of members at the time of their approval, and highly probable that some (eg the raising of the leaving age) were deeply unpopular. They reflected the views of the union leaders, who are generally articulate, committed, and to the left politically, rather than those of the typical teacher.

However, the policies of the teachers' unions have seldom been truly innovative. Even the most 'progressive' of them never presented original ideas. Rather, they have conveyed acceptance by the organization in question of ideas which originated outside the profession in political circles, or on its periphery, in colleges of education and within the Inspectorate. The true educational role of the teachers' unions has been that of a fifth column. It has consisted in making impossible effective resistance by teachers to ideas which have frequently been unpopular in themselves or impractical unless accompanied by massively increased resources. This fifth column has enabled the apparent pace of educational change to be much more rapid than might otherwise have been the case.

Should this be welcomed or condemned? It may be argued that if change had to await the mass support of classroom teachers it would invariably be postponed until years after it had become necessary. However, it may also be contended that the introduction of change in advance of its acceptance by the profession has been the cause of much of the *malaise* currently prevalent in the service, and of the phenomenon of 'innovation without change'.

Many of the educational changes of the past 20 years have been unpopular with large sections of the profession for genuinely educational reasons. There were, and are, many teachers whose outlook remains fundamentally academic and whose interests remain deeply rooted in book learning. At its best this outlook sees school education as an attempt to pass on the rudiments of a great cultural tradition: at its worst it reflects an unthinking hostility to change and to other traditions and backgrounds. In neither case is it friendly to the ethos of mixed-ability classes, or to schooling which is genuinely comprehensive. Above all, it has little time for the pastoral dimension now accepted by many to be an essential function of the school.

To many teachers the political implications of some of the changes are also unacceptable. Many of the innovations are perceived as originating in left-wing circles: their egalitarian aims are clear for all to see. To that substantial section of the profession which is both politically and educationally deeply conservative such ideas are anathema.

A further cause of unpopularity lies in the fact that almost all changes in curriculum and method have placed additional demands on teachers, who have not felt that sufficient support was provided by their employers. Teachers who were out of sympathy with the aims of the changes felt no motivation to remedy a lack of resources by increased effort on their own part. Matters were, of course, made worse by the fact that these additional demands were imposed at a time when, with one brief interruption, teachers' earnings were experiencing a substantial relative decline (EIS, 1979).

In these circumstances it is difficult to conclude that the educational policies of the teachers' unions adequately protected the interests either of their members or of the education service. They did not seek to put forward original ideas, nor did they succeed in substantially modifying the ideas of others. Still less did they succeed in resisting unpopular changes. On the contrary, they facilitated the imposition of changes for which the resources were not made available and which did not command the assent, still less the enthusiastic support, of the practitioners. As a result, bad ideas frequently obtained undeserved influence and good ones half-hearted implementation in unfavourable circumstances. The morale of the profession suffered a blow from which it has yet to recover. The education system has been exposed to ill-informed and reactionary attacks; its prestige is low and its finances threatened. Real benefits to pupils are hard to discern. It is a sorry story, from which lessons should be learned.

Some teachers have concluded that it is inappropriate for a teachers' union to have any educational policies at all. Instead, it should seek merely to exact a good price in return for agreeing to altered working practice. In its favour, this policy would certainly be less disastrous than its predecessors. Innovations could not easily be introduced on the cheap or without formal agreement from the organized profession. High costs would encourage deep consideration. The earnings of teachers would tend to increase and their status and the esteem in which the service is held would improve: thus the quality of recruitment would be enhanced. The buying and selling of goodwill would impose a type of accountability which is now lacking.

Nevertheless, this type of industrial trade unionism would have significant disadvantages. It would remove the teacher still further from the centre of educational decision-making and would thus exacerbate many existing failings. The professionalism of teachers would decline. The area of their personal discretion would be reduced and their role would approximate ever more closely to that of skilled operatives. Such a policy would fail to reflect a whole dimension in the proper aspirations of the profession. Teachers believe that they have a unique contribution to make to the management of education: a contribution which is practical yet committed, politically disinterested but intellectually honest. It is the duty of their unions to afford a channel whereby that contribution can be made effective.

There are three levels at which teachers need representation on educational issues: within the school, at the level of the individual employing authority, and at the point where national policy is determined. No teachers' union has made more than token demands for an effective voice for all its members in policy-making at their place of work. It would be wrong to suggest that the newly qualified probationer should wield an influence equal to that of his head of department or of the head teacher. Nevertheless the rigid hierarchical structure of the profession and the complete exclusion from any influence of its junior members is without parallel in other professions and is deeply unhealthy. Professionalism implies and requires a degree of personal autonomy for every practitioner which cannot be reconciled with the present-day organization of schools. Without that autonomy, the level of professional responsibility and commitment must remain low.

Every teacher, however junior, also has legitimate interests as a subject specialist which are perhaps best articulated at local authority level. There was a time when the unions supported a network of subject committees but these are today largely moribund, as teachers find it more rewarding, in all senses, to participate in the system of subject panels established and maintained by their employers. The elective nature of the old committees in any case defeated their main objective which must be the right and duty of every teacher to participate personally in the affairs of his profession. This is a need which cannot, however, easily be met by groups working to implement the policies of the employers — groups which are frequently seen as avenues to promotion. There is a need for a structure whereby teachers can articulate professional opinions regardless of their compatibility with the policies of the authorities. There is a role for the unions here.

Above all, there is a need for an effective teacher voice at national level. This should not solely consist, as in the past, in reacting to official pronouncements. It is also the job of an effective and responsible teachers' union to initiate — to expose educational deficiencies and to suggest remedies. Naturally, this involves admission that the state of the service is imperfect — something normally regarded as well-nigh sacrilegious. In reality, nothing would be conceded: the extreme defensiveness of the professional organizations towards any criticism of the service conceals little and deludes few. Rather, it causes teachers to be identified with failings which as individuals they are frequently ready to condemn.

Activists in control of their union's educational policies tread an uncertain path. They betray their trust if they use their position to advance individually held opinions, as in the past they have so often done by lending support to unpopular but 'progressive' notions. On the other hand, their educational pronouncements should not serve merely as the handmaidens of their salary policies or their demands for improved staffing. They should seek to make that contribution which only the organized voice of the profession can make. Practical experience and a faith in the abiding value of learning must be the starting point. Doubts must be articulated, implications pointed out, necessary resources demanded.

On occasion, though less frequently than they claim, this is just what the unions have done. What they have never done, however, is take any effective action in support of educational policies. Instead, representations have been made at opportune moments to authorities and government departments. The knowledge that no action will follow enables these authorities to accept assurances of support in general principle and disregard any reservations accompanying them. Teachers' organizations will never attain the influential position in the processes of educational decision-making which their members' claims to professional status demand until they are as willing to take effective action in pursuit of their educational policies as in pursuit of better salaries and conditions of work.

Conditions of service

One of the most difficult problems for any teachers' union is how to balance its aspirations about salaries with its policies on staffing and supply. Resources for education are limited, and always will be. The larger the number of teachers employed, the smaller the salary that can be paid to each. The lower the salary paid, the poorer the quality of the profession.

In reality, the choices are not quite so stark, the consequences not quite so determined. Budgets are not absolutely inflexible nor are the variables so few. Nevertheless the essential dilemma remains. Most of the educational changes recently promoted, and welcomed by the unions, require increased (and often also more highly competent) staff. Thus pupil: teacher ratios in Scottish schools improved from 25.2:1 in 1961 to 18.4:1 in 1979. In a service as labour-intensive as education, where roughly 70 per cent of the total expenditure is on wages and salaries, the financial implications of such an increase in staff were very great. In the absence of public willingness to increase spending on education at a similar rate, it necessarily imposed severe limitations upon the service in other ways. In particular it made almost impossible the kind of improvement teachers wish to see in their individual salaries. The full extent of this has yet to be felt: the total cost of an increase in staffing in a profession paid on lengthy age-related incremental scales is spread over a long period of time. Nevertheless, the increase in cost has been quite sufficient to leave the teachers' salary bill as the single most expensive salary bill in the public sector. Those groups who are better-paid — doctors, judges, higher ranks of the armed forces and senior civil servants — are much fewer in number: those who are more numerous — local authority manual workers, — the various categories of industrial civil servant — are substantially less well paid. Thus the money required to finance a 1 per cent increase in the salaries of teachers is sufficient to increase the pay of local authority manual workers by 1 ½ per cent or the pay of doctors by several times that amount. This is a point whose significance is hardly likely to be lost on government or local authorities. Indeed, to a government intent on restricting public spending there can be few options which have as large an immediate effect as depressing the level of the teachers' salaries award.

The relationship between teachers' earnings and their numbers can be seen in the fact that the period from the mid-1960s to the mid-1970s in which so much labour-demanding educational change occurred was a period of continuous and substantial decline in teachers' relative earnings. To a considerable extent, the expansion of staffing during this period was limited by shortages in the supply of new recruits largely attributable to the decline in salaries. Thus the total cost proved in part to be self-limiting. Were it not for the existence and enforcement of minimum standards of qualification for entry to the profession, it is doubtful if this would have been the case. In a more open market it is probable that a more rapid expansion of staff would have proved possible but at the cost of a decline in standards. As a result a downward spiral of both salary levels and standards would have been established.

The limitations placed upon this process by the insistence upon minimum qualifications were far from complete. The period was marked by an increasing subject imbalance among secondary teachers. Graduates in subjects with a high market value, such as mathematics and physics, were not recruited in sufficient numbers: the shortfall was partially compensated for by over-recruitment in social subjects. Even if there was no qualitative decline in intake (and there is perhaps some reason to believe that teaching was regarded at times as a haven — permanent or temporary — for those graduates whose degrees otherwise offered them little chance of employment) this trend was nevertheless damaging to the curriculum of secondary schools and the quality of the education they offered. Thus, even despite an apparent maintenance of standards through control of entrance the true situation was both more complex and less satisfactory. A fundamental conflict exists between quantity and quality in teacher staffing which poses problems for employers and unions alike.

Both have been slow to respond. All the unions remain committed to unrealistic proposals for increased staffing. These are of two types — the purely educational, and those related to conditions of service. The first category consists largely of echoes of, and enlargements upon, proposals which originated elsewhere, and are almost never followed by action of any kind. The second is much more significant in this context. For a period of five years (1973 to 1978), meetings of the unions were dominated by discussions of conditions of service and proposals for the imposition of contractual maximum class sizes. Changes, above all the raising of the school leaving age, and to a lesser extent

the introduction of the expanded promotion scheme, had generated a pressing
need for a substantial immediate increase in staff which was not being met. As a
result, individual teachers faced increased class sizes, reduced preparation time
and occasionally both.

Industrial action resulted in the negotiation of maximum class sizes and
minimum preparation time for all teachers. These agreements are probably the
most significant development of the past few years. They represent, at the same
time, the biggest recent improvement in working conditions and the biggest
retreat from professional standards. The implications for the organization of
schools and hence for the education they provide are profound. The total effect
of the agreements may be seen as an enforced reordering of priorities by
education authorities. Whereas, previously, protection of the working
conditions of teachers occupied a very low priority in comparison with
curriculum change, subject balance, curtailing costs etc, employing authorities
were suddenly placed under an absolute obligation to guarantee certain
minimum conditions and to provide the staff required to meet them. Within the
individual school the effect was to strengthen the position of the classroom
teacher against the promoted staff. The freedom of the head teacher to direct the
affairs of his school was much restricted.

The consequences of this contract of service for staffing levels were both
substantial and immediate. The cuts in government spending imposed in 1976
brought about a deterioration in pupil: teacher ratios in many parts of England
and Wales but only in a handful of the best-staffed areas of Scotland. In most of
Scotland, teacher staffing was increased to meet the new contractual
obligations. Difficulties in reconciling these with the national staffing standards
for primary schools led to further negotiations in 1978 which produced an
agreement prescribing minimum standards 13 per cent higher than those
previously enforced. By 1979 the contract of service had guaranteed around
5000-6000 teaching posts (about 10 per cent of the total) which would not have
existed had the government and the education authorities enjoyed the same
freedom of action as in England.

Educational policy, both at national and local level, is determined as much by
financial as by educational considerations. Therefore, guarantees of minimum
staffing levels, maximum class sizes and minimum facilities for preparation and
correction must be seen as essential to the interests of both pupils and teachers.
The unions now face a difficult decision: whether or not to respond to the
considerable pressure from members to negotiate further improvements in the
contract, thus imposing fresh restrictions upon the schools and increased
staffing requirements upon the authorities.

It would, of course, be unwise to argue that there are no points at which the
contract could be improved with benefit. However, the argument against
wholesale improvement is overwhelming. The implications for the academic and
professional standards of teachers of substantially increased numbers have been
discussed above. An almost equally serious objection arises from the restrictions
placed upon the activities of the individual teacher by contractual requirements
and the effect upon the collective attitude of the profession brought about by
frequent resort to such restrictive practices.

Salaries

If professionalism is to be encouraged it must be rewarded. Salary is as potent an influence upon the attitudes of teachers as of other workers. This is true of both external and internal differentials. Thus, if equivalent abilities and qualifications will attract generally greater earnings outside the teaching profession, teachers will inevitably feel undervalued. Staff turnover and wastage rates will be high; morale will be low and motivation poor. In practice, this has been the experience of the profession throughout most of the post-war period. Teachers' pay has almost invariably compared poorly with that of other groups such as lawyers and doctors with whom teachers have wished to compare themselves. Moreover, (other than in the years of exceptional increases such as 1974) it has been steadily falling relative to earnings throughout the community. This was true even during that period of the 1960s and early 1970s when society, or at least governments, appeared to see in education the vital means of achieving desired social and economic changes. If the true value which society attaches to any occupation or activity can be measured by what it is prepared to pay for it, then education has been falling in the market over the past 30 years.

This is as true within the profession as in the world outside. The internal salary structure may be seen as reflecting the priorities within education of local authorities, governments and of teachers themselves. The past ten years have seen a substantial extension of the promotion structure, increasing both the proportion of promoted to unpromoted staff and the salary advantage accruing to the promoted. The reasons for this increase have been only in small part educational. Thus, in 1971, a large number of 'guidance' posts were created with little previous thought about the role they were to fulfil. A whole new tier of assistant head teachers was brought into existence at the same time with no planned role at all. This was done so as to create the impression of massive salary increases at minimum cost: thus a sum which would have been quite inadequate to give a worthwhile increase to the whole profession was used to give large increases to a small minority.

The effect of this meaningless jobbery should not be underestimated. Most of the posts remain as irrelevant now as on the day they were created. The recent Inspectorate report on the guidance system is as near to a confession of failure as an official publication could ever be. No similar study exists on the effects of the promotion structure as a whole. Education authorities, however, are now universally disillusioned. Requests for additional promoted posts for primary schools — where they are thin on the ground — attract little sympathy. Many secondary teachers, including many holders of senior promoted posts, willingly admit that they would be hard put to identify any specific educational advance which can be linked to the explosion in promoted posts.

Less beneficial effects are, however, easy to see. A top-heavy career structure has necessitated an increase in staffing of a particularly sterile type. The amount of non-teaching time required for administration by each promoted teacher is such that an additional non-promoted teacher must be employed for every three or four additional promoted posts created. A substantial increase in staffing has thus taken place without any reduction in class sizes, any increase in subject choice, any improvement in the curriculum or in the preparation of the classroom teacher. As a use of limited resources, this is lamentable.

The considerable increases in salary paid to the promoted naturally raise the prestige of administration and reduce the prestige of teaching. Nothing could be more injurious to the long-term interests of either the profession or the service. It is absolutely vital that the classroom practitioner should be held in high esteem, that teachers should be encouraged to seek a long-term career in the classroom and that they should be encouraged to cultivate the skills of teaching to the highest level.

Nobody with ambition or family commitments, indeed nobody desiring a modestly comfortable standard of living, can afford to contemplate a lifetime career in the classroom. He is obliged to seek promotion which will inevitably entail a retreat, partial or complete, from class contact. The more successful promotion panels are in identifying talent, the greater the impoverishment of the most — indeed the only — essential part of service.

The effect upon individual teachers is scarcely less catastrophic. Self-esteem is diminished. Competition for promotion encourages toadying. An obsession with hierarchies replaces professional judgement and eclipses any real demonstration of academic freedom. It encourages the adoption of attitudes likely to be approved by those 'higher up'. This is as true of the attitude of the head teacher to the director of education as of the attitude of the youngest probationer teacher to his head of department. In a climate of rapid educational change and experiment the prevailing official attitude becomes one of unthinking and uncritical progressivism.

The hope of promotion acts as a powerful deterrent to militancy. Attainment of a senior post creates divided loyalties. Thus the effectiveness of the profession on its own behalf is reduced. The availability of substantial wage increases in the form of responsibility payments fosters the illusion of an alternative to an adequate basic rate for the job. In the long term, of course, the dependence of every teacher upon the basic scales as the foundation for his salary invalidates this as an altérnative. This, however, does little to reduce the effectiveness of the promotion structure as a device for buying off militancy and depressing the earnings and self-esteem of the whole profession.

Teachers in general have shown no more than a passing awareness of the failings of the present structure: no union has yet produced any strategy for improving it. The first essential must be to reward success as a *teacher*. It must be made possible for the talented educator to spend the bulk of his professional life in the classroom. He must not be forced into administration for financial reasons. Nor is it sufficient to abolish promoted posts and use the money to increase basic salaries. What is required is a system of inducements for real professional development. Means have to be devised whereby the able and effective teacher receives financial recognition. It will be objected that it is not possible to identify precisely the skills and qualities of the 'good teacher' or even to pinpoint the individuals in question. Such defeatism does not merit serious attention. The whole promotion structure rests upon the selection of individuals — a selection moreover to be based upon qualities largely peripheral to the job the individuals have hitherto been employed to perform. It will not be possible to identify infallibly the ablest teachers any more than it is possible to select infallibly the best potential head teachers, but there is no reason to believe that the success rate will be any lower.

Any teachers' union considering substantial changes in the salary structure can properly advance these ideas only at a pace which enables it also to protect the interests its members have in the existing structure. Thus a feeling that the existing promotion structure is inherently unprofessional and anti-educational does not absolve a union of its obligations to members in promoted posts. The EIS has tackled the general question of how change can be brought about while vested interests are protected by approving a salaries strategy which lays down three priorities. The protection and enhancement of the living standards of all teachers are given highest priority: proposals for structural change occupy third place. This ensures that structural changes can be made only with such money as may remain out of any award after every teacher has received an increase at least sufficient to protect him against inflation. Such a strategy has the merit of enabling a programme of reform to be pursued over a period of time without incurring the type of internecine strife which understandably breaks out whenever changes are made by increasing one teacher's living standards at the direct expense of another's. This strategy is not in itself a programme for increasing professionalism but it does provide the framework within which such a programme can be developed.

Conclusion

Teachers are most highly valued and their salaries and status are accordingly most favourable when the education service is commonly perceived as being successful. Apparent success may have various causes, but a high level of professional competence is certain to be one. High salaries may tend to produce commitment and efficiency but the reverse is equally true. Quite simply, it is in teachers' economic interests to ensure that the profession does its job well, and to support measures designed to improve its capacity to do so.

However, it is clear that at present the pattern and level of inducements and rewards offered to teachers, both as a group and within the profession, are not designed to ensure that the optimum balance is struck between numbers and individual excellence or that the maximum potential level of professional competence is attained by the existing workforce. Until both the external salary relativities and the internal salary structure offer positive encouragement to professional development, progress is unlikely.

Equally, however, progress depends upon making such alterations as are necessary to the decision-making processes of the education system to ensure that increased professionalism can find effective outlets. There is little point in teachers' unions pressing for professional levels of salary unless they simultaneously press for the right to perform a truly professional function. Unions have, on occasion, devised excellent policies to pursue some part of their members' interests: what is now required is an integral strategy comprising both educational and 'professional' elements.

References

Educational Institute of Scotland (1979) *Commission on Pay Comparability: EIS Submission* EIS: Edinburgh

Scottish Education Department (1977a) *The Structure of the Curriculum in the Third and Fourth Years of the Scottish Secondary School* (The Munn Report) HMSO: Edinburgh

Scottish Education Department (1977b) *Assessment for All* (The Dunning Report) HMSO: Edinburgh

Part 8: Bibliography and Biographical Notes

Bibliography

Agnes McMahon

The bibliography is divided into four sections. The first covers published books and pamphlets by individual authors, the second lists publications (books and documents) issued by official bodies, and the third includes articles, periodicals and working papers. These three sections include nearly all of the references cited in individual chapters; unpublished manuscripts, multi-media teaching packages, manuscripts and a few specialized references have been omitted.

In section IV a number of key references from sections I, II and III listed in the various chapters have been annotated. The asterisks and crosses which appear in sections I to III have the following meanings:

* indicates that the reference has been annotated in section IV.
+ indicates that the publisher's address has been included at the end of section III.

Section I: Books and Pamphlets

Abernethy, D (1969) *The Political Dilemma of Popular Education — An African Case* Stanford University Press: California

Adelman, C (1978) On first hearing *in* Adelman (1978)

Adelman, C (ed) (1978) *Uttering, Muttering* CARE: University of East Anglia, Norwich

Adelman, C and Walker, R (1975) *A Guide to Classroom Observation* Methuen: London

Allen, D and Ryan, K (1969) *Microteaching* Addison-Wesley: Reading, Mass

Allwood, L M (1975) *Australian Schools: The Impact of the Australian Schools Commission* Australian International Press and Publications: Melbourne

+ Anderson, G J and Lauwerys, J A (1978) *Institutional Leadership for Educational Reform: The Atlantic Institute of Education* UNESCO: Paris

*Anderson, R, Spiro, R and Montague, W (eds) (1977) *Schooling and the Acquisition of Knowledge* Lawrence Erlbaum Associates: Hillsdale, NJ

Bamijoke (ed) (1977) *Proceedings of the Seminar on Teacher Education in Nigeria* Institute of Education: Zaria, Nigeria

*Barnes, D (1976) *From Communication to Curriculum* Penguin Books: Harmondsworth

Bassett, G W (1978) *1978 Review of Teacher Education in Queensland* Report of the Committee appointed by the Board of Advanced Education and the Board of Teacher Education to advise on desirable developments in Teacher Education in Queensland: Brisbane

*Batten, M (1979) *Report of a National Evaluation of the Development Program* Schools Commission Evaluation Studies, Schools Commission: Canberra

Becker, H (1971) *Personal Change and Adult Life* Routledge and Kegan Paul: London

Beckne, R (1975) *The Working Environment in School: A Summary of the SIA Report* National Board of Education: Stockholm

+ Bélanger, M (1976) *Innovation in INSET: Canada* OECD: Paris

Belbenoit, G (1976) *Innovation in INSET: France* OECD: Paris

Bennett, W S and Hockenstad, M C (1973) Full time people — workers and concepts of the professional *in* Halmos (1973)

Berliner, D C and Rosenshine B (1977) The acquisition of knowledge in the classroom *in* Anderson *et al* (1977)

*Berman, P and McLaughlin, M W (1978) *Federal Programs Supporting Educational Change* The Rand Corporation: Santa Monica, Ca

Birdsall, L (1979) *Network: A Schedule of Activities for Spring-Summer 1979* California Staff Development Network: Sacramento, Ca

Bishop, A J and Whitfield, R C (1972) *Situations in Teaching* McGraw-Hill: London

Block, J H and Anderson, L W (1975) *Mastery Learning in Classroom Instruction* Macmillan: New York

Block, J H and Burns, R B (1976) Mastery learning *in* Shulman (1976)

Bloom, B S (1968) *Learning for Mastery* Centre for the Study of Evaluation of Instruction Programs: University of California at Los Angeles

Bloom, B S (1976) *Human Characteristics and School Learning* McGraw-Hill: New York

Bloomer, J (1975) OUTSIDER: pitfalls and payoffs of simulation gaming *in* Gibbs and Howe (1975)

Bolam, R (1973) *Induction Programmes for Probationary Teachers* A report on an action research project, School of Education: University of Bristol

*Bolam, R (1978) *Innovations in the In-Service Education and Training of Teachers* OECD: Paris

Bolam, R (ed) (forthcoming) *School-Focused INSET* Heinemann: London

Bolam, R and Baker, K (eds) (1975) *The Teacher Induction Pilot Schemes (TIPS) Project: 1975 National Conference Report* School of Education: University of Bristol

Bolam R, Baker, K and McMahon, A (1979) *Teacher Induction Pilot Schemes: Final National Evaluation Report* School of Education: University of Bristol

Bolam, R and Porter, J (1976) *Innovation in INSET: The United Kingdom* OECD: Paris

Bolam, R, Smith, G and Canter, H (1979) *LEA Advisers and the Mechanisms of Innovation* National Foundation for Educational Research: Slough

Bone, T R (1976) Current developments in teacher education in Scotland *in* Lomax (1976)

Borich, G (1978) *The Evaluation of INSET for Teachers in the United States* OECD: Paris

Bradley, H W (1978) *Cost and Efficient Utilisation of INSET Resources in England and Wales* OECD: Paris

Brameld, T B (1955) *Philosophies of Education in Cultural Perspective* Holt, Rinehart and Winston: New York

Brim, O and Wheeler, S (1966) *Socialization after Childhood: Two Essays* John Wiley and Sons: New York

Broudy, H S (1972) *The Real World of the Public Schools* Harcourt, Brace, Jovanovich: New York

Broudy, H S (1972) *A Critique of Performance-Based Teacher Education* PBTE Series, American Association of Colleges for Teacher Education: Washington, D C

Brown, G (1975) *Microteaching: A Programme of Teaching Skills* Methuen: London

Brubacher, J S (1962) *Modern Philosophies of Education* McGraw-Hill: New York

Butts, D C and Megarry, J (1977) Teaching educational technology at a distance *in* Hills and Gilbert (1977)

Cameron, P (1978) *Cost and Efficient Utilisation of Resources in Australia* OECD: Paris

Cameron, P (1978) *The Cost and Use of Resources for In-Service Education* Schools Commission Services and Development Program, Discussion/Review Paper No 2, Schools Commission: Canberra

Campbell, W J (1975) *Being a Teacher in Australian State Government Schools* Australian Advisory Committee on Research and Development in Education, Report No 5, Australian Government Publishing Service: Canberra

Campbell, W J, Evans, G T, Philp, H W S and Levis, D S (1977) *The STEP Project: A Study of Three-year Primary Teacher Education Programs* Report to the Commission on Advanced Education: Canberra

Campbell, W J and Robinson, N M (1979) *What Australian Society Expects of Its Schools, Teachers and Teaching* Department of Education, University of Queensland: Brisbane

Casciani, J and Megarry, J (1978) First steps toward a simulation of dialect change pp 101-9 *in* Megarry (1978c)

Castle, E (1970) *The Teacher* Oxford University Press: London

Clawson, J (1980) Mentoring in managerial careers *in* Derr (1980)

Claxton, G (1978) *The Little Ed Book* Routledge and Kegan Paul: London

Collins, C W and Hughes, P W (1979) Expectations of secondary schools: a study of the views of students, teachers and parents *in* Williams (1979)

Collins, J F, Porter, K, Beam, A and Moss, D (1979) *Sources and Resources: An Annotated Bibliography on Inservice Education* National Council of States on Inservice Education: Syracuse, NY

Conant, J B (1963) *The Education of American Teachers* McGraw-Hill: New York, Toronto, London

Coons, J E and Sugarman, S D (1978) *Education by Choice: The Case for Family Control* University of California Press: California

Cope, E (1971) *School Experience in Teacher Education* School of Education: University of Bristol

*Cope, E (1975) Research into the practical elements of teacher training, with special reference to the supervisory processes and student learning *in* Society for Research into Higher Education (1975) (see Section II)

Corrigan, D, Haberman, M and Howey, K (1979) *Adult Learning and Development: Implications for In-Service Teacher Education: An American Viewpoint* OECD: Paris

Cove, M (1975) Implications of the Australian Schools Commission for teacher development *in* Allwood (1975)

Cremin, L C (1976) *Public Education* Basic Books: New York

Cropley, A J and Dave, R H (1978) *Lifelong Education and the Training of Teachers* Pergamon Press and the UNESCO Institute for Education: Oxford

Cross, D (1979) Talking past one another's ears: a simulation debriefing dialogue pp 24-30 *in* Megarry (1979b)

Cruickshank, D R (1971) Teacher education looks at simulation: a review of selected uses and research results pp 185-203 *in* Tansey (1971)

Cruickshank, D R and Telfer, R A (1979) *Simulation and Games: An ERIC Bibliography* (Bibliographies on educational topics no 11) ERIC Clearinghouse on Teacher Education: Washington, D C

Dearman, N D and Plisko, V W (1979) *The Condition of Education* U S Government Printing Office: Washington, D C

Deen, N and Boeder-Rijdes, E S (1976) *Innovation in INSET: The Netherlands* OECD: Paris

Dennis, J R and Gaede, O R (1977) Simulation gaming in the teacher education curriculum *Illinois Series on Educational Applications of Computers Number 18:* Urbana, Ill

Dent, H C (1977) *The Training of Teachers in England and Wales: 1800-1975* Hodder and Stoughton: London

Derr, C (ed) (1980) *Work, Family and Career: New Frontiers in Theory and Research* Praeger: New York

Dow, G (1979) *Learning to Teach: Teaching to Learn* Routledge and Kegan Paul: London

Dreeben, R (1970) *The Nature of Teaching* Scott, Foresman and Company: Glenview, Ill
*Dunkin, M J and Biddle, B J (1974) *The Study of Teaching* Holt, Rinehart and Winston:
    New York

Eisenberger, K W (1979) *Demographic Change: The Cost of Decline* Washington, D C
Ekholm, M (1976) *Social Development in School: Summary and Excerpts* Reports from
    the Institute of Education, University of Göteberg **48**:13
Eklund, H (1978) *The Evaluation of INSET for Teachers in Sweden* OECD: Paris
Elam, Stanley (1971) *What is the State of the Art? PBTE Series* American Association of
    Colleges for Teacher Education: Washington, D C
Elliott, J (1976) *Developing Hypotheses about Classrooms from Teachers' Practical
    Constructs: An Account of the Work of the Ford Teaching Project* Study Group on
    Evaluation, University of North Dakota: Grand Forks, North Dakota
Elliott, J (1978) Classroom research: science or common sense *in* McAleese and Hamilton
    (1978)
Elliott, J and Adelman, C (1976) *Innovation at the Classroom Level* Course E203 Unit 23,
    Open University Press: Milton Keynes
Elliott, J and MacDonald, B (1972) *People in Classrooms* CARE Occasional Publications
    No 1: University of East Anglia, Norwich
Eraut, M (1972) *In-Service Education for Innovation* National Council for Educational
    Technology: London
*Etzioni, A (ed) (1969) *The Semi-Professions and their Organization* Free Press: New
    York
Evans, C (1979) *The Mighty Micro* Victor Gollancz: London

Fafunwa, B (1976) *The Six-Year Project Report (I)* University of Ife: Nigeria
Fafunwa, B (1977) The problem of recruitment retention, promotion, transfer and
    discipline of teachers *in* Bamijoke (1977)
Fedida, S (1978) Viewdata in education pp 78-86 *in* Howe and Romiszowski (1978)
Ferguson, S (1977) TORESIDE COMPREHENSIVE SCHOOL: a simulation game for
    teachers in training pp 148-59 *in* Megarry (1977)
*Flanders, N A (1970) *Analyzing Teacher Behaviour* Addison-Wesley: Reading, Mass
Freidson, E (1970) *The Profession of Medicine* Dodd, Mead and Co: New York
Freidson, E (ed) (1971) *The Professions and their Prospects* Sage Publications: Beverly
    Hills
Fullan, M, Miles, M and Taylor, G (1978) *OD in Schools: the State of the Art: Volume 1*
    Department of Sociology, Ontario Institute for Studies in Education: Toronto
Fuller, F and Brown, O (1975) Becoming a teacher *in* Ryan (1975)

Galloway, C (1976) *Psychology for Learning and Teaching* McGraw-Hill: New York
Garcia, G M J (1976) *La Universidad Nacional de Educacion a Distancia, Su
    Implantacion y Dessarrollo Inicial* Ediciones CEAC, SA: Barcelona
Gibbs, G I and Howe, A (eds) (1975) *Academic Gaming and Simulation in Education and
    Training* Kogan Page: London
Gleeson, D (1977) *Identity and Structure: Issues in the Sociology of Education* Studies in
    Education, Nafferton Press: Driffield
Gliessman, D, Pugh, R C and Perry, F L (1974) *Effects of a Protocol Film Series in Terms
    of Learning Outcomes and Reactions of Users* National Center for the Development
    of Training Materials in Teacher Education, Indiana University : Bloomington
*Goble, N M and Porter, J F (1977) *The Changing Role of the Teacher* UNESCO: Paris
Goldman, R J (1976) Innovations in teacher education in Australia *in* Lomax (1976)
Gosden, P H J H (1972) *The Evolution of a Profession* Basil Blackwell: Oxford
Gosling, W (1978) *Microcircuits, Society and Education* (CET Occasional Paper No 8)
    Council for Educational Technology: London
Graves, J *et al* (1980) Career stages *in* Derr (1980)
Gregersen, J (1978) *The Evaluation of INSET for Teachers in Denmark* OECD: Paris
*Gross, N, Giacquinta, J B and Bernstein, M (1971) *Implementing Organizational
    Innovations* Harper and Row: New York

Habermas, J (1972) Technology and science as 'ideology' *in* Habermas (1972) *Towards a Rational Society* Heinemann: London

Habermas, J (1974) *Introduction to Theory and Practice* Heinemann: London

Halmos, P (1965) *The Task of the Counsellor* Constable: London

Halmos, P (1970) *The Personal Service Society* Constable: London

Halmos, P (1971) Sociology and the personal service professions *in* Freidson (1971)

*Halmos, P (ed) (1973) *Professionalisation and Social Change* (The Sociological Review Monograph 20) University of Keele

Hamilton, D *et al* (eds) (1977) *Beyond the Numbers Game* Macmillan Education: London

Hanson, J (1964) The spirit of the teacher *in* Hanson *et al* (1964)

Hanson, J *et al* (1964) *Nigerian Education* Longman: Nigeria

Hanson, J and Brembeck, C (1966) *Education and the Development of Nations* Holt, Rinehart and Winston: New York

Hargreaves, D H, Hester, S K and Mellor, F J (1975) *Deviance in Classrooms* Routledge and Kegan Paul: London

Harker, W J (1979) *The Saanich Teacher Training Programme Innovation* UNESCO: Geneva

Harris, W J A (1975) *The Distance Tutor* (Manchester Monographs Number 3) University of Manchester

Harris, W J A and Williams, J D S (1977) *A Handbook on Distance Education* (Manchester Monographs Number 7) University of Manchester

Haug, M R (1973) Deprofessionalization: an alternative hypothesis for the future *in* Halmos (1973)

*Havelock, R G (1969) *Planning for Innovation through Dissemination and Utilization of Knowledge* Centre for Research on Utilization of Scientific Knowledge, Institute for Social Research: Ann Arbor, Michigan

Havelock, R G (1973) *The Change Agent's Guide to Innovation in Education* Educational Technology Publications: Englewood Cliffs, NJ

Havelock, R G and Havelock, M C (1973) *Training for Change Agents: A Guide to the Design of Training Programs in Education and Other Fields* Centre for Research on Utilization of Scientific Knowledge, Institute for Social Research: Ann Arbor, Michigan

Hemphill, J K *et al* (1962) *Administrative Performance and Personality* Bureau of Publications, Columbia University: New York

Hencke, D (1978) *Colleges in Crisis* Penguin Books: Harmondsworth

Henderson, E (1980) The evaluation of an Open University course *in* McCabe (1980)

Henricson, S E (1979) *Cost and Efficient Utilisation of INSET Resources in Sweden* OECD: Paris

Hercik, V (1976) European models of teacher education in developing countries *in* Lomax (1976)

Hills, P and Gilbert, J (1977) *Aspects of Educational Technology XI* Kogan Page: London

Holmberg, B (1977) *Distance Education: A Survey and Bibliography* Kogan Page: London

Holmberg, B (1979) Distance study in educational theory and practice *in* Page and Whitlock (1979)

Hooper, R (1977) *National Development Programme in Computer Assisted Learning: Final Report of the Director* Council for Educational Technology: London

Houston, W R (1972) *Performance Education: Strategies and Resources for Developing a Competency-Based Teacher Education Programme* New York State Education Department: Albany, NY

Howe, A and Romiszowski, A J (1978) *International Yearbook of Educational and Instructional Technology 1978/79* Kogan Page: London

Hoyle, E (1969) *The Role of the Teacher* Routledge and Kegan Paul: London

Hoyle, E (1969) The strategies of curriculum change *in* Watkins (1973)

Hubbard, G (1979) The need for diversity of provision pp 80-5 *in* Schuller and Megarry (1979)

Hudgins, G G (1974) *A Catalog of Concepts in the Pedagogical Domain of Teacher Education* State Education Department: Albany, NY

Hughes, E (1958) *Men and Their Work* Free Press: New York

Husén, T *et al* (1973) *Svensk Skola i Internationell Belysning: Naturvetenskapliga Amnen* (Swedish Schools: An International Comparison in Science) Stockholm

+ IEC (1979) *Writing for Distance Education*: *Manual* and *Samples* International Extension College: Cambridge

Illich, I (1971) *De-Schooling Society* Calder and Boyars: London

Ingvarson, L (1977) *Some Effects of the Teacher Development Program in Victoria* Monash University: Melbourne

Jackson, P (1968) *Life in Classrooms* Holt, Rinehart and Winston: New York

Jenkins, D (1977) Saved by the bell *and* Saved by the army *in* Hamilton *et al* (1977)

Jenkins, W I (1978) *Policy Analysis* Martin Robertson: London

Joyce, B (ed) (1978) *Involvement: A Study of Shared Governance in Teacher Education* National Dissemination Center: Syracuse University, NY

Joyce, B (ed) (1980) *Lessons Learned from the History of Change in Education* The University of Nebraska Press: Omaha, Nebraska

Joyce, B, Bush, R, Marsh, D and McKibbin, M (1979) *The California Staff Development Study: Instruments and Guidelines for Implementation in Schools* Booksend Laboratory: Palo Alto, Ca

Joyce, B, Bush, R, Marsh, D, Meyers, H and Birdsall, L (1979) *Recommendations for the Evaluation of Staff Development in California: Report of a Preparatory Study* Office of Program Evaluation and Research, California State Department of Education: Sacramento, Ca

*Joyce, B, Howey, K and Yarger, S (1976) *Issues to Face* ISTE Report I, National Dissemination Center: Syracuse University, NY

Joyce, B, Howey, K and Yarger, S (1977) *Preservice teacher education* Consolidated Press: Palo Alto, Ca

Judge, H G (1974) *School is not yet Dead* Longman: London

Katz, L G (1974) Issues and problems in teacher education *in* Spodek (1974)

Keller, F S and Sherman, J G (1974) *The Keller Plan Handbook* W A Benjamin: Menlo Park, Ca

Kirkland, G H K (1978) Managing innovation: simulations for potential innovators pp 116-24 *in* McAleese (1978)

*Koerner, J D (1963) *The Miseducation of American Teachers* Houghton Mifflin: Boston, Mass

Kolawole, D (ed) (1975-78) *Mobile Teacher Trainers' Reports* Institute of Education: Zaria, Nigeria

Kolawole, D (1976) *General Information on Primary Education Improvement Project* Institute of Education: Zaria

Kolawole, D (ed) (1977) *Proceedings of the State Co-ordinators' Conference* Institute of Education: Zaria

Kolawole, D (1978) *The Effects of Environmental Stimulation on Cognitive Learning in Creative Activities* Ahmadu Bello University Research Board: Zaria

Kuhn, T S (1970) *The Structure of Scientific Revolutions* (2nd Edition) Chicago University Press: Chicago

*Lacey, C (1977) *The Socialization of Teachers* Methuen: London

Lander, R (1978) *Profeter i Egen Skola* (Prophets in Your Own School) Report No 168, Institute of Education, University of Göteberg

Langford, G (1978) *Teaching as a Profession* Manchester University Press: Manchester

Larsson, T (1978) The Local School Development Planning and Evaluation Project *in* Eklund (1978)

*Lauwerys, J (ed) (1969) *Teachers and Teaching* Evans: London

Lawrence, G (1974) *Patterns of Effective In-Service Education* Department of Education: Tallahassee, Fla

*Lomax, D E (ed) (1976) *European Perspectives in Teacher Education* John Wiley and Sons: London

*Lortie, D C (1975) *Schoolteacher: A Sociological Study* University of Chicago Press: Chicago, Ill

*Lynch, J (1979) *The Reform of Teacher Education in the United Kingdom* Society for Research into Higher Education: University of Surrey, Guildford

Macleod, G and McIntyre, D (1977) Towards a model for microteaching *in* McIntyre, Macleod and Griffiths (1977)

Macmillan, C J B and Nelson, T W (eds) (1968) *Concepts of Teaching* Rand McNally: Chicago

Magoon, A J (1976) Teaching and performance-based teacher education *in* Lomax (1976)

Mangers, D *et al* (1978) *The School Principal: Recommendations for Effective Leadership* Assembly Education Committee: Sacramento, Ca

Marklund, S and Bergendal, G (1979) *Trends in Swedish Educational Policy* The Swedish Institute: Stockholm

Marklund, S and Eklund, H (1976) *Innovation in In-service Education and Training of Teachers: Sweden* OECD: Paris

Marklund, S and Söderberg, P (1967) *The Swedish Comprehensive School* Longman: London

Marsh, D and Carey, L (1979) *The Involvement of Universities in Inservice Education* American Association of Colleges for Teacher Education: Washington, DC

Mayhew, L B (1970) *Graduate and Professional Education 1980* McGraw-Hill: New York

*McAleese, R (1978) *Perspectives on Academic Gaming and Simulation 3* Kogan Page: London

McAleese, R and Hamilton, D (eds) (1978) *Understanding Classroom Life* National Foundation for Educational Research: Slough

McCabe, C M (ed) (1980) *Evaluating INSET* National Foundation for Educational Research: Slough

McIntyre, D, Macleod, G and Griffiths, R (eds) (1977) *Investigations of Microteaching* Croom Helm: London

McIntyre, D and Macleod, G (1978) The characteristics and uses of systematic classroom observation *in* McAleese and Hamilton. (1978)

Megarry, J (ed) (1977) *Aspects of Simulation and Gaming* Kogan Page: London

Megarry, J (1978a) Developments in simulation and gaming pp 22-3 *in* Howe and Romiszowski (1978)

Megarry, J (1978b) Retrospect and prospect pp 187-207 *in* McAleese (1978)

*Megarry, J (ed) (1978c) *Perspectives on Academic Gaming and Simulation 1 & 2* Kogan Page: London

Megarry, J (1978d) Computer-based educational games and simulations in schools: a feasibility study pp 169-78 *in* Megarry (1978c)

Megarry, J (1979a) Home environment and learning: educational technology at a distance pp 77-87 *in* Page and Whitlock (1979)

*Megarry, J (ed) (1979b) *Perspectives on Academic Gaming and Simulation 4* Kogan Page: London

Merrow, J M (1975) *Politics of Competence: A Review of Competency-Based Teacher Education* National Institute of Education, Department of Health, Education and Welfare: Washington, DC

Miles, M B (ed) (1964) *Innovation in Education* Columbia University Teachers' College: New York

Mitchell, P D (1978) EDSIM: a classroom in a computer for lesson planning practice pp 191-204 *in* Megarry (1978c)

Moore, W E (1970) *The Professions: Roles and Rules* Russell Sage Foundation: New York

Morris, Van Cleve (1961) *Philosophy and the American School, an Introduction to the Philosophy of Education* Houghton Mifflin: Boston, Mass

Mulford, W (1979) *The Role and Training of INSET Trainers: An Interim Report* OECD: Paris

Murdoch, R P (1978) *Professional Development: The Induction and Education of Beginning Teachers* Research Report, Christchurch Teachers' College: Christchurch, New Zealand

Musgrove, F and Taylor, P H (1969) *Society and the Teacher's Role* Routledge and Kegan Paul: London

Nduka, O (1964) *Western Education and the Nigerian Cultural Background* Oxford University Press: Ibadan, Nigeria

Niblett, W R, Fairhurst, J and Humphreys, D W (1975) *The University Connection* National Foundation for Educational Research: Slough

Nicholson, A and Joyce, B (1976) *The Literature on In-Service Teacher Education* (ISTE Report III) National Dissemination Center: Syracuse University, NY

*Nisbet, J (ed) (1974) *Creativity of the School* OECD: Paris

Olsen, T P (1978) The Lundebjerg Project: a study of school-based INSET *in* Gregersen (1978)

Omojuwa, R (1974) *MTT Conference Report* Institute of Education: Zaria, Nigeria

Ozmon, Howard (1972) *Dialogue in the Philosophy of Education* Charles E Merrill: Columbus, Ohio

Page, G T and Whitlock, Q (1979) *Aspects of Educational Technology XIII: Educational Technology Twenty Years On* Kogan Page: London

Parlett, M and Hamilton, D (1973) Evaluation as illumination *in* Tawney (1973)

Passow, A H *et al* (1976) *The National Case Study: An Empirical Comparative Study of Twenty-One Educational Systems* International Studies in Evaluation, International Association for the Evaluation of Educational Achievement: Stockholm/New York

+Perraton, H D (1973) *The Techniques of Writing Correspondence Courses* International Extension College/National Extension College: Cambridge

Perrott, E (1977) *Microteaching in Higher Education: Research Development and Practice* Society for Research into Higher Education: University of Surrey, Guildford

Perry, G and Perry, P (1969) *Case Studies in Teaching* Pitman: London

*Perry, W (1970) *Open University: A Personal Account by the First Vice-Chancellor* Open University Press: Milton Keynes

Peshkin, A (1978) *Growing Up American: Schooling and the Survival of the Community* University of Chicago Press: Chicago

Peters, R S (1968) Must an educator have an aim? *in* Macmillan and Nelson (1968)

Peters, R S (1977) *Education and the Education of Teachers* Routledge and Kegan Paul: London

Pigors, P and Pigors, F (1961) *Case Method in Human Relations: The Incident Process* McGraw-Hill: New York

*Race, P and Brooks, D (1980) *Perspectives on Academic Gaming and Simulation 5* Kogan Page: London

+ Read, G A (1978) *CYCLOPS — An Audio Visual System: A Brief Description* Open University Press: Milton Keynes

Rendell, F and Bell, H S (1980) Why topic studies? *in* Tymister (1980)

Richardson, E (1973) *The Teacher, the School and the Task of Management* Heinemann: London

Rogers, E M and Shoemaker, F F (1971) *Communication of Innovations: A Cross Cultural Approach* Collier-Macmillan: London

Rosner, B (1972) *The Power of Competency-Based Teacher Education: A Report* Allyn and Bacon: Boston, Mass

Roth, J (1963) *Timetables: Structuring the Passage of Time in Hospital, Treatment and Other Careers* Bobbs-Merrill: Indianapolis

Rowntree, D and Connors, B (1979) *Developing Self-Instructional Teaching* Open University Press: Milton Keynes

Rubin, L and Howey, K (1976) *Innovation in INSET: United States* OECD: Paris

*Ryan, K (1975) *Teacher Education* (74th Yearbook of the National Society for the Study of Education, Part II) University of Chicago Press: Chicago

Sakamoto, T (1980) Development and use of DESK TOP TEACHING simulation game *in* Race and Brooks (1980)

Schein, E H (1972) *Professional Education: Some New Directions* McGraw-Hill: New York

Schmuck, R A (1974) Intervention for strengthening the school's creativity *in* Nisbet (1974)

Schmuck, R A, Murray, D, Smith, M A, Schwartz, M and Runkel, P (1975) *Consultation for Innovative Schools: Organization Development for a Multiunit Structure* CEPM College of Education, University of Oregon: Eugene, Oregon

*Schmuck, R A, Runkel, P, Arends, J H and Arends, R I (1977) *The Second Handbook of Organization Development in Schools* Mayfield: Palo Alto, Ca

Schmuck, R A, Runkel, P, Saturen, S, Martell, R and Derr, C B (1972) *Handbook of Organization Development in Schools* National Press Books: Palo Alto, Ca

Schuller, T and Megarry, J (eds) (1979) *World Yearbook of Education 1979: Recurrent Education and Lifelong Learning* Kogan Page: London

Schutz, A (1967) *The Phenomenology of the Social World* Northwestern University Press: Evanston, Ill

Sherwin, S (1974) *Teacher Education: A Status Report* Educational Testing Service: Princeton, NJ

Shugre, M E (1973) *Performance-Based Education and the Subject Matter Fields* American Association of Colleges for Teacher Education (AACTE): Washington,DC

Shulman, L S (ed) (1976) *Review of Research in Education 1976* American Educational Research Association, Peacock: Itasca, Ill

Skilbeck, M, Evans, G T and Harvey, J (1976) *Innovation in INSET: Australia* OECD: Paris

Skilbeck, M, Evans, G T and Harvey, J (1977) *In-service Education and Training — Australian Innovations* Curriculum Development Centre: Canberra

Skilbeck, M, Ingvarson, L, Edgar, W, Merrill, P and Beacham, J (1979) *School-Focused and School-Based INSET in Australia* OECD: Paris

Smith, B O (1969) *Teachers for the Real World* American Association of Colleges for Teacher Education (AACTE): Washington, DC

Smith, B O (ed) (1971) *Research in Teacher Education: A Symposium* Prentice-Hall: New York

Smith, B O, Orlosky, D E and Borg, J (1973) *Handbook on the Development and Use of Protocol Materials for Teacher Education* Panhandle Area Educational Co-operative: Chipley, Fla

Smith, K C (1979) *External Studies at New England: A Silver Jubilee Review 1955-1979* University of New England: Armidale, NSW

Smith, L and Schumacher, S (1972) *Extended Pilot Trials of the Aesthetic Education Program: A Qualitative Description, Analysis and Evaluation* CEMREL Inc: USA

*Smith, L M and Keith, P M (1971) *Anatomy of Educational Innovation* John Wiley and Sons: New York, London, Sydney, Toronto

Solary, T (1964) *Teacher Training in Nigeria 1840-1960* Africana: New York

Spodek, B (1974) *Teacher Education* National Association for the Education of Young Children: Washington, D C

Stake, R (1976) *Evaluating Educational Programmes* OECD: Paris

*Stenhouse, L (1975) *An Introduction to Curriculum Research and Development* Heinemann: London

Stones, E A and Morris, S (1972) *Teaching Practice: Problems and Perspectives* Methuen: London

Stonier, T (1979) Changes in western society: educational implications pp 31-44 *in* Schuller and Megarry (1979)

Tansey, P J (ed) (1971) *Educational Aspects of Simulation* McGraw-Hill: London

Tawney, D (ed) (1973) *Evaluation in Curriculum Development: Twelve Case Studies* Macmillan Education: London

Tawney, D (ed) (1976) *Curriculum Evaluation Today: Trends and Duplications* Macmillan: London

Taylor, J K and Dale, J R (1971) *A Survey of Teachers in their First Year of Service* School of Education: University of Bristol

Taylor, W (1969) *Society and the Education of Teachers* Faber and Faber: London

Taylor, W (1969) Recent research on the education of teachers: an overview *in* Taylor (1969)

Taylor, W (ed) (1969) *Towards a Policy for the Education of Teachers* Butterworth: London

Taylor, W (1969 and 1973) *Heading for Change* Routledge and Kegan Paul: London

Taylor, W (1972) *Theory into Practice* Harlech Television Publications: Bristol

Taylor, W (1974) Teacher education *in Encyclopedia Brittanica*

*Taylor, W (1978) *Research and Reform in Teacher Education* National Foundation for Educational Research: Slough

Taylor, W and Moore, S (1970) *...And Gladly Teach* Harlech Television Publications: Bristol

Tisher, R P, Fyfield, J A and Taylor, S M (1978) *Beginning to Teach Vol I The Induction of Teachers: A Bibliography and Description of Activities in Australia and the UK. Report on Stage I of the Teacher Induction Project* ERDC Report No 15, Australian Government Publishing Service: Canberra

Tisher, R P, Fyfield, J A and Taylor, S M (1979) *Beginning to Teach Vol II The Induction of Beginning Teachers in Australia: Research Report on Stage II of the Teacher Induction Project* ERDC Report No 20, Australian Government Publishing Service: Canberra

Tropp, A (1957) *The School Teachers* Heinemann: London

Turner, R L (1973) *A General Catalog of Teaching Skills* State Education Department: Albany, NY

Turner, R L (1975) An overview of research in teacher education *in* Ryan (1975)

Turney, C, Clift, J C, Dunkin, M J and Trail, R D (1973) *Microteaching: Research, Theory and Practice* Sydney University Press: Sydney, NSW

Twelker, P A (1971) Simulation and media pp 131-4 *in* Tansey (1971)

Tymister, H J (ed) (1980) *Deutschunterricht im 5 bis 10 Schuljahr: Praxis und Theorie des Unterrichtens* (German Education from the Fifth to the Tenth School Year: Theory and Practice) Urban und Schwarzenberg: Munich

van Maanan, J (1980) The career game: organizational rules of play *in* Derr (1980)

van Velzen, W (ed) (1979) *Developing an Autonomous School* Dutch Catholic School Council: The Hague

Venables, P (1979) The Open University and the future of continuing education pp 271-84 *in* Schuller and Megarry (1979)

Vincente-Missoni, M (ed) (1978) *Teachers' Centres in Italy* OECD: Paris

Vinde, P (1967) *The Swedish Civil Service, An Introduction* Ministry of Finance: Stockholm

Walker, D R F (1978) Computer-based games and simulations in geography: a problem in innovation and diffusion pp 180-5 *in* McAleese (1978)

Waller, W (1932) *The Sociology of Teaching* John Wiley and Sons: New York

Watkins, R (ed) (1973) *In-Service Training: Structure and Content* Ward Lock Educational: London

Wheeler, S (1966) Structure of formally organized socialization settings *in* Brim and Wheeler (1966)

Whitty, G and Young, M F D (eds) (1976) *Explorations in the Politics of School Knowledge* Nafferton Press: Driffield

Wilder and Fodeke (1977) *PEIP Coordinators' Report* Ministry of Education: Sokoto, Nigeria

Williams, B R (1979) *Education, Training and Employment* Report of the Committee of Inquiry into Education and Training, Volume 1, Australian Government Publishing Service: Canberra

Wilson, J (1975) *Educational Theory and the Preparation of Teachers* National Foundation for Educational Research: Slough

Wirtz, W (1977) *On Further Examination* College Board: New Jersey

Yarger, S, Howey, K and Joyce, B (1980) *Inservice Teacher Education* Consolidated Press: Palo Alto, Ca

Young, E (1977) *Activities for Primary Classes* Oxford University Press: Nigeria

Young, M F D (ed) (1971) *Knowledge and Control* Collier-Macmillan: London

Zoll, A A (1969) *Dynamic Management Education* Addison-Wesley: London

Section II: Official Publications

Benue State Ministry of Education (1977) *Joint Consultative Reference Committee on Primary Education Report* Ministry of Education: Makurdi, Nigeria

Centre for the Study of Evaluation (1977) *Evaluation of the California Early Childhood Education Program* (Vol 1) UCLA Graduate School of Education: Los Angeles, Ca

Committee on Performance-Based Teacher Education (1974) *Achieving the Potential of Performance-Based Teacher Education: Recommendations* (PBTE Series) American Association of Colleges for Teacher Education (AACTE): Washington, D C

Commonwealth Foundation (1977) *Education for Development* Occasional Paper XLIV: London

*Department of Education and Science (1972) *Teacher Education and Training* (The James Report) HMSO: London

Department of Education and Science (1972) *Education: A Framework for Expansion* (Cmnd 5174) HMSO: London

Department of Education and Science (1975) *A Language for Life: Report of the Committee of Enquiry appointed by the Secretary of State for Education and Science under the chairmanship of Sir Alan Bullock* (The Bullock Report) HMSO: London

Department of Education and Science (1976) *Helping New Teachers: The Induction Year* (Report on Education 84) DES: London

Department of Education and Science (1977) *In-Service Training: The Role of Colleges and Departments* (Report on Education 88) DES: London

Department of Education and Science (1977) *Teacher Induction: Pilot Schemes' Progress* (Report on Education 89) DES: London

Department of Education and Science (1977) *Education in Schools: A Consultative Document* (Cmnd 6869) HMSO: London

Department of Education and Science (1978) *Special Educational Needs: Report of the Committee of Enquiry into the education of handicapped children and young people under the chairmanship of Mary Warnock* (The Warnock Report) HMSO: London

Department of Education and Science (1978) *Higher Education into the 1990s: A Discussion Document* DES: London and SED: Edinburgh

Department of Education and Science (1978) *Primary Education in England: A Survey by HM Inspectors of Schools* HMSO: London

Department of Education and Science (1978) *Statistics Bulletin 78: Induction and In-Service Training of Teachers: 1978 Survey* DES: London

Department of Education and Science (1979) *Developments in the BEd Course: A Study Based on Fifteen Institutions* (HMI Series: Matters for Discussion 8) HMSO: London

*Department of Education and Science (1979) *Aspects of Secondary Education in England: A Survey by HM Inspectors of Schools* HMSO: London

Educational Institute of Scotland (1979) *Commission on Pay Comparability: EIS Submission* EIS: Edinburgh

Federal Ministry of Education (1970) *Educational Statistics* Government Printer: Lagos

Government of British Columbia (1978) *The Education and Training of Teachers in British Columbia* (The McGregor Report): Victoria

Harvard (1966) *The Graduate School of Education: Report of the Harvard Committee* Harvard University Press: Cambridge, Mass

Institute of Education (1975) *Primary School Syllabuses* Institute of Education: Zaria, Nigeria

National Association of Secondary-School Principals (1979) *The Senior High School Principal* (3 volumes) The Association: Reston, Virginia

National Board of Education (1976) *Educational Research and Development at the NBE* Stockholm

National Board of Education (1977) *Standardprovsresultat i Arskurs 6 i Sju Län* (Results of Standardized Achievement Tests in Grade 6 in Seven Countries) Pedagogiska Nämndens Verksamhets-Berättelse för 1976/77, Skolöverstyrelsen: Stockholm

National Board of Education (1978) *Enhetlig Skolstruktur och Likvärdig Utbildningsstandard* (Unified School Structure and Equal Educational Standards) Anslagäskanden för budgetåret 1979/80 i sammanfattning, Skolöverstyrelsen: Stockholm

Scottish Education Department (1965) *Primary Education in Scotland* HMSO: Edinburgh

Scottish Education Department (1977a) *The Structure of the Curriculum in the Third and Fourth Years of the Scottish Secondary School* (The Munn Report) HMSO: Edinburgh

Scottish Education Department (1977b) *Assessment for All? Report of the Committee to Review Assessment in the Third and Fourth Years of Secondary Education in Scotland* (The Dunning Report) HMSO: Edinburgh

Scottish Education Department (1978) *Learning to Teach* (The Sneddon Report) HMSO: Edinburgh

*Society for Research into Higher Education (1975) *How Long is a Piece of String?* (Pamphlet 4) SRHE: University of Surrey, Guildford

State Education Department of New York (1975) *Teacher Education Program Proposals* New York

+ UNESCO (1970) *Practical Guide to In-Service Teacher Training in Africa* UNESCO: Paris

+ UNESCO (1978) *Educational Reforms and Innovations in Africa* UNESCO: Paris

Section III: Articles, Periodicals and Working Papers

Aleyideino, S (1973) Primary Education Improvement Programme: the production and installation of new curricular materials in the northern states of Nigeria *Institute of Education Bulletin* (Zaria, Nigeria) **8** 2:12-16

Archer, E G *et al* (1977) Inservice training and primary schools: some Scottish experiences *The European Teacher* **15** 2: 14-20

Atkin, J M (1977) The Cartter Report on the leading schools of education, law and business *Change* **9** 2: 44-8

Atkin, J M (1978) Institutional self-evaluation versus national professional evaluation *Educational Researcher* **7** 10:3-7

Atkin, J M (1979) Educational accountability in the United States *Educational Analysis* **1** 1

Bates, T (1975) Survey of student use of broadcasting *Teaching at a Distance* **5**: 45-52

Benne, K (1970) Authority in education *Harvard Educational Review* **40** 3

Bloomer, J (1973) What have simulation and gaming got to do with programmed learning and educational technology? *Programmed Learning and Educational Technology* **10** 4:224-34

Borg, W R (1971) The Minicourse — a milestone on the road to better teaching *British Journal of Educational Technology* **2** 1:14-23

Borg, W R (1975) Protocol Materials as related to teacher performance and pupil achievement *Journal of Educational Research* **69** 1:23-30

Borg, W R and Stone, D R (1974) Protocol materials as a tool for changing teacher behaviour *Journal of Experimental Education* **43** 1:34-9

Bradley, H W and Eggleston, J F (1978) An induction year experiment *Educational Research* **20**:89-98

Burton, A (1977) Competency-based teacher education in the USA *Compare* **7** 1

Bush, R N (1975) Teacher education in the future: focus upon an entire school *Journal of Teacher Education* **26** 2:148-9

Bush, R N (1977) We know how to train teachers: why not do so! *Journal of Teacher Education* **28** 6:5-9

Christiansen, K (1979) How the ABZ GAMES work *Simulation/Games for Learning* **9** 3:107-16

Cronbach, L J (1975) Beyond the two disciplines of scientific psychology *American Psychologist* **15**:116-27

Cross, D (1978) A little Bullock goes a long way: a college of education simulation exercise *British Journal of Educational Technology* **9** 3:193-200

Cruickshank, D R *et al* (1979) The state of the art of simulation in teacher education *Simulation/Games for Learning* **9** 2:72-82

Davis, J (1979) The Educational Policy Information Centre (EPIC): an introduction and a review of the background of European co-operation *Educational Administration* **7** 1: 107-22

Dennis, J R (1979) Undergraduate programs to increase instructional computing in school *Association for Educational Data Systems Monitor* Jan/Feb/March: 8-11

Diehl, B (1979) Current simulation gaming in Australia *Simulation and Games* **10** 3:265-74

Elliott, J (1978) What is action research in schools? *Journal of Curriculum Studies* **10** 4:355-7

Emmer, E (1972/74) Direct observation of classroom behaviour *International Review of Education* **18** Special No: 474-90

Fenstermacher, G D (1978) A philosophical consideration of recent research on teacher effectiveness *Review of Research in Education* **6**

Frazier, E (1960) Talent and the school environment *Elementary School Journal* **60**:88-92

Garvey, B (1978) Microteaching: developing the concept for practical training *British Journal of Educational Technology* **9** 2:142-8

Glandon, N (1978) The TOTALITARIAN CLASSROOM GAME: reflections on authority *SAGSET Journal* **8** 1:24-9

Good, T L (1979) Teacher effectiveness in the elementary school *Journal of Teacher Education* **30** 2:52-64

*Grugeon, D (ed) *Teaching at a Distance* Quarterly journal published by the Open University: Milton Keynes

Hopkins, D and Lassa, P (1977) An evalaution of the Primary Education Improvement Project in Maiduguri Centre *ABU Institute of Education Bulletin* **12** 1:27

Howe, J A M and du Boulay, B (1979) Microprocessor-assisted learning: turning the clock back? *Programmed Learning and Educational Technology* **16** 3:240-6

Hoyle, E (1974) Professionality, professionalism and control in teaching *London Educational Review* **3** 2:15-17

Hunt, D and Joyce, B (1967) Teacher trainee personality and initial teaching style *American Educational Research Journal* **4** 3:47-63

Joyce, B (ed) (1978) From thought to action *Education Research Quarterly* **3** 4

Joyce, B, Howey, K and Yarger, S (1977) Preservice teacher education: impressions from a national survey *Journal of Teacher Education* **19** 1

Joyce, B and Showers, B (1980) Training ourselves: the message of research *Educational Leadership* **37** 4

Joyce, G, Wald, R and Weil, M (1972) Content for the training of educators: a structure for pluralism *Teachers' College Record* **73**, February 1972:371-91

Judge, H G (1975) How are we to get better teachers? *Higher Education Review* **8** 1:3-16

Judge, H G ((1977) American history and schooling: an English view *Oxford Review of Education* **3** 3:235-45

*Keegan, D J and Mitchell, I McD (1980) *Distance Education*

Keller, F S (1968) Goodbye teacher...*Journal of Applied Behaviour Analysis* **1**:79-88

Kersh, B Y (1962) The Classroom Simulator *Journal of Teacher Education* **13**:110-11

Kirst, M (1979) Organizations in shock and overload: the California public schools 1970-1980 *Educational Evaluation and Policy Analysis* **1** 4:27-30

Kolawole, D (1975) Primary Education Improvement Project: activities *Institute of Education Bulletin* (Zaria, Nigeria) **10**

Lomax, D (1969) A review of British research in teacher education *Review of Educational Research* **42** 3

Marsh, C J (1979) Teacher education simulations: the CHALLENGE OF CHANGE example *British Journal of Teacher Education* **5** 1:63-71

McKibbin, M and Joyce, B (1980) Psychological states and staff development *Theory into Practice* **19** 4

McLaughlin, M W and Marsh, D (1978) Staff development and school change *Teachers' College Record* **80** 1:69-94

McMahon, H F *et al* (1977) Student response to differentiated learning tasks in CML *Programmed Learning and Educational Technology* **14** 2:168-75

McNamara, D (1976) On returning to the chalk face: theory not into practice *British Journal of Teacher Education* **2** 2:147-60

McNamara, D and Desforges, C (1978) The social sciences, teacher education and the objectification of craft knowledge *British Journal of Teacher Education* **4** 1:17-36

*Megarry, J (ed) *Simulation/Games for Learning* Quarterly journal published by Kogan Page: London

Nathenson, M B (1979) Bridging the gap between teaching and learning at a distance *British Journal of Educational Technology* **10** 2:100-9

Newbury, J Mc (1978) The barrier between beginning and experienced teachers *Journal of Educational Administration* **16** 1:46-56

Nisbet, J, Shanks, D and Darling, J (1977) A survey of teachers' opinions on the primary diploma course in Scotland *Scottish Educational Studies* **9** 2

*Orlosky, D E (1974) The Protocol Materials Program *Journal of Teacher Education* **25** 4:291-7

Otto, E P, Gasson, I S H and Jordan, E (1979) Perceived problems of beginning teachers *South Pacific Journal of Teacher Education* **7** 1/2:28-33

Porter, J (1977) Further and higher education: the future of teacher education *Journal of Further and Higher Education* Summer 1977

Reiff, R (1971) The danger of the techni-pro: democratizing the human service professions *Social Policy* **2** May/June 1971: 82-4

Stenhouse, L (1971) The Humanities Curriculum Project: the rationale *Theory into Practice* **10:**154-62

Taylor, W (1979) Universities and the education of teachers *Oxford Review of Education* **5** 1:3-11

Twelker, P A (1967) Classroom simulation and teacher preparation *School Review* **75:**197-203

Walker, D and Graham, L (1979) Simulation games and the microcomputer *Simulation/Games for Learning* **9** 4:151-8

Wilson, R (1979) Looking towards the 1990s *British Journal of Educational Technology* **10** 1:45-51

Woodley, C P and Driscoll, L A (1974) The University of Colorado Protocol Project: a case study *Journal of Teacher Education* **25** 4:314-22

Zidonis, F and Fox, S (1975) Protocols of children's language *Theory into Practice* **14** 5:312-17

+ For details of availability of International Extension College, OECD, Open University and UNESCO publications contact:

International Extension College,
18 Brooklands Avenue,
Cambridge CB2 2HN,
England.

The Director,
Centre for Educational Research and Innovation,
OECD,
2 Rue Andre Pascal,
Paris 16,
France.

The Open University,
Walton Hall,
Milton Keynes MK7 6AA,
Buckinghamshire,
England.

UNESCO,
7 Place de Fontenoy,
75700 Paris,
France.

Section IV

Anderson, R, Spiro, R and Montague, W (eds) (1977) *Schooling and the Acquisition of Knowledge* Lawrence Erlbaum Associates: Hillsdale, NJ
This is a collection of papers that were originally presented at a conference in San Diego in 1975. The conference membership was deliberately interdisciplinary and consisted of psychologists, educationists and philosophers, and the central questions were concerned with knowledge; how it is organized, how it develops, how it is received and used and what instructional techniques can facilitate its growth. Each chapter consists of a main paper, a formal response to that paper and some general comments. The paper by Berliner and Rosenshine on the acquisition of knowledge in the classroom contains a useful review of the literature in that area and it provokes an interesting response from Philip Jackson who argues for more research involving observation in classrooms.

Barnes, D (1976) *From Communication to Curriculum* Penguin Books: Harmondsworth
Douglas Barnes draws on his analysis of classroom conversations to make his argument that the pattern of communication established between teacher and pupil is of crucial importance in the learning process. For this reason he feels that there should be a shift in teaching style away from formal methods which can have an inhibiting effect on children and towards an interactive pattern which will allow pupils to take a greater responsibility for their own learning. In particular he recommends that some class time should be spent in small group work and he includes some useful guidelines for teachers on the organization of such groups.

Batten, M (1979) *Report of a National Evaluation of the Development Program* Schools Commission Evaluation Studies, Schools Commission: Canberra
This report draws on documentation, interview and questionnaire data to present a comprehensive picture of the work done in the Development Program which was started in 1974 by the Australian Schools Commission, and which was designed to increase the range of INSET opportunities available to teachers and to raise INSET participation rates. It had three principal features: people from non-governmental as well as governmental schools and agencies were to be involved in planning and implementing programmes; decision-making was to be devolved to regional, school and community levels; and there was to be a variety of INSET provision. The report shows that there was strong support for school centred in-service work and it highlights the need for schools to plan a continuing programme for professional development.

Berman, P and McLaughlin, M W, (1978) *Federal Programs Supporting Educational Change* The Rand Corporation: Santa Monica, Ca
In 1978 the Rand Corporation in California completed an important four-year, two-part study of federal programmes supporting educational change. The first part of the study was concerned with the initiation and implementation of local change agent projects and in the course of this the research team surveyed 293 projects and conducted 29 case studies. Their major conclusion was that successful implementation of a project was characterized by mutual adaptation, a process which involved 'modification of both the project design and changes in the institutional setting and individual participants during the course of implementation'. This work is written up in a series of reports, of which Volume 1 contains a literature review and proposes a conceptual model of factors affecting change processes in school districts; Volume 2 contains an analysis of the survey data on the 293 projects; Volume 3 an analysis of the case study findings and Volume 4, entitled 'The Findings in Review', summarizes the findings.

In the second part of the study the research team examined the institutional and project factors that influenced the continuation of innovations once special funding had ended. They identified four sets of factors which were crucial to the successful implementation of projects; 'institutional motivation, project implementation strategies, institutional leadership and certain teacher characteristics.' The findings from this phase of the study are contained in Berman and McLaughlin, *Federal Programs Supporting*

Educational Change Volume VII: Factors Affecting Implementation and Continuation. Two useful papers based on the project findings have been published in the *Teachers' College Record*: McLaughlin, 'Implementation as mutual adaptation: change in classroom organisation' **77** 3:339-52, and McLaughlin and Marsh, 'Staff development and school change' **80** 1:69-95

Bolam, R (1978) *Innovations in the In-Service Education and Training of Teachers* OECD: Paris
This is a report on the first stage of a major project on in-service teacher education (INSET) which began in 1975 and which is jointly sponsored by OECD and the US National Institute of Education. It contains a synthesis of the reports on INSET which were commissioned from teacher educators in Australia, Canada, France, Germany and Switzerland, Italy, Japan, the Netherlands, Sweden, the United Kingdom and the United States. Bolam has presented a provisional conceptual framework for professional development in education and and has identified the main policy issues that emerged; these were contextual issues at national, regional, local and institutional level, and issues concerned with INSET users, INSET tasks, resources, strategies and methods.

Department of Education and Science (1972) *Teacher Education and Training* (The James Report) HMSO: London
This report refers specifically to teacher education in England and Wales but many of its recommendations are more widely applicable. The authors suggested that teacher education should be organized into three broad cycles or phases; personal education, pre-service and induction, and in-service education. The first cycle would be a two-year course of study for a recognized qualification after which students could decide to continue with education, move to another field of study or leave. The second cycle would also last for two years, comprising one year of theoretical and practical study in a college and a second induction year teaching in a school with help and advice from a professional tutor, and at least one day a week release to a professional centre for further study. Students who successfully completed the second cycle would enjoy graduate status and be registered teachers. The central proposal for the third cycle was that every teacher should be entitled to release with pay for in-service education and training for at least one term in every seven years throughout his career. Finally, it was proposed that each school should designate a member of staff as professional tutor with responsibility for the co-ordination of all second and third cycle work affecting the school.

Department of Education and Science (1979) *Aspects of Secondary Education in England: A Survey by HM Inspectors of Schools* HMSO: London
This report is the result of a national survey conducted by HMI in a 10 per cent sample of the secondary schools in England in 1975-78. The focus of the study was on provision for children in the 14-16 age group, ie the last two years of compulsory schooling, and four main aspects of education were examined; the development of language skills, the development of mathematical understanding and competence, the development of scientific skills and understanding and the personal and social development of the pupils. The report raises important questions that have implications not only for the pattern of school curriculum and organization but also for teacher education.

Dunkin, M J and Biddle, B J (1974) *The Study of Teaching* Holt, Rinehart and Winston: New York
This book about the teaching process is based directly on research evidence and the authors have presented a comprehensive review of those studies which have involved systematic observation of teaching in classrooms. There are six core chapters, each of which discusses research findings on a particular theme, eg classroom climate, the classroom as a social system. In addition, there is an introductory section which sets out a model for classroom teaching and which contains some general guidelines on statistics and research methodology. The implications of the research findings for teaching are discussed in the final section, which also contains recommendations for future work. This is a valuable reference work for teachers and researchers.

Etzioni, A (ed) (1969) *The Semi-Professions and their Organization* Free Press: New York

This book is a collection of essays which focus on what Etzioni has termed the 'semi-professions' eg nursing, teaching, social work. These are all occupations where people have employee status in an organization, and where a large majority of the workforce is female, factors discussed by the various authors in their essays on the controls and limitations that have prevented these semi-professions from acquiring full professional status. Lortie's chapter on elementary school teaching compares teaching with established professions along four dimensions: how the individual relates to the market; the nature of knowledge and skill possessed by members of the occupation; the relations established to the polity; and the extent to which those performing similar activities influence the careers of members of the occupation. It is an important contribution to the current debate about whether teaching ranks as a profession.

Flanders, N A (1970) *Analyzing Teacher Behaviour* Addison-Wesley: Reading, Mass

Flanders' central concern is to help teachers to learn more about their own teaching behaviour by developing ways of recording accurate and objective data about verbal interaction in the classroom. This book contains a description of his own ten-category system for interaction analysis and a discussion of its application and use. Though a large number of alternative ways of recording classroom behaviour have been developed since it was published, this book is still deservedly widely influential.

Goble, N M and Porter, J F (1977) *The Changing Role of the Teacher* UNESCO: Paris

This book is based on the documents and discussions that emanated from the 1975 International Conference on Education when the theme was 'the changing role of the teacher'. In the first section Goble examines the new influences and pressures on the teacher's role and argues that in future, schools and teachers will have to adopt a more supportive, less authoritarian stance and become more involved with the community. Porter then considers how teachers might best be trained to meet these new challenges, and suggests a three-phase model for teacher education, consisting of personal education, initial training and continuing education. Throughout, both authors have referred to the situation in developing as well as developed countries.

Gross, N, Giacquinta, J B and Bernstein, M (1971) *Implementing Organizational Innovations* Harper and Row: New York

An important study of the change process, which is based on a study of a major innovation involving a change in teacher roles introduced into the Cambire elementary school. The authors argue that the failure of innovations has too frequently been attributed to initial resistance by the members of an organization and that the problems of implementation have not been fully considered. They identify several factors which they feel prevented the successful implementation of the innovation at Cambire. The teachers did not clearly understand the innovation; they lacked the necessary knowledge and skills to carry it out; they did not have the required materials and equipment; the organizational arrangements in the school were incompatible with the innovation; there were no feedback procedures and lack of success in the early stages made the teachers resistant to change. Above all, the study highlights the crucial importance of the role of management in the implementation of innovations.

Halmos, P (ed) (1973) *Professionalisation and Social Change* (The Sociological Review Monograph 20) University of Keele

This is a collection of papers dealing with recent trends in the professions. Although none is specifically concerned with the teaching profession, a number of the papers deal with issues of professionalization which are very relevant to teaching. Most of these papers take a radical perspective and challenge the quest for more power, increased autonomy and higher status which together constitute one aspect of professionalization. Many of the papers challenge assumptions about the knowledge base of professional practice, and argue for more 'common-sense' and less technical knowledge. They also argue for a greater power equalization between practitioner and client, with the relationship rather than the expertise becoming the central concern of professional practice. Finally, the case is argued for a greater degree of professional accountability both to clients and to the public generally with the professions consequently yielding their individual and collective autonomy. The implementation of the changes proposed would reverse the professionalizing trends in teaching which have led to longer training, higher academic qualifications, the expansion of the research and development infrastructure, and the power of the organized profession to modify policy.

Havelock, R G (1969) *Planning for Innovation through Dissemination and Utilization of Knowledge* Centre for Research on Utilization of Scientific Knowledge, Institute for Social Research: Ann Arbor, Michigan
This report examines the innovation process and the ways in which knowledge is disseminated and employed, ie how it is transferred from a resource system to users. The first section of the study contains a comprehensive review of the literature on this topic and from this Havelock has identified three models that have been used to describe the utilization process, namely the research development and diffusion model, the social interaction model, and the problem-solving model. He then suggests a fourth 'linkage model' which combines aspects of the other three, and clarifies the interaction process between users and resource systems. This is an important reference work, which helps readers to understand the change process.

Joyce, B, Howey, K and Yarger, S (1976) *Issues to Face* ISTE Report I, National Dissemination Center: Syracuse University, NY
This is one of five reports on the first phase of a major study of in-service teacher education (ISTE) which began in 1975 and which has been sponsored by the American National Center for Education Statistics and the National Teacher Corps. The first phase of the study was co-ordinated by Bruce Joyce and Lucy Peck and it had a two-fold purpose; first, to identify the type of data that needed to be gathered about in-service and secondly to develop a conceptual framework about the structure of in-service. To do this, the research team adopted three main strategies: they reviewed the literature on in-service education; they acquired position papers on some of the central issues from recognized experts in the field; and they interviewed about 1000 school administrators and teachers and college personnel about major issues in in-service.

   The researchers identify four main dimensions or interlocking systems that form a structure for ISTE and argue that this complex system will have to be studied as a whole if there is to be real improvement in in-service. This conceptual model is discussed in detail in the first report; Report II contains the interview data, Report III a review of the literature and Reports IV and V contain the position papers.

Koerner, J D (1963) *The Miseducation of American Teachers* Houghton Mifflin: Boston, Mass
Koerner's book results from his two year investigative study into the education of American teachers and draws on interview and questionnaire data gathered during his visits to some 63 training institutions. He presents a critique of the system as it existed in the early 1960s and raises issues for discussion that are still relevant today. Some of his recommendations were that the study of education should be made more academically rigorous, that teachers should be paid on a differential basis according to their individual performance in the classroom, that some system of standard qualifying examinations should be introduced, and that lecturers on teaching methods courses should regularly spend some time working in schools to ensure that they do not lose sight of the reality of the classroom.

Lacey, C (1977) *The Socialization of Teachers* Methuen: London
This book examines the socialization process for students entering the teaching profession. It is based on a study of postgraduate students at Sussex University and traces their reactions to the practical elements of the course. It analyses the students' ability to develop or adopt strategies appropriate to new situations and is an important study of how teachers 'learn to get by' in a period of rapid institutional change.

Lauwerys, J (ed) (1969) *Teachers and Teaching* Evans: London
This book contains the introductory essays from four previous volumes of the Year Book of Education: *The Secondary School Curriculum* (1958); *Higher Education* (1959); *The Social Position of Teachers* (1953) and *The Education and Training of Teachers* (1963). The last two in particular raise questions which relate directly to the issues discussed in the present volume.

Lomax, D E (ed) (1976) *European Perspectives in Teacher Education* John Wiley and Sons: London
This is a collection of 16 essays written around the general theme of change and development in teacher education. Though the contributors have all worked in European systems, they also draw on experience in Asia, Africa, North American and Australia. Some of the main themes are identified in a key essay on teacher professionalism by Marklund which also contains a useful review of research on teacher characteristics, teacher behaviour and teacher roles.

Lortie, D C (1975) *SchoolTeacher: A Sociological Study* University of Chicago Press: Chicago, Ill
A thought-provoking study about the nature of teaching and teachers' perceptions of their tasks, which is partly based on interview data. Lortie discusses the central issues of recruitment, socialization and career rewards and their influence on teacher opinion and attitude. He suggests that in future teachers will need to be more adaptable, to work more closely with their colleagues and to be more prepared to share knowledge and expertise. He argues that this would be facilitated by a stronger link between theory and practice in initial training, as well as by induction programmes for beginning teachers and by a greater emphasis on in-service education.

Lynch, J (1979) *The Reform of Teacher Education in the United Kingdom* Society for Research into Higher Education: University of Surrey, Guildford
This is an examination of the major changes that took place in teacher education in the United Kingdom during the 1970s. The introductory chapter contains a concise history of teacher education and Lynch then moves to an analysis of some central issues; the contraction of the system and consequent restructuring of the colleges, the introduction of BEd degree programmes, the growing influence of the Council for National Academic Awards as a validating body, the introduction of new curricula and the tendency of colleges to become more involved in research and in-service training. He identifies the division between the public and university sectors in teacher training as a major weakness and argues that many problems will not be resolved until a choice is made between mass and elite systems of higher education.

Nisbet, J (ed) (1974) *Creativity of the School* OECD: Paris
This report brings together six papers originally presented at an OECD Conference in Portugal in 1972. It discusses the creativity of the school which is described by Nisbet as 'its capacity to adopt, adapt, generate or reject innovations'. The need is stressed to find a balance between, on the one hand, passively responding to social pressures, and on the other hand, initiating processes of social change; nonetheless, the bulk of the papers are concerned with ways of increasing the school's capacity for generating innovations.

Orlosky, D E (1974) The Protocol Materials Program *Journal of Teacher Education* **25** 4:291-7
Protocol materials are films or video-tapes of particular episodes of classroom behaviour, each one of which illustrates a different teaching concept, eg giving encouragement, feedback, transitions. They have been developed in America since 1970 and now form an important resource for all teacher educators. This article by Orlosky is a very useful introduction to protocols as he outlines the history of the programme and presents an overview of the main developments. The entire journal issue is devoted to articles about protocol materials.

Perry, W (1970) *Open University: A Personal Account by the First Vice-Chancellor* Open University Press: Milton Keynes

A fascinating study of the Open University by its first Vice-Chancellor which traces its development from controversial beginnings to its present assured status in the educational world. Sir Walter Perry claims that the difficulties of teaching students at a distance through a variety of means, including written and broadcast materials, have been substantially overcome. The University's creativity as an institution has been marked by the quality and originality of its teaching materials, which have been widely influential as well as commercially successful.

Ryan, K (1975) *Teacher Education* (74th Yearbook of the National Society for the Study of Education, Part II) University of Chicago Press: Chicago

The National Society for the Study of Education publishes a two-volume yearbook; one volume is intended to be of general educational interest and the second is on a more specialized theme. The 19 contributors to this particular volume have reviewed recent developments in teacher education and made suggestions about future trends, and the book includes a chapter by Gage and Winne on performance-based teacher education, one by Corwin on teacher unionism and one by Joyce in which he explores the concepts of man that underlie various theories of teacher education. Information about the Society may be obtained from The Secretary, 5835 Kembark Avenue, Chicago, Illinois.

Schmuck, R A, Runkel, P J, Arends, J H and Arends, R I (1977) *The Second Handbook of Organization Development in Schools* Mayfield: Palo Alto, Ca

This handbook has been designed as a practical resource book for organization specialists and for teachers and administrators who want to work on the organization of their school. The authors state that 'the ultimate goal of organization development is organization adaptability, by which we mean planned and constructive adaptation to change, not merely adjusting or acquiescing to externally imposed change' and they describe numerous strategies for involving staff in the assessment, diagnosis and transformation of their own school. The chapters are organized around distinct themes, eg establishing goals or improving meetings, but they each have the same format: an information/advice section, some specific activities, background reading and an annotated bibliography.

Smith, L M and Keith, P M (1971) *Anatomy of Educational Innovation* John Wiley and Sons: New York, London, Sydney, Toronto

This is a detailed and perceptive study of an attempt to introduce a major innovation into an American elementary school. The teachers involved were asked to work in teams to develop individualized learning programmes for the children and to maintain a very flexible approach to the curriculum. The school was newly built and had been specifically designed to facilitate this style of teaching. The two authors were in the school as participant observers for the first year of its life and were able to chart the developments and the problems that occurred in the implementation of the innovation. They draw attention to some of the pressures and constraints that can hamper successful implementation of an innovation despite a high level of initial commitment by the people involved.

Society for Research into Higher Education (1975) *How Long is a Piece of String?* SRHE: University of Surrey, Guildford

This pamphlet contains two papers on the evaluation of teaching practice which were discussed at a SRHE conference in October 1974. In the first paper, Edgar Stones argues that pupil learning should be a key criterion in the assessment of student teachers. Edith Cope makes a case for more research into supervision practices, research which employs a range of evaluation techniques and so is better able to grapple with the complexities of classroom and school. Finally, James Ellis presents a review of the research on the assessment of practice teaching.

Stenhouse, L (1975) *An Introduction to Curriculum Research and Development* Heinemann: London

In this stimulating textbook, which is intended for those engaged in the study of curriculum and teaching, Lawrence Stenhouse draws upon his own experience as the director of the Humanities Curriculum Project and upon work done by himself and his colleagues in the Centre for Applied Research in Education. He defines the curriculum as 'an attempt to communicate the essential principles and features of an educational proposal in such a form that it is open to critical scrutiny and is capable of effective translation into practice' and argues that teachers should become researchers into their own classroom practice. He advocates a partnership of teachers and curriculum research workers as a means of fostering the growth of a research tradition in schools.

Taylor, W (1978) *Research and Reform in Teacher Education* National Foundation for Educational Research: Slough
This study reviews a wide range of relevant research and explores its significance for teacher education in Europe. A prime concern is to demonstrate the value of close relationships between a broadly-based conception of teacher education research and the practice of teachers and schools. An important outcome of the work is the identification of areas where the current needs of the educational system demand further research. These include the acquisition of new skills by experienced teachers, the development of techniques for the assessment of teacher effectiveness, and the comparative study of patterns of curriculum organization.

Serials:

Distance Education is a biannual Australian periodical scheduled to commence publication in March 1980. Its intention is to disseminate information about research and practice in distance education, including correspondence study, external studies, individualized learning and audio-visual and broadcast media. It carries articles, reports, surveys and book reviews and has an international editorial board.
>   Editors: Desmond Keegan, Open College of Further Education, Adelaide; Ian McD
>   Mitchell, Adelaide College of the Arts and Education.
>   Publisher:School of External Studies, Royal Melbourne Institute of Technology, 167
>   Franklin Street, Melbourne 3000, Australia.

Perspectives on Academic Gaming and Simulation is the series title of the annual conference proceedings of SAGSET, the Society for Academic Gaming and Simulation in Education and Training. They are published by Kogan Page each spring, and contain the proceedings of the conference held in all corners of the UK the previous September. The papers cover applications in a wide variety of education and training contexts and usually include some computer-based simulations and games in addition to 'manual' exercises. SAGSET's published proceedings cover annual conferences since 1975 (see Megarry, 1978; McAleese, 1978; Megarry, 1979; and Race and Brooks, 1980, in the section I entries).

Simulation/Games for Learning is the quarterly periodical of SAGSET, the (British) Society for Academic Gaming and Simulation in Education and Training, entering its tenth volume in 1980. It carries articles on the theory and practice of simulation/gaming in all subjects and at all levels in education and training, including the rationale, design, use and evaluation of these exercises. Articles are contributed from North America, Australasia and Europe as well as Britain; the editorial board consists of internationally known simulation/gamers. The journal also carries reviews of simulations and games and relevant books, abstracts and monitoring of other publications.
>   Editor: Jacquetta Megarry, Jordanhill College of Education, Glasgow G13 1PP,
>   Scotland.
>   Publisher:Kogan Page, 120 Pentonville Road, London N1.

Teaching at a Distance is the house journal of the Open University: in addition to covering theoretical and practical aspects of the OU's teaching, it also carries articles on developments along similar lines elsewhere in the world. It started publication three times a year in 1974, but has now become biannual. See also Grugeon, D and Tibberham, K

(1980) *'Teaching at a Distance:* a selective survey of articles from issues 1-16' in *Distance Education* **1** 1

    Editor: David Grugeon, Regional Tutorial Services, The Open University.
    Publisher:The Open University, Walton Hall, Milton Keynes MK7 6AA, Bucks.

Biographical notes

Keith Baker (Chapter 13) was a teacher and lecturer before joining the University of Bristol School of Education Research Unit in 1974. He worked as Research Fellow on the Teacher Induction Pilot Schemes (TIPS) Project, which was a national study of the induction of probationary teachers. Subsequently he became Director of the Schools and In-Service Teacher Education (SITE) Project investigating the school-focused approach to staff development. Within the broad field of in-service teacher education, he has a special interest in processes of implementing innovations within schools. He has published several articles on the research projects and been involved in international co-development work on the evaluation of in-service under the OECD/CERI project on in-service.

Keir Bloomer (Chapter 26) is a member of the National Executive of the Educational Institute of Scotland, Scotland's major teachers' union. Since 1976 he has been the Convener of the Institute's Salaries Committee and chief spokesman for the teachers' side in national salary negotiations. He has also been deeply involved in negotiating agreements about conditions of service and staffing standards for Scottish teachers.

Although he is mainly associated with the trade union aspects of the Institute's work, Mr Bloomer has also been active in the education field. As a member of the EIS Education Committee he has played a part in creating its educational policy. He is also a member of the Consultative Committee on the Curriculum, an official body set up to provide advice to the Secretary of State for Scotland on aspects of the school curriculum.

Since 1978 he has been a member of the General Teaching Council and in 1979 became its Vice-Chairman. The work of the Council is concerned with control of entry to the profession, the maintainance of professional standards and the supply and training of teachers.

Since 1971 Mr Bloomer has been principal teacher of history in a city comprehensive in Glasgow.

Ray Bolam (Chapter 5) taught English in a comprehensive school in London before lecturing in a teacher training college in Yorkshire. He has been a Research Fellow in the University of Bristol School of Education since 1966 where his work has been mainly concerned with action research studies, particularly in the field of teacher education, and studies of planned change in education. Thus, he has directed several projects, all funded by the Department of Education and Science, on ways of improving the induction of beginning teachers. In particular, he led the national evaluation team which studied the government-funded pilot schemes in Liverpool and Northumberland from 1974-8. He has published a study of Local Education Authority Advisers as agents of change, also as a result of a DES funded project. Currently, he is working with Keith Baker (Chapter 13) on a study of the problem-solving capacities of schools in the particular context of school-focused in-service education and training. His international experience includes leading a British Council team to advise the government of Pakistan on a national project to improve the training of primary school teachers. Since 1974 he has been a consultant for OECD working on a study of in-service education and training in ten countries and also on a project concerned with ways in which external support agencies can strengthen the problem-solving capacities of schools in the Netherlands.

Tom Bone (Chapter 3) taught in a grammar school for five years and has subsequently been engaged in teacher education for 18. Since 1972 he has been Principal of Jordanhill, the largest college of education in the United Kingdom.

He is currently Chairman of the Committee of Principals of Scottish colleges of education, Vice-Chairman of the Scottish Certificate of Education Examination Board, Convener of the Supply Committe of the General Teaching Council for Scotland, a member of the Education Committee and the Committee for Scotland of the Council for National Academic Awards, an Executive Member of the Commonwealth Council for Educational Administration and of the British Educational Administration Society, a member of the Independent Broadcasting Authority's Education Advisory Council, and on the editorial boards of the British Journal of Educational Studies and the Journal of Educational Administration.

He is the author of a book on school inspection in Scotland, the editor of a book of studies in the history of Scottish education, and has contributed chapters to six other books and articles to various educational journals.

Dr Bone has had particularly wide experience of teaching and speaking at conferences in other countries, including four different provinces of Canada, the United States, Australia, India, Bangladesh, Zimbabwe, Belgium, Germany, Norway, and Eire. He has also made educational visits to the Netherlands, Sweden and Denmark, and is a frequent speaker at conferences in the United Kingdom.

His professional interests are the education of teachers, the assessment of secondary school pupils, and the training of educational administrators.

Robert Bush (Chapter 25) is Emeritus Professor of Education and Director of the Center for Educational Research at Stanford. He has been a teacher, counsellor, teacher trainer, researcher and administrator. He received his initial degrees in history and political science from Northern Colorado University and received his doctorate from Stanford University in 1941 in the field of higher education.

The major portion of his academic career has been at Stanford University for the past 40 years between 1937 and 1979. His fields of specialization are in teacher education (both pre-service and in-service), evaluation, secondary education, and the administration of educational research and development.

He currently serves (1) as a consultant to SRI International on its five year national evaluation study of Teacher Corps; (2) as a member of the Task Force for the Office of Planning and Evaluation of the California State Department of Education which is planning a longitudinal evaluation design for in-service education and staff development in the State of California; (3) as an adviser to the Ministry of Education and Culture in Brazil on the improving of teaching in Brazilian universities, and (4) in an advisory capacity to the California Commission on Teacher Preparation and Licensing.

Joan Dean (Chapter 10) has taught in schools and colleges and has been headmistress of two primary schools. She was Senior Adviser for Primary Education for Berkshire and is currently the Chief Inspector for Surrey LEA which involves leading a team of 33 inspectors with a responsibility for supporting the work of heads and teachers, monitoring standards and advising the Chief Education Officer. She obtained her MEd degree from Reading University and has been an examiner in practical teaching for several universities and for the CNAA for which she is Chief Examiner for the In-Service BEd degree at the College of Saint Mark and Saint John. She is the author of a number of books and has written articles for most of the main educational periodicals. She is a member of the School Broadcasting Council, and was, until recently, a member of the Professional Committee of the Schools Council and of the Executive of the National Association of Inspectors of Schools and Educational Advisers, of which she was

President in 1971-2. She was awarded an OBE in the New Year Honours List of 1980.

Mats Ekholm (Chapter 14) is a researcher in the field of education, based at Linköping, Sweden. He was at the Institute of Education, University of Göteborg, Sweden, from the late 1960s until 1975. In Göteborg he has conducted research focused on school climate and sociology of youth. He studied social development in school during the early 1970s using action research strategies. At present he is occupied with a research project in which innovations in school are studied from the inside. Three separate schools, their cultures and development processes, are being examined over four to five years by social anthropological and sociological methods. Since 1975, he has been one of the managers of a compulsory educational programme for all school leaders in Sweden.

John Elliott (Chapter 22) is tutor in curriculum studies at the Cambridge Institute of Education, where he is also directing an SSRC sponsored project on accountability in secondary schools. Formerly a secondary school teacher, he worked on the Schools Council Humanities Curriculum Project and was Director of the Ford T Project and lecturer in applied research in education at the University of East Anglia.

Glen Evans (Chapter 12) was a high school teacher from 1952 to 1959, when he took a lectureship at the University of Queensland. Following his doctoral studies in mathematics learning, he developed interests in psychometrics and cognition, in which areas he taught at the University of Iowa and the Ontario Institute for Studies in Education. In 1972, he returned to Australia to a Chair in Education at LaTrobe University and in 1974 was appointed Professor of Teacher Education at the University of Queensland. He was for five years Chairman of the Council of the Australian Curriculum Development Centre, and has since 1974 been involved with research into teachers' roles in curriculum development and the effects of programmes of teacher education.

Eric Hoyle (Consultant Editor and Chapter 2) has been Professor of Education at the University of Bristol since 1971. His previous posts included teaching in two secondary schools, a college of education and a university. His interests and published works are in the areas of educational administration, the process of innovation, the professional development of teachers and the relationship between research and policy.

He is also interested in the sociology of knowledge and the sociological study of organizations and of the professions. He was founding co-editor of *Research in Education* and is on the editorial boards of a number of other journals including the *British Journal of Teacher Education*. He was research consultant to the Donnison Commission on direct grant schools, vice-chairman of the Educational Research Board of the Social Science Research Council and is currently a member of the Executive Committee of the Universities Council for the Education of Teachers and a co-opted member of Avon Education Committee. He has lectured in various colleges and universities in Africa, Australia, North America and Malaysia.

Bruce Joyce (Chapter 1) received his doctorate in education from Wayne State University and subsequently taught at the University of Delaware, the University of Chicago, and Teacher's College, Columbia University. In the mid-1970s he became a visiting scholar at Stanford University. He now resides in Palo Alto, California as a writer and researcher in teaching, curriculum development and teacher education. In the field of teaching his line of research has included descriptive studies of teaching styles, the contribution of various school organizations to differences in teaching behaviour, and relationships between varieties of teaching styles and pupil learning. In teacher education he has explored teachers' ability to acquire repertoires of teaching strategies or 'models of teaching'. Dr Joyce has published more than 40 books and monographs and over 100 articles dealing with education including: *Models of Teaching* with Marsha Weil (Prentice-Hall, 1972; second edition, 1980); *Alternative Models of Elementary Education* with Michael McKibbin (D C Heath, 1980); *Creating the School* with Greta Morine (Little, Brown and

Co, 1976); and *New Strategies for Social Education* (Science Research Association, 1972).

Harry Judge (Chapter 24) is at present Director of the University of Oxford Department of Educational Studies and a Fellow of Brasenose College, Oxford. His main professional interest is in defining and developing the place of such a department within a university and linking it to the work of schools in the neighbourhood. He is also the convener of the Oxford Educational Research Group.

Before going to Oxford his career was in secondary schools, both as a teacher and a headmaster. In the 1960s he was a member of the Public Schools Commission appointed by the Labour Government, and in the early 1970s of the Committee of Enquiry into Teacher Education and Training appointed by Margaret Thatcher.

He has contributed extensively to historical and educational journals, is the author of two books and is at present particularly interested in education and politics in twentieth century Britain. Dr Judge has made a number of study visits to the United States, where he has been a Visiting Professor at the Massachusetts Institute of Technology. He is Chairman of the School Broadcasting Council of the British Broadcasting Council for the United Kingdom.

Lilian Katz (Chapter 20) has been Professor of Elementary and Early Childhood Education at the University of Illinois since 1968. In addition to her professorial duties, she has been the Director of the ERIC Clearinghouse on Elementary and Early Childhood Education there since 1970. Dr Katz has been closely involved in developments in pre-school education in the US since the early 1960s. Within early childhood education she has specialized in the problems of teacher training and development. Her writing has been focused on the problems of teachers of very young children, including their development and their working conditions. She has also trained pre-school teachers and teacher educators all over the US and in many other countries. She has been a visiting scholar and professor in the United Kingdom and Australia and served as a pre-school consultant to UNESCO. In 1979 she was appointed chairman of the Department of Elementary and Early Childhood Education at the University of Illinois and became co-director of the Research Unit on Teacher Education in that department.

Eugenia Kemble (Chapter 11) has been a Special Assistant to the President of the American Federation of Teachers since October 1975. Her main responsibilities involve educational programme and policy, including staff direction related to career education, school finance reform, testing, teacher education, early childhood education, and in-service teacher education. Ms Kemble directs staff work for the AFT's Task Force on Educational Issues, a select group of AFT Vice-Presidents and other AFT leaders which develops position papers and policy statements for the organization. She also represents the organization at various education meetings and conferences.

Her previous experience includes eight years for the United Federation of Teachers, the AFT's local branch in New York City, first as Assistant Editor of its newspaper and later as Director of Special Projects.

David Kolawole (Chapter 17) is a Nigerian educationist who has been in the teaching service for 30 years. He trained as a teacher in Nigeria before going to the United States of America where he obtained his MA degree at Indiana State University and his Doctor of Philosophy degree in Education at Michigan State University.

His major professional interests are in teacher training and research in curriculum development, and his recent research has been on the effects of environmental stimulation on cognitive learning in creative activities. He is a member of several professional bodies in education and he has attended several national and international conferences in education.

Dr Kolawole taught and was head of primary schools in Nigeria. He also taught in teacher training colleges in Nigeria and was principal of Mokwa Teachers' College for four years. From that position, he joined the Ahmadu Bello University in 1970 and taught philosophy of education at its Advanced Teachers' College for four years. Since 1974, he has been the Head of Division of Primary Education at Ahmadu Bello University, Institute of Education Headquarters — a position which includes co-ordination of the Primary Education Improvement Project.

Geoffrey Lyons (Chapter 6) is principal lecturer in Education Management at the Anglian Regional Management Centre, North East London Polytechnic. He undertook the 'Head's Tasks' project for the Department of Education and Science and is currently engaged in research into staff management with schools and local education authorities, and in producing training materials for middle managers in secondary schools. He is the author of *Heads' Tasks: a Handbook of Secondary School Administration* (NFER, 1976) among other publications.

Sixten Marklund (Chapter 7) started his professional career as a teacher and supervisor of teacher training. During 1956-61 he was a state school inspector, and during 1961-78 head of department at the Swedish National Board of Education, first for compulsory education, later for teacher training, and finally for educational research and development. In his work he has been dealing with central administrative matters of implementation of recent school reforms both as chief administrator and as a member of government commissions. He obtained his PhD in 1962 at the University of Stockholm on studies of class organization and student achievement, and he has written a number of books and articles on teacher training, educational change and educational research planning. During 1972-4 he was chairman of the National Educational Research Committee at the Council of Europe. He has also acted as educational expert in a number of projects at UNESCO and OECD. He was appointed Professor of Education at the Swedish National Board of Education in 1971. Since 1978 he has been a research professor at the International Institute of Education at the University of Stockholm.

David Marsh (Chapter 8) is an Assistant Professor at the University of Southern California where he teaches courses in staff development leadership, curriculum change and programme evaluation. He is the author of several state and national level task force reports on staff development policies and evaluation, and has written about the implications of the RAND Change Agent Study for staff development. He is currently conducting research with Bruce Joyce and Robert Bush on state policy in staff development and on the ecology of staff development. He is also studying the dynamics of school-based programme planning within a comprehensive school reform programme in California.

One of his primary interests is the relationship of staff development to comprehensive school-centred reform efforts. In this context, staff development is seen as one of a complementary set of strategies for the improvement of school programmes.

Lloyd McCleary (Chapter 6) is Professor of Educational Administration and Director of the R & D Laboratory, University of Utah. He has served as director, team leader, or consultant to over 20 projects in third world countries since 1960. He directed the current Education Sector Study for Bolivia and led the team which planned the now operational Rural Development Project there. He was Chairman of the Research Committee and led the research teams for the National High School Principal Study in the US completed in 1979, and he is now directing a Rockefeller Family Fund project on community involvement in the schools. He has written six books and numerous articles, monographs, and research reports dealing with teacher and administrator preparation and in-service development and with administration of schools.

Donald McIntyre (Chapter 21) is Reader in Education at the University of Stirling. After taking degrees in Mathematics and in Education at Edinburgh University, he spent some time teaching secondary school mathematics. Since 1961 he has been engaged in teacher education and educational research, at Moray House College, Hull University, and, from 1969, at Stirling University. His research has mainly been concerned with teachers and teaching, and with curriculum and assessment in secondary schools. Among his publications are, with Arnold Morrison, *Teachers and Teaching* (1969, 1973), *Schools and Socialization* (1971) and *The Social Psychology of Teaching* (1972), and, with Gordon Macleod and Roy Griffiths, *Investigations of Microteaching* (1977).

Agnes McMahon (Bibliography) has been a research associate in the University of Bristol School of Education since 1976 when she joined the evaluation team for the Teacher Induction Pilot Schemes (TIPS) Project. She is currently working on the dissemination phase of this project, one aspect of which involves the production of induction handbooks for use by school and LEA personnel. Prior to this she taught history in secondary schools in London and then moved to Dublin where she was a member of the Humanities team in the Curriculum Development Unit in Trinity College. During this period she was a member of various writing teams and edited a unit of materials on Celtic Ireland.

Jacquetta Megarry (Series Editor and Chapter 18) is a lecturer at Jordanhill College of Education, Glasgow, holding a joint appointment between the departments of education and audio-visual media. The latter commitment is mainly to the in-service CNAA Diploma in Educational Technology described in her chapter. Her current interests include simulation/games and computer-assisted learning; methods and media for distance learning; curriculum innovation and evaluation; and sex-typing in education, into which she is currently carrying out research.

After teaching in secondary schools, she was a researcher on Project PHI at Glasgow University (1971-3), developing and evaluating multi-media materials for science teachers in the Highlands and Islands of Scotland. She has been at Jordanhill since 1973, but spent a year at IBM's Scientific Centre in Peterlee (1974-5) as researcher on a computer-based games and simulations project for schools. She has run summer schools in simulation/gaming at Loughborough University (1974 and 1975) and at Concordia University, Montreal (annually from 1975 to 1979).

Jacquetta Megarry has been closely associated with SAGSET (the Society for Academic Gaming and Simulation in Education and Training) since 1973. She was its Chairman (1973-6), has edited its Journal *(Simulation/Games for Learning)* since 1975, and three of its recent books (1978-9). Her other publications include articles, chapters, research reports and distance learning materials, mostly in the general area of educational technology, innovative learning techniques, evaluation and sex-typing in education. She has also edited the *World Yearbook* since its revival in 1979.

Donald Orlosky (Chapter 19) has demonstrated a continuing interest in the application of theoretical knowledge about teaching to the performance of teachers in the classroom. For his doctoral dissertation he studied factors that promoted or prevented the performance of recommended classroom procedures by student teachers. His post-doctoral work focused on the use of innovative practices in the classroom. His professional positions have included the department chairmanship of DePauw University's Education Department where he also served as Director of the Student Teaching Programme, and was a visiting lecturer at Indiana University for eight years in Educational Research. He is currently with the faculty of the University of South Florida. He has been Director of the National Leadership Training Institute for Educational Personnel Development, an agency funded by the United States Office of Education to supervise programmes in Performance Based Teacher Education, training materials development, Protocol Materials development, and the National Teacher Centre Programme. He is consulting editor for the Charles E Merrill Publishing Company for the Coordinated Teacher Education Series and has recently co-authored (with B Othanel Smith) two books on teacher education: *Socialization and Schooling: The Basics of School Reform* (Phi Delta Kappa, 1976) and *Curriculum Development: Issues and Insights* (Rand McNally, 1978).

Pauline Perry (Chapter 9) received her university education at Girton College, Cambridge. She has taught in secondary schools and in universities in Britain, Canada and the USA, and has had varied journalistic experience on television and in newspapers.

Her books include *Case Studies in Teaching, Case Studies in Adolescence* and *Your Guide to the Opposite Sex*. She has also published numerous articles in educational journals. She is currently a Staff Inspector in Her Majesty's Inspectorate and has a special interest in the in-service training of teachers and in higher education generally.

John Raynor (Chapter 16) is Dean of the Faculty of Educational Studies at the Open University. He was educated at the London School of Economics, University of Liverpool and received his doctorate from the University of Sussex. He has taught at every level of education from primary school through to university. He joined the Open University in 1971, was head of the Curriculum Studies group from 1975 to 1979, and was chairman of two courses produced in the Faculty, E351 *Urban Education* and E361 *Education and the Urban Environment*. His publications include *The Middle Classes* (Longman, 1969), *Linking Home and School* (Longman, 1967 and 1972), *The City Experience* and *Schooling in the City* (Ward Lock, 1977). His special interests fall into two areas: cultural analysis and education, and urban and multi-ethnic education.

William Smith (Chapter 15) is the 24th United States Commissioner of Education. As Commissioner, he heads the 113-year-old Office of Education through which more than 100 educational programmes are administered. Dr Smith's academic degrees include BA from Wiley College, Texas, 1949, MEd (Boston State College, Massachusetts, 1955) and PhD (Case Western Reserve University, Ohio, 1970).

Prior to joining the Office of Education, Dr Smith was executive director of Programmes of Action by Citizens in Education (PACE), an independent organization which promotes educational innovation in public school districts in Cleveland, Ohio. Since coming to the Office of Education in 1969, he has served in a variety of posts including Acting Deputy Commissioner for Development, Associate Commissioner for Educational Personnel Development, and Director for Improvement of Educational Systems. From 1973 until the beginning of 1980, he was Director of the Teacher Corps programme. It was during this period that Teacher Corps experienced its most significant change in focus — from a pre-service undergraduate teacher education programme to one which concentrates on the school's entire in-service educational staff.

William Taylor (Chapter 23) has been Director of the University of London Institute of Education since 1973. He was previously Professor of Education in the University of Bristol, and taught at the University of Oxford, in colleges of education and in secondary schools. He is the author and editor of several books on the sociology of education, including *Society and the Education of Teachers* (1969) and *Research and Reform in Teacher Education* (1978). From 1976 to 1979 Dr Taylor was Chairman of the Universities Council for the Education of Teachers.

Richard Tisher (Chapter 4) is a Professor of Education and Associate Dean, Faculty of Education, Monash University, Melbourne, Australia. Prior to coming to Monash in 1974 he was Reader in Education at the University of Queensland and before that he taught in secondary schools in New South Wales and lectured at Sydney and Armidale Teachers' Colleges. His academic qualifications — MSc, DipEd (Sydney), BA (New England), PhD (Queensland) — are diverse, but have prompted his research interests in teaching strategies, curriculum innovation, teacher induction, and educational evaluation. Recently he has been involved in school evaluation, studies of teaching styles and pupils' perceptions of their learning environment, and a national survey of the induction of Australia's beginning teachers. He was President of the Australian Association for Research in Education (1977), a visiting Fulbright Scholar in the USA (1969-70) and, more recently, an invited participant at a national conference on teacher education at the University of Texas (1979). As well as publishing widely in books and in national and international journals he has maintained close contact with local educational groups and schools through participation in regional conferences, in-service workshops and school evaluations. He enjoys teaching and has been responsible for training courses at pre-service as well as at Master's level.

Index